T5-ARD-529

FROM SCHOOL TO WORK

FROM SCHOOL TO WORK

*A Comparative Study of Educational
Qualifications and Occupational Destinations*

Edited by

YOSSI SHAVIT

and

WALTER MÜLLER

with the editorial assistance of
CLARE TAME

CLARENDON PRESS · OXFORD
1998

Oxford University Press, Great Clarendon Street, Oxford OX2 6DP

Oxford New York

Athens Auckland Bangkok Bogota Bombay
Buenos Aires Calcutta Cape Town Dar es Salaam
Delhi Florence Hong Kong Istanbul Karachi
Kuala Lumpur Madras Madrid Melbourne
Mexico City Nairobi Paris Singapore
Taipei Tokyo Toronto Warsaw

and associated companies in
Berlin Ibadan

Oxford is a trade mark of Oxford University Press

Published in the United States
by Oxford University Press Inc., New York

© Yossi Shavit and Walter Müller 1998

All rights reserved. No part of this publication may be reproduced,
stored in a retrieval system, or transmitted, in any form or by any means,
without the prior permission in writing of Oxford University Press.
Within the UK, exceptions are allowed in respect of any fair dealing for the
purpose of research or private study, or criticism or review, as permitted
under the Copyright, Designs and Patents Act, 1988, or in the case of
reprographic reproduction in accordance with the terms of the licences
issued by the Copyright Licensing Agency. Enquiries concerning
reproduction outside these terms and in other countries should be
sent to the Rights Department, Oxford University Press,
at the address above

British Library Cataloguing in Publication Data
Data available

Library of Congress Cataloging in Publication Data
Data available
ISBN 0–19–829322–4

1 3 5 7 9 10 8 6 4 2

Typeset by Hope Services (Abingdon) Ltd.
Printed in Great Britain
on acid-free paper by
Bookcraft (Bath) Ltd
Midsomer Norton, Somerset

HD
5707
.F76
1998

11726357

PREFACE

In all developed societies the occupational attainment of individuals is largely shaped by the amount and kind of education they obtain. How and extent to which success in schools and universities affects occupational prospects, however, varies in different countries. Our basic hypothesis is that these variations are produced by differences among societies in the institutional arrangements of education and work. Countries differ in the way they organize education and channel each new generation through their diverse educational systems. Countries also differ in labour-market institutions. This book is concerned with varying institutional characteristics of educational systems and their effects on occupational outcomes.

The hypothesis of institutional effects is far from new (e.g. Turner 1960; Kerckhoff 1995) and has been developed and tested in several recent studies on how education and labour-market outcomes are linked. Methodologically, these studies fall into one of three categories. The first consists of single society studies which explore the effect of educational structures and institutional forms on the occupational attainments of different social groups. For example, Shavit (1992) studied the consequences of track placement in Israel's secondary schools in shaping ethnic inequality in occupational attainment. The major difficulty with single case studies is that they try to infer from a single case to a hypothetical one. For example, studies of tracking can show that track placement amplifies educational inequalities between children from different social strata. However, they cannot know how inequalities might have been in a hypothetical society in which tracking did not exist.

The second category of studies consists of those which compare the process of stratification in several societies with differing institutional contexts, and relate the institutional variation to differences in the parameters of the stratification process. Some well-known examples of such studies are Rosenbaum and Kariya's (1989) comparisons of Japan and the USA, Maurice, Sellier, and Silvestre's (1982) comparison of Germany and France, the study of Haller et al. (1985) on Austria, Germany, France, and the USA, and Allmendinger's (1989a) work on Germany, the USA and Norway. The major difficulty with comparisons made between only a few countries is that one often wonders if differences between them are really due to differences in the institutions of interest or to some other source of variation. When similarities are found, one wonders if the two or three countries are really all that different in terms of the institutional context. For example, comparing processes of stratification in Japan to those in the USA and Britain, Ishida

UWEC McIntyre Library

DISCARDED

DEC 1 8 1998

Eau Claire, WI

(1993) finds remarkable similarity between them, despite presumed institutional and cultural differences between them. The results of our study (see Table 1.1.a) show that the educational institutions of these three countries are quite similar when compared to the range of differences existing among other countries. By contrast, when differences are found, one cannot be confident that they are due to the institutional variation focused upon.

The third group of studies attempts to overcome this problem by comparing a large set of cases which represents the existing variation in both the dependent and independent variables. When the number of cases is large, the researcher can also try to control for possible spurious factors which might be responsible for the correlation between them. Treiman and Yip (1989), and Ganzeboom, Luijkx, and Treiman (1989) are examples of such studies. The major difficulty here is that with many cases it is difficult to develop an intimate knowledge of the institutional context of each. Consequently, researchers often conceptualize the social context in terms of some aggregate measures which are available from statistical sources or can be generated from individual level data available. Thus, there is indeed, as Ragin (1989) underlines, an inherent tension in comparative research between the number of cases, on the one hand, and a detailed understanding of their institutional and historical context, on the other.

We sought to resolve this tension by asking experts working in a large number of countries, to cooperate in a comparative study on the association between educational qualifications and occupational outcomes early in workers' careers. From knowledge that we already had on these countries—which admittedly was rather superficial in part—we expected that the countries selected would exhibit variation in both the magnitude and shape of the association as well as in its institutional context. We knew that our colleagues would be able to provide rich and detailed information on the context of the school-to-work transition in their countries. We invited scholars from countries for which we knew appropriate data existed, and where we knew of scholars who would participate in a cooperative effort of this kind. Thus, the countries do not constitute a representative sample of all possible institutional contexts of the school-to-work transition, but they do exhibit substantial differences in their institutional context (see Chapter I).

Once the team was formed, we agreed on a common substantive and methodological research plan. Each chapter was to include both a 'compulsory' and a 'free-style' component. The compulsory part includes a description of the institutional features of the educational system and the labour market, as well an analysis of comparable empirical data using similar definitions of variables and a common set of statistical tools. We believe that we have obtained a standard of comparability sufficiently high to allow for a number of substantive conclusions on the impact of specific institutional arrangements for various aspects of the school-to-work transition. In the 'free-style' component the authors discuss special topics which are valuable for the understanding of their specific case. The only exception to this general format is Kariya's chapter which summarizes and extends his earlier exemplary comparative work on the institutional contexts of the school-to-work transition in Japan and the USA.

First drafts of most chapters were presented at a meeting of the team which was held at the European University Institute in Florence in March of 1995. The papers were then revised and, after thorough evaluations by several members of the team, final versions were completed by early 1996. At this stage the two of us began an integration and analysis of the thirteen 'cases' in an attempt to test hypotheses regarding the institutional embeddedness of the association between educational qualifications and occupational outcomes. The results of our comparative analysis, as well as the conceptual and methodological framework of the study as a whole, are discussed in Chapter I.

The analysis reported in the lead chapter focuses solely on the common components of the thirteen country-chapters while usually ignoring idiosyncratic information on the specifics of the thirteen individual cases. The country-chapters are rich with detailed information on the educational systems and labour-market processes of the countries involved and should constitute a valuable resource to students of comparative stratification.

ACKNOWLEDGEMENTS

The project was supported by generous grants from the Research Council of the European University Institute, the Japan Foundation, the Mannheim Centre of European Social Research at the University of Mannheim and by the grant of the German Research Foundation (Deutsche Forschungsgemeinschaft) for the project on Educational Expansion and Social Reproduction. Parts of the lead chapter were written, and the volume edited while Walter Müller was Fellow of the Netherlands Institute for Advanced Study in the Humanities and Social Sciences (NIAS), Wassenaar. We are grateful to all these organizations for their support and for their confidence in the project.

Marie-Ange Catotti provided invaluable secretarial and administrative assistance to the project. We are grateful to her for attending to administrative matters great and small and always with her usual efficiency and calm. We are also grateful to Clare Tame for the wonderful job she has done in editing the volume, improving the linguistic style of the individual chapters and organizing them into a coherent whole. Her attention to detail and very high professional standards are exemplary. Thanks too to Peter Ucen for moulding the tables and figures of the various chapters into a common format and for helping us produce most of the graphics for the lead chapter. We also thank Reinhard Pollak, Beate Rossi and Susanne Steinmann who took care of clarifying with the authors matters associated with copy-editing, proof-reading, and the final polishing of the references. Finally, we are grateful to our colleagues, the participants in the project. We thank them for helping formulate the common conceptual and methodological framework, and for then agreeing to work within its confines. We are fortunate to have such highly professional and supportive friends.

Yossi Shavit and Walter Müller

Florence and Mannheim
December 1996

CONTENTS

LIST OF FIGURES

LIST OF TABLES

NOTES ON CONTRIBUTORS

Richard ARUM is Assistant Professor of Sociology at the University of Arizona.

Richard BREEN is Professor of Sociology and Director of the Centre for Social Research, Queen's University, Belfast.

Marlis BUCHMANN is Professor of Sociology at the University of Zurich and the Swiss Federal Institute of Technology.

Sin Yi CHEUNG is a Research Officer at the Department of Applied Social Studies and Social Research, Oxford University.

Antonio COBALTI is Dean of Sociology at the University of Trento.

Paul M. DE GRAAF is Associate Professor of Sociology at the University of Nijmegen.

Renate ELL is Research Fellow at the Mannheim Centre for European Social Research.

Robert ERIKSON is Professor of Sociology at the Swedish Institute for Social Research in Stockholm.

Dominique GOUX is Research Fellow at the National Institute of Statistics and Economic Surveys (INSEE) in Paris.

Anthony HEATH is Professor of Sociology at the University of Oxford and Official Fellow of Nuffield College.

Michael HOUT is Professor of Sociology and Director of the Survey Research Center at the University of California, Berkeley.

Hiroshi ISHIDA is Associate Professor of Sociology at the Institute of Social Sciences, University of Tokyo.

Frank JONES is Professor of Sociology in the Research School of Social Sciences of the Australian National University.

Jan O. JONSSON is Associate Professor of Sociology at the Swedish Institute for Social Research.

Takehiko KARIYA is Associate Professor of Sociology at the Graduate School of Education, University of Tokyo.

Vered KRAUS is Associate Professor of Sociology at the University of Haifa.

Eric MAURIN is head of the Households Living Conditions division of the National Institute of Statistics and Economic Surveys (INSEE) in Paris.

Walter MÜLLER is Professor of Sociology at the University of Mannheim and Department Head at the Mannheim Centre for European Social Research.

Stefan SACCHI is Research Fellow in the Department of Sociology at the Swiss Federal Institute of Technology in Zurich.

Antonio SCHIZZEROTTO is Professor of Sociology in the Department of Sociology and Social Research at the University of Trento.

Yossi SHAVIT is Associate Professor in the Department of Sociology and Anthropology at Tel Aviv University.

Susanne STEINMANN is Research Fellow at the Mannheim Centre for European Social Research.

Shu-Ling TSAI is Research Fellow at the Institute of Sociology at the Academia Sinica in Taipei.

Wout C. ULTEE is Professor of Sociology at the University of Nijmegen.

Christopher WHELAN is a Research Professor at the Economic and Social Research Institute in Dublin.

Meir YAISH is Research Fellow at Nuffield College, Oxford.

Clare TAME (associate editor) is Research Associate in the Department of Social and Political Sciences at the European University Institute.

1

The Institutional Embeddedness of the Stratification Process

A Comparative Study of Qualifications and Occupations in Thirteen Countries

WALTER MÜLLER AND YOSSI SHAVIT

INTRODUCTION

Education is the single most important determinant of occupational success in industrialized societies. Employers rely on educational credentials when selecting individuals for specific work tasks, and individuals, accordingly, invest in education in order to improve their competitive advantage on the labour market. It is evident, that both individual investments in education and the use made by employers of qualifications, affect the pattern of association that we observe between education and labour-market outcomes. But it is far from clear how precisely this association is generated in various countries. There are large differences between countries in the way education is organized. Indeed, educational systems differ greatly cross-nationally. We therefore start from the premiss that the role of education in occupational attainment varies between societies. In some, education is valued for the specific vocational skills it represents, in others, for equipping workers with a level of general knowledge, while in others still, education is valued for sorting students by their scholastic ability or learning potential. The main objective of this book then, is to identify systematic differences among countries, in the relationship between education and occupational outcomes, and to relate them to their institutional contexts.

The book thus focuses on a specific aspect of the broader issue of social stratification and mobility in industrial societies. Education is a crucial intervening link between the social background of individuals and their later class destination (Carlsson 1958; Blau and Duncan 1967). From earlier research we know, that among the several processes generating the inter-generational transmission of advantage, the link between education

and occupational destination varies most across countries. Using the CAS-
MIN data-set, Müller and his colleagues compared nine European countries
in terms of the absolute magnitude of the relationship between social origin,
educational attainment, and later class destination (Müller et al. 1989). They
found only small differences between these countries in the extent to which
social origins affect educational attainment or occupational destination, but
large differences in the effect of schooling on occupational class (see also
Erikson and Goldthorpe 1992: ch. 8). What then are the reasons for the
apparent international variation in the association between educational qualifications and occupational destinations? Which factors account for stronger
or weaker associations between education and jobs?

Theories vary in the way they conceptualize the link between education
and occupational outcome, in their understanding of the role of credentials
in sorting, selecting, and placing of workers for jobs, and in the importance
they attach to the institutional embeddedness of these processes—the latter
being particularly important in understanding cross-national variations in
stratification and mobility. In this chapter we develop several hypotheses
regarding the specific ways in which the characteristics of educational
systems affect the relationship between educational credentials and the occupational outcomes of individuals. The hypotheses are then tested in a comparative analysis of the results from thirteen national case studies reported
in this volume. We begin, in the next section with a brief review of some of
the major theoretical arguments regarding national similarities and differences in the pattern and magnitude of the association between education and
occupational attainment. We then formulate the major hypotheses of the
study, describe its method, data, and variables, and proceed to a presenta-
tion of our results. We conclude with an evaluation of the hypotheses, a discussion of the findings, and some suggestions for future research.

PREVIOUS RESEARCH ON THE INSTITUTIONAL
CONTEXT OF THE PROCESS

There is little comparative research on national differences and similarities
in the relationship between educational qualifications and occupational allocation as this field of research is much less developed, both theoretically and
empirically, than comparative research on educational attainment (Blossfeld
and Shavit 1993; Müller and Karle 1993; Erikson and Jonsson 1996b; Breen
and Goldthorpe 1996). One excellent example of institutionally sensitive
research on the transition from school to work, however, is Rosenbaum and
Kariya's (1989) comparative study of Japan and the USA (see also Kariya's
chapter in this volume). The school-to-work transition process in Japan dif-

fers from that of most other countries in that there are strong institutional linkages between school and universities on the one hand, and firms on the other. Schools and universities recommend students to specific employers with whom they cooperate, and these relationships have important consequences on the qualitative nature of the school-to-work transition. School performance, for example, is an important predictor of occupational attainment among Japanese high-school graduates entering the labour market.[1]

Societies vary in the institutional arrangements that constrain the school-to-work transition (Kerckhoff 1995). That is, in the structure of educational institutions, the differentiation of school tracks, curricula, and diplomas, regulatory rules established by the state, employer recruitment and promotion practices, formal entry rules for specific occupations, in particular the professions, semi-professions, and civil service jobs, and the role of collective actors, such as unions and professional organizations, in shaping education, training, and guidelines for the recruitment and promotion of personnel.

The institutional framework existing at a given time in a particular society largely depends on solutions found in the past for the general problem of training and employment. It also depends on how conflicting interests have been reconciled in the past. Particular solutions used in the past may, however, generate new problems which call, in turn, for new solutions. Societal idiosyncrasies may thus evolve and persist over time despite convergence in other aspects of the social structure. In a recent historical study comparing France, Germany, and Britain, Müller (1994) investigated the process by which the feudal order of stratification, and the systems of social control and production were transformed into modern patterns involving markets, bureaucracies, and professions. He found that different traditions have evolved regarding the use of education in allocating people to jobs. In Britain, the Crown relied on the loyalty of the nobility and on the expertise available in society at large, and did not develop a system of professional training for the civil service and the professions until the twentieth century. As a consequence, British education is decentralized, and organized on local, and even private bases, and has often developed through grass-root initiatives. In France, by contrast, with the destruction of the *ancien régime*— under which public offices could be bought, sold, and inherited—by the Revolution, a new recruitment principle was introduced for the higher levels of public administration. A new type of educational institution, the *grandes écoles*, were created to select and train personnel to be used by the enlightened and rational state, and still largely serve this function today. The German states (Prussia, in particular) with their early development of state bureaucracies, established specific educational entry requirements for the different levels of the administrative hierarchy. These were implemented according to the principle 'no office without a proper examination'

(W. Fischer and Lundgreen 1975). To this day, the links between education and jobs in Britain, France, and Germany seem to mirror these historical roots: the association is weakest in Britain, strong in France in the allocation to the service class, and strongest in Germany throughout the occupational hierarchy.

Two Types of Institutional Contexts: Qualificational vs. Organizational Space

The exemplary study by Maurice, Sellier, and Silvestre (1982) was among the first to develop a general theoretical framework for the study of the links between educational qualifications and labour-market outcomes. Conducting a detailed analysis of work organization, job recruitment, and mobility patterns in French and German enterprises, they developed a theory of societal effects, arguing that the way in which qualifications are 'produced' in the educational system and their subsequent use by employers, lead to complex system-specific relationships between qualifications and jobs. They describe Germany as a system patterned along a *qualificational space*, while France is patterned in an *organizational space*. In Germany, vocational qualifications are used by employers to organize jobs and to allocate persons among them, whilst in France, education is less closely related to the workplace and vocational skills are mainly obtained on the job. Since organization-specific skills are often not recognized by other employers, the association between education and jobs tends to be looser in France than in Germany.[2]

The hypothesis, that firms adapt the organization of work, personnel recruitment policies, and training programmes, to the output of the educational system, can be extended to other countries where the educational system focuses on general education, such as in Ireland and the USA, and work-related skills are taught on the job. In such cases, skills tend to be firm-specific. By contrast, where the educational system produces vocationally relevant skills, firms tend to adapt the production process to the available skill pool. Consequently, in such countries, the organization of work is similar across firms, and workers can move more easily between organizations, and are less likely to experience a devaluation of their human-capital investments by shifting between employers.

General vs. Specific Vocational Education

The distinction between organizational and qualificational space is closely related to the debate on the pros and cons of vocational education. Virtually all educational systems differentiate between academic and vocational education. Some scholars hold that this differentiation increases the inequality of educational and occupational attainment, with working-class students being disproportionately placed in vocational programmes which teach useless skills and label their students as dull and unmotivated (see e.g. Shavit 1990*a*). Others suggest that vocational education enhances the occupational chances of working-class students, and that vocational qualifications facilitate both finding employment and attaining skilled, rather than unskilled, jobs (Arum and Shavit 1995; Blossfeld 1994; Müller et al. 1989).

The curricula of vocational programmes differ in the mix of general and vocationally-specific components. General skills include literacy, arithmetic, general cognitive skills (such as understanding and processing information, reasoning on logical grounds), and basic cultural and communication abilities. Specific skills are more instrumental to particular functional tasks and include skills such as accounting, computer programming, childcare, the mastery of specific crafts, tools, or machinery.[3] Skills vary according to their transferability and utility for various work tasks and employers. General skills are usually perfectly transferable between occupations, while the transferability of specific skills is more limited.

Most educational systems offer a mix of general and specific skills. Some offer primarily general education (e.g. Ireland), others (e.g. Sweden) also offer transferable vocational skills under broad headings, such as metalwork, and teach basic principles whilst avoiding specialization, and yet others offer more specialized skills for particular occupations. These last are the systems which offer vocational training for hundreds of occupational titles, as, for example, in the apprenticeship systems in German-speaking countries, where the teaching of occupation-specific skills is coordinated between vocational schools and the workplace in what is known as the dual system. In the Netherlands too, a large number of occupational specializations are taught in specific school tracks. In such systems, the occupations specialized for would not just be carpenter, but cabinet maker or construction carpenter; and not just mechanic, but industrial machine mechanic, car mechanic, or lorry mechanic.

Where the occupation-specific component of vocational education is large, graduates have few transferable skills, and can only cash-in on them by transforming them into the corresponding occupations in the labour market. Viewed from the demand-side, where job applicants are endowed with specific skills employers are likely to hire them for corresponding occupations where they can be 'up and running' immediately, rather than engage in expensive on-the-job training. Consequently, we would expect that where education is occupationally-specific, workers with vocational qualifications are more likely to be found in skilled, rather than unskilled, occupations.[4] By contrast, where education has a weak component of skill-specificity, vocational qualifications are less likely to affect this outcome.

By contrast, in countries, where vocational education tends to be general rather than specific, workers require on-the-job training before they can be useful to employers. In such countries, job allocation follows Thurow's (1976) *job queue* model, which assumes that most skills necessary for job performance are obtained on the job. Educational qualifications are not valued for the skills they represent but for the indirect information they provide about job applicants insofar as credentials give employers an indication of the intelligence (trainability), work habits, and discipline of job applicants. Viewed from this perspective, vocational education may be a handicap rather than an asset. Moreover, vocational education is less prestigious than academic education. The more successful students tend to attend the academic programmes, whereas the less successful turn to vocational education. Thus, having attended a vocational programme of education constitutes a signal that the job applicant is neither bright nor disciplined.

A related issue is the involvement of employers and trade unions in the organization of vocational training. The greater their involvement in defining curricula, setting standards, testing, and so forth, the more likely the programmes are to be relevant to employers' skill needs. This is quite apart from the fact that employers are more likely to rely on qualifications which they themselves award. Perhaps the greatest involvement of employers takes place in traditional apprenticeships, where they are directly responsible for training. Whether qualifications obtained via apprenticeships are generally recognized, however, will depend on the extent to which they are carried out under agreed and generally accepted standards. A clear distinction could be made in this respect, between the German and the British apprenticeship systems.

Standardization and Stratification

In her influential comparative study of school-to-work transitions in Germany, Norway, and the USA, Allmendinger (1989*b*) proposes a typology of educational systems based on two dimensions: the *standardization of educational provisions*, and the *stratification of educational opportunity*. Standardization refers to 'the degree to which the quality of education meets the same standards nationwide. Variables such as teachers' training, school budgets, curricula and the uniformity of school-leaving examinations are relevant in measuring standardization.' Stratification refers to the extent and form of tracking at the secondary educational level. Where stratification is high, e.g. in Germany, Switzerland, and the Netherlands, students are separated early on into tracks which differ greatly in the curricula and in the odds that students would continue to the tertiary level. In these countries there is also little or no mobility between tracks. By contrast, in less stratified countries (e.g. the USA and Ireland), tracking begins at a later age, the curricula of the various tracks are somewhat similar, there is more inter-track mobility and, consequently, smaller differences among tracks in the odds of continuation to tertiary education. Allmendinger argues that the coupling between educational qualifications and occupational attainment is strongest in stratified and highly standardized systems. Where stratification is high, credentials provide detailed signals about the educational achievements of job applicants (i.e. not just 'high-school graduates' but 'graduated from a vocational institute of textiles'). Where they are standardized, employers can rely on credentials to represent skill content reliably. In systems with a low degree of standardization employment decisions are less likely to be based on education because credentials are more ambivalent signals. Breen, Hannan, and O'Leary (1995) have shown that in Ireland—a weakly stratified system—employers rely on success in school because this is tested according to nationally standardized procedures, and thus workers' credentials represent their respective rank in the job queue.

Credential Inflation

Where the job queue is at work, there is a built-in incentive for young people to acquire ever more education in order to stay ahead of the queue. It is argued that as ever larger proportions of the population obtain a credential, the labour-market value of credentials declines. In qualificational spaces, by contrast, the value of a credential does not consist (solely or primarily) in its scarcity and position in the hierarchy of credentials, but rather derives from the specific skills it represents. Furthermore, in such systems there are natural points of exit from the educational process which correspond to specific entry portals into the labour market. Thus, in qualificational spaces we can expect there to be less pressure to attain ever higher credentials. When comparing Switzerland and Germany, two typical qualificational spaces, with the USA and Japan, two organizational countries, we see that in the former only about 10–15 per cent attain tertiary degrees, as compared with over 30 per cent in the latter. Thus, organizational spaces tend to produce an excessive supply of secondary and post-secondary graduates, thereby lowering the value of these credentials in the labour market. By contrast, in occupational spaces, the value of credentials is preserved because it is mediated by *skill* rather than the relative ranking of workers in a more or less *unidimensional* queue.

Clearly, the labour-market prospects of individuals with particular qualifications do not only depend on the number of competitors, with similar or higher qualifications, but also on the market's demand of such qualifications. Furthermore—as argued above—the demand for qualifications may adjust to their availability on the market. Unfortunately, we do not know how to measure demand for the different qualifications in a manner that is truly independent of their supply. Therefore, we focus solely on the supply side, admittedly a gross simplification, and test the hypothesis that the value of qualifications in the occupational attainment process is related to its scarcity.

Arguments for National Similarities

The arguments cited so far, focus on how national differences in educational institutions and firms can produce differences in the relationship between qualifications and occupations. By contrast, the *neo-institutionalist* approach focuses on the diffusion of similarities. Proponents of this approach (see e.g. J. Meyer, Ramirez, and Soysal 1992) argue that the essential institutional aspects of educational systems are growing increasingly similar across countries. For example, as mass compulsory education becomes increasingly universal, and school systems adopt similar curricula (Benavot et al. 1991). Scholars working in this tradition believe that the shape and content of educational institutions are:

[c]losely linked to the rise of standardized models of society . . . and to the increasing dominance of standardized models of education as one component of these general models. These modern models of society and education and their interrelation, are similar around the world and generate educational systems and school curricula that are strikingly similar. (Benavot et al. 1991: 86)

Extrapolating from this logic, one would hypothesize that the role of educational qualifications in determining occupational attainment will tend to converge across countries, as the latter move towards common institutional models in the domains of education and work. This hypothesis contradicts the results of the studies discussed earlier, which show interesting national variations in the institutional arrangements of the link between education and labour-force outcomes. It also contradicts the substantial diversity of institutional frameworks reported by the chapters of this volume. Nevertheless, it remains an open empirical question as to whether national institutional differences affect the pattern and magnitude of education's role in occupational allocation or not.

Another perspective predicting convergence is the *industrialization hypothesis* (Treiman 1970). This approach is not sensitive to institutional contexts but, rather, is cast in terms of general societal development. As a result of the rationalization of production, international competition, and the operation of multinational companies, societies are said to converge to a common pattern of occupational stratification (Treiman 1970). More specifically, it is expected that occupational attainment will grow increasingly dependent on educational qualifications. In the effect of education on occupational prestige, Treiman and Yip (1989) find that the variation among countries is related to the level of industrialization. Contrary to the assumptions of enduring and consequential differences of educational institutions, the industrialization hypothesis anticipates a similar magnitude of association between education and labour-market outcomes among societies of comparable levels of industrialization.

Thus, the two approaches, while arguing from different theoretical perspectives, predict convergence between countries in the processes under study. This prediction can be taken as a convenient null hypothesis against which to test the arguments discussed and developed in the preceding sections of this chapter.

Summary and Hypotheses

In sum then, we distinguish between two ideal-type regimes of school-to-work transitions, which, following Maurice, Sellier, and Silvestre, we label *qualificational* and *organizational spaces*. The qualificational space is characterized by a high rate of *specific vocational education*. More precisely, a large proportion of the graduating cohorts leave the educational system with specific skills and occupational identities. This is in contrast with organizational spaces where education is predominantly *academic* or *general*, and where occupational skills are learnt on the job or in courses taken after leaving school. The educational systems in qualificational spaces tend to be stratified, maintaining a clear distinction between academic and vocational tracks. Organizational spaces, by contrast, can be stratified to varying degrees. Some, like the USA and Ireland, are relatively unstratified, while others, such as Italy and France, maintain distinct tracking at the secondary level but allow graduates of most tracks some form of matriculation diploma and some form of post-secondary education. Another axis along which school-to-work regimes are differentiated is the *standardization* of the school curricula and diploma throughout the national space. In some countries the educational systems are centralized and highly standardized, while in others there are substantial variations between regions and among and within the categories of private and state schools. In addition to these institutional characteristics, countries also differ in the sheer rate of tertiary education. Since, in some countries, the size of the tertiary educational sector depends on explicit state policies to expand or limit education, this variable may also be considered, at least in a wider sense, an aspect of the institutional arrangement of education.

We hypothesize that these variables affect the pattern and strength of the association between educational qualifications and occupational outcomes as follows:

Hypothesis 1: Across countries, the strength of the association between qualifications on the one hand, and occupational status and class position on the other, is positively related to the *standardization* of educational systems.

Hypothesis 2: Across countries, the strength of the association between qualifications on the one hand, and occupational status and class position on the other, is positively related to the *stratification* of the educational systems.

Hypothesis 3: Across countries, the strength of the association between qualifications on the one hand, and occupational status and class position on the other, is positively related to the *vocational specificity* of the educational systems.

Hypothesis 3a: In particular, where vocational specificity is high, vocational education enhances the odds of entering the labour force in a skilled blue-collar, rather than an unskilled, occupation.

Hypothesis 4: The effects of educational qualifications on occupational outcomes are inversely related to the proportions attaining tertiary qualifications.

The hypotheses concerning the effects of stratification and standardization of educational systems directly follow from the earlier discussion. In stratified educational systems students are sorted early on into different educational tracks which lead to distinct qualifications. In such systems, the differences among qualifications are clear and they are well recognized in the labour market. This should strengthen the role of qualifications in the occupational allocation process. Standardization enhances the comparability of qualifications in the national space and allows employers to rely on them with confidence when recruiting workers. This should appear as a stronger effect of qualifications on occupational outcomes.

With increasing vocational specificity the school-to-work regime adopts the characteristics of a qualificational space and the links between qualifications and occupational destinations should become stronger. Historically, and to the present day, vocational training has concentrated in preparation of skilled manual workers. Thus, vocational qualifications should particularly enhance the chances of access to skilled rather than unskilled manual jobs, especially where the degree of vocational specificity is high. Furthermore, vocational specificity is a particular aspect of stratification. Where the educational system offers very specific vocational curricula they do so in tracks which are distinct from those in which other curricula, academic or vocational, are taught. Therefore, vocational specificity, through its relationship with stratification, affects the association between education and occupational allocation throughout the occupational structure.

Finally, countries vary quite substantially in their rates of tertiary education. Excessive expansion of tertiary education should lower the labour-market value of post-secondary qualifications. It should also depress the occupational prospects of labour-market entrants with secondary or lower qualifications because they would be forced into competition with job candidates who are ahead in the job queue.

These hypotheses will be contrasted against the null hypotheses suggested by the neo-institutionalist and industrialization approaches which would expect to find basic similarities between industrialized countries in the shape and magnitude of the qualification/occupation association.

THE COUNTRIES

Our research design is similar to that employed by Shavit, Blossfeld, and colleagues (1993). We invited scholars from fifteen countries for which we knew appropriate data existed—and where we knew of scholars who could, and would, participate in a cooperative effort of this kind—to analyse the transition from education to first job in their country. Thirteen national case studies were completed and are presented in this volume. Thus, the countries do not constitute a representative sample of all possible institutional contexts of the school-to-work transition, but do exhibit substantial variation along the four institutional dimensions discussed earlier. Some are *qualificational spaces* (Germany, Switzerland, the Netherlands), others are *organizational spaces* (the USA, Australia, Britain, Ireland, and Japan), and yet others are mixed (France, Italy, Israel, Sweden, and Taiwan).

Each chapter includes a description of the institutional features of the educational system and the labour market, together with a report on the statistical analysis of survey data on the association between educational attainment and occupational outcomes.

In Table 1.1.a we classify the countries by the three institutional variables and by the rate of tertiary education among young cohorts. The classification draws on information provided in the individual country chapters, as well as on OECD data (OECD 1995*a*). Column (1) pertains to specific vocational education. A '2' identifies countries in which a large proportion (40 per cent or more) of birth cohorts is typically taught specific vocational skills while in formal education. A '0' identifies countries with very little instruction of specific vocational skills (about 0–15 per cent), and a '1' is assigned to intermediate countries. In column (2), we classify the countries by the degree of standardization of their educational system. The third column classifies the countries by the degree to which their secondary education is stratified.[5] Finally, column (4) reports the cohort proportions who obtain a post-secondary qualification.

TABLE 1.1.a. *Summary of national institutional contexts*

Countries	Vocational specificity of secondary education[a] (1)	National standardization of education[b] (2)	Stratification of secondary education[c] (3)	Per cent with post-secondary qualifications[d] (4)
1. Australia (AUS)	1	0	0	19.00
2. Britain (GB)	1	0	0	18.90
3. France (F)	1	1	1	17.20
4. Germany (D)	2	1	2	15.00
5. Ireland (IRL)	0	1	0	13.00
6. Israel (IL)	1	1	1	33.50
7. Italy (I)	1	1	1	9.00
8. Japan (J)	0	1	0	28.00
9. Netherlands (NL)	2	1	2	23.20
10. Sweden (S)	1	1	0	23.80
11. Switzerland (CH)	2	1	2	22.00
12. Taiwan (TAI)	1	1	1	29.50
13. United States (USA)	0	0	0	25.70

[a] A '2' indicates that some large proportion of secondary qualified workers enter the labour force with occupationally-specific skills. This code is assigned to countries with well-developed apprenticeship programmes and/or school-based training in detailed occupations (Germany, Switzerland, Netherlands). A '0' is assigned to countries in which very few students complete the formal educational system with specific vocational skills. These are countries where vocational programmes are either very small or in which the curriculum is predominantly of a general nature (Ireland, the USA, and Japan). In the remaining countries (France, Israel, Italy, Sweden, and Taiwan) large cohort proportions attend vocational tracks at the secondary level but the programmes are not very specific. For example, in the late 1980s in Israel, over 60 per cent of all twelfth graders in secondary vocational programmes were concentrated in 5 vocational subjects (CBS 1988: 626). Thus, vocational programmes are defined at a general rather than specific level. We also assign Australia and Britain to this category. In both countries, most vocational qualifications are now obtained in post-school apprenticeship and vocational courses rather than in schools. Their specificity is of an intermediate nature.

[b] A '1' in this column indicates that irrespective of the school or region in which they were awarded, qualifications tend to represent the same skill level throughout the national space. A '0' indicates that the qualifications attest to different skills in different school and/or regions. Britain is an ambiguous cases. On the one hand, general secondary qualifications (the CSE, GCSE) are highly standardized there. On the other hand, however, vocational and post-secondary qualifications are very diverse and unstandardized in Britain. We decide to assign Britain a '0' on standardization. In Switzerland, there are considerable differences between the cantons in curricula and the structure of the educational systems. However, the vocational training system has a high degree of standardization throughout the country and the maturity examinations follow national regulations. Furthermore, the Swiss chapter in the book employs data for German cantons where the educational system is more standardized than in the country as a whole.

Japan is assigned a '1' on standardization because although there are large differences between schools in requirements and prestige, the quality of teachers, curriculum, and school facilities are quite homogenous throughout the country.

 c Stratification of secondary education is coded as follows: a '0' represents prevalence of comprehensive schools which may or may not practise curricular and/or ability-based tracking. A '1' represents a prevalence of between-school tracking such that those on the academic route usually attend separate schools from those on the lower or vocational route. Finally, a '2' represents an extreme form of stratification with very early differentiation among a plurality of programmes. Japan's upper-secondary education is very stratified by 'school quality' but this dimension is orthogonal to our educational classification.

 d The data reported in this column are taken from the individual chapters. For nine of the thirteen countries (Australia, Britain, France, Ireland, Italy, Japan, the Netherlands, Sweden, and Switzerland) the proportions reported by the authors are similar to those reported independently by the OECD (OECD 1995b: 196–7, 1995a: 218–19).

For Israel, the high proportion (33.5 per cent) reported by Kraus, Shavit, and Yaish is lower than the Central Bureau of Statistics reported proportion of 25–44 year olds with 13+ years of schooling (Israel, Central Bureau of Statistics 1993: table 22.1). The latter is as high as 38 per cent but includes an unknown number of orthodox Jews who typically continue religious education, full or part-time, throughout their adult life and count it when asked to report on their educational attainment. We prefer the more conservative estimate reported in the volume's Israeli chapter.

The estimate provided by Arum and Hout is lower than that reported by OECD (1995b: 196) for the USA, 34.9 per cent. Part of the difference between the two estimates is due to the fact that some of the cohorts studied by Arum and Hout had not completed post-secondary education at the time of interview. Another probable reason for the difference is the more inclusive definition of post-secondary education employed by OECD. We prefer Arum and Hout's more conservative estimate of 25.7 per cent even though this attenuates the negative effect we find for Percent with Post-Secondary Education on the association between qualifications and occupational attainment. When we substitute the OECD value for the USA, the results were similar to those reported in Tables 1.3.b, 1.4.a, 1.4.b, and 1.5.a but the negative effects of percentage with post-secondary education were always larger.

The estimate provided in the chapter on Germany is about 15 per cent. This is much lower than the OECD estimates ranging between 22.4 and 26 per cent. The latter however, include post-secondary apprenticeship programmes which do not correspond to the definition of tertiary qualifications that we apply to other countries. We suspect that, for the same reason, the figure for Switzerland (22 per cent) is also too high. However, since it appears in both the Swiss chapter and the OECD publication we kept it. Any lower value would have accentuated the negative effect of this variable in the regression analyses which are presented below. Finally, the data for Taiwan were compared by Tsai to independent publications of the Taiwanese Ministry of Education (1995) and we trust that the two sources are consistent.

Table 1.1.b cross-tabulates the countries by standardization and stratification. The degree of vocational specificity of secondary education is marked by asterisks. Low specificity is indicated with no asterisk next to the country acronym. One or two asterisks indicate intermediate or high degrees. Assuming our hypotheses to be true—but neglecting the cohort proportions of tertiary qualifications—the table anticipates in which countries we should expect weak or strong effects of education on occupational outcomes. According to their level of standardization and stratification we should

TABLE 1.1.b. *Thirteen countries by level of standardization, stratification, and prevalence of specific vocational education*

Standardization	Stratification		
	Low	Medium	High
High	(1) IRL J S*	(2) F* I* IL* TAI*	(3) D** CH** NL**
Low	(4) AUS* GB* USA	(5)	(6)

Note: asterisks indicate the degree of occupational specificity of vocational education; two asterisks indicate a high level of occupational specificity; one asterisk indicates an intermediate level; no asterisks indicates low level.

expect the weakest effects in the countries in cell (4), the strongest effects in the countries in cell (3), and intermediate effects in the other countries—those in cell (1) should be closer to the bottom, and those in cell (2) closer to the top. The position of a country in the rank-order of effects of education on occupational outcomes should be additionally differentiated according to the number of asterisk assigned to a country.

DATA AND ANALYSIS

The country chapters employ recent, large, and nationally representative data-sets. Most chapters employ data on cohorts of recent entrants into the labour force, men and women in their twenties and thirties. The study captures the relationship of educational qualifications and labour-market outcomes at the point in life when individuals move from education to their first employment. The main reason for this focus is the assumption that at the entry point to working life the relationship between qualifications and work position can be grasped in its purest form. Occupational positions in later stages of the career will depend on many other factors which, if not properly controlled, may disturb the effects of education.[6]

The analysis pursued in the country chapters consists of a common core and freestyle components. The core includes regression analyses of occupational attainment at the first job held after the last qualification was obtained (or a proxy for such a job). In order to grasp occupational attainment in several facets, three kinds of analyses are performed:

- standard occupational attainment regression equations, where the dependent variable is the occupational prestige (or an equivalent scale);

- multinomial logit equations predicting the odds of entering the labour force in different occupational classes;
- multinomial logit equations estimating the odds of being employed, unemployed, or not in the labour force.

The major independent variable in all these regressions is the highest educational qualification obtained, coded in the CASMIN educational schema (described below). The effect of education on occupational attainment is contrasted to factors representing respondents' socio-economic origins. Thus, the regressions also include several variables such as parental education and father's occupational prestige when respondents were in their teens. These components of the analysis are reported separately for men and women.

The freestyle components vary greatly from chapter to chapter, and deal with essential features of the school-to-work transition not captured by the common framework. In this chapter, we focus on the common components of the analysis, referring the reader to the individual chapters for the details of the country-specific analysis. In deciding on the elements of the common core, we hoped to reach a high degree of comparability between the individual studies. In reality, this could not be fully achieved in all instances.

In three of the country chapters (Ireland, the Netherlands, and Sweden) the authors used a proxy measure for first job, and instead of measures for the first job they used measures for the current jobs of respondents early on in their careers. The Dutch study employs a sample of individuals in their first ten years of work life, the Swedish sample consists of individuals aged 25–34, and the Irish sample of individuals aged 24–35. In many cases this will indeed be the first job, and in other cases it will be a job very similar to it. The Swedish and Dutch chapters provide estimates for the potential distortions introduced by these proxy measures for first job which show that they are probably minor. In any case, they are very small when compared to the systematic variations among countries.

Differences also occur between the country studies regarding the control variables used in the analysis. The chapters on ethnically heterogenous countries (the USA, Israel, Australia, and Taiwan) include controls for race or ethnicity in order to purge the estimated effects of education from those which might be due to ethnic stratification. Differences among studies in the controls for social background do not substantially affect the estimated effects of education on first job because the effects of origins, net of education, are always very small or insignificant. Studies included other controls as well, such as age at entry into first job, demand for labour at the time, or ability. We inspected the data in detail and are convinced that none of these additional controls biases the estimated effects of qualifications on

occupational outcomes in the early career or on current labour-force participation and employment.[7]

There are also differences among studies in the measures of occupational
prestige or status. While most studies use the best available national prestige
scales, Switzerland and Sweden use Treiman's International Occupational
Prestige scale, and Australia, France, Taiwan, and the USA use scales of
socio-economic status. It is known that the major difference between scales
of prestige and of the socio-economic status of occupations concerns the values they assign to farmers. As a consequence the correlation between education and socio-economic status tends to be somewhat higher than the
correlation between education and occupational prestige. However, among
the cohorts studied in this book the proportion of respondents employed in
agriculture is very small, and it is unlikely that the different measures of
occupations produced significant differences in the effects of education.

Thus, while there are clear deviations from an ideal comparative design,
we are confident that they do not distort or bias the conclusions of the comparative analyses which we report in this chapter.

The Dependent Variables

In the interests of comparability, we adopt existing and well-known concep-
tualizations of our most important variables. As noted, occupation upon
labour-force entry is measured on occupational prestige scales, or their
equivalents, which are available for virtually all countries (see e.g. Treiman
1977). Each occupation is assigned a score which represents its social standing or prestige relative to other occupations.

In addition to occupational prestige scores, we measure occupation at
labour-force entry by coding it into the familiar EGP class schema (Erikson
and Goldthorpe 1992). Some of the contributors to the project employed the
seven-class version of EGP reproduced in Table 1.2.a, while others, using
smaller data sets, merged categories I and II, and IIIa and IIIb.

A third dependent variable is labour-force status, consisting of the three
categories—employed, unemployed, and out of the labour force—and measured at the time of interview, rather than retrospectively for the time of
labour-force entry.

The Independent Variable

Our definition of qualifications employs the CASMIN schema (Müller et al.
1989) and is based on two classification criteria: the hierarchical differentiation of general education; and the differentiation between 'general' and

'vocationally-oriented' education. We employ a seven-category version of the schema as shown in Table 1.2.b.

Several of the chapters (see e.g. the Dutch and Swiss contributions) compared the predictive efficiency of the CASMIN educational schema to a linear measure of number of school years completed and show a marked improvement in the fit associated with CASMIN.[8] There are two important

TABLE 1.2.a. *The EGP class schema*

Classes	Includes
I	Higher-grade professionals and administrators, and officials in the public sector
II	Lower-grade professionals, higher-grade technicians, lower-grade administrators and officials, managers in small firms and services and supervisors of while-collar workers
IIIa	Routine non-manual employees in administration and commerce
IIIb	Routine non-manual workers in services
IVabc	Small proprietors and artisans with or without employees, and self-employed farmers
V+VI	Skilled workers, lower-grade technicians, and supervisors of manual workers
VIIab	Unskilled workers including agricultural labourers

TABLE 1.2.b. *The CASMIN educational schema*

Qualification	Description
1ab	This is the social minimum of education. Namely, the minimal level that individuals are expected to have obtained in a society. It generally corresponds to the level of compulsory education
1c	Basic vocational training above and beyond compulsory schooling
2a	Advanced vocational training or secondary programmes in which general intermediate schooling is combined by vocational training
2b	Academic or general tracks at the secondary intermediate level
2c	Full maturity certificates (e.g. the *Abitur*, Matriculation, *Baccalauréat*, A-levels)
3a	Lower-level tertiary degrees, generally of shorter duration and with a vocational orientation (e.g. technical college diplomas, social worker or non-university teaching certificates)
3b	The completion of a traditional, academically-oriented university education

non-linearities in the school-to-work association. First, vocational qualifications have consistent effects, relative to non-vocational qualifications of similar levels, on entering the skilled blue-collar, rather than the unskilled
classes. Second, in many countries, higher education is valuable with respect
to entering Classes I + II, but is of less (in some cases, even negative) value
with regard to placement in other classes.

The CASMIN schema is also useful because, with some adaptations, it is
applicable to a wide variety of educational systems. And yet, when applying
the schema to concrete national contexts, some adaptations are necessary. In
many countries, for example, including Israel, the USA, Taiwan, Japan,
Ireland, and Sweden, category 1c either does not exist, or includes very few
individuals.[9] Finally, in Japan there is a small category of secondary school
graduates who attend post-secondary vocational courses. Ishida labels this
category 2d because it neither corresponds exactly to 2a nor to 3a. In order
to avoid confusion we have omitted this category in representations of Japan.

COMPARATIVE ANALYSIS

In this section we analyse the results of the common components of the thirteen country chapters. Some chapters do not include all parts of the analysis—for example, the Swedish chapter does not include analysis on
unemployment because the data-set used in Sweden does not distinguish
between unemployment and not in the labour force—and consequently, the
number of countries varies from one part of our analysis to another.

The comparative analysis does not purport to be exhaustive. The country
chapters are rich with statistical and contextual information and could feed
numerous comparative analysis on such topics as the role of education in
inter-generational mobility, gender differences therein, and in the school-to-
work transition generally, on the role of vocational education in occupational
placement, on ethnic and racial inequalities of educational and occupational
opportunity, and much more. But this chapter concentrates on evaluating
the plausibility of the hypotheses listed earlier. We analyse the relationship
between qualifications on the one hand, and occupational prestige of first job,
class of labour-force entry, and labour-force participation and unemployment on the other. In discussing the results comparatively, we concentrate
on both the major common threads which emerge from the data and on
striking national differences.[10]

Qualifications and Occupational Prestige

Figures 1.1.a and 1.1.b plot the effects of qualifications on standardized occupational scores for twelve countries.[11] For both men and women, the pattern of effects of educational qualifications on occupational prestige at first job is similar across countries. For both gender groups we see that in all countries, secondary qualifications provide access to more prestigious occupations than those at the elementary level. We should also note the familiar upward swing of the curves between secondary and tertiary qualifications (Featherman and Hauser 1978; Kraus and Hodge 1990). This reflects the fact that in all societies, the very prestigious occupations—the professions—are accessed through tertiary, and especially university, education.

Against the backdrop of this overall similarity in their pattern, there are interesting national variations in the magnitude of the effects of qualifications on occupational prestige. This is illustrated in Table 1.3.a which summarizes the difference in standardized prestige between the highest and lowest qualifications. The countries are sorted by the size of the average of the male and female entries. The table indicates that the effect of qualifications on occupational prestige is nearly twice as large in Germany and Switzerland as in Britain, Japan, and the USA. The other countries are located between these extremes. The Netherlands and Australia are close to the top and the remaining countries are within a small distance of one another.

Figure 1.1.c presents the education's effects found for men and women in Table 1.3.a in the form of a scatterplot. In most countries, the pattern of

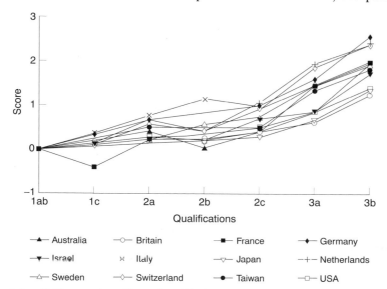

FIG. 1.1a. *OLS regression effects of qualifications on standardized occupation scores: men*

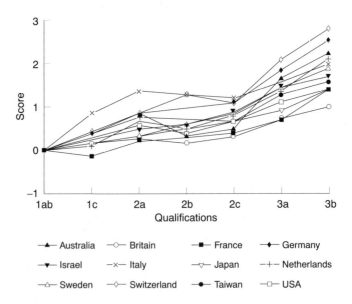

FIG. 1.1b. *OLS regression effects of qualifications on standardized occupation scores: women*

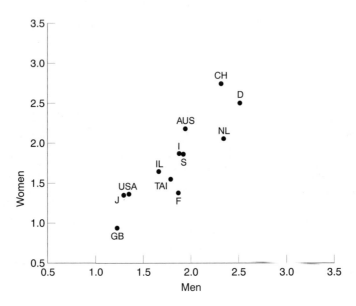

FIG. 1.1c. *Scatter plot of effects of education on standardized prestige scores for men and women*

TABLE 1.3.a. *Differences between highest and lowest qualifications in standardized occupations scores by gender*

Country	Women	Men	Average
Switzerland	2.76	2.33	2.55
Germany	2.51	2.53	2.52
Netherlands	2.07	2.35	2.15
Australia	2.21	1.96	2.08
Italy	1.88	1.89	1.89
Sweden	1.87	1.92	1.89
Israel	1.66	1.67	1.67
Taiwan	1.55	1.80	1.67
France	1.37	1.88	1.63
United States	1.37	1.35	1.36
Japan	1.36	1.30	1.34
Britain	0.97	1.21	1.13

effects of education on occupational prestige is similar for men and women, albeit weaker for women than for men. But the more important finding (reiterated in Figure 1.1.c) is the relative location of the various countries with regard to the magnitude of education's effects. The extreme position of Germany and Switzerland at the top of the list of countries, and the position of Britain, Japan, and the USA at the lower end are clear. This ranking at the extremes corresponds closely to the predictions we have derived from the institutional characteristics of the countries shown in Table 1.1.b. The location of the countries in the corners of the table corresponds to their location in the same corners of the scatterplot.

These country differences in the magnitude of the effect of qualifications on occupational prestige are due to differences among them in the societal-level variables. This is illustrated both in Appendix Figure 1.A and Table 1.3.b. In Figure 1.A, we group the countries by their values on three institutional variables, and compute the group mean effect of each qualification on standardized prestige. The figure shows that the mean effects are generally stronger where the educational systems are more stratified, standardized, and have a high degree of vocational specificity. The differences are most pronounced between countries of different degrees of vocational specificity.

Table 1.3.b reports the standardized effects of four societal-level variables on the magnitude of the effects of qualification on prestige.[12] The estimates are computed in linear regression models in which the dependent variables are the entries from Table 1.3.a for men and women. The independent variables are the four country characteristics shown in Table 1.1.b. In the first

Walter Müller and Yossi Shavit

four columns of the table we estimate simple regressions and find their effects to be similar for men and women. As hypothesized, the differences among the countries in the overall value of the effects of qualifications on occupational prestige at first job are positively related to the standardization, vocational specificity, and stratification of education, and, negatively, to the cohort proportions obtaining post-secondary qualifications. The effects of stratification and vocational specificity are stronger than those of the two other characteristics. However, since stratification and vocational specificity and standardization and stratification are highly correlated across countries, we also try to estimate three multiple regressions involving pairs of these three independent variables.[13] For both men and women the effects of stratification or vocational specificity are not affected when standardization is controlled for, but the effects of standardization, net of either of the two other characteristics are much reduced, and are even eliminated. The effects

TABLE 1.3.b. *The effects of university qualifications on prestige regressed on the institutional characteristics of countries, for men and women* (N = 12, t-statistics in parentheses, standardized coefficients)

Institutional variables	1	2	3	4	5	6	7
Men							
Stratification	0.82				0.28	0.82	
	(4.48)				(0.98)	(3.41)	
Standardization		0.49				0.00	0.19
		(1.77)				(0.02	(1.14)
% Post-secondary			−0.34				
			(1.15)				
Specificity of vocational education				0.87	0.64		0.80
				(5.67)	(2.23)		(4.91)
Adjusted R²	0.63	0.16	0.03	0.74	0.74	0.59	0.75
Women							
Stratification	0.66				0.14	0.72	
	(2.78)				(0.34)	(2.32)	
Standardization		0.32				−0.11	0.06
		(1.09)				(0.36)	(0.24)
% Post-secondary			−0.26				
			(0.85)				
Specificity of vocational education				0.73	0.61		0.71
				(3.38)	(1.46)		(2.90)
Adjusted R²	0.37	0.02	0.03	0.49	0.44	0.32	0.43

Note: Ireland has been excluded (see note 11).

of stratification also declines markedly when vocational specificity is controlled for, but the effect of vocational specificity is only slightly weakened by controls for stratification. We conclude tentatively, that the association between qualifications and occupations is stronger where educational systems offer a high level of vocational specificity, are stratified, and where the proportion attending tertiary education is low. The effect of stratification appears to be mediated by the prevalence of vocationally-specific training, and it seems questionable as to whether standardization has an effect which is independent of those of the other institutional characteristics considered.

Qualifications and Entry Class

In the country chapters, the relationship between qualifications and labour-force entry class is analysed as a multinomial logit which contrasts the log odds of entering the labour force in classes I, II, IIIa, IIIb, IV, and V + VI, with the odds of entering in the lowest class (i.e. VII). The independent variables in the model are educational qualifications controlling for various indicators of social origins, usually parental education and occupation. In this section, we focus on the effects of qualifications on selected class-of-entry contrasts. We ignore the analysis involving self-employment because in most cases, very few people enter the labour force directly into self-employment.

The Overall Effects of Education on Entry Class: Contrasting the Extreme Classes

Figures 1.2.a and 1.2.b represent the effects of the various qualifications at the extremes of the class structure. This was done by plotting their effects, relative to category 1ab, on the log-odds ratio of entering the labour force in Classes I + II, rather than Class VII.[14] The end-point of the curves on their right represent the effect of education on class placement measured at the extremes of the distribution of education. To facilitate visual inspection of the curves we separate them into two groups. Figure 1.2.a plots the eight countries for which the curves are more or less linear, while Figure 1.2.b includes five countries whose curves are less linear. Within each figure, the curves display substantial variation.

Beginning with the linear curves, the eight countries form two groups: Italy, Germany, Switzerland, and Taiwan; and the USA, Britain, Japan, and Sweden. The overall effect of education on the log-odds ratio of entering the service classes is about twice as large in the first group than in the second. A second important difference between the curves of the two groups is in the effects of lower-level vocational education on the log-odds ratio. In the top group, lower vocational education (1c and/or 2a) enhances the odds of

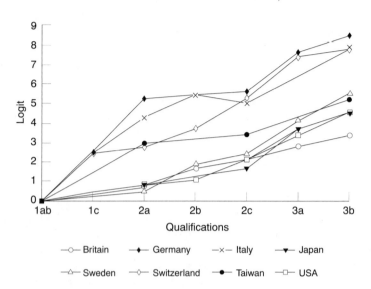

FIG. 1.2.a. *Logit effects contrasting entry Classes I + II (combined) and VII: men (linear curves)*

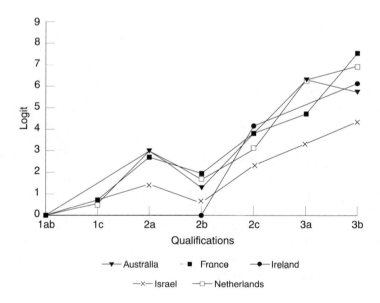

FIG. 1.2.b. *Logit effects contrasting entry Classes I + II (combined) and VII: men (non-linear curves)*

entering Classes I + II rather than the unskilled classes (VII). This is due, as we shall see later, to the benefit of these vocational qualifications for avoiding the unskilled class. The second group of countries (still in the 'linear' group) shares a very low effect of lower vocational education.

It is interesting to note that despite the large differences between the two groups in the effects of lower and secondary education, the slopes of the 2c–3b segments of the curves are generally similar. In other words, the effects of tertiary education on the log-odds ratio contrasting entry into the service classes and the unskilled classes, are more similar, in the two groups of countries, than the effects of elementary and secondary education. It would appear that the differences between the curves of the two groups are primarily due to the different role played by vocational secondary education in the occupational attainment processes. None of the countries in the second group has a sizeable apprenticeship or lower-level vocational programmes of the 1c type. Rather, vocational education in these countries is taught in separate programmes or tracks within schools.

We now turn to Figure 1.2.b and the five irregular curves. The Irish curve is irregular because Whelan and Breen merged qualifications 2a and 2b and imposed an equality constraint on the effects of qualifications 1ab and the combined 2ab. Substantively, this means that in Ireland, these lower qualifications have little value at this segment of the class-allocation process. Thus, Ireland is very similar to the lower group from Figure 1.2.a. In the other four countries, the odds ratio of entering the service, rather than the unskilled class, is higher for graduates of secondary vocational education (2a) than for those with only secondary academic education (2b). But once again, we find that in those three countries where the effects of 2a are largest (Australia, France, and the Netherlands), the overall effect of education is largest and is close to the magnitude of its effect in Germany, Switzerland, and Italy, the top group in the previous figure.

In sum, there are systematic national differences in the pattern and magnitude of the association between men's educational qualifications and their log odds of entering the class structure at the top rather than the bottom. The differences are related to differences among them in the role played by vocational secondary education in class allocation. In countries with a prevalence of specific vocational secondary education, the overall association tends to be stronger than in those with less specific vocational education. The marginal effects of post-secondary education (by which we mean, the difference between the effects of post-secondary and full secondary education) are less variable between countries despite differences among them in the structure of post-secondary educational institutions.

Figure 1.2.c plots the overall effect of qualifications on the log-odds ratio of placement at the extreme classes (I + II vs. VII) for men and women. The countries with relatively standardized, stratified, and vocationally-specific educational systems (Germany, Switzerland, and the Netherlands) tend to show high effects, and those with relatively unstratified and less standardized (Britain, the USA, and Japan) tend to appear at the bottom-left corner of the plot of the list. The intermediate countries, with regard to stratification, tend to occupy the central part of the figure. In Israel, a relatively standardized and stratified case, men's effects of qualification are lower than we would have expected, but women's effects are in the appropriate range. On the other hand, Ireland shows higher effects, especially for women, than we would have expected given the institutional characteristics of its educational system.

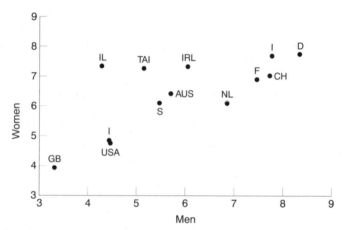

Fig. 1.2.c. *Scatter plot of overall effects of qualifications on the log odds contrasting entry Classes I + II and VII for men and women*

To formalize the analysis, we regress the two sets of effects on the institutional variables and present the results in Table 1.4.a. The results for men corroborate yet again the hypothesis that the magnitude of the association between qualifications and entry class is positively related to stratification, standardization, and the specificity of vocational education, and negatively to the percentage with post-secondary qualifications. As we have done in the analysis of occupational prestige, we also estimate three multiple regressions. Similar to the results of the analysis for prestige, controlling for standardization only slightly affects the estimates for the other institutional characteristics, but the 'net' effects of standardization are substantially reduced. From the equation including stratification and vocational specificity, we see that—contrary to the prestige analysis—stratification 'explains away' vocational specificity.

TABLE 1.4.a. *The effects of university qualifications on the log odds contrasting entry Classes I + II and VII, regressed on the institutional characteristics of countries, for men* (N = 13, t-statistic in parentheses, standardized coefficients)

Institutional variables	1	2	3	4	5	6	7
Stratification	0.71 (3.32)				0.75 (1.77)	0.60 (2.87)	
Standardization		0.51 (1.99)				0.20 (0.76)	0.38 (1.62)
% Post-secondary			−0.59 (2.45)				
Specificity of vocational education				0.59 (2.41)	−0.05 (0.12)		0.42 (2.05)
Adjusted R²	0.46	0.20	0.29	0.29	0.40	0.43	0.38

TABLE 1.4.b. *The effects of university qualifications on the log odds contrasting entry Classes I + II and IIIb, regressed on the institutional characteristics of countries, for women* (N = 13, t-statistic in parentheses, standardized coefficients)

Institutional variables	1	2	3	4	5	6	7
Stratification	0.61 (2.55)				0.28 (0.60)	0.59 (2.01)	
Standardization		0.35 (1.22)				0.03 (0.11)	0.19 (0.77)
% Post-secondary			−0.27 (0.93)				
Specificity of vocational education				0.63 (2.67)	0.39 (0.86)		0.58 (2.32)
Adjusted R²	0.32	0.04	0.00	0.34	0.30	0.25	0.31

Whereas for men, the unskilled blue-collar working class is a common destination for unqualified workers, for women it is usually the class of routine non-manual employees in services (IIIb). In Table 1.4.b we repeat the regression analysis but define the dependent variable as the effect of qualification 3b on the log odds contrasting Classes I + II with IIIb.[15] The results are quite similar to the male pattern seen earlier. The only difference is that the 'net' effect of vocational specificity is less affected by controlling for stratification.

In sum, national differences in the overall effects of educational qualifications on the log-odds ratios contrasting entry to the labour force in the top or bottom occupational classes, are systematically related to the four institutional variables under consideration. The effects tend to be larger in societies where the educational systems are stratified and standardized, and where there is a prevalence of specific vocational education. The effects of the prevalence of tertiary education are, as expected, negative. As in the analysis for the prestige outcomes, the effects of standardization appear to be smaller and more attenuated by controls than those of the other characteristics of the educational system.

Thresholds and Hierarchies

So far we have focused on societal differences in the *strength* of the association between educational qualifications and entry class. Another interesting aspect of the problem concerns the *shape* of the association. Most research on occupational attainment, especially some American, Dutch, and Israeli studies (see e.g. Blau and Duncan 1967; and Kraus and Hodge 1990) assume a *hierarchical* effect of education on occupational attainment. According to this model, any additional level of education enhances one's chances of getting ever better jobs in the job market. One cannot, according to this model, get *too much* education. In the context of a multinomial logit model of entry class, this hypothesis would imply that qualifications have positive effects on the log-odds ratios contrasting each entry class against a lower one. We illustrate this hypothesis with data for Germany and Sweden. Figure 1.3. plots the effects of qualifications on the logits contrasting entry Classes I, II, IIIa and IIIb against VII for men and women in the two countries. In both countries, and this is generally true in all others, the effects of education are stronger on contrasts involving the service and the unskilled classes and are weaker on the contrasts between the lower non-manual classes and VII.

Focusing first on the figure for Swedish men, the hierarchical hypothesis seems to be born out by the data: all four curves tend to rise more or less monotonously. The effect of qualifications is strongest on the logit of entering the class structure at the top, but also enhances the odds of entry in the lower non-manual classes. The hypothesis also applies to Swedish women, although university degrees (qualification 3b) do not enhance the odds of entering Class II above and beyond qualification 3a.[16]

The hypothesis does not apply to Germany where education has linear effects on the odds of entering the professional and managerial class (I), but displays a *threshold pattern* with respect to other class contrasts: the odds of entering an occupational class are greatly enhanced by having obtained the necessary qualification, but are not further improved by any additional

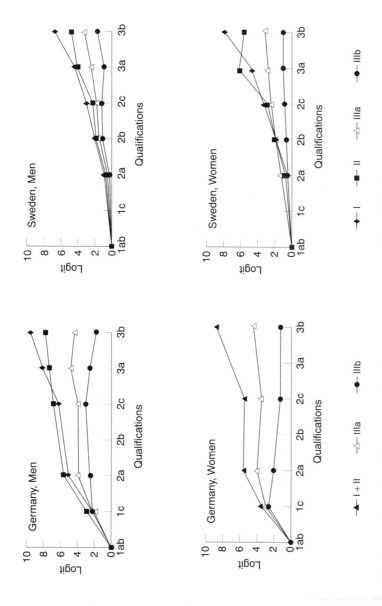

FIG. 1.3. *Logit effects of qualifications, contrasting various classes with Class VII, for men and women in two countries*

education. Entry into Class IIIa, for example, appears to be enhanced by qualifications 1c and 2a, whereas further education is of little additional value in this regard, and even has negative effects in some cases. The threshold pattern holds for both men and women in Germany.

These findings suggest the hypothesis that in countries with a low vocational specificity—as in Sweden—employers evaluate job applicants for general characteristics rather than for specific skills (Thurow 1976). The more education, the greater the attractiveness of the worker. By contrast, where specific skills are the norm—as in Germany—employers seek workers with precisely the appropriate training for the job, and do not value excessive qualifications.

A test of this hypothesis would have involved an inspection of, for example, Figure 1.3. for the remaining countries in the sample and an attempt to relate threshold and hierarchy patterns to vocational specificity. Unfortunately, we cannot test this hypothesis in data for other countries because the chapters for those with bona fide low vocational specificity (the USA, Ireland, and Japan) merged Classes I and II, and Classes IIIa and IIIb. In addition, Ireland and Japan are also countries for which several of the CASMIN educational categories are combined. Thus, rather than push the limits of the data, we opted to leave the true test of the hypothesis to future research.

The Effect of Vocational Education on Entering Skilled Blue-Collar Occupations

This part of the analysis focuses on the relationship between qualifications and the odds ratio of entering the labour force in a skilled or unskilled blue-collar occupation. It has only been carried out for men because in many countries, there are few women in the skilled and unskilled working classes, and the logits which contrast them often produce unstable estimates. We are concerned with three related questions: Does vocational education enhance the odds of employment in a skilled job? Do countries vary in the extent to which it does? Are national differences consistent with the institutional characteristics of their educational system?

For ease of visual inspection, we present the data for men in two figures. Figure 1.4.b includes countries where the effects are generally horizontal and Figure 1.4.a includes those with less regular patterns. We discuss the latter first. In all seven countries, vocational education at the secondary level enhances the odds of employment in skilled jobs relative to both the lowest educational category (1ab), and to general secondary qualifications (2b, 2c). Furthermore, in all cases except Switzerland, post-secondary, non-academic qualifications, which are often vocationally oriented, also have positive effects on the dependent logit. In Switzerland, qualification 3a prepares men for higher technical occupations and lower-grade professions. It should be noted that it enhances the odds of entering Classes I + II, but is not very relevant to entry into the skilled blue-collar class.[17] Thus, in the group of countries depicted in Figure 1.4.a we find a clear effect of—mainly vocationally oriented—qualifications for obtaining a skilled, rather than an unskilled, working-class job.

The German pattern deserves further comment. First, its effects are

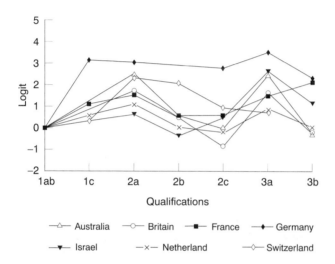

FIG. 1.4.a. *Logit effects contrasting entry Classes V + VI with VII: men (peaking curves)*

strongest. Specifically, there are marked differences between the least qualified and all other workers, because German workers with 1ab qualifications are effectively excluded from any skilled occupation. The curve shows that even qualification 2c enhances the odds of skilled employment. This reflects the fact that many people with 2c continue to obtain vocational qualifications which are not fully identified by the data.

In Figure 1.4.b the pattern is different: all effects are very weak, and the shape of the curves is generally horizontal although, in the USA and Sweden there are minor peaks associated with qualification 3a. Only in Italy, does any qualification above the social minimum, whether vocational or general, appear to help individuals avoid unskilled occupations.[18]

Summarizing these results, we can detect a correspondence between the availability of vocationally specific training in national educational systems

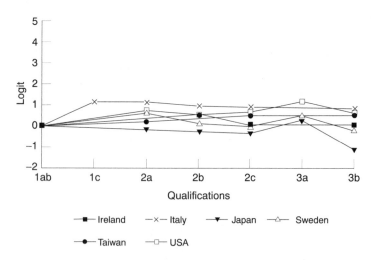

Fig. 1.4.b. *Logit effects contrasting entry Classes V + VI with VII: men (flat curves)*

and the impact of qualifications in allocating workers to skilled, rather than unskilled, positions. All seven countries in Figure 1.4.a, together with Italy (the exception in Figure 1.4.b) have substantial elements of vocationally-specific training (see Table 1.1.b). There are exceptions, however, and we would have expected stronger effects for Sweden and Taiwan given the nature of their vocational education.

In Table 1.5, we regress the effect of qualification 2a (vocational secondary) on the institutional characteristics of the educational system: stratification, standardization, percentage with post-secondary education, and the specificity of vocational education. The univariate equations indicate that in countries where education has a strong occupationally-specific component, vocational secondary education enhances the odds of obtaining a job in the skilled working class. In addition, the prevalence of tertiary education depresses these benefits. The gross effect of stratification is also substantial, however, when vocational specificity is controlled, it becomes negative due to multi-collinearity between these independent variables. The gross effect of standardization is zero and also becomes negative when other variables are controlled for. Thus, whereas the effects of percentage with post-secondary and vocational specificity appear consistent, those of standardization and stratification are unclear.

TABLE 1.5. *The effects of vocational secondary qualifications on the log odds contrasting entry Classes V + VI and VII, regressed on the institutional characteristics of countries for men* (N = 12, t-statistics in parentheses, standardized coefficients)

Institutional variables	1	2	3	4	5	6	7
Stratification	0.41 (1.43)				−0.47 (1.08)	0.83 (2.72)	
Standardization		−0.19 (0.62)				−0.69 (2.27)	−0.51 (2.39)
% Post-secondary			−0.61 (2.43)				
Specificity of vocational education				0.65 (2.73)	1.05 (2.39)		0.84 (3.96)
Adjusted R²	0.09	−0.06	0.31	0.40	0.38	0.35	0.57

Note: Ireland is excluded.

Qualifications, Labour-Force Participation, and Unemployment

So far, we have discussed the relationship between education and the occupational prestige and class position of respondents' first job. However, restricting the analysis to employment seriously limits the account on the returns to education. This is particularly true for societies with large-scale unemployment. Therefore, we now turn to a discussion of the consequences of education for labour-market participation and unemployment.[19] While we cannot enter into a detailed study of the intricate relationship between education on the one hand, and both unemployment and labour-force participation on the other, some basic findings are of interest.

The labour-force participation rates of men are very high in all the countries studied. The single most important reason for the non-participation of young men is educational attendance. It tends to be most prevalent among persons with a full secondary education (2c) who still move back and forth between work and tertiary education (not shown), less common among graduates of secondary vocational education, fewer of whom continue into further or higher education, and in all countries, women's labour-force participation is more optional in character than that of men (Gallie 1995; Lindbeck 1993). We assume that women's decision to participate involves weighing up the costs and benefits, and comparing expected employment income to the incurred costs of housekeeping. Education enhances women's participation rates because it enhances expected income from employment.

Figure 1.5.a plots the effect of each qualification, relative to the lowest, on women's log-odds ratio of being out of the labour force, rather than employed, at the time of interview. The original logit equations control for social origins and, often, for such other variables as age, region of residence, and ethnicity.[20] For all countries the lines in the figure generally decline from the lowest to the highest level of education, reflecting the tendency of educated women to participate in the labour force at higher rates than less educated ones. In some countries, however, notably France and Italy, the curves are not linear. In particular, secondary vocational qualifications (2a in France and 2a and 2b in Italy) enhance labour-force participation relative to both lower (1a and 1b) and higher qualifications (2c). But beside these exceptions, participation rates increase with the level of education.

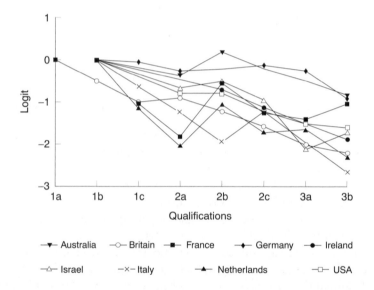

FIG. 1.5.a. *Logit effects of qualifications on labour-force participation: women*

Figure 1.5.b and Figure 1.5.c plot the logit effects of qualifications on men's and women's odds of unemployment. The most general finding is that in all countries represented in these figures, and for both sexes, education tends to reduce the risk of unemployment, and tertiary education is associated with much lower odds of unemployment than the very lowest qualifications. However, as before, the effects of education are not always linear. In several countries the risk of unemployment is lower for those with vocational qualifications than among those with general education of comparable or even higher levels. Among men, the advantages of vocational qualifica-

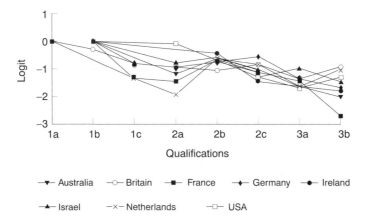

FIG. 1.5.b. *Logit effects of qualifications on unemployment: men*

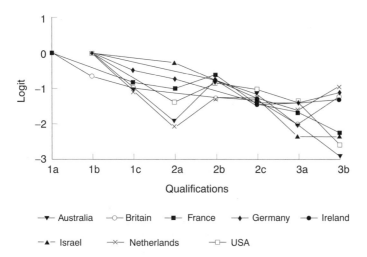

FIG. 1.5.c. *Logit effects of qualifications on unemployment: women*

tions appear in all countries with high or intermediate levels of specific vocational secondary education: Australia, Britain, France, Germany, the Netherlands, and Israel. Thus, although academic tracks are more demanding than the vocational programmes, they are associated with higher risks of unemployment. In the USA and Ireland, the two countries in our set of nations with a predominantly academic orientation at the secondary level, general secondary qualifications should not constitute a handicap relative to vocational qualifications. We suspect that employers in these two countries do not expect job applicants to come with ready-made skills. Rather, they are evaluated on the basis of their relative success in a one-dimensional educational hierarchy. A complete secondary education (2c) is considered a valuable credential even without tertiary qualifications. The findings for Ireland and the USA are consistent with these expectations: the effects of secondary education, on the log-odds ratio of unemployment, are more linear than in the other six countries.

For women the effects are, in general, similar to those of men, although they tend to be more linear. In particular, in fewer countries (Australia, the Netherlands, and—in contrast to men—the USA)[21] vocational qualifications reduce women's odds of unemployment relative to general qualifications of similar levels. Thus, women with general qualifications appear to be in a better competitive position relative to those with vocational qualifications in female labour markets.[22]

CONCLUSION

The single most important conclusion of this study is that the effects of education in the occupational attainment process, and its impact on employment chances in the labour force, are indeed systematically conditioned by the respective institutional contexts. Both the magnitude and the shape of the effects vary between countries and this variation is due, to a large extent, to differences in the social organization of education. In this section we summarize our findings by relating them to the main hypotheses of the study. We then highlight several implications of the results, and conclude by suggesting directions for further comparative research on the institutional context of the stratification process.

The *null hypothesis*, which derives from both the neo-institutionalist and industrialization perspectives,[23] suggested little difference between industrialized countries in the magnitude and patterns of association between educational qualifications and labour-force outcomes. The data reveal commonalities but also interesting variations. The commonalities are:

- For both men and women educational qualifications enhance the attainment of prestigious occupations.
- The marginal returns to education at the tertiary level are higher than returns at the lower levels of education.
- Educational qualifications are important determinants of whether one enters the service class or the unskilled working classes, but much less decisive for placement among the intermediate classes.

- In most countries, the odds of becoming a skilled rather than an unskilled worker are determined by whether one has a *vocational* qualification, rather than by the *level* of qualification.
- In all countries the odds of labour-force participation are related to educational attainment, more so for women than for men.
- In all countries, and for both men and women, the risks of unemployment are attenuated by education, especially by tertiary qualifications.

The most *striking differences* between countries are the following:

- The *magnitude* of the effects of qualifications on occupational outcomes vary greatly. When summarizing the prestige regressions we have seen that although the pattern of effects are similar for most countries, in Germany, the Netherlands, and Switzerland the overall effect is twice as large as in Britain, Japan, or the USA. National differences in the effects of qualifications on entry class are even more striking. For example, in Germany, Switzerland, and Italy, university graduates are about 2,000 times as likely as the least qualified, to enter the service class rather than the unskilled working class. In the USA and Israel the comparable odds ratio (for men) is less than 90, and in Britain it is less than 30.
- In some countries, vocational education enhances the odds of becoming a skilled, rather than an unskilled worker, while in others it is of little value when compared to academic education. For example in Germany, Switzerland, Israel, or Australia the odds of becoming a skilled rather than an unskilled worker are ten to thirty times greater for workers with vocational qualifications (2a or 3a) than for those with only general ones. By contrast, in Britain, Sweden, and Ireland the ratio is only two to four times greater.

Thus, we find considerable similarity alongside considerable variation between countries in the pattern of association between education and labour-force outcomes. Does this confirm or challenge the null hypothesis? The similarities mainly relate to the fact that education affects occupational allocation, and is particularly crucial for access to the professions and other service-class jobs. The differences relate to substantial variation in the *magnitude* and to the *shape* of education's effects. The latter is certainly the more relevant aspect of the issue and constitutes a serious challenge to the hypothesis of basic similarities.

The null hypothesis is challenged not just by the substantial variation in pattern and magnitude, which we found, but also by their systematic relationship with the institutional characteristics, as hypothesized.

Stratification, standardization, the occupational specificity of vocational education, and the relative size of the tertiary educational sector—taken as institutional characteristics of educational systems—are clearly related to the extent to which educational qualifications affect all but one of the occupational outcomes in the set of nations included in this study. The exception is that standardization does not affect the association between qualifications and the odds of entering the skilled working class.

The institutional variables also have substantial 'net' effects in most analyses except the following: the effect of standardization vanishes if either stratification or vocational specificity is controlled, and, in the analysis of access to the skilled working class it even becomes negative. In that analysis vocational specificity is dominant, and net of its effect, the effect of stratification is negative, due to the high multi-collinearities among these variables. Another exception is that for men, the net effect of vocational specificity vanishes (when stratification is controlled) in the contrast between the service class and the unskilled working class. This is surprising, since the case by case analysis reveals that it is intermediate vocational qualifications that play a major role in producing variation across countries. This apparent inconsistency could also be due to the large multi-collinearity among the institutional variables. The data are, however, also consistent with the following substantive interpretation: vocational specificity directly conditions the effect of vocational qualifications on the odds of entering the skilled, rather than the unskilled, working class, but its effect on the odds of entering the upper non-manual classes is indirect, via the stratification of the system.[24]

These findings beg a discerning evaluation of the hypotheses which have guided this comparative analysis. *Hypothesis 1* stated that the strength of association between qualifications, on the one hand, and occupational status and class position, on the other, is positively related to the standardization of the educational system. There is only limited and uncertain support for this hypothesis, since in none of our regressions do we find a positive effect for standardization when either of the other institutional characteristics is controlled. It is more likely that the positive bivariate effects found for standardization are spurious. Indeed, among the countries included in our study, most of those with a highly standardized educational system also have educational systems with an intermediate or high level of stratification and vocational specificity.

One possible reason for the weak effects of standardization may simply be due to the fact that we have only three countries with a low value on this variable. It may also be because, in several countries where the educational systems exhibit standardized curricular requirements, teaching standards, and examinations, there are still large, often informal, variations among various segments of the system. For example, in Japan, the system is nominally centralized and highly standardized but there are differences in implementation between private and public schools. In Israel, despite the highly centralized control of the educational system, there are large differences between Arab, Jewish, religious and secular schools in curricula, teaching practices, and accreditation procedures. Similarly, in Italy, regional differences may render the system less standardized than its centralized control intended it to be. It would appear then, that different educational systems introduce diversity through different backdoors, and that the concept of standardization is less useful than was initially imagined.

Hypothesis 2, relating to the stratification of educational systems, is clearly corroborated when we consider the full range of occupational outcomes. That is, when we study how education affects the placement of individuals on the differentiated ladder of occupational prestige, or how it influences the chances of access to the most advantageous, as opposed to the most disadvantaged class positions. Even net of other institutional characteristics, stratification enhances the magnitude of education's effects on both prestige of first job and entry into the service class. However, when it comes to the relevance of education for obtaining a skilled, rather than an unskilled, working-class position, the crucial factor appears to be the extent of vocational specificity of the educational system. The effects of standardization and stratification are less clear here.

According to *hypothesis 3*, vocational specificity strengthens the association between qualifications and labour-market outcomes, and, in particular, where vocational specificity is high, vocational education enhances the odds of entering the labour force in a skilled blue-collar occupation rather than an unskilled one. The results are consistent with these expectations. The effects of vocational specificity are strong for all outcomes and, in general, the net effects are less reduced by controls than those of any other characteristics. In most of the countries compared in Figures 1.4.a and 1.4.b, vocational qualifications do indeed improve the odds of employment in a skilled, rather than unskilled, working-class job, and, in Table 1.5 we find, that the extent to which this is the case depends systematically on the occupational specificity of vocational education. We also find that in countries, that do not have well-developed institutions of specific vocational training, not only do vocational qualifications matter less (which is not surprising), but also there is no educational alternative that clearly enhances access to a skilled, rather than an unskilled, working-class position. It is only in the countries with distinct vocational qualifications at the secondary level (see Figure 1.4.b) that some other qualifications (often of a tertiary kind) also enhance the chances of obtaining a skilled worker's job. The two sets of countries thus appear to differ in a more general way. In the countries lacking institutions of specific vocational training, the skilled and unskilled working classes are generally much less distinct by education than those with a marked vocational component in their educational systems.

Hypothesis 4 assumes that the effects of educational qualifications on occupational outcomes are inversely related to the cohort proportions attaining post-secondary qualifications. The hypothesis is confirmed in all univariate equations in which it was tested. The larger the national proportion with tertiary education, the weaker the effects of qualifications on occupational prestige, on the log odds of entering the service class, and the weaker the effects of vocational education on the odds of entering the skilled working class. Thus, educational qualifications would seem to play a less important role in labour allocation in countries with a large sector of tertiary education.

In addition to these generally positive conclusions with regard to our institutional hypotheses, the results suggest some additional insights. First, in our set of countries, stratification and vocational specificity are highly correlated. When school systems offer specific programmes, they tend to group students in distinct tracks. The more specific the training, the earlier the differentiation into track, and the higher the barriers to inter-track mobility. The literature on tracking has shown that stratification weakens equality of educational and occupational opportunity because, typically, lower-class students are placed in lower tracks which in turn deliver them to the least privileged classes (see e.g. Shavit 1990*b*). However, our findings suggest that stratification can also perform a positive role: when stratified systems provide occupationally specific vocational training, the credentials it confers are valuable and can enhance the occupational opportunities of students, in particular, by reducing the risk of dropping to the unskilled working class. In such systems, moreover, very few people tend to remain without a marketable qualification. Another aspect of the matter, however, is that in these cases—as, for example, in Germany—the group that remains without qualifications, although small, is likely to be concentrated in the unskilled working class and to encounter strong barriers to occupational advancement.

Second, in addition to the effects of vocational specificity on access to the skilled blue-collar jobs, it plays an important role for entry to the service class. We have seen that national differences in the effects of education on access to the service class is mainly due to differences among them in the structure of secondary education. Most of the countries with strong effects of education on access to the service class also have differentiated systems of secondary education. In most of these cases secondary *vocational* qualifications improve the odds of entry into the service class. Most of the other countries (notably Britain, Japan, Sweden, Britain and the USA) have less differentiated systems of secondary education which do little to enhance the odds of entering a service-class job.[25]

Third, in our set of nations, three represent the highest level of occupational specificity of vocational education: Germany, the Netherlands, and Switzerland. All three are marked by very large proportions of students who obtain vocationally oriented qualifications at the secondary level. In all three countries training is offered in hundreds of specific occupations. There is, however, a difference among them: in Germany and Switzerland, training is mainly organized according to the dual system of apprenticeships, whereas in the Netherlands most of the training takes place in schools, and apprenticeships are less common. Upon closer inspection of the data we find that in the Netherlands elementary or secondary vocational qualifications (1c and 2a) enhance the odds of obtaining a skilled rather than an unskilled, working-class job much less than in Germany and Switzerland. This is mainly due to the fact that in the Netherlands even workers with only the social minimum of education (1ab qualifications) have relatively good chances of obtaining skilled jobs. The finding is crucial, since it could imply that it is not the occupational specialization of the training that produces strong effects of vocational education, but the specific institutional *form* of the apprenticeship system in Germany and Switzerland (and in Austria, as known from other studies; see e.g. Haller et al. 1985). The Dutch case thus begs further scrutiny: what then, are the institutional or other mechanisms operating in the Netherlands that limit the competitive advantage of vocationally qualified workers over those with no qualifications?

Fourth, the analyses of occupational prestige and of class outcomes produce broadly similar results concerning the relative effects of the educational categories in the countries studied. They also show similar patterns with regard to the effects of the institutional variables. And yet, the analysis of class as an outcome enabled us to reveal interesting non-linearities in the effects of education on occupational outcomes. As noted, vocational education plays an interesting and non-linear role in the occupational attainment process. When a linear model is applied, one cannot detect the advantages associated with vocational education, and is tempted to conclude that this is simply another form of low educational attainment. Education matters differently for different outcomes, and different types of education are relevant for different kinds of outcomes in the class structure. Furthermore, we have suggested that in some countries, qualifications exert a threshold pattern of effects on occupational outcomes. Namely, in some countries, tertiary education does not enhance the odds of placement among the intermediate classes. This is in contrast to countries where 'the more the better' principle applies.

Which Way to Work?

We have pursued the comparative study of the relevance of education for first jobs both from a case-oriented and a variable-oriented perspective. In doing so, we have attempted to be sensitive to national context and yet to analyse a large number of countries. Thirteen countries represent perhaps the limit of what can be achieved in such an endeavour. And this was only possible because a network of colleagues and friends were willing to cooperate and to adopt common standards of analysis. Such a study cannot replace a project in which an even higher comparative standard can be achieved through the integrated analysis of individual data from several countries, but such studies have to be limited to a smaller number. For our own part, using a larger set of countries, we were able to draw a crude map whose contours are the institutional dimensions we have discussed. We were also able to place the various groups of countries in distinct regions of the map. Such a map should prove useful for future students who might want to add to it additional countries, and enable researchers to gain perspective when focusing on a limited number of cases, or even a single case. One can argue, for example, that Ishida's (1993) finding that Japan, the USA, and Britain display similar patterns of association between education and occupation is better understood in the light of the fact that the three countries occupy a similar location on such a map.

Such an approach has, needless to say, certain limitations. While focusing on the institutional characteristics of educational systems, we ignored many other factors of potential relevance, notably those related to employers, the workplace, and professional and other work organizations and their role in shaping the effects of education on the early work life of individuals. It is to be hoped that future research should answer the challenge thrown down by Kerckhoff (1995), and Hannan, Raffe, and Smyth (1996), and extend analysis in that direction.

Some of the chapters in the volume consider the roles of additional institutional characteristics of both schools and the workplace in their countries. For example, the Japanese chapters discuss the role of social networks among alumni as instruments in job search and placement, and the role of schools in selecting workers for firms. The Israeli contribution refers to the role of vocational training in the course of military service. The French chapter is rich with information on the legal educational requirements of occupations, on national employment policies, and on the institution of *cadres*—a select stratum of professionals and administrators—within French firms. Our attempt at a comparative analysis could not take these diverse institutional factors into account. We refer the reader to the, often fascinating, discussions in the country chapters of the volume.

Another serious limitation of our study derives from choosing first job as the point in career for which we study occupational outcomes of education. It is notoriously difficult to measure the first job in a comparable way. Countries differ in the prevalence of moves between education and employment in the early work life, and in the extent to which the first job sets the

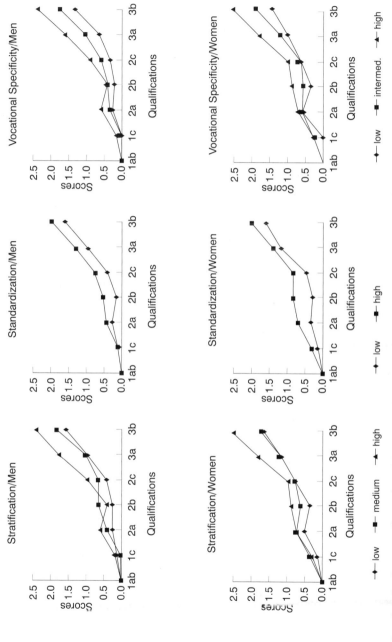

Fɪɢ. 1.A.1. *Average effects of qualifications on standardized prestige in groups of countries with varying levels of stratification, stan-dardization, and vocational specificity*

course for later occupational attainment (Erikson and Goldthorpe 1992). In addition, education probably has different effects on occupational outcomes in later stages of the career. Thus, we consider that this project is but a beginning towards a better understanding of how processes of stratification are embedded within particular institutional contexts.

NOTES

For their critical discussion and stimulating suggestions regarding the comparative analysis, we would like to thank Michael Hout, Hiroshi Ishida, Frank Jones, Robert D. Mare, Maurizio Pisati and the fellows of the 1996/1997 NIAS Nucleus, Stratification in Eastern and Western Europe in the 1990s, including Tom DiPrete, Robert Erikson, Harry Ganzeboom, Ruud Luijkx, Don Treiman, and Wout Ultee, as well as the members of the Tel Aviv Workshop on Social Stratification, especially, Haya Stier, Noah Lewin-Epstein, and Moshe Semyonov. We would also like to thank Peter Ucen and Karin Westerbeek for research assistance. Finally, we are grateful to Clare Tame for the excellent work done in editing the numerous versions of this chapter.

1. Ishida (1993) finds that the statistical association between occupation and education is not higher in Japan than in the USA and Britain, suggesting that different institutional mechanisms produce a similar stratification process.
2. This difference is also reported by other comparisons of Germany and France (Haller et al. 1985; König and Müller 1986). The institutional perspective is related to labour-market segmentation theory. It sensitizes us to the existence of two types of segmentation—organizational and occupational—and to their differential consequences for the association between education and occupational outcomes. Similar ideas have been proposed by Marsden (1990), and by Carroll and Mayer (1986). Soskice (1993b: 4) shows how the roles played by different systems of vocational training are associated with different modes of economic organization.
3. Human-capital theory (Mincer 1974) employs the term 'specific skills' to refer to firm-specificity. Namely, skills which are only relevant within a specific firm. We use the term to indicate occupational specificity.
4. More precisely, where the occupationally-specific component of training is large, we would expect workers to be found in the occupations for which they have been trained. The occupations which comprise the skilled working-class category (see the discussion on the class schema) are predominantly those kinds of occupations for which training is offered in vocational programmes. By contrast, the occupations grouped under the unskilled working-class category are those for which training is not necessary and, consequently, does not exist in most vocational education systems. Thus, when aggregating occupations into classes of skilled and unskilled occupations, the expectation as formulated here holds true
5. See the footnotes to the table for details on how countries were assigned to the various categories of vocational specificity, standardization, and stratification.

6. The way in which different education in different countries affects career progression would be an interesting subject for future research.
7. More specifically, the additional controls are as follows. The French chapter controls for year of entry to first job, but this variable has a rather weak effect. The chapter on Switzerland controls for demand for labour at year of entry, a variable which is only very weakly correlated with education. In neither case would these controls largely affect the estimates for the net effect of education. The chapter on Britain controls—in the linear regressions only—for school type and ability. In the models which we use for the comparative purposes (Model 4 of Tables 3.8 and 3.9 in the chapter on Britain) these variables have only weak direct effects on occupational prestige of first job. Therefore their possible attenuation of the net effect of education can again be only very small. Three chapters (Israel, Italy, and Taiwan) control for age at entry to first job. Age at entry to first job may be correlated with the level of education and therefore attenuate the effect estimated for education. In Taiwan the effect estimated for age is very small and statistically insignificant. It will therefore scarcely affect the estimate for education. The Israeli chapter includes both age and year of labour-force entry, two variables which are positively correlated with one another. The effect of age is positive while the effect of year is negative. When both variables are excluded from the analysis, the effects of education on the occupational prestige of first job and on the log-odds of entry class change very little. A similar phenomenon holds for Italy as well.
8. For more details on the CASMIN educational classification and its advantages relative to years of schooling, see Braun and Müller (1997).
9. Additional adaptations are the following: in Taiwan, there is no distinction between general (2b) and full (2c) secondary education, and both are coded 2c. In Germany, category 2b is virtually empty and is collapsed with 2a. The CASMIN classification fits Japan least well: the major form of stratification is between schools, rather than between academic and vocational programmes, and the CASMIN schema is not suited to capture this form of differentiation; there is very little vocational secondary education; and, as in Taiwan, the distinction between 2b and 2c does not apply. Furthermore, there is an ambiguity with regard to the classification of vocational education. Ishida does not use a 2a category because the completion of vocational high school offers a high-school certificate, a matriculation certificate, and some of the respondents were not asked the question on high-school type which is necessary to identify those who had attended vocational high schools. Ishida distinguishes between respondents who completed secondary education without any additional education (2c), and those who completed secondary education but continued on to non-university post-secondary education (2d). Category 2d refers to a lower level of post-secondary education which includes · technical training, whereas 3a refers to post-secondary, two-year junior colleges. In presenting the results of the Japanese case, we ignore category 2d as it does not correspond to any of our educational categories. Its effects, however on prestige and on the log-odds of entering Classes I + II and V + VI relative to Class VII (see the respective tables in the chapter by Ishida) are very similar to the effects of Ishida's 3a category. The Italian contributors to the project, Schizzerotto and Cobalti, assigned category 2b to *istituti tecnici*, a higher level of vocational secondary education than the

istituti professionali which are assigned to 2a. In Italy, therefore, category 2b refers to secondary vocational qualifications, in the same way as 2a, and not to general qualifications, as in other countries. Finally, in France, a large proportion (about 20 per cent in the most recent cohorts) do not complete compulsory education (1a), and an additional 5–10 per cent that do, but do not continue further in education (1b). The two categories often have distinct effects on occupational outcomes in France. Thus, rather than merge them into a single category (1ab) we prefer to define 1a (*Certificat d'études primaires*, now abolished or no diploma) as the social minimum of education in France, and recode 1b (*Brevet d'études du Premier Cycle* or *Brevet Elémentaire*) to 2b. The application of the CASMIN schema to the educational categories of the other countries is straightforward and is discussed in detail in the respective chapters.

10. In their chapter on Israel, Kraus, Shavit, and Yaish analyse data separately for Jewish men and women and for Arab men. The patterns of association between qualifications and occupational outcomes are very different for the three groups. Part of the difference is due to the interaction between ethnic discrimination and ethnic enclaves in the Israeli labour market. In the present analysis we only include data for Jews because we are not able to do justice to the important, but complex, issue of ethnic stratification in labour markets.

11. The means and standard deviations of prestige scales vary between countries. To adjust for these variations, we standardized all scales by dividing the coefficients by the national standard deviation of prestige. The figures plot the differences between the standardized coefficients of the various qualifications relative to qualification 1ab. Ireland is excluded from the comparative analysis because the Irish chapter does not include a separate analysis of occupational prestige for men and women.

12. The correlations between the four societal variables (n = 13) are:

	% with Post-Secondary Qualifications	Standardization	Stratification
Standardization	0.02	—	—
Stratification	−0.06	0.52	—
Vocational Specificity	−0.11	0.27	0.85

When computed for the set of twelve countries for which we estimate Table 1.3.b, the correlations are similar.

13. We dare not attempt three-variable regressions with the twelve cases at our disposal.

14. For nine countries, the chapters either included estimates for models which contrast the combined entry Class I + II with Class VII or such models were provided to us directly by the authors. However, for four countries we only had access to estimates from models in which Classes I and II were kept distinct. In such cases, the data shown in the figures are weighted means of the separate coefficients. The means are weighted by the relative sizes of the two classes.

15. For the four countries, in which Classes IIIa and IIIb were merged, the dependent variable is the logit contrasting I + II and IIIab. In unreported analysis in which we regressed, for women, the effects of qualifications on the same class contrast as for men (i.e. I + II/VII), we found that the gross effects were very

similar to those of men, but that about half of the net effects were either close to zero or negative.

16. One possible reason for this could be that in Sweden too there are specific matches between particular qualifications and particular occupational positions. A large proportion of Class II positions for women in the Swedish labour market are employed as nurses and kindergarten and primary school teachers. These jobs require a 3a qualification and nothing else. Additional qualifications do not improve the chances of access to these jobs.

17. The effect of qualification 3b on the log-odds ratio cannot be reliably estimated for Switzerland.

18. In the chapter on Ireland, Breen and Whelan find a remarkably strong effect of apprenticeships on the odds of becoming a skilled rather than an unskilled worker. However, apprenticeships are not common in Ireland and very few young people obtain them.

19. Several countries have been excluded from this analysis for various reasons. In Sweden, the database used does not include information on unemployment. In Italy, the coefficient estimates are generally insignificant and erratic, indicating instability. In Taiwan there are also very few unemployed cases in the sample.

20. Whereas, occupation and class of first job were measured in a uniform manner across countries, there are large differences among them in the age to which the measure of labour-force participation and unemployment pertain. In some cases (e.g. Britain, the USA, Ireland, France) these two variables were measured for very early stages of the career (typically for the twenties or early thirties), whereas in others (e.g. Germany, Israel, Italy) they were measured for later in the life course (typically the thirties and forties). Thus, we should expect to find considerable noise and random variation between countries in the relationship between qualifications and labour-force participation and unemployment, and we consequently should not over-interpret differences between countries.

21. In their chapter on the USA, Arum and Hout show that this is particularly due to the relatively good stake that women with vocational training in business and commerce have in the competition for service class and routine non-manual jobs.

22. We assume that education is an asset in the competition for jobs, and that it therefore reduces the risks of (involuntary) unemployment. However, the relationship between education and employment also involves considerations regarding 'reservation wages' (Lindbeck 1993): some people, especially among the more educated, may prefer unemployment rather than accept inadequate jobs, also because accepting a low-paying job may damage their prospects of obtaining better jobs in the future. The 'reservation wage' argument has two implications for the evaluation of our findings. First, we suspect that the negative effect of higher education on the involuntary component of unemployment is even larger than that seen in the data because voluntary unemployment is more common among the highly educated. Second, some of the apparent advantage of vocational relative to academic education may reflect reservation wage considerations among the latter. Namely, those with academic qualifications may be more likely to wait for the right job than vocational graduates.

23. We should add that the analysis in this chapter is not primarily designed to test the industrialization hypothesis for the simple reason that most of the countries included in the volume have all attained a high level of industrialization. What

we can show, however, is that in this set of highly industrialized countries, some differ quite substantially with respect to the association between education and labour-market outcomes. Furthermore, the systematic relationship of the strength of the association with the institutional characteristics does not disappear if we control—insofar as this is possible—industrialization level in our analyses. In analyses not reported here, we have added a measure of industrialization level (in the manner proposed by Erikson and Goldthorpe 1992: 383–4) to the regression equations reported in Tables 1.3–1.5. The results remain essentially unchanged.

24. The conclusions about the relative explanatory power of stratification and vocational specificity are indeterminate because of the multi-collinearity between them. In unreported analyses we estimated the regressions with two alternative definitions of the stratification and vocational specificity variables. First, we constructed an additive index of the two. The estimated effect of the index was slightly higher than the separate effects of its two components, but the effects of the other variable in the equations (standardization) did not change substantially. As a second alternative we created a dummy variable indicating those countries in which the value for vocational specificity differs from the value for stratification. This applies to Australia, Great Britain, and Sweden, which are low in stratification, but intermediate in vocational specificity. Comparing these countries to those which are low in both stratification and vocational specificity (Ireland, Japan, and the USA), we find systematically stronger effects of education in the former concerning two occupational outcomes: occupational prestige of first job and access to the skilled rather than the unskilled working class. Thus, even if we limit the analysis to countries with much less variation on stratification and vocational specificity (all low in stratification and either low or intermediate in vocational specificity), we find systematic effects of vocational specificity. The results of these analyses confirm the findings reported so far. Although we cannot precisely separate the effects of either of these variables, the results show that stratification and vocational specificity, taken together, strongly influence the effects of education on occupational outcomes in the early career.

25. Ireland and Israel are perhaps the most marked exceptions. In Ireland, the system of secondary education has a very low degree of differentiation, but we find a very strong contrast in the odds of obtaining a service-class position between those with an intermediate, and those with a full secondary, education. It may be that the low degree of differentiation is compensated by the very strong standardization of curricula and examination procedures. In Israel, we find a differentiated secondary school system, weak effects of education on Jewish men's odds of entering the service class, but stronger effects on the odds of women and of non-Jewish men. We suspect that in Israel's ethnically stratified occupational structure, the weak effects found for Jewish men reflects a floor effect on their occupational attainment. In other words, the odds that they would enter the service classes are relatively high even for those without tertiary education. Arab men have a greater risk of entering the unskilled working class and, indeed, the effects of education on their class placement are much stronger (see Chapter 7 in this volume).

2

The Transition from School to Work in Australia

FRANK JONES

INTRODUCTION

In their analysis of Australian patterns of status attainment up to the early
1970s, Broom et al. (1980: 41–51) were struck by the problematic nature
of the linkage between educational credentials and career beginnings. The
extent to which basic education affected the socio-economic status of first
job seemed to vary more than any other link in the chain of inheritance
of social inequality between the generations and over the life cycle.

Of the several processes underlying the basic model of status attainment, how successful or unsuccessful men are in converting their educational attainments into
initial occupational status seems the most problematic. Immigrants seem disadvantaged in this respect, whereas upper-middle class groups are decidedly advantaged. Urban groups are advantaged compared with those from rural origins.
Moreover, the nature of this process has changed. Schooling and first job have
become more closely linked since the end of World War II . . . the most vulnerable link [in the chain of status attainment] is entry to the labour force when educational resources are first traded for occupational status. (Broom et al. 1980: 51)

Starting from an entirely different standpoint, the late Paolo Ammassari
reached a similar conclusion. Ammassari (1969) was puzzled by the general lack of empirical evidence in support of the widely held view that economic growth in general, and industrialization in particular, should
promote upward occupational mobility. In his view, this expectation failed
to give adequate weight to the extent to which demographic and educational changes, and changes in values and attitudes associated with the
process of industrialization, are conditioned by existing social inequalities.

To be explicit, it forgets about the inertia of the social system represented by
established interests and its intrinsic capacity to develop equilibrating processes
that end by transforming what seem to be changes *of* the structure itself into
changes *within* the structure. (Ammassari 1969: 48)

So, while modernization brings with it greater occupational differentiation and specialization, it has—at most—contingent, rather than necessary, implications for greater openness in stratification systems. It is as though a shield cushioned the impact of a constantly expanding division of labour and societal openness, a shield representing what he termed 'societal control over occupational first choices' (Ammassari 1969: 53).

Ammassari developed his theoretical arguments on the basis of empirical results available at the time, the analysis of which was flawed. He relied on evidence from 'old' mobility ratios to conclude that the stratification order of modern industrial societies had failed to become more open in recent times (see his footnote 12, which relies heavily on Jackson and Crocket's 1964 overview of American data). However, more recent research relying on superior methods for dealing with structural change (namely, the log-linear model) has reached much the same conclusion. The extent to which occupational destinations depend on occupational origins seems to be remarkably stable over time and between countries (Erikson and Goldthorpe 1992; Jones 1992a; Jones, Kojima, and Marks 1994; for a dissonant view, see Ganzeboom, Luijkx, and Treiman 1989). Constancy, not change, in the strength of this association is the dominant pattern.

The analysis presented here does not address as fully as it might the question of change in the extent to which career beginnings depend on class origins and schooling. Although several national social surveys of the Australian population were conducted in the 1980s and early 1990s, few collected data on career beginnings. This analysis is therefore restricted to data collected in the first two rounds of the National Social Science Survey (NSSS), conducted by Kelley and others between 1984 and 1987 (Kelley, Cushing, and Headey 1987; Kelley, Bean, and Evans 1995).[1] These data sources are described more fully below. First, however, they need to be placed in the context of Australia's institutional structure around the time respondents in these surveys were completing their schooling and preparing to enter the labour market.

THE INSTITUTIONAL CONTEXT, 1965–1985

The Broom et al. study cited above was based on a survey conducted in 1973, just before the collapse of full employment at the end of the long postwar boom. Throughout the 1950s and 1960s, unemployment had been very low, averaging well below 2 per cent of the labour force for most of the period (Maddock and McLean 1987: 11). Indeed, a sharp rise in unemployment to over 2 per cent (Downing 1973: 123) around the time of the 1961 national election almost caused a change of government (Jupp 1964: 22).

This long post-war boom, and full employment, came to an abrupt end in 1973/74. Economic growth stagnated, and inflation and unemployment rose (Pagan in Maddock and McLean 1987: 106–9). To the extent that these problems resulted from the downturn in the world economy following the quadrupling of oil prices in late 1973 and early 1974, Australia was not alone in experiencing stagflation (Ormerod 1994: 133). Figure 2.1 highlights the sharp rise in unemployment rates beginning in 1974 and persisting throughout the 1980s. Youth unemployment, which is typically around three times the general rate of unemployment, rose from around 5 per cent in 1975 to over 20 per cent by the beginning of the 1980s.

The deterioration in job opportunities in the Australian labour market from 1974 onwards is self-evident. Comparing the period 1968–1973 with the period 1974–1979, we find that the general rate of unemployment at least doubled, not just in Australia, but also in such countries as Belgium, Germany, and the Netherlands. By the beginning of the 1980s, high unemployment regimes prevailed in most industrialized countries, except Sweden and Japan (Ormerod 1994: 118).

At the same time that the job market for school-leavers was deteriorating, educational retention rates were rising, especially among girls as Figure 2.2 shows.

Comparable official statistics do not exist for the period before 1967. However, Figure 2.2 shows that in the mid-1960s retention rates from the first to the middle years of secondary school were around 70 per cent and that, during the next two decades, they rose steadily. Midway through the period, however, retention rates for girls overtook those for boys. This crossover, which is more marked for the transition from first to final year, coincides with the deterioration in the youth labour market (see Figure 2.1 above). Also worth noting is the fact that, in 1973, the incoming Labor Government raised the youth unemployment benefit for 16 and 17-year-olds to parity with the adult rate. The government quickly abandoned this policy in order to remove any financial incentive to leave school early (Cass 1988: 18–22). This temporarily more generous treatment of young unemployed school-leavers may partly explain why retention rates to the end of secondary school did not rise among boys between 1972 and 1982. It does not, however, explain why they rose for girls. Perhaps more teenage boys tended to find the institutional constraints of the senior secondary years oppressive and at odds with their desire for 'adult' independence (even where the latter meant going 'on the dole'). On the other hand, this difference may simply indicate that the deterioration of the labour market was more severe for girls than boys (Keeves in Saha and Keeves 1990: 58). Certainly, youth unemployment was higher for girls in the second half of the 1980s (see Figure 2.1).

Frank Jones

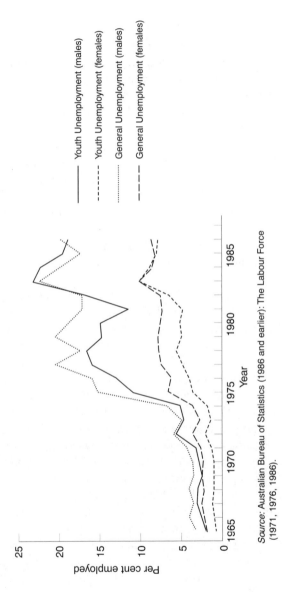

Source: Australian Bureau of Statistics (1986 and earlier): The Labour Force (1971, 1976, 1986).

Fig. 2.1. *Unemployment rates, 1966–1986*

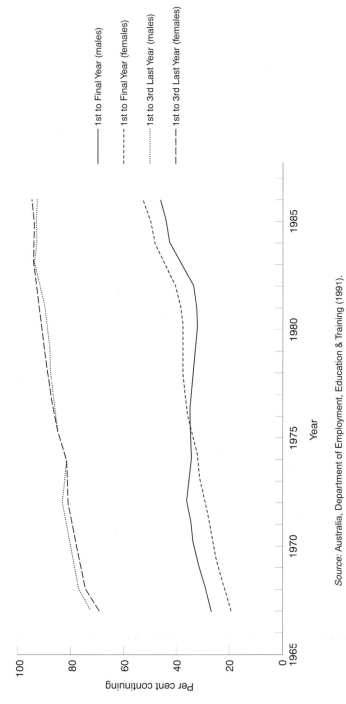

Legend:
——— 1st to Final Year (males)
– – – 1st to Final Year (females)
·········· 1st to 3rd Last Year (males)
— — 1st to 3rd Last Year (females)

Source: Australia, Department of Employment, Education & Training (1991).

FIG. 2.2. *Secondary school retention rates, 1967–1986*

The Australian educational system differs somewhat across administrative boundaries, but its general structure is described in Figure 2.3.[2]

For most of the period under consideration, children between the ages of 6 and 15 (16 in Tasmania) were required by law to attend school. Some states provided a year of pre-primary schooling for children aged 5, and about half of those aged 4 experienced some pre-school education. By the age of 5, nineteen out of every twenty children were in school, and much the same proportion was still at school ten or eleven years later (Keeves in Saha and Keeves 1990: 59). Thereafter, retention rates to the final two years of secondary school declined, with only about half the age cohort proceeding to the final year of secondary school (persons aged 17 or 18). Two out of five of those who completed secondary school (about 20 per cent of the age cohort) went on to tertiary education, mostly as full-time students, while the remainder sought to enter the workforce, either full-time or part-time. About one-third of the age cohort combined work and study.

In the 1960s, most Australian states reformed their secondary education systems. There was a movement away from single-sex, selective schools to coeducational, comprehensive schools. While some elite, selective state schools continued much as before, most schools became internally, rather than externally, stratified. Students were streamed within schools according to ability and performance rather than between schools that offered qualitatively different curricula. Although the final two years of secondary school still serve primarily as preparation for entry to higher education, some vocational training also takes place at school, especially in the technical high schools of some states (for an account of the extensive system in the state of Victoria, see Gilmour and Lansbury 1978: 58–9). Based on the British indentureship model, trade training typically combines on-the-job training as an apprentice, with some work release for further daytime or evening study at a technical training college. Credit is often given for vocational training undertaken while at school, especially at technical schools. In Australia, nearly all training for trade occupations involves an apprenticeship, combining components of both employment and training. As a system of employment, it involves contractual arrangements between an employer and an apprenticeship, enshrined in state regulations governing both parties in respect of wages and conditions. As a system of training, it involves the combination of work with both on-the-job training and prescribed courses, usually in a college of technical and further education (TAFE). To enter an apprenticeship, a person must normally be at least 15 years of age, and have completed the first three to four years of secondary school. Most indentureships last four years, and the great majority of apprentices are young men training in the metal, electrical and building trades (Australia 1985: 1 and table 2.10). The system of trade training for young women is less formalized and extensive.

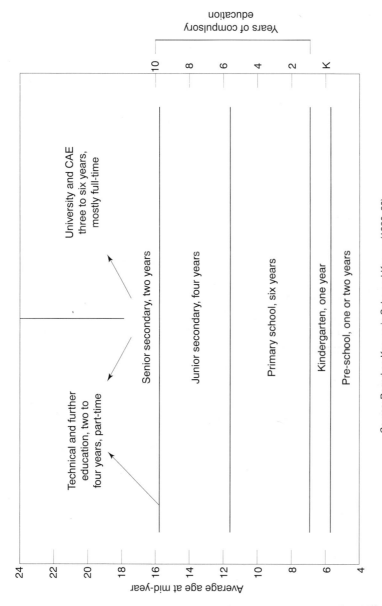

Source: Based on Keeves in Saha and Keeves (1990: 60).

FIG. 2.3. *Schematic structure of the Australian educational system, c. 1980*

As for the secondary school system in general, the movement towards comprehensive education means that schools tend to be stratified in terms of their geographical catchment areas and the socio-economic origins of their students, rather than by ability levels. However schools are also stratified according to type, that is, state, Roman Catholic, and private. About one-quarter of all Australian students study in private (non-state) schools, many operated by the Roman Catholic church. Private non-Catholic schools, who cater for about one-third of the pupils in the private sector, tend to charge high fees, and achieve very high retention rates to the final year of secondary school. Private Catholic schools also achieve relatively high retention rates. But whether private schooling improves occupational chances independent of other advantages of social origin is debatable (Keeves in Saha and Keeves 1990: 63). Research results tend to be equivocal because school system effects are difficult to separate from the effects of home background. We found no significant direct effect on the outcomes considered below and consequently have not reported these coefficients.

DATA SOURCES AND DEFINITION OF VARIABLES

As already indicated, the Australian data analysed below come from the first two rounds of the NSSS conducted between 1985 and 1987. Analysis is restricted to persons aged between 25 and 44 years at time of interview. Immigrants who arrived in Australia after their fifteenth birthday are excluded, because the primary focus is on how differences in Australian educational achievement affects early attainment. In this respect our analysis parallels that of Kraus, Shavit, and Yaish for Israel (see Chapter 7 in this volume), another country with substantial numbers of immigrants. Where possible, I distinguish Aboriginal Australians and persons born in Southern Europe.[3] The members of both groups suffer educational disadvantage (for a review of recent evidence, see Jones 1992*b*, 1993). However, in the case of Southern Europeans, most of their disadvantage appears to stem from the failure of Australian employers to take much notice of differences in education obtained *before* migration. So the exclusion of immigrants educated overseas may largely eliminate the effect of any such disadvantage. In fact, only one significant effect was found, and thus coefficients have not been given in the tables, despite the fact that these variables were included in the analysis. The final sample consists of 1,829 persons, approximately two-thirds of whom were interviewed in the first round of the NSSS and one-third in the second round.

Although the questions relating to education and jobs were similar in both rounds, there were some differences in methodology. For example, urban respondents in the first NSSS were interviewed personally, whereas rural respondents and all those in the second round were approached by mail. The personal interviews did not ask about the ages at which parents completed their schooling, only the highest grade of school they completed and their highest post-school qualification. To avoid sample attrition because of missing data on parental education, school-leaving ages were imputed conditionally on the basis of information about post-school qualifications, or at random (for those for whom no qualification was reported). Dummy variables signalling the presence of missing data or an imputed value are included in most analyses but the coefficients have not been reported in the tables because they are included to adjust for otherwise missing data in a multivariate analysis (Seber 1980: 72). This procedure was also used to deal with missing data on father's socio-economic status.

The educational categories used reflect the nature of the Australian educational system. Almost all parents received some secondary education. So the lowest parental category consists of those with no more than two years of secondary school. The next category consists of parents with more than two years of secondary education but no post-school qualifications. Parents with some post-school qualifications are divided into two groups: those with vocational or trade certificates and those with tertiary diplomas or degrees. In all cases, the reference person is the parent with the higher level of education. As Figure 2.4 shows, just over one-quarter of parents were in the lowest category; around 30 per cent had more than two years of secondary education; a similar percentage had some kind of trade or vocational qualification; and only about one in ten had a tertiary qualification.

The educational categories for respondents are defined in much the same way, except that persons with more than two years of secondary school have been further subdivided into those with three or four years of secondary education, and those with five or six years. The tertiary-educated are also subdivided into those with a tertiary diploma and those with at least a degree. As Figure 2.4 shows, women tend to be concentrated in the middle years of secondary school. At the tertiary level, fewer women than men have a degree but more have a diploma.

In terms of the CASMIN educational scheme that guides all analyses reported in this volume, what I term 'minimal education' corresponds to CASMIN categories 1ab (those who left school with no more than the social minimum of education required by law and who obtained no further qualification). My next category, 'some secondary', corresponds to the category 2b. CASMIN category 2a is represented by the 'trade qualified', which consists of all those who, after leaving school, obtained a trade qualification (from the Australian data, there is no means of knowing how much technical training a person obtained while still at school). 'Full secondary' comprises those who completed five or six years of secondary school and

Frank Jones

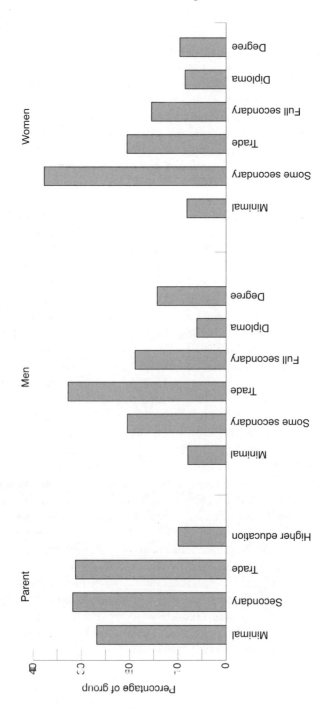

FIG. 2.4. *Educational level of parents and respondents by gender*

who—presumably—achieved a level of competence equivalent to the Higher School Certificate. However in the absence of explicit information on school certificates, it is not possible to define this group more precisely. At the tertiary level, the categories of diploma and degree are functionally equivalent to CASMIN categories 3a and 3b, respectively.

As for jobs, they have been classified into the revised class scheme described by Goldthorpe and Heath (1992), and scored according to the ANU3 status scale (Jones 1989). Table 2.1 provides descriptive background information on the continuous variables used in the analysis.

TABLE 2.1. *Means (and standard deviations) of continuous variables used in the analysis of the transition from school to work in Australia*

Variables	Persons	Women	Men
Father's occupational prestige	33.21	32.79	33.66
	(20.23)	(20.40)	(20.05)
Age at time of interview	33.82	33.83	33.81
	(5.44)	(5.49)	(5.39)
Age at first Job	17.39	16.98	17.82
	(2.65)	(2.36)	(2.86)
Year began first job	69.57	69.15	70.02
	(6.28)	(6.34)	(6.19)
First occupational status	30.56	30.70	30.40
	(17.33)	(16.35)	(18.35)
Current occupational prestige	35.94	33.52	38.33
	(19.94)	(18.19)	(21.26)
Number of cases (maximum)	1,829	945	884

The second round of the NSSS contained a specific question about the year in which respondents started their first regular job, that is, their first regular job after completing full-time education. The first NSSS did not include such a question. So for those respondents year of first job is an estimate based on age at completing secondary school plus an adjustment for any post-school education. A variable was also computed to measure the difference between (estimated) age at completing full-time education and the age at which respondents obtained their highest post-school qualification. I carried out sensitivity analyses which used current class position rather than entry class when this gap was large (that is, when the qualification was obtained several years after entry to the labour force). Results were essentially equivalent. Because substantive interpretation is not much affected by this problem, in what follows the relationship between qualifications and entry class is treated as unproblematic.[4]

The descriptive data of Table 2.1 need little explanation. So far as occupational prestige is concerned, because immigrants educated overseas are not included in the analysis, the spread of scores is slightly less than in the labour force as a whole (cf. Jones 1989: 195). As expected, there is more variation in the occupational statuses of respondents at the time of interview than at the time of their first job. Women tend to be clustered into fewer jobs at both points. The average respondent was in his or her early thirties at time of interview, and in his or her late teens at the time of labour-force entry. Women entered the labour market about a year earlier than men, on average. Age at workforce entry is low by comparative standards because many Australians combine work with part-time vocational training. As Figure 2.4 above shows, close to half the women in this sample left school with no more than four years of secondary schooling (by the time they were 16 years old). Another 20 per cent undertook vocational training leading to a trade certificate. Most of them would also have been under 16 when they entered the labour market. Half the sample (48.2 per cent) were already at work by the time they were 16 years old. As for year of workforce entry, the average was 1970 and the modal years were 1972–1973, when about 10 per cent of the sample started work. About one-quarter (26.1 per cent) started work in 1975 or later, after the collapse of full employment.

Labour-Force Status at the Time of Interview

Figure 2.5 and Table 2.2 provide information on the economic activities of respondents when they were interviewed in the mid-1980s. Nine out of every ten men were in paid employment, as was one in every two women. About one in twenty men was unemployed, compared with about one in fifty women. The implied unemployment rate for women is unrealistically low, in terms of figures from labour-force surveys conducted around the time (Australian Bureau of Statistics 1986). When we calculate unemployment rates in the normal way, by excluding persons not in the labour market, we find that male unemployment for this age group (5.5 per cent of the male labour force) is about the expected level, whereas the rate for women (3.3 per cent) is only about half that recorded in official surveys. So there must be a stronger discouraged worker effect in these data than in government surveys of labour-market activity.

Table 2.2 presents results from a multinomial logit regression of current labour-force status using a range of background characteristics. In the contrast involving unemployment, the only statistically significant effects are age and education. As is well-known, the risks of unemployment decline with age, at least until mid-career. Similarly, the risk of unemployment is greatest among those with the least education, and lowest among those with some

Fɪɢ. 2.5. *Current employment status by gender*

sort of post-school qualification. Note that the risk of unemployment is significantly greater among those with no qualifications (persons with a degree are the comparison group). The gender effect is not significant, and even if it were we would not be inclined to accept it at face value, for reasons given above.

As for the contrast between being in employment and being out of the labour market, the strongest effect, not surprisingly, is gender: women are much more likely than men to leave the labour market. But there are educational effects to be considered as well. Those with no post-school qualification are more likely to leave the labour market. Southern Europeans, on the other hand, have a high labour-force attachment, that is, they are less likely to leave employment.

Some of these effects cannot be reliably estimated when we carry out separate analysis for women and men because of sample size constraints. For unemployed women, only the lowest educational category has a statistically significant effect (as it does also for men). The effect of age is statistically significant for men, but not for women because of the small number reported as unemployed at the time of interview. Women with a degree or diploma are significantly more likely to remain in employment than women with lower levels of education, who are more likely to leave the labour market. Among men who left the labour market, the only significant effect is the contrast for men with the lowest level of education. However, men who completed secondary school but did not obtain a post-school qualification are more likely to leave the labour market, compared with men who obtained a degree.

TABLE 2.2. *Multinomial logit contrasting unemployment and being out of the labour force with being in employment in Australia, 1985–1986*

Independent variables	Persons		Women		Men	
	Unemployed	Not in labour force	Unemployed	Not in labour force	Unemployed	Not in labour force
Age	-0.080**	-0.013	-0.064	-0.006	-0.083**	-0.041
	(-0.027)	(0.012)	(0.050)	(0.013)	(0.032)	(0.034)
Sex (male)	0.556	-2.998**				
	(0.306)	(0.184)				
Father's SES	-0.011	-0.001	-0.003	-0.000	-0.014	0.002
	(0.008)	(0.004)	(0.015)	(0.004)	(0.010)	(0.001)
Parental education (relative to higher education):						
Minimal level	-0.470	0.291	-0.375	0.329	-0.648	-0.151
	(0.579)	(0.271)	(1.041)	(0.287)	(0.705)	(0.704)
Secondary level	-0.633	-0.036	-0.272	0.120	-0.854	-0.763
	(0.552)	(0.261)	(0.973)	(0.277)	(0.683)	(0.692)
Trade qualified	-1.078	0.173	-0.715	0.262	-1.318	-0.278
	(0.574)	(0.250)	(1.015)	(0.266)	(0.704)	(0.629)
Tertiary qualified	0	0	0	0	0	0
Own education (relative to degree):						
Minimal level	2.429**	0.897**	2.952*	0.840**	2.038*	1.727*
	(0.818)	(0.320)	(1.276)	(0.311)	(0.844)	(0.784)
Some secondary	1.777*	0.928**	2.172	1.002**	1.366	0.913
	(0.769)	(0.249)	(0.147)	(0.214)	(0.792)	(0.721)
Trade qualified	1.172	0.345	1.004	0.452*	0.829	-0.049
	(0.773)	(0.255)	(1.256)	(0.225)	(0.786)	(0.733)
Full secondary	1.506*	0.715**	1.760	0.616*	1.188	1.292*
	(0.772)	(0.266)	(1.195)	(0.242)	(0.794)	(0.664)
Diploma	0.723	-0.093	NRE	NRE	0.350	-0.109
	(1.012)	(0.319)	NRE	NRE	(1.246)	(1.173)
Degree	0	0	0	0	0	0
Intercept	-1.446	-0.371	-2.692	-0.825	-0.163	-2.074
	(1.281)	(0.528)	(2.148)	(0.546)	(1.446)	(1.484)

* significant at 0.05 level   ** significant at 0.01 level   NRE = not reliably estimated

The Transition from School to Work: Entry Status

Table 2.3 presents results from an ordinary least squares regression predicting the status of first job using much the same range of background characteristics, separately for women and for men, with and without the CASMIN education variables.[5]

TABLE 2.3. *Determinants of socio-economic status of entry job, for Australian women and men in the 1970s and 1980s*

Independent variables	Women		Men	
	(1)	(2)	(1)	(2)
Year of first job	0.523**	−0.093	0.330**	−0.073
	(0.082)	(0.073)	(0.101)	(0.088)
Father's SES	0.099**	0.050*	0.131**	0.064*
	(0.029)	(0.023)	(0.035)	(0.029)
Parental education (relative to higher education):				
Minimal level	−6.632**	−1.038	−8.608**	−4.658*
	(2.059)	(1.673)	(2.671)	(2.212)
Secondary level	−5.009*	−0.805	−6.349*	−3.182
	(1.982)	(1.602)	(2.512)	(2.075)
Trade qualified	−7.003**	−3.246*	−4.331	−3.846
	(1.894)	(1.535)	(2.440)	(2.005)
Tertiary qualified	0	0	0	0
Own education (relative to degree):				
Minimal level		−37.596**		−33.239**
		(2.174)		(2.439)
Some secondary		−31.981**		−32.653**
		(1.644)		(1.860)
Trade qualified		−23.540**		−26.495**
		(1.638)		(1.637)
Full secondary		−29.367**		−27.117**
		(1.707)		(1.762)
Diploma		−9.902**		−9.197**
		(1.896)		(2.429)
Degree		0		0
Intercept	−2.798	63.100**	7.154	59.848**
	(6.101)	(5.850)	(7.681)	(7.065)
R^2	0.164	0.466	0.116	0.409

* significant at 0.05 level   ** significant at 0.01 level

Taking first the results for women, we can see that where people start out on the occupational hierarchy depends on social origins, labour-market conditions at the time of labour-force entry, and their own stock of human capital.

The effects of year of labour-force entry (first job year) are interesting because they are significant when education is omitted (see Table 2.3, columns 1 and 3). These effects change sign and are reduced to statistical insignificance once education differences are taken into account. In other words, the results confirm the fact that younger cohorts received more education.[6] As for social origins, there is a significant effect of father's status on entry status over and above its indirect effects through the amount of schooling a child received. Educational effects on early status are strong. Women with a degree do best in terms of initial occupational status. However, the status disadvantage suffered by those with four or fewer years of secondary education is not much greater than it is for women who completed the full six years but did not obtain a post-school qualification.

A similar pattern of effects characterizes the early occupational attainment of men. Note, however, the differences in R^2 by gender. The occupational destinations of women are more predictable than those of men. Women enter a narrower range of statuses because of occupational segregation. Apart from this difference, the effects of year of entry, educational credentials, and origin are comparable. We should also note that there are some significant effects on entry status reflecting low levels of educational attainment in the parental generation. Having a father in the lowest educational category implies some status disadvantage for children, particularly for sons, irrespective of the children's own educational attainment.

The Transition from School to Work: Entry Class

Table 2.4 and Figures 2.6, 2.7, and 2.8 report analyses of how the entry class of young Australian workers depends on class origins, education, and qualifications. Figure 2.6 describes entry class, not in terms of a generalized scale of occupational requirements and rewards, but in terms of a class scheme representing salient differences in the market position of workers. The most common destination of young men is the class of skilled and semi-skilled manual labour, while for women it is the class of routine non-manual work. Comparable proportions enter one of the two higher service classes (I and II), but women are heavily concentrated in lower professional ranks (nurses and teachers rather than doctors and engineers). Such patterns are not unique to Australia.

Table 2.4 reports results from a multinomial logit analysis in which destination class depends on year of entry into the labour force, parental edu-

TABLE 2.4. *Multinomial logit of entry class, contrasted with Class VIIab, for Australian women in the 1970s and 1980s*

Independent variables	Entry class				
	I + II	IIIa	IIIb	IVabc	V + VI
Results for women:					
Year of first job	−0.005	−0.024	−0.026	−0.060	−0.057
Father's SES	0.026**	0.022*	0.020*	0.034*	0.016
Father self–employed	−0.179	−0.124	−0.251	0.819	−1.612*
Own education (relative to degree):					
Minimal level	−6.449**	−4.504**	−1.533	7.124	−4.609**
Some secondary	−4.586**	−1.731	0.134	8.627	−2.638*
Trade qualified	−2.540*	−1.785	0.325	9.298	−2.154
Full secondary	−2.837*	0.747	1.492	10.149	−2.677
Diploma	−1.109	−1.120	0.700	−0.330	−1.559
Degree	0	0	0	0	0
Intercept	3.577	3.331	3.122	−7.030	5.425
Results for men:					
Year of first job	−0.038	−0.103**	−0.051	−0.087**	−0.015
Father's SES	0.013	0.013*	0.005	0.029**	0.002
Father self–employed	−0.122	−0.619	0.246	1.593**	0.059
Own education (relative to degree):					
Minimal level	−5.726**	−3.214**	−1.301	−0.357	0.340
Some secondary	−4.527**	−0.737	−0.770	−0.176	0.843
Trade qualified	−2.682**	−0.689	−0.533	0.152	2.867**
Full secondary	−1.867**	1.137*	0.564	0.914	0.296
Diploma	0.560	1.165	−0.363	0.935	2.805**
Degree	0	0	0	0	0
Intercept	4.430*	7.164**	3.120	3.185	−0.155

* significant at 0.05 level   ** significant at 0.01 level

cation, father's job status and self-employment, and respondent's educational achievement. Estimates of effect are relative to the chances of entering semi-skilled and unskilled manual employment (Class VIIab). For interpretative purposes, it is useful to focus on the pattern of coefficients across entry classes, first for women and then for men.

The effects for year of labour force entry are negative, indicating worsening chances with the passage of time. This finding echoes the results from the full equation for socio-economic status (see Table 2.3 above). However, none

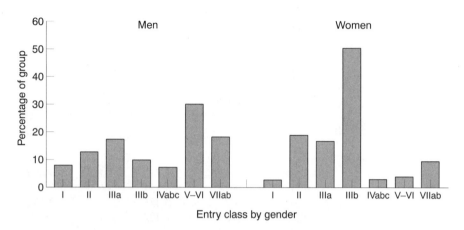

Fig. 2.6. *Entry classes among Australian workers*

of these contrasts reach statistical significance. We also see that coming from a higher status home improved a woman's chances of entering one of the non-manual classes and even self-employment (Class IV accounts for only 2 per cent of entry jobs among women). Having a self-employed father tends to reduce the chances of entering any class other than unskilled manual work, except for self-employment itself. However, this last effect is not statistically significant among women (it is among men). As for the effects of education, we need to bear in mind that these effects are relative to women with a tertiary degree. They show that a woman with a minimal level of education was less likely to enter any class except the comparison group (semi-skilled and unskilled manual workers). All effects for this educational category are negative, and statistically significant except for the (small) entry class of self-employed workers and the lower non-manual class.[7] A similar pattern characterizes the next educational level but in muted form. The following two lines of this panel contain only two effects reliably different from zero. The odds of a woman with a trade qualification entering the service class rather than Class VII are significantly worse than those of a woman with a degree. Similarly, women who completed secondary school without obtaining a tertiary qualification are also less likely to enter Classes I or II.

Turning now to the results for men, we find rather similar patterns. Being a more recent entrant to the labour force was something of a disadvantage, especially for entering the higher of the two routine non-manual groups and self-employment. Coming from higher status origins also affected entry class among men, but somewhat less strongly than among women. On the other hand, class inheritance among self-employed men was distinctly stronger. As was the case for women, a man's chances of entry to the service class largely depended on having a degree or a diploma. Possessing a specifically vocational qualification, such as a trade certificate or a diploma, favoured entry to the skilled and semi-skilled class (Class V + VI). Educational differences were not at all significantly related to the relative chances of becoming self-employed. Nor for that matter were they implicated in who entered the lower of the routine non-manual classes. Completing secondary school without obtaining a tertiary qualification increased the chances of entering the higher routine non-manual class, and decreased the chances of entering the service class (the same was true for women).

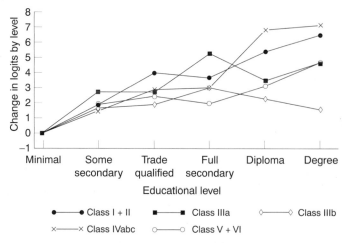

Note: Effects are relative to entering the lowest class (see Table 2.4).

FIG. 2.7. *Net effects of educational qualifications on the entry class of Australian women*

How education affects entry class among Australian women and men can be more easily seen when we display the change in logits reported in Table 2.4 on a graph, as is done in Figures 2.7 and 2.8. Note that the graphs show *changes* in logits in which the base for comparison (minimal education) has been set to the same initial point (zero) for all class comparisons. In practice, this involves plotting the *difference* between the effect of minimal education reported in Table 2.4 and the other effects for different educational levels. For example, the logits for women entering Classes I and II have been rescaled by subtracting -6.449 from the remaining educational effects in the first column, yielding 0, 1.863, 3.909, 3.612, 5.340, and 6.449, respectively). The reader should bear in mind that each line plots the change in (log) odds

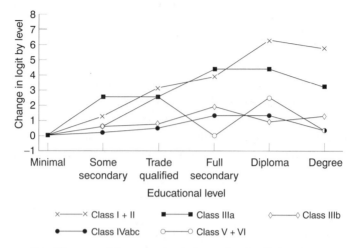

Note: Effects are relative to entering the lowest class (see Table 2.4).

FIG. 2.8. *Net effects of educational qualifications on the entry class of Australian men*

of entering a given class rather than the class of semi-skilled and unskilled labourers. In the above example, the odds of a woman entering Class I or II rather than Class VII are improved by a factor of 6.44 (the antilog of 1.863) if she had some secondary schooling. The improvement is more marked if she obtained a trade qualification (a factor of 49.85). They are vastly improved if she obtained a tertiary qualification (a factor of 632.07).

The figure points to the following conclusions. The (log) odds of entering the service class are enhanced primarily by obtaining a tertiary qualification. The (log) odds of entering any other class are improved simply by gaining an education above the social minimum. Among women, a specific vocational qualification (trade certificate) has utility mainly in promoting entry to the service class, but is also helpful in gaining access to all other classes (we ignore Class IVabc because the educational differentials are not reliable). Completing a full six years of secondary education is especially useful for entering the higher of the two routine non-manual classes and the lower service class. But it is also generally effective as a means of avoiding skilled and unskilled manual work. Apart from these specific results, differences in the level of education attainment seem rather unimportant in promoting access to lower non-manual work, self-employment, and skilled manual employment (as against entry to the lowest class), provided a woman obtained more than the social minimum of education. The lines connecting the changes in logit for these three classes are fairly flat from 'some secondary' to 'diploma/degree'.

The pattern for men is less clear-cut because men enter a wider range of class destinations than women (as Figure 2.6 above shows, half the women enter just one class destination, the lower routine non-manual class). So we can differentiate the process linking education to destinations with more precision. So far as the service class is concerned, the pattern for men is quite similar to that for women. A diploma or a degree is needed to materially improve a man's chances of entering this class rather than the class of semi-skilled and unskilled labour. The (log) odds of entering routine non-manual work (Class IIIa) are improved simply by having an education above the social minimum, whereas entry to Class IIIb and self-employment hardly depends on educational differences at all. Not surprisingly, the chances of entering skilled manual work are much improved by obtaining a trade certificate or a tertiary diploma. In other words, variations in acquired human capital are heavily implicated in gaining entry to the higher echelons of non-manual and manual work, but are less important for entering other classes, at least for those who acquired an education above the social minimum required by law.

CONCLUSION

The introduction to this analysis drew attention to other studies commenting on the problematic nature of the linkage between social origins, educational credentials, and career beginnings. For example, Broom et al. (1980) found that members of the early post-war cohorts fared better than their counterparts who started work between the two World Wars. We found comparable evidence of the detrimental effects of a worsening labour market on the early job status of Australian school-leavers in the 1970s and 1980s. As for the role of educational credentials, tertiary qualifications serve to control entry into the service classes of a modern industrial society like Australia. Among blue-collar workers, formal vocational qualifications govern entry into the aristocracy of labour. Persons who enter the labour market with no more than the socially required minimum of education are disproportionately likely to start their working lives as semi-skilled or unskilled labourers. On the other hand, the class destinations of other school-leavers are not much affected by school differences between these extremes, except for those who completed a full six years of secondary education. Their most probable destination was the higher of the two routine non-manual classes. One obvious implication of these findings is that lifetime education leading to a vocational qualification should provide an effective class mobility channel for those who failed to obtain one earlier in life.

NOTES

1. Needless to say, those who collected the data and made them available for wider use bear no responsibility for the analysis and interpretation presented here.
2. Primary and secondary schooling is provided by eight State and Territorial education departments, as is some further education in the technical and vocational area. Since 1973, however, university and tertiary college education has been funded almost entirely by the Federal government. For further detail, see Saha and Keeves (1990: 49–61), esp. Fig. 4.2 on which my Fig. 2.3 is based.
3. There are, unfortunately, very few self-identified Aboriginal Australians in the analysis (only a dozen or so). Given their lower rates of literacy and partial exclusion from mainstream Australian culture, those who did respond are likely to be a biased subset, especially in the self-completion components of the NSSS.
4. The main effect of this adjustment was to increase the relative size of each service class by around one percentage point. However, the effects of independent variables remained largely unchanged. One obvious by-product of this adjustment was to increase the average age at which respondents 'entered' the labour market.
5. School-type variables have been included in this model, but coefficients are not reported as no significant effects were found.
6. Year of entry is a continuous variable scored as the last two digits of the calendar year in question (i.e. an entry year of 1962 is scored 62; see Table 2.1 for means and standard deviations). The more recent the year, the larger the value this variable takes. So a positive effect like that in Table 2.3 implies that—net of other factors—those who started work more recently enjoyed a status advantage.
7. The coefficients for educational effects in Class IVabc may seem large, but are not estimated with any great precision.

3

Education and Occupation in Britain

ANTHONY HEATH AND SIN YI CHEUNG

INTRODUCTION

Over the course of the twentieth century, the character of educational stratification in Britain has gradually evolved from one primarily based on type of school to one based on academic certificates. In the early part of the century, for example, the major distinctions were between elementary, technical, grammar, and independent schools. Allocation to these types of school was partly financial and partly scholastic. Once pupils had entered these schools they were, to use Turner's terminology, 'sponsored' for different educational and occupational careers (Turner 1960).

At the bottom of the academic hierarchy came the elementary schools, which provided a basic minimum of literacy and numeracy, their pupils leaving at 14 without any formal certificates and typically entering manual work. These were the schools to which the majority of the population went. Technical schools (a far from homogeneous category) were relatively few in number and were more vocationally-oriented; they prepared pupils for various skilled industrial trades, sometimes entering students for vocational qualifications. Grammar schools prepared students for white-collar work or higher education, and their syllabus was oriented towards the school certificate, which was typically taken at the ages of 15 or 16. However, many pupils, particularly working-class ones left at the minimum-leaving age (which was age 14 between the two World Wars) without securing a school certificate. Even so, early leavers from grammar schools had improved chances of obtaining white-collar work compared with their contemporaries from elementary schools (Heath and Ridge 1983). On the other hand, pupils who stayed on and obtained passes in five subjects were deemed to have 'matriculated' and thus secured the qualification for entry to university. University, however, was largely the preserve of the private schools, and led to careers in the higher civil service and the elite professions.

Alongside these distinctions between types of school was a system of technical and professional qualifications that were obtained after leaving school. These vocational qualifications were geared towards specialized roles in the labour market. There was thus in essence a dual system of general education in schools and vocational training after leaving school.

For leavers from the elementary schools, there were apprenticeships in the skilled manual trades, as well as various basic clerical and technical certificates (for example the RSA and City & Guilds qualifications). For leavers from grammar schools, there were professional qualifications in law, accountancy, or teaching, which prepared students for the professions. These vocational qualifications were sometimes obtained by full-time study in specialized institutions of further education before entering work, the prime example of this being teacher-training. But more often they were obtained through part-time study while in paid employment, often in trainee positions. The model for this latter form of vocational training was of course the apprenticeship, but many white-collar qualifications had essentially the same character.

The pre-war picture, then, was of distinctions between types of school associated with differences in general educational level, together with a plethora of post-school specialized qualifications associated with particular types of employment. Correspondingly, political and educational debate at the time focused on access to the different types of schooling, and in particular on access to grammar schools. This culminated in the 1944 Education Act, which abolished fees at state-maintained grammar schools. Following the Act, the tripartite system of grammar, technical, and secondary modern schools was established, selection to the three branches depending upon the results of competitive examination at age 11 (the '11-plus'). The school-leaving age was also raised to 15 in 1947.

The institutional divisions between grammar, technical, and secondary modern schools remained throughout the 1950s. Some changes took place in the details of the school qualifications which pupils took: the General Certificate of Education at Ordinary level (GCE O level) replaced the School Certificate, and continued to be taken at 15 or 16. Two years later at age 17 or 18 pupils now took Advanced Level (GCE A level) examinations, which became the norm for pupils who stayed on into the sixth form. Eventually A levels became the standard entry requirement for university. But the basic character of British schooling throughout the 1950s remained that of a sponsored system. The 1944 reforms were intended to make selection more meritocratic, but in other respects the tripartite system of the immediate post-war period had a great deal in common with the pre-war arrangements.

In the last third of the century, however, the institutional arrangements of the tripartite system have largely been dismantled and replaced by a comprehensive system. The Labour-controlled House of Commons resolved:

That this House, conscious of the need to raise educational standards at all levels, and regretting that the realization of this objective is impeded by the separation of children into different types of secondary schools, notes with approval the efforts of local authorities to reorganize secondary education on comprehensive lines which will preserve all that is valuable in grammar school education for those children who now receive it and make it available to more children. (Department of Education and Science 1965)

This policy was implemented by the Labour Government's Circular 10/65 in 1965 which instructed local authorities to establish comprehensive systems of education in their areas. The Labour Government also proposed to raise the school-leaving age to 16, although this was not finally implemented until 1974.

In most local authorities, the distinctions between secondary modern, technical, and grammar schools were abolished over the next ten years and most state-educated children came to attend comprehensive schools. (A few grammar schools remained in authorities which were primarily organized on comprehensive lines, while two authorities continued to run a selective system divided between secondary modern and grammar schools.) Technical schools had declined during the post-war period and effectively disappeared at secondary school level, although Mrs Thatcher's Conservative Government tried to reintroduce them in the form of City Technology Colleges.

On the other hand, we should remember that private schools which were outside the state system remained largely untouched by these reforms. While there were a number of changes, such as the abolition by a Labour Government of Direct Grant status and the introduction by a Conservative Government of Assisted Places at private schools, there has been a large degree of continuity in the position, standing, and size of the private sector in British education. The private schools were, however, exposed to the trend towards credentialism that has marked the last third of the century.

In effect, credentialism has replaced school type as the basic principle of educational stratification in the comprehensive era. As in other countries, there has been a massive expansion in the number of pupils securing academic certificates and the system of certification has been extended to cover virtually the whole school population. In addition to the previous qualifications of O level and A level which were aimed at grammar-school pupils, a new examination called the Certificate of Secondary Education (CSE) became widespread. This certificate had been introduced some years before comprehensive reorganization, and was aimed at the less academic pupils in the secondary modern schools. The examination was set at a lower academic standard, and included more practical subjects. However, a grade 1 pass at CSE was widely regarded as equivalent to a pass at O level (and more recently the two examinations have been amalgamated into the GCSE). Comprehensive reorganization and the raising of the school-leaving age in 1974 gave a considerable boost to the numbers taking the CSE, and the majority of pupils subsequently left school with some kind of certificate—A level, O level, or CSE.

Alongside this expanded system of academic certificates, the multitude of post-school vocational qualifications has continued. Apprenticeships, however, have declined sharply in number and there has been some tendency for vocational training to shift out of the workplace and into colleges of further education and polytechnics (the latter recently renamed universities). A much greater range of subjects is now examined at GCSE, A level, and Degree level, including many more vocationally-oriented subjects. The dual system of general education (in schools), and vocational training (on the job) is thus beginning to blur. However, there continues to be a highly diverse system of vocational qualifications and various contradictory trends coexist: at the same time that, for example, nurse training is moving out of the hospitals and into colleges and universities, teacher-training and training for probation officers is being moved out of colleges and back into the workplace.

In summary, then, two main trends can be perceived in Britain in the course of the twentieth century: a shift from early selection at age 11 to comprehensive education and later decisions at age 16 (in effect a shift from sponsored to contest mobility); and a spread of certification to encompass virtually the whole of the school population.

However, it is important not to oversimplify the pattern of change. British education and training continues to have a complex and frankly rather disorganized character: important divisions between school types, especially between independent, grammar, and comprehensive schools, remain. Elements of selection, both financial and academic persist, and some recent initiatives of the Conservative Government have also reintroduced some less formal methods of selection (for example, for schools which have opted out of local authority control).

The consequence of these changes has been that employers now tend to recruit certificated school and university-leavers, whereas previously they would have recruited mainly unqualified school-leavers (many of whom would subsequently have gone on to acquire technical qualifications while at work). To use Ishida, Müller, and Ridge's (1995) terminology, certificates (especially the higher-level ones) have become a major means for occupational inclusion. Conversely, failure to acquire certificates has become a major means of occupational exclusion, the uncertificated having substantially higher chances of unemployment.

In terms of entry to the labour market, then, contemporary Britain can be expected to broadly resemble other contest systems, with a hierarchy of edu-

with new intake policies). Yet others went through local school systems that were in the process of reorganizing. For further details of the educational experience of the NCDS children, see Steadman (1980, 1983).

In addition to comprehensive reorganization, the school-leaving age was raised from 15 to 16 in 1974, just in time to catch the NCDS cohort, who had reached the age of 16 in March 1974. This brought them within reach of the public examinations of GCE O level and the CSE.

VARIABLES

Educational Qualifications

We use the data collected in sweep 5, variables N501441 to N501469,[1] to construct the following classification of highest qualification:

1a Social minimum: the respondent left school with no formal qualifications

1b Low-level school qualifications: left school with the CSE (except grade 1) or with grades at GCE O level below A–C (the standard 'pass' grades)

1c Basic vocational qualifications: obtained apprenticeship; JIB craft; RSA 1–3; City & Guilds, operative and craft; other technical and business qualifications of similar standard

2a Intermediate vocational qualifications: City & Guilds, advanced; ONC; OND; TEC; BEC

2b Intermediate academic qualifications: GCE O level (grades A–C), or CSE grade 1 (and equivalents such as the Scottish CEE or SCE O level)

2c Full secondary qualifications: GCE A level; SCE A level

3a Lower-level tertiary: teaching certificate; nursing certificate; professional qualification; HNC, HND, C&G Full; TEC/BEC Higher; equivalent diplomas and professional qualifications

3b Higher-level tertiary: university degree and equivalent.

The distribution of men and women with these qualifications is given in Table 3.2.

Table 3.2 shows the qualifications of all respondents for whom there were valid educational data in sweep 5. In subsequent analyses we shall exclude respondents who began a first job before completing their full-time education. Figures for this restricted sample are given in brackets.

Anthony Heath and Sin Yi Cheung

TABLE 3.2. *Highest qualification of the NCDS sample* (column percentages)

	Highest qualification	Men	Women
1a	social minimum	13.1 (12.4)	15.0 (14.0)
1b	basic academic	11.2 (11.5)	13.2 (13.4)
1c	basic vocational	8.7 (9.0)	4.3 (4.3)
2a	intermediate vocational	4.3 (4.5)	0.3 (0.3)
2b	intermediate academic	33.3 (34.4)	38.1 (38.9)
2c	full secondary	11.0 (10.6)	9.7 (9.8)
3a	lower tertiary	8.8 (9.3)	10.8 (11.2)
3b	university degree	9.6 (8.4)	8.6 (8.1)
N		5,205 (3,904)	5,455 (4,240)

School Type

Information on school type was collected in sweep 3 (Variables 2102 and 2103). We distinguish the following types of school: independent (including Direct Grant), grammar, comprehensive, secondary modern, and other.

The 'other' category contains a residual group of technical schools (very few respondents in our sample having attended these schools), and various LEA and non-LEA special schools.

The schools we have termed 'independent' were primarily fee-paying schools. We have however included in with them the Direct Grant schools. These schools were a kind of hybrid between the public and private sectors, offering free places (funded by the local educational authority), as well as fee-paying places. They were abolished in 1975 by the then Labour Government, and the great majority then became fully independent. However, the subsequent Conservative Government then introduced a scheme of 'assisted places' which in some respects restored state help to independent schools.

Note that Halsey, Heath, and Ridge (1980), and Heath and Ridge (1983) also distinguished major from minor independent schools, the former being members of the Head Masters' Conference. The NCDS does not allow us to make this distinction.

Father's and Mother's Education

Data were collected in sweep 3 on the age at which the respondent's father-figure or mother-figure left full-time education (variables N2396 and N2397). These variables were scored from 1 (under 13 years) to 10 (23 years or over). Note that ages 19 to 20, and 21 to 23 were grouped.

cational certificates leading to inclusion in, and exclusion from, more and less desirable positions in the labour market. As has been suggested this link between certificates and occupations may not be particularly strong in Britain, since the certificates, unlike the specialized vocational qualifications, are not closely geared to employers' requirements or to specific types of work. (On the other hand, it should be remembered that, under the old British system of vocational training, labour-market entry effectively preceded training, so the close link between the two has a quite different causal interpretation.)

In this chapter, we explore the transition from school to work of young people born in 1958. These young people were educated during the early stages of comprehensive reorganization, at the transition from sponsored to contest systems. They entered the labour market in the late 1970s and early 1980s, and were reaching occupational maturity in the early 1990s. They were participants in the credential revolution, and thus are in many respects close to the late twentieth-century system of educational stratification by credential. They are also of course representative of a major contingent within the current British labour force.

We ask how meritocratic were the processes to which these young people were exposed. Did ascribed characteristics such as social origins continue to be important? Did the old distinctions between types of school continue to influence their students' chances within the labour market? Independent and grammar schools have joined the credential society, so that league tables of school performance regularly show the socially most exclusive independent schools such as Eton heading the lists of A-level successes. Do these schools continue to give benefits in occupational placement over and above their success in securing examination results? In particular, do private schools (or for that matter grammar schools) help compensate their pupils in the labour market for their educational failures?

DATA

Our data come from the National Child Development Study (NCDS). This is a longitudinal study of children born 3–9 March 1958, designed to be nationally representative of all children in Great Britain (see Shepherd 1995 for full details). The NCDS had its origins in the Perinatal Mortality Survey (PMS), sponsored by the National Birthday Trust Fund. This was designed to examine the social and obstetric factors associated with stillbirth and death in early infancy among the 17,000 children born in Great Britain in that one week. Since then there have been five major follow-ups or sweeps designed to monitor the physical, educational, and social development of members of the birth cohort. Each was based on an attempt to trace all those who had participated in any earlier follow-up, excluding those known to have died, emigrated, or declined further cooperation. For each of the first three follow-ups, tracing through schools enabled the birth cohort to be augmented by including immigrants born in the relevant week.

The five follow-up sweeps were conducted in 1965 (when the children were aged 7), 1969 (aged 11), 1974 (aged 16), 1981 (aged 23), and 1991 (aged 33). The achieved sample size of the PMS was 17,414, and the sample has subsequently experienced the attrition that always occurs with panel studies of this sort (see Table 3.1). While Shepherd (1995) indicates that the attrition in the sample has not introduced major biases in the social profile of the respondents, we must be cautious in using these data. In particular, we should note the problem of 'informative dropout' (Diggle and Kenward 1994). In some of our analyses there are also substantial further reductions in the number of respondents—some due to missing data and some to exclusions (described below). Ideally, our results should be replicated wherever possible against other sources which have not suffered from attrition in this way. For some of the key analyses, however, alternative British data-sets with the necessary variables simply do not exist.

TABLE 3.1. *Sample sizes in the PMS/NCDS*

	PMS 1958 Birth	NCDS 1 1965 7 years	NCDS 2 1969 11 years	NCDS 3 1974 16 years	NCDS 4 1981 23 years	NCDS 5 1991 33 years
Target sample	17,733	16,883	16,835	16,915	16,457	16,455
Achieved sample	17,414	15,468	15,503	14,761	12,537	11,363

The NCDS children were growing up during a period of rapid educational change. As we noted earlier, in 1965 the Labour Government had introduced comprehensive reorganization through its Circular 10/65. But implementation of this initiative was gradual and affected different NCDS children in different ways. The NCDS children entered secondary school around 1969. A few attended independent schools, which were not affected by Circular 10/65. Some took the '11-plus' examination and entered grammar and secondary modern schools in authorities which had not yet reorganized, while others entered the new comprehensive schools (which were often of course simply renamed secondary modern and grammar schools

1970s, but it was given a dramatic upturn in 1980 when the new Conservative Government raised interest rates and taxes in an effort to control the rate of inflation, which had climbed to over 20 per cent in 1979 (when the Labour Government had been defeated at the polls). From 2.6 per cent of employees in 1974, the percentage unemployed grew slowly to 5.4 per cent in 1979 before leaping to 6.8 per cent in 1980, and 10.5 per cent in 1981. Detailed official figures on the unemployment rates of young people over this period are not available, but we know that in general new entrants to the labour markets have higher rates of unemployment. These adverse trends are therefore particularly likely to have affected the more qualified entrants, who left full-time education in 1980 or 1981.

The NCDS did not in fact collect usable data on the respondents' economic activity immediately after they left full-time education. What we use instead is the data on their economic activity in 1981. This in fact solves the major problem of changing unemployment rates over time, but leaves unsolved the lesser problem of length of experience in the labour market. Ideally, therefore we would control for length of labour-market experience.

Table 3.3 shows that, as expected, very few young men were looking after the home or were otherwise out of the labour market. A few men were still in full-time education—largely those with qualifications at full secondary level or above, who were presumably still in the process of acquiring further qualifications (such as post-graduate ones).

Leaving aside full-time education and the small numbers not in the labour market, how did qualifications relate to chances of being unemployed? We can see that the odds of being unemployed vs. employed were 1:4.0 for respondents with the social minimum, and then improved to 1:5.4 as respondents obtained the rather minimal 1b qualifications (largely the lower grades of CSE). Basic vocational qualifications gave a further marked

TABLE 3.3. *Qualifications and economic activity for men* (row percentages)

Highest qualification		In paid work	Unemployed	Full-time education	Other	N
1a	social minimum	76.5	18.9	0.4	4.3	540
1b	basic academic	83.8	15.6	0.2	0.4	488
1c	basic vocational	89.2	10.1	0.0	0.8	378
2a	inter. vocational	90.7	8.3	0.5	0.5	193
2b	inter. academic	90.4	7.3	1.0	1.2	1463
2c	full secondary	80.0	7.9	9.4	2.6	491
3a	lower tertiary	90.3	4.2	4.5	1.0	404
3b	university degree	77.2	7.4	13.1	2.3	434

improvement, the odds decreasing to 1:8.8. The monotonic improvement as one moves up the educational ladder is interrupted at full secondary level, and then peaks at the lower tertiary level, where the odds improve to 1:21.5. Graduates fare considerably worse with odds of 1:10.4—the same as at the intermediate vocational level. The relationship between qualifications and unemployment is not, therefore, a simple hierarchical one.

Some of these anomalies could of course be due to the length of time available for job search since leaving full-time education. Thus school-leavers with full secondary qualifications (which are typically taken at age 18) will have had, on average, two years fewer in the labour market than will leavers with intermediate qualifications (typically taken at age 16). Similarly, graduates will typically have left full-time education more recently than the holders of lower tertiary qualifications. They will moreover have been entering the labour market at a time when overall unemployment rates had dramatically increased. However, we suspect that this is not the full story and that new graduates in Britain do in general have less favourable odds of securing employment than do young people with lower tertiary qualifications (see Heath and McMahon 1997).

TABLE 3.4. *Qualifications and economic activity for women* (row percentages)

Highest qualification	In paid work	Unemployed	Full-time education	Other	N
1a social minimum	38.5	11.1	0.1	50.2	667
1b basic academic	54.0	7.9	0.2	38.0	624
1c basic vocational	65.5	5.0	0.0	29.5	200
2a inter. vocational	46.7	13.3	0.0	40.0	15
2b inter. academic	70.5	5.0	0.2	24.4	1,814
2c full secondary	76.1	5.2	8.1	10.6	481
3a lower tertiary	83.1	3.6	0.9	12.3	528
3b university degree	83.5	5.6	5.6	5.3	412

The same broad patterns of employment and unemployment apply to women just as they do for men. Among women who were economically active, the odds of being unemployed vs. employed were 1:3.5 for respondents with the social minimum education, and again were most favourable for people holding lower tertiary qualifications with odds of 1:23.1. As can be seen, these odds are rather similar to the ones for men (with the exception of 2a, where the N is too small for a sensible comparison to be made).

The pattern for full-time education is also quite similar to the male pat-

Economic Activity

We use the information collected in sweep 4 about the respondent's economic activity in 1981 (variable ECONSTAT). We distinguish the following categories: in employment; unemployed (including those awaiting jobs and those on youth training schemes such as TOPS); in full-time education; and other, mainly looking after the home but also including a small number of permanently sick and disabled, in prison, etc.

Social Class

The best measure of social class origins which is available in the NCDS is the socio-economic group (SEG) of the respondent's father when the respondent was aged 16, collected in sweep 3 (variable N2385). For full details of the SEG schema used by the NCDS at sweep 3, see OPCS (1970). It is possible to recode SEG so that it is a reasonable approximation to the Goldthorpe class schema. Unfortunately, however, the NCDS coding of SEG does not distinguish between small employers and small managers; small employers therefore have to be included in the service class, not in their proper home of the petty bourgeoisie. We thus use the following six classes for measuring social class origins:

Higher service class (SEGs 1, 3, 4)
Lower service class (SEGs 2, 5)
Routine non-manual (SEG 6)
Petty bourgeoisie (SEGs 12, 13, 14)
Foremen and skilled manual (SEGs 8,9)
Semi- and unskilled manual (SEGs 7, 10, 11, 15).

When measuring the class of the respondent's first job, we do have available in sweep 5 the 1980 version of the Goldthorpe class schema (VAR N530082). We use the following collapsed version:

Higher service class (Class I)
Lower service class (Class II)
Routine non-manual (Class III)
Petty bourgeoisie (Class IV)
Foremen and skilled manual (Classes V and VI)
Semi- and unskilled manual (Class VII)

A particular problem with measures of first job is that many people may take temporary jobs, either between school and university or during their time at university. In assessing returns to education such jobs which were obtained before the respondent achieved his or her highest qualification should clearly be excluded. We therefore exclude people who reported a first job earlier than their completion of full-time education. As we can see from Table 3.2, the number of respondents thus excluded is quite substantial, and we have rerun our main analyses on the full sample to check whether the exclusion introduces selection biases.

Social Status

To measure the occupational standing of the respondents' first job, we have used data from NCDS sweep 4 to construct the Hope-Goldthorpe scale. This scale is described by its authors as essentially a measure of occupational desirability (Goldthorpe and Hope 1974). Our results are very similar to those obtained by Kerckhoff (1990) using the Treiman prestige scores.

However continuous measures of father's SES were not coded by the NCDS and cannot be added to the data-set, since detailed occupational data (as opposed to socio-economic group) were never coded for fathers.

Cognitive Ability

Short tests of verbal and non-verbal ability were administered to the sample in sweep 2 when they were aged 11. The tests were designed specifically for the NCDS. We use standardized scores on the composite measure of general ability.

RESULTS

Our account of the results is divided into three sections. We first look at the relation between education and economic activity early in the career. In the second and third sections we look at first-job attainment, dealing with H-G scores first and then class positions.

Economic Activity

Members of the NCDS began to enter the labour market in 1974, when they were aged 16, and more cohort members followed them each year as they completed their full-time education. By 1981, the time of the fourth NCDS sweep, the great majority had left full-time education and were either in the labour market or were looking after the home. A very small proportion was out of the labour market for other reasons, for example permanently sick or disabled.

Over this period from 1974 to 1981, conditions in the labour market changed quite dramatically. Unemployment had been rising in the late

TABLE 3.7. *First-job scores by gender and qualification*

Highest qualification		Men	Women
1a	social minimum	33.8 (9.1) [518]	34.9 (5.2) [640]
1b	basic academic	36.3 (9.4) [481]	37.0 (6.1) [614]
1c	basic vocational	38.9 (8.9) [374]	38.0 (5.1) [197]
2a	intermediate vocational	40.8 (8.5) [191]	37.7 (2.2) [15]
2b	intermediate academic	41.3 (11.3) [1441]	38.8 (7.1) [1778]
2c	full secondary	45.2 (15.9) [433]	42.3 (11.1) [443]
3a	lower tertiary	47.9 (14.3) [376]	46.5 (14.4) [506]
3b	university degree	57.8 (17.2) [321]	54.9 (15.0) [355]

Note: Mean values are followed by standard deviations. Base Ns are given in square brackets.

for men, although (with the exception of lower tertiary qualifications) there is the suggestion that women obtain slightly poorer returns on their educational investments than do men. If we conduct a formal analysis of variance, we find that there is a statistically significant interaction between gender, qualifications, and first-job scores. We therefore in the following analysis treat men and women separately.

Finally, it is worth noting some elements of heteroscedasticity in the H-G scores for both the men and women. At the higher levels of qualifications the standard deviations in H-G scores are substantially larger than they were at the lower levels. In other words, these more highly qualified respondents enter jobs with a relatively wide variety of H-G scores. We shall see further evidence of this later when we move on to look at the class distributions of respondents in the next section.

We now move to a multivariate analysis of these data. We are interested in two questions here. First, what is the role of social origins in the attainment process? Do social origins have direct effects on first-job scores, even after controlling for qualification level, or is the impact of social origins wholly mediated by education? Second, what is the importance of the type of school one attended? At the time of the tripartite system, Heath and Ridge (1983) had shown, using 1972 data, that school type made a substantial difference to occupational attainment even after controlling for qualifications.[3] Does this still hold true in the comprehensive era covered by our NCDS respondents?

We use a series of linear regression models to explore these questions (although in view of the problem of heteroscedasticity described above, linear regression must be used with caution). We run the models separately for men and women in order to explore whether there are differences in the way the attainment process operates for men and women.

We begin with a simple model, the explanatory variables being measures of social origins. As we can see, father's class has large and significant effects on first-job score, while the measures of parental education also reach statistical significance.

In the second model we introduce dummies representing independent, grammar, secondary modern, and other schools, the omitted category being comprehensive schools, which had become the norm for pupils in the NCDS. As we can see, this leads to a significant improvement in fit. Grammar and independent schooling both have large and significant effects on first-job score, and their inclusion slightly reduces the impact of father's class. We should, however, be rather cautious in interpreting these school 'effects'. They could of course simply reflect the ability levels of the pupils who attended the different types of school. As we noted in the introduction, selection for grammar schools was essentially meritocratic, pupils taking a formal test (the '11-plus') in order to gain admittance, while the Direct Grant schools were also highly selective on academic criteria. In the third model we therefore control for measured ability at the age of 11. As we can see, measured ability has a major impact in Model 3 and its inclusion makes substantial inroads into the independent school and grammar school 'effects', the grammar-school parameter being more than halved.

The introduction of measured ability also leads to some reduction in the size of parameters for the parental variables; in the case of father's class the larger parameters fall by around one-fifth suggesting that the impact of social origins is partly mediated by the child's measured ability.

Finally, in the fourth model we introduce qualification level. This leads to a huge improvement in fit, but perhaps even more importantly it has some major consequences for other variables in the model. Thus qualifications reduce the Independent and Grammar school parameters well below conventional significance levels. The introduction of qualifications also leads to a further reduction in the size of the class-origin variables although, unlike type of school, service-class origins remain statistically significant in the fourth model. Perhaps most strikingly, however, we find that the effect of measured ability is substantially reduced, the parameter falling to almost one-third its original level, once qualifications are included. This in turn

tern, but there is of course a marked difference with respect to other activities outside the labour market—primarily looking after the home. There is a very strong hierarchical relation when we turn to the final column of the table: the higher the qualification, the lower the chances of a woman looking after the home at the age of 23. This is of course consistent with the evidence on the later age at marriage and first childbirth of more highly educated women.

We model these data with a multinomial logit, contrasting the unemployed and the economically inactive with those in paid employment. As expected, we find highly significant effects for educational level. Gender also has a highly significant effect, and there is a statistically significant interaction between gender and qualification. However, the addition of father's class and school type fail to make significant improvements in fit. (We run separate sets of models for father's class and for school type in order to minimize selection bias due to missing data.)

TABLE 3.5. *Fit of multinomial logit models of economic activity*

	School-type models	Father's class models
0. Independence	1307.3 (122)	1231.0 (188)
1. Qualifications	1033.7 (108)	991.4 (174)
2. Qualifications, gender	351.7 (106)	409.9 (172)
3. Qualifications, gender, gender* qualifications	107.9 (92)	183.1 (158)
4. Qualifications, gender, gender*qualifications, school type	98.9 (86)	
5. Qualifications, gender, gender*qualifications, father's class		167.4 (148)
N	6,592	5,714

The parameter estimates for Model 3 are shown in Table 3.6.[2] Inspecting the estimates we find that both the main effects of gender and the interaction effects are significant only in the case of the category 'not in the labour market'. In other words, if we excluded people who were not in the labour market, we would find that men and women had the same risks of unemployment at all educational levels.

TABLE 3.6. *Parameter estimates for Model 3*

	Unemployed	Not in labour market
Intercept	−2.20 (.07)	−2.33 (.09)
1a	0	0
1b	−0.48 (.14)	−0.68 (.33)
1c	−0.91 (.20)	−1.02 (.38)
2a	−0.39 (.40)	−0.88 (.55)
2b	−1.18 (.12)	−0.72 (.22)
2c	−1.12 (.17)	0.15 (.21)
3a	−1.65 (.19)	−0.53 (.23)
3b	−1.11 (.17)	−0.10 (.22)
Gender	−0.05 (.13)	−2.54 (.18)
Gender*ed	.38 (.28)	−0.33 (.66)
	.17 (.40)	0.09 (.76)
	−1.10 (.80)	0.05 (1.11)
	.21 (.24)	1.00 (.44)
	.45 (.33)	3.47 (.43)
	.55 (.39)	3.03 (.47)
	.29 (.34)	4.29 (.45)

Note: Employed is the omitted category.

Hope-Goldthorpe Scores

We turn now to the relation between qualification and first-job attainment. We begin with a simple overview of this relationship using the Hope-Goldthorpe (H-G) scale to measure the occupational standing of respondents' first jobs. This is shown in Table 3.7, where we display the mean H-G score for each qualification level. The table shows a clear monotonic relationship between qualifications and first-job scores. With the exception of women's intermediate academic qualifications, each step up the educational ladder leads to an increase in first-job score. However, the increments get bigger as we move up the educational hierarchy. There is relatively little difference, for example, between holders of basic academic and vocational qualifications in their first-job scores, or between intermediate academic and vocational qualifications.

   In contrast to these rather modest distinctions at the lower end of the scale, there is a notable jump at the top, men graduates obtaining an increment of ten points (and women graduates of eight points), compared with increments of typically two or three points lower down the educational hierarchy.

   Table 3.7 also shows that these patterns hold for women much as they do

Jarman, and Siltanen 1993). Alternatively, fathers may not use their social connections as vigorously on a daughter's behalf as they do on behalf of a son.

TABLE 3.9. *Regression models of first-job scores for women*

	Model 1	Model 2	Model 3	Model 4
Constant	33.8 (0.6)	34.7 (0.6)	30.6 (0.7)	32.8 (0.8)
Father's education	0.7 (0.1)	0.5 (0.1)	0.4 (0.1)	0.1 (0.1)
Mother's education	0.6 (0.1)	0.4 (0.1)	0.1 (0.1)	−0.1 (0.2)
Father's class:				
I	5.2 (0.6)	4.3 (0.6)	3.2 (0.78)	1.8 (0.7)
II	3.0 (0.5)	2.7 (0.5)	1.9 (0.5)	1.0 (0.6)
III	2.7 (0.7)	2.3 (0.7)	2.0 (0.7)	1.9 (0.7)
IV	0.9 (0.7)	0.7 (0.7)	0.3 (0.7)	0.0 (0.8)
V/VI	1.0 (0.4)	1.0 (0.4)	0.9 (0.4)	0.9 (0.4)
VII	0	0	0	0
School type:				
Independent		4.1 (0.8)	3.0 (0.9)	1.7 (0.9)
Grammar		4.4 (0.5)	2.7 (0.5)	1.0 (0.6)
Comprehensive		0	0	0
Secondary modern		−1.2 (0.4)	−1.0 (0.4)	−0.7 (0.4)
Other		−3.3 (1.1)	−2.4 (1.2)	−1.0 (1.3)
Ability (*100)			13.5 (1.2)	4.9 (1.4)
Credentials:				
degree				16.6 (0.9)
lower tertiary				9.9 (0.7)
full secondary				5.0 (0.8)
inter. academic				2.6 (0.6)
inter. vocational				1.3 (3.1)
basic vocational				2.9 (0.9)
basic academic				1.8 (0.7)
social minimum				0
R^2	0.07	0.09	0.12	0.25
N	4,264	4,264	3,801	2,982

Class Distributions

While measures of occupational desirability provide a useful overview of the process of occupational attainment, they have a number of important limitations. First, and perhaps most importantly, there are major conceptual differences between the hierarchical view of occupational attainment embodied in the models which we have used so far and the concept of discrete classes which are conceived as having distinct employment conditions—ones which cannot always be represented in continuous hierarchical terms. Second, the hierarchical view of the relation between education and occupation may be defective, and the evidence of heteroscedasticity which we have already seen suggests that there may indeed be problems. In particular, somewhat different processes may operate at the different levels of the labour market. Degrees, for example, may improve one's chances of entering the service class and of avoiding the working class, but they may not improve one's chances of obtaining skilled manual work and of avoiding unskilled manual work or unemployment (Heath and McMahon 1997).

Finally, conventional regression models are not well adapted to the analysis of interactions. As we have already seen from the analysis of variance, there are significant interactions between gender, qualifications, and first-job score. There are also theoretical grounds for supposing that there may be interactions between school type, qualification level, and class of first job: elite private or grammar schooling may help pupils with low educational qualifications but add little to the occupational fortunes of those with high qualifications. Similarly, there may be interactions between class origin, qualification level, and class: specific occupational destinations such as petty bourgeois ones may be only weakly related to formal credentials, recruitment depending on different social processes, such as direct inheritance.

We begin with a simple cross-tabulation which shows the pattern of association between credentials and class of entry. In order to reduce the number of sparse cells, we combine the two small categories of intermediate and basic vocational qualifications (1c and 2a).

As might be expected, Table 3.10 shows many of the same hierarchical features that we saw in the earlier regression analyses. Thus, the probability of reaching the higher service class increases as one moves up the educational ladder, 2 per cent of people with the social minimum reaching Class I compared with 37 per cent of those with degrees. The patterns for access

TABLE 3.10. *Credentials and class of entry for men* (row percentages)

	I	II	IIIa	IIIb	IV	V/VI	VII	N
1a social minimum	2.5	2.9	2.5	3.6	3.4	33.2	51.7	443
1b basic academic	1.8	2.5	11.7	4.4	2.5	41.8	35.2	435
1c/2a vocational	1.4	2.8	2.6	2.2	2.6	73.6	14.7	497
2b intermediate	5.4	9.3	17.0	3.6	1.2	45.1	18.4	1,297
2c full secondary	13.0	17.0	29.1	4.0	0.5	11.1	21.1	105
3a lower tertiary	13.8	17.7	17.4	0.9	0.9	33.7	16.6	350
3b university degree	33.3	26.7	11.1	1.8	0.9	6.0	20.1	333

indicates that the effects of ability on first-job score are largely mediated by qualifications. This is not perhaps very surprising, since measures of ability and British school examinations are largely measuring the same kinds of cognitive skills. However, it also has the fortunate side-effect that models which omit measured ability may not be seriously mis-specified.

TABLE 3.8. *Regression models of first-job scores for men*

	Model 1	Model 2	Model 3	Model 4
Constant	32.2 (0.7)	33.2 (0.8)	27.1 (0.9)	29.9 (1.2)
Father's education	1.0 (0.2)	0.8 (0.2)	0.7 (0.2)	0.3 (0.2)
Mother's education	0.6 (0.2)	0.4 (0.2)	0.2 (0.2)	−0.2 (0.2)
Father's class:				
I	7.4 (0.8)	6.7 (0.8)	5.3 (0.9)	2.9 (1.0)
II	5.7 (0.6)	5.2 (0.6)	4.1 (0.7)	2.9 (0.8)
III	3.5 (0.9)	3.1 (0.9)	2.3 (0.9)	0.6 (1.0)
IV	2.9 (0.9)	2.6 (0.9)	2.3 (0.9)	1.8 (1.0)
V/VI	2.5 (0.5)	2.3 (0.5)	2.1 (0.5)	1.2 (0.6)
VII	0	0	0	0
School type:				
Independent		4.6 (1.1)	3.3 (1.2)	1.2 (1.3)
Grammar		5.5 (0.7)	2.5 (0.8)	1.5 (0.9)
Comprehensive		0	0	0
Secondary modern		−0.3 (0.5)	0.5 (0.5)	1.3 (0.6)
Other		−2.9 (1.2)	−1.0 (1.3)	−0.4 (1.5)
Ability (*100)			19.8 (1.4)	7.9 (1.9)
Credentials:				
degree				19.3 (1.3)
lower tertiary				10.9 (1.1)
full secondary				7.3 (1.1)
inter. academic				5.5 (0.9)
inter. vocational				6.0 (1.3)
basic vocational				4.1 (1.0)
basic academic				1.6 (1.0)
social minimum				0
R^2	0.08	0.09	0.13	0.21
N	4,218	4,218	3,726	2,710

Perhaps the most interesting of these findings is that type of school does not have a direct effect on first-job score, once the other variables have been included in the model. This casts serious doubt on one of the prevailing myths about Britain, namely the advantage of the 'old school tie' in secur-. ing occupational privileges for pupils from independent schools. Certainly, linear regression provides at best a global test of the 'old school tie' hypothesis, and it is still possible that there are some specific effects that are swamped in the overall regression analysis. For example, the old school tie is expected to help the poorly qualified public schoolboys in particular, and a global test may fail to uncover this. We can test for specific effects of this sort when we move on to loglinear modelling in the next section.

In general, however, we suggest that the independent schools have now largely adapted to the new 'credentialized' regime operated by universities and now ensure that their pupils, who can no longer rely on connections to secure entry to privileged universities, acquire the A-level grades necessary. In other words, independent schools have adapted to a more credentialized world.

On the other hand, the spread of credentialism has not led to the complete disappearance of non-meritocratic factors in the attainment process. As we can see from the third model, the impact of father's social class, although somewhat reduced, remains highly significant even after controlling for school type, measured ability, and qualifications. In particular the parameters for Classes I and II remain around half their original size. Credentialism, then, does not mediate the effect of social background to the same extent that it mediates the effect of school type or of measured ability.

Broadly similar results are obtained for women: in the first model father's class has a significant effect, as does school type in the second model. In the third model, as with men, the introduction of measured ability reduces the school variables substantially. And in the fourth model the introduction of qualifications in turn reduces the effect of measured ability, as with men, to around one-third of its original level.

More interestingly, however, we find that father's education is also reduced to non-significance in the fourth model, while father's class is only barely significant. This suggests that there are some important differences in the ways in which ascriptive factors affect the attainment process for men and women. Various social processes could be at work here. One possibility is that women do not benefit from the inheritance of property in the way that men do; Goldthorpe and Payne (1986) for example have found that there is greater self-recruitment to the petty bourgeoisie among men than there is among women. But so few NCDS respondents of either sex entered the petty bourgeoisie as their first job that this is unlikely to be the explanation. Another possibility is that the kind of jobs which women typically enter are not ones where social connections are used in the recruitment process. Certainly there is a great deal of evidence in Britain that men and women enter different kinds of jobs, even at the same 'prestige' level, and these differences would need to be investigated in a full analysis of gender differences in the attainment process (see e.g., Hakim 1992; Blackburn,

latter may in effect become 'overqualified'—perhaps in their own eyes or in those of an employer—for this kind of skilled work.

Similarly, Class IIIa typically recruits men who leave school with O or A level. On the hierarchical principle, leavers with A level have an advantage over less-qualified candidates in gaining access to Class IIIa and avoiding lower-level work, but at the same time people who stay in full-time education beyond A level will become 'overqualified' for entry to routine white-collar work.

TABLE 3.12. *Credentials and class of entry for women* (row percentages)

	I	II	IIIa	IIIb	IV	V/VI	VII	N
1 social minimum	1.1	1.4	13.9	17.7	0.9	15.5	49.5	555
1b basic academic	1.8	2.8	40.2	18.2	0.6	13.6	22.9	545
1c/2a vocational	2.0	3.1	54.1	8.2	0.0	21.9	10.7	196
2b intermediate	1.4	4.7	60.4	13.7	0.0	9.3	10.4	1,608
2c full secondary	9.6	9.1	56.9	8.9	0.0	3.3	12.2	418
3a lower tertiary	5.0	16.7	48.6	9.8	0.2	4.2	15.4	479
3b university degree	18.6	39.7	20.3	5.1	0.3	5.1	10.9	350

The patterns for women are not greatly different from the male ones. Of course, women at all educational levels are less likely than men to be found in skilled manual work and are much more likely to enter routine white-collar work. Leaving this aside, there is a general pattern of hierarchy, with qualifications protecting one against entry into working-class jobs; the percentage entering Classes V–VII falls from 65 per cent at the social minimum to 16 per cent at graduate level. As with men, the odds of securing skilled rather than unskilled manual work follows a non-hierarchical pattern: the odds are most favourable for women with lower technical qualifications (1c/2a) and then deteriorate markedly higher up the educational ladder.

Perhaps the most notable departure from the male pattern is that lower tertiary qualifications do not protect women from unskilled manual work in the way that they protected men. This almost certainly reflects the kind of tertiary qualification that women secure. Unlike men, they will not be obtaining qualifications in engineering and related subjects. Instead they will be acquiring qualifications such as teaching and nursing ones that have little value in the working-class labour market.

Fitting a one-dimensional association model to Table 3.12, we again obtain a poor fit: Chi-square is 323 for 25 degrees of freedom and 90.8 per cent of cases are correctly predicted (slightly better than with the men). The intrinsic association (phi) also proves to be stronger for women (7.7), than

Anthony Heath and Sin Yi Cheung

for men (5.3). However, we should be very wary of interpreting parameter estimates from poorly fitting models.

The pattern of residuals from the one-dimensional association model show some parallels with those for men, but the parallels are far from exact. Leaving aside the extraordinarily high residuals for women with the social minimum qualifications (which are based on very small cell counts), perhaps the most striking phenomenon is that women with full tertiary qualifications tend to be over-represented (compared with the hierarchical model) in unskilled manual work and to be under-represented in routine white-collar work. Holders of lower vocational qualifications are over-represented in skilled manual work and holders of O level certificates in routine white-collar work. These two findings echo the male experience, but the male tendency for unqualified school-leavers to be over-represented in unskilled manual work is not repeated among the women.

TABLE 3.13. *Residuals from the one-dimensional association model for women*

	I	II	IIIa	IIIb	IV	V/VI	VII
1a social minimum	11.9	12.2	−3.2	−0.4	0.1	−0.6	1.8
1b basic academic	1.8	1.3	−1.9	1.3	1.4	1.2	−0.3
1c/2a vocational	−0.1	−0.8	0.5	−2.2	0.7	4.3	−1.6
2b intermediate	−3.8	−2.2	4.1	1.0	−1.9	−0.3	−5.0
2c full secondary	2.7	−2.3	1.0	−1.2	0.6	−2.9	1.5
3a lower tertiary	−1.0	1.8	−1.3	−0.7	0.6	−2.0	4.0
3b full tertiary	0.9	1.1	−5.0	0.5	2.6	2.7	8.5

Since the association models do not provide an acceptable fit to the data we now turn to multinomial logit models. A simple multinomial logit model will of course fit the data of Tables 3.10 and 3.12 perfectly, but they become more informative when we turn to check the effects of social origins and school type. We also wish to check for interaction effects: in particular do independent schools, or privileged social backgrounds, help less qualified respondents avoid undesirable class destinations, while they are of little extra help for the better qualified?

In order to keep the number of sparse cells to a minimum we combine Class I with Class II, and Class IIIa with IIIb. We also omit the petty bourgeoisie from the analysis, since so few respondents entered the petty bourgeoisie in their first job. Inspection of the parameter estimates from more detailed models also indicated that we could usefully reduce the number of categories for father's class and school type. We therefore simply distinguish manual from non-manual social origins and selective from non-selective schooling.

to Classes II and IIIa also follow the expected hierarchical pattern, peaking at full secondary educational level.

Few respondents enter petty bourgeois positions in their first jobs, as Goldthorpe has shown previously (Goldthorpe 1980). Very little can sensibly be said given the small numbers involved. But there does seem to be something of an educational gradient—the higher the qualification, the lower the probability of entering self-employment as a first job.

Access to the working class is rather more interesting. If we combine Classes V, VI and VII we obtain a striking change as we move up the educational ladder. Thus the percentages fall from 85 per cent of those with the social minimum entering working-class jobs to 26 per cent of graduates. However, there are notable exceptions to this hierarchical pattern, vocational qualifications leading to greater-than-expected working-class entry.

The vocational qualifications are strongly associated with skilled manual jobs, and when we distinguish within the working class between the skilled and unskilled levels, some interesting findings emerge. Thus the odds of reaching the higher rather than the lower working class are actually worse for graduates than they are for people with the lowest levels of qualification. In other words, for those graduates who have failed to reach Class IV or above, the chances of obtaining skilled work and of avoiding menial work are relatively poor. This is a finding that Heath and McMahon (1997) and Heath, McMahon, and Roberts (1994) have reported from quite independent data-sets (including the public use sample of the 1991 Census). We should note that this is not a consequence of students taking unskilled jobs while still in full-time education: Table 3.10 only includes jobs obtained after completion of full-time education.

A simple hierarchical view of the relation between credentials and class will not therefore adequately represent the data. We can show this more formally by using a Goodman association model (Goodman 1987; Becker and Clogg 1989). A one-dimensional association model essentially postulates that there is a hierarchical relation between the two variables in question, a relation that operates in the same way at all levels of the hierarchy, and in the one-dimensional case it is equivalent to an ordered logit model. More formally, it postulates that the ratios of the odds ratios are the same at different levels of the hierarchy.

If the model fails to fit, therefore, we must reject the simple hierarchical view of the relation between education and occupational attainment. Inspection of the residuals will also help us to locate where the hierarchical relationship breaks down.

Fitting a one-dimensional association model to the data we obtain a Chi-square value of 348 for 25 degrees of freedom. This is far from an acceptable fit to the data, and we therefore reject the hypothesis that hierarchy is the sole process involved in the education–occupation link. However, the hierarchical model would appear to have some value—the reduction in Chi-square from the independence model is 1388 to 348 for the loss of 11 df, and 88 per cent of the cases are correctly predicted.

TABLE 3.11: *Residuals from the one-dimensional association model for men*

	I	II	IIIa	IIIb	IV	V/VI	VII
1a social minimum	−0.8	−2.6	−5.1	0.6	2.4	−4.3	9.9
1b basic academic	−1.7	−2.6	0.7	1.3	0.9	−2.1	3.6
1c/2a vocational	3.0	3.0	−1.6	−0.7	−0.5	0.9	−1.8
2b intermediate	0.5	1.3	2.7	0.1	−1.5	2.8	−6.0
2c full secondary	−1.7	−1.1	3.5	0.7	−1.4	−2.0	0.9
3a lower tertiary	1.1	1.7	−0.3	−2.4	−0.1	3.2	−4.1
3b full tertiary	0.8	0.4	−3.4	0.3	1.8	−0.7	2.6

Inspection of the residuals from the association model confirms that there are significant deviations from hierarchy within the working class. As we had anticipated from our inspection of the cross-tabulation given in Table 3.10, graduates are significantly over-represented (in comparison with the hierarchical view of the education–occupation link) in the unskilled working class and are under-represented in the skilled working class. In contrast, holders of lower tertiary qualifications (which include many technical qualifications such as the HND) are relatively successful in avoiding unskilled manual work and in securing employment in the skilled working class. This pattern has clear parallels with the findings on unemployment reported in Table 3.3.

The other notable pattern in Table 3.11 is for certain educational groups to be markedly over-represented (relative to the hierarchical model) in specific entry classes. Thus men at the bottom of the educational ladder (with the social minimum or with basic academic qualifications) are markedly over-represented in the lower working class; men with intermediate qualifications are over-represented in routine non-manual positions and in skilled manual work; and men with full-secondary qualifications are markedly over-represented in the routine non-manual class.

One way to interpret these results is that certain classes represent the 'natural' entry categories for particular levels of qualification. Thus, Class V/VI is the natural entry class for school-leavers with intermediate qualifications; on the hierarchical principle, they have an advantage over less-qualified respondents in gaining access to the skilled work of Class V/VI and avoiding Class VII, but they also have an advantage over better qualified respondents who have stayed on at school to acquire higher qualifications. The

TABLE 3.16. *Parameter estimates for the multinomial logit models for women*

	Class I/II	III	V/VI
Intercept	−0.45 (.13)	0.85 (.09)	−0.81 (.15)
1a	0	0	0
1b	1.60 (.50)	1.62 (.23)	0.79 (.25)
1c/2a	2.31 (.65)	2.72 (.36)	1.70 (.39)
2b	2.48 (.45)	2.90 (.21)	1.07 (.23)
2c	3.21 (.48)	2.50 (.27)	−0.37 (.46)
3a	3.40 (.47)	2.38 (.26)	−0.20 (.40)
3b	4.76 (.50)	1.93 (.34)	0.60 (.46)
Father non-manual	0.54 (.18)	0.31 (.13)	−0.18 (.19)
Selective school	.02 (.22)	−0.27 (.18)	−0.33 (.30)

Note: Class VII is the omitted category.

more impact later in the occupational career, or brings benefits in a few occupational niches, such as the financial centre in the City of London, which could not be detected with the sample size that we have available. But in general it is level of qualification, not type of school, that matters.

We should emphasize that these conclusions apply only to the direct effects of school type, controlling for qualifications. Of course, it may still be true that elite schools have indirect effects insofar as these schools may help their pupils obtain good examination results and in this way assist their career chances. We did indeed find significant 'school effects' on examination results, although these largely disappeared once we controlled for measured ability. But it was the direct, rather than the indirect, effects that were central to the old school tie myth; that is, the myth held that certain types of schools gave occupational advantages to their 'old boys' (and possibly to their 'old girls'), irrespective of their educational success or failure. And analysis of the 1972 Mobility Survey suggests that, in the past, these direct effects were not in fact a myth.

We cannot strictly compare the NCDS results with those obtained from the 1972 survey, since there are many differences between the two data-sets regarding both structure and variables. We can, however, use the first, 1991, wave of the British Household Panel Survey (BHPS) to look at changes over time in the size of school effects. The 1991 wave of the BHPS is a representative sample of the British population; it contains data on first job, school type, and father's class, and we can of course divide the sample into birth cohorts enabling us to look at changes over time. When we do so, we find that, among men aged 50 to 65 in 1991, there were large and statistically significant effects of grammar and private schooling on first-job score (controlling for highest qualifications and father's class); but these school effects declined over time and were effectively zero in the cohort of men aged 16 to 29 in 1991.

The BHPS data therefore provided strong support for our conclusion that direct school effects have substantially weakened in Britain. It is likely that in Britain private schools (and selective schools generally) have joined the credential society. They prepare their pupils for the public examinations of GCSE and A level, and, reserving judgement on the question of causation, it is clear that their pupils fare well at these examinations. The schools themselves seem to share our view that it is qualifications, not the old school tie, that matter in contemporary Britain.

However, the way in which qualifications matter is not quite so straightforward as might be supposed. As we have seen, the relationship between qualifications and occupational success is not a simple hierarchical one. It is true that one's chances of reaching the service class increase as one moves up the educational ladder, and they do so perhaps more strongly for women than for men. In this sense the conventional hierarchical view is correct. The crucial point, however, is that graduates who fail to reach the service class do not have competitive advantages over their less qualified contemporaries. Thus, of men graduates who failed to gain service-class jobs on leaving university, half took Class VII jobs. In contrast, of respondents with lower tertiary qualifications who failed to enter the service class, less than one quarter had to make do with Class VII jobs. Similar patterns are evident with respect to unemployment.

Various social processes may lie behind this phenomenon. It could be due to period effects—to the particularly difficult labour market for graduates in the early 1980s. However, a similar result has been found for other samples entering the labour market at different periods (Heath and McMahon 1997), so this is unlikely to be more than a part of the story.

Another possibility is that the graduates see these Class VII jobs as temporary ones; they are simply waiting until more appropriate graduate-level employment comes along (the 'parking lot' interpretation). These Class VII jobs may be somewhat analogous to 'frictional' unemployment and may tell us little about the lifetime prospects of graduate labour. On this interpretation, we might expect to see these non-hierarchical patterns gradually disappear as men's careers develop (although women attempting to re-enter the labour market after child-rearing may exhibit a similar pattern).

But even if we accept the frictional interpretation, we still have to ask why graduates opt for these particular, financially unattractive positions in Class VII. One answer is that these positions are readily available; there is a high

TABLE 3.14. *Fit of multinomial models*

	men	women
0. Independence	957.2 (81)	818.6 (78)
1. Qualification	131.6 (63)	92.4 (60)
2. Qualification, father's class	102.2 (60)	73.3 (57)
3. Qualification, father's class, school type	59.6 (57)	71.6 (54)
N	2,152	2,110

Note that the degrees of freedom are reduced for women, since no women from selective schools obtained 1b qualifications. This should perhaps be thought of as a case of structural zeros.[4]

We begin with Model 1, in which class depends solely on qualification. As we can see, this leads to a big improvement in fit over the independence model. We then introduce father's class in Model 2. As with the linear regression analysis, this produces a significant improvement in fit. The change in Chi-square is 29.4 for the loss of 3 degrees of freedom in the case of men and a somewhat smaller 19.1 in the case of women. Adding school type in Model 3, we obtain a further significant improvement in fit for men, but not for women.

As can be seen, in the case of men Model 3 gives an excellent fit to the data (p = 0.38). We can therefore reject the hypotheses that the effects of school type and social origins vary for men with different educational levels. In the case of women, the fit is not quite so good but still acceptable (p = .055), and so again we can reject the hypothesis of interaction effects. Inspecting the residuals does not lead us to alter this conclusion.

Turning to the parameter estimates derived from Model 3, we find that the education parameters are much as we would expect from our analysis of the association model and its residuals. Thus there is a strong hierarchical picture in the case of access to Classes I/II; there is little gradient in access to Class III, and a curvilinear one in access to Classes V/VI. In particular, we see that graduates are little different from the most poorly qualified respondents in their odds of securing skilled manual rather than unskilled manual jobs.

The effect of social origins is also much as we would have expected, non-manual origins giving a major advantage in the competition to reach Classes I and II. However, the school 'effects' are at first sight paradoxical. Selective schools (that is, grammar and independent schools) are associated with poorer chances of reaching skilled manual rather than unskilled manual jobs and do not appear to give any positive benefits whatsoever.

This strange result may however reflect rather similar processes to those involved in graduate exclusion from skilled manual jobs. Pupils from selective schools may be thought to be 'over-educated' (even if they are not over-qualified) for skilled manual work. At any rate, these results seem to suggest that superior schooling and superior qualifications may involve exclusion processes as well as inclusion ones.

TABLE 3.15. *Parameter estimates for the multinomial logit models for men*

	Class I/II	III	V/VI
Intercept	−0.39 (.11)	−0.69 (.12)	−0.13 (.11)
1a	0	0	0
1b	−0.14 (.44)	1.77 (.45)	0.65 (.21)
1c/2a	0.68 (.42)	1.00 (.55)	2.04 (.22)
2b	1.58 (.31)	2.55 (.41)	1.46 (.18)
2c	2.00 (.34)	2.60 (.44)	−0.17 (.29)
3a	2.69 (.36)	2.96 (.47)	1.47 (.27)
3b	3.20 (.35)	1.94 (.49)	0.53 (.40)
Father non-manual	0.59 (.15)	0.29 (.16)	−0.09 (.13)
Selective school	.01 (.19)	0.32 (.20)	−0.99 (.21)

Note: Class VII is the omitted category.

The overall picture for women is fairly similar. We can see, however, that the qualification parameters for access to Classes I/II (relative to Class VII) are substantially steeper than they were for men (and this helps us to understand why the association models yielded a higher measure of intrinsic association for the women than for the men). We can also see that the parameter estimates for father's class are very close to the male ones (despite the fact that the reduction in deviance was rather less). And finally, while the school-type parameters are not significantly different from zero, the pattern of the signs is close to the male one.

CONCLUSION

Perhaps the most surprising result of this analysis of the NCDS data is that the type of school attended no longer affects one's occupational chances in Britain. The notion that the old school tie brings major benefits is one of Britain's favourite myths about itself, but we have failed to detect any evidence that the old school tie brought positive benefits to the members of the NCDS cohort, at least with respect to their first job. It may possibly have

4. One way to deal with this problem is to amalgamate educational levels 1a and 1b. We then have no empty cells. When we follow this procedure, the pattern of model fit is very close to that in Table 3.14 and the substantive conclusions are identical.

5. In his analysis of NCDS data Kerckhoff (1990) explains around 20 per cent of the variance in occupational prestige of first job. His model includes a number of variables such as number of siblings, attitudes to school and ability test scores which are not included in our basic model. The broad thrust of his results, however, is very similar to ours, and Kerckhoff also notes that comparable models to his would explain a great deal more of the variance in countries such as the USA (see Kerckhoff 1990: table 4.5).

6. Note that we cannot control for period effects in our models of the NCDS data, since year of labour-market entry will be formally equivalent to school-leaving age. One option would be—following Blossfeld (1986)—to use direct measures of the labour-market conditions rather than year of entry, but over the short period involved there is likely to be a major problem of multi-collinearity.

level of turnover in Class VII and so vacancies appear regularly. They are also positions which involve little commitment to in-firm training or the gaining of vocational qualifications. Psychologically, graduates may find it difficult to commit themselves to skilled manual work or even to routine white-collar work. Perhaps even more importantly, employers may be reluctant to take on graduates whom they believe will fail to repay investments in in-firm training.

The other major puzzle thrown up by our results is the relatively weak association, by international standards, between qualifications and occupational attainment. The variance explained in the linear regression models of first-job attainment was only 21.0 per cent for men and 24.6 per cent for women.[5] As well as being low by international standards, this is also a great deal lower than has previously been found for Britain. Thus Halsey (1977), using a very similar model to our own, explained 33.1 per cent of the variance in first-job scores in the case of men aged 25 to 39 in 1972.

There is some evidence that the link between education and occupation may have been weakening in Britain over the last quarter of a century (Heath, Mills and Roberts 1992), and this could perhaps be part of the explanation. Again, we can check the story from the BHPS data. What we find is that in the cohort of men aged 50 to 65 in 1991, 31.6 per cent of the variance in their first-job scores could be explained by father's class, school type, and highest qualification—very similar results to Halsey's. However, by the time we reach the youngest cohort, the variance explained had fallen to 24.9 per cent   a substantial drop but not as great as that suggested by the NCDS data.

Another important possibility, as we have already noted, is that the low variance explained in the NCDS data may reflect the changing labour-market situation in Britain over the period when these respondents were looking for their first jobs. In particular, the deterioration of the labour market during the late 1970s and early 1980s will have given the early (but less qualified) school-leavers competitive advantages over the later (but better qualified) school-leavers. Some of the variance in the NCDS data-set, therefore, may be explained by period effects, and it is probably unwise to make strict comparisons between the variance explained in the NCDS data-set and that obtained in the cross-sectional survey such as the 1972 Mobility Survey or the 1991 BHPS.[6]

Even if we make allowance for historically-specific changes in the labour market, it still appears to be the case that the education/first-job link is weaker in Britain than it tends to be elsewhere. As we saw in Table 3.10, 34 per cent of respondents with the social minimum moved into skilled manual jobs, and these respondents would have been leaving school at much the same age (and under much the same labour-market conditions) as those with basic academic or vocational qualifications. So the argument about changes in the labour market will not explain the apparent lack of credentialism among manual jobs.

The explanation surely has to do with the nature of recruitment to manual jobs in Britain. Traditionally, apprenticeships were linked with skilled manual jobs, and these apprenticeships would have been filled by unqualified school-leavers (since in the heyday of the apprenticeship most school-leavers, apart from those from grammar schools, left school with no formal qualifications). Apprenticeships have declined markedly in number in Britain, but traditions of on-the-job training have remained strong. In addition, the tradition of general academic education in schools, followed by vocational education after leaving school, has not been greatly changed. The NCDS data suggest that these vocational qualifications are often obtained after starting work, for example through 'day release' schemes, evening classes, and the like (see Kerckhoff 1990).

Career mobility may also tend to strengthen the association between qualifications and occupational attainment as the respondents' careers develop (Winfield et al. 1989). In Britain, as Goldthorpe (1980) has shown, young people move into a relatively narrow range of 'entry' occupations. Relatively few are recruited directly from schools and colleges into, for example, managerial posts in the service class; would-be managers are likely to start off in routine non-manual or skilled manual work in various trainee positions. This could explain why, in Table 3.10, so many men with lower tertiary qualifications began their careers in skilled manual work. The association between qualifications and eventual occupational attainment may therefore be a great deal stronger in Britain than it appears from this analysis of first jobs.

NOTES

1. We use the information collected in sweep 5 as this uses the categories needed to construct the classification of qualifications needed for this volume. In constructing the variable, however, we do not include all qualifications obtained by the time of sweep 5 but only those qualifications obtained during continuous full-time education.
2. Note, that the parameterization used here gives average effects for the main variables. The interactions then show the difference in the effects for men and women. We therefore have to divide the interaction effects by two to get the deviation from the main effect.
3. Heath and Ridge (1983) did not carry out a formal test of significance. We have however repeated their analysis of the 1972 data and have found highly significant school effects.

and economic mobility of young people entering the labour market, especially from the working time standpoint. That is, in relation to the number of hours worked weekly, and the difficulties encountered in trying to avoid part-time and short-term contracts.

Concerning the data, we make extensive use of the 1993 Education, Training, and Occupations Survey (Enquête Formation et Qualification Professionnelle) carried out by the French National Institute of Statistics and Economic Surveys (INSEE), and the annual Labour Force Surveys (LFS) for the period 1990–1995 (for details on the LFS and FQP surveys, see the Data Appendix to this chapter). The LFS fits the analysis of inter-generational mobility less than FQP, but its sample is larger and, above all, it allows us to analyse the terms of the labour contracts of young workers and the spread of involuntary part-time work.

THE FRENCH EDUCATION SYSTEM

Since 1975, the French system of general education has consisted of five years' primary school, four years' lower secondary school (*collège*), and three years' upper secondary education (*lycée*). The secondary course ends with the matriculation examination at the upper secondary level (*baccalauréat*) which entitles holders to seek access to university and post-secondary institutions (Figure 4.1). Under the previous system, inherited from the nineteenth century, there were two distinct tracks after compulsory primary school, namely an upper primary school and a lower secondary school. This system was highly selective, with pupils from the lowest strata of society being almost systematically oriented towards upper primary school and with little chance of reaching the upper secondary level where school fees were payable. From the early 1940s to the 1970s, a series of reforms progressively unified the system (see, for instance, Prost 1992). These transformations gave new opportunities to pupils from the lowest socio-economic strata, and contributed to the diffusion of basic general education, and the rapid increase of the general level of education in France.

However, such uniform democratization does not necessarily reduce social inequalities. In fact, during the past decades, the links between social origin and level of education have remained almost unchanged (see, for instance, Garnier and Raffalovich 1984; and Goux and Maurin 1995a, 1997). The paradoxical result of these recent trends is that, in spite—and because—of its uniform democratization, the French school is increasingly perceived as a direct cause of social inequality. In the 1950s and 1960s, inequalities in educational attainment were due to entry barriers of which the functioning of the school system was not deemed responsible. A low level of educational attainment simply meant that an individual had not had the *luck* to be born

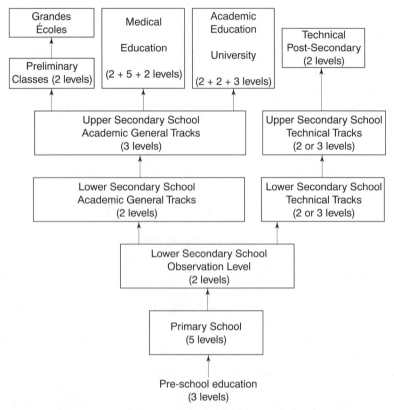

FIG. 4.1. *The French system of education: main articulations*

in the better strata of society, whereas today it tends to indicate a low level of *ability*, which is far more frustrating.

Stratification

The first important selection point in the modern French school system occurs after two years' lower secondary school. At around the age of 13, a number of pupils leave the general system and are oriented towards vocational tracks. More specifically, among French pupils born at the end of the 1960s, almost one-third left the general track before the end of lower secondary school (Table 4.2). The great majority of them are less academically able pupils who have already spent two years at the same school level.

4

From Education to First Job:

The French Case

DOMINIQUE GOUX AND ERIC MAURIN

INTRODUCTION

In France, as in many other Western countries, the educational system has been thoroughly transformed during the post-war decades. The 1950s and 1960s were years of rapid economic growth, and drastic shortages of qualified employees encouraged the French administration to open up the secondary school, and to encourage a broader diffusion of general education and qualifications. From a purely quantitative standpoint, this objective has undoubtedly been reached. Today, in each given birth cohort, the majority of French children pass their upper secondary examinations (51 per cent, as against 26 per cent in the 1960s), and France is no longer the lowest-ranking pupil in the classroom of industrialized countries (Table 4.1).

From a more qualitative standpoint, the current diagnosis is slightly more gloomy. The massive, and uniform democratization has not reduced inequalities in educational achievement between pupils from different social backgrounds, and the monetary and social returns to education seem to be declining (see, for instance, Baudelot and Glaude 1988; Goux and Maurin 1994). In short, the modern French school system, conceived in a period of rapid economic growth, now—in times of slow economic expansion—appears neither more fair, nor more economically efficient than its predecessor.

The purpose of this analysis is to make a simple, pragmatic re-evaluation of the French school system by focusing on the transition from school to the labour market. The first years after leaving school are a period of direct confrontation between labour supply generated by the educational system, on the one hand, and labour-market demand on the other. The way in which private and public organizations allocate young people among occupations, and compensate them differently, constitutes

Dominique Goux and Eric Maurin

TABLE 4.1. *Percentage rise in the share of qualified people*

Qualifications[a]	Birth cohort				
	1934–1938	1944–1948	1954–1958	1964–1968	1969–1973
1a	60.0	40.3	31.3	21.9	18.0
1b	4.7	8.9	10.3	8.6	5.9
1c	19.8	24.9	27.7	31.0	25.0
2a	3.3	5.2	5.5	9.2	11.3
2b, 2c	5.1	7.0	7.7	7.8	13.4
3a	2.8	5.6	9.4	12.3	15.1
3b	4.3	8.1	8.1	9.2	11.3

Field: All those born 1934–1938, 1944–1948, 1954–1958 or 1964–1968, living in France in May 1993, and those born 1969–1973, living in France in March 1995.

Lecture: Among people born between 1934 and 1938, 4.3 % reached a 3b educational level, against 9.2 % among those born between 1964 and 1968.

[a] In this table and the next ones, as in the text, we defined the international educational schema from the French system of education as follows: 1a: No diploma or *Certificat d'études primaires*—CEP—a primary-school leaving diploma, now abolished; 1b: *Brevet d'Études du Premier Cycle*—BEPC—or *Brevet Elémentaire*—BE—some lower secondary-school leaving diplomas; 1c: (short-course) Vocational training diplomas, gathering essentially *Certificat d'Aptitude Professionnelle*—CAP—and *Brevet d'Enseignement Professionnel*—BEP—(some of these holders are also BEPC graduates); 2a: Technical or professional *Baccalauréat*, which is the advanced high-school leaving diploma; a prerequisite for admission to university and other post-secondary education (not to be confounded with the English word 'bachelor') and other long-course vocational training diplomas (BEI, BEA, etc.); 2b, 2c: *General Baccalauréat*; 3a: Post-secondary degrees corresponding to two years of education beyond the *Baccalauréat*. Most of them are vocationally oriented diplomas, *Brevet de Technicien Supérieur*—BTS— *Diplôme Universitaire Technologique* -DUT-, the others correspond to the first university-cycle—DEUG, DUEL—and to social and paramedical diplomas; 3b: Post-secondary degrees corresponding to strictly more than two years' education beyond the *Baccalauréat*: Engineering qualifications (*Grandes écoles, écoles d'ingénieurs*), doctor's degrees, bachelor's degrees, thesis, Ph.D. in medicine, pharmacy, etc.

Source: FQP 1993 survey, INSEE, except for birth cohorts 1969–1973; Labour Force Survey 1995, INSEE.

an important indication of the ability of the educational system to match changing labour-market demand.

The chapter is organized as follows. First, we present the modern French system of education, its main stratifications, degree of centralization, and its main institutional relations with the labour market. Second, we analyse the links between the educational level of young people, on the one hand, and labour-market participation, socio-economic status of first job, and social class of first job, on the other. Finally, we study some aspects of the social

TABLE 4.2. *French general secondary school: main orientation stages* (in %)

Orientation during the lower secondary school	Birth cohorts				
	1944–1948	1949–1953	1954–1958	1959–1963	1964–1968
No secondary school[a]	48.0	42.8	20.8	9.1	9.9
Leave general lower secondary school after 2 years (at the end of 5ème)	6.0	7.6	11.8	17.1	15.4
Leave general lower secondary school after 3 years (at the end of 4ème)	3.0	4.0	7.8	8.2	6.6
Leave general secondary school at the end of lower cycle (at the end of 3ème)	12.6	11.9	21.3	26.9	27.5
Enter the upper secondary school	30.4	33.7	38.3	38.7	40.6

Field: Individuals born between 1944 and 1968.

Lecture: Among people born between 1944 and 1948, 48.0 % did never enter the secondary school (they left school during or after the primary cycle, or they entered the upper primary school). 30.4 % of them entered the upper secondary school (general track).

[a] Children who left school during or at the end of the first year of general lower secondary school are considered like those who did not enter the secondary school.

Source: FQP 1993 survey, INSEE.

Currently, when first oriented towards vocational tracks, pupils are on average one year older than those going on to the general track.[1]

The second important orientation/selection stage occurs at the end of lower secondary school and at the beginning of upper secondary school. Here again, pupils who do not go on to the general track are oriented towards apprenticeship or vocational tracks (provided they remain at school—school is only compulsory to the age of 16). Among pupils born at the end of the 1960s, around 27 per cent left the general track at this level of the secondary course (see Table 4.2). Here again, most of them are one or two years older than those who go on to the general track: in France, orientation towards vocational course generally occurs at the end of a progressive elimination from the general system.

In short, French secondary school is above all stratified upon the opposition general/vocational track,[2] this opposition being one of the basic principles of the stratification of French society. Today, among those aged between 30 and 40, two-thirds have either no qualification at all, a simple vocational qualification, or a lower secondary qualification (BEPC), and have undoubtedly experienced an early failure in the lower secondary school.

Post-Secondary Institutions

In France there are at least two very distinct institutions of post-secondary education: universities and the system of *Grandes Écoles* (GE). University entrance is open to all those with a *baccalauréat*, whereas access to the *grandes écoles* is highly selective. First, the student must be accepted into specific preliminary classes (*classes préparatoires*). At the beginning of the 1990s, among those who have passed the *baccalauréat* and continued studying in the post-secondary system, only 7–10 per cent were admitted to these highly selective institutions. Once admitted, the student then completes two to three years of intense preliminary competition—almost half of those admitted are eliminated during that initial obstacle race and transfer to university. At the end of this preliminary course, each selected pupil takes several entrance examinations. There is a clear hierarchy of *grandes écoles*,[3] so that it is generally not difficult to choose the one. Those graduating from the *grandes écoles* monopolize the highest levels within French firms' management, public administration, and universities. The coexistence of the *grandes écoles* and universities constitutes another basic stratification within the French system of education, and as a consequence, within French society. Among young people who began their working life in the 1990s, around 3–4 per cent are graduates from the *grandes écoles* as against 12 per cent of graduates from the second or third level of universities. At the other end of the educational hierarchy, around 50 per cent are either without a diploma or hold one of the (lower) secondary qualifications which are associated with an early elimination from the general system.

Centralization

The French educational system is highly centralized. Curricula and diploma are defined at the national level, mostly under the responsibility of the National Ministry for Education. There are several intermediate administrative levels between the Ministry and the different specific schools, namely twenty-eight regional *académies*, each of which is divided into elementary *inspections*.[4] Each *académie* is directed by a *recteur*, chosen and appointed by the Minister. *Académies* and *inspections* represent (administrative) intermediate levels of decisions which supervise the application of the general orientations given at the ministry level and which try to favour their concrete application. The existence of such an administrative organization may lead us to expect in France that local, idiosyncratic factors are less important than in other less centralized countries. But perhaps this is not the case. At the beginning of the 1990s, the OECD carried out comparative studies which show that in France (and in other centralized countries), the decision-making process is more balanced between local and national decisions than one might expect. The OECD estimated that in France nearly 33 per cent of the decisions are taken at the school level, 31 per cent at the intermediate level (*académies* and *inspections*), and 35 per cent at the national level (OECD 1992). In countries with a federal structure (like Switzerland, the USA), decisions are not taken at the national level, but the intermediate level is far more powerful than in France. In the USA, the intermediate level takes 80 per cent of the decisions, and in the last instance, schools are given less scope for own initiative than in France (OECD 1992). These raw figures suggest that centralization may actually lead to systems where local decisions and factors play an important role.

More specifically, let us consider pupils of the same social background and with the same level of performance at the end of primary school. It is now well established that their orientation and performance during lower secondary school can differ greatly from one school to another, even in a centralized system such as the French one (see Duru-Bellat and Mingat 1988). One of the key factors is the social 'tone' of the school. That is, the proportion of pupils from the lower socio-economic classes. However, the pedagogical choices have a great importance too. For instance, around half of the lower primary schools surveyed by Duru-Bellat and Mingat allocated pupils to different classes according to ability and level of performance.[5] Some concentrated pupils who had already remained two years at the same school level in the same classes, or those who opt to learn a foreign language (especially German) intensely. All other things being equal, these practices result in a higher rhythm of progression for those who stay in the general track during the lower secondary course (even the weakest), but generate higher (socially grounded) inequalities between pupils.[6]

We will not go further in the analysis of the importance of the choices made at the micro level. Let us just stress that in a 'centralized' system such as the French one, there are significant degrees of freedom at the micro level, and each given pupil destination can be significantly affected by the way his specific school makes use of these degrees of freedom. In other words, we would not be surprised to discover a significant level of heterogeneity of occupational destination between workers with the same level of educational achievement, even in such a centralized system as the French one.

Educational Requirements of Occupations

In France there are at least five types of institutional links between educational achievement and occupational destination. First, as in most industrialized countries, the educational requirements of many professions are formally defined by law, and individuals cannot become lawyers, doctors, architects, dentists, or chemists, etc., without having achieved a specific course in specific universities and without having passed a state examination.

Second, access to the various levels of the public sector is subordinated to formal examinations, each of which require a specific educational level. In France, the persistence of unemployment and the increasing difficulty in obtaining something other than short-term contracts make the public sector increasingly attractive for young graduates who prefer the employment stability of a lifetime contract to the higher, but less certain, compensation in the private sector (see, for instance, Goux and Maurin 1993).

Third, in the private sector, firms have inherited from the past, and especially from the different periods of war, rather rigid (military) categorizations of the different jobs and occupations their organizations are composed of. The notion of *cadre* is perhaps one of the most specific of these French categories. It has no genuine equivalent in the Anglo-Saxon or German traditions. The *cadres* generally belong to the managerial and professional staff of their firms, but it is not because of the occupational content of their jobs that they are appointed as *cadres*. When the firm chooses to hire (or promote) an employee at this level of its organization, it accords specific rights,[7] and imposes implicit duties that other members of the labour force do not have.[8] The different collective agreements often have precise, specific entry conditions (especially in terms of minimum educational level) for the category designated as *cadres*, so that the links between education and occupation are, at least partially, patterned by the existence of this institutional category.

More generally, each collective agreement includes specific definitions of several other important categories of employees. The categories of technicians and of skilled workers are often precisely defined.[9] Here again, the different specifications contribute to a genuine institutionalization of the link between education and occupation.

The fourth important institutional link concerns the less qualified young workers. Since the mid-1980s, the French Government has been helping and financing around one million hirings of young workers (i.e. less than 25 years old) each year, a large part being unqualified. Some of this state aid takes the form of apprenticeships in small private-sector businesses. Others are specific short-term contracts in the private sector (for which firms are exempted from social insurance costs). Another very important part consists in short-term contracts for young workers in the public sector (especially in local administration), the most popular being the CES (*Contrats Emploi Solidarité*). The young people who benefit from CES are on average less well qualified than those hired by private-sector firms and find it difficult to avoid going from one CES to another, so that one may speak of a kind of 'institutionalized' dual sector.

Last but not least, minimum wages in France concern a significant fraction of the labour force, especially among young workers, and may be thought as a real institutional constraint for firms. There is indeed in France an explicit social agreement that the purchasing power of lower wages should not drop. In 1995, among wage-earner workers who entered the labour market the two or three preceding years (i.e. with no more than three years' labour-market experience), around 45 per cent received no more than the minimum hourly wage. Half of these young low wage-earners benefited from state-aided employment contracts.

As a partial conclusion of the preceding section, in France, both the educational system and labour market appear to be strongly stratified and interrelated by multiple links. If economic growth were high and unemployment low, it would not be hard to predict a strong, direct, hierarchical, association between educational attainment and social status, but this is not the case. The French labour market is experiencing selective, mass unemployment. In such a period, the value of education becomes difficult to measure—the way it lowers unemployment risks becomes as important as the occupations it allows an individual to hold. In the following sections, our main concern is to describe, from a more empirical standpoint, the way educational attainment models affect both participation in the labour market and, above all, unemployment risks in France.

EMPLOYMENT CHANCES AND LABOUR-MARKET PARTICIPATION

One of the main features of the French labour market is the high level of unemployment among young workers. In France, most of the debate focuses on this specific drawback of the labour market. At the beginning of the 1990s, around 25 per cent of workers with less than three years' experience in the labour market were unemployed. That is, about two and a half times more than those with more experience.

In such a context, a good qualification remains an important passport—for both young men and young women who participate in the labour market, employment chances are strongly linked to educational attainment. For instance, two years after leaving school, nearly 40 per cent of boys and girls who entered the labour market at the beginning of the 1990s with no

TABLE 4.3. *From education to occupation: destination of young school-leavers in the 1990s* (in %)

Educational level	Unemployment	In work	Occupational destination							
			I	II	IIIa	IIIb	IVabc	V, VI	VIIab	All
1a	38.8	61.2	0.4	3.8	11.1	26.2	0.3	10.7	47.5	100
1b	30.9	69.1	1.9	8.0	24.0	29.0	1.3	11.6	24.2	100
1c	29.9	70.1	1.1	7.1	21.1	21.2	2.9	22.5	24.1	100
2a	24.4	75.6	1.8	18.6	34.3	16.0	2.5	13.6	13.2	100
2b, 2c	24.6	75.4	6.4	26.7	35.4	20.3	1.7	5.0	4.5	100
3a	18.2	81.8	5.0	58.1	24.5	4.9	0.8	4.3	2.4	100
3b	15.6	84.4	59.8	26.1	10.5	1.5	0.8	0.7	0.6	100
the whole	25.7	74.3	13.7	24.1	21.3	14.4	1.5	9.7	15.3	100

Field: Individuals, in work or unemployed, who entered the labour market two years ago between 1990 and 1993).

Lecture: Two years after first entering the labour market, 15.6% of individuals who have reached a 3b educational level are unemployed, while 84.4% are in work. Among the latter, 59.8% are higher-grade professionals, administrators, or managers (Class I).

Source: Labour Force Surveys, 1992 to 1995, INSEE.

educational qualification were still unemployed, as against 16 per cent of those who were highly qualified (Table 4.3).

A simple multinomial analysis confirms the extent of the initial disadvantage of not being qualified in France (Table 4.4). At the same time, it emphasizes the role of experience in the labour market—among young men as well as young women (under the age of 35), the more recent an individual's entry into the labour market, the smaller his or her chances of holding a job, and the higher the risks of unemployment (see also Figure 4.2). For instance, in 1995, among qualified male workers, the rate of unemployment one year after entry into the labour market is around 30 per cent, against 20 per cent after three years, 7 per cent after ten years.

Such relationships confirm that young workers' unemployment is primarily a problem of transition from school to work. That is, irrespective of educational level or age, young French workers cannot avoid a kind of waiting list before their progressive integration into the labour force.

The slowness of the transition process may explain why students delay their definitive departure from the school system, even though the returns of such a delay have become more and more uncertain. Between 1985 and 1995, the share of students in the population aged 20 to 25 almost doubled. For instance, in 1985, among those aged 22, less than 20 per cent were still in the school system, against one-third in 1990, and nearly 50 per cent in 1995 (see Figure 4.3).

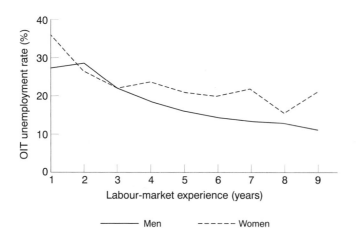

FIG. 4.2. *High unemployment rates at the onset of working life*

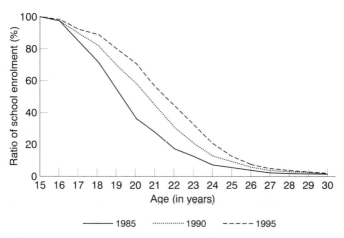

FIG. 4.3. *Increase in the rate of school enrolment, 1985–1995*

Unemployment, Educational Level, and Gender

Our multinomial analysis confirms a more traditional feature of modern labour markets, namely that the chances of finding a job are significantly higher for young men than for young women even where they have the same level of education (Table 4.4). Moreover, in France, the links between employment chances and qualifications are not exactly the same for young men and young women. For young men, unemployment risks are concentrated on those who have failed to obtain any qualifications. Apart from the unqualified young men, there are no significant differences between young men with a simple vocational qualification on the one hand, and young men with secondary qualifications or even tertiary short-course degrees, on the other.

On the contrary, among women who decide to participate in the labour market, one can observe a continuous increase of employment chances with educational level. What does this difference mean? One possible explanation is that women's employment chances specifically depend on employers who attach special importance to formal educational background. De facto, in 1995 as in 1990, 29–30 per cent of young French working women (under the age of 35) work in the public sector, versus only 19–20 per cent of young working men. In other words, young women's employment chances are particularly concentrated in the sector that accords the greatest importance to formal educational background in its selection process.

Then, the question becomes, why is there such a concentration of young women in these kinds of job? The reasons are not difficult to imagine. Women are concentrated in the sector where gender-based segregation is weakest. First of all, in the public sector, no initial gender-based segregation is possible. As already noted, public-sector recruitment (and initial job status) depends essentially on passing an anonymous *concours* or formal examination.[10] In 1995, 41 per cent of the tertiary graduated young women were working in the public sector, versus only 22 per cent of those who had no more than a primary certification. Similar rates are much lower for young men (27 and 13 per cent, respectively). Their employment chances are far less structured by the public sector, and also less dependent on their educational level.

The Increasing Labour-Market Participation of Women

So far, our picture is rather gloomy. Unemployment is widespread and high among young workers in France, and specifically hits inexperienced, unqualified workers (especially women) for whom a job may constitute the only way to attain social status. The increasing participation of women in the labour market cannot be considered a cause of this imbalance, but it has undoubtedly contributed to reveal the kind of difficulties that may face a labour market like the French one, in absorbing large supply shocks.

In France, as in most industrialized countries, young women's participation in the labour market has increased rapidly over the last decades. Among women aged 30 to 34, 20 per cent remained out of the labour market in 1995, as against 31 per cent in 1982 and 42 per cent in 1975 (Figure 4.4). First, given the increasing level of education of young women, it is likely that they will wish to capitalize on their corresponding skills, otherwise their efforts in the school system would make little sense. De facto, in France there is still a strong statistical association between women's educational level and their labour-market participation. Such a statistical relationship certainly reflects an actual direct causality between women's educational attainment and their desire and ability to hold a job. At the same time, one cannot exclude the possibility of some endogenous co-determination of both educational attainment and participation in the labour market. In short, a young woman wishing to become a job holder is more likely to make more of an effort at school and to achieve a good course, than a young woman who anticipates that she will stay at home and be (economically) inactive. Such endogenous co-determinations are rather hard to detect, and it is difficult to escape from the bias they create in the statistical diagnosis.[11]

Another possible explanation of women's increasing participation is that an increasing proportion of young women have grown up with a wage-earner mother. The corresponding model would spread from generation to generation. Our multinomial regressions confirm a statistically significant

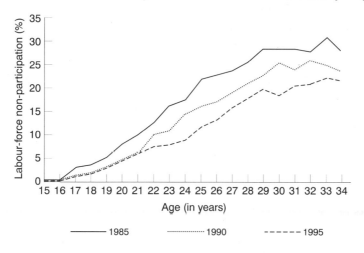

FIG. 4.4. *Rise in women's labour-force participation, 1985–1995*

relationship between daughters' and mothers' participation in the labour market.

A complementary explanation could have been an increasing participation at each level of the qualifications scale and in each type of family. To test this hypothesis, we have introduced an interaction variable (education x date of leaving school) in our multinomial analysis. If any, the observed trends are a slightly increasing participation of unqualified or primary qualified young women, and a slightly decreasing participation of the more qualified ones. Behaviour does not seem to change that much. The increasing participation of women mostly reflects the increasing level of their human capital.

Employment Chances, Labour-Market Participation, and Social Background

Concerning both employment chances and unemployment risks, it is clear that educational attainment is the key variable. Yet there remain slight but significant destination differences between young men and women who have reached the same educational level. A good social background is an a priori asset in the job search. Indeed, the set of useful information about the functioning of the labour market and social relationships tends to increase with the family's social status. At the same time, the higher parental income and status, the higher their ability to provide their children with the basic resources that help make unemployment periods less unpleasant and dramatic. Consequently, it is not clear whether a good social background favours labour participation and employment chances, or whether it simply tends to make unemployment periods softer and, tendentially, longer.

Interestingly, the statistical analysis provides mixed evidence on this point (Table 4.4). Fathers' status improves sons' employment chances, but has no significant effect on that of daughters'. Conversely, the higher the mothers' educational attainment, the lower their daughters' unemployment ratio, but the higher that of sons. Moreover, young women with qualified mothers participate in the labour market more than young women with unqualified mothers. Roughly speaking, each parent appears to favour specifically the employment chances of the children of the same sex.

As regards the link between mothers' education and daughters' participation in the labour market, there remains some ambiguity upon its actual significance. The first possible interpretation could be that the more educated the mother, the more likely she is to transmit to her child informal qualifications that the formal educational level does not reflect, but that the labour market pays for. The second possible mechanism is that highly educated mothers are those with the greatest labour-market experience which functions as an example and an encouragement to their female children.

In order to test these two competing hypotheses, we have introduced a

TABLE 4.4. *Multinomial logit contrasting unemployment and being out of the labour force with current employment*

Relative to employment	All		Women				Men	
			Model (1)		Model (2)			
(Standard error)	unemployed	not in LF	unemployed	not in LF	unemployed	not in LF	unemployed	not in LF
Intercept	−9.70	−4.77	−8.00	1.79	−8.05	1.51	−11.18	−32.72
	(1.24)	(1.26)	(1.69)	(1.41)	(1.65)	(1.38)	(1.90)	(3.68)
Date of leaving school	0.09	0.03	0.07	−0.04	0.07	−0.04	0.11	0.33
	(0.01)	(0.01)	(0.02)	(0.02)	(0.02)	(0.02)	(0.02)	(0.04)
Gender (contrasted against women) man	−0.50	−2.04	—	—	—	—	—	—
	(0.05)	(0.07)						
Qualifications (contrasted against 3b)								
1a	2.54	1.23	2.28	1.06	2.24	1.14	2.73	2.06
	(0.12)	(0.12)	(0.17)	(0.14)	(0.16)	(0.13)	(0.18)	(0.34)
1b	1.88	0.57	1.65	0.51	1.64	0.58	2.04	0.50
	(0.15)	(0.15)	(0.20)	(0.16)	(0.19)	(0.16)	(0.24)	(0.58)
1c	1.45	−0.00	1.44	0.03	1.45	0.12	1.40	0.06
	(0.11)	(0.12)	(0.15)	(0.13)	(0.14)	(0.13)	(0.18)	(0.39)
2a	1.29	−0.75	1.26	−0.74	1.18	−0.69	1.27	−1.18
	(0.17)	(0.23)	(0.21)	(0.25)	(0.21)	(0.25)	(0.28)	(0.74)

Dominique Goux and Eric Maurin

TABLE 4.4. *cont.*

Relative to employment	All		Women				Men	
			Model (1)		Model (2)			
(Standard error)	unemployed	not in LF	unemployed	not in LF	unemployed	not in LF	unemployed	not in LF
2b, 2c	1.14	0.27	0.82	-0.21	0.74	-0.06	1.59	1.51
	(0.18)	(0.16)	(0.24)	(0.20)	(0.24)	(0.19)	(0.29)	(0.32)
3a	0.87	-0.41	0.60	-0.37	0.52	-0.32	1.26	-0.08
	(0.16)	(0.17)	(0.21)	(0.19)	(0.21)	(0.19)	(0.25)	(0.38)
Father's class (contrasted against VIIab)								
I	-0.22	0.51	0.14	0.50	0.08	0.42	-0.79	0.55
	(0.19)	(0.18)	(0.26)	(0.22)	(0.22)	(0.19)	(0.30)	(0.32)
II	-0.39	0.13	-0.15	0.15	-0.15	0.23	-0.86	-0.01
	(0.19)	(0.19)	(0.24)	(0.21)	(0.23)	(0.20)	(0.30)	(0.38)
IIIa	-0.06	0.12	0.12	0.10	0.12	0.12	-0.34	0.11
	(0.15)	(0.16)	(0.20)	(0.18)	(0.20)	(0.18)	(0.24)	(0.36)
IIIb	-0.55	-0.39	-0.71	-0.24	-0.78	-0.34	-0.21	-6.47
	(0.48)	(0.50)	(0.63)	(0.51)	(0.639)	(0.50)	(0.72)	(∞)
IVabc	-0.34	0.02	-0.28	-0.02	-0.24	0.10	-0.42	0.16
	(0.14)	(0.14)	(0.19)	(0.15)	(0.18)	(0.15)	(0.21)	(0.31)
V, VI	-0.40	0.10	-0.45	0.07	-0.43	0.10	-0.39	0.20
	(0.12)	(0.13)	(0.17)	(0.14)	(0.16)	(0.13)	(0.19)	(0.27)

Mother's activity (contrasted with Always with no activity)								
with an activity	—	—	—	—	-0.28 (0.09)	-0.52 (0.08)	—	—
has had an activity	—	—	—	—	-0.17 (0.11)	-0.17 (0.09)	—	—
Father's education (contrasted against post-secondary)								
primary	0.02 (0.11)	-0.01 (0.11)	-0.22 (0.15)	-0.13 (0.13)	—	—	0.14 (0.17)	0.75 (0.25)
secondary	-0.08 (0.11)	-0.08 (0.10)	-0.38 (0.14)	-0.05 (0.12)	—	—	0.13 (0.16)	-0.06 (0.22)
Mother's education (contrasted against post-secondary)								
primary	-0.20 (0.11)	0.23 (0.12)	0.83 (0.18)	0.39 (0.14)	—	—	-0.96 (0.15)	-0.38 (0.26)
secondary	-0.19 (0.11)	0.07 (0.11)	0.82 (0.18)	-0.06 (0.14)	—	—	-0.99 (0.16)	0.47 (0.21)

Field: Individuals, men or women, aged 25–34.

Source: FQP 1993 survey, INSEE.

variable indicating whether the mother has or has not been economically active during her life (Table 4.4, Model 2). Interestingly, even roughly introduced, the mother's proximity to the labour market captured almost all the social background explanatory power. What really matters for a young woman is not whether her mother was qualified, but whether she made use of her qualifications and had some experience of the labour market.

SOCIO-ECONOMIC STATUS OF FIRST JOB

Education is an important asset to avoid unemployment and make the initial transition from school to work easier and shorter. Such a basic relationship between education and employment chances can partly explain why education (and more specifically, secondary and tertiary general education) remains so attractive in France, and why the French system of education has so many difficulties in absorbing the social demand for education. At the same time, it cannot explain the rising level of dissatisfaction among students and families alike, nor the fact that everybody agrees on the need for a necessary and pressing reform of the educational system.

One explanation of this paradoxical situation (i.e. a rising demand for something that is perceived as more and more unsatisfactory) is that while increasingly necessary to avoid unemployment and poverty, the value of educational attainment in the labour market is nevertheless decreasing. Students may be in a situation where education is necessary to guarantee them against total failure, but insufficient to improve their economic prospects and favour upward social mobility. To test this hypothesis, we built a score measuring the socio-economic status of first job (Table 4.5) and studied its net correlations with educational attainment.[12]

Education and Socio-Economic Status of First Job

At first sight, from a socio-economic standpoint, educational attainment appears a very decisive asset. The higher one's initial qualification, the higher one's initial position on the socio-economic scale. More than 50 per cent of the variance of socio-economic status of first job is explained by three basic factors: educational attainment, the date of entry in the labour market, and gender (Table 4.6). The initial gap is particularly large between graduates and non-graduates, on the one hand, between top graduates (3b) and other graduates (2c and 3a), on the other. As far as the socio-economic status is concerned, the two important things are whether an individual belongs to the elite or not, and whether he or she belongs to those who have completely failed or not. Intermediate distinctions are less important.

TABLE 4.5. *Average socio-economic status of first job*

Qualifications	Men			Women		
	Date of entry to labour market			Date of entry to labour market		
	1945–1959	1960–1974	1975–1989	1945–1959	1960–1974	1975–1989
1a	77.5	78.5	78.2	81.5	82.9	83.2
	(13.8)	(16.3)	(15.2)	(13.2)	(14.9)	(14.7)
1b	98.0	98.7	90.7	104.7	99.8	95.1
	(18.8)	(22.6)	(19.3)	(13.0)	(17.0)	(17.6)
1c	79.8	82.5	81.6	93.9	95.0	92.8
	(14.7)	(17.1)	(15.5)	(17.5)	(14.4)	(14.9)
2a	94.7	99.9	102.0	98.8	104.1	104.1
	(24.3)	(21.2)	(22.1)	(13.5)	(13.8)	(13.2)
2b, 2c	112.6	109.8	108.8	113.1	114.9	106.8
	(27.5)	(20.7)	(24.3)	(10.9)	(16.6)	(21.7)
3a	126.7	121.5	117.9	121.3	121.0	117.3
	(18.6)	(20.8)	(22.4)	(11.6)	(15.2)	(15.0)
3b	146.6	150.4	150.7	134.9	140.3	140.1
	(29.9)	(27.0)	(28.0)	(28.9)	(23.5)	(26.2)

Field: Every individual who entered the labour market between 1945 and 1989.

Lecture: The first job average occupational prestige of men endowed with a 3b educational level, and who entered the labour market between 1975 and 1989 is 150.7. The standard deviation is 28.0, which means that 95% of these men had a first job which occupational prestige was between 94.7 and 206.7.

Source: FQP 1993 survey, INSEE.

Dominique Goux and Eric Maurin

TABLE 4.6. *OLS analysis of socio-economic status of first job*

Models	All		Women		Men	
(Standard error)	(5)	(6)	(7)	(8)	(7)	(8)
Intercept	148.7	135.0	141.9	129.9	148.5	133.7
	(1.1)	(1.3)	(1.4)	(1.7)	(1.5)	(1.8)
Date of entry to the market	-0.001	-0.007	-0.033	-0.030	0.024	0.009
	(0.012)	(0.012)	(0.015)	(0.015)	(0.017)	(0.017)
Gender (ref = woman) men	-4.7	-4.7	—	—	—	—
	(0.3)	(0.3)				
Qualifications (ref = 3b)						
1a	-66.1	-61.5	-57.3	-53.3	-72.3	-67.4
	(0.6)	(0.6)	(0.8)	(0.9)	(0.8)	(0.9)
1b	-49.9	-46.9	-41.4	-38.6	-55.6	-52.6
	(0.7)	(0.7)	(1.0)	(1.0)	(1.1)	(1.1)
1c	-59.0	-55.0	-45.6	-42.4	-68.5	-64.0
	(0.6)	(0.6)	(0.8)	(0.9)	(0.8)	(0.9)

	(1)	(2)	(3)	(4)	(5)	(6)
	(0.8)	(0.8)	(1.1)	-32.3 (1.1)	-30.5 (1.1)	-47.2 (1.1)
2b, 2c	-37.0 (0.8)	-35.0 (0.8)	-29.9 (1.0)	-27.8 (1.0)	-40.5 (1.2)	-39.0 (1.2)
3a	-28.2 (0.7)	-26.7 (0.7)	-21.0 (1.0)	-19.9 (1.0)	-31.7 (1.1)	-29.6 (1.1)
Father's socio-economic status		0.11 (0.01)		0.09 (0.01)		0.12 (0.01)
R^2	0.527	0.540	0.486	0.498	0.567	0.581
Number of observations	15,871	15,348	7,909	7,630	7,962	7,718

Field: Individuals in work and formerly in work, aged 20–64.

Source: FQP 1993 survey, INSEE.

We have added to our initial regressions a simple interaction variable (education x date of entry in the labour market) in order to test whether the socio-economic return to education (at the beginning of the work career) has changed over time. The trend is that of a relative decline of the returns to low (1b), and medium (2c), secondary qualification, and of short-course tertiary qualifications (3a). The results hold for both men and women. Roughly speaking, the initial value of (now common) qualifications, such as the *baccalauréat*, is declining when contrasted with no qualifications, or with elementary vocational qualifications, while the initial value of the highest diplomas remains stable (3b).

From an occupational standpoint, the stagnation of the value of the highest qualification, together with the decline of the more common ones, reflect a kind of depreciation process, namely the progressive substitution of qualified workers for less qualified ones at all levels of public and private organizations. Nowadays, in the 1990s, nearly 40 per cent of the long-course graduates from the *grandes écoles* or universities are not *cadres* two years after leaving education, as against only 29 per cent at the beginning of the 1970s. To join the managerial and professional staff, it may still be necessary to hold one of the highest degrees of the French educational system, but it is less and less sufficient.[13] The same type of analysis could be made at the intermediate and lower levels of the occupational scale.[14] Twenty years ago, nearly all tertiary graduates had joined the upper classes of the society, as professionals, managers, administrators, or high-grade technicians within two years. Such a depreciation could be analysed as the result of the substitution of qualified for less qualified that induces the continuous increase of the supply of qualified workers in a labour market where wage-setting is institutionalized and wage hierarchy is stable (Goux and Maurin 1995*b*).

Socio-Economic Status of First Job and Social Background

Even if declining, the initial value of education remains important. Concerning young labour-force entrants, employers have no information other than their educational level and it is certainly why education is so decisive at this moment of the work career. Yet inequalities still remain among equally well-educated young workers, inequalities which are linked to the social and educational status of parents. Family background is not completely mediated through education. Statistically speaking, when social background variables are added to the basic regressions explaining socio-economic status of first job, we obtain a slight, but significant gain in the explained variance—Fisher tests are unambiguous on that point.

Indeed, the higher the socio-economic status of the father, the higher the initial status of the child—it is a quasi-linear relation. The parents' educational level itself is an asset. Moreover, all other things being equal, it seems to be more important to have a highly educated mother than a highly educated father. The introduction of the interaction term (father's class x date of labour-market entry) in the multinomial analysis gives interesting complementary results—a slight general decrease in the return to the father's own socio-economic status appears, but this decline is significantly less important for those whose father belongs to the upper service class, higher-grade professionals, managers, and administrators (Class I).

Finally, as far as the socio-economic status of first job is concerned, it becomes less and less important to be qualified, but more and more important to come from Class I. These two developments are certainly not completely independent, no doubt because declining returns to education stimulate Class I parents to make greater efforts to ensure their sons and daughters a good start in their work careers.

Gender Differences

Oddly, from the initial socio-economic status standpoint, both the total explained variance and its component due to education appear larger for men than for women. The first hypothesis would be that idiosyncratic (unobserved) resources exert more influence on women's initial social destination than on men's, making this initial destination less predictable for women. The second possible explanation is that women who participate in the labour market are not strictly representative. One can only study those whose (unobserved) abilities are sufficiently high to give them the opportunity to find a job (this would also explain why, all other things being equal, women tend to obtain a higher economic status in their first job).

To deal with selection bias, we followed the standard two-stage Heckman procedure. In doing so, we actually find out some selection effects, but they do not bias our estimations that much. Women's social destinations actually seem more dependent on unobserved factors than men's destinations.

EDUCATION, SOCIAL BACKGROUND, AND CLASS DESTINATION

One can easily argue that income or socio-economic status are but aspects of young workers' social identity. There are differences between manual and non-manual jobs, or between self-employment and wage-earning, that are sociologically relevant, but that cannot be captured through a single socio-economic scale. To take such differences into account, we have made complementary analysis using a class concept, namely that of Erikson,

Goldthorpe, and Portocarero (1979). We have studied the statistical association between education level (and social background) of young workers, on the one hand, and the classes that they join after leaving school, on the other one.

What does such an analysis show, what does it bring that our previous linear regressions do not show? In crude terms, it suggests that each social class has its privileged area of recruitment: upper service class/long-course tertiary education, middle service class/tertiary education, upper-lower service class/secondary general education, and so forth (Table 4.7).

For instance in order for your first job to belong to the upper service class (Class I) rather than to the middle service class (Class II), it is above all necessary to be highly qualified (i.e. 3b). In that specific area of social destinations, there are indeed no other important distinctions between the different qualifications. To be more specific, let us imagine that a 3a worker is competing with a 2b (or even a 1c) worker in order to reach a Class I rather than a Class II position. Our estimated odd ratios clearly suggest that the relative chances of the 3a candidate are not higher than those of his yet less graduate 2b competitors.[15] Such a *quasi-perfect* association between education and social destination can hardly be detected through simple linear regressions (which assume that social status is proportional to the level of education). It would reflect the strength of the institutional mechanisms that govern (in both private and public sectors) the allocation of young workers to different levels of the employment ladder. It suggests indeed that if you do not have the qualifications which are institutionally acknowledged to be adequate for a given social class, then reaching this given status is above all a question of luck (or of accident).

The global association between social background and initial social destination is somewhat less important than the association between education and social initial destination, but it is nevertheless significant. Once again, a detailed analysis suggests a quasi-perfect statistical association, with each social class constituting its own privileged area of recruitment. Let us for instance consider young workers, with similar levels of education but different social backgrounds competing for jobs in Classes I or II (i.e. upper or middle service classes). Our multinomial analysis suggests there is a significant specific advantage for those from the upper service class, and a significant specific disadvantage for those from other classes, especially the working classes and the lower service class (i.e. Classes IIIb, V, VI, or VII).[16]

More generally, the sociological area of recruitment for the upper service class, compared with that of other classes, is above all the upper service Class I itself. The same type of analysis would show, for instance, that the specific area of recruitment for Class IV (petty bourgeoisie + farmers' class) is Class IV itself. Such quasi-perfect patterns undoubtedly reflect the existence of specific social assets that favour transitions to your class of occupational origin. It may also reflect specific mobility costs, especially for those from modest backgrounds.

Finally, concerning trends, our multinomial analysis gives a perhaps more concrete picture of the depreciation process that our previous linear regressions suggested. All other things being equal, young women's initial positions belong more to Class IIIb and less to Class II. At the beginning of their working careers, men belong more to Class IIIb (and less to Class IV, for instance). The integration of young people in the social structure relies thus more and more heavily on the development of an *under service class*, which mostly corresponds to unskilled jobs in hotels, catering, and the retail industry.

The same figures confirm that women's initial opportunities are still more dependent on job opportunities in Class III. But they also show that these differences between young men and women are slowly diminishing. Such as log odds measured it, the rise in the importance of both Class IIIb and Class IIIa at the beginning of the working careers appears indeed quicker for young men than for young women. The basic reason lies undoubtedly in the decline of manufacturing industries and the rise in the share of services sector, which tend to make women's initial employment chances closer to those of men.

ECONOMIC AND SOCIAL MOBILITY

So far, we have built and analysed variables which give a good idea of the initial situation of workers, and the way it changes over time, from one generation to another. Such a picture has at least one drawback: it does not take initial social nor economic mobility into account. As suggested by the early analysis of unemployment, the first four or five years of the working career are years of intense mobility. It is important to understand the social and economic significance of this initial mobility. The present value of a given level of labour-market entry does indeed depend heavily on a worker's anticipated prospects. Our analysis of transition from school to work would remain incomplete if we omitted this complementary approach.

From Short-Term to Long-Term Contracts

One of the most direct measures of young workers' prospects is given by the terms which are set to their employment contracts. In France, nearly two-thirds of hirings are today for fixed-term contracts, lasting on average three to four months, and their transformation into indefinite-term contracts is far from systematic (according to raw estimations from the French Labour

TABLE 4.7. *Multinomial logit of entry class for men and women*

	Entry class, relative to Class VIIab (standard error)					
	I	II	IIIa	IIIb	IVabc	V, VI
Intercept	-0.01	1.66	1.11	-1.54	0.05	-0.24
	(0.38)	(0.26)	(0.22)	(0.24)	(0.42)	(0.23)
Date of entry to the market	-0.001	-0.003	0.008	0.026	-0.022	0.005
	(0.005)	(0.003)	(0.002)	(0.002)	(0.005)	(0.002)
Gender (contrasted against women)						
men	-0.54	-1.12	-2.20	-2.44	-0.46	0.70
	(0.05)	(0.04)	(0.03)	(0.03)	(0.06)	(0.03)
Qualifications (contrasted against 3b)						
1a	-8.08	-6.75	-3.96	-1.20	-2.82	-2.09
	(0.16)	(0.11)	(0.10)	(0.11)	(0.15)	(0.10)
1b	-6.54	-4.14	-1.72	-0.61	-2.39	-1.55
	(0.20)	(0.12)	(0.11)	(0.13)	(0.22)	(0.13)
1c	-7.69	-5.43	-2.56	-1.10	-2.74	-0.97
	(0.17)	(0.10)	(0.09)	(0.11)	(0.16)	(0.10)
2a	-6.17	-2.85	-1.06	-0.82	-1.85	-0.55
	(0.26)	(0.13)	(0.13)	(0.18)	(0.26)	(0.15)
2b, 2c	-4.47	-2.07	-1.00	0.00	-0.95	-1.00
	(0.19)	(0.15)	(0.16)	(0.18)	(0.24)	(0.19)
3a	-3.52	-0.81	-0.83	0.68	-1.29	-0.63
	(0.22)	(0.19)	(0.20)	(0.24)	(0.35)	(0.24)

against VIIab)						
I	2.13	1.30	1.43	0.72	1.77	0.40
	(0.17)	(0.14)	(0.13)	(0.15)	(0.29)	(0.15)
II	2.01	1.54	1.28	0.96	0.87	0.62
	(0.17)	(0.13)	(0.12)	(0.13)	(0.36)	(0.13)
IIIa	1.40	0.90	1.20	0.65	0.64	0.31
	(0.16)	(0.11)	(0.09)	(0.10)	(0.29)	(0.10)
IIIb	1.33	1.05	1.65	1.20	0.82	0.91
	(0.49)	(0.35)	(0.26)	(0.28)	(0.85)	(0.26)
IVabc	1.82	0.81	0.62	0.41	2.73	0.24
	(0.13)	(0.09)	(0.07)	(0.08)	(0.18)	(0.07)
V, VI	0.41	0.42	0.47	0.05	-0.11	0.18
	(0.15)	(0.09)	(0.07)	(0.07)	(0.24)	(0.07)
Father's education (contrasted against post–secondary)						
primary	-0.52	-0.36	-0.35	-0.63	-0.16	-0.34
	(0.11)	(0.09)	(0.08)	(0.09)	(0.16)	(0.09)
secondary	-0.29	-0.06	-0.04	-0.30	-0.05	-0.20
	(0.10)	(0.09)	(0.08)	(0.09)	(0.16)	(0.09)
Mother's education (contrasted against post–secondary)						
primary	-1.10	-0.61	-0.60	-0.39	-1.17	-0.42
	(0.12)	(0.10)	(0.09)	(0.11)	(0.16)	(0.10)
secondary	-0.70	-0.20	-0.21	-0.15	-0.90	-0.32
	(0.12)	(0.10)	(0.10)	(0.11)	(0.17)	(0.11)

Field: Individuals in work and formerly in work, aged 20–64.

Source: FQP 1993 survey, INSEE.

Ministry, only one-third of these contracts are changed into indefinite-term contracts).

Basic figures suggest that fixed-term contracts are primarily aimed at workers who are beginning their working career. One year after their entry into the labour market, around 40 per cent of young French workers have

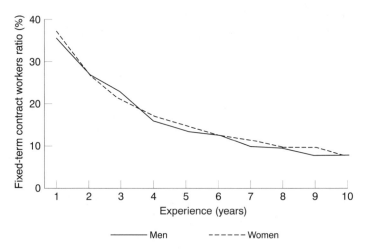

FIG. 4.5. *Rates of fixed-term contracts by experience*

only a fixed-term contract, as against 15 per cent of those with five years' experience (Figure 4.5).

A multinomial analysis confirms that the more recent the date of labour-market entry, the lower the likelihood of obtaining an indefinite-term contract (Table 4.8). The same econometric analysis shows that education is, together with labour-market experience, a key asset in obtaining an indefinite-term contract and stabilizes future prospects. Thus, education is not only a good way to avoid unemployment, it is at the same time a good means to stabilize an individual's market situation.

Interestingly, the links between education and types of employment contract are very close to those between level of education and the risk of unemployment—the more qualified an individual, the higher their chances of holding an indefinite-term contract, but, if an individual does not have such a long-term contract, the relative chances of holding a fixed-term contract (rather than being unemployed) do not depend on level of education. This suggests that, irrespective of qualificational level, the transition from unemployment to work begins with short-term contracts. They mostly aim at testing the fraction of the labour force which is seeking a job, before its definite selection into the organization's staff (for a specific analysis of this kind of process, see Lagarde, Maurin, and Torelli 1995).

An analysis which neglects the importance of these periods of trial under-estimates the role of education in the transition process from school to social and economic stability. The uncertainty linked to short-term contracts appears indeed almost as unequally distributed among the different cate-gories of workers as unemployment risks.

From Part-Time to Full-Time Jobs

The diffusion of short-term contracts is not the only aspect of the evolution of the French labour market towards a greater flexibility. A complementary dimension is the rise in the share of part-time jobs. Here again, it concerns above all inexperienced workers. In the early 1990s, around 25–30 per cent of young women and 10–15 per cent of young men with less than three years' labour-market experience were part-timers. That is, twice as many as a decade before. Most of this rise is corresponding to involuntary part-time,[17] i.e. most young part-timers would prefer to hold a full-time job (Figure 4.6). The basic logic of part-time's diffusion among young workers is indeed, in France, the one of economic efficiency: from the firms stand-point, part-time work (together with short-term contracts) represents an interesting way to minimize adjustment costs, namely the costs of testing inexperienced young workers, especially when they lack qualifications. As long as we study the transition from school to work, part-time may be con-sidered as a risk that young workers try to avoid.[18]

In France, another important feature of part-time work is that it remains more frequent among young women than young men, so that it is necessary to study men and women separately. If young women face more problems finding full-time employment, it is mostly because the demand for women's work force is highly concentrated in specific services sectors and occupa-tions, where part-time is both more adapted to the economic activity and more accepted than in manufacturing industries and/or manual occupations (where the introduction and the diffusion of part-time would represent a kind of cultural revolution).[19]

As regards young men, both raw figures and multinomial analysis yield interesting complementary indications. The fraction of part-timers is signifi-cantly higher among workers who do not have qualifications, and among those with low or medium general qualifications (1b or 2c). The fraction of part-timers is lower among highly qualified workers (3a or 3b), and among workers with a vocational or technical qualification (1c or 2a). Technical and vocational qualifications favour employment chances in the manufacturing industries, where the demand for part-timers is significantly less important than in the small businesses of the service sectors. For workers with general medium qualifications, the difficulty in access to full-time jobs is once again a

TABLE 4.8. *Multinomial logit contrasting unemployment and being employed in a short-term contract with employment in a long-term contract*

Relative to long-term contract (Standard error)	All		Women		Men	
	unemployed	short-term contract	unemployed	short-term contract	unemployed	short-term contract
Intercept	-0.37 (0.02)	-0.49 (0.02)	-0.32 (0.03)	-0.43 (0.03)	-0.33 (0.03)	-0.54 (0.04)
Gender (contrasted against women) men	-0.40 (0.01)	-0.18 (0.01)				
Labour-market experience	-0.21 (0.00)	-0.26 (0.01)	-0.18 (0.01)	-0.25 (0.01)	-0.25 (0.01)	-0.27 (0.01)
Qualifications (contrasted against 3b)						
1a	2.08 (0.04)	1.73 (0.05)	2.08 (0.06)	1.54 (0.07)	2.01 (0.06)	1.96 (0.07)
1b	1.32 (0.06)	1.55 (0.07)	1.38 (0.08)	1.44 (0.09)	1.25 (0.09)	1.72 (0.10)
1c	1.03 (0.04)	1.37 (0.04)	1.06 (0.05)	1.20 (0.06)	0.96 (0.06)	1.60 (0.06)
2a	0.87 (0.06)	1.49 (0.06)	0.90 (0.07)	1.29 (0.07)	0.87 (0.09)	1.79 (0.09)

2b, 2c	0.85	1.02	0.85	0.88	0.95	1.21
	(0.06)	(0.07)	(0.08)	(0.08)	(0.10)	(0.12)
3a	-0.06	0.53	-0.33	0.26	0.43	0.97
	(0.05)	(0.05)	(0.07)	(0.07)	(0.08)	(0.09)
Experience × qualifications (contrasted against experience × 3b)						
1a	0.018	0.051	0.017	0.063	0.035	0.034
	(0.007)	(0.008)	(0.009)	(0.012)	(0.010)	(0.012)
1b	0.019	-0.004	0.010	0.015	0.033	-0.033
	(0.010)	(0.012)	(0.013)	(0.016)	(0.016)	(0.019)
1c	0.019	0.007	0.023	0.026	0.023	-0.016
	(0.006)	(0.007)	(0.008)	(0.010)	(0.010)	(0.011)
2a	-0.044	-0.082	-0.044	-0.058	-0.054	-0.121
	(0.011)	(0.013)	(0.014)	(0.016)	(0.019)	(0.02)
2b, 2c	-0.023	-0.004	-0.032	0.005	-0.022	-0.020
	(0.011)	(0.013)	(0.014)	(0.016)	(0.020)	(0.023)
3a	0.011	-0.024	0.027	-0.010	-0.029	-0.055
	(0.010)	(0.012)	(0.013)	(0.015)	(0.017)	(0.019)

Field: Men and women, in work or unemployed, who entered the labour market for at most ten years (apprentices are excluded).

Source: Labour Force Surveys, 1990 to 1995, INSEE.

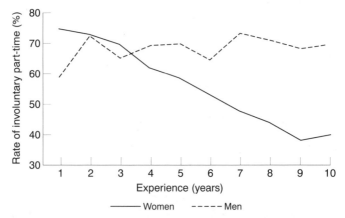

Fig. 4.6. *Involuntary part-time for young wage earners, 1992*

problem of transition. The relative disadvantage of being 1b rather than 1c (or 2c rather than 2a or, even, 3b rather than 3a), indeed vanishes progressively as careers go on. Around five or six years after their entry into the labour market, young qualified male workers are in the great majority full-time workers, whatever their qualifications.

Concerning women, the same analysis confirms the link between early labour-market experience and full-time employment: the more experience a woman has, the lower her risks of ending up as an involuntary part-timer (Table 4.9). At the same time, this suggests that the more qualified young women are, the higher their chances of holding a full-time job and the lower their risks of becoming involuntary part-timers. For women who participate in the labour market, technical or vocational qualifications are not oriented towards manufacturing industries or manual occupations and thus, from the working time standpoint, do not have the same return as for men. Finally, for young women, part-time employment appears to obey the same kind of logic as short-term contracts, namely it simply represents another feature of the transition from unemployment to a full-time, indefinite-term contract.

CONCLUSION

In France, the persistence of unemployment has led firms and policy-makers to encourage the introduction and widespread use of short-term and part-time contracts. Had we studied wages, we would have found that they are ever less a question of seniority, and ever more a question of performance. It has been easier to experiment with these new kinds of employment contracts within the population of young workers, than to negotiate them with the more experienced workers.

As shown by our study, one of the direct consequences is that in France, the transition from school to work has become a long and uncertain process. The deterioration of the relative situation of inexperienced young workers has two other, more indirect and undoubtedly less anticipated, consequences.

First, never—since the late 1960s—has the educational system come in for so much criticism. The central issue is no longer the social inequalities in educational attainment produced by the school system (which have not yet declined), but the inefficiency of the school system itself, its inability to provide young people with qualifications that would protect them against unemployment, short-term contracts, or involuntary part-time work. Both students and families feel bound to make efforts for diplomas that do not mean upward social mobility any more.[20]

Second, there appears to be a rising controversy about inequalities between generations. This very topic tends to supersede that of inequalities between social classes, which is still in France a very basic one. The feeling that solidarity between generations does not work is no doubt one of the starting points of the latest crisis that faces a lot of institutions in France (educational system, social security, unemployment benefits, retirements, etc.).

Young inexperienced workers lack social and economic status, and as such constitute a particularly exposed population. This is why society can dump its imbalances disproportionately on this group. At the same time, however vague their status, the young and inexperienced potentially depend on all important institutions. In a way, they are both students and workers, children and adults, and their problems can virtually become those of all the basic institutions of their society: school, labour market, and family.

In one sense then, French society has succeeded in confining most of its difficulties to this specific fragile population, more precisely, on this specific moment of the life of its members, but it results, nowadays, in a progressive, global questioning of its main institutions.

DATA APPENDIX

The Education, Training, and Occupations Survey

Our study is based on the latest Education, Training, and Occupations survey (FQP). This survey is conducted by the French National Institute of Statistics and Economic Surveys (INSEE), usually two to three years after each population census. The first was carried out in 1964, and the successive ones in 1970, 1977, 1985, and 1993. It covers all conventional

TABLE 4.9. *Multinomial logit contrasting unemployment, involuntary part-time employment, and voluntary part-time employment with full-time employment*

Relative to full-time employment	Women			Men	
(Standard error)	unemployed	involuntary part-time employed	voluntary part-time employed	unemployed	part-time employed
Intercept	-0.41	-1.10	-2.44	-0.59	-1.86
	(0.03)	(0.04)	(0.05)	(0.03)	(0.05)
Labour-market experience	-0.15	-0.16	-0.07	-0.22	-0.18
	(0.01)	(0.01)	(0.01)	(0.01)	(0.01)
Qualifications (contrasted against 3b)					
1a	2.06	1.72	1.26	1.61	0.91
	(0.06)	(0.08)	(0.11)	(0.05)	(0.09)
1b	1.29	1.49	0.84	0.99	1.01
	(0.08)	(0.10)	(0.15)	(0.09)	(0.13)
1c	1.02	1.36	0.50	0.63	0.02
	(0.05)	(0.06)	(0.09)	(0.06)	(0.10)
2a	0.77	1.21	0.08	0.50	0.00
	(0.07)	(0.09)	(0.13)	(0.09)	(0.15)

3a				
....	0.65	0.74	0.82	0.79
(0.07)	(0.10)	(0.12)	(0.10)	(0.14)
-0.43	-0.22	-0.70	0.26	-0.57
(0.07)	(0.97)	(0.11)	(0.08)	(0.14)

Experience × qualifications
(contrasted against experience
× 3b)

1a				
0.023	0.042	-0.132	0.069	0.017
(0.010)	(0.013)	(0.016)	(0.009)	(0.016)
1b				
0.015	-0.020	-0.124	0.058	-0.063
(0.013)	(0.017)	(0.021)	(0.015)	(0.025)
1c				
0.029	0.011	-0.070	0.054	-0.006
(0.008)	(0.011)	(0.013)	(0.001)	(0.017)
2a				
-0.032	-0.079	-0.051	-0.010	-0.009
(0.014)	(0.018)	(0.019)	(0.019)	(0.029)
2b, 2c				
-0.029	-0.019	-0.099	-0.009	-0.038
(0.014)	(0.018)	(0.017)	(0.020)	(0.027)
3a				
0.036	-0.019	0.063	-0.008	0.064
(0.013)	(0.020)	(0.015)	(0.017)	(0.026)

Field: Men and women, in work or unemployed, who entered the labour market for at most ten years (apprentices are excluded).

Source: Labour Force Surveys, 1990 to 1995, INSEE.

households in metropolitan France (mainland and Corsica). Around 18,000 persons, aged 20–64 were interviewed in May 1993. The survey records educational careers, training levels, and qualifications obtained. In France, the FQP surveys provide reference information on education and social mobility (for previous use of these surveys, see Erikson, Goldthorpe, and Portocarero (1979); Goldthorpe and Portocarero (1981); and Thélot (1982)).

Respondents retrace their school career, describing classes attended, qualifications obtained, and specializations taken. This allows us to determine the highest level and duration of education.

With respect to labour-market position (employed, unemployed, no occupation, student, soldier, retired, or at home), the exact occupational status of persons currently in employment and the last positions held by persons no longer in employment are indicated. The social position is described in the French class schema. Supplemented by other information available on the questionnaire, the French coding allow us to measure the class position with the EGP schema.

The 1993 FQP survey offers an even fuller description of the respondents' working careers. In addition to present occupation, it gives their occupational status at the time of labour-market entry—respondents give their first job occupation, the industry in which it is located, the terms of the labour contract, and their skills. Here again, entry class can be measured both according to the French class schema and the EGP class schema.

Last but not least, the FQP survey contains very detailed description of the respondents' social background. The socio-occupational categories of all the respondents' fathers are given. The information on educational attainment of both father and mother is also given.

In sum, the survey gives unique information on the social background, educational attainment, social status on labour-force entry, and present social status of each respondent.

The French Labour Force Surveys

The sample for the annual Labour Force Survey (LFS) is representative of the population aged over 15 years, with more than 140,000 people being questioned every year. The information available on every employed person is of the usual kind: educational level, age, occupation, experience, seniority in firm, and the industry of the employing firm.

Employment aspects are far more developed than in the FQP survey, and include the terms of the labour contract (indefinite, fixed-term, aided contract, interim, etc., full-time or part-time). Social background, however, is only known through the social class of the father, and educational attainment is not as precise as that in the FQP.

From one year to the next, one-third of the sample is renewed, so that individuals can be questioned up to three times. Consequently, by matching the different LFS, we built longitudinal data on every respondent. The panel dimension of this data allows us to take into account the individual unobserved abilities in the estimation of transitions.

In this study, we relied on the last six LFS conducted between 1990 and 1995, focusing on respondents who entered the labour market between 1980 and 1995 (entry date is approximated by the date of leaving school). The LFS also provides fairly full information on the length of the working week. In calculating the number of hours worked annually, we have relied as far as possible on the length of customary working weeks. For those who work irregular hours, we have used the number of hours worked in the week prior to the survey. Information is also available on individual earnings.

NOTES

1. Among those born twenty years earlier (1944–1948), 57 per cent had left the general track before the end of lower secondary school, including those who never went on to secondary school. These figures are taken from the FQP Survey, carried out by the French National Institute of Statistics and Economic Surveys (INSEE) in 1993. See also the Appendix to this chapter.
2. Since the end of the 1980s, however, efforts have been made to avoid too brutal an elimination of those who cannot go on to the general track. After two years' lower secondary school, direct orientation towards apprenticeship is no longer possible. New 'technical' classes have been created which theoretically lead to new *baccalauréat professionnel* (i.e. vocationally oriented degrees at the end of an upper secondary course).
3. The most prestigious *grandes écoles* are the École Nationale d'Administration, the Polytechnique, the Hautes Études Commerciales, and the École Normale Supérieure.
4. Each *inspection* is responsible for the primary and secondary schools of roughly one *département* or French administrative area, of which there are circa one hundred.
5. The work of Duru-Bellat and Mingat (1988) shows that the criteria which determine the process of orientation can themselves vary from one school to another. For instance, some schools attach greater importance to sciences, whereas others focus more on languages. The role of the demand of families and especially, the importance given to the wishes of the families is very different from one school to another.
6. It appears to be an efficiency vs. equality dilemma.
7. The cadres have their own pension funds, employment agencies, and trades unions.
8. Recent Labour Force Surveys show that the *cadres* work on average five to six hours more than the legal thirty-nine hours a week.

9. These categories are rooted in large firms of manufacturing industries where collective agreements are very important.
10. The French administration tries to promote part-time jobs that allow women to combine work and family life.
11. If both labour-market participation and educational level were perfectly explained by the same single unobservable variable, their statistical correlation would be a pure artefact. Ideally, in order to deal with such problems, in our specific case, it would be useful to observe some (instrumental) variables correlated with women's educational destination, but uncorrelated with their decision to participate in the labour market. We have tried to make such an instrumentation, making use of the fact that father's social class is a strong predictor of daughters' educational attainment, on the one hand, and an apparently poor one of daughters' decision to participate in the labour market, on the other. The corresponding estimators are not efficient enough to be useful.
12. The socio-economic scale referenced in the study is based on the estimation of the net impact of occupation (32 items) on the variance of household income. More precisely, we adjusted a gain function explaining household income level by standard variables, namely size, composition (number of employed, unemployed and economically inactive, number of children), localization (Ile de France, province), and occupation of head of household. Our socio-economic scale is derived from the estimated relative impacts of different occupations (of the heads of households) on the household income.
13. Before the end of their second year in the labour market, nearly 14 per cent of young French workers are high-grade professionals (11 per cent are *cadres*, 3 per cent are managers of large establishments or large owners). Among these sole new *cadres*, 28 per cent graduated from the *grandes écoles*, and 58 per cent from the second and third level of the different universities. The great majority of these young cadres are thus highly qualified people.
14. For instance, more than three-quarters of young technicians have a 3a educational level (i.e. *bacc.* + two years), but at the same time over 30 per cent of those who hold such a degree are but simple non-manual employees. Interestingly, the 'depreciation' rate is not lower among those who hold one of the new vocationally oriented technical diplomas (DUT, *Diplôme d'études Universitaires Technologiques*, or BTS, *Brevet de Technicien Supérieur*) than among those who hold a general degree from the first level of universities. These general qualifications are indeed more adapted than technical ones for those who try to pass entrance examinations in the public sector.
15. In Table 4.7, the corresponding log odds for the 3a worker are: $-3.52-(-0.81) = -2.71$ compared with $-4.47-(-2.07) = -2.4$ for a 2b worker, or $-7.69-(-5.43) = -2.3$ for a 1c worker.
16. In Table 4.7, the corresponding estimated log odds are $2.13-1.30 = +0.8$ for Class I contrasted with Class VII, while Class VI's relative chances are very close to Class VII (the estimated log-odd ratio is $-0.01 = 0.41-0.42$, not significant).
17. According to the Labour Force Survey, among young women who begin their working career with a part-time job, three-quarters would prefer to work for a longer time (including full-time work).
18. Later on in the working career, there is another factor which makes women's

part-time rate stabilize at around 20 per cent. Namely the fact that a number of women choose part-time because of family constraints. Both raw figures and multinomial analysis show that the share of involuntary part-time continuously decreases with experience, while the share of voluntary part-time continuously increases.

19. If one applies a logistic analysis to the part-time risks (compared with full-time chances), one finds that around half the differences between men and women may be explained by the basic occupational codes (32 items).

20. In 1993, over 26 per cent of French people have both a *higher* educational qualification than their father and a *lower* social position, as against 12 per cent in 1985.

5

Education and Labour-Market Entry in Germany

WALTER MÜLLER, SUSANNE STEINMANN
AND RENATE ELL

INTRODUCTION

In studies of labour-market organization, it is common to emphasize specific characteristics of the German education and training system and its relationship to the national labour market. In their seminal study, Maurice, Sellier and Silvestre (1982) describe the German labour market as patterned in a *qualificational space* in contrast to the organizational space of France. Using the vocabulary of labour-market segmentation, Marsden (1990) describes Germany as a typical case of a labour market, which is mainly segmented along *occupational lines* in contrast to labour markets mainly segmented between firms. The particular strength of occupations as lines of labour-market segmentation has been demonstrated in several publications from the Berlin life-history study (see Blossfeld and Mayer 1988; Mayer and Carroll 1987/1990). It is also a common topos of research that in Germany labour-market position is strongly predicted by the level and type of education. In the present contribution we focus on these assertions and examine whether they are still valid in the light of data relating to recent developments.

We begin by discussing the specific historical and institutional context in which the German education–labour-market relationship has developed. We then derive several hypotheses concerning this relationship. In the empirical section of the chapter we test these hypotheses studying three dimensions of labour-market outcomes: labour-force participation and unemployment, level of prestige obtained in first job, and class position of first job. We relate these outcomes to the educational and social background characteristics of labour-force entrants. We go on to examine for both men and women how, and to what extent, these relationships have changed during the last decades marked by several major relevant macrostructural changes. That is, the increasingly higher education of labour-market entrants; the increasing labour-force participation of women; the transition into an economy where the supply of jobs falls short of the demand for employment; and the transformation of the occupational structure from industrial to service-based.

THE INSTITUTIONAL CONTEXT OF EDUCATION AND WORK IN GERMANY

The education-labour-market relationship is conditioned by characteristics of the educational system and characteristics of labour-market institutions. Both are important for understanding education–job matches. The following discussion is organized by different types of education and vocational training. For each we discuss specific characteristics of the relationship to the labour market. In characterizing the educational system we draw on the two dimensions of standardization and stratification proposed by Allmendinger (1989*a* and 1989*b*), but at the same time, we stress the high degree of occupational orientation and differentiation. We also give a broad overview of how specific education-labour-market linkages have evolved over time. The discussion concentrates on secondary schooling, vocational training, and tertiary education.[1]

Secondary Schooling in Germany

Germany is one of the countries in Europe where secondary education has changed the least in the post-war period. The contemporary German system of general education is tripartite in structure. At the age of 10 pupils in most German schools opt for one of three separate school-types which differ in both orientation and ability levels. The *Gymnasium* (upper secondary school) traditionally leads children to the *Abitur* examination, and from there to university. The *Realschule* (middle school)—originally designed to prepare children for the more demanding intermediate technical and administrative occupations—leads to the *Mittlere Reife* examination after a total of ten years' schooling. The *Hauptschule* (lower secondary school) is attended by the least academically ambitious pupils and lasts until the end of compulsory schooling. In the 1970s in particular, attempts were made to soften this rigidly segregated structure and to integrate the tracks into a more comprehensive system of secondary education. However, with the exception of a small proportion of schools (concentrated in some of the federal states ruled by a long tradition of Social-Democratic governments), the tripartite structure still exists and continues to channel children through the school age, each track providing a distinct educational experience with little transition between tracks. Indeed, upward transitions are rare.

In spite of the continuation of the organizational and curricular differentiation between educational tracks, some change has occurred. Reforms have attempted to narrow the gap between the *Hauptschule* and the other tracks through prolongation of compulsory education from eight to nine years and by introducing additional subjects into the curriculum (e.g. foreign languages). Second, in their educational choices, an increasing number of pupils opted against the *Hauptschule* and switched to the less dead-end *Gymnasium* and *Realschule*. Today the *Hauptschule* has become the school for immigrant children and educational failures, with its concomitant problems of discipline and violence. This negative image of the *Hauptschule* increases the social disadvantage of its school-leavers, as can be seen in the growing difficulty of such children to obtain apprenticeships in attractive occupations or firms.

In sum, Germany's system of secondary education has not undergone any basic change that could throw doubt on Allmendinger's description of it as highly *stratified* (Allmendinger 1989*b*). It is also still valid to characterize it as *standardized*, even if the variation of curricula and school organization has increased since the 1970s—and more variation has been introduced through the addition of the new *Länder*. In spite of the different approaches to schooling among the federal states—which have legislative competence in educational affairs—the coordinating educational boards have ensured relatively similar examination standards. In all federal states there remain clear distinctions between school-leavers from the *Hauptschule, Realschule*, and *Gymnasium*.[2]

The German System of Vocational Training

Continuity is also a mark of the development of Germany's system of vocational training. The core of vocational training in Germany is its so-called dual system of apprenticeship. It evolved from the tradition of training and personnel recruitment in the guilds and developed into an institution which still shapes in determining ways Germany's educational system and its relationship to the labour market. This could only occur under specific historical conditions. Among the most important was the fact that in Germany the guild system was never abolished,[3] and the laws regulating the duties of the guilds in the German states in the early nineteenth century emphasized the obligations of the guild masters to provide a thorough training for their apprentices (Stratmann and Schlüter 1982). The master was obliged to allow any apprentice to participate in school (parallel to workplace training), to improve the more general skills of reading, writing, mathematics, technical drawing, and religion. This constituted the beginning of what is today known as the dual system, that is, training for practical skills in the workplace and learning more formal abilities in school.

A further crucial step in the development of the apprenticeship system was its adaptation by industry. This was most straightforward in those sectors which grew from craft production and where master craftsmen continued to employ journeymen and to train apprentices. In other industries, such as mining, a craftsman-like system of training evolved relatively early. In others, earlier patterns of on-the-job training for semi-skilled labour (e.g. in the heavy metal or chemical industries) sooner or later developed into the apprenticeship system for skilled workers. Finally, the system was adopted almost everywhere where the need for new kinds of qualified labour arose in the car and electronics industries, commerce, private and public administration, financial services, and public welfare, and even in the civil service. The German version of the apprenticeship system has various peculiarities which enable it to channel individuals into specific segments of the labour market (Blossfeld 1992, 1994).

First, it incorporates a large fraction of each entry cohort. Compared to the inter-war period and the first post-war decades it has even increased in quantitative coverage.[4] The dual system became the primary instrument of providing young people with vocational qualifications. Even if tertiary education strongly expanded at the same time, the crucial role played by the apprenticeship system is visible from the fact that increasing proportions of school-leavers, entitled to enter tertiary education, only took this step after having completed an apprenticeship (for risk aversion and as a kind of safety-net; Büchel and Helberger 1995). Although special school-based forms for providing vocational qualifications did emerge in the decades after World War II, no serious attempts were made to replace the apprenticeship system by other forms of vocational training.[5]

It is interesting to note that even in large industrial firms becoming a foreman or master craftsman is not simply a matter of on-the-job training or promotion within the firm, but generally presupposes the successful completion of an apprenticeship and an additional formal examination taken in an authorized training institution and awarded by an official body of examiners.

In contrast to apprenticeship systems in other countries, the German system has a relatively high degree of formal standardization, with norms governing the content and length of training, formal examinations, standards for workplaces licensed for training, and required qualifications for training personnel. In practice, however, there are marked variations in the quality of training, depending on characteristics of the firm, the workplace and training personnel, the organization of training, and the availability of specialized in-house training workshops (see e.g. Franz and Soskice 1994).

The apprenticeship system is strongly horizontally segmented. In 1950 it included particular apprenticeships in more than 900 different officially recognized occupations. Since then many occupations have become obsolete in the course of economic transformation, and apprenticeships in these occupations have disappeared. Reforms also successfully attempted to concentrate training—focusing on polyvalent key qualifications in a smaller number of specializations. However, in 1970, 600 different apprenticeships still existed and the present number of officially recognized and formally enacted training regulations for specific occupations is slightly below 400.

As Marsden (1990) has aptly analysed, the evolution and persistence of an apprenticeship system, in particular the industry-wide recognition across firms of apprenticeship qualifications, depend on a number of conditions. The German system includes many of the elements that help guarantee the broad recognition of qualifications and hence to give them a labour-market value, and a flexibility within the vocational training system for innovations and adaptations to changing market demands. For example, both employers and worker representatives (mainly trades unions) are strongly involved in a corporatist negotiation system with the state concerning the definition of curricula and other training requirements, the control of training, and the examination and certification process. Moreover, the chambers of trades, industry, and commerce are authorized to administer the day-to-day running of the training and certification process. Another important aspect is a kind of built-in feedback mechanism: as the labour market is built on the notion that qualifications are to a large extent acquired through general training before entry into regular employment, rather than through on-the-job training, there must be continual pressure to adapt the production of qualifications to changing needs. The German system of industry unions, which negotiate work contracts on an industry-wide basis, consistently presses for standardized rules for personnel recruitment, job allocation, and pay. As union membership is dominated by skilled workers, there is pressure to guarantee the pay-offs for the training investments made by their members by the use of exclusionary practices, and by making job allocation and pay scales dependent on educational credentials (Streeck and Hilbert 1990; for consequences of industry-wide coordination, see Soskice 1993*b*).

The general availability of occupationally-specific skills on the labour market encourages employers to organize work so as to maximize available skills without incurring additional training costs. That is to say, they try to recruit workers whose skills already fit the job. Workers, on the other hand, who have invested several years in acquiring skills, should be motivated to find a job that meets their qualifications. Indeed, there is a high probability that a worker moves into a regular job with the same employer after completion of the apprenticeship.[6] Although the likelihood of such transitions varies according to type of employer, occupational specialization, local levels of unemployment, and other conditions (Soskice 1993*b*), the German vocational training system leads to relatively low levels of early work life mobility for finding a job that matches worker qualifications (Allmendinger 1989*a*). The strong occupational specialization of apprenticeships and the expectation of employers to find workers with the required qualifications reinforces the occupational segmentation of mobility opportunities of individual workers.

In principle, not much has changed in the pattern that apprenticeships are taken up as a first step into the labour market, and that this is done immediately after leaving school. The school level from which the transition to apprenticeship is made has, however, continually increased. In the 1950s the transition into apprenticeship was generally made after the completion of compulsory education at the lowest track of general schooling (*Hauptschule*). From the 1960s onwards, increasing numbers of those entering an apprenticeship did so only after the *Mittlere Reife*; and beginning in the 1980s it became even more common to enter an apprenticeship after completion of full secondary education. Fewer and fewer apprentices combine vocational qualifications with only minimal schooling. As apprenticeships are more often added to higher levels of general education, the value of higher levels of 'pure' general education (without an apprenticeship added) will decrease more and more.

In contrast to other countries, in Germany the use of *formal* educational criteria—mostly from vocational training—even extends to large parts of self-employment. In particular, in many crafts, the setting up, registration, and practice of a business on one's own, is dependent on having acquired the relevant master craftsman qualification or diploma.

Tertiary Education

Tertiary education in Germany is characterized by specific features that affect its linkages with the labour market. In contrast to countries with a well-marked differentiation of institutions of tertiary education (e.g. the USA, England, or France), German state universities are quite homogenous. There is no system of elite universities, nor are there universities generally rated as sub-standard. Differentiation exists between different disciplines *within* institutions and in the quality of disciplines *across* institutions. The university system is *unstratified*. At the same time it is bound by legal and administrative provisions to provide *standardized* educational products throughout the country. Thus, the possession of a university degree should enhance occupational homogeneity, without being disturbed much by the self-selection of students, differences in the quality of education, or the public recognition of an institution's rank in a hierarchy of excellence.

Until the 1970s, university education at large had an exclusive status as only small proportions of a cohort reached it, but the relatively homogenous quality of training has given its students quite differentiated career prospects with only minor variation for graduates from different institutions.

Together with the development of the colleges of higher education or *Fachhochschulen*, since the mid-1970s major changes took place in the area of tertiary education. Before, with the exception of teacher training colleges, hardly any other institution of tertiary education existed beyond the classical and technical universities. With the increasing demand for higher education, however, the *Fachhochschulen* at the lower level of tertiary education expanded rapidly. They replaced the earlier schools of advanced vocational training (e.g. engineering schools or schools for social work). While studies at the latter typically served to upgrade apprenticeship-based qualifications (Müller 1978), the formal entry requirements to the *Fachhochschule* have been considerably raised and are much more school-based. It seems that the *Fachhochschule* has significantly weakened a workplace-oriented and step by step approach to acquiring higher-level occupational qualifications.

As with the lower levels of education, the German system of tertiary education also has a marked *occupational orientation*. In contrast to, for example, the United States, where curricula are broad and often of a general orientation, most of the curricula in German tertiary education prepare students for specific professions and careers. In the *Fachhochschule* the occupational orientation is even more pronounced than at university. The university system also shows many marks of occupationalism. Many professional organizations, covering disciplines taught at universities, include university professors and the graduates who work in the profession for which they have been trained. The close links between university education and occupational destination can be traced more specifically for the civil service and the professions.[7]

In the early eighteenth century, Prussia established an elaborate system of recruitment and promotion for its civil service based on educational certification. The patronage system was never as common in Germany as it was in France or Italy, and was checked much earlier through the introduction of examination rules. The rules for recruitment to the civil service were laid down in concise terms, and the King himself looked to it that they were strictly applied. For the training of qualified civil-service personnel, the King established a special faculty—the *Staatswissenschaften*—where the disciplines necessary for admission to public offices were studied. Training for the civil service included academic studies at university and—normally unpaid—in-service training.

Recruitment to the lower ranks of the German civil service was less stringent than for the senior positions. Yet, according to the principle of, 'no office without proper examination', which dates back to the nineteenth century, successful candidates had to pass state examinations before being admitted to office (Henning 1984: 127). Although such requirements were later reduced, they constituted an important element in perfecting the German civil service as a bureaucratic structure in which the hierarchical levels and career lines were tightly bound to a system of specific credentials which in turn circumscribed recruitment and promotion.

The development of professions is also tightly bound to university education and state-controlled examinations. The universities are responsible for the general educational part of training and certification. The state administered and certified the practical side in the form of *Referendariat*. The traditional professions—doctors, lawyers, the clergy and the *Studienräte*[8]—were trained in this way and most of them later employed by the state as civil servants. As Abbott so succinctly notes: 'State certification, rather than association membership [*as in England*] identified professionals in Germany, a situation that persisted long after the appearance of the (professional, the authors) associations' (Abbott 1988: 197).[9]

With the creation of technical universities and the gradual extension of the university curricula to cover new fields, new professions (architects, engineers, chemists, dentists, etc.) also became part of the regime of university certification and state recognition. The fact that the system of higher education was neither hierarchically segmented nor regionally concentrated contributed to broadly similar educational requirements for various professions throughout the country. The German state considered it its duty to guarantee the proper pursuit of professions by a strict examination system. With the strong involvement of the state in the professionalization process, the professional associations developed in a corporatist direction, in which they partly act with state-delegated authority.

Finally, part of the distinctiveness of the German development in university education and its relations to the labour market and society at large can be grasped from two particularly German terms: *Akademiker* and *Bildungsbürgertum*. Both social realities designated by these terms are intimately linked to education and the fact of their representation in the public language by specific terms underlines their social significance. *Akademiker* is a social category which includes all persons who have successfully completed an academic training. To belong to this category used to be of considerable significance for the social identity of a person. *Bildungsbürgertum* refers to that part of the German bourgeoisie which included the social groups distinguished by higher education (not necessarily linked to a university degree), as opposed to the *Wirtschaftsbürgertum* (Lepsius 1987). This class was strongest between the second part of the eighteenth century until the end of the nineteenth century, when it started to loose its significance, until it was finally eliminated under the Third Reich (see Conze and Kocka 1985; Kocka 1987).

However, there is no doubt that in Germany education played a stronger role than in other countries in constituting a network of families which were identified through the close links to the universities and to the higher civil service and which conceived themselves as a distinguished group in social life.

HYPOTHESES

To summarize then, we can say that in the light of the institutional characteristics of the German educational system and its links to the labour market, that it is highly standardized at all important levels and types of education. As regards stratification, the system of secondary education is highly stratified, whereas the traditional system of tertiary education has been relatively unstratified until the development of a second level within tertiary education (with the new *Fachhochschulen* as an institutional setting clearly separate from the universities) has moved it in a more stratified direction. In addition, access to tertiary education has been relatively restricted, not by a special point-of-entry selection procedure, but by the rigid and highly stratified structure of secondary education. In consequence, tertiary education has been an area of exclusion and privilege.

At all levels the educational system is occupationally oriented, most strongly in the area of vocational training at the post-compulsory and secondary level. Except for those, who follow the direct pathway through the *Gymnasium* to tertiary education, the great majority of school-leavers pass through the vocational training system, most of them through the apprenticeship system. The latter, through its dual organization and mechanisms to involve employer representatives and other collective labour-market actors, enforces especially close links between the training obtained and the occupationally segmented structure of jobs.

Bearing in mind these conditions, we now derive several hypotheses concerning the significance of education in Germany for the chances of finding employment, and for prestige and class position in first job.

Education and Unemployment

Given the German institutional context we expect two kinds of consequences for unemployment risks—one concerning their distribution over age groups, and the other concerning their relationship to type and level of education.

From the dominance of the occupational type of labour-market segmentation, where young labour-market entrants have previously acquired standardized and generally recognized skills and qualifications, we can expect them to have a relatively competitive position vis-à-vis already employed workers. Training costs for employers will be limited, and those who completed an apprenticeship have often already been with their employer during the apprenticeship. In the competition for jobs they are more or less insiders, like other workers. Under such conditions it should be easier for young workers to find regular employment than under conditions of the dominance of an internal labour market within a firm, where employers should expect higher training costs for new recruits, where young workers are generally outsiders, and where insiders have higher incentives to protect themselves from outsiders, because their firm-specific skills are less transferable than in occupational labour markets. As a consequence, unemployment risks should be less concentrated among young labour-market entrants in Germany than in countries with more firm-specific labour markets.

A strong occupational segmentation of qualifications and labour markets on the other hand implies that employers, who use qualificational criteria in recruitment decisions, will use both the level of qualification and the occupational fit of the training for the job when they screen job applicants. The likelihood of recruitment will not only depend on the level of qualification but also on supply-demand balances in specific occupational fields. In the German context therefore, the level of qualification should be a less determining factor for unemployment risks than in countries with a less occupationally segmented labour market.

In Germany, only a small proportion of labour-market entrants failed to complete at least vocational training beyond compulsory education, and these 'unqualifieds' tend to be judged negatively in terms of potential trainability, work motivation, discipline, and productivity. Therefore, having received a vocational training is a considerable advantage in competition for jobs, even where specific training is not functionally relevant. This 'extra-functional significance' (Dahrendorf 1992) of vocational training will affect unemployment risks. Those who have obtained vocational training should clearly be in a better position than those who enter the labour market with only compulsory schooling.

Education and Prestige/ Class of First Job

Given the German institutional context we should expect strong impacts of educational qualifications on the quality of jobs accessible on the labour market. Each type and level of education should distinctively affect the prestige and class position of first job. In particular, educational criteria should also strongly determine access to skilled as opposed to unskilled manual work. This is one of the main areas in which a system dominated by occupational labour markets should differ from systems structured more along firm-internal labour markets.

Because of the high level of credentialism in access to jobs (as concerns both the level of general education obtained and the occupational specialization of vocational training), we expect that the association pattern between educational qualification and job obtained will be quite similar in different population groups. In the German context we therefore expect rather limited gender differences in the effect of education on job placement. This should be particularly true at the stage of entry into employment. Whether stronger gender differences evolve in occupational careers will not be studied here. Further consequences for gender differences, not investigated here but relevant in an occupationally segmented system, probably derives from gender-specific educational *choices* rather than from *effects* of the chosen education.

From the institutional developments we have sketched, we do not expect that, by and large, differences in returns to different kinds and levels of education have declined over time. There are instead indications that they may have increased, for instance as a consequence of the more significant institutional differentiation at the tertiary level (universities and *Fachhochschulen*). However, we may find changes in the relative labour-market value of specific educational credentials. In particular, several developments can be observed which should have an impact on the value of the *Abitur*. With the increased significance of the lower level of tertiary education, the competitive advantage of the *Abitur* may decline. As more *Abiturienten* take up apprenticeships, the general education certified by the *Abitur* may drop in value, and the vocational component of the apprenticeship will take precedence. Particularly at the point of labour-market entry, the type of apprenticeship, rather than the level of general education, will tend to determine job prospects.

In earlier work, studying the effects of educational expansion Blossfeld (1985*a*) and Handl (1986, 1996) have argued that educational expansion leads to a reduced competitive advantage of tertiary education and to the displacement of the less qualified. These findings are contested by Däumer (1993). The following analysis is not intended primarily to decide between these competing hypotheses about educational expansion. By including the time component in the analysis we intend to verify whether the peculiar characteristics of the German pattern of education-labour-market links discussed in the literature persist across specific institutional changes, and to provide the empirical basis to find out how Germany remains peculiar when compared to the other countries studied in this volume.

DATA AND VARIABLES

Database

The data used in the following analyses come from a database which uses two different types of surveys representative of West German households: the German General Social Survey (ALLBUS) 1984, 1994 with N = 5346; and the German Socio-Economic Panel (SOEP), wave 1986 with N = 8023. These surveys use practically identical procedures for the collection of information from which the variables included in the present analyses are derived, and use similar sampling procedures. In an earlier analysis (Müller and Haun 1994), in which we used a compilation of ALLBUS and SOEP for the study of social inequality in educational transitions, we found only negligible differences in results produced by ALLBUS and SOEP. For the present analyses we have no indications that the surveys should systematically differ in their results.

Only West German citizens are included in the following analyses—as the inclusion of citizens of East Germany or foreign immigrants would introduce complexity which cannot be dealt with here for reasons of space. Due to selective refusal rates in survey participation, the working classes are slightly underrepresented in both surveys. However, no weighting procedures have been applied. We excluded all cases with missing values in any of the variables used from the analyses.

Definition of Variables

Cohort/Period: We define cohorts according to the year of entry to first job (see below) and then aggregate years of labour-market entry into periods of decades, or into an entry period either before 1960, or in 1960 or later. About 9 per cent of the cases entered first job before 1930; 0.3 per cent entered before World War I. The period before 1960 is clearly more heterogeneous in terms of economic and labour-market conditions than the period after 1960. Economic crises and breakdowns (the Great Depression, war conditions, and the post-war economic collapse) have affected labour-market entrants much more seriously than even the high levels of unemployment in some of the years since 1980.

Social Class: For father's class and class of respondent's first job the German version of the EGP coding schema developed in the CASMIN project is used (Erikson and Goldthorpe 1992).
Prestige: Prestige is measured with Wegener's (1985) Magnitude Prestige Scale (MPS). We used this—rather than the Treiman scale—because it is a national scale, more adequate to the specific prestige hierarchy in Germany,

and because it appears to have better measurement qualities than Treiman's international prestige scale. The scale extends within the range 20.0 to 186.8.

Education: The variables are coded according to the CASMIN educational classification (König, Lüttinger, and Müller 1988). Due to the small numbers of cases some of the categories have been collapsed. For *parental education* the higher code for either father or mother is used (according to the sequence 1ab, 1c, 2ab, 2c, 3a, 3b).

First Job: In both surveys, the respondents were asked to give the age (or year) in which they started first-time regular employment as their *main* activity. Because an apprenticeship is often conceived as employment in Germany, the respondents were asked to exclude apprenticeships or other forms of vocational training from consideration. In the SOEP survey, the respondent is explicitly asked for his or her first employment *after* vocational training.

We assume that first job is reasonably well measured, excluding short-term, casual work (such as vacation or student jobs). However, a more serious problem is that we do not know whether a person re-entered the educational system after his first job and only then reached the educational level which is measured in the surveys. In such cases a respondent may have a higher educational code than that which corresponds to the education received *before* entering the first job. In order to correct such mis-measurements we included in all the multivariate analyses several dummy variables which indicate whether a person entered the labour market earlier than can be expected if he entered immediately after the shortest possible number of years to obtain his educational level.[10]

RESULTS

Changing Distributions in Educational Participation, Social Background, and First Job

We begin the analysis by briefly discussing the basic distributions of the most important variables used in this chapter. The figures in panel A of Table 5.1 shows one of the peculiarities of the German educational system and how it changed in the course of the massive educational expansion Germany experienced in the post-war period. What makes Germany really different from many other countries with respect to labour-force qualifications is the very large proportion who have received a vocational training in addition to compulsory schooling before entering the labour force. This was true for men as far back as the cohorts born in the early decades of this century, while far more women from the same cohorts left the educational system with only compulsory education. Beginning with the post-World War II period, however, women steadily increased their participation in vocational training. From the 1980s the numbers entering the labour market with only compulsory education were similarly low for both sexes (see Handl 1986; Müller and Haun 1994). Among those obtaining a vocational qualification, the proportion of those classified at the intermediate level (2a compared to 1c) has strongly increased between the two cohorts distinguished here. The proportion of 2a qualifications is particularly large among women. The proportions with a full secondary or tertiary qualification also strongly increased for both sexes. While the gender gap in educational qualifications clearly decreased from the older to the younger cohort, still substantially fewer women than men obtain the most advantageous educational qualification—a university degree.

The increased educational participation is partially due to a changing composition of parental education and parental class. As panel B of Table 5.1 shows, the distribution of parental education and father's class have taken a direction more favourable for children's education. From the cohort which entered first job before 1960 to the cohort which entered in 1960 or later, the proportion of parents with only compulsory education has decreased, and the proportions with secondary and tertiary education have increased. In the distribution of father's class the proportion, in particular of farmers, within the petty bourgeoisie has decreased, and the proportion of fathers who belong to the service class has grown.

Other distributional changes in the variables used in the present analyses can be seen from panel C of Table 5.1. Consistent with the changes in the class distribution, the mean of father's occupational prestige has increased. Due to the increased educational participation, the average age of respondents at the point of entry into their first employment has increased by about two years (slightly less than two years for men). But even in the younger entry cohort men start their regular working life about a year later than women. This difference may be due to military or society (i.e. civil) service, which is compulsory for men. Finally, Table 5.1 also shows a substantial increase in occupational prestige at first job, which is slightly greater for women than for men. In both entry cohorts the standard deviation of prestige of first job is considerably larger for men than for women.

TABLE 5.1. *Distributions of variables used in the analysis*

A: Percentage distribution of respondent's educational level and entry class by gender and job entry period

	Men		Women	
	before 1960	1960 and later	before 1960	1960 and later
Educational level:				
1ab	13	6	42	14
1c	59	43	34	35
2a	12	21	13	28
2b	1	1	4	3
2c	5	9	3	8
3a	5	6	1	3
3b	5	14	3	9
Entry class:				
I	4	9	2	5
II	9	15	10	21
IIIab	11	13	40	47
IVabc	5	2	6	1
V	4	6	1	3
VI	47	45	11	11
VIIab	20	10	30	12
N	1,841	2,013	1,871	1,992

B: Percentage distribution of parents' education and father's class by cohort

	Before 1960	1960 and later		Before 1960	1960 and later
Parental education:			Father's Class:		
1ab	26	15	I	5	10
1c	59	59	II	8	10
2ab	9	12	IIIab	6	8
2c	2	4	IVabc	27	16
3ab	4	10	V	10	11
			VI	26	28
			VIIab	18	17
N	3,712	4,005		3,712	4,005

TABLE 5.1. *cont.*

C: Means (and standard deviations) of continuous variables

	Men		Women		Total
	before 1960	1960 and later	before 1960	1960 and later	
Age at job entry	18.1	19.9	17.0	19.0	18.6
	(3.8)	(4.1)	(3.4)	(3.7)	(3.9)
Occupational prestige	50.6	59.8	46.9	58.7	54.2
of first job	(22.5)	(29.5)	(19.6)	(24.8)	(25.1)
Father's occupational	52.3	57.1	52.1	55.1	54.2
prestige	(22.6)	(28.5)	(22.3)	(27.3)	(25.5)
N	1,821	2,031	1,869	2,022	7,743

D: Percentage distribution of current employment status by gender (aged 30–55)

	Men	Women
Employed	93	50
Unemployed	5	4
Not in labour force	2	46
N	2,120	2,006

Labour-Market Participation and Unemployment

In this first analytic section we consider the consequences of educational resources for *employment preferences* and *exclusion from employment opportunities*. Employment preferences are measured by the proportion of men and women employed in contrast to those not in the labour force between the ages of 30 and 55. Exclusion from employment is measured by the proportion of men and women who are unemployed.[11] In the patterns of employment preferences and exclusion from employment, Germany has several characteristic features: although unemployment rates rose in particular in the recessions of the 1980s and 1990s, since 1950 Germany always has had comparatively low rates of unemployment. Unemployment rates in Germany were constantly below the OECD average (OECD 1994, 1995a). At the same time, Germany has been, and still is, among the countries with a low level of female employment. The rates of unemployment, relevant for the first hypothesis formulated above, are given in Figure 5.1. Germany has one of the lowest levels of youth unemployment in Europe. Exclusion from the labour market is concentrated on the other end of the working life. Germany has higher than average levels of unemployment among persons aged 50 or above, and is among the countries with high rates of early retirement (Kohli et al. 1991).[12] These well-established findings of German labour-force statistics are consistent with the general hypotheses derived above on the variation of unemployment risks across the working life. Compared with the major problems of finding employment encountered by school-leavers in many other countries, the transition from school to work is relatively smooth in Germany, and the specific system of vocational training and labour-market organization most likely plays an important role in producing this outcome.

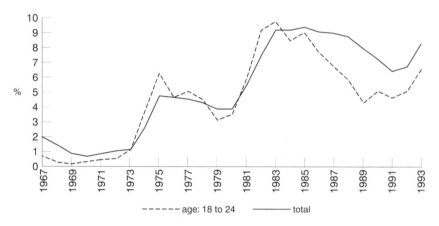

Source: Digitales Informations system 1995.

FIG. 5.1. *Unemployment rates in West Germany, 1967–1993*

Based on the ALLBUS and SOEP data, panel D of Table 5.1 shows the distribution of men and women among the three types of labour-market participation. The results are consistent with what we know from public labour-force statistics. Noteworthy is the high proportion of German women who are not in the labour force. But this is in agreement with many studies which show that in Germany large proportions of mothers with young children still quit paid employment (see e.g., Müller 1986; Tölke 1989; Kurz 1995; Lauterbach 1994). The proportions of the unemployed are slightly underestimated, due to biases in survey participation. If—according to panel D of Table 5.1—the proportions of those unemployed are larger among men than among women, this should not be mistaken as an indication of higher risks of unemployment for men—it is mainly the consequence of the much smaller employment rates among women.

160   *W. Müller, S. Steinmann, and R. Ell*

The multinomial logistic regression analysis in Table 5.2 takes into account these differences in labour-force participation rates. The figures indicate the effect of father's social class and of the respondent's education on the likelihood of being unemployed or not in the labour force rather than being currently employed (the latter representing the reference category of the dependent variable). The effects of the respondent's education and father's class are measured as contrasts to the reference group of respondents with the most disadvantaged conditions, that is, those who obtained only compulsory education (1ab), and whose fathers were unskilled workers at the age of 16. (In all later analyses we will follow a similar strategy in choosing reference categories). The first two columns of the table relate to the combined sample of men and women, including sex as a control variable. The following columns show the estimates separately for the female and male sample.

Three main findings are evident from Table 5.2. First, the much lower labour-force participation among women than among men is reflected in the parameter for sex in the combined regression (column 2) and in the intercepts in the separate regressions. The coefficient for gender relating to unemployment is also negative for men. The effect, however, is statistically not significant.

Second, social background affects labour-market participation almost exclusively indirectly via education. We have tested various models including parental education and father's occupational prestige and models with other specifications of father's social class. All lead to the same conclusion as that is evident in the model presented here. That is, that there is only one possible instance of a direct effect of social background—compared to the sons of unskilled workers, the sons of self-employed fathers run less risk of becoming unemployed during their working life. This finding is corroborated in a study focusing on labour-market entry (Steinmann 1994). Steinmann finds that in the transition from school to work, the children of self-employed fathers have a shorter waiting time to find employment after leaving school and have shorter spans of unemployment during their working lives.

Investments in education and educational resources significantly increase employment preferences among women and improve employment chances for both men and women. All women with education beyond compulsory education are more often in the labour force than the least educated women, but only university education makes a large and significant difference. As to the risks of unemployment, these appear to decrease consistently with level of education. For men, the risk of unemployment decreases linearly (on a logarithmic scale!) with the level of education.[3] The pattern is slightly different for women, and obtaining the *Abitur* or tertiary education seem to be the crucial educational resources for protection against unemployment.

Whether education—in the context of German educational and labour-market institutions—constitutes a relatively weak or relatively strong protection against unemployment can only be judged in comparison with other countries. The evaluation of the respective hypothesis proposed above thus must await the findings from comparable analyses in other countries. The hypothesis, however, relating to the crucial role of vocational training and the particular vulnerability for unemployment of those who enter the labour market with no more than compulsory education is supported by the present analysis. According to all three equations vocational training, even on an elementary level (1c), attenuates unemployment risks almost as much as additional education up until a tertiary degree.

Occupational Prestige of First Job

We now turn to the quality of first job and begin with an indicator of its status or general desirability: prestige. Figure 5.2 shows the raw prestige average at first job for men and women by qualification and period of entry into the labour market. The figures for men and women look similar. However, at each level—except for 1ab—women obtain slightly more prestige-conferring jobs than men. The returns on education are also similar in the two periods before and after 1960. With the exception of the *Abitur*-level, returns to each level of education slightly increase in the second period. In the earlier period the disadvantage for men compared to

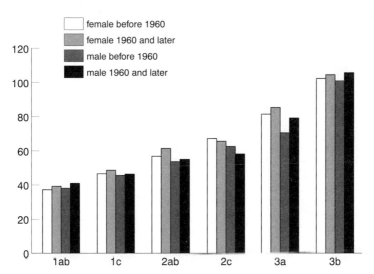

FIG. 5.2. *Mean occupational prestige of first job by sex, job entry period, and education*

TABLE 5.2. *Multinomial logit contrasting unemployment and being out of the labour force with current employment for men and women aged 30–55*

	All		Women		Men	
	unemployed	not in labour force	unemployed	not in labour force	unemployed	not in labour force
Intercept	-1.50***	-.18	-1.32*	-.04	-2.39**	-5.48***
	(.49)	(.29)	(.71)	(.31)	(.86)	(1.04)
Social origin (relative to Class VIIab):						
I, II, IIIab, V, VI	-.13	-.00	.07	-.02	-.27	.33
	(.20)	(.12)	(.34)	(.13)	(.25)	(.47)
IVabc	-.40	-.09	-.07	-.16	-.69**	.59
	(.26)	(.15)	(.41)	(.15)	(.36)	(.51)
Educational level (relative to 1ab):						
3b	-1.38***	-.81***	-1.15**	-.90***	-1.71***	.50
	(.38)	(.22)	(.54)	(.23)	(.53)	(.76)
3a	-1.29**	-.33	-1.44	-.28	-1.36**	-.42
	(.52)	(.30)	(1.09)	(.33)	(.61)	(1.14)
2c	-.83*	-.03	-1.43*	-.14	-.56	1.18
	(.44)	(.24)	(.81)	(.26)	(.55)	(.84)

2ab	−.79*** (.28)	−.28* (.15)	−.74* (.39)	−.30** (.15)	−.96** (.41)	.00 (.67)
1c	−.61*** (.23)	−.01 (.13)	−.50 (.33)	−.04 (.13)	−.80** (.32)	.22 (.49)
Sex (1 = male)	−.19 (.17)	−3.65*** (.16)				
Year of study (relative to 1984):						
1986	−.15 (.19)	−.29*** (.11)	.47 (.37)	−.32*** (.11)	−.45* (.24)	.36 (.40)
1994	−.65** (.28)	−.45*** (.15)	−.52 (.51)	−.57*** (.16)	−.61* (.34)	1.08* (.52)
Log likelihood		−2233.07		−1601.24	−595.29	
Chi²		1405.66		101.23	87.08	
df		36		34	34	
Pseudo R²		.24		.03	.07	
N		4,126		2,006	2,120	

* p ≤ .10   ** p ≤ .05   ***p ≤ .01

women is particularly marked at levels 2c and 3a. In the second period the prestige returns to tertiary education increase a little more for men than for women, and thus the gap between men and women is narrowed.

Table 5.3 examines how occupational prestige in first job depends on conditions of social origin and educational attainment, and it shows to what extent the former are mediated through education. According to the summary R^2 measures, over 50 per cent of the variance in first job is explained by these variables for both men and women, and 25 per cent among women and 30 per cent among men is added by education to the variance explained by social background. Both total variance explained and the component added by education seem large by international standards.[14]

The educational component seems to be larger for men than for women. However, this is an artefact of the chosen comparisons of models: even the equations which do not include education—the models of columns (1) and (3)—contain some correlated education effects in R^2 through the cohort variable. These education components in R^2 of columns (1) and (3) are larger for women than for men. This can be seen from the parameter estimates for the cohort variables in the last panel of Table 5.3.

If education is not controlled for, more recent cohorts receive first jobs with increasingly higher prestige. If we control for education these differences between cohorts mostly disappear. This is because the younger cohorts received higher education and could convert their educational investments into higher status jobs. This pattern is particularly striking for women. Women who entered the labour market before 1970 received considerably lower status jobs at entry than women entering in 1980 and later (Mayer 1991). Their improved educational participation in the more recent cohorts puts them on an equal footing with men.

Education obtained has a huge impact on status of first job. What really counts is tertiary education, particularly university education. Compared to the educational minimum, the educational credentials earned on the way to the *Abitur* have significant effects on first job status, but remain substantially less than what can be gained with a university education after the *Abitur*. For women each educational level beyond compulsory schooling, except for university, provides larger gains than for men. The similar findings from the simple prestige averages in Figure 5.2 are thus corroborated with the multivariate analysis. As additional analyses (not documented here) show, prestige returns also depend on the *type* of vocational training obtained. Apprenticeships in agriculture, in a craft or trade provide less prestigeful jobs (on average five points on the MPS scale) than apprenticeships in commerce or other non-manual occupations.

For social background the models include all three variables: parental education, father's occupational prestige, and father's class membership.

Excluding any of these variables would underestimate the total effect of social background and would lead us to overestimate the unique contribution of education. Family background is not completely mediated through education. The effects of father's occupational prestige are only reduced by slightly more than half when respondent's education is included into the equation. Parental education also affects the first job status of the respondents, independent of their education. This, however, is barely the case for father's social class: its effect is substantial when the respondents' education is not controlled for, but declines sharply when education is taken into account.

How did the effects of the various factors related to prestige of first job change over time? Table 5.4 contrasts the cohorts entering employment before 1960 to those entering in 1960 and later. Although the basic pattern of coefficients appears unchanged, we observe a number of differences between the two periods worth mentioning. First, variance explained increases for both men and women. The increase in predictability of prestige of first job is particularly large for men. Second, some of the parameter estimates change in non-negligible ways. The intercepts for both men and women become larger. Thus, even persons with the least advantageous resources receive first jobs of slightly higher prestige in more recent years. Direct effects of father's class decline for men and women. Direct effects of parental education disappear almost completely for women. Only for men father's occupational prestige appears to affect prestige of first job more in the years after 1960 than before. Thus, at large, direct effects of social-background characteristics rather decline than increase.

As to prestige returns to education two, quite substantial changes occur—returns to lower-level tertiary education (3a) increase, while the value of a full secondary education (2c) clearly declines. This is true for both sexes, but the changes are stronger for men than for women. As returns to university education (3b) also increase slightly, the differential in returns between any type of tertiary education and all other educational qualifications increased. Below tertiary education the gap between intermediate and full secondary education declines for both men and women, in the case of men because of reduced returns to the *Abitur*, in the case of women both because of decreased returns to the *Abitur* and increased returns to intermediate secondary education. The improved position of women at first employment is notable in this table again. As the intercept shows, even women with minimum education receive slightly better jobs after 1960 than before, and—with the exception of the *Abitur* and elementary vocational training (1c), the prestige returns to education increase.

If, as we did in analyses not documented here, we split the data into more narrowly defined entry cohorts, the observed trends of a stronger

W. Müller, S. Steinmann, and R. Ell

TABLE 5.3. *OLS regressions of occupational prestige in first job*

	Men		Women	
	(1)	(2)	(3)	(4)
Intercept	40.49***	33.27***	46.21***	33.96***
	(1.78)	(1.63)	(1.45)	(1.26)
Father's occupational prestige	.16***	.07***	.12***	.06***
	(.03)	(.02)	(.02)	(.02)
Social origin (relative to Class VIIab):				
I	8.78***	1.75	7.08***	3.09*
	(2.73)	(2.15)	(2.26)	(1.84)
II	6.36***	.82	6.28***	1.13
	(1.96)	(1.55)	(1.66)	(1.36)
IIIab	6.13***	1.87	5.15***	1.24
	(1.93)	(1.52)	(1.57)	(1.28)
IVabc	3.20**	1.20*	3.59***	1.48*
	(1.38)	(1.09)	(1.15)	(.94)
V/VI	-.74	-.38	1.56	1.28*
	(1.27)	(.99)	(1.06)	(.86)
Parents' education (relative to compulsory or less):				
post-secondary	22.93***	3.73**	22.00***	3.88**
	(2.35)	(1.89)	(1.96)	(1.65)
higher secondary	18.56***	3.16*	15.47***	2.36
	(2.63)	(2.10)	(2.19)	(1.80)
lower secondary	13.79***	3.18***	12.43***	2.24**
	(1.60)	(1.29)	(1.33)	(1.11)
compulsory + apprenticeship	5.06***	1.46*	4.71***	1.75**
	(1.13)	(.90)	(.93)	(.76)

	(1)	(2)	(3)	(4)
Educational level (relative to 1ab):				
3b			63.31*** (1.55)	62.65*** (1.45)
3a			38.65*** (1.72)	45.17*** (2.09)
2c			24.11*** (1.69)	26.32*** (1.42)
2ab			16.58*** (1.33)	20.82*** (.87)
1c			8.22*** (1.12)	9.53*** (.73)
Job entry cohort (relative to 1980–1994):				
before 1930	-7.04*** (2.08)	.30 (1.65)	-18.47*** (1.53)	-3.56*** (1.31)
1930–1939	-3.62** (1.71)	2.23* (1.35)	-15.98*** (1.35)	-2.07** (1.16)
1940–1949	-4.04*** (1.52)	1.42 (1.21)	-12.52*** (1.27)	-.43 (1.09)
1950–1959	-3.65*** (1.42)	.73 (1.13)	-13.25*** (1.20)	-.83 (1.04)
1960–1969	1.02 (1.40)	1.96* (1.11)	-9.34*** (1.18)	.48 (1.00)
1970–1979	2.53* (1.39)	1.81* (1.09)	-4.67*** (1.15)	.87 (.94)
R^2	.24	.53	.27	.52
N	3,852	3,852	3,891	3,891

* $p \leq .10$ ** $p \leq .05$ *** $p \leq .01$

TABLE 5.4. OLS regressions of occupational prestige in first job by job entry period

	Men		Women	
	before 1960	1960 and later	before 1960	1960 and later
Intercept	33.72***	35.92***	31.16***	35.18***
	(1.71)	(2.28)	(1.22)	(1.61)
Father's occupational prestige	.05	.08***	.06***	.06***
	(.03)	(.03)	(.03)	(.03)
Social origin (relative to Class VIIab):				
I	3.68	-.38	1.80	2.61
	(3.19)	(2.90)	(2.56)	(2.61)
II	3.98*	-1.93	2.49	-.64
	(2.23)	(2.15)	(1.84)	(1.97)
IIIab	4.82**	-.59	1.10	.90
	(2.17)	(2.13)	(1.77)	(1.85)
IVabc	3.39**	.62	3.32***	-.89
	(1.40)	(1.71)	(1.16)	(1.50)
V/VI	2.18*	-2.58*	3.04***	-.39
	(1.32)	(1.47)	(1.14)	(1.27)

Parents' education (relative to compulsory or less):				
post-secondary	4.77*	3.18	8.87***	1.73
	(2.90)	(2.58)	(2.48)	(2.28)
secondary	2.95*	3.76**	4.23***	1.67
	(1.74)	(1.84)	(1.46)	(1.60)
compulsory + apprenticeship	.18	2.76*	1.33	2.30*
	(1.09)	(1.47)	(.90)	(1.27)
Educaticnal level (relative to 1ab):				
3b	60.16***	63.74***	61.04***	63.90***
	(2.32)	(2.35)	(2.49)	(1.93)
3a	33.51***	41.95***	42.52***	46.51***
	(2.26)	(2.67)	(3.26)	(2.82)
2c	27.16***	21.68***	28.53***	26.36***
	(2.39)	(2.53)	(2.37)	(1.90)
2ab	15.86***	15.68***	18.55***	21.97***
	(1.72)	(2.16)	(1.12)	(1.37)
1c	8.80***	6.64***	9.73***	9.46***
	(1.29)	(1.20)	(.86)	(1.29)
R^2	.45	.56	.46	.51
N	1,821	2,031	1,869	2,022

$* \ p \leq =.10$ $** \ p \leq =.05$ $*** \ p \leq =.01$

determination of prestige in first job and an increased advantage of tertiary education appear to be even stronger. In the cohort entering first job between 1980 and 1994, R^2 increases to .61 for men, and .55 for women; the estimated prestige returns for higher tertiary education (3b) increase to 71 points for men and to 78 for women.

In sum, education became a stronger determinant of prestige in first job. The variance explained clearly increased and tertiary education also provided higher prestige returns for the entry cohorts after 1960, and even more so in late 1982 and the early 1990s. As increasingly larger fractions among the younger cohorts moved into the highly differentiated area between full secondary education and a university degree, these changes in educational participation became one of the main reasons why variance explained by education in prestige of first job increased.[15] As long as higher education does not become significantly devalued, the continued increase in the proportion of labour-market entrants with tertiary education should continue to reinforce the trend of a stronger (statistical) determination of prestige at labour-market entry.

Class of First Job

The labour market is strongly sex-segregated and the distributions of jobs for men and women vary substantially. This is only one reason for complementing the study of educational outcomes with dimensions which are more sensitive to the sex differences in first jobs than are prestige scores. One such dimension is social class. The huge difference between men's and women's class distribution at first job is very clear from panel A of Table 5.1. Men are much more often in working-class jobs, in particular, in the skilled sections of the working classes (Classes V and VI), whereas women are more often in routine non-manual jobs. Between the two periods, the change in class distributions was larger for women than for men. The proportion of women in the unskilled working classes decreased drastically, and the proportions in the skilled working classes and all non-manual classes increased. After the transformations, there is still a perceptible difference in the shares of service class jobs of men and women—men more often obtain jobs in Class I, and women in Class II.

The differences in class distributions of men and women help us understand one particular finding of the prestige regressions above, that is, why women, on average, have higher prestige scores than men, and why they receive slightly higher prestige returns for education than men. The main reason being that jobs in Class III (mostly held by women) tend to have higher prestige scores than jobs of unskilled or even skilled workers (mostly occupied by men). For instance, in the period after 1960, the average prestige of jobs in the routine non–manual class is 54 points, in the skilled working class it is 46, and 35 points in the unskilled working class. Jobs held by men and jobs held by women within these classes have almost identical average prestige scores. The possible (symbolic) advantages that women have compared to men in terms of job prestige appears in a more realistic light when we analyse outcomes in terms of class position. Even in the more recent period almost twice as many men than women obtain their first job in the most advantageous class position, the upper service class.[16]

Because of the specific class destinations of women, some of the models we would have liked to test cannot be estimated reliably for women, because some education–job–destination combinations occur very rarely (for instance virtually no women with tertiary education enter a working-class job in their first employment). We therefore first present a more detailed model for men and then compare men and women with less detailed data. The model presented for men in Table 5.5 (see pp. 174–5) is itself the result of extended tests to obtain a model which is as parsimonious as possible. The model used is a multinomial logit model in which we compare the chances of access to one of the more desirable class destinations to the risks of entering the labour market as an unskilled worker. Father's social class, parental education, and the respondent's education, plus the various control variables mentioned in the methods section above are used to predict these risks. Initially the model also included father's prestige as well as more detailed classifications of father's class and parental education. For father's class each of the Classes I, II, and IIIab were considered separately and not collapsed as in the final version in Table 5.5. For parental education, two levels of education (2ab/2c vs. 1c) were distinguished. The various tests carried out showed that the social background effects can be represented without loss of substantial information with the few parameters shown in Table 5.5.

For father's class and parental education the model basically is a levels model, in which the figures in the non-zero cells indicate the extent to which a given origin condition improves the likelihood of access to a given class rather than of becoming an unskilled worker. As indicated by the blocks drawn into the table, some of the origin effects are constrained to be the same for various destinations. The cells which include no entry are constrained to form zero log-odds ratios with the corresponding reference categories. For a given variable, the inclusion of zero-constraints generally depresses the estimates for the parameters in the non-zero cells.[17] In a non-constrained model the estimates for effects of specific conditions of father's class and parental origin are therefore generally somewhat larger than they appear in our models. The parameters in our models, however, have smaller standard errors; and the tables are much clearer to read. Detailed inspection of non-constrained models did not suggest any interpretations or conclusions different from those of the constrained models. In particular, effects of the respondent's education are almost identical in a constrained or unconstrained model.

According to the estimates of these models in Table 5.5, social background affects class of men's first job directly, that is, beyond its effects mediated through education. Similar to the prestige regression, we find positive effects of parental education. However, in the prestige regressions we found effects of father's prestige but not of father's social class. Here the results are reversed. We find effects of father's class but not of father's prestige. We find significant effects from father's to son's job only if we represent and measure the job of both in the same dimension (either prestige or class).

Three kinds of class effects can be identified: white-collar inheritance, petty bourgeoisie inheritance, and skilled worker inheritance.

White-collar inheritance pertains to origin Classes I to IIIab and destination Classes I to V. We include destination Class V within the white-collar block, because most of the cases with first job in Class V are qualified technicians (see note 16). White-collar inheritance thus means that sons of white-collar origin find ways of starting working life within the world of white-collar work with higher probabilities than one would expect from their education. They avoid working-class jobs.

The effect of petty bourgeoisie inheritance is particularly high. It mainly pertains to farmers' sons who work as family helpers on the parental farm or who become farmers very early in life. But the effect also derives from a few offspring of the non-agricultural petty bourgeoisie who follow their fathers' footsteps.

Skilled-worker inheritance is somewhat less strong than white-collar inheritance. Like the other two effects, it points to class maintenance, but also indicates differentiation in the job prospects of sons from working-class families—the sons of skilled workers have some degree of protection against starting their working life as unskilled workers, whereas this is not the case for the sons of unskilled workers.

As concerns parental education, Table 5.5 reveals two areas of zero cells, but for completely different reasons. First, access to the petty bourgeoisie class (rather than to the unskilled working class) does not depend directly on parental education. As far as parental background directly affects access to this class, this is exclusively (and—as we have seen before—massively) through direct inheritance of class position. Second, tertiary education of parents does not have a direct effect on the entry class of children. However (as other analyses not presented here show) parental tertiary education has a strong indirect effect, mediated through the respondents' education. Almost all children of highly educated parents follow their parents' educational routes, thus mainly profiting through their competitive advantages in education from their background for a promising entry into working life. The other two levels of parental education—an apprenticeship beyond compulsory schooling or any kind of secondary education—provide a clear direct advantage for sons at the beginning of their working life. Compared to parents with only compulsory education, elementary vocational or secondary education enhance the likelihood of access into skilled manual work (rather than unskilled work) and even more access to any form of non-manual work. For both destinations secondary education of parents ensures slightly better chances than only vocational training added to compulsory schooling.

The effects of the respondent's education on entry class again are high. The figures could be interpreted in a gradualistic-linear way in the sense that the more education you have, the better the prospects for an advantageous class position in first job. However, beyond this, the figures also show that specific levels and types of education are *particularly* associated with *specific* class destinations.

Consider first access to Classes I and II. Education effects increase almost linearly. As the effects are measured in logits, the exceptional pay-offs found for tertiary education in the prestige analyses are confirmed here. Though the increments in pay-offs for tertiary education, in particular, for university education, are only really marked in the case of access to Class I. The competitive advantage of tertiary education compared to (full) secondary education is substantially smaller if we turn to Class II, and it vanishes altogether for Class IIIab. Access to Class II and III is dependent on education in the form of a two-step function: having at least vocational training in addition to compulsory education; and obtaining intermediate secondary education. The latter provides a larger gain for access to Class II than to Class III.

Education is almost irrelevant for access to the petty bourgeoisie. (The crucial factor here is father's class!). As regards access to Classes V and VI, the main split is between school-leavers from compulsory schooling and those who went further, either through an apprenticeship or through secondary or tertiary education. Even a 1c qualification, however, appears to be a sufficient condition to become a skilled worker rather than an unskilled worker. Additional or higher-level qualifications do not enhance these chances. For access to Class V a formal vocational training is an even stronger precondition. But here, in contrast to access to the skilled working class, secondary and tertiary, in particular, lower level tertiary education considerably enhance the chances of access beyond those given with 1c qualifications.[18] This is entirely plausible as first employment in Class V can mainly be found in qualified technical occupations, which often are trained in institutions assigned to the lower level tertiary category (schools of engineering or technical colleges; *Fachhochschulen*) or—if obtained through an apprenticeship—presuppose higher/high-level general education. Education

TABLE 5.5. *Multinomial logit for men contrasting entry-class positions I, II, IIIab, IVabc, V, and VI, with VIIab*

	I	II	IIIab	V	VI	IVabc
Intercept	-6.65*** (1.05)	-5.58*** (.64)	-3.90*** (.36)	-6.81*** (1.05)	-1.83*** (.23)	-4.20*** (.50)
Social origin (relative to Class VIIab):						
I, II, IIIab			.66*** (.17)			.66*** (.17)
IVabc						2.88*** (.24)
V/VI				.38** (.16)	.41*** (.10)	
Parents education (relative to compulsory or less):						
secondary			.94*** (.22)		.45** (.21)	
compulsory + apprenticeship			.77*** (.14)		.37*** (.12)	

Educational level (relative to 1ab):

3b	9.38***	7.68***	4.15***	5.87***	1.96***	1.08
	(1.08)	(.71)	(.50)	(1.12)	(.47)	(.78)
3a	7.98***	7.20***	3.98***	6.69***	3.39***	1.58**
	(1.09)	(.70)	(.50)	(1.09)	(.42)	(.74)
2c	6.13***	6.72***	4.58***	6.00***	3.16***	1.71***
	(1.11)	(.67)	(.42)	(1.08)	(.35)	(.56)
2ab	5.07***	5.54***	4.04***	5.47***	2.97***	1.32***
	(1.05)	(.62)	(.32)	(1.03)	(.23)	(.39)
1c	2.17**	2.87***	2.27***	4.47***	3.08***	.92***
	(1.08)	(.61)	(.28)	(1.01)	(.17)	(.27)

Log likelihood   −4377.61
Chi²   3162.87
df   104
Pseudo R²   .27
N   3,725

* $p \leq =.10$ ** $p \leq =.05$ *** $p \leq =.01$

also appears to be more important for access to Class V than for access to the routine non-manual class, mainly due to the fact that (not surprisingly) it is relatively easier for someone with minimum education to enter Class IIIab than Class V.

The finding that specific types and levels of education are specifically relevant for specific outcomes is underlined by additional analyses, in which we use educational information in a way that is more congenial to the German educational system, but was not adopted here for reasons of comparisons with other countries. These analyses show that the chances of access to the various class positions are also conditioned by type of vocational training. If non-tertiary education is combined with a commercial apprenticeship the chances of access to the non-manual classes, in particular, to Class II, improve markedly. Apprenticeships in a craft or trade occupation impact strongly on access to Classes V and VI, but are of only minor value for access to any of the non-manual classes.

Having discussed the findings for a detailed analysis for men and for data referring to the total observation period, we now move to a somewhat less detailed analysis to compare men and women in two periods of time. Since only a very small number of women belong to Class IVabc in their first employment these women are excluded from the analysis. Furthermore, in the case of women we collapsed educational categories 3a and 3b because of the very low frequencies in some of the destination classes. As in the previous analyses we have carried out numerous tests in order to find a model which represents the effects of social background as parsimoniously as possible. For these variables effects of the same size have been constrained to be identical. The results for this analysis are given in Table 5.6a for men and Table 5.6b for women.

As measured by pseudo R^2, the independent variables scarcely allow better predictions of the distributions in the class destinations for the younger cohort than for the older cohort. This is in contrast to the prestige regression analysis where R^2 increased for both men and women.

Consistent with the results in Table 5.5, we find direct effects of social background. These effects, however, differ for men and women. For men, as before, we mainly find effects of father's class. Effects of father's occupational prestige are not significant. From the earlier to the later entry period the direct effects of father's class decline. While, as in the previous analyses, for the older cohort we find special effects for the 'inheritance' of white-collar, petty bourgeoisie, and skilled worker positions from fathers to sons, these effects disappear in the younger cohort with the exception of the petty bourgeoisie. For women we do not find significant effects of father's class, but significant effects of father's occupational prestige. Some of these prestige effects appear to be slightly smaller in the second period. As to parental education:

for men the effects have the same pattern as we found before, but tend to be stronger in the second period. For women, direct effects of parental education (in particular, of secondary and post-secondary education) were stronger than for men in the earlier period, but declined clearly in the second period. The only effect of parental education which remains significant for women who entered the labour market after 1960 is that for category 1c.

In summary, the direct reproduction of social-background advantages at the stage of entry into first employment differs for men and women. This may be explained by the fact that fathers and sons operate in the same male labour market, social reproduction largely occurs through inheritance of the main labour-market segments, blue-collar work, white-collar work, and self-employment, whereas many daughters operate in a different, sex-segregated labour market to that of their fathers. It is thus likely that for daughters social reproduction occurs less through inheritance of class position, but rather within a more marked hierarchical dimension as expressed by parental education or by father's occupational prestige.

Although social reproduction for men and women occurs on somewhat different grounds and through different mechanisms, direct influences of social background on class position at entry into first employment have declined from the earlier to the more recent period for both sexes. For men, direct inheritance of class disappeared with the exception of the petty bourgeoisie, while direct effects of parental education slightly increased. For women direct effects of parental education and father's prestige decreased.

As to the effects of the respondent's own education, we need not comment in much detail on the general pattern of associations, because they are consistent with the more differentiated analysis already discussed for men. Much the same results appear for men and women. This is true for the general pattern of association between education and class as well as for the changes in the association over time. The exception is that the *Abitur* appears to provide better first job prospects for men than for women.

No significant change over time occurs in the advantages of tertiary education for obtaining a service-class first job. The relative advantage of tertiary education, however, slightly declines for both sexes for the less typical destination of tertiary education: Classes III, V, and VI.[19] Consistent with the findings in the prestige regressions we observe a marked decline of the labour-market value of the *Abitur*. While in the earlier period its value for access to the combined service classes was relatively close to tertiary qualifications, it has become rather similar to intermediate secondary qualifications in the post-1960 period. For men, but not for women, the intermediate secondary and the vocational qualifications on the elementary level also appear to provide slightly smaller advantages against the educational minimum in the more recent period.

TABLE 5.6.a. *Multinomial logit for men contrasting entry-class positions I + II, III, IVabc, and V + VI, with VIIab*

	I + II		IIIab		V + VI		IVabc	
	before 1960	1960 or later	before 1960	1960 or later	before 1960	1960 or later	before 1960	1960 or later
Intercept	-4.57***	-3.99***	-3.32***	-2.49***	-1.67***	-1.43***	-3.72***	-4.00***
	(.72)	(.73)	(.37)	(.38)	(.20)	(.26)	(.35)	(.60)
Social origin (relative to Class VIIab):								
I, II, IIIab	.73***		.73***					
	(.17)		(.17)					
IVac		-.61***		-.61***		-.61***	2.98***	2.26***
		(22)		(.22)		(.22)	(.31)	(.42)
V/I			.41***		.41***		.41***	
			(.13)		(.13)		(.13)	
Parents' education (relative to compulsory or less):								
secondary	.56**	.92***	.56**	.92***	.56**	.92***		
	(.29)	(.277)	(.29)	(.28)	(.29)	(.28)		
compulsory + apprenticeship	.36***	.78***	.36***	.78***	.36***	.78***		
	(.15)	(.18)	(.15)	(.18)	(.15)	(.18)		

Educational level (relative to 1ab):								
3b	8.05*** (.93)	8.39*** (.88)	4.56*** (.75)	3.82*** (.65)	2.85*** (.67)	2.27*** (.60)	.69 (1.03)	2.10* (1.26)
3a	7.38*** (.87)	7.58*** (.96)	3.18*** (.78)	4.35*** (.75)	4.06*** (.51)	3.49*** (.68)	.39 (1.16)	3.39*** (1.11)
2c	8.25*** (.98)	5.60*** (.81)	5.88*** (.77)	3.59*** (.52)	4.28*** (.68)	2.74*** (.43)	.20 (1.25)	3.18*** (.77)
2ab	5.71*** (.78)	5.20*** (.76)	4.48*** (.47)	3.62*** (.44)	3.06*** (.33)	3.05*** (.33)	.71 (.51)	2.19*** (.69)
1c	3.07*** (.743)	2.56*** (.76)	2.46*** (.40)	2.15*** (.40)	3.10*** (.21)	3.16*** (.27)	.50 (.32)	1.52** (.61)
Log likelihood (Model: before 1960)		−1713.95						
Log likelihood (Model: 1960 +)							−1741.81	
Chi²		1270.7					1424.30	
df		45					44	
Pseudo R²		.27					.29	
N		1,784					1,941	

* p ≤ =.10   ** p ≤ =.05   *** p ≤ =.01

TABLE 5.6.b. Multinomial logit for women contrasting entry-class positions I + II, III, and V + VI, with VIIab

	I + II		III		V + VI	
	before 1960	1960 or later	before 1960	1960 or later	before 1960	1960 or later
Intercept	-4.47***	-4.21***	-1.59***	-1.45***	-3.50***	-2.91***
	(.37)	(.48)	(.223)	(.29)	(.32)	(.38)
Father's ocupational. prestige	.02***	.02**	.01**	.01*	.01*	.01
	(.01)	(.01)	(.00)	(.01)	(.001)	(.01)
Parents' education (relative to compulsory or less):						
post-secondary	2.05*	.53	2.05*	.53	2.05*	
	(1.09)	(.40)	(1.09)	(.40)	(1.09)	
secondary	1.52***	.29	1.52***	.29	1.52***	
	(.40)	(.21)	(.40)	(.21)	(.40)	
compulsory + apprenticeship	.57***	.69***	.57***	.69***	.57***	.69***
	(.14)	(.18)	(.14)	(.18)	(.14)	(.18)

Educational level (relative to 1ab):						
3ab	7.83***	7.76***	3.43***	3.03***	2.81**	2.09*
	(1.12)	(.87)	(1.09)	(.80)	(1.48)	(1.08)
2c	6.46***	4.81***	3.48***	2.47***	3.12***	2.32***
	(.88)	(.57)	(.82)	(.43)	(1.08)	(.56)
2ab	5.26***	5.21***	3.29***	3.10***	3.06***	3.08***
	(.43)	(.46)	(.32)	(.29)	(.42)	(.38)
1c	3.22***	3.23***	2.25***	2.59***	3.58***	3.35***
	(.34)	(.44)	(.18)	(.21)	(.26)	(.31)

Log likelihood (Model: Entry before 1960) −1653.7
Chi² 971.8
df 30
Pseudo R² .23
N 1,714

Log likelihood (Model: Entry 1960 or later) −1784.2
Chi² 1085.3
df 30
Pseudo R² .23
N 1,879

* p ≤ .10   ** p ≤ .05   *** p ≤ .01

For men, finally, access to the petty bourgeoisie becomes more dependent on education. This is probably due to the sharply declining proportion of agricultural jobs in the changing mix of the agricultural and non-agricultural sectors in the combined IVabc class. Outside agriculture the likelihood of starting working life on one's own account appears to increase with education.[20]

The findings on changes of educational effects over time are largely consistent with those found in the prestige regressions. However, the latter show increasing competitive advantages of tertiary education for both men and women. The logistic regressions reveal no such change. For access to the service classes the advantages of tertiary education remain unchanged and for access to the less typical class destinations they may have even declined. One explanation for this seeming discrepancy is that within the classes most frequently entered by those with tertiary education, the prestige composition of jobs has changed. Indeed, in the post-1960 period, the average prestige of jobs held in all non-manual classes has increased.[21] Given this fact both findings can be reconciled: the relative chances of access to the non-manual classes could remain constant (or even decline slightly as with Class III) and returns in terms of prestige still increase.

CONCLUSION

The expectations formulated at the beginning of this analysis have been largely confirmed. The findings on the significance of general and vocational qualifications for the chances of obtaining employment, and the quality of first job are largely compatible with the initial discussion on the specific educational and labour-market institutions in West Germany and the links between them.

We have attempted to show that the German system of vocational training leaves its marks in a specific pattern of the risks of unemployment. While it generally does not expose (except for particular conditions of demographic imbalances) young labour-market entrants to overproportional risks, it tends to concentrate unemployment among those without—at least—an elementary vocational training.

As to the impact of education on the quality of first job, we find differences in prestige and class position between holders of different types and levels of education that are very marked in comparison with other countries (see, in particular, the chapters on Britain and the United States). We find large proportions of variance of prestige in first job explained by education and large effects of different levels and types of education in the competition for the more or less desirable class positions. The pay-offs are particularly large for tertiary education.

It is also a characteristic feature of the German system that the education–class linkages do not correspond to a simple linear model. Rather, specific types and levels of education provide specific competition advantages for access to specific classes. Upper tertiary education, for instance, provides a specific advantage in access to service-class positions, in particular, the *upper* service class. But it does not provide advantages over less advanced levels of education in access to non-service class positions. At the lower end of the education and training system, an apprenticeship in addition to compulsory schooling is a more or less necessary and almost sufficient condition to become a skilled worker. The chances of becoming a skilled worker are not particularly increased by any higher educational qualification. However, Germany is not only marked by 'level credentialism', but also by 'occupational credentialism' (Konietzka and Solga 1995). This is indeed a core element of the occupationally segmented structure of the German labour market, whose basis is strongly shaped not only by the occupational differentiation of the vocational training system, but also by the occupational orientation of parts of tertiary education. One indicator of this occupationalism is that the occupational specialization of an apprenticeship has a marked effect on prestige and class of first job. Apprenticeships in a craft or trade strongly improve the chances of becoming a skilled worker, but only slightly improve any chance of obtaining a routine non-manual job or a service-class position. Access to non-manual class positions is only made easier by commercial apprenticeships.

In terms of the chiefly symbolic dimension of prestige, women receive slightly higher returns to education than men. Women are able to turn education into more prestigeful jobs, mainly because occupations in the female routine non-manual labour market tend to have a higher prestige than occupations in the working classes, mainly held by men. When outcomes are judged in terms of class position obtained, and when differences in the distribution of jobs typically held by men and women are controlled for, the pattern of more favourable returns to education for women disappears. Furthermore, even in the more recent period clearly more men than women obtain their first job in the upper service class. But again, this is not a result of different returns to education for men and women. It is instead a result of the fact that at the highest levels of education women still fall short of male participation rates, and that women opt for different substantive fields of education than men. In Germany higher education for women has been significant in improving their job prospects, but in the higher tertiary level of education women still are less present than men.

It is important to qualify the conclusion of only minor gender differences in returns to education in at least two additional respects. First, we analysed outcomes in first jobs. Conclusions may differ when we follow men and women along their further steps in the work career. Secondly, even for first job we have neglected one important dimension—that is, that women may receive less income than men for their level of education.

The basic patterns of the effects of education have not fundamentally changed over time. At any rate there are no indications of a substantial decline in the general significance of education for prestige or class of first job. The results for the two dimensions differ somewhat. For prestige of first job variance explained increases across cohorts and the gap in prestige returns between labour-market entrants with the lowest education and entrants with tertiary education, in particular lower level tertiary education increases. No such tendencies appear for class of first job. The most simple and plausible explanation for these discrepant results is that within both service classes the average prestige of jobs increased through changes in the composition of jobs belonging to each class.

Though we do not find indications of a marked devaluation of education in general, this is clearly true for one specific educational level: the *Abitur*. The prestige as well as the class analyses indicate declining returns to the *Abitur*. In France, the old saying about the value of the Baccalauréat (*'sans le bac on est rien'*), now takes into account its devaluation, and has become, *'le bac, c'est ne rien'*. Less drastically, this seems to be the case for Germany as well. In earlier decades the *Abitur* was not only the entry ticket to university, but also constituted a good-starting point for several careers, such as journalism or banking. Careers within these areas increasingly became professionalized and access dependent on tertiary educational credentials. Most likely two changes within the educational system have contributed to the devaluation of the labour-market value of the *Abitur*, which was and still is, the major educational credential based on higher *general* education in Germany. Both these changes are in the German tradition of stressing the vocational/occupational orientation of education. The first concerns an institutional reform and innovation: the establishment and strong expansion of a new layer of lower level tertiary educational institutions (*Fachhochschulen*) which have a clear practical orientation towards a broad set of semi-professional occupations. The second is the use (or misuse, see Büchel and Helberger 1995) of the *Abitur* as an educational preparation for apprenticeships in more demanding or prestige-conferring occupations.

The devaluation of the *Abitur* cannot alter the conclusion that Germany continues to be a society in which education plays a very large role for the kind of job a young person obtains when entering the labour market. Instead, one could say that within the ensemble of our results the developments causing the devaluation of the *Abitur* underline the findings of earlier work elaborating the qualificational space as the crucial dimension of the German labour market (Maurice, Sellier, and Silvestre 1982; Haller et al. 1985; König and Müller 1986; Müller et al. 1990; König 1990; Allmendinger 1989*a*). But we have to stress the strong occupational component of this qualificational space, both in education and training and in the organizational division of labour. Neither educational expansion nor the gradual transformation of the occupational structure from industrial to service occupations have fundamentally changed these characteristic features of education–labour-market linkages in Germany. Interestingly, based on common historical roots and institutions, the developments during the communist regime in Eastern Germany followed rather similar lines as in the West—and as far as occupational credentialism is concerned its manifestations in the East were apparently even stronger than in the West (Konietzka and Solga 1995).

The large effects of education on first job notwithstanding, social background affects prestige and class in first job, not only indirectly through education, but also directly. Father's prestige appears to be more important for daughters than for sons and when first job is measured in terms of prestige. Father's class is more important for sons and when first job is measured in terms of class. The class effects mainly contribute to the inter-generational reproduction of non-manual class, petty bourgeoisie, and working-class positions. Parental education also directly influences first job of children, in particular, of daughters. However, at large we find that these influences declined from the earlier to the more recent period. As this is true for both direct effects of social background and total effects, we conclude that at least until entry into the labour market the inter-generational reproduction of social inequalities seems to have declined.

What do these findings tell us about more general theories or beliefs on the development of social structures in German society. Some authors— most prominently among them Beck (1984)—see social structures largely dissolving through increasing tendencies of individualization. Structural position at one point in time, or in one social arena, is increasingly less linked with structural position at another point in time or in another arena because individual *opportunities for options* multiply as well as the *risk of failure*. As a concrete instance of such developments the bonds between education and work position are assumed to become weaker. Clearly our data do not support such assumptions and confirm earlier critical evaluations of these theses (Mayer and Blossfeld 1990). Rather than strengthening the post-modern variant of modernization theory the present results could be taken in support of the more conventional version of modernization theory formulated in stratification research (Blau and Duncan 1967; Treiman 1970). Conditions of social origin have a smaller effect on prestige or class of first job while education becomes a more powerful predictor at least of prestige in first job. However, first job is but the entry position in the labour market. Even though in Germany first job has a strong impact on later careers (König and

Müller 1986; Mayer and Blossfeld 1990; Blossfeld 1989), the reduced effects of social background on first job could be compensated by stronger effects of the resources of the parental family on the career development. The effects of education which are strong at the transition from school to work might become weaker as other factors also influence the work career. A final evaluation must therefore await the study of further career mobility over the working life.

NOTES

This study is part of the project 'Educational Expansion and Social Reproduction in Europe' at the Mannheim Centre of European Social Research funded by the German Research Foundation (Deutsche Forschungsgemeinschaft).

1. Other important developments, such as adult education or the emergence of a wide variety of specific training programmes, both within and outside firms, also merit attention, but have not been dealt with in the present analysis for reasons of space (see CEDEFOP 1991: 151–63).
2. For a schematic picture of the contemporary German educational system, see OECD 1995a: 277.
3. Whereas, in France, for example, the French Revolution and the Napoleonic reforms effectively swept away the traditions of vocational training together with the guilds.
4. In the 1950s, approximately 50 per cent of a cohort had completed an apprenticeship, while this figure rose to nearly 70 per cent in the 1980s, mainly due to the increased participation of women in apprenticeships. According to Tessaring (1993: 136), in 1990, 67 per cent of men and 63 per cent of women aged 16 to 19 years entered vocational training in the dual system.
5. At least three types of school-based alternatives have to be distinguished: a real alternative to apprenticeships developed in some areas of business and social services, in particular in occupations chosen mostly by women (secretaries, kindergarten nurses, medical aides, and other health-related occupations). The second kind is a temporary substitute for cases where the apprenticeship system is deficient: for school-leavers unable to become apprenticed due to a shortfall of such places (for example, in the early 1980s, when school-leavers from the baby-boom birth cohorts met with an economy in crisis), or for school-leavers who lack abilities (in this case, vocationally oriented school programmes attempt to provide the qualificational preconditions for entry into an apprenticeship). The third kind are training programmes which follow and build on the successful completion of an apprenticeship—for example, in becoming a master craftsman in a traditional craft area, or in a more modern context, in supporting the career transition from skilled worker to highly qualified technician.
6. According to recent data, the average proportion of such smooth transitions from apprenticeship to regular employment is 52 per cent for male apprentices (Bender and Dietrich 1994).

7. For a more detailed discussion, see W. Fischer and Lundgreen (1975); and Müller (1994).

8. This title for German secondary school teachers is telling as it indicates both the academic orientation of the profession and its civil-service status.

9. The italics are the authors'.

10. The control variables used indicate how many years earlier than expected the labour market is entered. For instance, by the inclusion of dummy variables in the prestige regressions of Table 5.3 we compensate for the artificially lower prestige of first job for those who entered first job *before* they had obtained their highest level of education (used in the analysis to predict first job).

11. These measures of employment preferences and exclusion from employment are at best poor proxies, since we cannot control for the 'discouraged workers', that is, those classified as 'not in labour force' who abandoned, or never started, a job search because they expected to fail.

12. In 1992, for instance, male labour-force participation stood at 74 per cent for those aged 55 to 59, and 31 per cent for those aged 60 to 64; the respective figures for women were 42 and 10 per cent.

13. The exception of education group 2c is probably an artefact, arising from the fact that some of the younger members in this group are still fluctuating between education and employment and are not yet integrated in a stable way into the labour force, as indicated by the large proportion 'not in the labour force'. If we only include those aged 35 to 55 in the analysis, the irregularly high proportion of men 'not in the labour force' in education group 2c disappears and the effect for unemployment becomes more like—albeit still lower—those for groups 2ab, 3a and 3b.

14. The figure for total variance explained exactly corresponds to an earlier finding by Müller (1978), but is considerably greater than in the models by Mayer and Blossfeld (1990), who use a different measure of sons' education and exclude parents' education.

15. The results of a simulation study not documented here in detail show that the increases in R^2 mainly result from changes in the distribution of education and not from changes in returns to given levels of education.

16. At this point, we should also try to understand why the proportions in Classes IV and V are so large. Indeed, neither self-employment nor positions for men are typical class positions for first jobs. More detailed inspection of the data shows that the relatively large proportions observed for these classes partly derive from the coding conventions of the Erikson-Goldthorpe class schema, and partly from the fact that we have collapsed agricultural and non-agricultural jobs in Class IV. In fact, the majority of jobs in Class IV are in agriculture, more so in the older than in the younger cohort; others are small retail shopkeeping, the self-employed in trade, commerce or the crafts. In addition, a substantial part of Class IVabc first jobs are as family helpers (among women close to 60 per cent in the older cohort and about 20 per cent in the younger cohort, among men about 20 and 10 per cent, respectively). As to those coded into Class V, indeed only small proportions are foremen. At entry into the labour market, Class V is mainly composed of 'technician' jobs of various kinds. The most frequent single category is technical drawing, particularly among women.

17. Due to the zero constraints, the parameters of the constrained variables cannot

188   *W. Müller, S. Steinmann, and R. Ell*

be interpreted as a straightforward difference to one specific reference category (such as Class VII for father's class, or compulsory education for parental education). The reference is defined by the zone of all zero cells. However, in constructing the model, we only constrained parameters to be zero for cells, which in a non-constrained model did not differ significantly from the reference category. As the reference category in the non-constrained model was chosen as the least advantageous origin condition (VII for father's class and 1ab for parental education), the parameters for the cells later constrained to zero generally had positive, although not significantly positive, values. Constraining them to be identical with the reference category generally raised the value of the baseline (expressed in the intercept), and in consequence depressed the estimates for the parameters in the non-zero cells.

18. None of the differences between the effects of education 1c and any higher educational category is statistically significant for access to Class VI, whereas for access to Class V all these differences are highly significant.

19. Inspection of the component parts of the respective odds ratios, however, shows that the declining competitive advantages of those with tertiary education, compared to those with minimum education, in obtaining a job in Class III rather than in Class VII, is not because relatively more labour-force entrants with tertiary education had to take a job in Class VII in the more recent period. The declining odds ratio is rather due to the fact that those with minimum education had relatively better chances in the more recent period to obtain jobs in Class III, V, or VI.

20. The non-significant effect of higher tertiary education is probably due to the fact that the self-employed with this level of education would generally be assigned to Class I.

21. The average prestige score of jobs held in Class I increased from 117 to 122; from 76 to 79 for service class II; and from 49 to 53 for the routine non-manual class.

6

Investment in Education

Educational Qualifications and Class of Entry in the Republic of Ireland

RICHARD BREEN AND CHRISTOPHER T. WHELAN

INTRODUCTION

In this chapter we investigate the relationship between educational qualifications and class of entry in the Republic of Ireland, using data on entrants to the labour market in the period since 1967. Our goal is to show how macro-social and institutional factors condition the nature of the link between qualifications and entry class. We begin, therefore, by outlining some salient institutional features of the Irish educational system and labour market.

The Irish educational system has a tripartite structure in which pupils transfer from primary to secondary level education around the age of 12, and some students subsequently enter third-level education generally at the age of 18. Post-primary education takes place in either secondary or vocational (or, to a lesser extent, comprehensive or community) schools, and has conventionally been divided into two cycles: the junior cycle, usually lasting three years, and culminating in the Junior Certificate examination; and the senior cycle, usually lasting two years, leading to the Leaving Certificate examination.

Before the reforms of the 1960s, the great majority of the Irish population experienced only primary education provided through the national school system. Both national and secondary schools are predominantly denominational in character. The secondary schools provide a grammar school type of education concentrating on non-technical subjects. Such schools were not oriented to labour-market demands: as Tussing (1978: 12) puts it 'the major function of secondary education was religious, moral and intellectual', and the products of such education were (if male) destined for jobs in professional and other white-collar occupations. The less numerous vocational schools, on the other hand, were specifically orientated to providing practical training and the curriculum was explicitly linked to the perceived labour demands of the local economy.

The impetus for change in the system came from the publication in 1965 of the OECD/Irish Government funded report, *Investment in Education* which itself was the product of concern about the articulation of the existing school system with the needs of a newly industrializing economy. Two issues raised in that report were particularly relevant in accounting for subsequent policy developments. The first of these was the finding that there existed large social class and regional disparities in educational participation rates. The reforms of the second half of the 1960s were intended to reduce these disparities through the abolition of fees for post-primary education, the introduction of school transport, and so forth. The second objective was to improve the level of trained manpower by an expansion of enrolment in broadly defined vocational subject areas.

The blanket introduction of free secondary education in 1967 has now come to be seen as a blunt instrument; expanded provision was made largely without regard to pre-existing differences between pupils in terms not only of their financial but also their cultural resources. Perhaps more surprising is that it was the academic rather than vocational side of education that benefited from increases in pupil enrolments. The relative position of the vocational sector has actually worsened since 1960 and a large number of senior cycle school-leavers continue to lack qualifications in vocational subjects.

One reason why vocational subjects remained relatively unpopular among secondary school students after the reforms of the 1960s relates to the nature of the labour market and the kinds of jobs available to those leaving schools after the senior cycle. During the 1970s far from manufacturing industry demanding large inflows of vocationally trained young people, employment in white-collar work expanded dramatically while in manufacturing it grew more slowly than in the 1960s. Service-sector growth was most rapid in the public sector and in the insurance and finance area of private services. Consequently, labour-market demand and educational supply remained roughly in equilibrium up to the 1980s recession. However, at this point the stable relationship between the educational system and the labour market was threatened by large-scale youth unemployment. The emergence of these difficulties led to a focus on deficiencies in labour supply. Secondary level education became seen by many as 'inflexible' and as having an 'over-academic bias'. One consequence was the establishing of post-school training schemes.

Despite the proliferation of such schemes there is, in fact, little evidence that skilled labour is in short supply. Indeed, although unemployment is disproportionately concentrated among those with low levels of educational qualifications, one effect of the expansion of the education and training system over the past two decades has been to help produce a surplus of labour at the higher levels. However, as O'Connell and Lyons (1995) note, while such evidence indicates that there is no shortage of people to fill particular jobs, Ireland still suffers from specific qualification gaps relative to other leading industrial societies. Thus, although Ireland has a relatively large share of educationally well-qualified persons, with 20 per cent of the 25 to 34 age group having third-level qualifications, only 50 per cent of Irish men and 60 per cent of Irish women in the same age group have completed upper secondary education. Notwithstanding the trend towards higher educational attainment, 20 per cent of secondary school-leavers continue to leave school with either no, or inadequate, qualifications.

The low level of demand for skilled labour in Ireland arises largely as a consequence of its industrial structure. Agriculture, much of it based on small family farms, continues to be much more important in the Irish economy than many other European economies. For historical reasons Ireland lacks a large indigenous industrial base and large manufacturing enterprises. Industrial development has been relatively recent and based on the attraction of foreign multinationals. As a consequence apprenticeship training in Ireland is relatively insignificant, accounting for no more than 5 per cent of labour-market entrants. The bulk of training is carried out at the place of work. However, widespread scepticism has been expressed about the quality and efficacy of such training (O'Connell and Lyons 1995).

As Soskice (1993*a*: 102) has argued: '[w]hat is notable about all the advanced economies such as the UK in which business is weakly collectively organised . . . is that none has effective initial training systems in which private companies play a major part.' This is certainly true of Ireland. It is the existence of powerful employer organizations which facilitates the creation of an external training agency, a system of wage determination which makes poaching difficult, and a governance structure within organizations that ensures workforces do not exploit their power to the full. In Ireland these elements are absent. Despite the existence of a series of tripartite (state, employer and trade union) national agreements inter-organizational and intra-organizational tensions set limits to the capacity of employer organizations to commit their members to agreed common strategies. Rather, the pattern of Irish industrialization ensured that employers' interests were diverse. One important reflection of this is the clear preference of multinational organizations for conducting their own wage and labour negotiations and an associated emphasis on internal 'human resource development' strategies (Hardiman 1988).

The pattern of linkages between education and the labour market does not fit neatly into either the 'qualification mobility space' or 'organizational mobility space' ideal types which have been proposed in the literature

(Maurice, Sellier, and Silvestre 1986). The link between types of educational pathways and job entry is much looser in Ireland than in countries such as Germany. However, unlike the United States, where a similarly weak relationship between educational courses and job entry exists, Ireland possesses a national curriculum and a set of standardized examinations which are widely used by employers for recruitment purposes. The system is thus characterized as involving a high degree of standardization but a low degree of stratification (Allmendinger 1989*b*). As a result, although horizontal differentiation (in terms of the type of educational qualifications a job seeker possesses) is relatively unimportant, vertical differentiation (the level of educational attainment) has a powerful influence. The examination system provides a mechanism that, despite the absence of any clear institutionalized connection between education/ training institutions and job entry paths, allows for a close link between educational success and labour-market prospects. In Ireland educational qualifications, as demonstrated in examination performance, act:

[a]s a signal of the potential productivity of job seekers thus . . . [enabling] . . . employees to minimise their recruitment costs and allowing them to make as fine distinctions as are required in order to select among a possibly large field of job applicants in a very slack labour market. (Breen, Hannan, and O'Leary 1995, parentheses added)

Given such a situation we should expect parents to place a heavy emphasis on their children's level of educational attainment, and, in particular, we should expect the relationship between class of origin and educational achievement to be conspicuously strong because such achievement is critical in a number of respects. In the first place the cost of educational failure is particularly high because it involves not only location at the bottom of the class hierarchy, but also a high probability of being unemployed. In addition, in the absence of horizontal differentiation, vertical differentiation is extremely important with employers using quite fine distinctions in examination results in deciding who to hire and how much to pay. Finally, it is the same criterion—overall educational performance—that determines access to higher or third-level education.

   In addition, there is a comparatively limited degree of career mobility (that is, from entry class to current class) in Ireland. Compared with England and Wales career immobility in the service class is substantially higher in Ireland while long-range upward mobility into the service class is substantially lower (Breen and Whelan 1996). Thus, entry class takes on a position of considerable importance in the entire process of inter-generational mobility, serving to reinforce further the significance that is attached to educational qualifications. Furthermore, Erikson and Goldthorpe (1992) have argued that while it is necessary to make a clear conceptual distinction between absolute and relative mobility this does not mean that relative mobility patterns are independent of the absolute mobility flows. Thus, in Ireland the possibility exists that the long-term situation of an excess of labour influences class strategies and the outcome of these strategies, and the series of competitions arising from them are then reflected in the pattern of relative mobility rates.

DATA DESCRIPTION AND OUTLINE OF ANALYSIS

The survey of Poverty, Income Distribution and Usage of State Services carried out by the Economic and Social Research Institute in 1987 provides the database for our analysis. A detailed description of this survey is provided in Callan et al. (1989). The survey was designed to provide a national sample of the adult population of the Republic of Ireland resident in private households. In this chapter we use data on all respondents aged 24 to 35 at the time of the survey: in other words, who were born between 1952 and 1963 and who therefore would have entered the labour market in the period 1967 to around 1985. This gives us 659 men and 635 women.

In the remainder of this chapter we report four sets of analyses. We first examine the relationships between class origin and education; between class origin and class of entry; and between education and class of entry. We then investigate the relationship between class of entry, on the one hand, and the effects of both class origins and education. The results of these analyses then enable us to investigate the strength of the various bivariate relationships and also to assess the extent to which the relationship between class origins and entry class position is mediated via the educational system. We also briefly report the results of a comparable OLS analysis employing Hope-Goldthorpe prestige scores and of an analysis of the impact of class origins and educational achievement on current economic status distinguishing between being at work, unemployed, or not in the labour force. In the concluding parts of the chapter we return to the institutional context and explain what our results tell us about this.

Class and Educational Categorizations

Both class of origin and class of entry are operationalized using the following six-category class schema: I + II service class; III routine white-collar; IVa I b petty bourgeoisie; IVc farmers; V/VI skilled manual; and VII non-skilled manual. In the case of education we start from the eight-category CASMIN schema which distinguishes education according to level and—to some degree—type. Certain of the distinctions in the schema, however, are not mirrored in the Irish educational system or cannot be distinguished in our data. For example, we do not separate CASMIN categories 1a (inadequate completion of elementary education) and 1b (completed elementary education) since, although our data allow us to identify those with no educational qualifications, it would be of no value to distinguish between those among this group who dropped out of school before the minimum school-leaving age and those who did not. Similarly, category 1c (elementary education plus vocational training) does not exist in Ireland, and category 2a (general intermediate education plus specific vocational training) does not exist within the school system. The closest approximation to this is apprenticeship training which usually follows completion of general intermediate education. However apprenticeships are almost exclusively taken by men and the numbers involved are small.

Accordingly, we use four educational categories that correspond to distinctions between educational level that, as we argue below, are of central importance in understanding the link between the educational system and the labour market in Ireland. These categories (with their CASMIN counterparts in parentheses) are: no formal educational qualifications (1a, 1b, and 1c); lower or intermediate secondary level education (2a and 2b); higher secondary level education (2c); and third-level education (3a and 3b). We also, however, define a further variable to indicate whether or not an apprenticeship had been pursued. This variable, which we enter into our later analyses, then serves to distinguish between CASMIN categories 2a and 2b.

Educational Selectivity

In order to provide a context for our subsequent analysis we provide details in Table 6.1 of the degree of educational selectivity in Ireland in terms of both class of origin and father's education. In panel A the dramatic increase in educational participation is reflected in the discrepancies between the marginal distributions of highest educational qualifications for fathers and respondents. While 85 per cent of the former had no formal qualifications, the figure drops to 27 per cent for the latter. It is therefore inevitable that a substantial majority of those who themselves have completed upper secondary or tertiary education have fathers who lack any qualifications. Selectivity in the system is reflected at the bottom of the hierarchy: those with less than an upper secondary level education are drawn almost exclusively from the origin group possessing no qualifications. When we consider selectivity in terms of class origins, as set out in panel B of Table 6.1, we find that two-thirds of third-level graduates are drawn from the service class and the property-owning classes. The substantial expansion of the system

TABLE 6.1. *Educational selectivity by father's education* (in-flow %) *and class origins* (% by column)

	No qualifications	Lower secondary level	Upper secondary level	Third level	Total
A. Father's education:					
no qualifications	97.4	95.3	73.2	64.8	85.3
lower secondary level	1.7	2.6	9.1	5.0	4.6
upper secondary level	0.3	0.7	13.3	15.8	5.8
third level	0.6	1.4	4.3	14.4	4.3
B. Class origins:					
service class	1.1	3.1	13.0	27.3	8.7
routine non-manual	5.4	4.1	8.7	5.2	6.0
petty bourgeoisie	2.8	4.8	8.7	9.9	6.1
skilled manual	18.5	21.4	16.7	15.1	18.4
non-skilled manual	53.4	36.7	20.1	13.4	33.3
farming	18.8	29.8	32.8	29.1	27.6
TOTAL %	27.2	30.3	29.2	13.3	100.0
TOTAL at each educational level	352	392	378	172	1,294

has led to a situation where the distribution of those completing post-primary education comes relatively close to mirroring the overall distribution. Once again it is the lowest educational destination which provides the sharpest differentiation with nine out of ten of those who terminate their education at the primary or lower secondary level—approximately 60 per cent of the age group—having working-class or farming origins.

Educational Inequalities

In Table 6.2 we document the outflows from class origins to educational destination broken down by gender. Consistent with our previous discussion, the most striking feature is the scale of the inequalities observed between those originating at the extremes of the class hierarchy. The observed odds ratio summarizing the competition between the service class and the non-skilled working class to achieve third-level education and avoid the absence of qualifications reaches 117:1 for men and 110:1 for women.[1] The pattern of results suggests the operation of strong hierarchical class resources in attaining more desirable educational destinations. Another interesting feature of the results is that they are consistent with our expectations that within

TABLE 6.2. *Educational level by class origins, by gender* (out-flow %)

Educational level	Service class		Routine non-manual		Petty bourgeoisie		Skilled-manual		Non-skilled manual		Farmers	
	Men	Women	Men	Women	Men	Women	Men	Women	Men	Women	Men	Women
No qualifications	2.0	4.8	22.0	27.8	8.6	15.9	26.4	28.2	38.2	49.1	25.1	10.5
Lower secondary	14.0	8.1	19.5	22.2	20.0	27.3	40.5	29.9	43.3	23.4	37.9	26.5
Upper secondary	44.0	43.5	46.3	38.9	42.9	40.9	24.8	28.2	12.0	23.4	24.1	47.5
Third level	40.0	43.5	12.2	11.1	28.6	15.9	8.3	13.7	6.5	4.2	12.8	15.4
TOTAL	7.6	9.8	6.2	5.7	5.3	6.9	18.4	18.4	32.9	33.7	29.6	25.5
N	50	62	41	36	35	44	121	117	217	214	195	162

the petty bourgeoisie and farming groups different strategies are pursued in relation to sons and daughters. We take up this point in more detail later. Finally, consistent with the evidence of gender segregation in pursuit of apprenticeship training and, indeed, more generally in access to skilled work, working-class men display a much higher tendency to terminate their education at the lower secondary level than do their female counterparts.

THE RELATIONSHIP BETWEEN CLASS ORIGINS AND EDUCATIONAL LEVEL

We model the outflow from class origins to education by means of a topological or levels model (Hauser 1978, 1979). The model we have applied is set out in Table 6.3. Our starting-point involves distinguishing three levels in order to reflect the hierarchical differences in resources and desirability to which we have previously referred. Thus focusing first on men, the strong tendency for men from the service class to complete third-level education is captured by assigning the corresponding cell to level 3. The sons of the petty bourgeoisie are hypothesized to display the second strongest tendency towards such movement and are allocated to level 2. The expectation of modest differentiation between Classes III, IVc, and V/VI and of a lower rate of movement into this level is reflected in the allocation of all three cells to level 1. The levels defined thus far prove inadequate to capture the barriers to entry into third-level education experienced by the non-skilled manual class. It is therefore necessary to distinguish a fourth level referring solely to this cell. Allocation of all but one of the remaining cells to the original three levels allows us to capture a variety of hypothesized outcomes which are consistent with our understanding of the manner in which hierarchical influences operate. These include:

1. the increase in the tendency to leave the educational system at the lower secondary level as one moves from the white-collar classes to the property-owning classes, and finally to the working class;

2. the fact that the tendency to leave the system at the upper secondary level is strong for the white-collar classes and the petty bourgeoisie but somewhat weaker for all other classes;

3. a strengthening of the tendency to leave the system without qualifications as one shifts from the service class and the petty bourgeoisie to the routine non-manual class, and a further strengthening for the skilled manual class.

There is, however, a further hierarchical effect which requires that we extend the number of levels in our models. This is the distinctive tendency

TABLE 6.3. *Levels model for out-flow from class origins in educational destination*

	Education			
	No qualifications	Lower secondary	Upper secondary	Third level
Men				
I + II	1	1	3	3
III	2	1	3	1
IVa+b	1	2	3	2
IVc	3	2	2	1
V/VI	3	3	2	1
VII	5	3	2	4
Women				
I + II	1	1	3	3
III	2	1	3	1
IVa+b	1	2	3	1
IVc	1	2	3	1
V/VI	3	2	2	1
VII	5	2	2	4

of the non-skilled manual class to leave the educational system without qualifications. To accommodate this effect it is necessary to allocate the relevant cell to a fifth level.

The pattern of levels for women is the same as that for men in both the white-collar classes (I + II and III) and the working classes (V/VI and VII), except that in the latter women are rather less likely to leave school at the lower secondary level, a decision which is linked to barriers to entry into apprenticeships. However, among those classes that own the means of production (IVa+b and IVc) there are more substantial gender differences. These arise largely because of the distinction between the child (or children) who inherit the family farm or business, and those who will not. This distinction is particularly important among farm families because farm inheritance in Ireland is impartible. Inheriting children are likely to be male and to receive a relatively low level of education—though quite how low will depend on the size of the enterprise and the associated need for specialist theoretical knowledge. Women from farm origins, being non-inheritors, are much less likely than men to leave without educational qualifications and are correspondingly more likely to leave education after the Leaving Certificate. In the case of the petty bourgeoisie, the gender difference relates to the fact that men are more likely to complete tertiary education than women. This difference may well reflect the fact that, more than in the case of farming, at least some small business sectors are perceived to require increasingly sophisticated human-capital inputs.

This model, which views the class-origin–education relationship in broadly hierarchical terms but which allows for certain gender interactions associated with property ownership and patterns of occupational segregation, fits the data with a G^2 of 26.1 with 26 df. The parameters of the levels model are reported in Table 6.4.

TABLE 6.4. *Class origin to educational destination out-flow: parameter estimates for levels model*

Level	B	SE
2	0.792	(.135)
3	1.263	(.116)
4	−0.611	(.245)
5	1.932	(.167)

THE RELATIONSHIP BETWEEN CLASS ORIGINS AND CLASS OF ENTRY

In Table 6.5 we show the outflow from class origins to class of entry by gender. The most striking feature is the degree of class segregation between the sexes in their first job. Just over six out of ten women are found in the routine white-collar class compared to one in five men. Conversely, seven out of ten men are found in the manual classes compared to one in four women. However, the extent of class differentiation is exaggerated, since almost two-thirds of the routine white-collar positions are located in Class IIIb—in other words they are in positions which in terms of employment relationships are in many ways more like those of Class VII than of IIIa. Furthermore, very few men and no women are found in Classes IVa+b or IVc. It is necessary, therefore to keep in mind, when considering the results of our attempts to model relative mobility, that the range of occupational destinations, especially in the case of women, displays a great deal less variation than that observed in the conventional mobility table.

The model we develop of the outflow from class origins to class of entry is based on the following set of expectations. We anticipate direct entry into Classes IVa+b and IVc only among men and only among those whose class origins are here. We also anticipate some downward mobility from farm origins into Class VII, some of which will be compensated for by subsequent counter-mobility (into agricultural labouring prior to inheriting a farm). We

TABLE 6.5. *Class at first job by class of origin by sex* (% by column)

Class at first job	Service class		Routine non-manual		Petty bourgeoisie		Skilled-manual		Non-skilled manual		Farmers		Total	
	Men	Women	Men	Women	Men	Women	Men	Women	Men	Women	Men	Women	Men	Women
Service class	30.0	32.3	7.3	2.8	14.3	20.5	9.1	10.3	4.6	5.1	9.7	16.7	9.6	13.5
Routine non-manual	28.0	62.9	36.6	83.2	20.0	68.2	22.3	57.3	17.5	58.4	12.8	65.4	19.1	60.9
Petty bourgeoisie	2.0	1.6	0.0	0.0	5.7	0.0	0.8	0.0	0.0	0.5	0.0	0.6	0.6	0.2
Skilled-manual	20.0	1.6	22.0	8.3	40.0	4.5	42.1	12.0	33.6	13.1	23.1	7.4	30.7	9.2
Non-skilled manual	20.0	1.6	34.1	5.6	20.0	6.8	24.0	20.5	44.2	22.9	46.7	9.9	37.5	16.1
Farming	0.0	0.0	0.0	0.0	0.0	0.0	1.7	0.0	0.0	0.0	7.7	0.0	2.6	0.0
TOTAL	7.6	9.8	6.2	5.7	5.3	6.9	18.4	18.4	32.9	33.7	29.6	25.5	100	100
N	50	62	41	36	35	44	121	117	217	214	195	162	659	785

further expect movement from farm origins into Class V/VI: once again part of this may be associated with counter-mobility but it may also arise as non-inheriting men are provided with an education that permits them to enter skilled manual jobs. A similar pattern of movement into Class V/VI should also occur among young men of petty-bourgeoisie origins. Among the non-inheriting sons from larger farms and businesses we should expect to find direct class inheritance in the cases of Classes I/II, V/VI, and VII.

This model was operationalized using the design matrices shown in Table 6.6. N1 and N2 fit parameters N11 and N21 which capture direct inheritance in Classes IVa+b and IVc, respectively. N3 fits a single parameter, N31, for the flows into Class I/II from origins I/II, IVa+b and IVc. N4 then fits a single parameter, N41, to capture all the other flows discussed above—namely to V/VI from IVa+b, IVc and V/VI, and to VII from IVc and VII.

This model, however, fails to fit the data by a considerable extent, due entirely to its underestimation of the upwardly mobile flow from Class VII origins into Class V/VI. In other words, the distinction between skilled and semi-skilled or unskilled workers is less clear than expected. One possible explanation for this concerns the importance of sectors such as construction in providing manual employment. Here the distinctions between skilled and non-skilled work are somewhat tenuous so that skilled manual workers are less of an 'aristocracy of labour' than in other countries. This conclusion is supported by the evidence that skilled manual workers actually have higher rates of unemployment that semi-skilled (Whelan, Breen, and Whelan 1992). Adding an extra term to the N4 matrix, yields the matrix N4A shown in Table 6.6. This places the cell representing the flow from Class VII to Class V/VI at the same level as the other flows into V/VI. Taken together the four matrices yield a model having G^2 of 17.28 with 21 df.

For women the model is much simpler. Matrices N1 and N2 can be omitted because of the lack of any movement of women directly into Classes IVa+b or IVc. N3 is retained to reflect the advantage in access to Class I/II associated with origins in Classes I/II, IVa+b or IVc. Matrix N4A is also simplified (and labelled N5) first by removing the flows from Classes IVa+b and IVc. This is done because neither counter-mobility nor education for skilled manual employment are of any significance for women born into these classes. Second, an extra cell is included at level 2 of the matrix: this is the flow from Class V/VI to Class VII. The result, as Table 6.6 shows, is a matrix that in effect establishes a sectoral barrier between the working classes (V/VI and VII) between whom perfect mobility holds, and the remaining classes.

This model returns G^2 of 23.31 with 23 df. The parameter estimates for both men and women are given in panel A of Table 6.7. The similarity between them is quite striking.

TABLE 6.6. *Design matrices for origin-class/entry-class model*

N1	N4
1 1 1 1 1 1	1 1 1 1 1 1
1 1 1 1 1 1	1 1 1 1 1 1
1 1 2 1 1 1	1 1 1 1 2 1
1 1 1 1 1 1	1 1 1 1 2 2
1 1 1 1 1 1	1 1 1 1 2 1
1 1 1 1 1 1	1 1 1 1 1 2
N2	**N4A**
1 1 1 1 1 1	1 1 1 1 1 1
1 1 1 1 1 1	1 1 1 1 1 1
1 1 1 1 1 1	1 1 1 1 2 1
1 1 1 2 1 1	1 1 1 1 2 2
1 1 1 1 1 1	1 1 1 1 2 1
1 1 1 1 1 1	1 1 1 1 2 2
N3	**N5**
2 1 1 1 1 1	1 1 1 1 1 1
1 1 1 1 1 1	1 1 1 1 1 1
2 1 1 1 1 1	1 1 1 1 1 1
2 1 1 1 1 1	1 1 1 1 1 1
1 1 1 1 1 1	1 1 1 1 2 2
1 1 1 1 1 1	1 1 1 1 2 2

Note: Matrices refer to cross-tabulation of origin (rows) by entry class (columns). Rows and columns are ordered: I/II, III, IVa+b, IVc, V/VI, VII.

TABLE 6.7. *Parameter estimates for education to entry class and origin class to entry class models* (standard errors in parentheses)

	Men	Women
A. Origin class to entry class:		
N11	2.825 (1.02)	—
N21	3.329 (0.76)	—
N31	0.956 (0.27)	1.074 (0.26)
N41	1.155 (0.17)	—
N51	—	1.106 (0.21)
B. Education to entry class:		
M11	6.273 (1.03)	6.075 (1.13)
M12	1.057 (0.36)	2.226 (1.04)
M21	1.188 (0.23)	0.803 (0.34)
M22	4.275 (1.03)	2.497 (0.59)
M31	0.501 (0.21)	—
M41	—	1.645 (0.28)

THE RELATIONSHIP BETWEEN EDUCATION
AND CLASS OF ENTRY

In Table 6.8 we set out the details of the outflow from educational destination to class of entry. The observed pattern is consistent with the expectation that a strong hierarchical effect will be the dominant feature of the relationship. Given the fact that the CASMIN educational categories do not distinguish between different types of university or other third-level courses, the only aspect of horizontal differentiation which will be discernible in our analysis relates to the requirement of an apprenticeship for certain skilled manual jobs. Even then it will be relevant only among young men. On the other hand, vertical differentiation is extremely important.

In modelling the education/entry-class relationship we begin by making the distinction between those classes where access is substantially determined by formal educational qualifications—namely Classes I/II, III, and V/VI[2]—and those in which inheritance of the means of production is required—Classes IVa+b and IVc (and, to a much smaller extent, Class I/II: see Breen and Whelan 1993; Ishida, Müller, and Ridge 1995; Jonsson 1993). This latter requirement is sufficient to ensure that very few people enter these classes as their first destination. Taken together this yields a threefold distinction of first destination classes: those regulated by educational qualifications; those regulated by inheritance; and those to which neither sort of barrier applies (Class VII).

With the exceptions noted earlier, educational resources can be conceived of as a simple hierarchy. When measured in CASMIN categories it is simply a case of the higher the better.

The foregoing considerations suggest the following linkages between education and first class. For boys we expect a direct link between having undertaken an apprenticeship (and thus having acquired a lower secondary level education) and entry to Class V/VI. We expect a lack of educational qualifications to be associated with entry to Class VII and also to Class IVc and, to a lesser extent, IVa+b. Beyond this we anticipate a relatively simple hierarchical effect, with upper secondary and tertiary education being linked to entry to Classes I/II and III.

We operationalized this model using the design matrices shown in Table 6.9. The matrix M1 deals with the outflow from third-level education. It specifies two parameters, M11, which reflects the flow to Classes I/II, and M12 which captures the flow to Class III. We expect the coefficient for M11 to be larger than that for M12 so illustrating the stronger link between third-level education and entry to the salariat. Matrix M2 deals with the outflow from upper secondary level education, and its two parameters relate to the

TABLE 6.8. *Class at first job by educational level* (% by column)

	No qualifications		Lower second level		Higher second level		Third level	
	Male	Female	Male	Female	Male	Female	Male	Female
Service class	0.6	0.0	0.0	3.3	11.9	11.9	51.2	55.7
Routine non-manual	15.8	44.0	13.4	70.6	32.7	79.5	16.7	43.2
Petty bourgeoisie	0.0	0.6	0.1	0.1	1.9	0.0	0.0	1.1
Skilled manual	25.4	22.9	45.2	9.8	22.0	2.3	16.7	0.0
Non-skilled manual	54.8	32.6	39.3	15.7	28.3	6.4	13.1	0.0
Farming	3.4	0.0	1.7	0.0	3.1	0.0	2.4	0.0
TOTAL in educational category	26.9	27.6	36.3	24.1	24.1	34.5	12.7	13.9
N	177	175	239	153	159	219	84	88

flows to Classes I/II (M21) and III (M22). But in this case, of course, we
expect the coefficient for M22 to exceed that for M21. Lastly matrix M3
captures the link between lower secondary level education and entry to Class
V/VI using the single parameter M31. In large part this arises because of
the movement of young people from lower secondary level education into
apprenticeships and thence into skilled manual work.

TABLE 6.9. *Design matrices for education/entry-class model*

M1	M3
1 1 1 1 1 1	1 1 1 1 1 1
1 1 1 1 1 1	1 1 1 1 2 1
1 1 1 1 1 1	1 1 1 1 1 1
3 2 1 1 1 1	1 1 1 1 1 1
M2	**M4**
1 1 1 1 1 1	1 1 1 1 2 2
1 1 1 1 1 1	1 1 1 1 1 1
2 3 1 1 1 1	1 1 1 1 1 1
1 1 1 1 1 1	1 1 1 1 1 1

Note: Matrices refer to cross-tabulation of education (rows) by entry class (columns). Latter
are ordered: I/II, III, IVa+b, IVc, V/VI, VII.

This model uses five parameters to capture the education/first-job class
relationship. By default primary education only or no qualifications are associated with entry into Classes IVa+b, IVc and, to the greatest extent, VII.

Fitting this model to the cross-tabulation of education by entry class for
men yields a G^2 statistic of 11.88 with 10 df, which is not significant at $p <$
.05. The parameter estimates, shown in column 1, panel B of Table 6.7, are
all in the expected direction and have the expected orders of magnitude.

Among women the inflows into first job classes are somewhat different,
but we hypothesize a basically similar pattern in the education/first-class
relationship. In our data almost no women enter Classes IVa+b or IVc
directly from education, and very few enter an apprenticeship. In addition,
among all those in Class III a much greater proportion of women than of
men are in Class IIIb. As a consequence, although the absence of the specific apprenticeship–Class V/VI link means that the effect of education is
almost entirely simply hierarchical among young women, this hierarchy is a
little different from that observed among young men. While upper secondary
and tertiary education are once again linked to entry to Classes I/II and III,
lower secondary education is linked to entry to Class III, while primary education is linked to entry into the manual classes, V/VI and VII.

This model was operationalized using three design matrices. M1 and M2
were as specified in the case of men. The matrix M4 (which was used instead

of M3) was then specified to have a single parameter, M41, which captures the link between a primary level education and entry into the manual classes, V/VI and VII.

Fitting this model to the cross-tabulation of education by entry class for women yields a G^2 statistic of 14.33 with 10 df, which is not significant at $p < .05$. The parameter estimates, shown in column 2, panel A of Table 6.7, are all in the expected direction and once again have the expected orders of magnitude.

THE JOINT EFFECTS OF CLASS ORIGINS AND EDUCATION

We now turn to the question of the extent to which the relationship between class origins and class of entry to the labour force is mediated via the effects of educational qualifications. To this end we examine the three-way relationship between class origins, education, and entry class.

We begin by investigating the way in which class origins and educational qualifications combine to influence entry class position. Specifically, is their relationship additive or interactive? A test of the three-way interaction between origins, education, and entry class was insignificant for both men ($G^2 = 62.68$ with 75 df) and women ($G^2 = 25.00$ with 60 df)[3], suggesting that the link between educational credentials and entry class is the same across all origin classes.

The second question we asked was 'Do the models of educational and class origin effects that we developed above prove adequate when used to model their partial additive effects in the three-way cross-tabulation?' To investigate this issue we tested the relative goodness-of-fit of our education and origin models against the full (saturated) set of education and origin effects. The results are shown in Table 6.10. The model reported on line 1 includes the additive effects of education and class origins on entry class, with these effects modelled using all the education by entry class and origin class by entry class interaction terms. In line 2 the former set of terms is replaced by the education effects shown in the matrices of Table 6.9. Similarly, in line 3 the latter set of terms is replaced by the origin effects shown in the matrices in Table 6.6. Lastly, line 4 fits both sets of reduced effects.

The G^2 difference between lines 1 and 2 provides a test of the adequacy of the reduced education effects model and that between lines 1 and 3 of the reduced class effects model. In neither case, for either men or women, are these statistics significant. Similarly, model 4 is not a significantly poorer fit to the data than model 1.

TABLE 6.10. *Goodness-of-fit of models of origin class and education effects*

	Men G²	df	Women G²	df
1. All education and all origin-class effects	62.68	75	25.00	60
2. Reduced education model and all origin effects	70.92	85	39.10	67
3. All education effects and reduced origin model	86.12	96	42.42	78
4. Reduced education and origin models	94.79	106	56.51	85

We can then compare the parameter estimates of the model shown on line 4, given in Table 6.11, with those reported in Table 6.7 to investigate the extent to which the origin class effects are changed through controlling for education. We see that, for both men and women, while controlling for origin class has virtually no impact on the education parameters (as we should expect), some of the class origin parameters do change in value. Broadly speaking, these changes are as we would have anticipated. Among men the class inheritance parameters in the petty bourgeoisie (N11) and farming classes (N12) remain unchanged, but both the parameter capturing advantageous access to Class I/II on the part of those who originate in Classes I/II or IV (N31) and the parameter that captures the various flows into V/VI and VII from Classes IV, V/VI and VII (N41) decline in size compared with

TABLE 6.11. *Partial education and origin-class effects* (standard errors in parentheses)

	Men	Women
Origin class effects (controlling for education):		
N11	2.997 (1.02)	—
N21	3.183 (.076)	—
N31	0.102 (0.33)	0.595 (0.30)
N41	0.870 (0.17)	—
N51	—	0.509 (0.24)
Education effects (controlling for class origins):		
M11	6.089 (1.04)	5.848 (1.13)
M12	0.908 (0.36)	2.146 (1.04)
M21	1.013 (0.23)	0.741 (0.34)
M22	4.080 (1.04)	2.315 (0.59)
M31	0.523 (0.21)	—
M41	—	1.520 (0.28)

those shown in panel A of Table 6.7. Indeed, N31 is now not statistically significant, suggesting that the greater ease of access on the part of those born into Classes I/II or IV to an entry position in Class I/II is wholly the result of their greater likelihood of gaining higher educational qualifications. Among women the picture is similar. The two class origin effects (N31 and N51 which captures the reciprocal flows between Classes V/VI and VII) shown in panel A of Table 6.7 are halved when we control for educational qualifications.

In Tables 6.12 and 6.13 we report the parameter estimates for two multinomial logit models relating to the log-odds of being found in any entry class relative to being found in Class VII. The first, model (a), is the same as the model whose coefficients are reported in Table 6.11, except that we have here estimated the full set of additive class origin and education effects on class of entry *with the constraints implied by the levels models specifications for these two effects.* This means that the parameter estimates in Tables 6.12 and 6.13 are all either equal to some linear function of the levels parameters shown in Table 6.11 or are constrained to be zero.[4] The reference category for class origins is Class I + II and for education is level 1.

The results shown in Tables 6.12 and 6.13 for model (a) have exactly the same interpretation as for the levels model specification. In some cases this extends to identical interpretations for specific parameters, as is the case with the class inheritance effects among men, given by N11 and N21 in Table 6.11 and the effects of origins IVa+b on access to Class IVa+b and of origins in IVc on access to IVc in Table 6.12. In other cases the relationship between the two parameterizations is less direct. For example, the constrained zero effects of origins in Class IVa+b on the log-odds of entering Class I + II mean that children born into Class IVa+b have as good a chance of access to Class I + II as those who are born into that class (holding education constant). However, the levels specification N3 shows that this advantage also extends to Class IVc, but in Table 6.12 origins in this class are linked to a negative coefficient (−0.870) showing that, relative to Class I + II, children from such a background have a poorer chance of entering Class I + II. But the reason for this is that the levels effect N4 shows that origins in the farmer class are also associated with a stronger tendency to enter Classes V + VI and VII. The net result is the lower chance of access to Class I + II reflected in the parameter value -0.87. But in Table 6.13 we see that for women, Classes IVa+b and IVc, because they always have zero coefficients, have the same partial log-odds of being found in all entry classes as do women from social-origin Class I + II.

Turning to the education coefficients, we see that for men education has no effect at all on the chances of access to Class IV. Among men the only effect of a lower secondary level education (2a + 2b) is to improve their

TABLE 6.12. *Multinomial logit estimates of the log odds of being in various entry classes relative to Class VII for men aged 24–35 (standard errors in parentheses; * indicates statistically significant at p < .05)*

	Entry class									
	I + II		III		IV a + b		IVc		V + VI	
	a	b	a	b	a	b	a	b	a	b
Intercept	-4.629* (1.02)	-4.637* (1.02)	-0.506* (0.19)	-0.527* (0.20)	-4.200* (0.72)	-4.243* (0.72)	-3.978* (0.72)	-3.997 (0.72)	-0.519* (0.12)	-3.285* (0.30)
Class origins:										
III	-0.102 (0.33)	-0.051 (0.33)	0	0	0	0	0	0	0	0
IVa + b	0	0	0	0	2.997* (1.02)	3.025* (1.02)	0	0	0.870* (0.17)	0.791* (0.18)
IVc	-0.870* (0.17)	-0.791* (0.18)	-0.870* (0.17)	-0.791* (0.18)	-0.870* (0.17)	-0.791 (0.18)	3.183* (0.76)	3.089* (0.76)	0	0
V + VI	-0.102 (0.33)	-0.051 (0.33)	0	0	0	0	-0.870* (0.17)	-0.791* (0.18)	0.870* (0.17)	0.791* (0.18)
VII	-0.972* (0.37)	-0.842* (0.38)	-0.870* (0.17)	-0.791* (0.18)	-0.870* (0.17)	-0.791* (0.18)	0	0	0	0
Education:										
2a +2b	0	0	0	0	0	0	0	0	0.523* (0.21)	0.358 (0.24)
2c	4.080* (1.04)	4.040* (1.04)	1.013* (0.23)	0.963* (0.23)	0	0	0	0	0	0
3a + 3b	6.089* (1.04)	5.989* (1.04)	0.908* (0.36)	0.791* (0.37)	0	0	0	0	0	0
Apprenticeship	—	0	—	0	—	0	—	0	—	2.135 (0.21)

Likelihood ratio Chi-squared and degrees of freedom
Model a: 268.86, 226
Model b: 152.98, 225

chance of access to Classes V + VI rather than VII. Among women the hierarchical nature of the effect of education is very evident. Here there is a basic
distinction between Classes V + VI and VII, and all other classes. Entry to
the former is associated with education at level 1: education above this
affords access to Classes I + II, III, and IVa+b. Education at successively
higher levels (2c and 3) acts to improve the chances of access to Classes I +
II and III.

In model (b) in Tables 6.12 and 6.13 we add a single parameter that links
the possession of an apprenticeship training with entry to Class V/VI. Our
expectation in fitting this was that its effect should be very strong among
men but almost non-existent among women, and that its inclusion should
considerably reduce the effect of lower secondary level education on the log
odds of entry to Class V/VI rather than VII. These expectations were born
out: among men this parameter is weakened (from 0.523 to 0.358) to the
point of non-significance, while the extra variable has a very marked effect
(possession of an apprenticeship qualification greatly increases the log odds
of being found in Class V + VI rather than VII). At the same time the intercept for Class V + VI is reduced (from −0.519 to −3.285) indicating that it
is difficult to enter Class V + VI without such a qualification. The Chi-
squared value for model (b) is also much lower than for model (a), indicating the importance of this route for access to the skilled manual class.[5]
Among women, however, the extra parameter is not significant. It has no
impact on the education or origin class effects in the model nor does it
reduce the model's Chi-square value by a significant amount.

Because certain of the levels parameters included in our model are meant
to capture the flows between several pairs of origin and entry classes, it is
possible to disaggregate these by fitting each of these flows using a separate
parameter. So, for example, the level N41 among men remains significant in
our model when we control for educational level and an apprenticeship
because of the large parameters for the flow from Class IVc to VII and from
VI to VII. When we fit them separately the other four flows subsumed under
the N41 parameter—such as that from IVc to V/VI—are not statistically significant. Among women, the parameter N51 remains significant chiefly
because of downward mobility from Class V/VI to Class VII.

ANALYSIS OF PRESTIGE OF FIRST JOB

In Table 6.14 we show a comparable analysis using Hope-Goldthorpe prestige scores. Here the dependent variable is the prestige score of the first job
and the explanatory variables are father's occupational prestige and a set of
three dummy variables for educational level. The OLS results show that the

TABLE 6.13. *Multinomial logit estimates of the log odds of being in various entry classes relative to Class VII for women aged 24–35* (standard errors in parentheses; * indicates statistically significant at p < .05)

	Entry class							
	I + II		III		IV a + b		V + VI	
	a	b	a	b	a	b	a	b
Intercept	-1.606* (0.55)	-1.601* (0.55)	2.238* (0.29)	2.244* (0.29)	-2.270* (0.62)	-2.267* (0.62)	-0.460* (0.16)	-0.799* (0.64)
Class origins:								
III	-0.595* (0.30)	0.595* (0.30)	0	0	0	0	0	0
IVa + b	0	0	0	0	0	0	0	0
IVc	0	0	0	0	0	0	0	0
V + VI	-1.104* (0.37)	-1.107* (0.37)	-0.509* (0.24)	-0.512* (0.24)	-0.509* (0.24)	-0.512* (0.24)	0	0
VII	-1.104* (0.37)	-1.107* (0.37)	-0.509* (0.24)	-0.512* (0.24)	-0.509* (0.24)	-0.512* (0.24)	0	0
Education:								
2a +2b	1.520* (0.28)	1.523* (0.28)	1.520* (0.28)	1.523* (0.28)	1.520* (0.28)	1.523* (0.28)	0	0
2c	3.835* (0.56)	3.829* (0.56)	2.261* (0.29)	2.255* (0.29)	1.520* (0.28)	1.523* (0.28)	0	0
3a + 3b	7.368* (1.12)	7.367* (1.12)	3.666* (1.03)	3.665* (1.03)	1.520* (0.28)	1.523* (0.28)	0	0
Apprenticeship	—		—		—			0.321 (0.58)

Likelihood ratio Chi-squared and degrees of freedom
Model a: 74.187, 187
Model b: 73.907, 180

size of the parental prestige coefficient is reduced to almost one-third its original size when education is entered into the equation. Furthermore, although it remains statistically significant the origin variable contributes less than 1 per cent to the explained variance when entered after the educational dummies. No interaction between origin or education and gender is observed and many of the subtleties revealed by class analysis are hidden from view.

TABLE 6.14. *OLS determinants of prestige score of first occupation* (standardized coefficients)

	(i)	(ii)
Prestige score for father's occupation	.28	.11*
Education:		
2a+2b		.13*
2c		.25*
3a+3b		.52*
R^2	.080	.270
N	1,294	1,294

* p < .001

CLASS ORIGINS, EDUCATIONAL QUALIFICATIONS AND LABOUR-MARKET STATUS

Our final analysis examines the labour-market position of the 24 to 35 age group at the time of the survey. Here we distinguish between those who have a job, those who are in the labour market but unemployed, and those who are not in the labour market. While some of the younger members of the cohort may still have been in their first job at the time of the survey, for the majority this measure of their current position will relate to a point beyond that of entry to the labour market. As a result the distribution of respondents over the current position variable reflects very clearly the different career paths followed by men and women. Almost all men in our sample were currently in the labour market: 133 were unemployed, 517 were working, and only 9 were not in the labour market. On the other hand, women were almost evenly divided between those who were in the labour market (285 in a job and 46 unemployed), and those who were not (304).[6] Overwhelmingly those women who were not in the labour market were engaged in some form of household work, generally associated with child-rearing.

These distinctions are evident in the results presented in Table 6.15 which contains parameter estimates for the log odds of being either at work or not

TABLE 6.15. *Multinomial logit estimates of log odds of being in work or not in the labour force relative to being unemployed, at the time of survey, for men and women aged 24–35* (standard errors in parentheses; * indicates statistically significant at p < .05)

	Men		Women	
	At Work	Not in labour force	At Work	Not in labour force
Constant	2.709*	−10.793	1.098*	2.371
	(1.04)	(335.6)	(0.71)	(0.71)
Class origins:				
III	−1.996	9.411	−0.978	−1.241
	(1.11)	(335.6)	(0.83)	(0.83)
IV a + b	−1.390	−1.375	0.124	0.068
	(1.19)	(516.6)	(0.98)	(0.98)
IVc	−0.942	9.297	−0.032	−0.349
	(1.06)	(335.6)	(0.72)	(0.73)
V + VI	−2.257*	8.651	−0.714	−0.643
	(1.05)	(335.6)	(0.72)	(0.73)
VII	−2.314*	7.396	0.027	−0.459
	(1.04)	(335.6)	(0.72)	(0.73)
Education:				
2a +2b	0.450	−0.934	0.798	−0.081
	(0.26)	(1.09)	(0.47)	(0.46)
2c	1.494*	−10.998	1.511*	0.098
	(0.34)	(203.4)	(0.43)	(0.42)
3a + 3b	1.818*	−10.371	1.343*	−0.801
	(0.54)	(280.9)	(0.55)	(0.57)
Apprenticeship	−0.016	0.095	11.320	11.380
	(90.23)	(0.76)	(170.0)	(170.0)
Log-likelihood, parameters	−323.83	20	531.05	20
zero-slopes log likelihood, parameters	−376.96	2	573.00	2

in the labour force relative to being unemployed. For both men and women, the chances of being at work rather than unemployed depend upon education, although among women there is no significant difference between upper secondary level and tertiary education. When we control for education, class origin effects play no part among women, although they do play an important role for men. Here, unlike the situation with regard to class position at first job, the crucial distinction is not between the propertied classes and all others. Rather the partial odds on being at work decline

TABLE 6.16. *Multinomial logit estimates of log odds of not being in the labour force relative to being in the labour force, at the time of survey, for women aged 24–35* (standard errors in parentheses; * indicates statistically significant at p < .05)

Constant	0.946	
	(0.33)	
Class origins:		
III	−0.448	
	(0.45)	
IVa + b	−0.037	
	(0.42)	
IVc	−0.314	
	(0.33)	
V + VI	−0.042	
	(0.35)	
VII	−0.456	
	(0.33)	
Education:		
2a + 2b	−0.712*	
	(0.25)	
2c	−1.157*	
	(0.22)	
3a + 3b	−1.903*	
	(0.31)	
Apprenticeship	0.300	
	(0.41)	
Log-likelihood, parameters	−410.02	10
zero-slopes log likelihood, parameters	−439.57	1

gradually as one moves from the service class to the propertied groups to the routine non-manual class, and finally to the manual classes. The statistically significant contrast is between the service class and the manual classes. The resources used by service-class families to increase the odds of sons being at work go beyond the educational advantages which provide an adequate explanation of the relationship between such origins and class position on entering the labour market.

The virtual absence of men who are not in the labour force means that the coefficients for this outcome are uninterpretable. Among women none of the coefficients is significant, suggesting that neither class origins nor education serves to distinguish between being unemployed and out of the labour force. However, this result owes much to the choice of unemployment as the reference category. If, instead, we look at whether women are in or out of the labour force at the time of the survey (as reported in Table 6.16), we see clear and significant education effects, such that the higher a woman's level of educational attainment, the more likely she is to be in the labour force. Such a finding is compatible with a situation in which household and individual decisions about whether a woman will leave the labour force to go into home duties are made in the light of the labour-market position and opportunities open to her. There is, as a result, a tendency for those with more education, and hence better labour-market prospects, to remain there and for those with less education and poorer prospects to choose home duties. It follows, therefore, that the salient distinction among women is, in fact, between those who are at work (who tend to have higher levels of educational qualifications), and those who are either unemployed or outside the labour force, whose educational qualifications tend, on average, to be lower.

CONCLUSION

The models fitted help us build up a reasonably clear picture of the relationship between class origins, educational qualifications, and entry class in contemporary Ireland. In general terms, among both men and women the impact of education is chiefly hierarchical. That is, a model that distinguishes between four different levels of educational attainment, without making any distinction by type, is adequate to capture the nature of the link between qualifications and class of entry to the labour force. There is one exception to this: among men having followed a specific apprenticeship, training is linked to entry into the skilled manual classes, V/VI. These findings serve as further evidence to reinforce the by now well-known conclusion about the nature of the link between the Irish educational system and the labour market.

[t]he educational system is not highly horizontally or qualitatively differentiated, in the sense that there does not exist a close link between specific educational tracks (or even combinations of subjects studied) and specific occupations (Hannan and Shortall 1991). Rather, most vocational training (at any rate for those who enter the labour market without going on to university or other third-level institution) is undertaken within firms. On the other hand, there does exist a set of national school examinations that have very general currency . . . employers make use of relatively fine gradations in exam performance in deciding which school leavers to employ and how much to pay them. This occurs because they view exam performance as a good indicator of recruits' potential general productivity. Within the very slack labour market that exists in Ireland, employers can select what appear to be the best applicants at a very low cost by making use of the readily available (and widely accepted as valid and reliable) criterion of exam performance. (Breen, Hannan, and O'Leary 1995: 1)

In our case, in the absence of information about specific examination performance, we find that educational level plays a similar role, allowing employers to use level of educational attainment as a signalling device for 'potential general productivity'.

We would argue that the Irish case provides a contrast to both models of the education–labour-market link analysed by Müller and Karle (1993). They distinguish between credentialist countries, such as Germany and France, in which differentiation within the educational system is mirrored by differentiation in occupations, and the less credentialist countries, such as Britain, where the link is weaker. They also suggest that mobility is likely to be greater in the non-credentialist countries. Ireland is clearly not a credentialist country in the same way as Germany or France: in particular, horizontal differentiation is of little significance, as we have noted. However, education and occupation are nevertheless strongly related: higher levels of qualification lead to better jobs. Furthermore, we know that rates of social fluidity in Ireland are particularly low (Breen and Whelan 1985, 1992; Whelan 1994). Thus Ireland presents an example of a country in which educational qualifications are closely linked to the position one can occupy in the labour market and in which social fluidity is low. But this link is founded upon vertical rather than horizontal educational differentiation. The reasons for this can be found in the facts of Irish history and the nature of the Irish labour market. On the one hand, the roots of the modern Irish educational system are to be found in the period of British rule and the system incorporates elements of the British system such as a national curriculum and a national examination system. At the same time, the Irish system retains some distinctive characteristics, such as the voluntary and denominational character of much post-primary education. As a result the system is highly centralized in terms of curricula and examinations but remains substantially in the hands of religious denominations. The results of national examinations have long been accepted as a yardstick of educational attainment and thus of the 'potential general productivity' of the individual job seeker. This is reinforced by the nature of the Irish labour market in which an excess supply of labour has led to high rates of emigration and unemployment. Under these circumstances the ready availability of public examination results makes them a convenient means by which employers can screen large numbers of job seekers at minimal cost.

If we turn from the question of the articulation between the educational system and the labour market to the issue of the extent and nature of the linkages between class origins and class of entry, then we find a set of results that once again tell a largely familiar story. To a considerable extent the specific mobility channels that exist between origins and entry class operate through the educational system. There are exceptions, but, by and large, we find these where we would expect them. Most notably, of course, although the amount of movement into the classes that own the means of production (Classes IVa+b and IVc) is very limited when we consider first destination, nevertheless such movement as occurs is not mediated via education: rather, it is the result of direct inheritance. Similarly, the flow from farm origins into the unskilled working class, which is to some degree part of the process of counter-mobility on the part of young men who will later inherit their parents' farm, is also independent of educational qualifications. Once again, this is not unexpected. We also hypothesized two other flows of men from farm origins which we suggested should be mediated by education. These concern upward mobility for non-inheriting sons into Class V/VI and into Class I/II. And indeed we found that such channels of mobility did exist but, once educational qualifications and apprenticeship were entered into the model, they became statistically non-significant. We also hypothesized similar channels of movement among young men of petty bourgeoisie origins. Once again we found that the channel into Class I/II was mediated through education and that, as for men of all other class origins, entry into Class V/VI was linked to the acquisition of a lower secondary level education and/or an apprenticeship. The only remaining class origin effect among men that is not wholly mediated through education is the tendency for class inheritance in Class VII. This effect is entered into our models as part of the N41 parameter and although its magnitude is substantially less than that of the class inheritance effects for Classes IVa+b and IVc it does suggest the existence of particular barriers, operating over and above educational effects, to the movement of young men out of this origin class.

Among women, the parameter that captures the advantages in access to Class I + II among those born in this class or in Classes IVa+b or IVc remains significant when we control for educational level, while the levels parameter N51 remains significant because of downward mobility from Class V/VI to Class VII. Both these flows must, therefore, operate to some extent independently of education. More generally, however, among women class origin effects are halved when we control for educational level and flows such as that from Class VII to Class V/VI or class inheritance in either of these classes seem to take place wholly through educational channels.

Almost all the channels of mobility from class origins to first-job class that are not mediated via education have their origin in the classes that own the means of production. Such channels of mobility are characterized by the direct inheritance of property and by specific strategies linked to this (such as counter-mobility). However, not all mobility from these origins operates independently of education and virtually all mobility from origin classes that do not own the means of production takes place through the medium of the educational system. Understanding the relationship between class origins and entry class is thus very largely a question of understanding how educational qualifications are distributed according to class origins. In Ireland, however, because of the nature of the links between the educational system and the labour market we can be a little more specific. The crucial issue, from the point of view of success or failure in the labour market, concerns the level of education that an individual acquires and only in restricted instances its type. Because of the relatively low level of intra-generational (first to current class) mobility in Ireland, entry-class position takes on a particularly high degree of importance. Vertical educational differentiation acts as the chief criterion for selection to such positions. It is therefore hardly surprising that we find close links between educational outcomes and class origins as families seek to maximize their children's prospects through investing in education.

The situation in relation to the odds of currently being at work is somewhat different. For women it is true again that the impact of class origins is entirely mediated by education. Indeed education is the factor which distinguishes between those women who are working outside the home and those who are either unemployed or in full-time home duties. The evidence thus is consistent with the interpretation that decisions to leave the labour market are based on a realistic assessment of labour-market opportunities.

For men education once again plays a substantial role in determining current economic status but we continue to observe independent class origin effects. In the absence of any evidence for an interaction between class origin and educational qualifications, what appears to be involved is not a differential return to education by class but rather the persistence of a set of class influences which operate independently of the educational system. Furthermore, such effects are no longer simply a consequence of property effects. Instead it is membership of the service class which confers the greatest advantage and location in the manual class provides the sharpest contrast. The advantages enjoyed by those originating in the service class go beyond those associated with educational qualifications, suggesting that we need to take into account a range of other potential factors including social networks and, possibly, employers' use of class origins as a proxy for skills or characteristics that employers seek—such as social or communications skills. With the exception of access to the propertied classes, the Irish evidence suggests that for men aged 24 to 35 class position on entry to the labour market is meritocratically determined, at least in the sense of reflecting educational qualifications—but this is not true of the basic life-chance represented by the opportunity to be in paid work.

NOTES

1. Note that because of the relatively small numbers involved these odds ratios will have large standard errors.
2. This is particularly true when considering first destination. Later access to these classes is less closely linked to formal educational qualifications.
3. The model for women has fewer degrees of freedom because entry Class IVc had to be omitted due to the small number of women who enter it directly.
4. So, if we compare, say, the parameter estimates shown in the (a) columns of Table 6.12 (which refers to men), we see that the effect of being born into Class III, rather than Class I + II, on the log odds of entering Class I + II rather than VII, is equal to the negative of the levels model parameter N31. The same parameter for origins in Class VII is equal to N31–N41. The most complicated relationship between the levels parameters and the multinomial logit parameters is found in the education effects for women (Table 6.13). These effects are each made up as the sum of the M41 levels parameter given in Table 6.11 and the other levels parameters. Thus, for example, the effect of education at level 3a or 3b on the log odds of being found in Class I + II is equal to M41 + M11.
5. All the models reported in Tables 6.12 and 6.13 were estimated separately for men and women using for each the four-way cross-classification of origins by education by whether or not an apprenticeship qualification had been obtained by entry class. Thus, the Chi-squared values and degrees of freedom relate to this four-way table, in contrast to Table 6.10 where they refer to the three-way cross-tabulation of origins, by education, by entry class.
6. Though some of those women who considered themselves not in the labour market may nevertheless have been prepared to take employment if it were available.

7

Gender and Ethnic Differences in the Transition from School to Work in Israel

VERED KRAUS, YOSSI SHAVIT, AND MEIR YAISH

INTRODUCTION

This chapter examines the pattern of association between educational qualifications and labour-market outcomes for men and women in Israel. We compare the effects of academic and vocational qualifications on occupational prestige and class of labour-force entry, and study the relationship between qualifications and unemployment. In addition to gender comparisons, we also examine ethnic differences in the relationship between educational qualifications and occupational outcomes. Previous Israeli research on ethnic differences in the stratification process focused on comparisons of Sephardi and Ashkenazi Jews (see e.g. Kraus and Hodge 1990; and Shavit 1990a),[1] whereas our major ethnic focus is on inequalities between Arabs and Jews in the occupational attainment process. Most Arab workers are employed in the Jewish-controlled economy where they suffer severe labour-market discrimination. This is best indicated by their disproportionate concentration in unskilled blue-collar occupations. One of the mechanisms of discrimination against Arabs is the requirement imposed by many firms, that job applicants have a military discharge certificate. Since Arabs—with the exception of the Druse—do not serve in the Israeli military, they are de facto excluded from the better jobs in the Jewish-controlled labour market. The literature on Arabs in the Israeli economy, however, reveals another interesting pattern. Israeli Arabs and Jews usually live in separate villages, towns, and neighbourhoods, and Arabs who find employment within the Arab ethnic enclaves enjoy advantages in the conversion of educational resources to occupational outcomes (Shavit 1992; Semyonov and Cohen 1990) because jobs catering to members of that enclave, such as teaching, social services, health care, and public administration are usually reserved for members of the enclave who are shielded from competition from members of the Jewish majority. The occupational returns to education within the enclave are thus higher than those of Jews, or other Arabs, employed outside the enclave.

Previous studies on the occupational attainment process in Israel measured the dependent variable on unidimensional scales of prestige (Kraus 1976) and SEI (Tyree 1981). In doing so, they ignore several qualitative aspects of the process. More specifically, they ignore the distinction between employees and the self-employed, and between skilled and unskilled occupations, but most importantly—from the standpoint of gender differences—they ignore the distinction between blue-collar and pink-collar unskilled work. Men with low or no educational qualifications are likely to find employment in blue-collar occupations while their female equivalents are most likely to enter unskilled service occupations (Yaish 1995) and hence women appear to attain better occupations than men when measured on a prestige scale (Kraus and Hodge 1990: 159).

Regarding the conceptualization and measurement of education, most Israeli studies follow the example of American status attainment research and define educational attainment as a hierarchical variable indicated by years of schooling or similar measures. This ignores important qualitative differences, however, especially between vocational and academic qualifications at the secondary and tertiary levels. The results of previous research (Kraus and Hodge 1990) suggest that in Israel—as in the USA—primary education carries little weight in the occupational attainment process, but that the effects of secondary, and especially tertiary, education are strong. We will show that the pattern of the relationship between education and occupational outcomes is even more complex: it is linear for Jews, and exponential for Arabs, reflecting the interaction between discrimination and the benefits of the ethnic enclave.

THE ISRAELI CONTEXT

The School System

The basic structure of the Israeli school system is outlined in Figure 7.1. Compulsory education now lasts until the age of 15, and is free. Since the early 1970s, the system has been undergoing a reform intended to shift the educational sequence from the old $1 + 8 + 4$ system (one year of compulsory pre-school for 5-year-olds, followed by eight years of compulsory primary school, and up to four years of secondary education), to the new $1 + 6 + 3 + 3$ system (one year of pre-school, six years of primary school, followed by three years of lower secondary school, and three years of upper secondary education). The reform was never fully implemented, however, and today about one-third of all school children still attend eight-year pri-

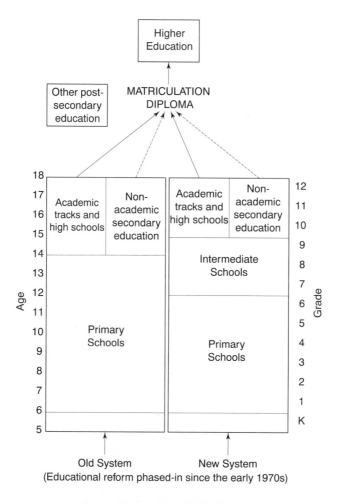

Source: Shavit and Blossfeld (1993: 340).

FIG. 7.1. *The structure of the Israeli school system*
From *Persistent Inequality: Changing Educational Attainment in Thirteen Countres,*
ed. Yossi Shavit and Hans-Peter Blossfeld. Copyright © 1993 by WestviewPress.
Reprinted by permission of WestviewPress.

mary schools. The upper secondary level is differentiated into academic and
vocational education. The former prepares students for the matriculation
examinations and paves the way to university, whereas the latter, most of
which are targeted at the less able students, are in effect educational culs de
sac.[2] The student body is about equally divided between the two tracks.

Nominally, the curriculum at the primary and lower secondary schools is not stratified, but research has shown that ability grouping is widespread, and that group membership at the lower secondary level is an important determinant of track placement at the upper secondary level (Yogev 1981). Most researchers would agree that grouping at the primary and lower secondary levels, together with track placement at the upper secondary level, take place primarily on the basis of students' prior achievements (Yogev 1981; Shavit 1984). And yet among Jews there has been a strong correlation between ethnicity and group and/or track placement. Oriental Jewish students, namely those originating in Muslim countries, are far more likely to be placed in lower ability groups and in the vocational rather than academic tracks. As a consequence, they are less likely to obtain the matriculation diploma and to continue to university. The statistical relationship between ethnicity and placement is due to the large mean ethnic differences in measured scholastic aptitude and achievement.[3]

In general, the Israeli system may be characterized as centralized. Teachers are certified by the Ministry of Education—with the exception of those working in ultra-orthodox schools—curricula are developed by the Ministry, matriculation and university admission examinations are centrally administered, and—until the late 1980s—all universities were publicly and centrally funded. At the same time, however, the system is differentiated along multiple lines. Hebrew and Arab language schools cater to Jews and Arabs, respectively. Jews do not attend Arab schools, and very few Arabs attend Jewish schools. Within the Jewish system, there are several streams catering to the different shades of religious orthodoxy, and additional lines of differentiation reflecting cultural and ideological differences especially Christian denominational schools serving the Arab population, and regional schools serving *kibbutzim* and *moshavim*, all subject to central supervision.

In the Jewish sector, the vast majority of students in primary and secondary education attend state schools (private education is only prevalent at the pre-school level). In the Arab sector by contrast, denominational Christian schools are more common, especially in the larger urban areas of Haifa, Jaffa, and Nazareth. These schools have a better reputation than state schools and are preferred by those Arab families who can afford them. Although owned and operated by the various Christian churches, these schools are subject to the supervision of the Ministry of Education and comply with its guidelines regarding curricula and teachers' certification. Thus, although the Israeli system is centrally controlled and supervised, it consists of numerous educational subsystems which are organizationally and culturally distinct and is best described as a system of centrally sanctioned pluralism.

In the Jewish sector, about half of all secondary school students attend vocational tracks, whereas in the Arab sector only about 20 per cent do so.

Vocational education is about twice as expensive as academic education because it requires investment in well-equipped workshops and skilled vocational instructors. Historically, Israeli governments have been reluctant to invest in the development of vocational education in the Arab sector, and as we shall see below, Jewish men are three times as likely as Arab men to hold vocational secondary qualifications.

Vocational secondary education is differentiated along three dimensions: subject, study track, and organizational affiliation of the school. Table 7.1 presents the joint distribution of subject and track. The matriculating vocational track refers to the programmes leading to both a vocational certificate and to the matriculation examinations (although only a minority of students actually pass all the examinations necessary to obtain the matriculation diploma). The

TABLE 7.1. *Vocational twelfth grade pupils by subject and study track* (percentage distributions)

Subject	Total	Study track		
		Matriculating	Non-matriculating	Practical track
Metal Work	11.5	32.8	40.1	27.1
Mechanics	8.2	33.8	44.9	21.3
Electricity, Instrumental Mechanics and Refrigeration	12.5	64.5	30.2	5.3
Electronics	14.8	91.8	8.2	—
Data Processing	—	100.0	—	—
Wood Work	1.4	18.6	33.9	47.5
Drawing and Planning	2.9	63.7	31.6	4.7
Building and Architecture	2.5	85.9	12.4	1.7
Laboratory Assistants	2.0	68.0	32.0	—
Sewing and Fashion	8.0	43.5	29.5	27.0
Applied Art	1.9	62.0	30.7	7.3
Clerical Work	25.4	46.8	35.9	17.3
Hotel Keeping, Home Economics and Tourism	2.5	50.9	22.1	27.0
Nursing	4.7	67.7	20.5	11.8
Other	1.7	65.8	14.3	19.9
TOTAL	100.0	55.8	29.5	14.7

Note: The percentages refer to vocational students in Hebrew language schools (i.e. to Jews). Half of all Jewish twelfth graders attend vocational tracks. In Arab language schools, vocational education is much more limited in scope. For example, among Arab twelfth graders in 1985/6, only about 20 per cent attended vocational education (Shavit 1990*b*). The distribution of subjects of study in Arab vocational tracks is not reported in the Statistical Abstracts.
Source: State of Israel, CBS, 1986; table XXII/23.

normal track leads to the vocational certificates and to some matriculation examinations. Finally, as its name suggests, the practical track places a premium on practical training with less emphasis on academic studies.

The number of subjects offered by upper secondary vocational schools is limited. About 60 per cent of vocational twelfth graders are concentrated in four subjects (metalwork, mechanics, electrical mechanics, and other electrical training). If we were to present date separately by gender, we would see that the majority of girls study clerical work and the majority of boys study the first four subjects. Clearly, the degree of occupational specificity (see the Introduction to this volume) of the skills acquired from such a limited number of programmes cannot be very high, and the specific skills required by most occupations in the labour market are not taught in schools.

The Role of the Military

For Jews, the military provides an important link between vocational education and the labour market. Research carried out in the late 1970s and early 1980s at the Sald Institute examined the usefulness of vocational education at the secondary level. More specifically, researchers were concerned with the extent to which graduates of vocational programmes find employment in occupations corresponding to their area of training. They found that the correspondence rate varied from 25 to 50 per cent, depending upon how liberally 'correspondence' is defined. An important finding of these studies is that the correspondence rate increases significantly for graduates who practice their vocation while in the military. Military service is an important arena for the accumulation of both on-the-job and classroom-based training in a variety of occupations. In some civilian occupations there are large concentrations of individuals who acquired their vocational skills while in the military (radar operators, mechanics for heavy-duty construction equipment, air-conditioning technicians, paramedics, and so forth). The military in turn attempts to minimize training costs by assigning graduates of upper secondary vocational programmes to 'corresponding' roles in the army. The vast majority of Arab men do not serve in the Israeli army, and therefore— although we do not know what proportion of the labour force is affected by their military experience in their job allocation—we would expect the effects of vocational qualifications on the odds of entering the labour force a skilled worker to be stronger for Jews than for Arabs.

The Educational Requirements of Occupations

In Israel as elsewhere, the professions are formally defined by educational requirements, either legally or through ministerial decree. To illustrate this, about 70 per cent of our respondents who were employed in Class I or II hold university of other post-secondary qualifications. However, since a large proportion of Israelis hold post-secondary qualifications (34.6 per cent of our sample of 25–44 year olds), only about 65 per cent of them are employed in Class I or II. By contrast, in Germany and Italy, where a smaller proportion have post-secondary credentials, the comparable proportions are in excess of 85 per cent (Shavit et al. 1994). Thus, in Israel, although the professions are very selective on higher education, the latter does not guarantee entry into the professions.

In Israel, apart from the professions, the institutionalization of formal educational requirements for occupational practice have been motivated primarily by a concern for public safety. Thus, ministerial decrees legally define the educational requirement for all medical and para-medical occupations, for construction engineers and technicians, electricians, drivers, pilots, and many other occupations.[4] De facto, the educational requirements for most jobs are determined by individual employers' hiring practices. However, over half the Israeli labour force is employed in largely publicly owned, bureaucratic organizations (i.e. the state, local authorities, the *Histadrut* or Federation of Labour, and the Jewish Agency) where the educational requirements of jobs are clearly indicated. Kraus (1992) has shown that the effect of education on occupational prestige is stronger in the public sector than elsewhere.

DATA AND VARIABLES

Our data is drawn from the 1991–1992 National Mobility Survey conducted by Kraus and Toren (1993) in which 4,800 Jewish households and 900 Arab households were interviewed face to face. The present analysis employs a sub-sample of Jewish men and women, and Arab men aged 25–44, who were born in Israel or immigrated there before the age of 15. Arab women have been excluded from the analysis as their labour-force participation rates are very low (12.3 per cent as compared with 46.4 per cent for Jewish women in 1990) (Lewin-Epstein and Semyonov 1993: 89), and consequently few of them have non-missing values on the dependent variables used in the study.

What is a First Job?

Social mobility researchers are often faced with the dilemma of defining 'first job'. There are several issues involved including, duration of employment, number of hours worked, and timing of entry. For the purposes of this project, we have focused on jobs entered (or held) after the completion of the last known educational qualification obtained.

Respondents were asked about their first full-time job, a full-time job held in 1985, and their current job. In addition, they were asked for the year in which they started and ended each job, and for information on the occupational title and employment status while in each job. We also know when each respondent attained their last qualification. With this information we proceeded to construct our dependent variables.

Among Jews, about 70 per cent began their first job *after* obtaining their last educational qualification. The corresponding figure for Arab men is 88 per cent. Respondents who started their first jobs *before* completing their last qualification, were asked whether they had entered their 1985 job within five years of ending their last spell in education. If so, we consider their 1985 job as their first job (about 6 and 8 per cent of Jewish women and men, respectively, and 2 per cent of Arab men). For those who did not meet this condition (22 per cent of Jews and 8 per cent of Arab men), but started their current job within five years after completing school, first job was defined as that held at the time of the interview (4.3 and 5.2 per cent, respectively for Jewish women and men and 1 per cent for Arab men). For those who did not meet any of the above conditions, but *continued* their first occupation for at least three years after the last exit from formal education, we assigned the first job information (nearly 6 per cent for Jews and 5 per cent for Arab men). Finally, about 12 per cent of Jewish respondents and about 4 per cent of Arab men did not meet any of the above four conditions.

Regarding the respondents for whom we could not identify first job, we considered whether to exclude them from the analysis altogether, or to assume that the characteristics of their current job reflect those of their first job after school completion. Analyses of the data indicated that these respondents were more likely to have entered the labour force later in life and to have tertiary qualifications—the implication being, that exclusion of these cases would bias the results against the more highly educated. Consequently, we decided to retain them in the analysis measuring the dependent variable by assigning them information on current job. We also replicated some of the analyses on a sub-sample excluding these cases with little difference in the results. This is probably due to their small number, and to the fact that most graduates of post-secondary education move directly into permanent occupations. The distribution of respondents by time of measurement of first job is presented in Table 7.2.

In common with other chapters in this volume, we recoded occupation of first job into both a continuous occupational prestige score and a class schema. The former was measured on the Vered scale of occupational prestige (Kraus 1976), and the latter on the Israeli version of the EGP class schema (Goldthorpe, Yaish, and Kraus, forthcoming). The mean prestige score is 43.6 for Jewish respondents—somewhat higher for women than for

TABLE 7.2. *Percentage distribution of first jobs by time of measurement*

	Jewish men	Jewish women	Arab men
First job reported	69.3	72.1	88.4
Job held in 1985	8.3	6.1	2.4
Current job	5.2	4.3	0.9
Extended first job	5.7	5.5	4.7
Extended current job	11.6	12.1	3.6

TABLE 7.3.a. *Means and standard deviations of continuous independent variables*

Variables	Jewish men	Jewish women	Arab men
Father's occupational prestige	31.5	31.8	25.0
	(26.4)	(26.4)	(19.3)
Age at time of interview	35.6	34.8	33.8
	(5.4)	(5.7)	(5.5)
Age began first job	23.2	22.7	18.4
	(5.6)	(5.1)	(5.8)
Year began first job	78.6	78.9	76.1
	(6.8)	(7.0)	(7.7)
Own occupational prestige	40.3	46.7	31.8
	(27.0)	(25.2)	(30.2)
Number of cases	1,705	1,773	576

TABLE 7.3.b. *Percentage distribution of categorical independent variables*

Variables	Jewish men	Jewish women	Arab men
Religious orthodoxy			
Orthodox	10.6	10.3	5.9
Traditional	35.2	36.0	44.4
Secular	54.1	53.6	55.6
Parental education			
Primary or less	56.7	53.0	90.8
Secondary	24.8	27.8	5.6
Tertiary	18.5	19.2	4.4
Ethnicity			
Sephardim	46.7	48.2	—
Ashkenazim	53.3	51.8	—
Muslim	—	—	84.4
Christian	—	—	15.6

men—and much lower for Arab men (see Table 7.3a). The distribution of
EGP classes are shown in Table 7.4. Jewish men are more likely than Jewish
women to enter the labour force in Class I and as skilled manual workers
(Class V + VI). Women are more likely to be found in Classes II, IIIa and
IIIb. In other words, Jewish men are over-represented in the professions and
skilled and supervisory manual classes, while women are more often found
in the semi-professions and service occupations. Jewish men are also more
likely than Jewish women to begin their careers as self-employed workers.
Arab men are twice as likely as Jewish men to enter the labour force as
unskilled blue-collar workers (Class VII), and one and a half times as likely
to be self-employed, i.e. small-scale artisans in the construction sector, truck
and taxi drivers, and small contractors. Arab men are less likely than Jewish
men to be in Class I, and in Class IIIa, but—like Jewish women—they are
more likely to be found in Class II. Educated Arab men who cannot find
work in their profession often turn to teaching, a typical Class II occupation.[5]

TABLE 7.4. *Distribution of entry class by gender and ethnicity*

Class	Jewish men	Jewish women	Arab men
I	25.8	9.4	11.2
II	4.3	17.5	10.1
IIIa	7.7	15.7	2.8
IIIb	4.8	30.9	5.4
IV	9.0	3.3	14.5
V + VI	33.3	12.5	24.9
VIIab	14.9	11.0	31.1

Current Employment

The third dependent variable is current employment status. As shown in
Table 7.5, there is a large difference between men and women in the rates
of employment, unemployment (defined as not having a job but having
looked for one during the week preceding interview), and of being out of the
labour force. Men in the 25–44 age group are more likely to be employed
and less likely to be unemployed or out of the labour force. Arab and Jewish
men are about equally likely to be employed. Our estimate of the labour-
force participation rate for Jewish women is quite close to the estimate of 70

TABLE 7.5. *Percentage distribution of current labour-force status*

	Jewish men	Jewish women	Arab men
Employed	93	69	95
Unemployed	4	8	2
Not in labour force	3	23	3

per cent provided by the Central Bureau of Statistics for that age group in 1991 (Israel, CBS 1991: 369).

Historically speaking, Israeli Governments have maintained aggressive employment policies keeping the unemployed rates well below international standards. During and since the mass immigration from the former Soviet Union—about 500,000 immigrants arrived within a 3–4 year period beginning in the late 1980s—the unemployment rate peaked at about 12 per cent of the total labour force but was soon brought down to 6–7 per cent as economic activity was invigorated by the demands generated by immigration itself, and by foreign and domestic investments attracted by the prospects associated with the peace process. Our data were collected when immigration was at its peak. The average unemployment rate was well above that estimated in our data. For example, for men and women aged 25–34 in 1990 the unemployment rates were 8.7 per cent and 11.7 per cent, respectively (Israel, CBS 1991: 352), higher than our estimates of 4 and 8 per cent circa. The bias is due, first and foremost, to the exclusion of very recent immigrants from our sample. Data from the Central Bureau of Statistics show that overall, the unemployment rate for non-immigrants is 5.5 per cent as compared with the national rate of 9.6 (Israel, CBS 1991: 353). In addition, groups hard hit by unemployment are often under-represented in probability samples.

Qualifications

Most respondents attended school under the old educational system in which primary education consisted of grades one to eight. We define the CASMIN qualification 1b (the social minimum of education) as a complete primary education indicated by the completion of eight years of schooling. Category 1a includes respondents who dropped out before the eighth grade. CASMIN category 1c is very rare in Israel, and given that the study did not ask respondents about apprenticeships they might have had, this category has been left empty. Categories 2a and 2b are operationalized as having attended, respectively, vocational and academic secondary schools, but without having obtained a matriculation diploma. Matriculants are assigned to category 2c. Category 3a includes respondents with post-secondary, non-university education. Among men, this refers primarily to one and two-year technical programmes which are offered as extensions to secondary vocational education. Among women, it refers primarily to teacher training colleges and nursing schools (both have since been redefined as academic programmes). University graduates are assigned to 3b.

TABLE 7.6. *Distribution of educational qualifications by gender and ethnicity*

	Jewish men	Jewish women	Arab men
1a	2.7	1.5	7.6
1b	20.7	17.8	35.1
2a	21.8	16.5	7.2
2b	4.5	6.2	7.8
2c	13.8	18.8	14.1
3a	14.2	19.7	11.0
3b	22.3	19.5	17.1

Table 7.6 presents the percentage distributions of the educational categories for the three groups. Among Jews, women are slightly less likely than men to be found in the lowest educational categories (1a and 1b), and among university graduates (3b). They are more likely than their male counterparts, to obtain non-academic tertiary qualifications (3a) such as in teacher training or nursing, and to have a matriculation diploma with no further education (2c). Jewish men are more likely than women to attend vocational secondary tracks and to obtain vocational qualifications (2a).

A comparison of Arabs and Jews reveals several interesting patterns. First, the proportion of Arab men in the lowest educational categories is much larger. This is a well-known difference between Arabs and Jews in Israel (Shavit 1989). Second, Arab men are also less likely than either Jewish group to obtain a vocational secondary qualification. This reflects the sparsity of vocational education in the Arab sector (Shavit 1990*b*). Third, of those who went on to secondary education (76.6, 80.8, and 57.2 per cent for Jewish men Jewish women and Arab men, respectively), the proportion of Arabs who obtain university qualifications is slightly higher than those of either Jewish group (29.1, 24.2, and 29.8, respectively). Shavit (1990*b*) attributes this pattern to the prevalence of academic, secondary education in the Arab sector. In the Jewish sector about half of all secondary students attending vocational tracks are diverted away from the matriculation diploma and from tertiary education. By contrast, in Arab secondary schools, where vocational education is scarce, a larger proportion of students remain on the path leading to university education.

For all three groups, qualification category 2b, which includes those who completed academic upper secondary education did not obtain the matriculation diploma, is small because the vast majority of those entering academic upper secondary tracks obtain the diploma.

Social-Origin Characteristics

We measure social origins by father's occupational prestige measured on the Vered scale (see Tables 7.3a and 7.3b). Parental education was taken as the higher of the father's or mother's education measured on a three-point scale: primary or less, secondary, and post-secondary. Father self-employed is a dummy variable indicating that the father was self-employed when the respondent was in his or her teens. Religious orthodoxy distinguishes between very orthodox, traditional, and secular. Among Jews, ethnicity contrasts between those of Sephardi and Ashkenazi origins on the basis of their own and their father's country of birth. Of Jewish respondents, 9 per cent are second-generation native Israelis and were assigned to the Ashkenazi category. Among Arab men ethnicity distinguishes between Muslims and Christians.

In addition, we employ three variables measuring time—age at the time of interview, age at entry into first job, and calendar year at entry into first job, which are used in the analysis of current employment status, occupational prestige and class position at labour-force entry, respectively.

ANALYSIS

Education and Current Unemployment

Table 7.7 presents the results of multinomial logit regressions contrasting unemployment and not being in the labour force against being employed. Arab men are excluded from this analysis because among non-missing Arab cases there were only fourteen who were unemployed and eighteen who were not in the labour force.

The results show marked differences between men and women in the determination of labour-force status. Among women, education tends to reduce the odds of both unemployment and being out of the labour force. The effect of education on these odds for women is roughly monotonous.

TABLE 7.7. *Multinomial logit contrasting unemployment and being out of the labour force with current employment for Jews*

Independent variables	Jewish women		Jewish men	
	Unemployed	Not in labour force	Unemployed	Not in labour force
Intercept	-2.056*	-1.252*	-1.940	-1.677
	(0.834)	(0.259)	(1.422)	(1.280)
Age	-0.053**	-0.032**	-0.060	-0.045
	(0.018)	(0.012)	(0.031)	(0.029)
Parental education (relative to post-secondary):				
Primary or less	0.570	0.182	-0.631	-0.593
	(0.429)	(0.257)	(0.658)	(0.509)
Secondary	0.598	-0.140	-0.687	-1.066
	(0.414)	(0.249)	(0.668)	(0.546)
Ethnicity(AA)	-0.207	0.020	0.972*	-0.502
	(0.233)	(0.163)	(0.444)	(0.366)

	(1)	(2)	(3)	(4)
Religious orthodoxy (relative to secular):				
Orthodox	0.411	0.602**	-0.951	0.666
	(0.330)	(0.229)	(0.757)	(0.430)
Traditional	-0.417	0.253	-0.266	-0.232
	(0.233)	(0.155)	(0.342)	(0.375)
Father's occupational prestige	-0.000	0.002	-0.006	-0.006
	(0.004)	(0.003)	(0.008)	(0.007)
Education (relative to 3b):				
1ab	2.383**	1.753**	1.491*	1.211*
	(0.472)	(0.274)	(0.690)	(0.598)
2a	2.093**	1.068**	0.703	0.776
	(0.451)	(0.271)	(0.714)	(0.608)
2b	1.561**	1.199**	0.904	0.108
	(0.557)	(0.323)	(0.944)	(1.116)
2c	1.092*	0.762**	0.136	1.729*
	(0.455)	(0.256)	(0.840)	(0.534)
3a	-0.007	-0.409	0.481	-1.146
	(0.533)	(0.303)	(0.786)	(1.109)

* Significant at the 0.05 level   ** Significant at the 0.01 level

Among men, by contrast, education has less consistent and smaller effects. It is negatively related to being out of the labour force but only one contrast—i.e. between the lowest and highest qualification—is significant. In addition, the effects of education on unemployment are much smaller than those seen for women. For men, the odds of being out of the labour force are largest for those with a 2c qualification. We assume that many of them are still attending post-secondary education.

Current employment status is also affected by the age of the respondent. As one would expect, older individuals have had time to find stable employment are thus less susceptible to unemployment. In addition, older women are more likely to have completed the early stages of motherhood and may be returning to—or entering for the first time—careers in the labour market. Furthermore, orthodox women are less likely to be in the labour force while ethnicity has no significant effect on either contrast. Similar trends are reported by Ben-Porath (1983).

Educational and Occupational Attainment

Our next objective is to document the relationship between educational qualification and the attainment of occupational prestige. In Table 7.8 we present the results of linear regression analysis of occupational prestige of first job for Jewish men, Jewish women, and Arab men. For each group we present a reduced form equation, which includes social-origin variables, and an extended equation which also includes qualifications, age, and year of labour-force entry. Comparing the effects of social origins for the two equations would tell us to what extent education mediates the effects of social origins on occupational prestige in first job.

For Jewish men, education mediates most of the ethnic effect on occupational prestige, about half the effects of parental education, and some of the advantages due to father's occupation. The results for Jewish women are similar. Education explains the ethnic differences in the prestige of first job, and mediates the advantages associated with parental education. By contrast to men, among women, the direct effect of father's occupational prestige net of education is insignificant.

For both Jewish men and women, the advantage associated with religious orthodoxy is not mediated by education. The higher occupational prestige attained by orthodox Jews in Israel is due to their monopolization of religious services, i.e. employment as rabbis, cantors, mohels, teachers and instructors in yeshivas, kashrut supervisors, teachers in religious schools, and the like. These occupations usually score in the middle to high segments of the prestige scale. Non-orthodox men are completely excluded from these occupations. Orthodox women who join the labour force are probably over-represented in teaching in orthodox and religious schools (medium-range occupational prestige), and under-represented in low-status service occupations. In sum, the advantages associated with Jewish orthodoxy, especially that enjoyed by orthodox men, is a reflection of the orthodox niche in the Israeli economy. By contrast to the orthodox 'traditional' Jews do not benefit from their compromising observance as is indicated by the negative effect of this dummy variable. Being 'traditional' does not give access to the niche. In addition, this social category is disproportionately Sephardi, geographically peripheral, of low social strata, and its negative effect probably reflects unmeasured heterogeneity involving ethnicity and socio-economic origins.

Among Arab men social origins scarcely affect occupation attainment. The proportion of variance explained by the reduced form equation is much lower than those explained by the equation for Jews. This is partly due to the low levels of variance among Arabs in several of the independent variables. Specifically, very few Arab parents had more than primary education. Therefore, the effects of this variable could not be estimated and is not included in the equations in Table 7.8. By contrast, the effect of father's occupational prestige is larger than among Jews, but its effect is fully mediated by education. We suspect that this reflects the fact that the recent resurgence of Muslim orthodoxy in the Arab population in Israel is most prevalent among the lower socio-economic classes.

Turning to the full equations, we find that a late age of entry into the labour market slightly enhances the prestige of first job. We suspect that this is an indirect effect of tertiary qualifications and that if we were to distinguish among academic degrees (i.e. between BAs and MAs or their equivalents) the advantage of age of entry would be explained. In addition, entering the labour market at a later period lowers the occupational prestige attained. This apparent decline in occupational opportunities during the 1970s and 1980s may reflect the oversupply of skilled labour brought about by the massive immigration of skilled workers from the ex-Soviet Union.

The predicted prestige scores for each group by qualification are shown in Figure 7.2.[6] The extreme educational categories are separated by about 40 prestige points for Jews and by about 60 points for Arabs, about two standard deviations within each group. For Jews the effects of CASMIN educational categories on occupational prestige are quite linear.

In general, within each qualification, women attain higher prestige scores than men, with the exception of university degrees. Their advantage is most pronounced at the 2a/2b and 3a levels. Women with 2a/2b qualifications are usually found in pink-collar occupations (Class IIIb on the EGP schema) whose prestige scores are somewhat higher than the occupations to which comparably educated men turn (namely, occupations in Class VII). For women, 3a qualifications usually mean qualifications in nursing and teaching,

V. Kraus, Y. Shavit, and M. Yaish

TABLE 7.8. *Regressions of occupational prestige in first job*

Independent variables	Jews				Arab men	
	Men		Women			
	(1)	(2)	(1)	(2)	(1)	(2)
Age of entry		1.03*		0.64**		0.83**
		(0.16)		(0.13)		(0.17)
Year of entry		-0.36**		-0.38**		-0.11
		(0.10)		(0.09)		(0.13)
Parental education (relative to post-secondary):						
Primary or less	-7.38**	3.07	-9.32**	1.61		
	(2.18)	(1.90)	(1.91)	(1.76)		
Secondary	-2.41	1.08	-1.38	1.89		
	(2.12)	(1.83)	(1.78)	(1.61)		
Ethnicity[a]	-8.77**	-1.58	-9.00**	-1.63	-1.40	-0.95
	(1.44)	(1.23)	(1.26)	(1.16)	(3.56)	(1.90)

Religious orthodoxy (relative to secular):						
Orthodox	7.77**	6.87**	4.10*	4.10*	-8.99	-0.85
	(2.11)	(1.84)	(1.91)	(1.72)	(5.49)	(2.94)
Traditional	-6.14**	-2.45*	-3.61**	-1.09	-0.68	0.42
	(1.46)	(1.20)	(1.29)	(1.14)	(2.70)	(1.47)
Father's occupational prestige	0.11**	0.07*	0.07*	0.03	0.34**	0.05
	(0.03)	(0.02)	(0.03)	(0.02)	(0.07)	(0.04)
Education (relative to 3b):						
1ab		-43.47**		-43.27**		-62.17**
		(2.00)		(1.97)		(2.03)
2a		-37.17**		-30.51**		-59.02**
		(1.85)		(1.85)		(3.00)
2b		-39.26**		-29.17**		-62.88**
		(2.82)		(2.39)		(2.98)
2c		-26.07**		-22.02**		-54.93**
		(1.90)		(1.69)		(2.45)
3a		-21.94**		-6.34**		-16.72**
		(1.84)		(1.64)		(2.65)
Constant	46.99**	70.04**	54.90**	82.62**	25.34**	69.61
Adjusted R^2	0.13	0.47	0.14	0.44	0.05	0.74

* Significant at the 0.05 level   ** Significant at the 0.01 level

[a] Indicates Sephardi for Jews and Muslim for Arabs.

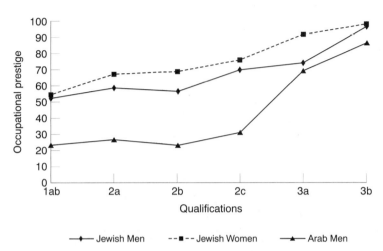

Fig. 7.2. *Predicted mean occupational prestige by qualifications, gender and ethnicity*

whereas for men they usually mean post-secondary technical certificates (especially technicians). The former enjoy higher prestige scores than the latter. Among university graduates there are very small gender differences in occupational prestige.

The pattern for Arab men is very different and more interesting. First, the curve is not at all linear. For Arab men, primary and secondary qualifications do not enhance occupational attainment. By contrast, the occupational prestige attained by Arab men with tertiary qualifications are similar to those of Jews. This pattern reflects differences between the two groups in the labour market to which they turn for work. Arab men with tertiary qualifications usually find work within the Arab enclave as teachers, administrators, doctors, and the like. Semyonov and Cohen (1990) and Shavit (1992) have shown that Arab men employed in the ethnic enclave obtain higher occupational returns for their education than other groups of workers in the Israeli economy. However, the Arab enclave private economy is very limited and, for historical and political reasons, including the discriminatory practices of the government vis-à-vis Arab communities, consists mainly of small-scale businesses (Lustick 1980; Lewin-Epstein 1993: ch. 2). Most Arab workers are employed in the Jewish sector or in small firms which provide services to the Jewish sector. When employed by Jews, Arabs face occupational discrimination and are often recruited for unskilled occupations irrespective of their educational credentials (Shavit 1992; Semyonov and Cohen 1990). This reality is consistent with the pattern in Figure 7.2. Most Arab men are employed in the least prestigious occupations irrespective of their qualifications. Only those with tertiary education, many of whom work in the Arab enclave, are rewarded for their qualifications.

Multinomial Logit Regressions of the School-to-Work Transitions

In this final empirical section, we employ multinomial logistic regressions to further explore the nature of the relationship between qualifications and occupation early in the career. Whereas in the previous section occupations were measured on a unidimensional prestige hierarchy, we now examine labour-force entry into distinct occupational classes. As noted earlier, we have used an Israeli adaptation of the EGP class schema (Goldthorpe, Yaish, and Kraus, forthcoming) which differentiates among classes along three dimensions: a hierarchical dimension representing skill and authority levels; a sectoral dimension distinguishing between white-collar and blue-collar workers; and a distinction between employees and self-employed workers.

The analysis for Jewish men and women (Tables 7.9 and 7.10) uses a seven-category class schema, as required by the guidelines for the comparative project (Müller and Shavit 1994). Unfortunately, we do not have sufficient cases for such detail for Arab men, and have combined Class I and II, and Class IIIa and IIIb (Table 7.11). The list of independent variables in the models is the same as in the analysis of occupational prestige with three exceptions. First, in the exploratory analysis we found that the effects of parental education on the log-odds ratios of entry class were never significant. Subsequently, we excluded this variable from the final analysis. Second, father's self-employment is included because it is an important determinant of the odds that young men and women will enter the labour force as self-employed workers themselves. Third, very few women with tertiary qualifications turn to unskilled blue-collar occupations. Consequently, we can estimate the separate effects of post-secondary (3a) and university (3b) qualifications on women's entry class logits and merged these two categories.

Jewish Men and Women Compared

We begin by comparing the results for Jewish men and women. First, the effects of education on the log odds contrasting entry Class VII with I and II are much stronger for women than for men. This may reflect the fact that men have alternative routes into the service class. Specifically, they may become managers of low-level professionals by climbing the ranks in the military before formally entering the labour force and then cross over to similar civilian occupations. Some men also move directly into managerial positions in medium-sized or large family businesses. These routes are less

TABLE 7.9. *Multinomial logit of entry class contrasted with Class VIIab for Jewish women*

Independent variables	Entry class					
	I	II	IIIa	IIIb	IVabc	V + VI
Intercept	4.13*	5.66**	2.46	1.76	1.50	3.61*
Age	0.11**	0.11**	-0.02	0.02	0.07	-0.06
Year of entry	0.04	-0.05*	0.01	0.01	-0.02	0.01
Ethnicity (AA)	-0.77*	-0.354	-0.10	-0.47	-1.03**	-0.64*
Father's occupational prestige	0.01	0.01	0.01	0.00	0.01	0.00
Religious orthodoxy (relative to secular):						
Orthodox	0.95	1.44**	0.20	0.31	0.65	0.11
Traditional	-0.25	-0.19	-0.55*	-0.38	0.26	0.13
Father self-employed	0.25	0.22	0.14	0.26	0.65	0.12
Qualifications (relative to 3ab)						
1ab	-6.95**	-7.97**	-3.22**	-2.24**	-2.97**	-2.88**
2a	-5.08**	-5.08**	-2.05**	-1.39*	-2.55**	-2.00**
2b	-3.20**	-4.60**	-1.11	-0.65	-1.82*	-2.56**
2c	-2.90**	-2.88**	-0.50	-0.45	-1.11	-1.31

* Significant at the 0.05 level   ** Significant at the 0.01 level

TABLE 7.10. *Multinomial logit of entry class contrasted with Class VIIab for Jewish men*

Independent variables	Entry Class					
	I	II	IIIa	IIIb	IVabc	V + VI
Intercept	8.02**	3.26	5.16**	0.16	2.15	3.73**
Age	0.03	0.12**	0.04	-0.02	0.07*	0.02
Year of entry	-0.07**	-0.07**	-0.06**	-0.01	-0.04*	-0.04*
Ethnicity (AA)	0.12	-0.11	0.10	0.25	0.16	0.43*
Father's occupational prestige	0.00	0.02**	0.01	0.01*	0.01*	0.00
Religious orthodoxy (relative to secular):						
Orthodox	0.46	0.02	0.69	-0.02	0.15	-0.37
Traditional	-0.15	-0.23	-0.27	-0.49	-0.52*	0.04
Father self-employed	-0.14	0.56*	-0.07	0.11	1.33**	0.24
Qualifications (relative to 3b):						
1ab	-4.83**	-3.21**	-3.24**	-0.60	-2.13**	-1.11*
2a	-3.22**	-2.24**	-1.98**	-0.72	-1.41**	-0.47
2b	-4.07**	-3.86**	-2.36**	-0.40	-1.50*	-1.46*
2c	-2.30**	-1.06	-1.05	0.62	-0.73	-0.66
3a	-1.40*	-0.13	-0.25	1.30	-0.21	1.42*

* Significant at the 0.05 level   ** Significant at the 0.01 level

TABLE 7.11. *Multinomial logit of entry class contrasted with Class VIIab, Arab men, Classes I + II and IIIa + IIIb combined*

Independent variables	Entry class			
	I + II	IIIab	IVabc	V + VI
Intercept	−9.52*	−2.58	−6.48**	1.17
Age	−0.08	0.05	0.10	−0.06
Year of entry	−0.08	0.03	−0.06*	0.02
Religion (Muslim)	0.04	1.18	0.47	1.30**
Father's occupational prestige	0.03*	0.01	0.02	0.00
Religious orthodoxy (relative to secular):				
Orthodox	−0.03	−1.45	−0.15	−0.81
Traditional	0.24	−0.30	−0.32	−0.47
Father self-employed	0.35	−0.23	0.82*	0.02
Qualifications (relative to 3b):				
1ab	−8.70**	−2.15*	—	−0.52
2a	−6.33**	−2.07	—	−0.79
2b	—	−1.61	—	−0.45
2c	−6.21**	−0.90	—	−0.33
3a	−0.40	2.27	—	1.99

* Significant at the 0.05 level   ** Significant at the 0.01 level

common among women who are more dependent on qualifications for entry into the top two classes.

Second, among women, the effect of education on the log odds involving Class IIIa are clearly weaker than those involving Class I and Class II. There is a clear hierarchy of these three classes with respect to their educational requirements among women. By contrast, among men, Class II and Class IIIa are not distinguishable in this regard. It would seem that whereas among women the boundary between Class II and Class III is quite clear, among men it is not. Turning our attention to the intercepts of the models presented in Tables 7.9 and 7.10, we note that among women the intercept of the contrast between entry Classes II and VII is larger than that involving Classes I and VII. Among men, by contrast, the latter is larger than the former. This means that men are more likely to enter Class I than Class II, whereas women are more likely to enter Class II than Class I. The same pattern appears in the comparison of entry to Class IIIa and IIIb—men are more likely to enter IIIa while women are more likely to enter Class IIIb. In sum, men are more likely to enter the more advantageous of each pair of non-manual classes.

Third, among men, the educational requirement of Class IIIb and Class VII are indistinguishable from one another. This is indicated by the fact that none of the effects of education in the fourth column of the table for men is significant. Both classes recruit men with very low educational attainments. By contrast, among women Class IIIb recruits more educated women than Class VII.

Fourth, the effects of education on the odds of entering the labour force as a self-employed worker are weak but significant for both men and women.

Fifth, men with a general secondary education but without a matriculation diploma are more likely to become unskilled workers than those with a vocational secondary qualification (in four of the columns of the table the effects of 2b are more negative than the effects of 2a). This is an important finding because it indicates that general secondary education involves a risk—failure to obtain the diploma may leave a young person with few marketable skills. On the other hand, it leads to the matriculation diploma, to university, and to the service class. Interestingly, we do not find the same pattern among women. The effects of qualification 2b are always higher than the effects of 2a, and always lower than the effects of 2c. The reason for the gender differences in this regard probably relate to the nature of the distinction between vocational and general secondary education for men and women. The most common form of vocational secondary education for women prepares them for clerical occupations, but women with no vocational qualifications end up in the same occupations, and we suspect that employers do not distinguish between the two groups of women.

Finally, for men, non-academic tertiary qualifications, most of which are technical, significantly enhance the odds of becoming a skilled, rather than an unskilled worker. Among women, we are not able to evaluate the role of qualifications 3a because they are merged with 3b.

Comparing Arabs and Jews

We now add Arab men to the comparison. To this end, we re-estimated the model for Jewish men and women, using the merged class categories employed for Arab men. In the interest of space, we do not present the numeric results of this analysis but, rather present a graphic comparison of the effects of qualifications on entry classes for the three groups. As we have seen before, for Jewish women, the effects of qualifications on the log odds of entering the service classes (I + II) are positive and linear (Figure 7.3), and for Jewish men the overall effect of qualifications are weaker than those of women. We also see the familiar dip associated with qualification 2b for Jewish men.

For Arab men the effects are not linear. Secondary qualifications enhance

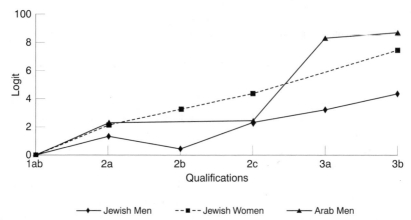

FIG. 7.3. *Effects of qualifications on logit contrasting entry Classes I + II and VII*

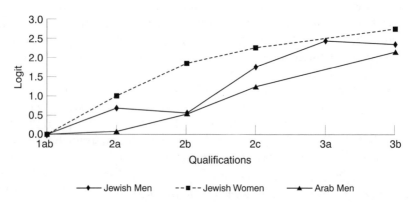

FIG. 7.4. *Effects of qualifications on logit contrasting entry Classes IIIab and VII*

the log-odds ratio when compared to lower qualifications. However, workers with a matriculation diploma are as likely to enter the service classes as those with just a vocational secondary diploma. The steepest effect for Arabs is associated with tertiary education. This pattern is similar to that of the effects of qualifications on occupational prestige and probably reflects the same processes we discussed earlier—discrimination in the Jewish economy and the benefits of employment in the ethnic enclave.

The effects of qualifications on the log odds contrasting entry Class IIIab and Class VII (Figure 7.4) are much weaker than those seen in Figure 7.3.

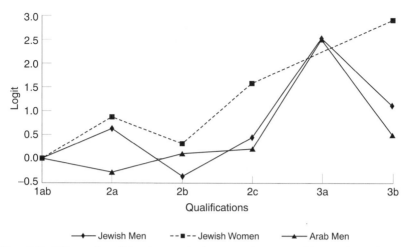

Fɪɢ. 7.5. *Effects of qualifications on logit contrasting entry Classes V + VI and VII*

They are also quite similar for Jewish men and women except that once again we see a dip in the men's curve associated with qualification 2b. For Arab men education is somewhat less effective in enhancing the odds of entering the labour force in Class III rather than Class VII.[7]

Turning finally to Figure 7.5 and the contrasts involving the skilled and unskilled working class, we find that for men, both Arabs and Jews, the odds are greatly enhanced by having obtained a post-secondary vocational quali-fication. In addition, while both Jewish men and women benefit from hav-ing obtained a vocational secondary qualification, Arabs do not. This is similar to the pattern we have seen in the analysis of occupational prestige: the Israeli labour market does not reward secondary qualifications of Arab workers. Interestingly, for men of both ethnic groups, university qualifica-tions do not enhance the odds of becoming a skilled, rather than an unskilled, worker. University graduates who fail to obtain white-collar jobs fare no better than those with lower-level qualifications. For women, by con-trast, the effect of tertiary education is large, but we cannot tell whether this is due to its academic component (3b), its vocational component (3a), or both.

CONCLUSION

Our findings may be summarized as follows. First, regarding the effects of educational qualifications on labour-force participation and unemployment, for Jewish women, education tends to increase the odds of employment. By contrast, among Jewish men, the least educated are least likely to be employed but otherwise the effects of education on employment and on labour-force participation are limited. It would seem that men have little choice but to offer their labour irrespective of their skill level and, presumably, expected income. For women, by contrast, labour supply is more elastic, and educated women who can obtain desirable employment are more likely to offer their labour than less educated women who presumably prefer traditional household duties to the alternatives that the labour market has to offer. Unfortunately, we were not able to analyse the relationship between qualifications and labour-force status for Arab men because our sample of Arabs is very small and their employment rate is very high, leaving very few cases unemployed or out of the labour force.

Second, qualifications are very strongly related to the occupational prestige of entry job. For both men and women, about 45 prestige points (nearly two standard deviations) separate the most, from the least, educated.

Among Arab men, education explains a much larger percentage of the variance in occupational prestige than it does for Jews of either sex. We have suggested, following previous research (Semyonov and Cohen 1990), that this is due to the interaction between education and ethnic labour markets: most Arabs are employed in the Jewish-controlled economy and are allocated to the working classes irrespective of their qualifications. However, those with tertiary qualifications often find service-class jobs in the ethnic enclave, primarily in the public services catering to the enclave. Thus the enclave facilitates the transformation of qualifications into the new service class in the Arab population.

Stratification theory usually posits that a strong effect of education on occupational attainment indicates meritocratic social allocation and is indicative of a universalistic social system. In our case, the strong effect seen for Arabs is due to a particular interaction between education, discrimination, and the ethnic labour market. It results from discrimination rather than from meritocratic occupational selection.

Third, for both Jewish men and women, education is the major mechanism through which educated and Ashkenazi families manage to enhance the occupational prestige of their children. In other words, education mediates fully the positive effects of parental education and ethnicity on occupational prestige. However, whereas among women, it also fully mediates the positive effect of father's occupational prestige, among men, it does not. The direct net effect of father's occupation on sons' occupational attainment reflects the other assets, besides education, that well-placed fathers can draw upon to assist in the good placement of their sons. Our results show that they are either less able, or less interested, in doing the same for their daughters. In a gender segregated labour market, daughters are less likely than sons to follow their fathers' footsteps into male-typed occupations, and fathers may be unable to exert informal pressure or to 'pull strings' in the limited occupational niches where women compete for jobs. The best they can do is to provide daughters with an education which will help them in the competition.

Among Arab men, by contrast, the association between their social origins and their occupational attainment is very weak. Most members of the old Palestinian elites left the country during the war of 1948, and the population that remained consisted predominantly of the poor peasantry. Thus, during the 1950s and 1960s, when our respondents were growing up, the Arab population in Israel was homogeneous from a stratification point of view. The weak association between father's and sons' socio-economic characteristics is due to the socio-economic homogeneity of the parental generation.

Fourth, with the exception of university graduates, employed women enjoy a higher mean occupational prestige score than men. This is primarily due to the fact that women with primary and secondary qualifications are disproportionately found in occupational classes IIIa and IIIb, whereas men of similar qualifications are over-represented in the skilled and unskilled blue-collar classes. The mean prestige of the former is substantially higher than that of the latter.

Fifth, a related finding is that the effects of education on the log-odds ratio of class placement of Jewish women are generally stronger than for Jewish men. We suggested that the weaker effects of education on the occupational and class placement of Jewish men is due to the unmeasured effects of skill formation while in military service where many recruits receive training in technical occupations. In addition, those men and women who are promoted to ranks of authority gain experience in managerial roles. Unfortunately, there is very little Israeli research on the role of military service experience in shaping patterns of labour-force entry and occupational attainment (see Mangum and Ball 1987; and Fredland and Little 1985; for American research on this topic), and we can only hypothesize that the vocational and managerial skills acquired while in military service affect occupational choice. We also hypothesize that their effects are stronger for Jewish men whose rates of conscription are higher than those of either Jewish women or Arabs. The effects of education on the occupational attainment and class placement of Jewish men are weaker, so we would hypothesize, because the military service constitutes an alternative route into the labour force.

Finally, we have found consistent, if modest, benefits of vocational education at both the secondary and post-secondary levels: holders of secondary,

and post-secondary vocational diplomas are more likely than adjacent qualification categories to become skilled, rather than unskilled, blue-collar workers. There are also indications that non-vocational secondary education can
be a hindrance to occupational attainment when it does not lead to post-
secondary qualifications or to white-collar jobs. The implications of these
combined findings are important: students who embark on the academic
route risk penalties for non-completion. Vocational education blocks the road
to university education thereby setting a ceiling on the attainment of its students. However, it also provides them with a safety net which reduces their
odds of falling to the least desirable class positions. This finding is consistent with those reported by Arum and Shavit (1995) for the USA.

The study of which this chapter is a part examines the hypothesis that the
institutional context of the school-to-work transition conditions the pattern
and magnitude of the association between education and occupations. The
Israeli case reminds us that processes of occupational stratification are also
embedded in the context of ethnic relations. One can hardly assume that the
stratification process is homogeneous within the national space. Rather, it
often displays substantial variation between groups within a given society. In
Israel, the association between education and occupation of Jews and non-
Jews is probably as diverse as between the countries represented in this
study. Interestingly, the association is stronger for Arabs despite the less
meritocratic nature of the attainment process, and precisely because they are
split between the two labour markets we discussed. Clearly, future development of the comparative agenda in stratification research should develop the
conceptual tools with which to incorporate ethnic differentiation into the
comparative model.

NOTES

Funding for this research was provided by the Research Council of the European
University Institute and the Japan Foundation. We would also like to thank Walter
Müller for detailed comments on an earlier draft of this chapter.

1. The results of previous research indicate that inequalities between these two
   groups in occupational attainment are primarily due to differences in educational
   attainment, and this result is repeated in findings reported below.
2. Recently, vocational education has been undergoing a reform intended to increase
   the proportion of students obtaining the matriculation diploma and continuing to
   post-secondary education. These reforms, however, will not have affected the
   cohorts for which we have data.
3. See also Shavit 1984, 1990*b*; and Dar and Resh 1991, and citations therein.
4. The decrees which define the requirements of the various occupations, services,

and economic activities are issued by government ministries, and it is difficult to know for certain how many, of the 400 or so occupations listed in the Standard Classification of Occupations are subject to decrees. We interviewed an expert at the Ministry of labour who estimated that only 60–100 occupations are subject to one decree or another pertaining to formal educational requirements.

5. Traditionally, teaching has been an all-male profession among Arabs, and even today about half the teachers in Arab schools are men (Israel, CBS 1992: 630).

6. The predicted values are computed for the group-specific means of age at entry and father's occupational prestige for the earliest year of entry, for parents with primary education, and for secular respondents. Among Jews they were computed for Sephardim and among Arabs for Muslims.

7. We did not plot the logit effects of qualifications on the contrast involving Class IV because these were not reliably estimated for Arab men.

8

Occupational Returns to Education in Contemporary Italy

ANTONIO SCHIZZEROTTO AND ANTONIO COBALTI

INTRODUCTION

This chapter examines the linkage between education qualifications and social position of first job and current employment status, respectively, in Italy from the mid-1950s to the mid-1980s. In no society are the work outcomes of individuals determined solely by intellectual ability and/or professional skill, and even in post-industrial societies, with their high rates of social mobility and educational enrolment, social origin and gender still condition the occupational position both directly, via occupational inheritance and the gender segmentation of the labour market, and indirectly, by differentiating among educational opportunities (Blau and Duncan 1967; Goldthorpe 1980; Halsey, Heath, and Ridge 1980; Schadee and Schizzerotto 1990; Erikson and Goldthorpe 1992; Müller and Karle 1993; Shavit et al. 1994; Cobalti and Schizzerotto 1994).

The weight of ascribed and acquired characteristics in determining the occupational destinations of individuals is influenced by a society's degree of openness. And this is in turn linked with the institutional regulations and operational forms of its educational system and labour market.

THE ITALIAN EDUCATIONAL SYSTEM AND LABOUR MARKET

Until the early 1960s, the features of the Italian educational system were shaped by the 1922 educational reform (see Figure 8.1a). Compulsory education was established as primary school (*scuola elementare*), lasting five years for children aged 6 to 10. The secondary level was divided into two distinct tracks—academic and vocational. Moreover, at the lower secondary level, a dead-end school (*scuola complementare*) was created, while the selectivity of the educational system was increased by introducing

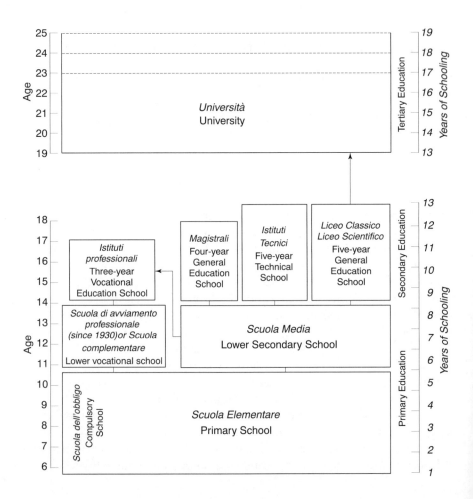

Fig. 8.1.a. *Italian educational system, 1922–1961*

admission and school-leaving examinations. In the early 1930s, the *scuola complementare* was replaced by the *scuola di avviamento professionale* (lower vocational school), with some limited opportunities for transfer to higher secondary school.

The Italian school system remained largely unchanged until 1962, when the *riforma della scuola media unica* (compulsory lower secondary school) came into force (see Figure 8.1b). The distinction between the *scuola di avviamento professionale* (lower vocational school) and the *scuola media* (lower

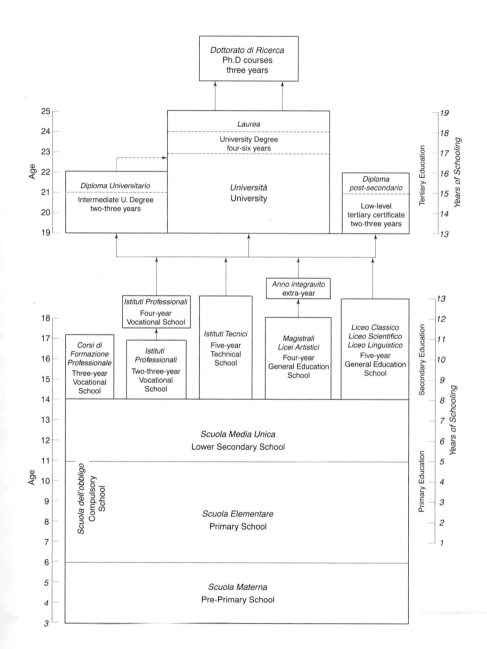

F<small>IG</small>. 8.1.b. *Current Italian educational system*

secondary school) at the lower level of secondary education was abolished, the school-leaving age was set at 14 where it has remained, and the *scuola media unica* (three-year lower secondary school) became part of compulsory education. In the late 1960s, the traditional tendency of the *istituti tecnici* to favour theoretical over practical vocational training was reinforced as a result of reforms which gave diploma holders from these schools access to university.[1]

Operating parallel to the school system are vocational training courses (*corsi di formazione professionale*), which cater to skilled manual and lower non-manual positions in the local labour market, and a proportion of drop-outs from the initial years of upper secondary school transfer to these courses.

The raising of the school-leaving age to 14, the unification of the two streams of lower secondary education, and the reduced differentiation between the various segments of the upper secondary school have been matched by a substantial increase in the school population. In addition to its impact on the lower secondary school, this growth has also been pronounced—albeit to a lesser extent—at the upper secondary school and university levels: between 1960 and 1981, upper secondary school enrolments tripled and university enrolments almost quadrupled.[2]

As shown elsewhere (Schizzerotto 1988; Cobalti and Schizzerotto 1993 and 1994), the expansion of the Italian post-compulsory school population has principally benefited the sons and, even more so, the daughters of blue-collar workers, the urban petty bourgeoisie and the rural petty bourgeoisie. Nevertheless one cannot claim that this has led to the democratization of Italian upper secondary and university education. First, because the majority of the children of the economically and culturally less advantaged classes have entered the less prestigious branches of upper secondary education, namely the *istituti tecnici* and *istituti professionali*. Second, because the growth of the school population has been paralleled by an increase in the levels of educational selection and, more precisely, in the proportion of students failing at the end of the school year. These selective processes have been most evident in the early years of university and high school tracks attended by the children from lower socio-economic families of origin. In 1960/61 the percentage of students repeating their first year of upper secondary school was nearly 20 per cent. By 1980/81 this figure had risen to nearly 26 per cent, and was accompanied by a parallel expansion of students who, after failing a school year, left school altogether instead of repeating the year (from nearly 9 per cent in 1960/61 to just over 17 per cent in 1980/81). These average rates, however, conceal major disparities, in values and in trend, between the more and less prestigious branches of secondary education. The drop-out rate in the passage from the first to the second year of *liceo* (the academic track of upper secondary school), dropped from 12.2 per cent in 1960/61 to 8.1 per cent in 1980/81. By contrast, the rate at *istituti tecnici* more than tripled (from 5.1 per cent to 18.8 per cent). The same phenomenon occurred in the *istituti professionali*, where the drop-out rate increased from 19.2 per cent to 24.1 per cent. Rates of educational wastage in the Italian universities are even more striking. In the twenty-year period 1960/61–1980/81, the drop-out rate between the first and second years of university almost tripled (from 10.6 per cent to 28.9 per cent), and the proportion of students still attending university beyond the legal duration of their courses due to failure to fulfil examination requirements increased sharply (from 14.2 per cent in 1960/61 to 24.4 per cent in 1980/81).[3]

High drop-out rates and the incidence of irregularity in educational careers have considerably slowed—compared with the rate of growth of the secondary school and the university population—the increase in the number of Italians holding a certificate of higher secondary or tertiary education. In the period 1971–1981, enrolments at higher secondary schools increased by approximately 800,000, but the number of higher secondary school-leavers only rose by circa 160,000 (Alessi and Bruni 1990: 148). The pattern is similar for university graduates. In the period 1971–1981, the university population increased by 354,000, but the number of graduates increased by less than 10,000 (Alessi and Bruni 1980: 148).

The relatively small and slow increase in diploma holders and university graduates, however, should not be regarded as an effect of higher educational wastage alone. It has also stemmed, among those born in the 1960s, from a decline in both gross transition rates to higher secondary school and university (de Lillo and Schizzerotto 1982), and in the proportion of diploma holders and university graduates (Shavit and Westerbeek 1995).[4]

Clearly, it is not solely the distribution of educational qualifications that determines the occupational positions reached. The links between level of education and occupational position are also affected by the economic system's demand for an educated labour force and by the institutional features of the labour market (Müller 1994).

As regards the latter, it should be borne in mind that in Italy educational qualifications have legal validity and that access to many occupations is regulated by law. Consequently, major segments of the Italian labour market— the public sector, the professions, and semi-professions—have almost always been subject to cast-iron credentialism. Only enrolment on the professional register—subject to possession of a university degree and the passing of the appropriate state examinations—entitles an individual to practise in a wide variety of traditional and new professions.[5] The same applies to the less prestigious, semi-professions in the field of technical and administrative consultancy, which are reserved for diploma holders from certain *istituti tecnici*.

And in the public sector the formal hierarchy of occupational roles has invariably corresponded to the hierarchy of educational qualifications.

This correspondence between level of education and occupational position is much less rigid in the private sector, except, as already stated, the professions and semi-professions. First, because many small and medium-sized Italian firms have had scant need for a highly educated workforce. Second, because the Italian educational system has always neglected—even in the short-term vocational training sector administered by the regions—the needs of the economy and firms in terms of a skilled workforce. Finally, because the likelihood of owning one's own firm depends more on the possession of the means of production than on educational credentials.

Of course, this state of affairs has varied considerably over time. Until the mid-1950s, the weak Italian economy, still based mainly on agriculture, had little need for a highly educated labour force. The situation changed rapidly between the mid-1950s and the early 1970s. True, the accelerated industrialization of Italy until the mid-1960s was characterized, in both large and small firms, by the use of labour-intensive technology and Fordist organizational models. Nonetheless, industrialization also expanded the technical and administrative occupations practised by the more highly educated labour force.

In the second half of the 1960s, the pace of economic development began to slacken, while the number of diploma-holders and university graduates continued to increase, albeit slowly. However, the effect of the inflation of higher educational qualifications was apparently minor. First, because an attempt was made to counter the risk of under-employment among diploma holders and university graduates by artificially expanding the public sector. Second, because contractual agreements and labour legislation made the Italian labour market extremely rigid, and this in turn penalized firms, even large and medium-sized ones, hiring diploma holders or university graduates for jobs deemed inconsistent with (i.e. inferior to) their educational qualifications. Firms therefore found it not in their interest to replace their old, poorly educated workforces with young and more highly educated personnel. The latter, therefore, found themselves quite simply unemployed (Barbagli 1974; de Lillo and Schizzerotto 1982).

The decline in the occupational prospects of the more highly educated was to some extent counteracted by the fact that—even as the economic boom petered out—the Italian economic system had started along the road of tertiarization and of post-Fordist technological and organizational innovation. However, it was only after the late 1970s that this transformation got fully under way. Unfortunately, in terms of the absorption of educated manpower, its effects were somewhat limited. Because of the rigidity of the labour market and because of the economic crises of the previous decade, the few large Italian companies that operated, mainly, on the basis of diversified quality production and flexible mass production, reduced their workforces. They consequently increased the number of employees with secondary and tertiary education only slightly relative to supply. Conversely, medium-sized and small firms increased their workforces. A proportion of these firms introduced diversified quality production, flexible mass production and—in particular—flexible specialization (Regini 1996), and consequently absorbed a larger number of highly-educated workers compared with the past. However, purely for reasons of size, their ability to absorb diploma-holders and university graduates was necessarily limited.

Moreover, the Italian budgetary crisis, and the consequent impossibility of using the public sector to absorb those with high levels of education has attenuated the positive effects of tertiarization and post-Fordism.[6]

THE RESEARCH HYPOTHESES

In summarizing the foregoing discussion, we may say that, between the mid-1950s and the mid-1980s, Italy experienced a limited and fluctuating rise in the proportion of diploma holders and university graduates; an equally limited increase in demand for highly educated workers; strong educational credentialism caused by the rigid institutional rules governing the Italian labour market; and, as a consequence of these phenomena, a longer period of unemployment/non-employment by the more highly educated before finding their first job.

Despite the almost complete absence of effective vocational training policies, the above phenomena should have established close links between educational and occupational stratification. However, hypothesizing the presence of a strong association between level of education and occupational position is not the same as saying that contemporary Italian society is meritocratic in the allocation of individuals to occupational destinations.

On the contrary, we know—and we shall later show in detail—that in Italy the distribution of educational qualifications is closely conditioned by social origin and gender (Cobalti and Schizzerotto 1993 and 1994; Shavit and Westerbeek 1995). Moreover, we suggest that the same holds true, albeit to a lesser extent, for the social position of first job.

Let us first take the influence of social origin. Employers and the self-employed can hand down their businesses to their children by inheritance, and something similar may occur, though less frequently, among the sons and daughters of employees in high-grade positions. The reason for this phenomenon is that, in Italy, *internal* labour markets prevail over *occupational* labour markets (Marsden 1990). Italian firms seldom compete to hire the most highly skilled labour available, but instead tend to hire young people and to give them on-the-job training. And the same applies in the public sector. Thus, although the public administration and firms select applicants for posts at various occupational levels (mainly) on the basis of their educational qualifications, the hiring strategy provides room for a particularistic selection procedure. In other words, the lack of any vocational training among young people looking for their first job allows employers (both in the private and public sector) to select—level of schooling being equal—more on the basis of social origin than intellectual ability.

Turning now to the influence of gender on first job, in Italy, as in many contemporary societies, the asymmetrical division of domestic responsibilities between men and women has created a gender-based segmentation of the labour market. In the past this segmentation harmed women, whereas today, the traditional conception of the social role of women is changing, and women are now far more highly educated. These phenomena, together with the expansion of the tertiary sector, provide women with greater opportunities to obtain desirable occupations. We may therefore expect to find a complex segmentation by gender of the Italian labour market which is sometimes to the advantage of men and sometimes to that of women.

The last hypothesis deals with the association between educational qualifications and current employment status. Given the prevailing social conception of gender roles and the dominant pattern of the domestic division of labour, Italian men tend to work, or to look for a job, irrespective of their level of education. By contrast, only highly educated Italian women possess the cultural resources and economic tools with which to move beyond the household and into the labour market (Schizzerotto and Bison 1994).[7] We contend, therefore, that the differences in employment status linked to educational qualifications are best observed among women.

More precisely, we believe that these differences mainly concern the risk of exclusion from the labour force. Italian trade unions provide nearly all dependent workers—whatever the social position of their jobs—with a high level of protection against the risk of losing their jobs. This protection is more effective among the most privileged jobs, usually obtained by more highly educated women. Even if these women lose their jobs, they are still strongly motivated to look for a new one. By contrast, poorly educated women are more liable to abandon hope of finding a new job after becoming unemployed. One should bear in mind, moreover, that women with low levels of education are often confined to menial jobs, with rigid working hours, low wages, and little job satisfaction. Therefore, even if they are not laid off, they may still consider leaving the labour market a viable option. We then hypothesize that women with low levels of educational qualification are not in the labour force much more frequently than their more highly educated counterparts.

As already stressed, both highly and poorly educated women are much more closely involved in household work and childcare than men, and these responsibilities weigh more heavily on married than on single women. As a consequence, we suggest that marital status also influences the risk of exclusion from the labour force for women.[8]

DATA, VARIABLES, AND METHODS

The data for the analyses reported here were taken from the Italian Social Mobility Survey conducted in 1985 by Barbagli, Capecchi, Cobalti, de Lillo and Schizzerotto (Cobalti and Schizzerotto 1994). The sample (a multi-stage probability sample) for the survey was composed of 5,016 Italians, men and women, aged 18 to 65, employed and unemployed. Only those born in 1941–1960 and who had worked in the past or were working at the time of the research were selected for the analyses presented here (1,715 cases).

As stressed in the Introduction, our intention has been to study various social determinants of first job and 1985 employment status, with the latter being defined according to a threefold scheme: employed, unemployed, and not in the labour force.

The first job was defined by two variables: an occupational score and a class scheme. The score was measured on the Italian occupational scale drawn up by de Lillo and Schizzerotto (1985), and representing the overall social desirability of an occupation, ranging from a maximum of 90.20 (for senior civil servants in central government), to a minimum of 9.97 (for dependent manual workers without qualifications).

For class of first occupation, we adopted a variant in six positions of the CASMIN scheme. In accordance with this new scheme, the two fractions of the petty bourgeoisie (urban and agricultural) were collapsed; the same was done for the urban and agricultural fractions of the unskilled working class. Class IIIab was split into IIIa and IIIb. Note that Class IIIb (lower grade of routine non-manual occupations) includes numerous service proletariat positions (Esping-Andersen 1993) which were much closer—in terms of work and market situation—to those of the unskilled working class than to those of the lower grade of the service class. Class IVabc also comprised family workers (i.e. those employed in the family business).

Education was the first independent variable considered. More precisely, the interviewees' level of education prior to first job was used, coded into six levels according to a variant of the CASMIN scheme (König, Lüttinger, and Müller 1988). The six levels were as follows: 1ab—compulsory education or less; 1c—basic vocational qualification, including those who had obtained a vocational certificate (*attestato di qualificazione professionale*), after two to three years' further education; 2a—intermediate vocational qualification, this sector was represented by *istituti professionali* (five years' duration); 2b—technical qualification, including those who had obtained a diploma at an *istituto tecnico* (five years); 2c—general qualification, including those who had obtained the most academically oriented diploma (*liceo classico* and *liceo scientifico*), and those with a diploma from the *istituto magistrale*—a school originally intended to train primary school teachers, but in which general education overwhelmingly prevails over vocational training; 3ab—tertiary education, including the very few interviewees with a low-level tertiary qualification and those with a university degree (obtained after four to six years of university, depending on the faculty).

As the second independent variable, parental education was taken as father's level of education or (when this information was unavailable), mother's level of education, and divided into compulsory education or less; lower secondary education; and higher secondary and tertiary education.

We then turned to father's occupation, which was measured with the same scale and scheme as for interviewees' occupation. A further set of three dummy variables was used: (1) employers and the self-employed vs. employees; (2) employers, the self-employed, and employees in agriculture vs. employers, the self-employed, and employees in other sectors; and (3) employers, the self-employed in agriculture vs. all other employers, the self-employed, and employees.

Birth year was assigned a value, ranging from 1 (those born in 1941) to 20 (those born in 1960). Occasionally, interviewees were split between two birth cohorts: those born in 1941–1951 and those born in 1952–1960. The second cohort had experienced the 1962 and subsequent educational reforms.

In studying the associations between educational credential and employment status, we also considered interviewees' marital status, which was divided into two categories: married (comprising those in consensual unions, the separated, and divorced), and singles.

Our data were analysed using ordinary least squares (OLS) regressions and multinomial logistic (ML) regressions.

EDUCATIONAL ATTAINMENT, OCCUPATIONAL DESTINATIONS, AND SOCIAL ORIGINS

Starting with the marginal distributions and simple cross-tabulations of the variables described in the previous section, more than two fifths of the sub sample had entered the school system after the introduction of compulsory lower secondary education in the form of the *scuola media unica*. However, bearing in mind the scant effectiveness of the Italian educational reforms of the 1960s, few respondents obtained upper secondary school qualifications (2a, 2b, and 2c), and even fewer attended university successfully (3ab). Furthermore, given the weak ties between the Italian educational system and the needs of the economy, the proportion of those with basic (1c), and inter-mediate (2a) vocational qualification is very low.

TABLE 8.1. *Distribution of first occupational destinations by educational qualification and gender* (out-flow percentages)

Education	Destinations						
	I–II	IIIa	IIIb	IVabc	V–VI	VIIab	All
All (n = 1,715)							
1ab	1.2	1.7	15.8	13.1	12.1	56.1	58.2
1c	19.5	16.1	19.5	6.8	20.3	17.8	6.9
2a	35.1	17.5	8.2	8.2	15.5	15.5	5.7
2b	47.7	15.9	9.7	8.5	8.5	9.7	10.3
2c	59.5	12.9	7.6	11.8	3.5	4.7	9.9
3ab	93.0	2.6	.6	3.2	.6	—	9.0
All	23.1	6.2	12.8	10.9	10.6	36.4	100.0
Males (n = 977)							
1ab	1.0	1.2	10.8	14.5	19.3	53.2	60.7
1c	5.2	12.1	6.9	8.6	37.9	29.3	5.9
2a	23.8	20.7	4.8	7.9	23.8	19.0	6.4
2b	50.4	12.8	8.0	6.4	12.0	10.4	12.8
2c	40.0	15.0	5.0	20.0	10.0	10.0	6.1
3ab	88.6	3.8	—	6.3	1.3	—	8.1
All	18.5	5.6	8.6	12.5	17.7	37.1	100.0
Females (n = 738)							
1ab	1.5	2.5	23.0	11.0	1.7	60.3	55.3
1c	33.3	20.0	31.7	5.0	3.3	6.7	8.1
2a	55.9	11.8	14.7	8.8	—	8.8	4.6
2b	41.3	23.5	13.7	13.7	—	7.8	6.9
2c	70.0	11.8	9.1	7.3	—	1.8	14.9
3ab	97.4	1.3	1.3	—	—	—	10.2
All	29.3	7.0	18.4	8.9	1.2	35.2	100.0

Because of the limited supply of highly educated labour and the effects of credentialism on the Italian labour market, the inequalities among those with different levels of educational qualification in the class positions of their first jobs correspond almost linearly to the hierarchy of educational qualifications. In fact, the percentage of those reaching the ranks of the service class

(Classes I and II) markedly and regularly declines from university graduates (3ab), to those with only compulsory education or less (1ab). By contrast, the proportion of interviewees belonging to the category of unskilled manual worker (VIIab) increases monotonically from no university graduates to almost three-fifths of those with only compulsory education. The same applies to the middle classes. Those with intermediate vocational qualifications (2a), record the highest percentage of subjects in the category of high-grade routine non-manual employees (IIIa). Lastly, those with basic vocational qualifications (1c), exhibit the largest proportion of low-grade routine non-manual employees (IIIb), and skilled workers (V–VI).

Only the arrivals in the petty bourgeoisie (IVabc) diverge from this pattern. The percentage of interviewees with compulsory education who began their working lives as artisans, shopkeepers, or (small) farmers comes close to the corresponding percentage of those with *liceo* and *istituto magistrale* diplomas (2c), and the proportions of the petty bourgeoisie among those with basic vocational qualifications (1c), intermediate vocational qualifications (2a), and technical qualifications (2b) are similar. In short, the chances of entry to petty-bourgeoisie positions are independent of level of education. The reason being, that in order to achieve low-level self-employment positions, the possession—albeit limited—of the means of production is more important than the possession of educational credentials.

This overall picture, however, conceals substantial gender disparities (see Table 8.1, middle and lower panels). Beginning with educational credentials, it is evident that women stop their education at the compulsory level less frequently, and hold university degrees more often, than men. Moreover, a technical qualification is more frequently obtained by boys, while girls are over-represented at the *liceo* level. This latter effect is mainly due to the inclusion of those who attended the *istituti magistrali*—institutions with one of the largest female student bodies of any type of school in Italy.

Turning to first jobs, one notes that men have less polarized occupational destinations than women. Furthermore, women end up more frequently in the service class and in routine non-manual occupations—both high and low grades—than men; while men almost entirely make up the skilled working class.

However, gender differences in occupational returns to education appear to be much more than simply the effects of the educational system and of labour-market segmentation. Compulsory education pushes a greater proportion of women than men towards unskilled manual occupations. But this is offset by the fact that any other qualification virtually frees women from confinement to working-class occupations. It is worth noting that at each level of schooling over and above compulsory education (except technical education), the percentage of women in service-class positions is invariably higher than the corresponding percentage of men. By contrast, a relatively large proportion of men with basic vocational education, but also with higher secondary diplomas, belong among the unskilled manual worker class.

Can these results be interpreted as showing that women are systematically more privileged than men? Only partially. First, because—-given the gender disparities in labour-market participation—we are not referring to women in general, as we were in the case of men, but only to a fraction of them, and a fraction within which the proportion of highly educated women is greater than in the sub-sample of women with no work experience.[9] Second, because, in practice, only women graduates reach the upper stratum of the service class, and even among graduates, the percentage of women in this position is half the corresponding percentage of men.[10] Third, because in Italy, low-grade routine non-manual positions, in which women are over-represented, often occupy a worse market and labour situation (Lockwood 1958; and Goldthorpe 1980) compared with that of the skilled working class, in which men are over-represented. Clearly, women who have arrived in Class II enjoy a much better overall occupational position than that of men in both the skilled and unskilled working class.

Yet, irrespective of how one interprets gender inequalities in the distribution of first jobs by educational qualifications, the higher a man or woman's educational qualifications, the more frequently they will enter upper positions in the occupational stratification and escape from lower ones.

Ascertaining whether upper educational qualifications guarantee access to the most desirable first jobs (for both women and men), or whether they simply *mask* the influence of privileged family backgrounds, requires an examination of the distribution of educational qualifications and occupational destinations by social origin.

Beginning with the level of education, we can see from our sub-sample that the distribution across classes of origin varies considerably (see Table 8.2, upper panel). It is the children of the service class, followed by the off-spring of high-grade routine non-manual employees, who record the largest proportions of graduates and the lowest rates of subjects with only compulsory schooling. One-third of the offspring of the service class, and one-sixth of the children of high-grade routine non-manual employees obtain a tertiary-level qualification, while not even one-tenth of children from other classes are able to do so. The opposite is true for the lowest levels of education: less than one-fifth of those from upper class families of origin (Classes I and II), and slightly more than one-third of the children of higher-grade routine non-manual employees go no further than compulsory education, while this occurs for more than half of those with fathers in other occupational positions (and indeed, for three-quarters of the children with working-class origins).

TABLE 8.2. *Distribution of educational qualifications by social origin and gender* (out-flow percentages)

Origins	Education						
	1ab	1c	2a	2b	2c	3ab	All
All (n = 1,715)							
I–II	14.9	4.6	6.3	17.8	23.6	32.8	10.1
IIIa	34.8	9.3	4.7	14.0	20.9	16.3	2.5
IIIb	57.0	6.9	6.9	15.5	10.3	3.4	3.4
IVabc	61.3	5.3	5.0	10.3	9.9	8.2	34.1
V–VI	52.0	11.6	7.5	13.3	8.4	7.2	20.1
VIIab	76.1	6.1	4.9	4.7	5.3	2.9	29.8
All	58.2	6.9	5.7	10.3	9.9	9.0	100.0
Males (n = 977)							
I–II	16.8	2.2	7.9	23.6	16.8	32.7	9.1
IIIa	39.2	4.3	8.7	17.4	13.0	17.4	2.4
IIIb	59.4	3.1	9.4	25.0	3.1	—	3.3
IVabc	66.4	3.3	4.5	11.3	5.9	8.6	34.4
V–VI	51.2	11.5	8.1	18.7	4.8	5.7	21.4
VIIab	76.1	6.6	6.6	5.2	3.8	1.7	29.4
All	60.7	5.9	6.4	12.8	6.1	8.1	100.0
Females (n = 738)							
I–II	12.9	7.1	4.7	11.8	30.6	32.9	11.5
IIIa	30.0	15.0	—	10.0	30.0	15.0	2.7
IIIb	53.8	11.5	3.8	3.8	19.2	7.7	3.5
IVabc	54.3	8.1	5.7	8.9	15.4	7.7	33.5
V–VI	52.9	11.8	6.6	5.1	14.0	9.6	18.4
VIIab	76.3	5.4	2.7	4.0	7.1	4.5	30.4
All	55.3	8.1	4.6	6.9	14.9	10.2	100.0

Closer scrutiny of Table 8.2 reveals interesting differences in the educational attainments of the sons and daughters of each class. Those from Classes I, II, and IIIa display the largest proportions of subjects with higher secondary general education. And the sons and daughters of Class V–VI show the highest percentages of individuals obtaining both basic and intermediate vocational qualifications.

Aside from the already-mentioned sex segmentation of education, the general pattern of class inequalities in educational outcomes changes very little when one passes from men to women (see Table 8.2, middle and lower panels). Only the petty bourgeoisie seems to follow a specifically gender-based strategy of educational investment. Indeed, within this class the difference between the proportion of daughters who go beyond compulsory education and the corresponding proportion of sons is much higher than in all other classes. This finding is not new, and stems from a petty bourgeois reproductive strategy, which assigns the family firm to the son while compensating the daughter with a higher level of education (Schadee and Schizzerotto 1990).

To return to the general features of the links between class of origin and education, our analysis clearly shows that the distribution of levels of education systematically changes from one class of origin to another. Therefore, despite the close association between educational qualifications and the social position of first job, we cannot say that the latter is entirely independent of family background. Hence it follows that contemporary Italy cannot be defined as a society in which only achievement and personal ability determine occupational destinations. Nonetheless, it should be noted that the distribution of levels of education by social origin is less unequal than the distribution of classes of occupational destination by education. Thus, one can tentatively say, that education has an effective influence on occupational destinations, net of social origin.

In the following section, we try to establish the validity of this statement in a stricter and more formal way, concentrating on whether, and to what extent, occupational destinations vary according to social origin.

The degree of occupational inheritance is higher at the extremes of the class structure (see Table 8.3). About two-thirds of the sons and daughters from service-class families begin their working lives in service-class positions, and less than one-tenth of them fall into the category unskilled manual workers. Conversely, almost three-fifths of the children of the unskilled working class remain in the same position as their fathers, and few manage to reach service-class occupations. Interviewees from other classes are much more inter-generationally mobile. Nevertheless, our data show a clearly structured pattern of inter-generational transition from class to class. Leaving aside children from service-class backgrounds, it is the children of high-grade routine non-manual employees who reach the top of the class structure. And apart from the children of unskilled manual workers, it is the offspring of the petty bourgeoisie and skilled manual workers who most often begin their careers in unskilled manual positions. Finally, and not surprisingly, our data show that the offspring of each class display the highest percentages of subjects with first jobs belonging to that same class.

The basic features of inter-generational mobility undergo some changes according to the interviewee's sex (see Table 8.3). Given the previously described disparities of occupational destination between men and women, the latter are more often inter-generationally mobile than the former.[11] For the same reason, women are more frequently immobile in the service class than their brothers.

TABLE 8.3. *Distribution of first occupational destinations by social origin and gender*
(outflow percentages)

Origins	Destinations						
	I–II	IIIa	IIIb	IVabc	V–VI	VIIab	All
All (n = 1,715)							
I–II	66.1	8.0	5.2	6.3	6.3	8.0	10.1
IIIa	30.3	16.3	20.9	11.6	4.6	16.3	2.5
IIIb	20.7	12.1	27.6	3.4	8.6	27.6	3.4
IVabc	20.5	5.8	12.0	21.9	8.4	31.4	34.1
V–VI	22.0	8.4	17.7	4.0	16.5	31.4	20.1
VIIab	11.9	3.1	10.8	5.3	11.3	57.6	29.8
All	23.1	6.2	12.8	10.9	10.6	36.4	100.0
Males (n = 977)							
I–II	62.9	7.9	1.1	4.5	12.4	11.2	9.1
IIIa	26.2	21.7	8.7	13.0	8.7	21.7	2.4
IIIb	15.6	6.2	31.4	3.1	15.6	28.1	3.3
IVabc	16.9	4.7	7.1	26.7	13.9	30.7	34.4
V–VI	15.8	7.6	13.4	4.8	25.8	32.6	21.4
VIIab	8.4	3.1	6.6	4.5	18.8	58.6	29.4
All	18.5	5.6	8.6	12.5	17.7	37.1	100.0
Females (n = 738)							
I–II	69.5	8.2	9.4	8.2	—	4.7	11.5
IIIa	35.0	10.0	35.0	10.0	—	10.0	2.7
IIIb	26.9	19.2	23.2	3.8	—	26.9	3.5
IVabc	25.5	7.3	18.6	15.4	.8	32.4	33.5
V–VI	31.6	9.6	24.3	2.9	2.2	29.4	18.4
VIIab	16.5	3.1	16.1	6.2	1.8	56.3	30.4
All	29.3	7.0	18.4	8.9	1.2	35.2	100.0

Generally speaking, the variations in the occupational destination class by social origin are almost as pronounced as the corresponding inequalities in educational qualification (but less marked than the inequalities of destination by level of education). Therefore, we cannot rule out that the above-described disparities in occupational destinations are fictitious, and that they may disappear after controlling for the effects of social origin on educational attainment. Nevertheless, in the light of remarks made in the section dealing with the research hypotheses, we believe that some direct effect of social origins on occupational destinations remains even if their indirect effect, via education, is taken into account. We shall seek to verify this statement by means of multivariate analysis.

THE EFFECTS OF EDUCATION AND ASCRIPTIVE CHARACTERISTICS ON FIRST JOB: OLS AND ML ANALYSES

OLS regressions confirm that, in Italy, educational qualifications are the most influential factor affecting the social position of first job (see Table 8.4).[12] By and large, the analysis confirms that the influence of each level of education, over and above compulsory schooling, is stronger among women than among men. Yet the differences between men and women are only conspicuous in the case of basic and intermediate vocational qualifications. Instead, the advantages afforded by a technical qualification, a general education, and a university degree appear similar among men and women.

Moreover, the results of OLS regressions show that, according to our hypotheses, educational qualifications are not the only social characteristic to influence the score of first job. The latter is also affected by the man or woman's family of origin. Indeed, our model reveals that fathers (or mothers) with either a higher secondary qualification or a university degree enhance the social position of their sons' and daughters' first job. It also reveals that the father's occupational score influences their sons' first occupational status. And finally, fathers employed in agriculture and self-employed fathers in the same economic sector lower and raise, respectively, the starting-point of their daughters' work careers.

In completing the picture emerging from OLS regression, we may add that there is a straightforward explanation as to why the score for women's first job is not affected by their father's score on the occupational scale. Suffice it to recall the heavy concentration of women in the service class, in high-grade and in low-grade routine non-manual employee occupations (see Table 8.1). Even so, as we have shown, the first job of women is not completely independent of their father's occupational position.

The model departs from our hypotheses in only one respect: it shows a decline over time in the score for interviewees' first job. It is well known, however, that OLS regressions are sensitive to marginal distributions (Mare 1981). We cannot rule out, therefore, that this result disappears when a methodologically more sound statistical model is adopted. And this is what we tried to do using ML regressions. As the dependent variable, we used the log odds of entering Classes I and II, Class IIIa, Class IIIb, Class IVabc, Classes V and VI, instead of Class VIIab.

Before commenting on the results of the ML regression models for men and women, it should be borne in mind that we added fictitious cases to the data for men and women in order to handle the problems caused by the zero-cells.[13]

Generally speaking, the ML regressions confirm the main results of our enquiry. They show that both education and social origin affect the class of first job, and that the former is much more often, and more deeply, influential than the latter. In addition, in accordance with our suspicions and contrary to the results of OLS regressions, the ML models prove that there is

TABLE 8.4. *OLS regression of male and female first-job scores: coefficients and standard errors*

Variables	Males	Females
Intercept	23.027**	23.348**
	(1.388)	(1.531)
Father's occupational score	.153**	.053
	(.037)	(.041)
Father's occupation:		
Autonomy (relative to dependent workers)	1.903	−1.876
	(1.228)	(1.334)
Father's occupation:		
Agriculture (relative to workers in other sectors)	−2.293	−5.815**
	(1.972)	(1.912)
Father's occupation:		
Autonomy in agriculture (relative to workers in other categories)	1.363	6.794**
	(1.972)	(2.399)
Father's education (relative to compulsory school):		
Lower secondary	.865	2.540
	(1.489)	(1.619)
Higher secondary and university	6.124**	7.667**
	(1.985)	(1.972)
Educational level (relative to 1ab):		
1c	6.706**	16.122**
	(1.747)	(1.742)
2a	14.408**	25.731**
	(1.704)	(2.240)
2b	21.770**	23.667**
	(1.302)	(1.905)
2c	17.390**	21.871**
	(1.836)	(1.443)
3ab	35.833**	36.983**
	(1.660)	(1.693)
Age	−.196**	−.205*
	(.072)	(.083)
R^2 (adj.)	.552	.603
N	977	738

* $p < .05$ ** $p < .01$

no systematic age-effect on first job. More precisely, the ML regressions show that in only one case do the odds of arriving in a given class for the youngest birth cohort change, in comparison with the corresponding odds for the oldest birth cohort, among both men and women (see Tables 8.5 and 8.6).

Closer scrutiny of the above models yields a more complex picture. Let us begin with education. It is immediately evident that the higher the level of education, the greater the odds of entering Class I or Class II. This is truer for men than for women, however. Among the former the effects of education are almost ordinal: they increase from basic to intermediate vocational qualifications, they are more or less the same for each higher secondary school diploma (2a, 2b, and 2c), and they rise dramatically in the case of tertiary education (see Table 8.5). Among women, by contrast, the effects are similar for basic vocational, intermediate vocational and technical qualifications, and then increase, but the influence of general education is close to that of a university degree (see Table 8.6). Moreover, the advantages afforded by a basic vocational education in the competition to arrive in Classes I and II, rather than Class VIIab, are much more substantial among women than among men (see Tables 8.5 and 8.6). This result agrees with that obtained with OLS regressions. But ML models do not fully confirm the gender disparity in the influence of intermediate vocational education. Rather, it is general education that displays a stronger effect among women than among men (see Tables 8.5 and 8.6). There is a simple explanation for the difference between the two statistical procedures in this respect. The OLS regressions refer to the general effects of each educational qualification on the first job score, while ML models consider the competitive advantages in entering one specific class rather than another. At any rate, it should be remembered that the proportion of women with general education belonging to Classes I and II is higher than the proportion of men with the same educational qualification (see Table 8.1).

Educational credentials after compulsory education also increase the odds of beginning one's career from Class IIIa, though to a lesser extent than Classes I and II. However, whereas the effects of each level of education are similar among men, among women, tertiary education exerts less influence than other educational credentials (see Tables 8.5 and 8.6). This clearly means that women graduates are more likely to enter the desirable Classes I and II than to end up in the less privileged Class IIIa.

By and large, the odds of ending up in Class IIIb, Class IVabc, and Class V–VI are independent of level of education. There are few exceptions to this general pattern. Among men, having basic or intermediate vocational qualifications increases the relative chances of becoming a member of the skilled working class. For women, access to the same class is only facilitated by having basic vocational qualifications. The same type of education also favours

TABLE 8.5. *ML regression of male log odds of entering all occupational classes relative to Class VIIab: parameters and standard errors*

	Class of first job				
	I–II	IIIa	IIIb	IVabc	V–VI
Constant	-4.287**	-4.551**	-2.377**	-2.960**	-1.634**
	(.551)	(.601)	(.384)	(.384)	(.279)
Father's occupational score	.007	.021	.014	.015	.020
	(.017)	(.020)	(.017)	(.014)	(.013)
Father's occupational class (relative to VIIab):					
I–II	.950	-.011	-1.187	-.990	.088
	(1.040)	(1.230)	(1.418)	(1.032)	(.841)
IIIa	.394	1.810	.314	.966	-.494
	(1.009)	(1.023)	(1.012)	(.922)	(.938)
IIIb	.525	.800	1.933**	.164	.309
	(.754)	(.938)	(.540)	(1.102)	(.596)
IVabc	.519	.460	.361	2.016**	-.083
	(.580)	(.693)	(.532)	(.460)	(.390)
V–VI	-.095	.442	.904*	.002	.420
	(.482)	(.569)	(.422)	(.515)	(.311)
Father's education (relative to elementary school):					
lower secondary	.596	.154	.960*	.500	.277
	(.456)	(.565)	(.453)	(.483)	(.402)
higher secondary or university	.491	.579	-.575	2.021**	-.455
	(.681)	(.807)	(1.176)	(.695)	(.714)

Educational level (relative to 1ab):					
1c	2.420**	3.046**	−.001	.546	1.166**
	(.759)	(.609)	(.591)	(.559)	(.350)
2a	4.227**	4.017**	−.041	.715	1.111**
	(.586)	(.581)	(.681)	(.582)	(.416)
2b	5.417**	3.889**	.944**	.655	.893
	(.531)	(.557)	(.468)	(.507)	(.407)
2c	4.982**	3.879**	.848	1.400*	.849
	(.644)	(.693)	(.748)	(.590)	(.612)
3ab	7.795**	4.434**	1.480	2.302*	.752
	(1.101)	(1.238)	(1.430)	(1.128)	(1.426)
Birth cohort 1952–1960 (relative to cohort 1940–1951)	−.508	−.760*	−.231	−.007	−.054
	(.284)	(.346)	(.266)	(.237)	(.199)
Chi²			805.93		
N			979		

* p < .05   ** p < .01

TABLE 3.6. *ML regression of female log odds of entering all occupational classes relative to Class VIIab: parameters and standard errors (in brackets)*

	Class of first job				
	I–II	IIIa	IIIb	IVabc	V–VI
Constant	−4.809**	−5.568**	−2.607**	−2.641**	−4.387**
	(.609)	(.683)	(.380)	(.460)	(.909)
Father's occupational score	.063**	.092**	.062**	.031	.040
	(.021)	(.025)	(.017)	(.021)	(.040)
Father's occupational class (relative to VIIab):					
I–II	−2.450	−2.982*	−1.792	−1.068	−.788
	(1.280)	(1.503)	(1.099)	(1.257)	(2.223)
IIIa	−1.781	−1.183	.382	−.208	−10.952
	(1.235)	(1.381)	(1.014)	(1.243)	(306.8)
IIIb	.175	1.844*	.691	−.064	−10.219
	(.909)	(.850)	(.609)	(1.125)	(297.0)
IVabc	−1.654*	−1.592	−.915	.475	−1.499
	(.674)	(.829)	(.491)	(.600)	(1.323)
V–VI	−.226	.068	.159	−.695	.414
	(.571)	(.683)	(.383)	(.669)	(.921)

Father's education (relative to elementary school):					
lower secondary	.929	.628	.258	.965	.412
	(.607)	(.657)	(.560)	(.655)	(1.255)
higher secondary or university	.613	−.252	−.409	1.723*	1.146
	(.764)	(.898)	(.752)	(.730)	(1.241)
Educational level (relative to 1ab):					
1c	5.270**	4.075**	2.232**	1.355	2.701**
	(.703)	(.687)	(.576)	(.802)	(.982)
2a	5.343**	3.032**	1.123	1.146	2.004
	(.784)	(.876)	(.762)	(.898)	(1.294)
2b	5.409**	4.180**	1.281	1.945**	1.929
	(.718)	(.712)	(.664)	(.697)	(1.257)
2c	7.216**	4.709**	2.216**	2.707**	2.426
	(.853)	(.864)	(.806)	(.838)	(1.381)
3ab	7.687**	2.803	.597	1.078	2.811
	(1.112)	(1.478)	(1.437)	(1.451)	(1.571)
Birth cohort 1952–1960 (relative to cohort 1940–1951)	−.481	.062	.231	−.711*	−.052
	(.330)	(.385)	(.238)	(.334)	(.620)
Chi^2	736.15				
N	744				

* $p < .05$ ** $p < .01$

their entry into Class IIIb. Finally, access by women to the petty bourgeoisie is facilitated if they have technical, upper secondary, or *liceo* level diplomas.

We now turn to the effects of social origin. As stressed above, these influences are displayed—albeit infrequently—by both men and women. Nonetheless, the effects seem to differ greatly between the sexes. As stated, only among men is there a strong inheritance effect regarding the odds of remaining in Class IVabc. An immobility effect—though one which is not easy to understand—can also be discerned for the sons of Class IIIb. Finally, it is worth noting that father's occupational score has no significant influence on the sons' odds of arriving in any class (see Table 8.5). Conversely, the entry of women into Classes I and II, Class IIIa and Class IIIb is enhanced by their father's occupational score (see Table 8.6).[14]

On the contrary, the effect of father's education is the same for both men and women. Generally speaking, it does not systematically affect the occupational destinations of either the former or the latter. The only exception is the odds of entering the petty bourgeoisie, which are higher, for both sons and daughters, when the father has a higher secondary or university level of education (see Tables 8.5 and 8.6).

On reviewing the overall results, it appears that ML models favour our hypothesis concerning the influences of social origin on the class position of first job to the same extent (not to say a lesser one) as OLS regressions. This is a surprising outcome because ML regressions should allow a more reliable treatment of data arranged on a class scheme. It may be the result of the splitting of the effect of origins between a hierarchical component (occupational score), and a power relation component (class position *strictu sensu*).[15] Moreover, one should bear in mind that ML models do not compare the frequency of arrival in a given class with the corresponding frequencies of arrival in any other class. On the contrary, they only match each class against the reference class. It might thus be thought that using solely a class scheme, and modelling the data in such a way as to account for all possible pairwise comparisons among destination classes, would yield less surprising results.

One should also consider that neither OLS nor ML regressions possess specific parameters expressing the strength of the two-way association between social origin and level of education. Unfortunately, without this information it is difficult to ascertain whether, in contemporary Italy, ascriptive characteristics affect, both directly and indirectly, individuals' occupational destinations more profoundly than education, or vice versa. Results from previous analyses carried out using log-linear models (see Cobalti and Schizzerotto 1994) indicate that, taking simultaneously into account both direct and indirect effect, social origins exert more influence on first job than education. Yet, from these analyses too education emerges as the independent variable with the highest direct effects on the social class of first job.

EDUCATION AND EMPLOYMENT STATUS

As stated in the Introduction to this chapter, besides occupational destinations, we also analysed the impact of educational qualifications and ascribed attributes on 1985 employment status.

For the sake of brevity, we report and comment on the distribution of employment status only by level of educational attainment and sex (see Table 8.7). Nearly all men, but only two-thirds of women, were employed at the time of the survey. Among the men, the proportions of those employed, unemployed, and not in the labour force vary randomly across educational qualifications. Among the women, by contrast, employment status systematically

TABLE 8.7. *Distribution of current employment status by educational qualification and gender*

Education	Employment status			
	employed	unemployed	not in labour force	all
All (n = 1,715)				
1ab	77.8	3.5	18.7	58.2
1c	83.0	5.1	11.9	6.9
2a	88.6	6.2	5.2	5.7
2b	94.4	2.8	2.8	10.3
2c	82.9	5.3	11.8	9.9
3ab	96.8	.6	2.6	9.0
All	82.7	3.6	13.7	100.0
Males (n = 977)				
1ab	95.1	3.2	1.7	60.7
1c	98.3	1.7	—	5.9
2a	92.1	7.9	—	6.4
2b	96.8	2.4	.8	12.8
2c	88.3	6.7	5.0	6.1
3ab	100.0	—	—	8.1
All	95.3	3.3	1.4	100.0
Females (n = 738)				
1ab	52.7	3.9	43.4	55.3
1c	68.4	8.3	23.3	8.1
2a	82.4	2.9	14.7	4.6
2b	89.3	3.9	7.8	6.9
2c	80.0	4.5	15.5	14.9
3ab	93.3	1.3	5.3	10.2
All	66.0	4.1	29.9	100.0

changes according to level of education. With the exception of those with *liceo* level educational qualifications, the percentage of employed women increases *pari passu* with the level of educational qualifications, and the opposite is true of women not in the labour force: (again with the above exception) this decreases linearly from compulsory to tertiary education.

These figures bear out our hypothesis concerning the association between education and employment status. However, in order to test its validity better, we once again used ML models.[16] Using the same set of independent variables as in the ML models regarding the class of first job, we added—in the light of our hypothesis that social attributes affect labour-market participation—a new variable expressing interviewees' marital status.

In accordance with the above remarks, ML regressions show that, among men, birth cohort and educational credentials have no direct effect on the risk of being unemployed or of not being in the labour force. Nor does father's occupational class and score display any association with men's occupational status (see Table 8.8).[17] And nor again, among women, does social origin influence the odds of their being either unemployed or not in the labour force. Educational credentials, however, do strongly affect the likelihood of leaving the labour market. More precisely, the possession of a technical qualification, a general education, and a fortiori a university degree, strongly reduce this substantially (see Table 8.8). Moreover, it is worth noting that among women, birth cohort also affects employment status. Women in the youngest age cohort, in comparison with those from the oldest one, run a higher risk of being unemployed and a lower risk of not being in the labour force (see Table 8.8). This result is because in recent years Italian women enter the labour market more often than in the past, and for precisely this reason their risk of unemployment increases. Yet, even in the case of women, it is marital status, rather than education and age, which is the single most important attribute affecting the odds of not being in the labour force. According to our hypothesis, this risk is much lower among single than among married women.

Somewhat surprisingly, there is also a strong association between *men's* marital status and their employment status. But in this case the effect of marital status moves in the opposite direction to that displayed by women. That is, unmarried men are the most likely to be either unemployed or not in the labour force. These results are more understandable when one considers the (still) predominant definitions of gender roles in contemporary Italy. Since married women are perceived mainly as homemakers, they encounter considerable obstacles when they seek to enter the labour market. Conversely, men without jobs are less likely to marry because they are unable to present an image of themselves as successful breadwinners.

CONCLUSION

Thus, we can say that in contemporary Italy, education exerts a strong and direct influence on the social position of first job. Both statistical models used support this point. The OLS regressions show a positive, and monotonic, relation between the level of education and an individual's occupational score, and the ML regressions reveal that the higher the educational qualification, the greater the odds of entering higher social classes, rather than the unskilled working class. University graduates enjoy a marked advantage in the competition to arrive in the service class, while those with only compulsory education or less are both much more likely to end up in the unskilled working class and to be excluded from the service class and high-grade routine non-manual occupations.

Yet, despite the strong links between education and occupational position, contemporary Italy is not a fully meritocratic society as regards the allocation of individuals to occupational classes. Both OLS and ML regressions show that the social position of the first job is affected, albeit to a limited extent, by social origins. Moreover, one has to remember that social origins have a greater indirect effect on occupational destinations because of their strong impact on educational qualifications. We may say therefore that the tight bond between level of education and first job is due not only to meritocracy, but also to the presence of a still pervasive credentialism—where the *attainment of educational qualifications* counts more than the *achievement of professional skills*—on a limited supply of well-educated people, and a rigid labour market.

The distance of contemporary Italy from the concrete pursuit of equality of opportunity increases further if we take the disparities between men and women into account. Both OLS and ML regressions indicate the existence of substantial variations by gender in the influences of education and social origin on occupational destination. Gender influence is crucial, while the effect of social origin disappears, when employment status is considered. More precisely, the ML regressions show that the influence of education on the chances of being employed, or otherwise, varies considerably by sex. Men's employment status is independent of education, while the educational qualifications of women profoundly affect their risk of exclusion from the labour force. The higher the level of a women's education, the less likely she is to leave her job voluntarily.

These results depict the outcome of certain peculiarities in the Italian situation which concern the educational system, the labour market, and the family, with the connected gender disparities.

Starting with the school, although this is no longer organized so as to produce an elite, is still not fully responsive to the vocational training needs of

TABLE 8.8. *ML regression of male and female log odds of being unemployed or not in the labour force relative to being employed: parameters and standard errors* (in brackets)

| | Gender and Employment Status | | | |
| | Males | | Females | |
	unemployed	not in labour force	unemployed	not in labour force
Constant	-3.916**	-3.783**	-3.037**	0.113
	(.611)	(.708)	(.615)	(.275)
Father's occupational score	-.037	-.031	.014	.015
	(.026)	(.030)	(.026)	(.013)
Father's occupational class (relative to VIIab):				
I–II	-.698	1.787	-1.266	-1.036
	(1.629)	(1.686)	(1.462)	(.778)
IIIa	1.649	2.073	-.082	-.338
	(1.004)	(1.465)	(1.318)	(.711)
IIIb	0.901	1.277	-.413	-.443
	(.881)	(1.169)	(1.100)	(.514)
IVabc	1.155	1.017	-.733	-.617
	(.759)	(.951)	(.794)	(.383)
V–VI	.645	.105	-.660	-.521
	(.655)	(.994)	(.681)	(.326)
Father's education (relative to elementary school):				
lower secondary	1.199**	-.283	-.131	-.310
	(.561)	(1.178)	(.713)	(.375)
higher secondary or university	1.971**	1.444	.887	.525
	(.844)	(1.049)	(.833)	(.461)

Educational level (relative to 1ab):			
1c	−1.009	.202	−.702*
	(1.066)	(1.081)	(.354)
2a	.728	−.219	−1.311**
	(.564)	(1.103)	(.545)
2b	−.827	−1.086	−2.059***
	(.691)	(1.115)	(.5598)
2c	.131	.730	−1.283***
	(.734)	(.810)	(.326)
3ab	−1.065	−1.096	−2.822***
	(1.095)	(1.198)	(.564)
Birth cohort: 1952–1960 (relative to cohort 1940–1951)	.308	−.433	−.448**
	(.419)	(.548)	(.194)
Civil status: singles (relative to consensual unions, divorced, etc.)	1.719**	.808	−2.258***
	(.406)	(.557)	(.363)
Chi²	59.342		192.264
N	982		738

* p < .05   ** p < .01

the economy. It is true that the number of diploma holders and university graduates is still lower than in many post-industrial societies. But it is also true that in recent years this proportion has grown to a greater extent than that required for the pure and simple reproduction of the country's economic, political, and cultural elites. If we inspect the trend of enrolments, indeed, we have to conclude that the Italian training system has started down the road of mass schooling. Nevertheless, neither the upper secondary schools, which should provide training for the labour market (i.e. the upper technical and vocational school), nor the universities, have training curricula geared to occupational reality. In the main they impart a mix of basic cultural and social skills (which vary according to track) which can be used in the exercise of a variety of more or less similar occupations. Nor are these basic technical skills completed by attendance on vocational training courses preparatory for specific trades. Very few individuals, in fact, attend courses of this kind on completion of their studies. And even if the majority were to do so, the situation would not change to any great extent. In Italy, vocational training is not managed jointly by the public administration, private sector firms and the trade union organizations (as in Germany), but by the local public administration, which, generally adopts training criteria similar to those of the upper secondary schools (and universities). As already pointed out, in Italy it is almost exclusively large and medium-sized enterprises that systematically provide vocational training and re-skilling, but only for their own employees. And even in this case, as in that of small firms, on-the-job training predominates over formal instruction, at least at the middle and lower levels of the occupational hierarchy.

Although the Italian school system does not transmit specific vocational skills, it does convey certain social skills, such as ability to cope with daily life, a readiness to adapt to change, and the capacity to take initiatives and which facilitate the organization of work, especially in the small and medium-sized firms that constitute the bulk of the Italian economic system and whose success stems precisely from the flexible specialization that they require of a flexible and adaptable workforce.

The prevalence of small and medium-sized enterprises, together with the organizational dysfunctions of upper secondary schools and universities, helps explain why there are relatively few diploma holders and university graduates in Italy compared with other market economy countries. As already stated, small and medium-sized enterprises, even when they adopt post-Fordist organizational models, do not require large and highly skilled workforces.

This relatively small number of diploma holders and university graduates partly explains the close links between position of first job and level of education. But these links are mainly the consequence of the credentialism of the Italian labour market. In fact, the inflation of educational credentials typified by the United States and most European countries is almost absent in Italy, where intellectual unemployment rather than the underemployment of diploma holders and university graduates has been the main outcome of the (albeit limited) growth in the supply of educated labour.

Contractual agreements in the private sector, and labour law in the public one regulate occupational positions associated with educational qualifications. These rules have a double social closure effect (Parkin 1979). First, they make it highly unlikely that a dependent worker without a high-level educational credential will be able to move into top level positions, even if he or she has acquired the required skill on the job. Second, they obstruct, even if they do not prevent, the hiring of university graduates and diploma holders for 'subordinate jobs'. It is thus difficult to replace older and less educated personnel with younger, better qualified workers and explains why Italy is one of the industrialized nations with the lowest rates of career mobility and the greatest inequalities in the corresponding chances of relative mobility (Schizzerotto and Bison 1996).[18]

The close relationship between educational qualifications and occupational position and the connected phenomena of intellectual unemployment are fostered by two other features peculiar to Italy. The strong job security—stronger than in most other European countries enjoyed by those already in full-time, tenured employment which makes dismissal of an employee in order to replace them with a better qualified and more able worker practically impossible. The second feature touches on the occupational expectations of diploma holders and graduates, many of whom prefer to wait a considerable amount of time, for a job that matches their educational qualifications and personal expectations rather than accept one of 'inferior' status. This strategy is facilitated by the fact that young Italians stay in the parental home much longer than their counterparts in other market economy countries, and even those who do not live at home often receive economic assistance from their parents. Moreover, the social networks to which middle and upper class families belong assist their children in their search for a first job. Hence young Italian graduates and diploma holders do not confront the labour market on their own—behind them stand their families of origin which strongly attenuate the effect of intellectual unemployment and help them in their search for a job which matches—at least as regards occupational status—their expectations.

In Italy, as elsewhere, it is the nuclear family that predominates—albeit with the prolonged cohabitation of parents and children—and at least in recent generations women have markedly reduced the educational and labour-market inequalities that once separated them from men.

Although the Italian educational system has not eliminated the disparities in educational chances linked to social origin, it has ensured equality in such chances between men and women, and since the 1970s more women have obtained diplomas and degrees than men and in the same period female activity rates have slowly but steadily increased. It is true that in contrast to many other European countries and the United States, female labour-market participation is still much lower than that of men, that there is still a marked degree of occupational segregation, and that in order to increase their activity rates Italian women have not only had to become better educated than men but also to reduce their marriage and fertility rates. It is also true that women with diplomas and university degrees have begun to move into decidedly advantageous positions and sometimes as we have seen one more advantageous than those obtained by men with similar qualifications. One should also bear in mind that women work full-time and for life spans as long as those for men, and that this is not solely the case of single or childless women. After all, Italian maternity legislation for employed women is among the most advanced in Europe, and almost all children aged 3 to 6 years attend pre-school. Neither can one say that these considerations only touch a small minority of Italian women as the proportion of women—independent of educational qualification—in full-time work is higher in Italy than in the United States, Germany, England, or Sweden.

NOTES

The authors would like to thank Luisa Saviori and Ivano Bison for their help in handling the data analysed in this chapter, and in the construction of the figures.

1. In the mid-1980s, the Italian university system underwent two additional changes: the creation of a three-year Ph.D. course (*dottorato di ricerca*); and the creation of an intermediate university degree, the so-called *diploma universitario*, awarded after two to three years' study.
2. In 1960/61, secondary school enrolments numbered 761,831, but by 1980/81 this figure had risen to 2,415,325. In the same period, university enrolments rose from 268,181 to 1,035,876.
3. There are five reasons why Italian university students take so long to complete their degrees: teaching is often organized haphazardly; attendance is not compulsory; there is no time limit for graduation; tuition and fees are very low; and finally, young Italians stay in the parental family for a long time and are not pushed to look for a job.
4. The reason for the decline in the social demand for higher education among those born in the 1960s is not entirely clear. On examining the drop in the gross transition rates from compulsory education to upper secondary school, and from upper secondary school to university, de Lillo and Schizzerotto (1982) cite the long wait for a first job experienced by diploma holders and university graduates during the mid-1970s and early 1980s. Shavit and Westerbeek (1995), in a

stimulating and methodologically sophisticated paper, examined the odds of completing higher secondary education and university. Rather than the occupational problems of well-educated young Italians they point to the overcrowding of the Italian school system and its consequent inability to lower the 'cultural and economic barriers which determine the educational aspirations and possibilities' of the children of the less privileged classes as the main reason for the fall in demand for higher education during this period.

5. In Italy, social closure by educational credentials and professional associations, which affects entry to the professions touches not only the learned professions, but also many recent technical professions such as engineering, agronomy, geology, psychology, financial services, commerce, fiscal consultancy, and so forth.

6. Our description of the Italian labour market applies more to the northern and central regions than to the southern ones. For the purposes of this analysis, we decided not to take express account of the dual character of the Italian economy, because of the reduced size of the sub-sample used in subsequent analyses. We have dealt with the question elsewhere (Cobalti and Schizzerotto 1994).

7. That is to say, more highly educated women usually obtain jobs with medium to high salaries and are more likely to have flexible working hours, which in turn enables them to adjust work and family commitments and to pay for domestic help.

8. Under the label 'married' we have grouped all men and women with any kind of family tie. Children constitute the main obstacle to women's labour-market participation, but unfortunately we do not know whether the women in our sample have children or not. Nonetheless, we can say that despite the recent decline in birth rates, the great majority of Italian 'married' women have at least one child. At any rate, we have shown elsewhere (Schizzerotto and Bison 1994) that even after controlling for the number of children, marital status affects women's occupational chances.

9. The percentage distributions of educational qualifications among women with no work experience are as follows: 1ab (73.3), 1c (2.1), 2a (1.8), 2b (4.9), 2c (12.3), 3ab (5.6). The difference between this distribution and that reported in the lower panel of Table 8.2 is smaller than the actual disparity between women with work experience and those without. In fact, the level of education of the latter corresponds to the highest level obtained. By contrast, in our analyses we necessarily refer to the qualifications possessed by women with work experience on obtaining their first job. During their working lives some of these women have earned higher educational qualifications. Indeed, inspection of the highest educational levels attained by the women in question shows that the proportion of those with only compulsory education declines from 55.3 per cent to 52.2 per cent, while the percentage of university graduates rises from 10.2 to 13.1.

10. On average, 5 per cent of Italian men and 2.3 per cent of Italian women began their work careers in Class I. The percentage of graduate men observed in Class I is 41.8 per cent, and that of graduate women, 21.3 per cent.

11. It is interesting to note that the proportion of women from manual working-classes families—both skilled and unskilled—who reach service-class positions is twice that of men.

12. This is evident from the values of the parameters given in Table 8.4. As

further evidence, we add that a regression model with all variables, expressing
the family of origin effect, but with no variable expressing the effect of education, explains only one-quarter of the overall variance. More precisely, the
adjusted—R^2 of this simpler regression model is 0.265 for men and 0.260 for
women.

13. More precisely, we randomly selected one case from the male, and six from the
female sub-samples. We then replicated these, assigning a new educational qualification to each, so that every empty cell in the middle and lower panels of
Table 8.1 was filled with one case. We were thus able to estimate the parameters—otherwise inestimable—that express the effect of tertiary education (for
both men and women), intermediate vocational qualification for women, and
general education (for women) on the (log-) odds of attaining each occupational
class. This—admittedly heterodox—procedure highlights the strong competitive
advantages secured by university degrees and upper secondary diplomas on
entry into the Italian labour market, and does not cause any real change among
the remaining estimable parameters. Several alternative solutions were tried
prior to adopting this procedure (e.g. estimating six separate models, one for
each possible comparison with Class VIIab, computing the (log)-odds of university degree relative to classes different from VIIab, and so forth), but none
proved satisfactory.

14. This result, too apparently contradicts the OLS regressions. As stressed above,
the latter indicated the fathers' occupational scores affect only the scores of sons'
first jobs and not those of daughters. One should bear in mind, however, that
ML regressions refer, not to occupational scores, but to the odds of arriving in
one class rather than another.

15. To test this statement, we repeated the ML regression of Table 8.6 omitting
father's occupational score. It turned out that, in the male sub-sample, the number of significant parameters expressing the influence of class of origin rose from
three to eight. And more importantly, six of the significant parameters are
immobility parameters. In the case of the female sub-sample, the significant
parameters rise from three to six, half of which are immobility parameters.

16. In this case too, we avoided the problem of inestimable parameters by adding
one case to the empty cells of Table 8.7. See also note 13.

17. Surprisingly, the ML model in questions shows that being a father with a lower
secondary education raises the odds of being unemployed, and that a father with
either a higher secondary diploma or a university degree increases the odds even
more. We are unable to give a satisfactory explanation for this result, but tentatively suggest that being the son of a well-educated father raises occupational
expectations, leading to a greater reluctance to accept a job which falls short of
such expectations.

18. In the article quoted in the main text, Italy was compared with England, France,
Sweden, Poland, Hungary, Japan, the USA, and Australia. From the analysis it
turned out that both Italian rates of career mobility and intra-generational
mobility were very close to those of Poland, Hungary, and Japan but differed
markedly from those of the other countries listed above.

9

Educational Credentials and Labour-Market Entry Outcomes in Japan

HIROSHI ISHIDA

INTRODUCTION

Japanese education is characterized by apparently contradictory features of equality and stratification. Compulsory education, which combines six years of elementary school and three years of lower secondary education, is known for its high degree of uniformity and equality (Cummings 1980). During compulsory education, most Japanese students are enrolled in state schools on the basis of residence. Educational facilities, personnel, and curricula are highly standardized, with students learning by and large the same material at approximately the same time and pace throughout Japan. There is virtually no tracking or ability grouping at this level. Since neither skipping a grade for fast learners nor repeating a grade for those who are behind is allowed, each grade is virtually age-homogeneous. However, many students supplement their school work with after-school programmes financed by their families. These help slow learners catch up with course work, and fast learners prepare for entrance examinations, thus introducing an unequal ingredient into a seemingly egalitarian system.

After the completion of compulsory education, approximately 95 per cent of students go on to upper secondary education. At this transition students are sorted into different high schools, ranked hierarchically (Rohlen 1983). Japanese school districts usually consist of several high schools of different academic quality, with a refined ranking and stratification among schools, in stark contrast to the egalitarian nature of compulsory education. At the top of the hierarchy we find elite schools which send their students to prestigious four-year universities. At the bottom we find night schools and vocational schools whose graduates move directly into the labour market. Goals, curricula, and the quality of instruction vary across schools, causing de facto tracking between, but not within, schools.

Upon graduation, high-school students are sorted into different career tracks. Slightly less than 30 per cent enter the labour force directly, about 36 per cent attend an institution of higher education, about 30 per cent continue in some form of further education (e.g. technical schools or preparatory colleges), and the remaining percentage neither work nor continue in education.

Japanese colleges and universities are also ranked hierarchically on the basis of the difficulty of entrance examinations (Cummings, Amano, and Kitamura 1979; Koike and Watanabe 1979; Takeuchi 1981). Four-year national universities are generally more prestigious and provide better quality education at a lower cost than their private counterparts. The latter are generally located at the lower end of the scale, with a few high-quality private universities at the top alongside the national ones. However, Japanese higher education is heavily dependent on the private sector, and almost three-quarters of the students in four-year universities are enrolled in private institutions.

Junior colleges normally offer two-year programmes for a limited range of subjects and are ranked below the four-year universities. These are mostly small private institutions attended predominantly by women, and three-quarters of them offer a single curriculum in non-vocational subjects, such as music, home economics, and English literature. Less than 5 per cent of junior college graduates go on to attend four-year universities.

There is a marked gender stratification in higher education. Over 90 per cent of junior college students are female, but this figure drops to 30 per cent for four-year university students. Furthermore, women students tend to concentrate on the humanities, home economics, and education, with very few taking up engineering or science subjects.

The Japanese educational system is therefore characterized by a relatively high degree of standardization at the compulsory stage, and a relatively high degree of stratification at the post-compulsory stage. According to Allmendinger (1989*b*), these features—standardization and stratification—should encourage employers to use education for the selection of future employees (see also Müller and Karle 1993; Kerckhoff 1996). Indeed, job opportunities in Japan are highly segregated by educational level. Young people with different educational qualifications rarely compete for the same job, and most jobs specify the level of education required of applicants. Many jobs are also gender segregated even though the 1986 Equal Employment Opportunity Law officially prohibits the recruiting of men and women separately for different jobs.[1] Furthermore, there is a strong institutional linkage between schools and employer institutions in Japan, and particular employers and high schools often establish long-term recruiting relationships (Rosenbaum and Kariya 1989; Rosenbaum et al. 1990).

As far as the recruitment of high-school students is concerned, Japanese employers take into account the ranking of high schools and rely heavily on schools themselves to pre-select students (Kariya 1991; Okano 1995). Local employers tend to recruit predominantly from a small number of high schools which they have relied on in the past, and the latter act as a stable supplier of prospective employees. Rosenbaum and Kariya (1991) emphasized the role of the universalistic criterion—school grades—in selecting students for jobs within each school. Okano (1993) and Kinney (1995) found that non-achievemental factors, such as gender and social background, are also considered in the selection procedure.

The important feature of this transition is that jobs are unevenly distributed between high schools, and students compete for jobs within schools since it is the schools that help them obtain jobs.[2] Employers delegate the selection to schools, and the latter act as a gatekeeper in the linkage between school and work. The transition from education to the labour market is a serious matter for high schools because their reputation depends on successful job placements. Therefore, it is important to examine employment prospects of high school graduates from schools of differing ranks.

The recruitment of junior college and university graduates is less structured than that of high schools. Japanese colleges and universities do not play a decisive role in the pre-selection of students, except for a few cases where employers require a university recommendation. Although college seniors obtain information from school placement services, they can contact prospective employers directly. Professors (especially in engineering and science departments) sometimes play a mediating role of helping students contact firms or provide recommendations (Watanabe 1987).

Alumni networks are also important avenues for finding employment with prestigious universities generally having more extensive networks which help university graduates. Furthermore, in the 1970s, it was common practice among Japanese firms to openly limit job applicants to graduates from particular universities (Hashizume 1976; Kariya 1995). This pre-selection of job applicants has persisted into the 1990s, although many companies—mainly large ones which can attract candidates from prestigious universities—do not formally admit that they pre-select applicants by college ranking (Takeuchi 1995; Ishida, Spilerman, and Su 1995). The larger the firm, the more prestigious the universities from which it recruits. Therefore, one can argue that there is a close connection between employment opportunities and stratification in higher education in Japan.

One of the most important aspects of the transition from schooling to work in Japan is that, for most Japanese, this takes place only once in a life time (Ishida 1993; Brinton 1993). In other words, it is rare for Japanese workers to return to education once they have entered the labour market.

Unlike some industrialized countries where entry and re-entry together with marginal entry into the labour market occur, in Japan we find a 'rigid structural barrier between the educational system and the labour market' (Ishida 1993: 250). The preparation for college entrance examinations is usually too demanding to be combined with full-time work, and the system of internal promotion and on-the-job training discourages workers from interrupting their work careers for additional education. Hence it is difficult for Japanese workers to accumulate additional educational credentials once they leave the school system, and the first—and last—entry into the labour market immediately following school completion becomes crucial.[3] Therefore, the linkage between education and the entry position in the labour market appears to be stronger in Japan than in some other industrial countries (Ishida 1993).

Another important aspect of the transition from education to work in Japan is the relationship between what is learned at school and job prospects. Japanese schools teach the basic skills of reading, writing, and arithmetic very efficiently (Lynn 1988), but vocational, technical, and other work-related skills are often considered unimportant or even harmful at the time of job search (with the exception of candidates for engineering and highly specialized professions). Employers are generally interested in hiring intelligent but inexperienced students and training them on the job (Spilerman and Ishida 1996). Although Japan has vocational high schools, these are located towards the bottom of the educational hierarchy and the skills they produce are not always appreciated by employers. The latter appear to be more interested in non-cognitive traits such as punctuality, diligence, and trainability (Takeuchi 1995). These features lead us to believe that the association between education and labour-market outcomes is partly based on the fact that employers utilize education as a signal of higher productivity, rather than as a direct measure of cognitive skills which increase productivity (Sakamoto and Powers 1995).

Our analysis uses nationally representative samples of Japanese men and women residing in Japan in 1985 and investigates the pattern of transition from schooling to work. It uses class and educational schema which allow cross-national comparisons with the studies in other chapters, and focuses on the gender differences in the effects of education on first entry positions and cross-cohort comparisons of the pattern of transition from schooling to work in Japan.

Furthermore, we have attempted to focus on the institutions within which job allocation takes place, and examine the effect of high-school quality and college quality on the entry job attainment. Because jobs are allocated to high schools first—before they are matched to individual students—high schools of differing quality are likely to receive job offers from different kinds of firms. Higher ranking high schools are more likely to have linkages with large firms which offer stable employment and good working conditions. In the same way, since many large Japanese companies only interview candidates from prestigious universities, we expect that the graduates from these institutions will enjoy an advantaged position in the Japanese labour market.

DATA AND VARIABLES

The data-set used in this chapter are taken from the 1985 Social Stratification and Mobility Survey (1985 SSM). The survey consists of three separate samples (two male and one female). The two male samples were combined to form a total sample of 2,473, and the female sample contains 1,474 respondents.[4] Our analyses focus on the respondents who first entered the labour force in 1960 or later, with the pre-1960 cohort being used in some sections for comparative purposes. The section which examines the effect of high-school quality and college quality includes all respondents educated in the post-war educational system irrespective of the year of labour-market entry.[5]

Our dependent variables—labour-market entry outcomes—are social class of first job, socio-economic status of first job, and firm size of first job. Firm size is introduced as a dependent variable because employees working in differing firm size typically experience different financial returns and working conditions in Japan. Present employment status, that is, the distinction among employed, unemployed, and out of the labour force, is not available in the Japanese data-set, as the employment status question does not distinguish unemployment from out of the labour force.

Social class is measured by a six-category version of the EGP class schema (Erikson, Goldthorpe and Portocarero 1979; Erikson and Goldthorpe 1992): service class (I + II); routine non-manual (III); petty bourgeoisie (IVab + IVc + VIIb); skilled manual working class (V + VI); and unskilled manual working class (VIIa). We combined Class VIIb with Class IVc, rather than with Class VIIa, because almost all members of Class VIIb are family workers, rather than agricultural employees, and their employment situation is more closely related to Class IVc (independent farmers), than to Class VIIa (unskilled manual workers) (see Ishida, Goldthorpe, and Erikson 1991).

Socio-economic status is measured by the Japanese occupational prestige scores, developed by the SSM researchers (Okamoto and Hara 1979; Naoi 1979). Firm size for first job is divided into three groups: small (0 to 99 employees); medium-sized (100 to 999 employees); and large (1,000 and over and the public sector).[6]

Survey questions related to education are used to construct cross-nationally comparable CASMIN educational categories (Müller, et al. 1990):

social minimum of education (compulsory education) (1ab); full secondary education, including both academic and vocational (2bc); full secondary education plus some additional schooling (2d); lower tertiary education (two-year junior college) (3a); and higher tertiary education (four-year university) (3b). Because the largest category of respondents belongs to that of the completion of full secondary education, these were further differentiated into those without any further schooling (2bc), and those with some additional technical or vocational schooling (2d).[7]

Social background variables include father's occupational status (measured by the Japanese occupational prestige scores), father's social class (measured by the EGP class schema), and father's education (1ab, 1c, 2bc, and 3ab).

ANALYSIS

Before turning to multivariate analyses, let us examine the univariate statistics. Tables 9.1.a and 9.1.b present the distributions of educational credentials and entry class positions by gender and cohort. Educational upgrading is apparent both for men and women between the younger cohort (which includes respondents who first entered the labour force in 1960 or later), and older cohort (which includes respondents who first entered the labour force before 1960). In the younger cohort, very few left schooling after compulsory education, with upper secondary education subsequently becoming almost universal. Furthermore, clear evidence of gender differences is noticeable in the attainment of tertiary education among the younger cohort members. Men are much more likely to attend four-year rather than two-year institutions, while women are more likely to attend two-year junior colleges.

The distributions of entry class differ between the two cohorts. For both men and women, there is a trend of a decline in self-employment (Class IVbc/VIIb), especially in farming, and a corresponding expansion of the white-collar sector. Among the younger cohort members, the majority (57 per cent) of women respondents are found in Class III, while a third (33 per cent) of male respondents are found in Class III. Clerical work is highly feminized in many industrial countries, but in Japan an almost equal proportion of men and women occupy clerical positions (Shirahase and Ishida 1994). In other words, the extent of feminization of clerical work is much less marked in Japan because it is used as a training ground for male workers (Cole and Tominaga 1976). Consequently the proportion of both male and female school-leavers who entered Class III positions are high in Japan.

Tables 9.2.a and 9.2.b report the results of multinomial regression analyses predicting EGP entry class (using the unskilled manual working class as

TABLE 9.1.a. *Frequency and percentage distributions of educational credentials and EGP entry class by cohort for men*

	1960 or later		pre-1960	
	N	%	N	%
Educational credentials:				
1ab	160	13	614	55
2bc	538	45	331	29
2d	101	9	38	3
3a	32	3	51	5
3b	364	31	91	8
EGP entry class:				
I + II	212	18	115	10
III	390	33	203	18
IVabc/VIIb	79	7	297	26
V/VI	324	27	321	29
VIIa	190	16	189	17

TABLE 9.1.b. *Frequency and percentage distributions of educational credentials and EGP entry class by cohort for women*

	1960 or later		pre-1960	
	N	%	N	%
Educational credentials:				
1ab	133	18	346	59
2bc	336	45	172	30
2d	119	16	48	8
3a	103	14	11	2
3b	57	8	5	1
EGP entry class:				
I + II	110	15	54	9
III	429	57	177	30
IVabc/VIIb	24	3	156	27
V/VI	79	11	88	15
VIIa	106	14	107	18

the base) by education and social background variables.[8] Several findings stand out from Tables 9.2.a and 9.2.b. First, for both men and women, educational credentials play a decisive role in determining the chances of entry into white-collar class positions (Class I + II and Class III) as opposed to unskilled manual positions (Class VIIa)—the higher the educational level, the more likely the respondents are to enter white-collar positions. Second, for both men and women, the chances of entry into self-employment (IVabc/VIIb) and the skilled manual class (V/VI), as opposed to the unskilled manual class (VIIa), are generally not affected by educational credentials. To begin one's work career as self-employed is probably influenced more by access to physical capital (e.g. by inheriting a family business) than by education. Indeed, among men the likelihood of entry into self-employment is affected by father's self-employment.

Third, male and female samples follow a very similar pattern. However, attendance in an institution of higher education appears to have a greater impact on obtaining a service-class position for women than for men. This suggests the privileged position of female graduates of four-year universities in the labour market, since the number is much smaller than that of male graduates (see Tables 9.1.a and 9.1.b). In summary, educational credentials seem to be effectively used by the employers to recruit into white-collar positions, while the allocation of self-employment and manual positions are not much affected by these credentials.

Table 9.3 shows the results of running OLS regression models of first occupational status on education and social background variables. Occupational status returns to education are significant and large for both men and women. The effect of education on occupational status is more or less linear: the higher the level of education, the higher the level of occupational prestige. In particular, a degree from a four-year university boosts occupational status for men and women by more than 12 points, compared to those with only compulsory education.

As regards gender, there are some interesting differences. First, the total variance in first occupational status explained by education and social background is greater for men than for women. Entry job prestige is more likely to be a function of achieved education and ascriptive social background characteristics among men than among women. Second, cross-cohort differences in the effect of educational credentials are apparent among women but not among men. The occupational status advantages enjoyed by graduates from junior colleges and four-year universities appear to be greater among women in the older cohort than among those in the younger cohort. The proportion of women who went on to higher education increased noticeably from the older to the younger cohort, and, as a consequence, the market value of higher education may have diminished across the cohorts.

It should be noted that there is no comparable decline in the occupational status returns to college education among men even though both men and women benefited from the rapid expansion of tertiary education. There is, however, an important difference in the way men and women are affected by the expansion of higher education. The increased level of attendance in

TABLE 9.2.a. *Multinomial logit of EGP entry class on educational credentials and social background for men*

	I + II	III	IVabc/VIIb	V/VI
Intercept	−5.681**	−3.368**	−3.667**	.196
Age	.038**	.022**	.055**	−.001
Father's education:				
1c	.274	.341	.160	.101
2bc	.375	.538*	.021	.098
3ab	.372	.321	−.125	−.241
Father's EGP class:				
IVabc/VIIb	.205	.045	1.427**	.119
Father's prestige	.031**	.029**	.001	.012
Sons' education				
2bc	1.671**	1.322**	−.147	−.421*
2d	2.660**	1.396**	−1.287	.155
3a	3.678**	2.362**	.436	.190
3b	4.483**	3.110**	.280	−1.233**

Note: Class VIIa is the reference category.

* p < .05
** p < .01

TABLE 9.2.b. *Multinomial logit of EGP entry class on educational credentials and social background for women*

	I + II	III	IVabc/VIIb	V/VI
Intercept	-3.844**	−1.389*	−4.707**	−.587
Age	.045**	.010	.094**	.003
Father's education:				
1c	−.097	.264	−.342	.224
2bc	.645	.738*	.807	.486
3ab	.618	.150	.190	−.737
Father's EGP class:				
IVabc/VIIb	−.253	−.433	.440	.139
Father's prestige	−.006	.014	−.013	−.001
Daughters' education:				
2bc	1.609**	2.214**	−.359	.070
2d	3.546**	2.663**	.608	1.035*
3ab	4.844**	2.686**	.491	−.028

Note: Class VIIa is the reference category.

* p < .05.
** p < .01.

TABLE 9.3. *OLS regression of first occupational status on educational credentials and social background by cohort and gender*

	Men		Women	
	1960 or later	Pre-1960	1960 or later	Pre-1960
Intercept	32.592**	29.390**	39.470**	31.464**
Age	.075	.104**	−.017	.105*
Father's education:				
1c	−.097	1.308*	.545	.505
2bc	.064	1.526	.467	.283
3ab	−.426	1.939	2.275	1.309
Father's EGP class:				
IVabc/VIIb	−.152	−.864	−1.576*	−1.303
Father's prestige	.095**	.116*	.023	.049
Sons'/daughters' education:				
2bc	2.379*	2.561**	5.925**	6.367**
2d	3.121*	5.551**	7.182**	7.794**
3a	5.944**	8.567**	8.179**	19.213**
3b	12.314**	12.646**	12.821**	17.104**
R^2	.285	.314	.200	.297

* $p < .05$.
** $p < .01$.

higher education among women is the result of increased attendance in junior colleges and four-year universities, while among men it was primarily in four-year institutions. Indeed the occupational status returns to the junior college category showed a dramatic reduction from 19 points in the older cohort to 8 points in the younger cohort among female respondents, while the reduction in the effect of four-year university is much more modest. It is, therefore, junior colleges where the market value is most likely to have declined.

The third difference between men and women lies in the effects of social background. Among female respondents, there is no significant effect of social background, except for the negative effect of father's self-employment in the younger cohort. On the other hand, among male respondents, father's occupational status and father's completion of primary education significantly increase the sons' first occupational status. This suggests that parents with considerable resources successfully influenced their sons' occupational attainment independent of sons' education, but the same parents did not, or could not, influence their daughters' attainment in the same way. The observation that Japanese parents are more concerned with the occupational attainment of their sons than that of their daughters (Brinton 1993) is consistent with the lack of direct effects of father's education and prestige on occupational attainment among women.

Tables 9.4.a and 9.4.b present the results of multinomial regression analyses of entry firm size on education and social background (using the small firm as the base category). The analysis is restricted to respondents employed in an organization. The most striking finding here is the gender difference in the effects of education on entry firm size.

Among male respondents, educational credentials generally affect the chances of being hired by large or medium-sized firms, especially in the younger cohort. Education beyond compulsory level increases the chances of employment in larger firms. Among male respondents in the older cohort, educational credentials increase the chances of employment in large firms (as opposed to employment in small firms) but not in medium-sized firms. The only exception pertains to university graduates who have better chances of working in either a medium or large-scale firm rather than in a small firm.

Among female respondents, the effects of educational credentials are not straightforward. Education does not distinguish the employment chances in small versus medium-sized firms. The chances of working in a large firm increase when the respondent had a high-school diploma with no additional schooling or a university degree.[9] High-school graduates are usually allocated to jobs through the school-referral system, which probably increases the chances of employment in large firms. A university education benefits both female and male graduates by opening employment opportunities in large firms. The attendance in a junior college, however, does not increase the chances of employment in large firms. Junior colleges provide assistance in the process of job search, but play a much less decisive role than high schools in influencing occupational outcomes, and they may not have established sufficient channels to direct many of their graduates to jobs in large firms.

In summary, the chances of employment in larger firms are more closely related to educational credentials among men than among women. Furthermore, the effects of education are not linear for men and women. Employment prospects in larger firms do not necessarily increase as the level of education increases. Although graduates from four-year universities are most advantaged in obtaining jobs in large firms, female high-school graduates, for example, have better access to these jobs than junior college counterparts. These findings may be related to the existence of long-term relationships between particular high schools and large firms, and suggest the need to examine the institutional settings where the job allocation process takes place.

In order to pursue the issue of the influence of institutional settings on occupational outcomes, we examine the effect of type and quality of high

TABLE 9.4.a. *Multinomial logit of entry firm size on educational credentials and social background by cohort for men*

Cohort Firm size	1960 or later		Pre-1960	
	Medium	Large	Medium	Large
Intercept	−2.456**	−3.093**	−1.758	−4.156**
Age	.020	.039**	−.009	.077**
Father's education:				
1c	.071	.218	.376	.431
2bc	.157	−.016	.287	.062
3ab	.275	.448	.112	.730
Father's EGP class:				
IVabc/VIIb	−.111	−.233	−.331	−.608**
Father's prestige	−.004	−.003	.004	−.011
Sons' education				
2bc	1.097**	1.987**	.589	1.372**
2d	.968*	1.700**	.766	1.089*
3a	−.504	2.286**	.006	1.929**
3b	1.616**	2.562**	1.901**	2.133**

Note: Small firms are the reference category.

* p < .05
** p < .01

schools and colleges on entry class and entry firm size. This part of the analyses includes respondents who attended senior high schools or colleges and universities under the post-war educational system without reference to the year of labour-market entry because the sample size becomes too small when we focus on the respondents who first started work in or after 1960.[10]

First, we focus on what happened to students who graduated from high schools of different quality, that is, to examine the educational and occupational destinations of high-school graduates by high-school type and quality. In order to determine the educational and occupational destinations, our respondents who graduated from high school are first divided into two groups: those who entered the labour market without further schooling after the completion of high school; and those who continued in some additional form of schooling. Three different kinds of further schooling are distinguished by taking into account the type and quality of post-secondary education. Therefore, four categories of educational or occupational destinations are created: attendance in highly competitive or competitive four-year universities; attendance in other universities and two-year junior colleges, attendance in (one or two-year) technical schools; and entry into the labour

TABLE 9.4.b. *Multinomial logit of entry firm size on educational credentials and social background by cohort for women*

Cohort Firm size	1960 or later		Pre-1960	
	Medium	Large	Medium	Large
Intercept	.028	−.742	−3.509*	−4.877**
Age	−.029	−.008	.052*	.061**
Father's education:				
1c	.388	.574	.043	.437
2bc	.293	.278	.978	.614
3ab	−.060	.185	.079	.423
Father's EGP class:				
IVabc/VIIb	−.191	−.610*	.280	.200
Father's prestige	.002	.004	−.017	.015
Daughters' education				
2bc	.536	1.051*	.713	.823*
2d	.286	.170	.109	.045
3a	−.328	.201	—	.321
3b	.468	1.796**	—	1.694

Note: Small firms are the reference category.

* $p < .05$.

** $p < .01$.

— The number of cases is too small to compute reliable estimates.

market. We employ slightly different categorization for female respondents as few of them attended highly competitive or competitive four-year universities, and few male respondents attended two-year junior colleges: attendance in four-year universities; attendance in two-year junior colleges; attendance in (one or two-year) technical schools; and entry into the labour market.

In order to distinguish the quality of high schools attended by our respondents, the schools are first divided into two types, academic and vocational/night schools. Academic schools are further divided into three groups by converting the names of the schools into one of three quality scores.[11] Therefore, four categories of high-school quality are constructed: highly competitive academic high schools; competitive academic high schools; other academic high schools; and vocational or night schools.

Tables 9.5.a and 9.5.b show the distribution of educational and occupational destinations of high-school graduates by gender and the distribution of high-school quality by gender. Over 50 per cent of both male and female high-school graduates in our sample entered the labour force without any

TABLE 9.5.a. *Educational and occupational destinations of high-school graduates and the distributions of high-school and college quality for men*

	N	%
Educational and occupational destinations of high-school graduates:		
Highly competitive/competitive 4-year universities	145	20
Other 4-year universities/2-year junior colleges	141	19
Technical schools	67	9
Labour-market entry	374	51
Distribution of high-school quality:		
Highly competitive academic high schools	117	17
Competitive academic high schools	119	17
Other academic high schools	125	18
Vocational and night schools	326	48
Distribution of college quality:		
Highly competitive 4-year universities	37	13
Competitive 4-year universities	108	38
Other 4-year universities/2-year colleges	141	49

TABLE 9.5.b. *Educational and occupational destinations of high-school graduates and the distributions of high-school and college quality for women*

	N	%
Educational and occupational destinations of high-school graduates:		
Four-year universities	80	10
Two-year junior colleges	117	15
Technical schools	153	20
Labour-market entry	435	55
Distribution of high-school quality:		
Highly competitive academic high schools	81	11
Competitive academic high schools	146	19
Other academic high schools	291	39
Vocational and night schools	231	31
Distribution of college quality:		
Highly competitive/competitive 4-year universities	39	20
Other 4-year universities	41	21
Two-year junior colleges	117	59

further schooling. Male graduates are more likely to attend highly competitive or competitive four-year universities, while female graduates are more likely to enter two-year junior colleges or technical schools. As to the distribution of high-school quality, a much larger proportion of male respondents attended vocational or night schools than female respondents.

Tables 9.6.a and 9.6.b give the results of multinomial regression analyses predicting the educational or occupational destinations of high-school graduates (using labour-market entry as the base) by high-school quality (using vocational and night schools as the base) and social background variables. The effects of high-school quality are striking. The decision to enrol in an institution of higher education of any quality or direct entry into the labour market is significantly affected by the quality of high school attended for both men and women.

In addition, among female respondents, high-school quality affects the chances of whether high-school graduates attended technical schools or entered the labour market directly without any further schooling. Because

TABLE 9.6.a. *Multinomial logit of educational and occupational destinations of high-school graduates on educational credentials and social background for men*

	Highly competitive and competitve four-year universities	Other four-year universities and two-year colleges	Technical schools
Intercept	−5.125**	−2.660**	−.895
Age	.001	−.021	−.026
Father's education:			
1c	−.014	.405	−.058
2bc	.997*	.858*	.522
3ab	2.543**	1.505**	.847
Father's EGP class:			
I + II	−.721	.078	−.377
IVabc/VIIb	−.318	−.012	−.609
Father's prestige	.022	.024	.004
High-school quality:			
highly competitive academic	5.065**	2.224**	.756
competitive academic	4.207**	2.155**	.587
other academic	2.500**	1.034**	.392

Note: Labour-market entry is the reference category.

* p < .05
** p < .01

TABLE 9.6.b. *Multinomial logit of educational and occupational destinations of high-school graduates on educational credentials and social background for women*

	Four-year universities	Two-year colleges	Technical schools
Intercept	−4.624**	−.672	−1.997**
Age	−.079**	−.104**	−.018
Father's education:			
1c	.491	.015	.314
2bc	.712	.372	.087
3ab	1.664**	.992*	.563
Father's EGP class:			
I + II	1.535*	.100	.309
IVabc/VIIb	1.394*	.065	.593*
Father's prestige	.035*	.031*	.013
High-school quality			
highly competitive academic	3.467**	1.607**	1.126**
competitive academic	3.351**	2.124**	1.126**
other academic	2.136**	1.485**	.632*

Note: Labour-market entry is the reference category.

* $p < .05$.
** $p < .01$.

the proportion of female respondents who attended a four-year university or a junior college is much smaller than that of male respondents (25 as against 39 per cent), technical schools, which include secretarial schools and English language schools, appear to attract many female high-school graduates. Furthermore, these schools were as important as junior colleges for female students to gain access to clerical positions (see Table 9.2.b). It is not surprising, therefore, that the effect of high-school quality on the chances of attending technical schools is present among female respondents.

The effects of social-background variables on the educational and occupational destinations of high-school graduates are apparent in Tables 9.6.a and 9.6.b. The odds of attending institutions of higher education (as opposed to entering the labour market directly after high-school education) are significantly affected by father's attendance in the same institutions for both male and female respondents. These effects are noteworthy because they are independent of high-school quality. Although social background variables affect the quality of high school attended, their significant direct effects on the educational and occupational destinations of high school graduates suggest that fathers with considerable cultural resources (that is, attendance in higher education) are able to increase the chances of their sons' and daughters' attendance in higher education, irrespective of the type and quality of the high schools attended by their children.

Furthermore, father's occupational status affects daughters' attendance in four-year universities or junior colleges, and the daughters of the service class or the self-employed are advantaged in their attendance of four-year universities. These effects suggest that over and above affecting the attainment of secondary education, some aspects of social origin influence the attainment of post-secondary education.

The next set of analyses focuses on high-school graduates who entered the labour market without any additional schooling, and examines the effects of high-school quality on various features of first job. The quality of high schools attended does not have any significant effect on first occupational status and first entry EGP class. The average occupational status score for high-school graduates is about 42 points for men, and 45 points for women. However, when we compute the average scores separately by high-school quality, they show little difference for both male and female samples. Similarly, the most frequent class position obtained by male high-school graduates is Class V/VI (33 per cent), followed by Class III (29 per cent), irrespective of high-school quality. The most frequent class destination for female graduates is Class III (72 per cent), irrespective of high-school quality.

The effect of high-school quality, however, appears to have an impact on the size of the firm where male high-school graduates found employment.[12] As shown in Table 9.7.a, male graduates from highly competitive academic high schools have a better chance of starting employment in a large or medium-sized firm than in a small firm: by converting the coefficients into odds ratios, students who graduated from highly competitive academic high schools are more than five times as likely to start work in a medium-sized or large firm as those who graduated from vocational or night schools. The magnitude of these effects is substantial although these effects are not significant at the .05 level probably due to the small number of students who graduated from highly competitive schools and entered the labour force immediately after graduating from high school. A similar effect cannot be found among the female graduates of highly competitive academic high schools. The gender difference may be related to the proportion of students entering the labour market. Only 16 per cent of male graduates from highly competitive academic high schools began work without any further schooling, whereas the figure for female graduates is 33 per cent. Because there was a relatively small pool of male graduates of highly competitive schools who sought employment, it was not difficult to find employment in either large or medium-sized firms for most of them. Indeed, almost 90 per cent obtained employment in such firms.

The final set of analyses examines the effect of college quality on first entry position and includes only those respondents who attended four-year universities and two-year junior colleges. The college quality variable is constructed on the basis of type of institutions of higher education (two-year junior colleges or four-year universities), and the difficulty of entrance examination. Three categories of college quality for male respondents are: highly competitive four-year universities; competitive four-year universities; and other four-year universities and two-year junior colleges. Because the number of female respondents who attended highly competitive four-year institutions is small, the college quality variable for female respondents has the following three categories: highly competitive universities or competitive four-year universities; other four-year universities; and two-year junior colleges. The distribution of college quality by gender is shown in Tables 9.5.a and 9.5.b.

The pattern of the relationship between college quality and first entry position is very similar to that of the relationship between high-school quality and first entry position. The average occupational status and the entry EGP class position are not significantly different among graduates of differing college quality for men and women. The average occupational status score is 53 points for male graduates and 51 points for female graduates, irrespective of the quality of college attended. Among both male and female graduates, about 42 per cent started as the service class, and about 47 per cent as the routine non-manual class, irrespective of college quality.

The size of the firm in which college graduates were employed, however, is affected by the quality of college attended. As shown in Table 9.7.a, male graduates from highly competitive four-year universities had significantly better chances of starting employment in either large or medium-sized firms as opposed to small firms. Similarly, in Table 9.7b female graduates of highly competitive or competitive four-year universities had better chances of being hired by large firms than by small firms.[13] Therefore, it is the highly competitive institutions which confer a distinctive advantage for labour-market entry.

CONCLUSION

Educational credentials are a powerful determinant of labour-market entry position. They influence the socio-economic status and social class of first job, and firm size at entry. The effects of educational credentials are most apparent on first occupational status. For both men and women, occupational prestige scores increase more or less linearly with the level of education, with a degree from a four-year university producing particularly large returns.

TABLE 9.7.a. *Multinomial logit of entry firm size on high-school/college quality and social background for men*

Firm size	Medium	Large	Medium	Large
Intercept	−1.691	−1.480	−1.013	−.181
Age	.049*	.084**	.003	.034
Father's education:				
1c	−.077	.615	.333	−.360
2bc	−.345	.105	.313	−.121
3ab	−1.382	.221	−.864	−.386
Father's EGP class:				
IVabc/VIIb	−.740	−.404	−.553	−.718
Father's prestige	−.004	−.037	.022	−.002
High-school quality:				
highly competitive academic	1.686	1.739		
competitive academic	−.760	.137		
other academic	.664	.365		
College quality				
highly competitive 4-year			2.143	2.534*
competitive 4-year			.252	.234

Note: Small firms are the reference category.

* p < .05.
** p < .01.

The chances of employment in white-collar positions are greatly affected by educational credentials. Attendance at a four-year institution of higher education, in particular, increases the likelihood of entry to service-class or routine non-manual positions for both young men and women. However, educational credentials do not distinguish employment opportunities in self-employment or skilled manual or unskilled manual sectors. Self-employment as the first job is likely to be affected by factors unrelated to education, such as access to physical capital and entrepreneurial spirit.

The lack of the effect of education on distinguishing employment chances between skilled and unskilled manual positions is worth noting. Although there are vocational high schools which teach technical subjects in Japan, these skills are not much appreciated by employers. The emphasis on internal promotion and on-the-job training in Japanese companies (Koike 1988) means that employers probably do not use education to sort applicants by technical skills, and, as argued in the introduction, appear to be more concerned with non-cognitive—as opposed to cognitive and technical—skills in recruiting school-leavers. Educational credentials are likely to be used as a signal of trainability and the potential to become productive skilled workers,

TABLE 9.7.b. *Multinomial logit of entry firm size on high-school/college quality and social background for women*

Firm size	Medium	Large	Medium	Large
Intercept	.707	−.469	.117	−1.299
Age	−.035	−.022	−.081	.007
Father's education:				
1c	.387	.521	.130	.298
2bc	−.311	−.001	1.108	.658
3ab	−.513	−.096	−.387	.327
Father's EGP class:				
IVabc/VIIb	−.137	−.590	−.239	−.424
Father's prestige	.005	.034	.019	.008
High-school quality:				
highly competitive academic	1.160	.194		
competitive academic	.299	.143		
other academic	−.089	−.013		
College quality:				
highly compet./compet. 4–year			1.557	1.689*
other 4–year			.343	.896

Note: Small firms are the reference category.

* p < .05.
** p < .01.

rather than an indicator of technical skills, and the initial allocation of newly hired employees to skilled vs. unskilled jobs is probably not based on education.

Firm size is a crucial variable in differentiating the life chances of Japanese employees (see e.g. Ujihara and Takanashi 1971; Odaka 1984; Koike 1988). Wages, fringe benefits, and other rewards are distributed unequally among employees of differing firm size, and the differences by firm size appear to be greater in Japan than in, for example, the United States (Ishida 1993). Therefore, given the relatively low inter-firm mobility into and out of large Japanese firms (Cole 1979), to begin employment in a large firm constitutes a considerable advantage in the Japanese labour market. Our analyses show that the chances of employment in large firms are affected by the levels of education especially among males. Male university graduates and high-school graduates of highly competitive academic schools have particularly greater chances of employment in large firms.

In contrast, access to jobs in large firms for young women does not seem to be closely related to education. The only clear exception being female university graduates from highly competitive or competitive institutions who have better chances of employment in large firms. The gender difference may occur because many Japanese companies hire female workers with the expectation that they will leave employment upon marriage or childbirth. Large Japanese companies which attract candidates of all educational levels have the advantage of choosing those who best meet their needs, and sometimes prefer female high-school graduates to those who went on to higher education (with the exception of graduates from highly competitive institutions) for clerical jobs, since high-school graduates tend to have a longer working period until they leave the labour market at marriage or childbirth. This may well explain why female high-school graduates have better chances of employment in large firms than junior college graduates (see Table 9.4.b).

In order to examine the effect of institutional settings on occupational outcomes, this study has focused on the type and quality of high schools and universities. Because many Japanese high-school graduates find their first job using the school's job-referral system and the schools themselves establish long-term relationships with particular firms, it was hypothesized that students who graduated from high schools of differing type and quality would have differential chances of employment (Kariya 1991; Okano 1995). Similarly, the selective recruitment practices based on college ranking by many Japanese firms are believed to result in differential job opportunities for college seniors who graduated from different quality institutions (Takeuchi 1995; Kariya 1995).

Our analyses show that the type and quality of high schools and colleges do not affect entry class or first occupational status, primarily due to the limited variance in these two dependent variables among either high-school or college graduates. Because the entry positions open to high-school graduates are concentrated in skilled manual or routine non-manual kinds and those open to college graduates are primarily the service class or routine non-manual class positions, there was little differentiation among those with the same educational level. By contrast, a first employment opportunity in large firms seems to be affected by the type and quality of high schools and colleges attended by male students, so that young men from highly competitive academic high schools and universities have better chances of employment in large firms. Similarly, female graduates of highly competitive and competitive universities enjoy access to employment in large firms. These results are consistent with the notion that job vacancies in large firms are unevenly allocated among schools of differing quality and that graduates' career chances are influenced by the type of high school or university attended.

The results of this study suggest that in Japan the unequal distribution of occupational outcomes is related not only to different levels of educational credentials, as measured by our comparative educational schema, but also to the differentiation by type and quality within the same level of educational credentials (that is, among high-school and college graduates). The stratification in higher education and upper secondary schools plays an important role in differentiating the life chances of young people in Japan.

NOTES

An earlier version of this paper was presented at the meeting of the International Sociological Association, Research Committee 28 (Social Stratification) in Stockholm, Sweden, 29 May–2 June 1996. I am grateful to the participants of the meeting and in particular to Walter Müller and Yossi Shavit for valuable comments. The analyses reported here were conducted as part of the 1995 SSM project, and I am grateful to the 1995 SSM Committee for permission to use the 1985 SSM survey.

1. There is, however, no legal penalty for violation of this law, and although firms may not advertise jobs for men and women separately, many restrict women from applying for career-track jobs informally.
2. A cross-national survey of young people in Japan, England, and the USA shows that over 60 per cent of high-school graduates in Japan were assisted by their schools in finding their first job, while only 42 per cent of school-leavers in England, and less than 15 per cent of high-school graduates in the USA, sought school assistance (Koyo Shokugyo Sogo Kenkyusho 1989).
3. Some women workers, however, have a pattern of exit and re-entry into the job market, and some of those who left work later obtain additional education. However, it is unlikely that this additional schooling affects job prospects on re-entry to the labour market.
4. High-school and college types and names were only available in one of the male samples, and the sample size is therefore reduced in the analysis of the effect of high-school and college quality on first entry position.
5. This is because the sample size becomes too small if we restrict our analysis to those who entered the labour force in 1960 or later.
6. Respondents who described themselves as employees were included in the analysis. Employers and family workers were excluded from the analysis of firm size.
7. These additional schools include a wide range of schools, such as secretarial schools, schools for medical technicians or cooks, and English language schools. We should add, however, that we cannot distinguish respondents from educational categories 2b and 2c because the question of high-school type (academic or vocational) was not addressed to all male respondents (see note 4).
8. Multinomial regression analyses were carried out using STATA. I am grateful to Walter Müller and Susanne Steinmann for their advice in running STATA. The analyses predicting entry EGP are not conducted separately by cohort because very few cases are found in particular cells of the multiway table if we divide the sample by cohort. Similarly, educational categories 3a and 3b have been combined for the female sample due to the small number of female respondents with a university degree in the old cohort.

9. Although the effect of a university degree on the odds of employment in a large firm for the old cohort (1,694) is not significant at .05 level the magnitude is substantial and the small number of cases involved in computing the coefficient probably accounts for the non-significance.
10. Respondents who did not attend high school were excluded from the analyses, as were respondents who attended pre-war educational institutions, given that high-school quality scores are not easily computed for these schools.
11. I am grateful to Takehiko Kariya, Yuko Nakanishi, and Hirokazu Ouchi for providing me with the procedure to convert high-school names to quality. However, I have made a few alterations to their procedure, and am alone in being responsible for any remaining errors.
12. The analysis is limited to high-school graduates employed in an organization at their first job. Those who became employers, self-employed, or family workers have been excluded from the analysis.
13. The effect of attendance at a highly competitive four-year university among male respondents, and that of attendance at a highly competitive or competitive four-year university among female respondents on the odds of employment in a medium-sized firm are not significant at the .05 level. However, the magnitude of these effects is substantial, and the small number of cases used to compute these coefficients probably account for the non-significance.

10

From High School and College to Work in Japan

Meritocracy through Institutional and Semi-Institutional Linkages

TAKEHIKO KARIYA

INTRODUCTION

It is a well-known fact that educational qualifications have a great impact on first job placement, and that the higher an individual's level of educational attainment, the more likely he or she is to acquire a 'good' job—higher salary and fringe benefits, training and promotion opportunities, and prestige. In fact, in industrialized countries, higher educational qualifications are often a precondition for entry to a 'good job'.

Sociological research on social stratification and mobility provides two major explanations. On the one hand, technical functionalists regard educational qualifications as a signal of an individual's job competence or human capital (Collins 1971, 1979). Through education, individuals acquire knowledge and skills for jobs. The more education individuals have, the more human capital they obtain. Thus, according to this view, employers will tend to seek highly educated workers for highly skilled jobs.

On the other hand, conflict or reproduction theorists view education as an apparatus which reproduces inequality (Bowles and Gintis 1976; Bourdieu and Passeron 1977; Collins 1979), and contest the view that education increases human capital, contending that employers use educational credentials to exclude people who do not share their own dominant status or class culture.

Whether or not education provides human capital and/or class culture, neither functional nor abstractive relationships explanations focus sufficiently on the process of an individual's transition from educational institutions to work.

How do school and college graduates find jobs? What leads them to first jobs? How does an individual's socio-economic background influence the allocation of first-job opportunities? To answer these questions, we need to pinpoint substantial processes in the school–work transition.

Individuals enter employment through a variety of institutions: high schools, colleges, apprenticeships, and so forth. Perhaps because traditional status attainment studies focus on individuals, studies of the school-to-work transition have tended to ignore institutional factors (Althauser and Kalleberg 1990). Ironically, while status attainment research calls education-to-first-job attainment connections 'paths', it does not examine whether various institutions make actual 'career pathways' and thus define career options.

The analysis presented here differs from other chapters in this volume insofar as we do not use the same analytic framework, or a nationally sampled data set. Instead, using survey data on Japanese college and high-school graduates, we examine in detail the mechanisms of the school-to-work transition. What institutional relationships are involved in the transition from high school to work? Do they differ from those in the college-to-work transition? Does family background affect first-job entry? If so, to what extent? And how does this affect the transition from educational institution to work?

In Japan, universities and high schools are ranked by students' academic achievements. It is believed that school rank determines graduates' chances of getting 'good' jobs. According to such widely accepted views, Japan is generally regarded as a meritocratic society. By contrast, Japanese sociologists have shown that an individual's family background has a considerable impact on their chances of entering highly ranked educational institutions (Kikuchi 1990; Ishida 1993), and first-job attainment (Ishida 1993; Ishida, Müller, and Ridge 1995). Sociologically speaking, Japan is not a meritocratic society insofar as meritocracy is restricted by ascriptive factors such as parental education and occupation.

However, previous studies have their limitations. The first relates to the way of measuring meritocracy. To test whether first-job assignment in Japan is meritocratic, previous studies have tended to concentrate on levels of educational attainment (higher, secondary, or elementary), and rarely focus on more detailed criteria of meritocratic occupational selection, such as school's rank, and students' academic achievement. Thus, we do not yet know about interrelations among rank of educational institutions, students' family background, school grades, and first job-attainment. To what extent does school rank have an impact on an individual's first-job opportunities, net of family background? Do academic grades affect transition to first jobs even after controlling for students' social origins? And how does family background influence the school-to-work transition, independent of achievement factors? These questions still remain unanswered by previous studies.

More importantly, past studies use input–output models to explain first-job attainment. Previous research rarely focuses on substantial processes of school-to-work transition. As shown later, Japan provides an interesting case of linkages between supply and demand sides of labour. But previous studies tend to employ an input–output model between education and first-job attainment as in other societies, where linkages are not as important. Because of this limitation, previous Japanese studies on social mobility fail to offer an alternative model to the conventional input–output model to explain the association between education and first-job attainment.

In this chapter, in addition to introducing more detailed meritocratic criteria into analyses, we present two linkage models to explain the relationships between education and first-job attainment: an institutional linkage model for high-school graduates; and a semi-institutional model for college graduates.

The institutional linkage model explains how high-school students transfer to work through continuous and reliable relationships between high schools and employers. On the other hand, college graduates rely on more informal relations with their alumni to get good jobs. These alumni-student relationships appear informal, but are in reality partly supported by universities and employers. Thus, we refer to them as 'semi-institutional linkages' between colleges and employers.

Do these two types of linkage limit or promote meritocracy in first-job attainment? Which factors carry more weight in the transition from school to work—school performance or family background? Does 'opportunism', through institutional or semi-institutional linkages, intervene in the transition from education to employment (Williamson 1975)? Can parents influence their children's odds of finding 'good jobs' through linkages? Irrespective of family influence, do linkages work on meritocratic criteria? And most importantly, whether linkages increase or decrease meritocracy in the transition from education to employment?

DATA

We have used three data-sets in this analysis. The first is based on the Japanese High School and Beyond survey (JHSB 1982) (see Yoshimoto et al. 1984), a national longitudinal survey including information on high-school graduates' first jobs, school performance, and family background. The survey allows us to examine whether grades actually have a marked impact on jobs in Japan, and to what extent father's occupation and non–cognitive factors influence early job assignments. A nationwide sample of Japanese high-school seniors in 1980 were surveyed again in 1982 (NSK 1984) (see

Yoshimoto et al. 1984). From the JHSB survey, we select a total of 1,206 high-school graduates who answered the original survey and the first follow-up survey, and who did not continue with either part-time or full-time education or training.[1]

The second data-set is from a survey of 977 senior students at seven high schools in the Kanto area. We call the data-set 'local high-school survey'. The survey was carried out in January and February 1995. These seven high schools selected are the same as those chosen by Rosenbaum and Kariya (1989) for their analysis of school-to-work transitions using the survey data of the 1984 seniors. The data were collected more recently than the Rosenbaum and Kariya study, and the JHSB. Therefore, we can examine contemporary states of school-to-work transition with this data-set. The data-set does not contain information about students' family background.[2] But does include information on whether students find jobs from employers with which high schools maintain linkages. Thus, by combining results from analyses of these two survey data (that is, the JHSB and the local high-school survey), we can conduct analyses of transition from school to work in detail.

The third set of data are taken from a questionnaire survey of 704 business major senior students at nine universities. The survey was carried out in January and February in 1993, when senior students finished job-hunting, and already had 'promises to be hired' (*neitei*) from employers for the coming April.[3] The sampled students are mostly business majors, such as economics, commerce, and business management. The survey includes information on students' first jobs, family background, GPA, and job-search methods including semi-institutional linkages. Therefore, this third data-set allows us to examine operation of semi-institutional linkages for college-to-work transition.

School-to-work in Comparison

To understand how Japanese students find a job, it is useful to compare them with their counterparts in other countries. An international comparative study (Koyo Shokugyo Sogo Kenkyusho 1989) shows distinctive features of Japanese students' transition to work, the greatest difference being that most Japanese graduates both from secondary and higher education began their job search much earlier than their counterparts in the USA or Britain.[4] In Japan, 61.7 per cent of secondary school graduates started their job search more than three months before graduation, whereas only 24.7 per cent of their American, and 34 per cent of British, counterparts did so. The same is true for higher education where only 35.5 per cent of American, and 50 per cent of British higher education graduates started to look for employment more than three months before graduation, whereas 77.4 per cent of their Japanese counterparts did so. Job search is usually completed before students leave schools in Japan, whereas most graduates in England and the USA start job search after graduation.

In addition to earlier job search, Japanese graduates apply to fewer employers to find a job than their American or English counterparts. For their first jobs, Japanese college graduates applied to 2.6 employers on average. The average for secondary school graduates is 1.3—half that of Japanese college graduates. On the contrary, American higher education graduates applied to 8.6, and secondary school graduates to 3.3 employers for their first jobs. In Britain, the figures are 8.2 and 3.8, respectively. In fact, Japanese graduates find their work place with much less difficulty than their American and British counterparts. Japanese students find their first jobs with fewer employer contacts than their American or British counterparts.

Third, Japanese graduates use school placement services more often than their American and British counterparts: 46.6 per cent of American and 36.2 per cent of British higher education graduates answer that they used their educational institutions for their first-job search. On the other hand, 59.6 per cent of the Japanese counterpart did so. The difference among countries is larger for secondary education level. The percentages of those who used schools' placement service are 62.6 per cent in Japan, 13.8 per cent in the USA, and 42.3 per cent in Britain.

In summary, the Japanese transition to work is characterized by earlier job search during school years, contact with fewer employers, and heavier reliance on school placement services.

From High School to Work—Institutional Linkages between Schools and Employers

As shown, we find distinctive features of the school-to-work transition which distinguish not only the Japanese school graduates from their counterparts in the USA and Britain, but also within Japan, where the paths of college and high-school graduates differ greatly—the main difference being the types of linkage between schools and employers. In the following sections, we will examine the differences in more detail.

As Rosenbaum and Kariya (1989, 1991) show, Japanese high schools are deeply committed to job placement for their graduates, and high schools and employers create long-term relationships through which high-school graduates are led into jobs. Employers require high schools to recommend students, and schools select and recommend students to employers. In such circumstances, employers rarely turn down recommended students. Thus, high schools play a crucial role in the transition of students into the labour force.

Furthermore, employers prefer to recruit continuously from specific high schools. Recruitment and job placement from high school to work can be stabilized by relying on highly trustworthy relationships, or *jisseki kankei*, literally 'relationship based upon past results or record'. Although there is no formal or written contract, each school has an ongoing relationship with specific employers ('linkage employers') with whom they deal every year, and each employer retains relationships with specific schools ('linkage schools'). As a result, Japanese students only have to apply to a limited number of employers and hence obtain their first job more rapidly.

These high-school–employer connections are a good example of institutional linkages in labour transaction. Japanese high-school students make the transition to work not only through personal ties, but also through stable relationships between schools and employers. These connections tend to remain irrespective of the presence of particular high-school teachers in charge of job placement or personnel staff in a company, and labour transactions are conducted continuously between organizations. The repetitiveness of the transitions from specific schools to specific employers creates a pathway through which future job seekers will be led to those employers again. In this sense, these linkages differ from personal ties, and we refer to them as 'institutional linkages'.

Through these linkages, the transition from high school to work takes place in the following stages (Hida 1983; Iwanaga 1984*a*, 1984*b*; and Kariya 1988, 1991). First, employers distribute job offers to high schools, offering more and better jobs to higher ranked schools. Kariya's regression analyses show that the higher the rank of the school, the more job offers they receive for desirable jobs from large firms (Kariya 1991). As Iwanaga (1984*a*, 1984*b*) and Kariya (1991) found, employers prefer to recruit from the same high schools, as they know what to expect from the schools' graduates. These links impose obligations on both schools and employers to satisfy one another. Schools must select students who satisfy employers to keep on receiving their job allocations in the future. Employers must continue to hire a school's graduates in order to guarantee a reliable source of good-quality employees.

Moreover, schools nominate students for particular jobs (see Hida 1983; Amano et al. 1988; Kariya 1988, 1991). Early in their senior year, students choose among jobs offered to the school, and teachers allow students to apply for the school's nomination if their choice is appropriate. A committee of teachers nominates and ranks students for these jobs. Although this system is not a market, employers cannot choose among all interested students, but only among those nominated by the school, and students cannot apply to an employer without the school's nomination. Thus, students compete for jobs even before they enter the labour market.

What selection mechanisms are involved in high-school students' transition to first jobs through these institutional linkages? Do these linkages advance meritocratic occupational selection? Or, does family background still intervene in these processes? We will answer these questions in the next section.

Meritocracy in the Transition from High School to Work: Multivariate Analyses

The following analyses test to what extent school grades, non-cognitive behaviour, and father's occupation affect the first-job assignment of high-school graduates in Japan.[5] From the Japanese High School and Beyond survey (JHSB), we selected 1,206 work-bound students for the following analyses. The variables used are: days absent from school, discipline problems, and participation in school activities. In addition, we examine the influence of grades and father's occupation. Since these influences may operate differently for young men and young women, we conduct separate analyses for each.

Two levels of grade achievement are used: the top quartile (Grades 1), and the second quartile (Grades 2). The distribution of grades comes fairly close to dividing by quartile. That is, 26.8 per cent of boys and 26.1 per cent of girls had grades in the top three categories, and 27.4 per cent of boys and 28.4 per cent of girls had grades in the fourth category. Then we make two dummy variables: Grades 1 and Grades 2.

Among the jobs available to those non-college young people, white-collar jobs are generally more desirable than other kinds of jobs in Japan (Kariya 1991). Therefore, our first dependent variable is the distinction between white-collar (clerical) jobs and others.

Another distinction affecting job desirability in Japan is firm size. Large firms offer more opportunities for training, promotion, and job security, and as surveys show, young people in Japan have a marked preference for jobs in large firms (Kariya 1988, 1991).

As regards blue-collar jobs, young Japanese men prefer manual jobs in large firms. Thus, our analyses of blue-collar jobs compares selections of young Japanese men from large and small firms.

Is hiring in Japan based upon students' school grades, or less on grades and more on non-cognitive behaviour? Does father's occupation affect these outcomes? Logit analyses examine what factors explain which students have desirable first jobs after graduation. The results are reported separately for men and women in Table 10.1.

From Table 10.1, we find that grades have a very strong, significant impact for young men and women. Top grades (Grades 1 and Grades 2) strongly affect which students obtain white-collar jobs. But absences, discipline,

TABLE 10.1. *Logit analysis of 1982 white-collar jobs for 1980 high-school graduates*

| | Clerical jobs | | Clerical jobs in large firms | | Manual jobs in large firms |
	Males	Females	Males	Females	Males
Grades 1	.564*	.463*	.717*	.409*	.527*
	(.225)	(.135)	(.292)	(.175)	(.186)
Grades 2	0.156	.325*	0.354	.357*	.411*
	(.270)	(.139)	(.340)	(.182)	(.192)
Absences	−0.104	−0.172	−0.181	−0.229	−0.233
	(.256)	(.166)	(.338)	(.238)	(.191)
Discipline	0.029	−0.132	0.044	−.248*	−.232*
Problems	(.139)	(.081)	(.172)	(.092)	(.114)
Activities	.730*	0.170	.687*	.476*	0.169
	(.261)	(.114)	(.332)	(.163)	(.160)
SES1(prof/mgr)	−0.081	0.283	0.086	.424*	−0.119
	(.304)	(.179)	(.351)	(.201)	(.245)
SES2	0.169	−0.007	0.291	0.172	0.164
(white collar)	(.316)	(.174)	(.362)	(.209)	(.167)
Constant	3.333*	4.948*	2.901*	4.497*	3.974*
	(.358)	(.183)	(.464)	(.240)	(.26)

Note: Entries indicate unstandardized coefficients, standard errors in parentheses.

   * indicates coefficients which are over 1.96 times their standard error.

participation in activities, and father's occupation mostly have no effect for young men and women. The exception being extra-curricular activities which has a significant positive effect for young men.

To analyse the more selective attainment of white-collar jobs in large firms, we repeat the above analyses to examine which students find white-collar jobs in large firms (vs. other jobs). We find that large firms rely even more on top grades for young men, but not for young women. Participation in activities has a significant positive effect for males and females, and discipline problems have a significant negative effect for young women (but not young men), but school absence continues to have no significant effect. Father's occupational status (where this is high) has a significant positive effect for girls, but not for boys. Thus, for these more desirable selections, several factors have a stronger impact in large firms than they do for white-collar jobs in general.

Finally, we turn to the analyses of desirable blue-collar jobs — manual jobs in large firms. As shown in Table 10.1, first and second quartile grades have large, significant effects on the blue-collar attainments of men. Discipline problems also have significant negative effects. None of the other variables have significant influence on blue-collar attainments, including father's occupation.

In summary, we find that grades have a great effect on high-school students' chance to get desirable jobs both for boys and girls. Most non-cognitive behavioural factors have smaller effects than academic performance, except for extra-curricular activities for young men. These results indicate that even among non-college youth, academic performance is used as an important selection criterion. Among young people with only a high-school diploma, fine-grained measurement of merit (i.e. grades) makes a difference in finding a good job. In this sense, the selection of high-school students for desirable jobs is based on a meritocratic principle.

In contrast, except for female white-collar jobs in large firms, father's occupation has a small and insignificant effect on students' transition to desirable jobs. Among young people with the same level of non-college degree, socio-economic background has little influence on the transition to first job. But, of course, we should not neglect the exceptional case: selection for the most selective jobs for female students. Our analysis indicates that students with fathers in professional or managerial occupations are more likely to enter white-collar jobs in large firms. Moreover, such direct effects of father's occupation are as large as academic grades, after controlling for other independent variables. That is, the school-to-work transition cannot avoid the influence of family background. Accordingly, we conclude that for the very selective jobs, both achievement and ascriptive factors affect high-school-to-work transition in Japan.

Although the Japanese High School and Beyond data-set allows us to examine the effects of achievement and ascriptive factors on the transition to work, we cannot test how much institutional linkages affect the transition from high school to work. Using survey data from seven high schools in a prefecture, Rosenbaum and Kariya (1989) show that institutional linkages—far from weakening meritocratic selection by introducing opportunism—mean that students need to have better school performances in order to enter desirable jobs with linkage employers.

The Rosenbaum and Kariya study used a data-set from the early 1980s. Do we obtain the same results using more recent survey data? To answer this, we use a new data-set collected in 1995 from the same high schools. Unfortunately, the data lack information on students' family background, and we cannot examine how much students' social origins mediate the high-school-to-work transition through institutional linkages. But the data do include information about linkages allowing us to investigate how linkages are involved in the transition from high school to work. Therefore, analyses of this local high-school survey are used to supplement the results from the JHSB analyses above.

We tested how desirable jobs are assigned according to students' school performance, using a similar model to the previous analyses. Table 10.2 shows a list of variables used. The results of logit analyses for determinants of opportunities to obtain desirable jobs are presented in Table 10.3 for women, and Table 10.4 for men.

TABLE 10.2. *Variables in logit analysis for desirable job plans*

Dependent variables:

The chance to obtain desirable jobs, such as clerical jobs in a large firm, for female students in general or commercial high schools, and clerical jobs for male students in general or commercial high schools, and technical jobs in large firms for male industrial high school students.
−1 if students have a desirable job, 0 otherwise.

Independent variables:
Grades:
  Top5: 1 for top5 students in 40–45 students of a class, 0 for otherwise.
  Top6–10: 1 for top 6 to 10 students in 40–45 students of a class, 0 for otherwise.
RULE: 1 for students violated school rules often, 0 for otherwise.
LATE: 1 for students who were often late for school, 0 for otherwise.
LEADER: 1 for students who were a representative in student council, or leader of extra-curricular activities or home-room[a] class, 0 for otherwise.
EXTRA: 1 for students active in extra-curricular activities, 0 for otherwise.

[a] In Japanese high schools, home-room is the unit of classes, which usually include 40 to 45 students.

For female students in general and commercial high schools, we find results which are very similar to those of the previous analysis of the JHSB. Students with better school grades have better chances of obtaining clerical jobs, whereas non–academic school performance in the model has a small and insignificant effect. For jobs in large firms, none of the independent variables is significant. The odds of being employed in a large firm cannot be explained by school performance for female high-school students. Finally, to obtain the most desirable jobs, that is, clerical jobs in large firms, only the top grades (TOP 5) have a large and significant effect. Unlike the case for clerical jobs in general, the estimated effect of the second highest grades (TOP 10) is not as large and is not significant. Thus, only the top academic achievers can have access to these most selective jobs. Using the more recent survey data, we can see that the transition from high school to work has meritocratic characteristics.

The results for male students differ slightly. For male students in general and commercial high schools, none of the variables in the regression equation is significant. This result differs from that of the JHSB data. On the contrary, to obtain jobs in large firms for male students in general, commercial, and industrial high schools, better grades (TOP 10) have a significant and positive effect.[6] Better academic achievement also affects the odds of obtaining technical jobs in large firms for male students in industrial high schools. For these desirable jobs for male students, academic performance is used as an important selection criterion.

How do linkages work through the transition? Logit analyses examine determinants of opportunities for jobs in 'linkage' as opposed to non-linkage

TABLE 10.3. *Logit analysis for chances of entering desirable jobs for female students* (N=392)

Variable	Clerical jobs		Jobs in large firms		Clerical jobs in Large Firms	
	B	SE	B	SE	B	SE
TOP5	1.158	0.315***	0.407	0.362	1.224	0.469**
TOP10	0.900	0.250***	0.241	0.308	0.722	0.441
RULE	−0.211	0.441	−0.981	0.666	−6.780	18.002
LATE	−0.415	0.395	0.468	0.465	0.220	0.789
LEADER	−0.035	0.234	0.179	0.285	0.182	0.402
EXTRA	−0.326	0.216	−0.178	0.267	−0.165	0.380
Constant	−0.196	0.190	−1.547	0.243***	−2.775	0.377***

* Sig. <0.05   **<0.01   ***<0.001

TABLE 10.4. *Logit analysis for chances of entering desirable jobs for male students*

Variable	Clerical jobs (N = 195)		Jobs in large firms (N = 418)		Technical jobs in large firms (N = 223)	
	B	SE	B	SE	B	SE
TOP5	0.370	1.145			1.233	0.630+
TOP10	0.901	0.641	0.881	0.247***	1.549	0.488**
RULE	0.658	0.715	0.268	0.395	0.854	0.947
LATE	−0.794	0.689	−0.511	0.315	−1.146	1.120
LEADER	0.530	0.609	0.296	0.234	0.098	0.462
EXTRA	0.319	0.556	0.443	0.229	0.574	0.457
Constant	−2.336	0.416***	−1.261	0.192***	−2.928	0.444***

* Sig. <0.05   **<0.01   ***<0.001 +<0.10

firms. Table 10.5 shows a result for female students in general and commercial high schools. For this analysis, we selected female students with clerical jobs, and examined the distribution of the odds of being hired in linkage employers (vs. non-linkage employers).

TABLE 10.5. *Logit analysis for chances of entering jobs in 'contract firms' for female students with clerical jobs*

Variables	Jobs in 'contract firms' (N = 194)	
	B	SE
TOP5	1.371	0.415***
TOP10	0.288	0.342
RULE	−0.623	0.785
LATE	−0.592	0.723
LEADER	0.362	0.334
EXTRA	−0.111	0.317
Constant	−0.534	0.279

* Sig. <0.05   **<0.01   ***<0.001

From Table 10.5, we find that the top-level grades (TOP 5) have a considerable impact on the odds of obtaining a clerical job with linkage employers. Students with higher grades are more likely to be hired in firms with which their high schools have institutional linkages. In other words, to obtain jobs, better grades are required by linkage employers more strongly than others. This indicates that institutional linkages do not discourage meritocratic selection. Rather, these linkages appear to promote meritocracy based on students' academic achievement.

For the case of male students, our analysis includes all students (Table 10.6). So that the logit analysis for males contrasts jobs in linkage vs. non-linkage employers irrespective of occupation. Table 10.6 shows that better grades (TOP 10) have a significant positive effect. The better the grades, the more likely students are to be hired by linkage employers. This finding again shows that institutional linkages tend to strengthen meritocratic selection for first-job assignment.

The present analyses reinforce the findings of Rosenbaum and Kariya's research (1989) insofar as both male and female students, higher grades are required to find jobs through institutional linkages rather than without them.

TABLE 10.6. *Logit analysis for chances of entering jobs in 'contract firms' for male students*

Variables	Jobs in 'contract firms' (N = 418)	
	B	SE
TOP10	0.515	0.240*
RULE	0.226	0.366
LATE	−0.553	0.285+
LEADER	0.172	0.223
EXTRA	0.047	0.215
Constant	−0.595	0.172***

* Sig. <0.05   **<0.01   ***<0.001 +<0.10

From College to Work

In contrast with high-school students, Japanese college students are given more freedom to apply to companies for jobs. Especially, for students in the humanities and social sciences, who constitute the majority of Japanese college students,[7] colleges play a smaller role of job placement than for high-school students and for engineering and science majors (Yoshimoto et al. 1992). College-to-work transition for humanities and social sciences major students do not rely on institutional linkages.

Nonetheless, this does not necessarily mean that Japanese college graduates' job search is conducted without any linkages. To understand what types of linkages are involved, we need to look at a brief history of the relationship between colleges and employers for the last three decades. Pursuing the history leads us to find a more subtle mechanism for college students' entry into first jobs.

Previously, Japanese universities were more heavily involved in the selection and recommendation of their graduates to potential employers (Brinton and Kariya, forthcoming).[8] Until the late 1970s, most large Japanese companies limited their 'port of entry' for white-collar employees to a handful of elite universities in what was known as the 'reserved university system' or *shitei-kou-sei*. College professors or administrators in charge of job placement sent letters of recommendation to employers. Because of such a policy of restricting recruiting to specific institutions, job seekers from other educational institutions could not even apply to these companies, because the latter only accepted application forms from particular universities.

According to a survey conducted in 1975, among samples listed in the First Rank of the Tokyo Stock Market, 35.1 per cent of large firms adopted this 'closed-door' policy for managerial and clerical jobs, and 46.6 per cent for engineering and technical jobs for college graduates (Keizai Doyukai 1975).[9]

This closed-door system of hiring college graduates has, however, come in for substantial criticism, probably because college graduates were seen as a prospective elite. Social critics criticized those practices, and the mass media claimed that the closed-door policy was unfair and was the main reason for the exacerbation of the famous Japanese 'examination hell'. Complaining on behalf of students 'rejected at the front door', they blamed this closed-door policy for unfairness (Ogata 1975).

Responding to such criticisms against 'degreeocracy', companies began opening their doors to students from other universities from the late 1970s. This 'free application policy', which allowed students from any college to apply to those companies, then, became a more common hiring arrangement among large companies.

Those free-market arrangements set out in the late 1970s have prevailed widely through the 1980s. Under these arrangements, it was assumed that Japanese college students were in a free market without institutional linkages. But, in fact, despite the introduction of a 'free application policy', more subtle linkages between colleges and employers, alumni–student networks, replaced the old closed-door policy.

A content analysis of graduates' reports about their job-hunting experiences at a university indicates that this really happened (Kariya et al. 1993);[10] the analysis shows that frequencies of reports referring to school recommendation decreased from 35 per cent in 1975 to zero in 1980. Instead, the number of reports mentioning contacts with alumni rapidly increased. In 1975, only about 40 per cent of graduates referred to their relations with alumni in their reports, but the rate increased to higher than 60 per cent in 1980, and reached 80 per cent in 1981.

Documents from university placement offices also indicate that during the early 1980s students' meeting with alumni became an integral part of job-hunting activities. A guidebook of job search for students published by a placement office of a private university referred to the importance of visiting alumni for the first time in 1980. Earlier versions of the guidebook published before that year mentioned nothing about meeting with alumni as a part of job-search activities. But in the guidebooks published after that year, senior students are encouraged to meet their alumni to find a job. According to these students' and institution's reports, we infer that alumni–student relations have become important during the 1980s and these relationships have created bridges between universities and employers even after the introduction of the free application policy.

Indeed, it is not unusual that alumni convey information about jobs and firms to current students. Alumni also transmit information about job applicants to employers. Although the old boy network exists in other industrial countries, Japan is different from other countries, especially in the degree of organizations' involvement. Both universities and firms are active in Japan to utilize alumni–student relations. Universities' placement offices, on the one hand, file lists of alumni's current positions, firms, and their addresses and phone numbers of offices and show them to job seeking senior students. Career offices also encourage students to make a contact with alumni who work for a company in which the student wants to get a job.[11]

On the other hand, firms use alumni–student relations for recruitment. Many firms, especially large ones, use young employees with less than ten years' work experience as recruiters or *rikuruuta* as they are known, who are temporarily given roles to make contact with job-seeking senior students from their old universities. Some companies even authorize them to screen candidates. Graduates often reported their roles in selection processes in companies.[12]

As shown, young employee-recruiters are involved in the hiring process and their involvement in hiring decisions is more formal and better organized by companies than the case of old boy networks in other countries, which are more implicit and less accepted socially in formal recruitment processes.

Both universities' placement offices and students note that visiting alumni is a crucial part of job hunting. Thus placement offices are organizationally involved in those processes. Unlike Japanese high schools, universities do not recommend students to employers, but do help students meet alumni.

The nature of these alumni–student relations lies in its semi-formality (Brinton and Kariya, forthcoming). Meeting with alumni is partly an informal activity for students. But both universities and firms are actively involved in creating these relationships for their formal purposes. In fact, both employers and students regard these relations as neither fully formal nor completely informal. Accordingly, alumni–student relationships in Japan may be referred to as semi-formal linkages.

To what extent do these semi-formal linkages affect transition of college students to first jobs? Does the use of these linkages increase students' chances to acquire a good job? How do other factors such as college rank, students' GPA, and their family background influence first-job assignment through these linkages? Do these linkages strengthen or weaken meritocracy for selection of students into 'good' job opportunities? These questions will be answered in the next section.

Meritocracy in the Transition from College to Work: Multivariate Analyses

To examine what factors influence transition of business major students to the first jobs, we conduct logit regression and path analyses, which estimate effects of students' family background, semi-institutional linkages, and academic achievements on desirable job allocation.

We used a data-set from a survey of 704 male college students in business-related majors in nine Japanese universities, carried out a few months before graduation when students had already found jobs where they would begin their work career upon graduation. We excluded those who obtained jobs in public-sector employment. Thus, our sample to be analysed are those with private firms' jobs. Samples with missing values are also eliminated from the analyses. Finally, 572 male students are our target for analyses here.

The variables used for analyses are shown in Table 10.7. Because large firms are believed to provide higher salaries and better work conditions, we use company size as a dependent variable.[13] Then we make a dummy vari-

TABLE 10.7. *Dependent and independent variables for analyses of the college-to-work transition*

Independent variables:
Dummy variables:
Father's occupation:
 FMAN: those whose father is a manager in a large firm or public office
 FPROF: those whose father is a professional
 FWHITE: those whose father is a white-collar worker in a large firm or public office
Parental education:
 FHIGH: those whose father had university education or higher
 MHIGH: those whose mother had higher education (4-year or 2-year college)
University Rank:
 TOPUNIV: those in top-ranking universities with Z-score (HENSACH) 70 or higher
 SECUNIV: those in second-ranking universities with Z-score (HENSACH) 60 to 69
Job Search Methods:
 PERSONAL CONNECTION: those who used personal connections to find a job
Number of OBs: the number of 'old boys' (i.e. alumni) respondents met for job search
GRADE: Grade at university. 1 = more than 70% of subjects obtained As; 2 = 50–69%; 3 = 30–49%; 4 = less than 30%

Dependent variables (first-job opportunities):
LARGE: those who have jobs in large firms

---

able of the dependent variable (large vs. smaller firms) to examine the distribution of the likelihood of obtaining jobs in a large firm.

Independent variables used are also listed in Table 10.7. As for family background, we used three dummy variables of father's occupation, and two dummy variables of parents' education. For other independent variables, two dummy variables of university's rank, two variables of job-search methods, and students' grades are included in the analysis. As for the two job-search method variables, we have one dummy variable for personal connection (1 if students used personal connections to find jobs, otherwise 0), and the other variable indicating the extent to which students used the alumni network measured by the number of alumni whom students met during their job search. The means and standard deviations of the variables are shown in Table 10.8.

TABLE 10.8. *Means and standard deviations of variables used in the analyses*

Variable	Mean	Std Dev
Large	.50	.50
FMAN	.21	.41
FPROF	.06	.23
FWHITE	.10	.30
FHIGH	.36	.48
MHIGH	.19	.39
TOPUNIV	.16	.36
SECUNIV	.28	.45
GRADES	1.97	.89
N. OF OBs	13.95	20.59
PERSONAL CONNECTION	.17	.37

Before going on to the analyses for college–work transition, let us examine to what extent chances to enter top-rank universities are determined by students' family background. A logit regression produces the outcome that parents' education and father's occupation have a significant effect on the chances of being admitted to a top-rank university (Table 10.9). Those whose parents have higher educational qualifications are more likely to be top-rank university students. Students whose fathers are managers in large firms or public offices are also given more chances to enter top universities. Thus, the chance to enter top-rank universities is greatly influenced by students' family background. It is worth keeping this in mind, when we interpret results from analyses for the college-to-work transition.

TABLE 10.9. *Logit analysis of the chances of attending a top-ranking university*
(N = 572)

Variable	B	SE	Sig
FMAN	.6099	.2794	.0291
FPROF	−.3116	.5814	.5919
FWHITE	.1452	.4153	.7266
FHIGH	1.0558	.2842	.0002
MHIGH	.7580	.2911	.0092
Constant	−2.5619	.2111	.0000

*Dependent variable is chance to attend top-ranking universities with Z-score (HEN-SACHI) higher than 70

Now let us look at the results from logit regression for the chances of being hired by a large firm (Table 10.10). Four different models are employed. Model 1 takes students' family background as the only independent variable. From this, we find that those students whose parents have higher education degrees and those whose fathers are in managerial positions in large firms or public offices have a greater likelihood of obtaining a job in a large firm.

We add two dummy variables of university rank to the analysis (Model 2). The result shows that the effects of family background decrease greatly, while only FMAN (fathers are managers) remains significant. Instead, the two dummy variables of university rank show very strong positive effects on the chance to be hired in large firms. In particular, students from top-rank universities have a great advantage in obtaining jobs in large firms. These results suggest that a large part of influence from family background is transferred to university rank, and that a hierarchy of higher education institutions determines students' job opportunities greatly. In this sense, academic performance plays an important role in the college-to-work transition in Japan. But the effect of FMAN (manager-fathers) is still significant. This outcome also indicates that father's managerial position has a direct influence on the chance of being in a large firm. We will test whether this direct influence comes through personal ties or semi-institutional linkages later.

In Model 3, students' grades are put into the equation. But the results do not change greatly. Grades within a college do not have a significant effect, and other variables' coefficients do not change much from the result of Model 2 analysis. Unlike high-school students' transition to work, grades in college do not have a clear influence on job opportunities. This result indicates that a rank order of colleges rather than grades within a college is used as a meritocratic selection criterion to screen students to large firm jobs.

TABLE 10.10. *Logit analysis of the chances of being hired by a large firm*

Variable	Model 1		Model 2		Model 3		Model 4	
	B	SE	B	SE	B	SE	B	SE
FMAN	0.852	0.234***	0.586	0.267*	0.596	0.297*	0.532	0.277
FPROF	−0.126	0.384	0.077	0.440	−0.042	0.442	−0.206	0.479
FWHITE	−0.110	0.292	−0.265	0.338	−0.249	0.340	−0.281	0.347
FHIGH	0.646	0.208**	0.342	0.237	0.286	0.241	0.319	0.247
MHIGH	0.609	0.266*	0.356	0.308	0.371	0.312	0.368	0.321
TOPUNIV			2.999	0.399***	3.131	0.422***	2.433	0.464***
SECUNIV			1.840	0.220***	1.838	0.223***	1.278	0.266***
GRADES					0.192	0.115	0.138	0.118
No. of OBs							0.028	0.009**
PERSONAL CONNECTION							−0.485	0.283
Constant	−0.477	0.121***	−1.156	0.153	−1.152	0.282***	−1.370	0.296***

* Sig. <0.05   **<0.01   ***<0.001

330   *Takehiko Kariya*

When we include two variables of job-search methods into the equation, we obtain very interesting results (Model 4). All the family background variables become insignificant. University ranking still has a marked and significant effect. The number of old boys contacted during job search has a significant effect: the more students meet, the more likely they are to be hired by a large firm. Thus, semi-institutional linkages increase the likelihood of employment in large companies. In contrast, the use of personal connections has a negative and insignificant effect. This result suggests that a direct influence from father's managerial positions (FMAN) may not occur through personal ties. Rather, we speculate that a socio-cultural environment of a family, where fathers are managers in large firms, may transmit preferable business-cultural-milieu to their offspring.

To investigate how semi-institutional linkages works in more detail, we carried out a path analysis. In place of the dummy variable, firm size, we used the number of employees as a dependent variable, and excluded some independent variables in order to simplify the path diagram (see Figure 10.1 and Table 10.11).[14]

The same findings are repeated from the above logit regression. University ranking has a great effect; the number of old boys also has a considerable influence, father's occupation (managerial positions in large firms or public offices) has a positive and significant direct effect, but grades and personal ties do not have significant direct effects on the dependent variable. University ranking has both direct and indirect effects, and the indirect effect comes through alumni–student relationships. High-ranking universities produce more students in large firms, year after year, than lower ranking institutions, and the 'stock of alumni' in these large firms constitutes a social resource for future students from the same colleges. By these direct and indirect effects, students from higher ranking universities have an advantage in acquiring those good jobs.

On the contrary, personal ties have a significant, negative effect on old-boy contacts, insofar as students who used personal ties tended to meet less alumni for job search. This indicates that the use of personal ties is incompatible with the use of alumni networks in the search for a job. Furthermore, father's occupation has no influence on the use of personal ties. From this finding, we infer that the direct effect of father's occupation (managers) does not go through those personal ties.

In summary, logit and path analyses support our hypothesis that semi-institutional linkages are involved in the college-to-work transition. The more students use alumni-connections for job search, the greater their chances of finding employment in large firms. Moreover, these linkages are not embedded in family-related ties. Linkages by personal ties and the old-boy network are thus incompatible.

TABLE 10.11. *Regression analysis for college-to-work transition*

Independent Variables	Dependent variables				
	Firm Size	No. of OBs	Personal Connections	Job Plan	Univ. Rank
Father's Occ.(FMAN)	470.02*	1.82	0.01	0.06	3.88***
Univ. Rank	48.54**	1.50***	0.00	0.02***	
Grades	4.06	0.71*	−0.02*	0.00	
Job Plan	462.30**	2.95*	−0.04		
Personal Connection	−83.95	−5.19**			
No. of OBs	16.38**				
Constant	−2009.45*	−82.73***	0.46**	−0.68***	60.58***
R^2	0.18***	0.46***	0.02*	0.09***	0.05***

$N = 464$ $p < .05$ ** $p < .01$ *** $p < .001$

Father's Occ.(FMAN): 1 for those whose fathers are managers, otherwise 0

Univ. Rank: Z-score of university

Grades: 1.5 for those with 10–20% of grades are As; 3.5 for 30–40% are As; 5.5 for 50–60% are As; 8.5 for 70% or more are As

Job Plan: 1 for students who had job plan to enter large firms in March of junior year, 0 for otherwise

Personal Connection: 1 for those who used personal connections for job search, 0 for otherwise

No. of OBs: the number of 'old boys' students met for jobs search

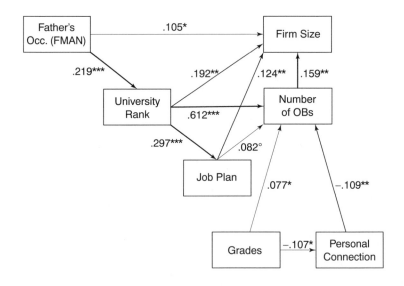

N = 464, Arrows are shown only when the coefficients are significant 5% level.
Sign. * < 0.05, ** < .001, *** < .0001.

FIG. 10.1. *Path analysis for college to work transition*

Our analyses also indicate that the college-to-work transition is strongly influenced by university rank which can be regarded as a meritocratic selection criterion. But from the analysis, we find that the odds of entering a top-ranking university is partly mediated by family background. Our analyses also show that the transition from college to large firms is partly influenced by ascriptive factors such as father's occupation. Students whose fathers are managers in large firms or public offices have a greater chance of working for a large firm. Despite the fact that these influences do not occur through personal ties, the ascriptive principle still remains in the selection of college students into 'good' jobs.

CONCLUSION

This chapter scrutinizes the transition mechanisms from high school and college to work in Japan. Two linkage models, institutional and semi-institutional linkages, were tested to explain how first-job entry from educational institutions is carried out. Analyses elucidated that institutional linkages between high schools and employers operate for high-school students' transition to work. We found that semi-institutional linkages between colleges and employers play an important role in allocating desirable jobs to college students.

These two linkages do not undermine the meritocratic component in job allocation, and indeed may even promote labour allocation based on academic achievement. From the same level of educational attainment, academic achievements (that is, high-school grades and institutional rank for college students) make a difference in first-job attainment both for high school and college students. In this sense, our analyses support a widely accepted image of Japanese society as meritocratic.

However, the allocation of Japanese students to first jobs is not altogether independent of the impact of social origin. Parental education and occupation have a substantial impact for entry to top-ranking universities. Family background also has a moderate and significant effect on the high-school-to-work and college-to-work transitions. High-school female students and male college students, whose fathers are managers, have a greater chance of finding better jobs, suggesting that ascriptive factors are partly involved in the transition from education to employment in Japan. But we also find that the effect of father's occupation works directly rather than indirectly through linkages for male college students. Thus, we conclude that ascriptive factors' influence do not derive from linkages. How family background affects the transition still remains an unanswered question for further research.

From those results of our analyses, which focus on substantial processes of school-to-work transition in Japan, we can discuss how educational attainment is associated with first-job opportunities. So far as educational attainment is used as a screening device for recruiting employees, it should be interpreted by employers. What meanings are given to educational achievement? The answer depends on how employers can collect what information about job applicants from educational achievement. Linkages provide a way of conveying such information to employers.

A close overview of the processes of the transition from education-to-employment in Japan reveals how meritocratic and non-meritocratic factors work through linkages. Japanese high schools and colleges have developed two types of linkages with employers, both of which give employers access to detailed information about job applicants. Where linkages transmit information about the merit of potential job applicants, they promote meritocratic labour allocation. Through these linkages, educational attainment is connected with job opportunities. In such cases, educational performance and job opportunities are not associated in abstract and functional relations. Instead, it is the substantive school-to-work transition processes that connect education and first-job attainment by giving real meanings to educational achievement.

NOTES

1. See Rosenbaum and Kariya (1989).
2. We did not include questions on family background, as this is difficult to obtain from Japanese high-school students given that schools try to maintain student privacy.
3. Japanese students graduate from school in March and begin work in April.
4. The sampled youth categorized originally as 'secondary and elementary education graduates, and higher education graduates' (JIL 1989), but because young people in the former category are from secondary schools in these three countries, for simplicity, we have changed the terms to just 'secondary school'.
5. The following analyses are reproduced from Rosenbaum and Kariya (1991).
6. Because the chances of male students to be hired in large firms are less selective than for women students' clerical jobs, we use only TOP 10 as grades variable here. In this analysis TOP 10 includes top-level grades from the best to the tenth in a classroom.
7. In 1994, about 65 per cent of students were studying in the humanities and social sciences in Japan.
8. The description of the college-to-work transition is based on Kariya et al. (1993); and Brinton and Kariya (forthcoming).
9. In the late 1960s, more large firms adopted the closed-door hiring policy. A survey revealed that in 1968, 24 per cent of firms hired exclusively from 'reserved' universities, and among large companies with more than 5,000 employees, this figure rose to 91.3 per cent (Tokyo Shoko Kaigisho 1968, cited from Ogata 1975). A student from a 'second-class' university reported in 1976 that '[I] telephoned the personnel office of a firm I'm interested in. But as soon as I told the person the name of my university, he hung up the phone call suddenly without even listening to me' (Nobi Nobi 1976).
10. Each year university placement offices collect and accumulate senior students' reports of their job-search experiences which are then distributed to future students. We collected one of these annual reports from 1975 to 1990 from a private university in Tokyo, and counted the number of cases (i.e. former students) containing references to university recommendations.
11. One graduate reported in 1981 that '[i]n September, the placement office is crowded with senior students, all struggling to get a list of the alumni to make contact with them' (Kariya et al. 1993).
12. '[I] was told by a personnel officer in a company to meet their younger employees, so I did. Afterwards, I realized they evaluated me and reported it to the personnel office' (graduate from a private university, 1980).
    '[I]t is not unusual for a recruiter's evaluation to lead to hiring' (graduate from a private university, 1981).

'[Y]ou should visit OBs ("old boys"). Those visits will qualify you to go forward to official job interviews' (graduate from a private university, 1983).

13. As we do not have exact numbers of employees for each firm, we have given crude figures for the four categories of firm size as follows: 5,000 for top-ranking companies in a given industry; 1,000 for companies listed on the Tokyo Stock Market; 500 for second-ranking companies in a given industry; and 300 for small and medium-sized enterprises.

14. This analysis is taken from Kariya (1995). The analysis was already reported by Hirasawa Kazusi in Kariya (1995), but the interpretation presented here is that of Kariya.

11

Education and Early Occupation in the Netherlands around 1990

Categorical and Continuous Scales and the Details of a Relationship

PAUL M. DE GRAAF AND WOUT C. ULTEE

INTRODUCTION: SCALES AND DETAILS

It has, somewhat facetiously, been remarked that there is a great divide in the literature on social stratification. On the one hand, there are various studies regarding the social scale as one long continuum. On the other hand, although two-class schemas are no longer used, a great many analyses still treat a society's structure as a limited number of discrete classes. Consequently research conducted against the background of the first assumption primarily employs linear regression techniques, and research involving the second assumption log-linear models and multinomial logistic regression techniques. Linear regression was quite influential in the 1960s (Duncan and Hodge 1963) and yielded the status attainment model. Recently, log-linear modelling has been on the ascent (Erikson and Goldthorpe 1992). This type of analysis has resulted in a core model of social fluidity for industrial societies in general, with distinctive deviations from this model for particular combinations of certain classes in specific countries. Log-linear techniques are applied when studying an association between two categorical variables without assuming one variable being a condition for the other; when various variables are assumed to cause a variable comprising more than two categories, multinomial logistic regression techniques are favoured.

Status attainment models were initially criticized as being too concerned with testing hypotheses holding that some individual characteristic accounts for a person's occupational status. That is, these models were deemed individualistic. At one time it also was held that log-linear models describe a country's mobility pattern and for that reason are holistic.

However, as Hauser (1978: 922) remarked, 'the important distinction is not between units of analysis, but between levels of measurement and of detail.' Status attainment models also depict what is going on in a society, since 'a scalar measure of association between status variables is no less an indicator of "mobility structure" than is a set of coefficients pertaining to the interior cells of a mobility table'. Erikson and Goldthorpe's finding of a core model of social fluidity with specific deviations for particular classes in certain countries has made clear that the relation within a country between the origin and the destination of its inhabitants cannot be summarized by a single measure, as in status attainment models. The core model of social fluidity comprises several parameters, and to apply this model fruitfully to specific countries, additional parameters have to be introduced.

Accepting the value of testing the hypothesis that the relation between origin and destination can be summarized with only a single parameter, against the hypothesis that several parameters are necessary to characterize it, the question arises of how to describe the relation between origin and education and the relation between education and destination. After all, a status attainment model not only incorporates measures for social origin and destination, but also for education, the variable supposed to mediate between origin and destination. The question of how to capture for various contemporary industrial countries the relation between origin and education has been addressed by Shavit and Blossfeld (1993). This chapter addresses the question of what is gained for the contemporary Netherlands if the relation between the education and the destination of its inhabitants is not captured by a single parameter of a model regressing a continuous variable on a continuous variable, but is instead summarized into several parameters of a model regressing a polytomous variable on a polytomous variable. As middle cases we consider the regression of a continuous variable on several dichotomies, and the regression of a polytomous variable on a continuous variable. The data analysed cover those who left school less than ten years ago, and pertain to the period around 1990. The latter restriction was made so as to focus the transition from education to occupation.

Our interest in this question is not simply methodological, but primarily substantive. A perusal of the International Standard Classification of Occupations by the International Labour Office (ILO 1990) makes clear that both a continuum as well as some polychotomy might be projected behind its zillion occupational titles. However, a glance at for instance the International Standard Classification of Education devised by the United Nations Educational, Scientific and Cultural Organization (UNESCO 1976) suggests that a schema comprising a limited number of categories might be more appropriate than some continuous scale. Education has a limited number of levels—lower, intermediate, higher—and within levels usually no more than two directions—general and vocational—are distinguished. Any attempt to turn such a classification into a more or less continuous scale pertaining to, say, the number of years usually spent in school to obtain certain credentials, masks possible differences which merit empirical study rather than automatic elimination. Indeed, one guess is that when analysing the relation between education and occupation within a country at some point in time, those with vocational education are placed more tightly into some slot of a country's occupational structure than those with a general education.

TRENDS IN DUTCH STRATIFICATION

Recent quantitative studies of long-term changes in the Dutch stratification system almost without exception have led to the conclusion that this system has become more open (Ganzeboom and Luijkx 1995). The association between father's and sons' occupational prestige—as measures on a prestige scale from the 1950s—has decreased gradually between 1954—the first year for which a prestige table is available—and the early 1990s. The association between father's social class and sons' social class according to the class schema of Erikson, Goldthorpe, and Portocarero (1979) has decreased since 1970, the first year for which a class table can be constructed.

Status attainment models distinguishing the Dutch population into cohorts born since World War I (De Graaf and Luijkx 1995) have led to the conclusion that both for men and women the direct effect of father's occupational status on their level of education has decreased, and the direct effect of father's occupational status on the occupational status of these men and women has almost completely disappeared. The effect of social background on education weakened gradually from the turn of the century onwards, telling against hypotheses holding that specific legal changes had straightforward effects. For men, the direct effect of education on occupation increased, for women it slightly decreased. The explanation proffered for the finding that for women the relation between education and occupation has become weaker invokes a selective increase of the labour-force participation of Dutch women. These status attainment models regressed continuous variables for occupation on continuous variables for education.

Erikson and Goldthorpe applied their core model of social fluidity to a Dutch father–son class mobility table for the 1980s. They found some indications that the Dutch pattern of fluidity is distinctive: there was more mobility than predicted by the core model between the routine non-manual class and the service class, and less mobility than expected between the non-skilled industrial workers and the routine non-manual classes (Erikson and

Goldthorpe 1992: 171). In a study of thirteen industrial countries, the Netherlands and Sweden were the only ones to show in recent decades a decreasing relation between origin and education, with education being taken as a categorical variable and origin as a continuous variable (Shavit and Blossfeld 1993).

Until now, models of the relation between education and occupation in the Netherlands deployed continuous measures. Given models for this country of the relation between origin and destination and between father's occupation and education involving categorical variables, it is desirable for the Netherlands to establish the relation between education and occupation as obtained with categorical variables for education and occupation, and compare it with the association between education and occupation as measured on continuous scales. This comparison is the aim of this chapter.

Given Erikson and Goldthorpe's (1992) seminal study, it is obvious that in the present analysis the classes making up a country's social structure will be distinguished by way of the schema developed by Erikson and Goldthorpe. As a standard for levels of education, a schema recently developed by Müller et al. (1989) has been proposed. In the following section we gauge the applicability of this classification as part of a review of the history of Dutch educational institutions. This is followed by a description of the institutions underpinning the Dutch labour market, especially the institutions governing the transition from school to work. We then go on to outline the nature of our Dutch data, and take a brief look at the relation between education and employment. Subsequently, we model the relation between education and destination by linear-regression techniques, and apply logistic models to characterize the relation between education and destination using social origins as a control variable, before going on to discuss our results in the concluding section.

EDUCATION IN THE NETHERLANDS

In the sixteenth century the Low Countries—then ruled by Spanish kings—became the first colony ever to become politically independent of an imperial power, when a combination of a religious protest and a tax revolt led to the formation of the Republic of the Seven United Dutch Provinces. The political ascent of the Dutch Republic went hand in hand with the emergence of Amsterdam as the centre of the emerging world economy (Wallerstein 1974), and the flowering of the Dutch system of what now is called tertiary education.[1] The emphasis placed by Protestantism on the need for all believers to be able to read the Bible for themselves probably accounts for the fact that primary schooling was widespread in the Dutch Republic.[2]

The main change in the Dutch educational system during the nineteenth century was a reform of secondary education. The Dutch secondary education was traditionally built around Latin and Greek which were prerequisites for university entry, but in the 1850s, the Dutch Government founded the *Hogere Burger Scholen*, a type of secondary education more attuned to the demands of commerce and industry and consisting of modern languages, mathematics, and physics.

In the twentieth century, three changes must be mentioned. The first regarded school financing. In the nineteenth century, primary schooling was state funded. Schools taught—apart from arithmetic, reading, history, and geography—Christian virtues, but since most schools were attended by both Protestants and Catholics, Bible reading was not always part of the curriculum. This motivated orthodox Protestants and Catholics to set up their own privately financed schools. This led to the so-called *Schoolstrijd*, an issue that was settled during World War I with the introduction of full state financing of 'special schooling' (Lijphart 1968). The number of pupils attending these schools increased rapidly, from about 30 per cent of all primary school pupils in 1900, to about 45 per cent in 1920, and to 70 per cent in 1938.

The second change was the introduction of an umbrella law on education, the *Mammoetwet*, at the end of the 1960s (Dronkers 1983). Although this law did not do away with selection of students at the end of primary school (at the age of 12) for the three types of secondary school (lower vocational, intermediate general, and higher general education (academic and non-academic)), it did provide new ways of moving within and between levels, and gave vocational education a more prominent place compared with general education. The structure of the present Dutch system of education is shown in Figure 11.1.

As regards subjects taught at intermediate level and the occupations catered for by vocational schooling, in vocational schools of whatever level, general schooling is included such as foreign languages and mathematics—the former sometimes being geared to specific vocations. Students at all types of schools have a great deal of choice in examination subjects.

In lower vocational schooling an effort was made to cater to both the industrial (welding, bricklaying, decorating, and tailoring) and service sectors (care of the elderly, baking and confectionery making, and retail clothes selling). Intermediate vocational education may consist of car maintenance, producing chemical reactions and surveying chemical processes, bookkeeping, stock management, and salary administration. Higher vocational education comprises nursing, training for naval officers, social work and teaching. Engineering in the sense of design and calculation is taught in technical universities; supervision and execution of the construction of roads and boats is taught in intermediate vocational schools. Most vocational schools

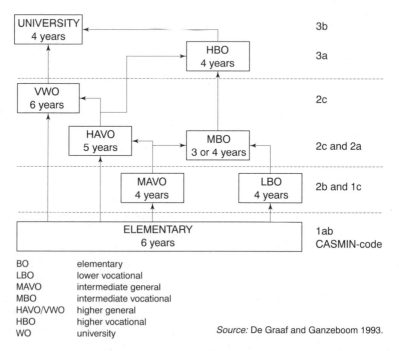

BO   elementary
LBO   lower vocational
MAVO   intermediate general
MBO   intermediate vocational
HAVO/VWO   higher general
HBO   higher vocational
WO   university

Source: De Graaf and Ganzeboom 1993.

FIG. 11.1. *Contours of the Netherlands' educational system*

do not simply have various shorter periods of apprenticeship outside school with an employer, but so-called practice-years. In the councils overseeing the various types of vocational education, employer organizations are represented. At the tertiary level, universities are a curious mix of vocational (engineering, law, and medicine) and classical (history, languages, etc.) studies. Current school-leaving age in the Netherlands is 16 years. Until the age of 18, working adolescents attend compulsory schooling for several days a week organized by their employment branch.

The third change regards the gradual lowering of the financial barriers to post-compulsory education. Prior to World War II, fees were not payable for secondary schooling, and schools funded books for special social categories. During the post-war period, a grants system was introduced for the children of low-income parents studying at university, and high-income parents could obtain tax breaks if their children remained in post-compulsory education. Since the 1980s, all people aged 18 or over in any type of education have been entitled to a grant covering the living and studying costs. This system was subsequently tightened up by lowering the number of years for which a grant could be obtained, partial replacement of grants by loans, and proof of progress while being registered at a school.

This overview of the Dutch educational system and the way it took its present shape, indicates that although it confronts students with a large number of choices, it also allows for flows between its various levels. A hypothesis about this feature might hold that the gradient of the relation between education and occupation will not show sharp breaks. This review also suggests that if a core pattern of the relation between education and occupation were proposed for contemporary industrial societies using the schema of levels of education proposed by Müller and his colleagues for international comparisons (Müller et al. 1989), the Netherlands would show particular specifications of this pattern. The schema most fundamentally has three sub-levels: primary, secondary, and tertiary education. The primary level consists of three levels: inadequate completion of primary education (1a); completed primary education (1b); and primary education plus some vocational training (1c). At the secondary level, there are three sub-levels: some intermediate general education plus additional vocational education (2a); full intermediate general education not leading to academic education (2b); and higher secondary education leading to academic education (2c). At the tertiary level there are two sub-levels: higher vocational education (3a); and academic education (3b).

When applied to the Netherlands, this international schema seems to place Dutch secondary lower vocational education below Dutch secondary intermediate general education. In addition it gives Dutch intermediate general education and Dutch intermediate vocational equal ranking. However, the rules of the Dutch educational system are such that secondary lower vocational education (1c), more or less equals intermediate general education (2b), and that intermediate vocational education (2a), is above intermediate general education (2b). After primary school, the choice is between lower vocational education, intermediate general education, and higher general education. After lower vocational education people may enter the labour market, but they also may continue into intermediate vocational education. In addition, after intermediate general education, people may start working, continue into intermediate vocational education, or enter higher general education. The relations between the Dutch system of education and the schema of Müller and colleagues are indicated in the last column of Figure 11.1.

THE DUTCH LABOUR MARKET AROUND 1990

Educational expansion has been very strong in the Netherlands and the upgrading of the labour market has not kept the same pace (Huijgen 1989).

Although the proportion of jobs requiring higher education has grown and the average job level of the younger generations has generally increased, the value of all educational qualifications has decreased at the same time, with the value of lower level qualifications dropping more rapidly than that of higher level credentials. Those with higher level qualifications have moved into jobs previously reserved for the less educated, while those with the lowest qualifications have been pushed into badly paid and insecure jobs, or unemployment. Although it is difficult to predict which developments will take place in the coming years, these trends are likely to continue. The value of educational qualifications will corrode, and especially so for the newcomers with the lowest qualifications.

One feature of the present Dutch labour market contrasts somewhat with the marked devaluation of the lowest qualifications and the smaller devaluation of higher level qualifications. This is the high unemployment rate among those with tertiary academic education in the population at large. As of the early-1990s, the unemployment rate for university graduates has been higher than that for people with higher or intermediate vocational education. A prime hypothesis about these differences is that universities cannot refuse students unless explicitly authorized by the Ministry of Education, whereas intermediate secondary and higher vocational schools may do so on their own, and in actual fact do refuse students in this manner. Another hypothesis is that the high unemployment rate itself prolongs educational careers for want of job prospects. Indeed, the unemployment rate for those leaving school without a qualification is lower than for those leaving school with a qualification. A third explanation is that, with cutbacks on government spending, the universities, as the prime pool for (semi-)government employees, have suffered most.

This somewhat unexpected relationship between education and unemployment is one of several developments in the Netherlands since the 1980s that made clear that the institutions regulating the Dutch labour market presumed full employment and that these institutions have to be changed to cope with a situation of structurally high unemployment and to ward off the emergence of a two-tier society.

Judging by its unemployment rate, the Netherlands weathered the first oil shock of the 1970s quite well, whereas the second oil shock of the early 1980s was accompanied by a dramatic rise in the unemployment rate. Whereas the unemployment rate was below 5 per cent at the end of the 1970s, according to the European Union definition it was 8.1 per cent in 1981, 11.9 per cent in 1983, 12.4 per cent in 1984, and 10.5 per cent in 1985 (the corresponding percentages for the EU-10 being 7.0, 8.9, 9.4, and 9.5). What a lot of people guessed at that time, and what became authoritative after a parliamentary inquiry in the early 1990s, was that the official unemployment rate understated the prevalence of unemployment, the main reason being that older workers facing lay-off were declared disabled.[3]

The brunt of structurally high unemployment was borne by young people. First, because given the strong influence of trade unions and work councils in employer–employee relations, in leaner times a policy of no firing and no hiring was followed. Second, because until the early 1980s the relative position of young people in Dutch society had been improving. This happened as a consequence of a lowering of the voting age from 23 during most part of the twentieth century, to 21 in 1967, and 18 in 1972. In an attempt to incorporate young people into the political system, regulations stipulating lower wages for those under a certain age were scrapped, regulations with respect to the chances of obtaining a stipend for studies become easier with the amount of money awarded by a stipend increasing, and social-security regulations were changed so that school-leavers who did not immediately find work, obtained state benefits for an indefinite period without a lot of strings attached to them. This strong position of young people vis-à-vis the Dutch welfare state system has to some extent been responsible for high levels of youth unemployment. In addition, it became much easier for young people to leave the parental home as social housing programmes allocated housing to single persons and allowed them to draw rent subsidies if their income was below a certain level.

At the end of the 1980s, in an effort to clamp down on the cost of social security and youth unemployment, these regulations began to change. Young people to some extent had responded to the structurally high unemployment rate by extending the period they attended school, and thus postponing unemployment and increasing government expenditure on educational grants. The official number of years necessary to complete a university programme was lowered from five to four in the second part of the 1980s, and the system of educational grants became decidedly less liberal in the 1990s. Starting around 1990, school-leavers who did not find work were more often pressed by governmental employment offices into work-experience places, made available by employers as a part of collective bargaining. In addition, in an attempt to entice employers, in collective wage agreements youth wages were reintroduced. In addition, the level of unemployment and disability benefits was lowered, as well as the length of the period people could claim unemployment benefits. People under the age of 50 in disability schemes are re-examined, with the definition of a suitable other job having widened. Until now, the Minister of Education still has not seduced the universities into a stronger selection of students. This would be something of a feat in times where the absolute number of students for demographic reasons is falling and universities are being paid for both the number of students entering university and the number of students obtaining a degree.

DATA

Two sets of data are analysed in this analysis. The first set is taken from the Netherlands Mobility File 1985–1992, a collection of smaller surveys undertaken for various purposes in these years comprising major variables in status attainment research and class analysis. We selected from this file all those with less than ten years out of school and ever employed. This resulted in rather small data set for 1,021 men and 1,084 women. This perhaps somewhat heterogeneous file contains variables on social origin and will be used mainly for the purpose of estimating the effects of family background. The second and more reliable set of data is extracted from the Labour Market Survey 1991 undertaken on a permanent basis by the Netherlands' Bureau of Statistics (CBS) to establish, among others, the structure of the Dutch labour market and the monthly unemployment rate for the Netherlands. It comprises 7,199 men and 7,663 women which left school less than ten years ago and which are not drafted into the military. Of these men, 6,499 are currently employed, and of these women 5,864. This comparably coded file lacks data on social origins. Our research strategy will be to employ the Netherlands Mobility File just to find out whether the omission of social origins in the Labour Market Survey of 1991 biases our findings on the value of education.[4]

Table 11.1 presents the frequency distributions for educational attainment for both the Netherlands Mobility File and the Labour Market Survey 1991. For the latter survey the table presents distributions for all those who left education between 1981 and 1991, and for a selection of persons who are currently employed. We distinguish between primary education (1ab), lower vocational secondary (1c), intermediate vocational secondary (2a), intermediate general secondary (2b), higher secondary general (2c), higher vocational (3a), and academic education (3b). The table makes clear that a large proportion of those who finished their educational careers in the 1980s have had vocational training. According to the Labour Market Survey of 1991 only about 22 per cent of the men and about 27 per cent of the women have no vocational training. The average educational attainment of employed persons is higher than the educational attainment of the whole sub-population which left school between 1981 and 1991, which shows that the probability to be employed is dependent on schooling.

A further inspection of Table 11.1 makes clear that the Netherlands Mobility Survey 1985–1992 sample somewhat over-represents those with higher levels of education. As a result, especially the category with intermediary vocational training is under-represented in the file. We do not know to what extent this is due to a response bias or to coding difficulties. It has

TABLE 11.1. *Distribution of educational attainment according to Labour Market Survey (CBS/EBB 1991) and Netherlands Mobility File (NMF 1985–1992)*

	Labour Market Survey 1991 selection: less than ten years after leaving school, not in military service		Labour Market Survey 1991 selection: less than ten years after leaving school, employed		Mobility File 1985–1992 selection: less than ten years after leaving school, ever employed	
	men	women	men	women	men	women
1ab: elementary (BO: Basis Onderwijs)	9.0%	8.0%	7.1%	4.2%	5.8%	6.0%
1c: lower vocational (LBO: Lager Beroeps Onderwijs)	22.4%	14.7%	22.7%	13.1%	17.9%	14.7%
2a: intermediate vocational (MBO: Middelbaar Beroeps Onderwijs)	31.9%	35.4%	33.5%	39.5%	20.4%	23.7%
2b: intermediate general (MAVO: Middelbaar Algemeen Voortgezet Onderwijs)	7.5%	11.0%	7.0%	9.9%	12.0%	14.1%
2c: higher general (HAVO: Hoger Algemeen Voorgezet Onderwijs VWO: Voorbereidend Wetenschappelijk Onderwijs)	5.9%	7.7%	5.7%	8.0%	12.2%	14.1%
3a: higher vocational (HBO: Hoger Beroeps Onderwijs)	14.6%	18.3%	15.2%	19.9%	19.7%	21.3%
3b: university (WO: Wetenschappelijk Onderwijs)	8.6%	4.8%	8.8%	5.4%	11.9%	6.1%
Number of individuals	7,199	7,663	6,499	5,864	1,021	1,084

to be said that the present schema for coding educational qualifications presses older and newer types of education into one, and that the Dutch Central Bureau of Statistics partly for that reason abandoned computer coding of educational qualifications. It is likely that this merged file consists of files with different coding procedures. We must rely on the assumption that the relationship between family background, educational attainment and occupational achievement will not be biased.

EDUCATION AND EMPLOYMENT

Before analysing the relation between education and early occupation in the Netherlands around 1990, it might be good to have a quick look at the relation between education and various aspects of employment in our samples. What is the relationship between educational attainment and employment status, that is, being employed, unemployed, or outside the labour market?

In order to answer this question, our Labour Market Survey 1991 sample is broken down in Table 11.2 by sex, education, and current employment status. We observe that the employment status is strongly associated with educational attainment. For both men and women, the categories with only general training (1ab, 2b and 2c) show the highest probabilities of being out of the labour force. Women of whatever level of education are less likely to be currently employed than men. At all levels of education, women who have left school less than ten years before, are more likely than men to be outside the labour force. About 25 per cent of all women and about 3 per cent of all men who left school between 1981 and 1991 are out of the labour force.

As expected, we observe that for both men and women who left school less than ten years ago, unemployment is strongly associated with educational attainment. Unemployment rates are highest among those with primary school only, and lowest among those with intermediate or higher vocational education. In general, vocational training (categories 1c, 2a, and 3a) protects against unemployment, but university training (3b) offers lower employment probabilities than higher vocational training (3a). We argued that in the Netherlands there is no feedback process which limits participation in university education in times of labour-market saturation for academics, whereas such processes do exist for intermediate and higher vocational programmes. It is striking that even among those with lower vocational schooling (finished at the age of 16) unemployment is lower than among university graduates.

In Table 11.3 these findings are refined by a multinomial logit regression analysis. The table shows the effects of education on the log odds to be employed or unemployed relative to the log odds to be out of the labour market. The advantages of vocational training are clear, but the specific level of vocational training seems to be unimportant. The table also shows that the association between educational attainment and unemployment and the association between education and a position out of the labour market are comparable. Only a university degree gives a higher probability of being

TABLE 11.2. *Employment status by educational attainment and sex*

	Educational attainment							
	1ab	1c	2a	2b	2c	3a	3b	all
Men								
Employed	74.0%	93.9%	96.1%	85.8%	88.5%	95.2%	93.1%	92.0%
Unemployed	15.5%	4.6%	2.8%	8.1%	5.2%	3.0%	5.3%	5.1%
Not in labour force	10.5%	1.6%	1.1%	6.1%	6.3%	1.8%	1.6%	2.8%
Number of individuals	650	1,610	2,298	543	426	1,050	622	7,199
Women								
Employed	35.9%	63.6%	81.6%	63.4%	76.1%	75.0%	82.5%	71.7%
Unemployed	7.2%	4.7%	2.6%	3.0%	3.7%	3.6%	6.0%	3.7%
Not in labour force	56.9%	31.7%	15.9%	33.6%	20.2%	20.5%	10.7%	24.6%
Number of individuals	615	1,130	2,716	842	590	1,405	365	7,663

Selection: less than ten years after leaving school, not in military service, no missing information
Source: Labour Market Survey 1991 (EBB/CBS)

unemployed (and seeking employment), as compared to being out of the labour market (i.e. unemployed and not seeking employment), especially for women. This may suggest that people with university degrees do not accept a position out of the labour market and prefer to be unemployed, even if this does not bring them unemployment allowances.

TABLE 11.3. *Effects of educational attainment on employment status, relative to being out of the labour market, multinomial logit models*

	Employed	Unemployed
Men (N = 7,199)		
Intercept	1.870	0.260
1ab: elementary	0[a]	0[a]
1c: lower vocational	1.919	0.504~
2a: intermediate vocational	2.243	0.299~
2b: intermediate general	0.739	0.064~
2c: higher general	0.573	−0.468~
3a: higher vocational	2.261	0.605~
3b: university	1.991	0.944
Degrees of freedom	12	
Chi²	318.6	
Women (N = 7,663):		
Intercept	−0.475	−1.963
1ab: elementary	0[a]	0[a]
1c: lower vocational	1.147	0.094~
2a: intermediate vocational	2.068	−0.049~
2b: intermediate general	1.090	−0.189~
2c: higher general	1.739	0.439~
3a: higher vocational	1.690	0.052~
3b: university	2.330	1.353
Degrees of freedom	12	
Chi²	608.2	

Note: Out of labour force is the reference category.

Selection: less than ten years after leaving school, no missing information
    ~ denotes insignificance (p > .05)
    [a] denotes reference category

Source: Labour Market Survey 1991 (EBB/CBS).

Table 11.4 displays cross-tabulations of the sample by sex, education, and having a temporary or indefinite work contract, and by sex, education, and having a part-time or full-time job (working less or more than thirty-four hours). This table shows the labour-market attachment by education and sex. According to the first panel of Table 11.4, the number of men with a tem-

TABLE 11.4. *Labour-force attachment by educational attainment and sex*

	Educational attainment								Number of individuals
	1ab	1c	2a	2b	2c	3a	3b	all	
Proportion with temporary job:									
Men	14.0%	10.9%	8.4%	14.1%	16.3%	7.1%	22.9%	11.3%	6,112
Women	12.5%	11.9%	9.5%	11.1%	15.6%	10.9%	27.8%	11.8%	5,648
Proportion with part-time job (less than 34 hours):									
Men	9.3%	6.8%	3.9%	8.3%	9.8%	6.7%	8.0%	6.0%	6,104
Women	40.3%	32.5%	23.8%	31.8%	28.7%	34.9%	39.3%	28.7%	5,642

Selection: less than ten years after leaving school, employed (not self-employed or working family member), no missing information

Source: Labour Market Survey 1991 (EBB/CBS).

porary job as a percentage of all employed men hardly differs at all from the proportion of employed women. The lowest proportion can be observed among those with vocational education. For both men and women the proportion with a temporary job is highest among those with an academic qualification. Once more it is clear that those with vocational training—irrespective of level—are the most in demand on the labour market.

The second panel of Table 11.4 shows that women are more likely to have a part-time job than men, which of course is a result of women's responsibilities for childcare. In the Netherlands most women have full-time jobs after they finish education, but almost none of them continue to work in full-time jobs after they have got their first child (De Graaf and Vermeulen 1997), with no exception for the higher educated. The proportions of women in part-time jobs presented in this table therefore resemble the relationship between educational attainment and the timing of the first child, and the suggestion of a strong connection of part-time work to educational attainment is not warranted. The same holds for men: the proportion of men with a part-time job does not seem to be associated strongly with educational attainment, although we see that those with general education (1a, 2b, 2c) and university training have a greater likelihood of entering part-time jobs. To sum up, those with vocational education have a higher labour-force attachment. No level stands out with respect to weak labour-force attachment, although the opportunities for those with low or intermediate general education and for university graduates are relatively small.

EDUCATION AND LEVEL OF OCCUPATION

In Table 11.5 we present the mean occupational prestige for the seven educational categories for both men and women, for both the Labour Market Survey 1991 and the Mobility File 1985–1992. Educational categories again are ranked according to the CASMIN schema for international comparisons. Prestige scores were assigned to occupational titles according to a scale developed for the Netherlands by Sixma and Ultee (1984). This scale ranges from thirteen for occupations with the lowest prestige to eighty-seven for occupations with the highest prestige.

In each of the four distributions, the gradient of the relation between levels of education and occupation prestige is less than fully smooth. As expected, in all four cases, those with low education (1ab and 1c) have less occupational prestige than those with the intermediate level of education (2a, 2b and 2c), whereas those with higher education (3a and 3b) have the highest occupational prestige. Within the intermediate and high-level categories some differences can be observed, but on the lowest level we observe that the average prestige of those with only primary education and those with low vocational training are very much alike. At the intermediate level, general education gives the smallest returns, followed by vocational training and higher general training. Intermediate vocational training (2a) clearly offers better labour-market opportunities than an intermediate general education (2b). This is hardly surprising because it takes three or four extra years of schooling to finish intermediate vocational training than intermediate general education. Intermediate vocational training and intermediate general education are both finished approximately at age 18 or 19. At the highest level of education we see that university education brings higher prestige jobs than higher vocational training.

TABLE 11.5. *Mean occupational prestige by education and sex*

	Labour Market Survey 1991		Mobility File 1985–1992	
	Men	Women	Men	Women
1ab: elementary	27.6	30.0	32.4	33.4
1c: lower vocational	30.1	31.8	32.2	33.4
2a: intermediate vocational	39.6	42.2	42.5	42.9
2b: intermediate general	35.1	38.7	40.7	42.6
2c: higher general	46.0	43.8	47.4	46.7
3a: higher vocational	61.9	54.1	57.3	55.7
3b: university	70.0	67.3	64.5	65.3
All	42.7	43.8	46.0	45.5
Standard deviation	19.8	16.2	19.1	17.0
Number of individuals	6,495	5,863	1,021	1,084

Selection: less than ten years after leaving school, employed (Labour Market Survey) or ever employed (Mobility File), no missing information

Occupational prestige: Dutch Ultee/Sixma prestige scale (Sixma and Ultee 1984)

Source: Labour Market Survey 1991 (EBB/CBS) and Mobility File 1985–1992.

Comparing men and women with the same level of education, we see that at the lower levels women have more occupational prestige than men, and at the higher levels less prestige than men. This is the result of the sex-specific occupational segregation: on average men and women have the same prestige, but women are concentrated in a relatively low number of occupations around the average. This corresponds to the lower standard deviation of the occupational prestige of women (16.2) when compared to the standard deviation of men (19.8). We regard the higher prestige for women with university education compared with men with university education according to the Mobility File 1985–1992 as a statistical fluke.

In Table 11.6 we regress, separately for men and women from our Mobility File 1985–1992, occupational prestige on a dummy version of our seven-level educational schema. In the first two columns we present the total effects of family background on occupational prestige. In the third and fourth columns no controls for father's occupational prestige and father's education are included, and in the last two columns both family background and educational attainment are taken into account. The models show that family background effects on occupational prestige are intermediated completely by educational attainment. Between the equation with only educational attainment and the equation with controls for both education and family background, the adjusted R^2 hardly improves and the coefficients for the indicators for family background are insignificant. These results display that the effects of educational attainment are not biased in the model without family background, which implies that an analysis of the larger and more representative Labour Market Survey 1991, which does not include variables for social origin, will not be far off the mark.

Therefore, in Table 11.7 we return to the far larger and more reliable Labour Market Survey 1991 and seek to establish the extent to which it is possible when predicting occupational prestige, to replace the six dummy variables for level of education by a continuous measure for the number of years spent in school to obtain a certain level of education. Is it just the length of the educational career which affects the level of the first job? The number of years spent in education by people with a certain level of education, is taken from Figure 11.1, giving each educational category the minimum years of education to complete it.

The adjusted R^2 of the linear regression of occupational prestige on six dummies for level of education for men is 0.467 and for women 0.310. When the six dummies have been replaced by the measure for years of education, the model deteriorates markedly, and the adjusted R^2 for men is 0.386 and for women 0.260. A comparison of these adjusted R^2 implies that the relation between education and a continuously measured occupation, is better described by a six-dummy version of educational attainment than by a continuously measured education. The parameter for years of schooling in Table 11.7 (columns b) indicates that one year of additional schooling has a return of 4.19 points of occupational prestige for men and of 3.16 points for women. This gender difference of about 25 per cent in the returns of schooling is statistically significant.

The regression equations of Table 11.7 repeat the results of Table 11.5 in which the mean occupational prestige score was broken down by educational attainment. We observe that the difference in mean occupational prestige

TABLE 11.6. *Effects of educational attainment on occupational prestige with and without controls for family background*

Education	Total family background effects		No controls for family background		Controls for family background	
	Men	Women	Men	Women	Men	Women
1ab: elementary	—	—	0[a]	0[a]	0[a]	.0[a]
1c: lower vocational	—	—	-0.0~	0.0~	-0.3~	0.0~
2a: intermediate vocational	—	—	10.4	9.6	9.8	9.1
2b: intermediate general	—	—	8.2	10.1	7.7	9.8
2c: higher general	—	—	14.9	12.5	14.0	11.5
3a: higher vocational	—	—	25.6	22.8	24.9	21.6
3b: university	—	—	30.3	31.7	29.4	30.3
Father's prestige	0.17	0.15	—	—	0.06~	0.06~
Parents' education	1.03~	2.88	—	—	-0.81~	0.39~
Intercept	36.6	35.1	32.1	33.1	30.9	30.5
R^2 adjusted	0.040	0.062	0.310	0.286	0.311	0.289
Number of individuals	684	693	684	693	684	693

Selection: less than ten years after leaving school, ever employed, no missing information

Occupational prestige: Dutch Ultee/Sixma prestige scale (Sixma and Ultee 1984)

~ denotes insignificance ($p > .05$)

[a] reference category

Source: Mobility File 1985–92.

TABLE 11.7. *Effects of educational attainment on occupational prestige*

Education	Men		Women	
	a	b	a	b
1ab: elementary	0[a]		0[a]	
1c: lower vocational	2.5		1.9	
2a: intermediate vocational	12.0		12.2	
2b: intermediate general	7.5		8.7	
2c: higher general	18.4		13.9	
3a: higher vocational	34.3		24.1	
3b: university	42.4		37.3	
Years of education		4.19		3.16
Intercept	27.61	−9.04	29.98	3.53
R^2 adjusted	0.467	0.386	0.310	0.260
Number of individuals	6,495	6,495	5,863	5,863

Selection: less than ten years after leaving school, employed, no missing information

Occupational prestige: Dutch Ultee/Sixma prestige scale (Sixma and Ultee 1984)

~ denotes insignificance (p > .05)

[a] reference category

Source: Labour Market Survey 1991 (EBB/CBS).

between the intermediate and the higher level is considerably larger than the difference between the lower and the intermediate level. On the lowest level of education there is only a small difference in occupational prestige between those with only primary education and those with low vocational training. On the intermediate level higher general education appears to be superior to intermediate vocational education, which takes about the same number of years of schooling, whereas intermediate general education is inferior. On the highest level, university training gives access to higher prestige jobs than higher vocational training. It is clear that the relationship between educational credentials and occupational prestige is not equal to the relationship between educational attainment and employment rates. Whereas vocational training gives better chances to find a job, it does not bring higher job levels. This last conclusion is limited to the lower and intermediate levels of education, because at the higher level the distinction between general and vocational training cannot be made.

All in all, it has to be said that a depiction of the relation between education and occupational prestige by way of dummies for level of education yields a more detailed picture than by way of a variable for years spent in education. In the Netherlands, the relationship between occupational prestige on a continuous scale and educational attainment is not captured well by taking education as a continuous variable according to the average number of years spent in school by those with a certain level of education. There are three major reasons for this observation. First, low vocational training does not bring much additional occupational prestige if compared to the returns of primary education, and the same more or less holds for intermediate general education. Second, on the higher levels of education the gain in occupational prestige brought by an additional year of education is decidedly higher than at the lower levels. Third, although the duration of higher vocational training and a university education are comparable, on average university degrees give access to higher status jobs.

EDUCATION AND CLASS

Tables 11.8 and 11.9 report on a multinomial logit model applied to the sample from the Mobility File 1985–1992, in which it is possible to control for family background. In these the seven levels of education are cross-classified against a five-class version of the schema developed by Erikson, Goldthorpe and Portocarero (1979). Class I/II is the service class, and Class III refers to the routine non-manuals; Class IVabc refers to the small self-employed (farmers and petty bourgeoisie); Class V/VI are the skilled manual occupations, and Class VIIab (the reference category in the model) refers to the semi-skilled and unskilled manuals.

Table 11.8 shows the total effects of father's class on first occupational class. The probability of entering the service class is dependent on having a father in this class. All other classes are not different with regard to the odds of finding a first position in the service class. The probability of having a first job in the routine non-manual class is clearly lower for the sons and daughters from manual origins. The odds of obtaining a position in the self-employed class is especially affected by having a father in this class. No immobility effects can be observed for the skilled manual class.

In Table 11.9 we add educational attainment to the model. The prime purpose of Table 11.9 is to establish the consequences of the omission of father's class in later models for the relation between education which are based on the Labour Force Survey 1991. For men, 14 of the 16 coefficients for father's class turn out to be insignificant, and for women 10 out of the 16. Given these findings, we can safely assume that the effects of educational attainment on occupational class are not seriously biased by the absence of family background and we can limit attention to multinomial logit models for tables taken from the Labour Market Survey 1991 file. The few significant effects show that some direct class inheritance effects are present,

TABLE 11.8. *Total effects of father's class on occupational class, relative to Class VIIab, multinomial logit models*

	I/II	III	IVabc	V/VI
Men (N = 1,021)				
Intercept	0.083	−0.550~	−2.079	−0.314
Father's class:				
I/II	1.023	0.748	−0.025~	0.126~
III	0.381~	1.043	−0.318~	−0.475~
IVabc	0.114~	0.359~	1.988	−0.424~
V/VI	−0.010~	−0.053~	−1.198~	0.314~
VIIab	0[a]	0[a]	0[a]	0[a]
Women (N = 1,084)				
Intercept	−0.180~	0.602	−2.071	−2.053
Father's class				
I/II	1.495	0.675	2.017	0.631~
III	0.483~	0.692	1.165~	−0.781~
IVabc	0.459~	0.225~	2.052	−1.280~
V/VI	0.262~	0.397~	1.183	0.443~
VIIab	0[a]	0[a]	0[a]	0[a]

Selection: less than ten years after leaving school, ever employed, no missing information

~ denotes insignificance (p > .05)

[a] denotes reference category

[b] denotes no person in category entered occupational class

Source: Mobility File 1985–1992.

especially with regard to the small self-employed, and to some extent also for the non-manual classes, and more so for women than for men.

In Table 11.10 we cross-classify, for both men and women, social class by educational attainment. In this and all further tables we present statistics based on the Labour Market Survey. Now we use a class schema comprising seven classes. In contrast to Tables 11.8 and 11.9, we no longer merge Classes I and II, and we divide Class III into Classes IIIa and IIIb. Classes I and II consist of higher-grade and lower-grade professionals (controllers), respectively, and the distinction is mainly one based on necessary schooling and job level. Class IIIa refers to routine non-manual occupations in administration and commerce, whereas Class IIIb refers to routine non-manual occupations in value and services. The latter difference may be important for establishing differences in occupational achievement between men and women. Going from the lowest to the highest level of education, on the

TABLE 11.9. *Effects of educational attainment and father's class on occupational class, relative to Class VIIab, multinomial logit models*

	I/II	III	IVabc	V/VI
Men (N = 1,021)				
Intercept	−2.011	−1.756	−2.071	−1.107
1ab: elementary	0ᵃ	0ᵃ	0ᵃ	0ᵃ
1c: lower vocational	−0.034~	0.181~	−0.039~	1.048
2a: intermediate vocational	2.078	1.312	−0.040~	1.095
2b: intermediate general	1.538	1.722	−0.592~	0.609~
2c: higher general	2.408	1.830	0.472	0.032~
3a: higher vocational	4.171	2.285	−0.481	0.948~
3b: university	4.574	2.555	ᵇ	−0.192~
Father's class:				
I/II	0.278~	0.374~	−0.027~	0.162~
III	−0.179~	0.724	0.329~	−0.439~
IVabc	−0.345~	0.215~	2.027	−0.471~
V/VI	−0.263~	−0.146~	−1.189~	0.303~
VIIab	0ᵃ	0ᵃ	0ᵃ	0ᵃ
Women (N = 1,084)				
Intercept	−2.343	0.028~	−4.516	−3.323
1ab: elementary	0ᵃ	0ᵃ	0ᵃ	0ᵃ
1c: lower vocational	0.204~	−0.175~	−0.175~	1.616~
2a: intermediate vocational	1.844	0.697	0.121~	0.513~
2b: intermediate general	1.588	1.294	1.520~	1.468~
2c: higher general	2.301	0.893	0.543~	1.275~
3a: higher vocational	4.472	1.261	1.579	1.743~
3b: university	5.312	1.384	ᵇ	2.500~
Father's class:				
I/II	0.786	0.505	1.938	0.659~
III	−0.467~	0.490	1.011~	−0.834~
IVabc	0.110~	0.168~	2.017	−1.230~
V/VI	0.269~	0.361~	1.914	0.530~
VIIab	0ᵃ	0ᵃ	0ᵃ	0ᵃ

Selection: less than ten years after leaving school, ever employed, no missing information

~ denotes insignificance (p > .05)
ᵃ denotes reference category
ᵇ denotes no person in category entered occupational class

Source: Mobility File 1985–1992.

whole the proportion of those in a semi-skilled or unskilled manual job drops, and the proportion in the service class rises.

On the lowest level we observe again that more than half of men with some vocational training (1c) attain positions in the skilled manual class, and 31 per cent find their first jobs in the semi-skilled and unskilled classes. Only a small fraction finds a non-manual occupation. In general the occupational positions of those with lower vocational training are not distinctively different from persons with only primary education, although they have completed four more years of schooling. The enormous educational expansion which has taken place in the Netherlands turned intermediate and higher vocational training into something of a standard. Those with only lower vocational qualifications are pushed down to lower job levels. It has been shown that employers prefer more highly educated workers for the same jobs (Huijgen 1989), and those with primary schooling and low vocational training have to compete for the remaining lower grade jobs. However, it is remarkable that 40 per cent of those without any qualification enter a skilled manual job. Apparently in the Dutch case, the link between educational qualifications and jobs in manufacturing is quite weak.

Sex segregation in the Dutch labour market is such that women never have worked in skilled manual jobs. Women with lower education who entered the labour market in the 1980s found jobs in either semi-skilled and unskilled jobs or in the routine non-manual jobs. For women too the difference between those with only primary education and those with low vocational training is small. Yet some vocational training seems to increase the probability of entering a job in administration or in personal services (hairdressers, cleaners, etc.).

On the intermediate level we see important differences between those with intermediate vocational training (2a), intermediate general education (2b), and higher general education (2c). The chances for a higher class job of people with intermediate general education are significantly worse than those for the two other categories, which holds for men and women, although they are somewhat better than those of people on the low levels of education (1ab and 1c). People with intermediate general education are more likely than those with intermediate vocational education to be found in semi-skilled or unskilled manual occupations and in routine non-manual jobs. Intermediate vocational training brings opportunities to enter the non-manual class, but mainly so in routine jobs. About 15 per cent of all men and women with intermediate vocational training enter Class II of lower controllers. For men, a higher general education brings more occupational chances than for women. About 25 per cent of them obtain jobs in the service class, as opposed to only 14 per cent of women with higher general education. On the other hand, we observe that higher general education is far

TABLE 11.10. *Occupational class by educational attainment and sex*

	Educational attainment							
	1ab	1c	2a	2b	2c	3a	3b	all
Men								
Higher controllers (I)	0.7%	0.7%	3.7%	2.2%	4.6%	22.2%	50.9%	9.8%
Lower controllers (II)	2.4%	2.8%	15.7%	8.0%	20.4%	52.1%	38.2%	19.1%
Administration/commerce (IIIa)	2.2%	3.7%	12.4%	17.3%	35.4%	13.6%	7.5%	11.1%
Sales/personal services (IIIb)	2.6%	4.0%	6.9%	11.8%	6.5%	4.0%	1.0%	5.3%
Self-employed (IVabcd)	7.2%	6.6%	7.5%	4.4%	4.1%	1.1%	0.2%	5.2%
Skilled manual (V/VI)	40.0%	51.4%	39.5%	27.1%	12.0%	4.7%	1.0%	31.0%
Semi/unskilled manual (VII)	45.0%	30.8%	14.3%	29.3%	16.9%	2.2%	1.2%	18.5%
Number of individuals	458	1,464	2,076	451	367	980	574	6,370
Women								
Higher controllers (I)	0.4%	0.1%	0.8%	1.2%	1.9%	5.4%	41.3%	3.9%
Lower controllers (II)	3.6%	3.5%	15.5%	6.7%	12.2%	50.1%	43.8%	20.7%
Administration/commerce (IIIa)	13.0%	20.2%	29.9%	41.3%	51.5%	25.1%	11.4%	28.8%
Sales/personal services (IIIb)	19.8%	27.3%	32.4%	25.0%	19.2%	14.8%	1.3%	24.2%
Self-employed (IVabcd)	4.0%	4.0%	1.7%	1.9%	1.9%	0.6%	0.0%	1.8%
Skilled manual (V/VI)	9.3%	9.0%	3.1%	4.0%	3.6%	0.4%	0.3%	3.6%
Semi/unskilled manual (VII)	49.8%	35.8%	16.6%	20.0%	9.6%	3.5%	1.9%	16.9%
Number of individuals	247	766	2,312	581	468	1,165	315	5,854

Selection: less than ten years after leaving school, employed, no missing information

Source: Labour Market Survey 1991 (EBB/CBS).

from a guarantee for success on the labour market. Large proportions end up in routine non-manual jobs (women more than men) or in semi/unskilled jobs (especially men).

For men, higher education is almost a guarantee to find a job in the service class. However, differences between higher vocational training and a university degree are salient insofar as the former prepares for a job in Class II, and the latter for a job in Class I. The chances for women with higher vocational education to enter the highest social class are much lower than for men with the same level of education. At the university level, the opportunities of men and women are more equal, although even here men are in a somewhat better position in the labour market.

In Table 11.11 we use a multinomial logit model to analyse the cross–classification of occupational class by educational attainment. The model in Table 11.11 uses all the available degrees of freedom and estimates 36 effects. These 36 effects in the model are very significant for both men and women. The Chi-squared test against the hypothesis that all effects are zero has 36 degrees of freedom and yields for men in a Chi^2 of 4,067 points, and for women in a Chi^2 of 2,415 points. The number of parameters is too high to interpret them tidily, but of course the results of this bivariate analysis resemble the outcomes of the descriptive Table 11.10 to a large extent. Once again, the difference in occupational achievement between primary education and low vocational training is small, but it is now clear that those with low vocational training have a somewhat better chance of entering the non-manual Classes IIIa and IIIb than persons with only primary education. The occupational opportunities of those with intermediate education are much higher, but we see clear differences within this level. Intermediate vocational training and higher general schooling give more chances than intermediate general schooling, especially for entry to the service classes, Classes I and II. Higher vocational training and university education have superior value on the Dutch labour market, and from a class perspective the higher value of a university education above a vocational training is clear. Apparently, the lower employment rates of academics are compensated by higher job levels. These patterns are similar for women and for men, but on the whole the returns of education are higher for men.

In Table 11.12 we again focus on the contrast between educational attainment as a nominal variable (a set of dummy variables), and the measure of years of schooling. This model estimates only 6 effects, and the Chi-square test with 6 degrees of freedom tells that these effects are significantly different from zero. For men the Chi^2 is 3,383 points, and for women 1,935 points. A comparison of the models in Table 11.12 and those in Table 11.11, shows that the 30 extra effects in the model with educational attainment as a categorical variable are significant ($Chi^2 = 684.1$ for men, and 479.7 for

TABLE 11.11. *Effects of educational attainment on occupational class, relative to Class VIIab, multinomial logit models*

	I	II	IIIa	IIIb	IVabc	V/VI
Men (N = 6,370)						
Intercept	−4.229	−2.930	−3.025	−2.843	−1.831	−0.118
1ab: elementary	0[a]	0[a]	0[a]	0[a]	0[a]	0[a]
1c: lower vocational	0.420~	0.532~	0.903	0.809	0.284~	0.631
2a: intermediate vocational	2.883	3.023	2.884	2.122	1.191	1.139
2b: intermediate general	1.649	1.631	2.499	1.930	−0.056~	0.040~
2c: higher general	2.935	3.120	3.766	1.894	0.412~	−0.225~
3a: higher vocational	6.553	6.075	4.825	3.415	1.138	0.856
3b: university	7.960	6.373	4.841	2.689	−0.115~	−0.036~
Degrees of freedom	36					
Chi^2	4067.0					
Women (N = 5,854)						
Intercept	−4.812	−2.615	−1.346	−0.920	−2.510	−1.677
1ab: elementary	0[a]	0[a]	0[a]	0[a]	0[a]	0[a]
1c: lower vocational	−0.801~	0.298~	0.777	0.650	0.330~	0.298~
2a: intermediate vocational	1.752~	2.545	1.935	1.588	0.223~	0.003~
2b: intermediate general	2.005	1.525	2.073	1.144	0.154~	0.059~
2c: higher general	3.203	2.851	3.025	1.614	0.900	0.703~
3a: higher vocational	5.242	5.271	3.310	2.360	0.742~	−0.427~
3b: university	7.888	5.750	3.138	0.515~	[b]	−0.115~
Degrees of freedom	36					
Chi^2	2414.9					

Selection: less than ten years after leaving school, employed, no missing information

~ denotes insignificance (p > .05)
[a] denotes reference category
[b] denotes no person in category entered occupational class
Source: Labour Market Survey 1991 (EBB/CBS).

women, ndf = 30). This means that for both men and women a multinomial logit model predicting the odds of being in one of the seven occupational classes with a continuous variable for years of schooling describes the pattern of association between education and occupation worse than a multinomial model predicting class from a categorical level of education. The parameters of the model with years of education show that the ranking of the classes from I to VII is strictly ordinal with regard to years of education. The more years of education, the greater the likelihood of entering a job in a 'higher' class, going from Class VII to Class I.

Paul M. De Graaf and Wout C. Ultee

TABLE 11.12. *Effect of years of education on occupational class, relative to Class VIIab, multinomial logit models*

	I	II	IIIa	IIIb	IVabc	V/VI
Men (N = 6,370)						
Intercept	−15.964	−10.328	−6.056	−4.737	−3.088	−0.836
Years of education	1.149	0.823	0.475	0.310	0.168	0.127
Degrees of freedom	6					
Chi²	3382.9					
Women (N = 5,854)						
Intercept	−18.540	−9.232	−2.811	−2.247	−2.639	−1.341
Years of education	1.224	0.727	0.282	0.223	0.037~	−0.019~
Degrees of freedom	6					
Chi²	1935.2					

Selection: less than ten years after leaving school, employed, no missing information

~ denotes insignificance (p > .05)

Source: Labour Market Survey 1991 (EBB/CBS).

CONCLUSION

In the Netherlands the relationship between education and occupational position is far from tight for the cohort which entered the labour market in the 1980s. Occupational class is very scattered, especially for those with intermediate levels of education: those with low levels of educational attainment arrive in the skilled or unskilled manual class (men), or in the routine non-manual and unskilled manual class (women); those with high levels of educational attainment obtain positions in the service class, be it the class of the high controllers (university graduates), or the class of the low controllers (higher vocational schooling); but people with intermediate levels of education, who form half of the labour force in this labour-market cohort, are already widely dispersed in this early phase of their working life. One of the most important reasons for this finding is in the developments on the Dutch labour market, where supply and demand of educational qualifications are not balanced. The highly educated so far have not experienced major disadvantages of these developments, because they could enter service-class jobs previously occupied by some of those with intermediate education. On the other side of the spectrum, it is obvious that the lower educated are being pushed to the lowest jobs, or out of the labour market altogether. Those with intermediate education are now in a dubious position. If the changes in the qualitative structure of the Dutch labour market do not keep pace with the growth of individuals with higher educational qualifications, the position of those with intermediate schooling will deteriorate disproportionately in the future, and the—still high—value of higher education will also diminish.

In the mid-1990s, about 75 per cent of the newcomers on the Dutch labour market have vocational training. Intermediate and higher vocational training offer large advantages with regard to employment and job security, but low vocational training now hardly offers more chances than primary education alone. The worth of an academic degree is somewhat ambiguous insofar as it facilitates entry into the highest occupations, but carries a greater risk of unemployment than vocational training. In addition, university graduates work more frequently in temporary and part-time jobs. This suggests that employers are sometimes uncertain as to the value of this qualification.

Two other findings on the Netherlands deserve attention. First, we have shown that value of educational qualifications is lower for women than for men, also for the young cohort featured in this study, which should be explained by demand and supply effects. In the Netherlands, childcare is a woman's job, and more than 90 per cent of women stop full-time work on the birth of their first child. Anticipation of, and concentration on domestic duties and limited work hours have a negative impact on career development. Demand side effects may also be present. Employers tend to treat all women alike which leads to statistical discrimination. Second, we observed (again) that these days direct effects of father's occupation on the occupational attainment are hardly present in the Netherlands. It is education which links origin and destination nowadays.

This analysis started by accepting the issue of testing the hypothesis that in a highly industrialized country such as the contemporary Netherlands the relation between education and occupation during the first years of the working life can be captured by a single parameter between two continuous variables, against the hypothesis that this association is a relation between two categorical variables best described by a multitude of parameters. The result of the analyses performed here is that the relation between education and occupation in the Netherlands around 1990, is depicted less well by one parameter between two continuous variables, than by all the parameters possible for a relation between two categorical variables.

The proposed educational schema for educational attainment devised for comparative purposes for application fits well to the education–occupation link in the Netherlands, but must be specified in one respect. Whereas the proposed schema places intermediate general education and intermediate vocational education on the same footing, in the Netherlands intermediate vocational education ranks above intermediate general education. This ranking is not only indicated by the choices people have to make within the Dutch educational system—intermediate vocational education comes logically after intermediate general education but also by the relation between education and occupational prestige. People with intermediate vocational education have on average more occupational prestige than people with intermediate general education.

In the Netherlands, the relation between educational attainment and occupation as both a continuous variable (prestige), and as a categorical variable (class), is described better by treating education as a nominal variable (a set of dummy variables), than by education continuously measured. However, we do not want to abandon the linear approach, because this issue brings us back to Featherman and Hauser's (1978: 261) attempt to describe the relation between continuous education and continuous occupational status not by one linear function, but by a spline function combining two linear functions. Casual inspection of Table 11.4 makes clear that one additional year of education at first does not contribute much, but more at later levels of the educational scale. Perhaps the relatively slow structural change on the labour market and the much faster educational expansion make the difference in value between qualifications on the lower and the intermediate level much lower than the value difference between qualifications on the intermediate and the high level.

NOTES

1. It is estimated that in around 1650, between 4 to 5 per cent of Dutch men had at some time studied at an athenaeum or academy. At the end of the seventeenth century this percentage had dropped to 2.5, and at the end of the eighteenth century to 1.3 (Otterspeer 1992: 19).
2. The percentage of men who signed their marriage certificate in Amsterdam by writing their name was 57 in 1630, and rose steadily to 85 in 1780 (Hart 1976: 131). The percentage of women who did so rose in the same period from 32 to 64.
3. Employers, labour unions, and staff of organizations overseeing disability schemes colluded to an inflow in disability schemes well above what under conditions of full employment would have been the case. The regulations were such that a disabled person has a higher income than a long-term unemployed person.
4. In our sample, respondents in all educational categories have between zero and ten years of labour-market experience by design, and there will be no association between educational attainment and experience. Therefore, the effects of educational attainment on occupational outcomes are not attenuated by the effects of experience and we can estimate an overall effect of education on occupation for those who have not been in the labour market for more than ten years. One may

wonder, however, whether the effect of education changes during the first ten years on the labour market. In Table 11.7, we report the effect of years of education on occupational prestige to be 4.7 for men and 3.2 for women. A breakdown of this effect by experience reveals that the effect does not vary strongly over the early career, with one exception—for respondents with no experience the effect is only 3.3 for men and 2.2 for women. The reason for the small effects for those who only just arrived on the labour market may be that they will often have temporary, and less serious, jobs. The relationship between education and occupation stabilizes after one to two years on the labour market, and the overall effect for those who have been between zero and ten years in the labour market gives a reliable estimate of the effect of education on occupation.

12

Qualifications and the Allocation Process of Young Men and Women in the Swedish Labour Market

ROBERT ERIKSON AND JAN O. JONSSON

INTRODUCTION

Social stratification is a phenomenon that relates to the allocation of people to positions in the class structure. If the rewards connected with different social positions are perceived as trophies, then the allocation process is the competition. One must not necessarily adhere to the view of life as a rat-race to acknowledge the crucial role that agencies which shape the allocation regime play for individuals in a given society. Individuals adjust to these agencies, often try to play the game according to what they perceive the rules to be, and sometimes seek, individually or collectively, to change those rules.

In modern Western societies, the agencies that shape the allocation regime are, first and foremost, employers. They, or their representatives, make decisions about hiring and firing. By doing so, they determine the greater part of the allocation principles. The state is the second most important agency. Through regulations regarding authorization, legitimation, licensing, diplomas, and other formal requirements, it is responsible for (or at least, superintends) well-defined and important principles governing job eligibility.

In many capitalist countries, the power of employers to hire and fire is circumscribed not only by state intervention, but also by the activity of employees' representatives (trade unions and occupational associations) with whom they often collaborate, negotiate, or fight. Organized employees' interest groups also try politically to change state regulations, for example in order to protect their profession from competition from 'outsiders' (cf. Parkin 1979; Collins 1979). Since allocation principles are almost always contested, they vary over time and across nations, mainly due to differences and changes in power resources among allocation agencies and interest groups, but also due to other macro phenomena, such as technological change.

Despite this, however, allocation principles may still be expected to show a great deal of invariance across nations insofar as organizations competing in a market employ, by and large, similar allocation principles in the pursuit of efficiency. Such principles can be assumed to be fairly stable over time within societies. The struggle between divergent interests is often institutionalized—this could be a rational strategy because the costs of overt conflict are high and since a predictable environment is important for actors. Historically rooted allocation principles may also carry a great deal of inertia because of tradition or habit (cf. Müller 1994).

Besides personal recommendations, the most frequently used allocation criteria are educational credentials (or qualifications) and experience because they signal competence, productivity, and personality traits required by employers. Needless to say, education counts more than experience for labour-market entry. Since rigorous tests and interviews on a large scale are expensive, recruitment decisions are often based on imprecise information regarding personal characteristics for which formal qualifications and experience are poor measures, for example, social skills, ability to cooperate, sense of judgement, and creativity. Such qualities, however, are not easy to change, so individual strategies are normally focused on achieving educational merits that are demanded by employers.

What status do educational credentials have as an allocation criterion in present-day Sweden? We discuss this question below with reference to the allocation agencies and their relations to the educational system, and with reference to features of the educational system itself. Especially when studying young people, the institutional links between the educational system and the labour market are of great importance (cf. Rosenbaum et al. 1990). Subsequently, we outline in what way the association between level of education and labour-market outcomes is structured by other factors, such as social origin, sex, type of education, and labour-market characteristics. As our discussion unfolds, assumptions about such structuring effects are presented and then tested empirically on recent data for young Swedes. The chapter ends with a discussion of the main results.

ALLOCATION AGENCIES

We think three aspects of the relations between allocation agencies and the educational system are important to highlight in the Swedish context.[1] First, a historically strong state has meant that educational institutions have always been tightly connected to the state, while private schools have received little state support, either financially or politically. For a long time, the main task for universities was to educate the clergy, civil servants, teachers, and doctors. In the 1960s, when both the public sector and universities expanded dramatically, this traditional bond remained, as a large part of university expansion was directed towards the public sector (even if the public sector expansion did not primarily occur in the state sector, but at county and municipal levels, which are responsible for childcare and health care).

The mirror image of this connection between educational institutions and the state is the weak relationship between the private sector and the educational system. Historically, there have been recurrent complaints that secondary and tertiary education are 'too academic', and too little concerned with the practical problems of industry. The private sector has—with some exceptions—not been involved in, or directly supported, schools. One of the upshots of this lack of involvement is that there is only a weak link between industry and vocational training, although there are cases where this is strong locally.

Second, there have been few formal or informal restrictions on access to private-sector jobs in Sweden, except at the higher professional level; the guilds lost their influence early in Sweden, and craft organizations are almost without any influence today; and blue- and white-collar trade unions have for a long time been organized by industry, rather than by occupation. Unions organizing university graduates, however, are mainly structured according to occupation.

One consequence of the weak relationship between the school on the one hand, and the private sector and organized labour on the other, is that vocational education—important as it is today in the Swedish school system—is almost entirely disconnected from interest groups in the labour market. The exception is that employers in the public sector exert strong influence on some types of education, running schools for nurses, police education, and internally organized education for railway and post-office employees, among others.[2]

Third, trade unions have been powerful in Sweden at least since the 1930s, with very high membership rates and exert considerable influence on decisions regarding personnel policies, mainly on a local basis. By and large, they tend more than employers to promote internal candidates in order to ensure career ladders for their members. Perhaps even more important, trade unions have pursued a policy of 'last-in-first-out' in cases of redundancy. As a consequence, it is the unions rather than employers, who emphasize work-life experience as opposed to formal qualifications in decisions about hiring and firing.

One upshot of the trade unions' way of organizing interest on an industrial basis, and their strong position in negotiations with employers, is that 'closed employment relationships' (cf. Sørensen and Kalleberg 1981) dominate in Sweden. Job competition mainly concerns vacancies, and when an employee has achieved a position, it is in principle not possible for an outsider to compete for it by offering the employer to do the job for a lower wage. 'Open' employment relationships, where such wage competition is prevalent, do probably exist only in the intersection between product and labour markets, that is, for consultants and other self-employed (and then it is not really an employment relationship, though it may lead to one). Trade unions have also acted to narrow income differences, and have promoted the institutionalization of collective bargaining, which may be one reason behind the internationally small income variation in Sweden (Hibbs 1991). The absence of an organizational division between skilled and unskilled workers has contributed to small wage differentials even within the manual working class.

In addition to these features, it is worth noting that until recently, the state had a monopoly on labour exchange in Sweden, with a government agency (*arbetsförmedlingen*) covering the labour market almost completely,[3] except for internal promotion and recruitment to higher grade jobs. It is difficult to say whether this organization has had an impact on allocation *principles*, though one could assume that it has promoted universalistic characteristics, and it is likely that it has made the recruitment process more homogeneous and less haphazard across organizations, providing employers with cheap and accessible information on job applicants.

THE SCHOOL SYSTEM

Four features of the Swedish school system are particularly important for the allocation process. First, one consequence of the weak relationship between vocational schooling and labour-market actors is that mainly general, occupational skills are taught in vocational programmes. Firm-specific skills are almost exclusively a matter for on-the-job training, whereas industrial, branch-specific skills may be taught in school locally. Apprenticeships are uncommon in Sweden, and there never existed anything like a widespread apprenticeship system.

Second, the Swedish comprehensive and secondary school systems are highly standardized and centralized with similar economic resources, and a national curriculum. The state also provides detailed regulations governing teacher training, school hours and organization, the teacher/student ratio, study guidance, and health-care provisions for pupils.

Third, the reformed Swedish school is characterized by a low grade of stratification, and an absence of final examinations and ability tests. The comprehensive school reform in the 1960s introduced mixed ability classes up to the ninth grade, i.e. age 16 (Swedes start school at the age of 7) with some exceptions.[4] For the transition to the *Gymnasium*, there are three main options, namely an academic branch of study, a semi-vocational branch, and a vocational programme. The first option is normally three years, and the two latter two years, and it is mainly the academic branch—upper secondary school—that provides opportunities for university studies.[5] The other branches contain an element of academic subjects too, so students stand a fairly good chance of continuing onto tertiary schooling, and with some complementary, and easily accessible, courses also to traditional university studies. Admission to the *Gymnasium* and university are, in case of shortage of places, dependent on grade-point averages—previously examinations were used at the entrance to secondary schools (ability tests were never tried in the Swedish school system apart from at university entrance). There are some types of education, e.g. medical schools, where the entry requirements in terms of grades are quite high, but it is generally possible to continue on to the next level in the educational system even with low grade-point averages. Thus, transitions from one level to the next are fundamentally based on the students' own choices.

The fourth characteristic of the reformed Swedish educational system is the absence of educational dead-ends. Vocational branches of study give comparatively good opportunities to continue to further education. There is also a large-scale system of adult education which provides a 'second chance' for those who leave school early. In many cases, state financial support facilitates adults' studies at secondary level.

Regardless of any specificities in the Swedish school system, we expect there to be a general and strong association between levels of education, on the one hand, and labour-market rewards, such as occupational prestige and social class positions, on the other. When considering the particular links between level of education and social-class positions, we assume first and foremost that there is a strong association between university education and jobs in the upper service class, especially in the public sector. This is because of the heritage of a close relationship between schools of higher education and the state administration, and later, county and municipal councils. Second, we expect the reverse situation for those with compulsory education only: strong dissociation with the upper service class, especially in the public sector. The features of the Swedish educational system and the characteristics of allocation agencies suggest a particular configuration of associations between educational qualifications and labour-market outcomes. For example, we assume that there is a positive association between vocational education and skilled work, but that this association is fairly weak, because of the weak link between vocational schools and industry and because of the lack of exclusionary practices towards unskilled workers in Sweden.

STRUCTURING FACTORS IN THE ALLOCATION PROCESS

Allocation agencies shape the nation-specific pattern of the association between education and occupational position in their interaction with the school system. There is, however, nothing resembling a nationally homogeneous 'allocation regime'. What we observe as associations are averages—in practice, several factors may mediate between education and position, and/or may interact with education in producing labour-market outcomes. Previous research and theory points to a number of potential structuring variables. Below, we will consider some of these pertaining to the educational system, to the labour market, to the sexual division of labour, and to the social-class system. An overriding aim of this chapter is to study to what extent the association between level of education and social position is structured by these factors, or, to put it differently, to what degree the association between qualification level and social position must be understood as working through a different (or in any case a rather diverse) 'signal system' than what is normally acknowledged in human capital and credential models.

Educational Structuring

One set of structuring factors refers to what is often termed 'education', defined as years of education completed (in human-capital models), or as qualification level (in credential models). Credential models are appropriate in many European educational systems (cf. Braun and Müller 1996; Jonsson 1996a), where the level of education, typically defined by formal examinations and diplomas, is an essential signal to employers of skills, knowledge, productivity, and personality traits. Still, information on an individual's level of education conceals differences in ability and school performance, as well as differences in the type of education attained within a given level, factors that also may signal characteristics that employers use for occupational selection.

Information on school achievement, measured as teacher-assigned grades, is readily available at no cost in Sweden because it is included in job applicants' diplomas which are normally requested by employers. Grades are also easy to interpret, and, because of the centralized Swedish school system, comparable across the nation. Indeed, insofar as employers value diligence, cognitive abilities, academic excellence, or similar personality traits, grades must be considered significant information in the hiring process. We therefore assume that grade-point averages have a positive effect on occupational prestige.

Education may be subdivided into different types, with differing consequences for labour-market opportunities. Generally, the relation between supply and demand of persons at a given level of education will depend on such an 'educational sector' because of the inherent qualities of certain types of education—some may be taken for their consumption value rather than for their market value—or on varying difficulties in passing through them. Even given school performance and academic ability, some types of tertiary education will be held in high regard by employers.[6] Hence, we expect occupational opportunities of a given level of education to differ between educational sectors. While general education and the small sector of humanities and liberal arts probably give less than other sectors, technology could be expected to give large returns.

Labour-Market Structuring

A second set of structuring factors concerns the arena in which educational credentials are put to use. Labour-market theories maintain that various segmentations in the labour-market structure individuals' mobility and rewards (cf. the reviews by Kalleberg and Sørensen 1979; Baron 1984). Such segmentation occurs, among other things, along the lines of industrial branches and firm sizes. Previous research shows that some branches offer better career opportunities than others (for Sweden, see le Grand 1993), and such opportunities are also positively related to firm size (Brown and Medoff 1989), probably partly because larger firms offer more hierarchical levels facilitating internal promotion (Hedström 1988). These labour-market characteristics can be assumed to mediate between education and social position because higher educational qualifications and education of specific types entail better opportunities to find a job in a sector or firm in which higher social positions are more easily attained.

Industrial branch and firm size can also be assumed to interact with education: educational differences may mean more for occupational and income attainment in some labour-market segments if the institutional structure in these segments promotes meritocratic principles. Following Bell (1973), one can assume, for example, that educational credentials are most important in the emerging service sector of the economy, in particular in its public-professional branch. Larger firms with more bureaucratic organization may also follow more formal guidelines in hiring and promotion, which in turn may strengthen the link between education and jobs (cf. Stolzenberg 1978).

Sex Differences

In analysing the allocation process, sex differences are of the utmost interest. Not only can we expect differences in returns to additional education to affect men's and women's propensity of 'investing in' more education; the labour-market opportunities for men and women are highly consequential for emerging sex differences in economic standing and life-chances generally. Thus, we will in this chapter try to unravel whether the allocation process, defined in the more extended model alluded to above, is different between men and women.

Both vertical and horizontal sex segregation in the labour market is preponderant in Sweden, as in other societies—the horizontal segregation is comparatively strong in the Scandinavian countries (Charles 1992; Jacobs and Lim 1992), probably due to the very high labour-market participation which was made possible through the expansion of traditionally female occupations in the public sector. But what should we expect with regard to the association between education and social position? Discrimination against women, and an unequal division of household labour between men and women may on average affect women's occupational returns negatively, but we find it less plausible that such discrimination would be more severe among women at higher levels of education than at lower ones.

Indeed, we believe that the returns for taking additional education may be greater for women, and that the association between level of education and social position is stronger than for men. At labour-market entry, this may occur because of the strong horizontal sex segregation in Swedish schools and in the Swedish labour market (Table 12.1), which means that women's choice of education and work channel them into branches of industry where we assume that the importance of formal merits is greatest. Moreover, we expect the education–position bond to weaken more with age for men than for women. This is partly due to the fact that women tend to be employed in industrial branches where occupational labour markets are more pronounced than internal labour markets—in Sweden, this is particularly true of the health care and educational branches (le Grand 1993). Partly, such a pattern could also be produced by restrictions on women's promotion opportunities—following their greater responsibility for family and home, or due to employer discrimination—while career moves based on non-credential characteristics such as work-life experience are more common among men (cf. Baron, Davis-Blake, and Bielby 1986; le Grand 1993).

Social Origin

A standard assumption in theories of social change in stratification is that *achieved* characteristics, chiefly education, will assume an ever-increasing influence on an individual's social position and living conditions, and that the importance of *ascribed* characteristics, such as those relating to the family of origin, will vanish as societies become industrialized and modernized (Blau and Duncan 1967; Treiman 1970). In general, this assumption is more often adhered to than supported by empirical evidence. At least, most studies, independently of which society is studied, conclude that there is a lingering effect of social origin on 'destination', even when comparing people at the same level of education. For Sweden—in spite of evidence that it has weakened somewhat over time (Jonsson 1996*a*)—this 'direct' effect of origin is still substantial for people born into the urban and, in particular, the rural petty bourgeoisie, and it is prevalent also for children from the upper service class (Jonsson 1993). This result is a reminder that education is not the sole determinant of social-class destination, and that, for example, 'inheritance effects', or social immobility, may often depend upon the inter-generational transmission of land, capital, or a business. Thus, if we do not control for social origin, we risk over-estimating the association between education and class position because children born into more privileged classes tend to attain both higher education and higher social positions.

We may moreover risk obtaining a distorted picture of career mobility, if the effect of family background on career development is not accounted for (Erikson and Goldthorpe 1992). In addition, and perhaps more interestingly, social background may also *interact* with education in the allocation process. It may be the case, for example, that family resources in higher classes are particularly effective up to a certain limit, which can help children of these classes if they drop out of school more than if they take a university degree— the incentives are strong since a loss in status may be quite costly (Keller and Zavalloni 1964; Erikson and Jonsson 1996*b*). Alternatively, the social network of parents who qualified for higher positions by attaining higher educational credentials may be most important for those children.

We expect to find an effect of social-origin class on social position even when comparing people at the same level of education, particularly for those in the primary sector, and the self-employed. We will in addition test whether there is an effect of social background on the association between education and social position, and, if so, whether it shows the advantage of higher social origins to be greater at lower, or higher levels of education.

DATA AND VARIABLES

The data were collected by Statistics Sweden for the Swedish Commission on Educational Inequality (Erikson and Jonsson 1993, 1996a). The present data-set consists of almost 214,000 men and women born in Sweden (or immigrated before the age of 7) between 1956 and 1965, and who held a job in 1990.[7] Information on their grade-point averages,[8] and educational attainment was gathered from educational registers. Parents' characteristics were collected from the 1960, 1970, 1980, and 1990 censuses. Respondent's job, social class, and industrial branch, as well as size of establishment for employees were taken from the 1990 census. Descriptive information on the variables is given in Table 12.1.

Occupational prestige is measured by Treiman's prestige scores (Treiman 1977: appendix A). Prestige may, of course, be interpreted directly as the status connected to various social positions, but it can as well be seen as an indicator of the material rewards connected to the positions and of the educational qualifications required in them. Respondent's social class is classified according to the EGP class schema (Erikson and Goldthorpe 1992), whereas parent's social class is measured on a similar, but not identical, social class schema (SCB 1989; Erikson and Jonsson 1996a).

Respondents' educational level is coded to the CASMIN schema (Müller et al. 1989).[9] Parents' level of education is coded on a similar scale, having seven hierarchically ordered categories, while educational sector is coded according to a Swedish standard classification (SCB 1988).

We identify fourteen industrial branches according to a classification developed within a comparative project on allocation mechanisms (Erikson and Jonsson 1996c). Establishment size is a rank-ordered variable with eight values. Work-life experience is constructed by taking the year of the census (1990) minus the registered year of a secondary level or university examination. When such information was lacking, we constructed a school-leaving year from the reported level of education by adding the typical number of years of schooling at that level to the birth year plus seven (at which age nearly all our respondents started school). An additional year was subtracted for male non-graduates to account for military service, which is compulsory in Sweden.

RESULTS

Educational Qualifications and Occupational Prestige

We start by analysing the association between educational attainment and social position, or, to be precise, the effect of qualification level on occupational prestige. Table 12.2 shows regression estimates of prestige on level of education, entered as dummy variables with compulsory schooling (1b) as the reference category, with control for other factors. Since one of our main aims is to study whether the allocation process differs between the sexes, we show separate analyses for men and women.

Model 1 is our baseline model. It includes work-life experience and origin measures in addition to level of education (the origin effects make almost no difference to the education parameters). As expected, educational careers pay off in terms of occupational prestige. Once we take work-life experience into account, the 'return' to taking a lower vocational education in addition to compulsory schooling is around 4 prestige points for women and less than 3 for men. This must be considered a small gain. The next two levels (2b and 2c) lead to occupations of noticeably, though not substantially, higher prestige (7–11 points). Having a tertiary level education, however, leads to markedly higher prestige (about 18 points for lower tertiary education, and around 25 for degree level).

Ten years of work-life experience adds, on average, no more than one prestige point for women, but about two and a half for men. This result is, however, difficult to interpret, since the measure of experience is less accurate for women. For men and women alike, class origins outside the unskilled working class, and parental education above the compulsory level have positive, but weak effects on occupational prestige at the beginning of their work-life careers.[10] At the same time, origin does not add very much to the variance explained by the model (not shown in Table 12.2). All in all, one is more impressed by the overwhelmingly achieved character of the early occupational attainment process, at least when defining ascription in terms of social origin. The strongest ascribed effects—related to the difference between having an origin in Class I compared to one in Class VII, and having at least one parent with a post-graduate education compared to both being on compulsory level only—adds together merely 4–5 prestige points, controlling for the respondents' own education.[11]

In Model 2, school performance, measured as grade-point average (GPA), is added along with type of education. One step on the GPA ladder (which ranges from 1 to 5) returns around 2.5 prestige points, controlling for level of education. As displayed in Table 12.2, school performance is behind some of the effect of educational qualification on prestige; 1–3 points are due to differences in GPA at a given level of education.[12] Our conclusion is that the credential value of education is high in the Swedish labour market, whereas good school performance which does not lead to higher education is not particularly important for employers' recruitment policies—it may be that though such information is both available and comparable it is either not trusted or considered irrelevant for job performance (cf. Rosenbaum et

TABLE 12.1. *Descriptive statistics of variables used in the analysis*

	Percentages		%
	Men	Women	All
Respondent's level of education:			
1b Compulsory	18.7	13.4	
2a Vocational secondary	40.7	38.6	
2b Lower secondary	8.5	11.1	
2c Upper secondary	9.5	11.8	
3a Lower tertiary	13.5	15.9	
3b University degree	9.1	9.2	
Respondent's social-class position (destination):			
I Upper service class	11.4	8.1	
II Lower service class	17.5	21.0	
IIIa Lower white-collar	8.1	15.0	
IIIb Unqualified white-collar	6.8	24.6	
IV Self-employed	5.4	2.5	
VI Skilled workers	26.6	12.4	
VII Unskilled workers	24.1	16.4	
Parents' highest level of education:			
Compulsory			42.4
Elementary			7.6
Lower vocational			25.1
Matriculation			10.8
Lower tertiary			5.4
University degree			8.1
Post-graduate			0.7
Parents' highest social class:			
I Upper service class			8.5
II Lower service class			20.0
III Lower & unqualified white-collar			10.0
IVab Self-employed			8.7
IVcd Farmers			6.1
VI Skilled workers			24.3
VII Unskilled workers			22.4

	Men	Women
Type of Education:		
General (non-directed)	32.1	34.5
Humanities and liberal arts	0.5	0.8
Teaching	2.2	8.3
Business, administration, social science, law	11.6	22.1
Engineering, natural science, crafts	44.6	4.3
Transports and communication	2.2	1.0
Medicine and care	2.0	20.5
Agriculture, forestry, fishery	2.4	0.8
Personal service, military and police	2.5	7.6

	Men	Women
Industrial Branch:		
Service, Public, Professional	8.7	48.1
Service, Public, Administration	4.3	3.8
Service, Public, Other	4.5	3.5
Service, Private, Professional	4.8	3.4
Service, Private, Administration	2.0	3.4
Service, Private, Other	14.1	12.6
Trade sector:	12.4	10.9
Industrial prod., Process, Protected	1.1	0.3
Industrial prod., Process, Comp. Hi-tech	3.3	1.5
Industrial prod., Process, Comp. Lo-tech	2.1	1.4
Industrial prod., Craft	20.3	3.2
Industrial prod., Manufacturing, Hi-tech, large scale	5.4	1.9
Industrial prod., Manufacturing, Lo-tech	13.3	4.7
Primary sector	3.6	1.2

Metric variables	Men		Women	
	Mean	Std.dev.	Mean	Std.dev.
Occupational prestige	42.53	13.48	42.13	12.88
Grade-point average	2.94	0.67	3.17	0.67
Work-life experience	9.61	3.72	10.15	3.93
Establishment size	4.05	2.71	4.14	2.77

TABLE 12.2. *OLS regression estimates of occupational prestige on level of education and other variables in 1990 for women (N = 102,530) and men (N = 110,365)*

Background variables	Model 1		Model 2		Model 3	
	Women	Men	Women	Men	Women	Men
Level of education:						
1b Compulsory schooling	0.00	0.00	0.00	0.00	0.00	0.00
2a Lower vocational	4.14	2.58	2.02	0.94	2.30	0.83
2b Semi-vocational	7.53	7.06	5.56	5.64	5.44	5.23
2c Matriculation	11.04	9.26	8.53	7.92	8.02	7.47
3a Lower tertiary	18.37	18.76	14.93	16.72	14.09	15.23
3b University degree	24.50	25.17	20.23	22.35	19.16	20.29
Work-life experience*10	1.18	2.45	1.32	2.80	1.29	2.77
Class origin:						
I	2.05	2.63	1.69	2.30	1.55	2.30
II	1.57	2.11	1.33	1.96	1.15	1.87
III	1.32	1.51	1.07	1.41	0.94	1.46
IV	0.97	1.54	0.79	1.47	0.83	1.49
VI	0.43	0.84	0.32	0.69	0.26	0.61
VII	0.00	0.00	0.00	0.00	0.00	0.00

Parental education:						
Compulsory	0.00	0.00	0.00	0.00	0.00	0.00
Low vocational	0.52	0.65	0.47	0.66	0.45	0.66
Matriculation	0.69	0.72	0.60	0.67	0.56	0.64
Lower tertiary	0.82	0.58	0.67	0.46	0.71	0.45
University degree	1.33	0.88	1.03	0.48	1.10	0.46
Post-graduate	2.50	2.53	2.03	1.47	2.02	1.37
Grade-point average			2.51	2.55	2.30	2.33
Type of education						
General			0.00	0.00	0.00	0.00
Humanities			-3.01	-5.58	-1.78	-3.71
Teaching			(0.25)	-1.71	2.59	-1.89
Administration/social science			2.45	-0.33	1.48	-0.42
Technical/craft			2.79	1.07	1.78	0.97
Communication			2.18	-1.52	1.02	(-0.17)
Care			2.44	4.65	2.71	3.57
Agriculture			-0.82	-1.31	-1.35	-1.22
Service			-1.90	(0.26)	-1.91	(-0.33)
Industrial branch					Included[a]	Included[a]
Firm size					0.63	(-0.00)
R^2	0.35	0.38	0.38	0.40	0.42	0.42

Note: [a] 3 dummy variables (cf. Table 12.1). Parameters not shown.
Estimates in brackets not significant at the 1% level.

al. 1990 for the United States). We should note, however, that our measure of GPA stems chiefly from secondary school, and that subsequent grades may be more important for those with a tertiary level education.

The independent variable introduced in Model 2, characterizing the type of education taken, is a set of eight dummy variables with general education as the reference category. There are clear differences between 'educational sectors' in occupational attainment. Humanities/liberal arts, for example, has a negative effect for men and women alike (close to 6 and 3 points, respectively). The education/teaching sector has a negative effect for men (less than 2 points), as has the service sector for women, whereas an education in the care sector has a fairly strong positive effect for men (almost 5 points) and is less strong for women. The latter sex difference probably appears because men with this type of education often become doctors, and thereby attain a high prestige also compared with others at the same educational level. A more detailed analysis in which type of education was entered before GPA (not shown), showed that the effects of type of education modify the effects of levels of education only slightly.

From the results in Model 3 we can see that including industrial branch and firm size into the analysis has hardly any impact on the effect of education on prestige. Thus, the educational effect is only to a very small extent attributable to the fact that higher levels of education facilitate young people to find a job in a sector with favourable occupational opportunities. On the other hand, industrial branch and, for women, also firm size, have net effects on occupational prestige. Working in the private, professional service sector, for instance, adds more than 5 points for both men and women as compared to manufacturing, whereas those who are employed in the non-professional, non-administrative segment of the private service sector ('skin trades', i.e. personal service such as hairdressers or cosmetologist; the media, etc.) on average 'lose' 3–4 prestige points. Jobs in the protected process industry are connected with prestige 'gains' of the same magnitude. (Estimates for labour-market segments are not shown in Table 12.2.)

Furthermore, we tested whether the association between level of education and occupational prestige varies by industrial branch (results not presented). The overall impression is that the effect of education on prestige is very similar across industrial branches—higher levels of qualification lead on average to higher occupational prestige, and to much the same extent. Thus, there is no support for the assumption that allocation to positions within the service sector *in general* are more dependent on formal merit than in other industrial branches.[13] We also tested whether origin effects on occupational prestige varies by industrial branch, not of education, and found some support for the hypothesis that origin effects are relatively strong for men in the primary sector, almost as strong as those of education.

Finally, does the allocation process differ between sexes? The effect of work-life experience is greater for men, which probably would be true even if we could have used a better measure of experience (le Grand 1994 finds greater wage returns to experience for men on other Swedish data). There are some sex differences with regard to the effects of type of education—for instance, education in the humanities has a stronger negative effect for men than for women and the effect of education for teaching is negative for men while being positive for women. The total effect of social background is, as already mentioned, about the same for both sexes, however. Also, differences between men and women in the effect of level of education, as well as of grades, on occupational prestige are very small indeed. Thus, our hypothesis that the link between education and occupational attainment would be stronger for women is not supported by tests on occupational prestige.

We can conclude from Table 12.2 that a model predicting occupational attainment should first and foremost include level of education. All other variables of Model 3 are fairly unimportant in comparison. They all have significant effects, which is not surprising given the huge sample size, but controlling for these variables does not change the education effects very much; and their own effects are, with some exceptions, weak.[14] One exception is that studies in humanities/liberal arts lead to less prestigious jobs than other types of education; another is that finding a job in the professional (especially private) service sector is conducive to occupational prestige, while miscellaneous service jobs in the private sector (in the media or the skin trades, for example) are related to less prestige for employees at a given level of education. The 'prestige gaps' between these alternatives correspond to the difference between a semi-vocational secondary education and matriculation; or to the difference between matriculation and lower tertiary level education.

It is expected that there should be a strong effect of education (especially at tertiary level) on prestige, since the prestige of an occupation to some degree depends on the formal qualifications of its incumbents. Replacing occupational prestige with income does not change the main results, however (Erikson and Jonsson 1996*c*).

Educational Qualifications and Social-Class Position

Next, we analyse, as the second measure of labour-market position, in which social classes people with different educational credentials start their working careers. We do not assume that social classes, in contrast to prestige ratings, can be ordered in one vertical dimension. We use a class schema with seven classes, and the educational schema with six levels, as above. To study whether the allocation process differs between the sexes, we again make separate analyses for men and women.

Modelling the Allocation Process for Men and Women

The analyses are made with a kind of topological loglinear model (Hauser 1978; Erikson and Goldthorpe 1992), in which the pattern of interaction in a table is described by a levels matrix. The levels correspond to interactions of different strength and are located in different areas, or cells, in the table. The interaction in cells at the same level is expected to be of the same strength, which means that independence should hold within each level.

What interactions between education and class do we expect, then? First of all negative associations between lower levels of education—defined as compulsory and lower vocational schooling—and the most privileged class positions in Class I and II (the upper and lower sections of the service class): there is a well-protected gateway to these classes, and the code-word is educational credentials. Furthermore, those with intermediate secondary education (2b) will have difficulties entering the higher service class (Class I). We also generally expect negative interactions between the tertiary level of education and positions outside the service class. Here, the credential value of tertiary education functions as a safety-net.

We expect positive associations between academic education, that is, the three highest levels (2c, 3a, and 3b) and service-class positions (Classes I and II); and between compulsory and lower vocational schooling (1b and 2a) and working-class and unskilled non-manual jobs (Classes VI, VII, and IIIb). Since the latter levels of education constitute weak resources for obtaining a white-collar job, the main career route for those with no additional qualifications will be self-employment (IV)—therefore, we expect a positive interaction in these cells too. We also take into account that routine non-manual positions (IIIa) will typically be filled by those with only secondary level education.

Based on these considerations, we constructed a seven-level matrix, where the cells for which we expected the lowest interaction—university graduates taking manual jobs—are placed at level N3, cells where we expect slightly lower barriers to be operating on level N2, and so forth, up to cells where we expect a strong positive interaction, which are assigned to level P3. This levels matrix was then fitted to the education by class tables for men and women. This topological model made a major improvement in fit compared to the independence model, but was still not acceptable as a way to describe the interaction patterns. On the basis of the deviations between observed and fitted values, we adjusted the levels matrix, while still trying to keep to the ideas that governed the construction of the original one. Thus, no cell was moved more than one step in the matrix. This procedure resulted in different matrices for men and women, displayed in Table 12.3.

Fitting these levels matrices to the data returns a G^2 of 459 for the whole

TABLE 12.3. *Design matrices for the association between education and class position in the early career among men and women*

Education	Class						
	I	II	IIIa	IIIb	IV	VI	VII
Men							
1b	N2	N2	0	P1	P2	P1	P2
2a	N2	N1	0	P1	P1	P2	P1
2b	N1	0	P1	P1	0	0	0
2c	P1	P1	P2	P2	P1	0	0
3a	P1	P2	0	N1	N1	N2	N2
3b	P3	P1	0	N2	N2	N3	N3
Women							
1b	N2	N2	N1	P2	P1	0	P2
2a	N2	N2	0	P1	0	P2	0
2b	N1	0	P1	P2	0	P1	0
2c	P1	P1	P2	P1	0	0	N1
3a	P1	P3	0	N1	0	N2	N2
3b	P3	P1	N1	N2	N2	N3	N3

group of men aged 25 to 34, and a G^2 of 439 for the corresponding group of women, as reported in the first and fourth panels of Table 12.4 (Model B). With 24 degrees of freedom the models thus fit very badly, given that the G^2s are nearly twenty times larger than the degrees of freedom. Whether the deviations from the models carry any sociological significance is questionable however, since there is such a large number of cases. A more 'normal' sample size of one-tenth of the present, would produce G^2s of around 65—still not fitting but with a less cumbersome deviation. Dissimilarity indices of around 2 suggest that the models capture the most essential interactions between levels of education and social-class positions.

The interaction parameters from Model B in Table 12.4 are reported in Table 12.5. The effects are quite substantial—the difference between parameters for the lowest and the highest level is 4.89 for men and 5.11 for women. The expected odds ratio for a man with a university degree to obtain a job in Class I rather than one in Class VII, compared to the corresponding odds for a man with only compulsory education, is 1,236. The corresponding odds ratio for women is 1,686. Thus, we find for Sweden, as elsewhere, a very strong association between education and social-class position, at least in the early career. As follows from the levels matrices, this

TABLE 12.4. *Loglinear models for the association between level of education and social-class position, and for the interaction between this association and age, for men (N = 105,239) and women (N = 98,306), respectively*

	G^2	df	DI	Bic
Men, 25–34 years of age				
A. Independence	58604	30	28.8	58357
B. EGP+CASN+7 levels	458.7	24	2.0	181
C. EGP+CASN+15 levels	250.3	16	1.1	65
Men, 6 classes of origin by 5 levels of parental education (= 30 education by class tables)				
D. Conditional independence	47343	900	24.4	56113
E. ORIG*EDUC*(EGP+CASN)+EGP*CASN	1099	870	2.8	−8962
F. UNIDIFF	1012	841	2.7	−8713
G. UNIDIFF(ORIG)+UNIDIFF(EDUC)	1049	861	2.7	−8908
Men, 10 cohorts				
H. Conditional independence	58477	300	28.8	55008
I. AGE*(EGP+CASN)+EGP*CASN	599.9	270	2.3	−2522
J. UNIDIFF	505.6	261	2.0	−2513
Women, 25–34 years of age				
A. Independence	72351	30	32.0	72007
B. EGP+CASN+7 levels	439.1	24	1.8	163
C. EGP+CASN+15 levels	264.9	16	1.1	81
Women, 6 classes of origin by 5 levels of parental education (=30 education by class tables)				
D. Conditional independence	64518	900	29.7	53812
E. ORIG*EDUC*(EGP+CASN)+EGP*CASN	1128	870	3.1	−8874
F. UNIDIFF	997.8	841	2.8	-8670
G. UNIDIFF(ORIG)+UNIDIFF(EDUC)	1015	861	2.8	−8883
Women, 10 cohorts				
H. Conditional independence	72542	300	32.3	69093
I. AGE*(EGP+CASN)+EGP*CASN	438.1	270	2.1	−2666
J. UNIDIFF	427.5	261	2.1	−2573

Key: EGP Class position (destination)   CASN Level of education   ORIG Class origin
EDUC Parents' highest education   UNIDIFF Uniform difference model

association is primarily based on strong barriers preventing those with lower education from entering the service class, and a safety-net making it possible for those with tertiary education to avoid manual and unqualified white collar positions. An important conclusion from Table 12.5 is that the association between education and class position is stronger for women.

TABLE 12.5. *Parameter estimates (β) and standard errors (se) from level models (7 levels) of the association between level of education and class position for men and women*

Parameter	Men		Women	
	β	se	β	se
N3	−2.68	(0.07)	−2.75	(0.08)
N2	−1.21	(0.02)	−1.41	(0.03)
N1	−0.55	(0.02)	−0.49	(0.02)
P1	0.68	(0.01)	0.66	(0.01)
P2	1.02	(0.01)	0.91	(0.01)
P3	2.21	(0.03)	2.36	(0.02)

Note: Estimates based on Table 12.4, Model B.

Sex Differences in the Allocation Pattern

Is the stronger association between education and position for women a general feature, or is it due to some specific link between particular levels of education and particular social classes? In order to compare the detailed interaction pattern among women with the pattern prevailing for men, we have to fit the same model for both sexes. This is done by creating a level matrix where each separate combination of levels in the matrices for men and women defines one unique level. This procedure generates fifteen different levels. Such a model may seem to be overdetermined, but we believe that the results can be interpreted thanks to the large sample size. In Table 12.6 we report the interaction parameters resulting from fitting this levels model to men and women simultaneously, with separate parameters for the two sexes.[15]

The stronger association for women, as displayed by the general interaction terms in Table 12.5, occurs, with some exceptions, through a *generally* tighter link between level of education and class position. First, it appears to be almost impossible for women to obtain a service class job without relatively high qualifications. As hypothesized, then, women's lower chances of working their way up are reflected in the weaker associations between lower levels of education and positions in higher classes.

Second, the entry to skilled working-class jobs also appears more dependent upon the requisite qualifications for women than for men. The parameters relating compulsory and lower vocational training to skilled and unskilled working-class jobs are fairly similar for men, regardless of vocational training and skill requirements. They clearly differ for women, however, for whom those without vocational training encounter problems in

TABLE 12.6. *Parameter estimates from level models (15 levels) of education by class destination for men and women*

Education	Class position												
	I		II		IIIa		IIIb		IV		VI		VII
	m	w	m	w	m	w	m	w	m	w	m	w	m	w
1b	-1.1/-1.5		-1.1/-1.5		0.1/-0.5		0.7/ 0.8		1.1/ 0.6		0.7/ 0.0		1.0/ 0.9	
2a	-1.1/-1.5		-0.6/-1.2		0.0/ 0.0		0.6/ 0.7		0.7/ 0.0		1.0/ 0.9		0.7/ 0.0	
2b	0.1/-0.5		0.0/ 0.0		0.6/ 0.7		0.7/ 0.8		0.0/ 0.0		-0.1/ 0.4		0.0/ 0.0	
2c	1.1/ 0.6		0.6/ 0.7		1.0/ 0.9		1.1/ 0.6		0.7/ 0.0		0.0/ 0.0		0.1/-0.5	
3a	1.1/ 0.6		1.0/ 2.3		0.0/ 0.0		-0.7/-0.5		-0.6/-0.3		-1.1/-1.5		-1.1/-1.5	
3b	2.6/ 2.4		0.6/ 0.7		0.1/-0.5		-1.1/-1.5		-1.1/-1.5		-2.7/-2.8		-2.7/-2.8	

Note: Estimates based on Table 12.4, Model C.

acquiring skilled jobs, while those with such training have better chances than men of avoiding unskilled jobs. Thus, the odds ratio relating compulsory and lower vocation schooling to skilled and unskilled manual jobs is 1.8 for men, but 6.0 for women. In a similar way, women with higher secondary (2c), or tertiary education (3a) end up in unskilled jobs in Class VII less often than men. Likewise, the parameters for university graduates (3b) entering Class III and Class IV are clearly lower for women.

In sum, the results suggest that the association between formal qualifications and social-class positions is stronger for women. This comes about in two ways: first, women with a low level of education have, as expected, less opportunities of obtaining a more advantageous position than men. Second, and not anticipated, higher education also gives women better protection against having to take an unskilled manual job than is the case for men. Below, we try to find out whether this is due to the sex segregation in types of education, or to labour-market segmentation.

Education, Class, and Social Origin

It is well known that social origin influences the class positions attained, both via educational attainment and 'directly', that is, for those at a given level of qualification. This is the case also for social-class attainment in the early career in Sweden in the late twentieth century. In Tables 12.7 and 12.8, we apply multinomial logistic regression models to study the effect of education on social-class position for men and women, respectively. The results show that this effect is reduced when class of origin, parental education, and prestige of origin are taken into account, but that the effect of education remains very strong indeed. Thus, dividing the odds of a man with a degree to obtain a job in Class I, rather than one in Class VII, with the corresponding odds for a man with only compulsory education gives an odds ratio of 1,313. The odds ratio when the three factors of social origin are controlled for is nearly halved to 788—the association is still obviously substantial. The corresponding odds ratios for women are 2,724 and 1,556, respectively. Less extreme odds ratios are not reduced to the same extent.[16]

It may be worth noting that if a man with a degree has to take a working-class job, it is more likely to be unskilled than skilled. This result is in line with the idea that one risk with continuing to university is that other occupational skills are small if one fails to obtain a job related to the education attained (cf. Breen and Goldthorpe 1996). The corresponding effect does not appear for women, however.

We also find that the direct effects of the various aspects of social origins all appear with the expected signs. Thus, the higher the level of parental education, the higher the probability of entering a more qualified job than

TABLE 12.7. *Parameters from multinomial logistic regression models for men*

	I	II	IIIa	IIIb	IV	VI	VII
Model: Entry class on education							
Interc.	-3.32	-2.11	-2.01	-1.73	-1.53	-0.28	0.00
Education:							
1b	0.00	0.00	0.00	0.00	0.00	0.00	0.00
2a	0.46	0.70	0.32	0.26	-0.04	0.62	0.00
2b	2.13	2.00	1.65	1.12	-0.09	0.14	0.00
2c	3.11	2.44	1.95	1.32	0.23	0.01	0.00
3a	4.55	4.33	2.61	1.05	0.65	0.51	0.00
3b	7.18	5.08	3.52	2.02	1.24	-0.18	0.00
Model: Entry class on education, parental education, parental class, and parental occupational prestige							
Interc.	-3.26	-2.02	-1.99	-2.84	-2.55	-0.33	0.00
Education:							
1b	0.00	0.00	0.00	0.00	0.00	0.00	0.00
2a	0.38	0.63	0.25	0.16	-0.07	0.59	0.00

2b	1.87	1.79	1.43	0.87	-0.17	0.07	0.00
2c	2.73	2.15	1.67	0.96	0.10	-0.07	0.00
3a	4.21	4.07	2.35	0.71	0.52	0.43	0.00
3b	6.67	4.72	3.17	1.52	1.04	-0.27	0.00
Parental education:							
1b	0.00	0.00	0.00	0.00	0.00	0.00	0.00
2a	0.21	0.19	0.29	0.35	0.20	0.08	0.00
2c	0.28	0.24	0.33	0.36	0.07	0.12	0.00
3a	0.29	0.30	0.36	0.78	0.19	0.05	0.00
3b	0.62	0.44	0.37	0.93	0.41	0.15	0.00
Parental class:							
I	0.00	0.00	0.00	0.00	0.00	0.00	0.00
II	-0.24	-0.04	-0.07	-0.02	-0.07	0.21	0.00
III	-0.24	-0.12	0.09	0.37	0.07	-0.03	0.00
IV	-0.76	-0.71	-0.62	-0.38	0.95	-0.40	0.00
VI	-0.62	-0.40	-0.43	0.03	-0.23	0.21	0.00
VII	-0.92	-0.65	-0.61	0.17	-0.23	-0.14	0.00
Parental occupational prestige	0.01	0.01	0.01	0.02	0.02	0.00	0.00

TABLE 12.8. *Parameters from multinomial logistic regression models for women*

	I	II	IIIA	IIIB	IV	VI	VII
Model: Entry class on education							
Interc.	-3.79	-2.50	-1.64	-0.20	-2.30	-1.67	0.00
Education:							
1b	0.00	0.00	0.00	0.00	0.00	0.00	0.00
2a	0.79	0.96	1.35	0.71	0.30	1.81	0.00
2b	2.19	2.18	2.09	0.88	0.47	1.37	0.00
2c	3.63	3.22	2.78	1.16	1.08	1.42	0.00
3a	4.92	6.30	3.15	1.35	1.80	1.53	0.00
3b	7.91	5.97	3.60	1.38	2.25	1.54	0.00
Model: Entry class on education, parental education, parental class and parental occupational prestige							
Interc.	-4.28	-2.83	-2.28	-0.86	-2.72	-1.56	0.00
Education:							
1b	0.00	0.00	0.00	0.00	0.00	0.00	0.00
2a	0.71	0.91	1.30	0.68	0.22	1.79	0.00
2b	1.95	2.03	1.94	0.78	0.29	1.26	0.00

2c	3.20	2.94	2.52	0.97	0.75	1.21	0.00
3a	4.55	6.06	2.93	1.19	1.51	1.36	0.00
3b	7.35	5.60	3.27	1.14	1.81	1.26	0.00
Parental education:							
1b	0.00	0.00	0.00	0.00	0.00	0.00	0.00
2a	0.36	0.20	0.28	0.13	0.17	0.09	0.00
2c	0.46	0.16	0.23	0.10	0.23	0.22	0.00
3a	0.60	0.44	0.38	0.44	0.33	0.50	0.00
3b	1.03	0.66	0.58	0.57	0.89	0.73	0.00
Parental class:							
I	0.00	0.00	0.00	0.00	0.00	0.00	0.00
II	-0.09	-0.01	0.00	0.05	-0.19	0.00	0.00
III	-0.01	0.05	0.21	0.26	-0.08	0.00	0.00
IV	-0.57	-0.45	-0.51	-0.33	0.02	-0.66	0.00
VI	-0.46	-0.31	-0.14	0.02	-0.41	-0.26	0.00
VII	-0.45	-0.34	-0.15	0.07	-0.43	-0.37	0.00
Parental occupational prestige:	0.02	0.01	0.02	0.02	0.02	0.00	0.00

one in Class VII. In the same way, the odds are higher for entering a non-manual job—it may be indicative that the odds for someone taking a job in Class IIIb rather than in Class VII are quite high, if at least one of the parents has a tertiary education. Along the same lines, the odds of avoiding unskilled manual jobs and of acquiring jobs in the service class are clearly higher for persons with service-class origins than for others. It is worth noticing that the odds of a man (but not a woman) with self-employed parents to enter self-employment is quite substantial, irrespective of his education and his parents' education and prestige. Furthermore, the higher the level of parental prestige, the higher the odds of not being employed in an unskilled manual job.

In sum, the importance of the family of origin on the early career class position is still substantial, even when we compare individuals at the same level of education. The inheritance effect among the self-employed—pointing to the transmission of physical resources across generations—is fairly strong for men but non-existent for women. Thus, it appears that the patrilineal forms of inheritance within this class will carry on well into the next millennium.

The fact that the class of origin affects the class position of adult persons, even when educational differences between social classes are taken into account, is in accordance with numerous studies in industrialized societies (Kurz and Müller 1987). A less often considered question is if there is, in addition, an interaction between social origin and the association between education and class of entry, i.e. whether this association is of different strength for different social origins. Such an impact could, among other things, shed light upon family strategies of how to support children's occupational attainment (cf. Erikson and Jonsson 1996*b*).

We test for this interaction effect by fitting uniform difference models to the thirty tables of the individual's education and social class formed by the combination of six classes of origin by five levels of parental education. With this model one assumes that the pattern of interaction is the same in the tables compared, while the strength of the association may vary from table to table. The model produces one parameter for each table, indicating the relative strength of that association (Erikson and Goldthorpe 1992; Xie 1992).

The results from this fitting exercise have already been reported in Table 12.4. A model (E) in which it is assumed that the interaction is the same in all thirty tables fits fairly well for both men and women, but the uniform difference model (F) gives significant improvements to that fit. However, we may assume that differences between the effects of class of origin are the same at all levels of parental education and vice versa. Such an assumption is made in Model G in Table 12.4. It turns out that the difference in fit from the uniform difference model (F) is not significant for women and just significant for men (p = 0.01). The relevant parameters from Model G are reported in Table 12.9. The association between education and class of entry is relatively weak among those from the higher service class (Class I), and relatively strong among those from the class of unskilled workers (Class VII). Furthermore, the higher parental education, the weaker the association between education and entry class.[17] This holds for both men and women.

TABLE 12.9. *Parameter estimates from uniform difference models of the education by class association for different combinations of class of origin and parental education for men and women*

Parameter	Men		Women	
	β	se	β	se
Origin class:				
I (ref. cat.)	0.00		0.00	
II	0.03	(0.02)	0.03	(0.02)
III	0.02	(0.03)	0.03	(0.02)
IV	0.06	(0.03)	0.05	(0.02)
VI	0.03	(0.03)	0.10	(0.02)
VII	0.06	(0.03)	0.10	(0.02)
Parental education:				
1b (ref. cat.)	0.00		0.00	
2ab	−0.03	(0.01)	−0.04	(0.01)
2c	−0.07	(0.02)	−0.06	(0.02)
3a	−0.02	(0.02)	−0.04	(0.02)
3b	−0.07	(0.02)	−0.05	(0.02)

Note: Estimates based on Table 12.4, Model G.

One could perhaps interpret this result in the vein that sons and daughters of workers have no other resources for advancement than education—if they have only a low level of education they will have correspondingly low chances of finding a job outside their class of origin—while children from the service class have, to a larger extent, other options available, e.g. the transmission of physical capital (cf. Erikson and Jonsson 1996*b*). However, that high levels of parental education tend to reduce the association between education and class, even given class of origin, suggests that also other processes are operating, perhaps that younger people from the higher classes can rely on social networks in finding jobs.

The Early Occupational Career

How does the association between education and class position change during the early career? We hypothesized above that, especially for men, the association would decrease over time as positions will be progressively less determined by education over the career. In Table 12.4 we show the result from tests of this issue by fitting models to a data matrix of education by class by age for men and women.

A model of constant interaction between education and class over age (Model I)—from looking at G^2, DI, and Bic—gives a better fit for women than for men.[18] A model of uniform difference produces a larger improvement in fit for men than for women. The reduction in G^2 from Model I to Model J is actually not significant for women while clearly being so for men. The parameters from Model J indicating change between cohorts for men and women are reported in Table 12.10. While the parameters for women do not change, as would be expected from the difference in G^2 between Models I and J, the association between education and class clearly decreases with age for men. This could be a cohort effect, but it is more probably an effect of work-life experience. Such experience decreases the importance of education for the class positions of men, in line with our expectations. More interesting, however, and according to our assumptions, is perhaps the lack of change for women. Obviously, work-life experience between the ages of 25 and 35 does not improve their chances. One reason for this difference between men and women may be that the occupational careers of women under the age of 35 are often interrupted by childbirth (Felmlee 1993), another—which we test below—that women are employed in labour-market segments where work-life careers are difficult to pursue.

Sectoral Cleavages

As discussed earlier we expect to find different patterns of association between education and class depending upon the type of education attained, and labour-market segment. In order to study such possible interactions, we divided our sample according to type of education, employment sector, and branch of industry. We distinguish three types of education: general education (including education for agriculture, the police, and military occupations); studies in liberal arts/humanities, the caring professions, and teaching; and education for administrative, economic, social, and technical occupations. We identify two employment sectors—private and public—and three branches of industry (service, trade, and production). Since we make all combinations separately for men and women, the result is thirty-six education by class tables to which we fitted a uniform difference model. This

TABLE 12.10. *Parameters (β) and standard errors (se) from a uniform difference model of possible change in the association between education and class by age for men and women*

Age	Men		Women	
	β	se	β	se
34 (ref. cat)	0.00		0.00	
33	0.02	(0.02)	0.01	(0.02)
32	0.04	(0.02)	−0.00	(0.02)
31	0.03	(0.02)	−0.03	(0.02)
30	0.09	(0.02)	−0.03	(0.02)
29	0.10	(0.02)	−0.03	(0.02)
28	0.13	(0.02)	−0.01	(0.02)
27	0.11	(0.02)	0.00	(0.02)
26	0.16	(0.02)	−0.00	(0.02)
25	0.11	(0.02)	0.00	(0.02)

Note: Estimates based on Table 12.4, Model J.

model fits very badly, however, suggesting that the assumption of a common pattern of interaction is untenable. Instead we fit an independence model to each individual table, calculating G^2/n as a measure of association, and using these measures as dependent variables in ordinary least square regressions. The results are reported in Table 12.11.

Model 1 in Table 12.11 just compares the association between education and class for men and women and reproduces our earlier result that this relation is stronger for women. In Model 2 we add type of education. The association among those with social science and technical education is stronger than that among those with general education, and much stronger in the category having an education for teaching, caring and medical occupations. Interestingly, once we control for type of education, the effect of sex is no longer significant, presumably because many more women than men take the latter type of education (cf. Table 12.1).

When employment sector is added in Model 3, we find, in accordance with our hypothesis above, that the allocation to class positions is more structured according to formal merit in the public rather than the private sector. The other effects remain unaltered. Finally, Model 4 shows that the lack of meritocratic structure is especially pronounced in organizations involved in trade—an almost completely private branch of industry—a result also found in our analysis of occupational prestige reported in connection with Table 12.2.

Robert Erikson and Jan O. Jonsson

TABLE 12.11. *OLS regression estimates of the association between education and class (G²/n) on sex, type of education, employment sector, and branch of employment*

Variable	Factor	Models			
		1	2	3	4
Sex	Men (ref. cat.)	0.00	0.00	0.00	0.00
	Women	0.18*	−0.03	−0.05	−0.04
Type of Education	General (ref. cat.)		0.00	0.00	0.00
	Social science + Technology		0.30*	0.32*	0.31*
	Arts and care		0.79*	0.73*	0.73*
Employment Sector	Private (ref. cat.)			0.00	0.00
	Public			0.19*	0.16*
Industrial Branch	Service (ref. cat.)				0.00
	Trade				−0.16*
	Production/primary				−0.07

Notes: Model 1 is based on two tables; Model 2 on six; Model 3 on 12 and Model 4 on 36 tables.
Each table is weighted by the number of observed cases in it.

 * Significant at the 5 per cent level

To conclude, the high association between education and class among women appears to follow from their choice of educational and occupational sector. A relatively large proportion of women aim at jobs in the medical and caring sectors and in schools, where most jobs are in public-sector employment and where well-defined qualifications are often formally required.

CONCLUSION

In this chapter, we have studied how individuals with different formal qualifications are allocated to differently rewarded positions in the labour market and class structure in Sweden. We began with a number of assumptions about the pattern and strength of the association between educational credentials and social positions. We also outlined possible ways in which this association may be dependent on, or structured by, other factors, such as type of education, industrial branch, firm size, sex, and social origin.

What conclusions can be drawn? First, naturally, there is generally a substantial association between formal qualifications, on the one hand, and occupational prestige and social-class positions, on the other. This association is pervasive in that it exists in all subgroups identified by our structuring variables. Moreover, the effect of education on position is on the whole unmediated by industrial sector and firm size, although these factors have independent effects on labour-market outcomes. This goes to show that the education—position link is in general not produced because higher education leads to jobs in sectors and establishments which are characterized by a more favourable opportunity structure.

Second, even if the pattern of association between education and social position is much as expected, it is not simply a matter of 'the higher the level, the higher the position'. A university degree produces the most predictable outcome with a strong positive association with the upper service class and a similarly strong negative one with manual work. At the other end of the educational hierarchy, those with only compulsory or low-level vocational education, face fairly high entry barriers to service-class occupations, while barriers to unqualified white-collar positions, self-employment, and manual work are low. As anticipated, in Sweden there is little difference between the two lowest levels of education in terms of access to social positions and occupational attainment. Matriculation or lower tertiary education tend often to lead to service-class positions, and the higher of these qualifications rarely to other social positions. The great divide in the educational structure when it comes to social-class positions is, in spite of this, between those with a degree and all others. However, for occupational prestige the divide is between those with any tertiary level education and those with less education.

Third, we proposed that the study of the association between educational attainment and labour-market rewards should ideally also include measures of *type* of education and of school achievement (grades or other measures of 'ability'). At least in Sweden, grades have an impact on occupational prestige at a given level of education, though the effect is not particularly strong and the effects of level of education on outcomes do not change very much, when grades are taken into account. When scrutinizing the credential value of a qualification, the level attained is essential, but our empirical analyses show that type, or sector, of education is also important to consider in order to give an accurate picture of the allocation process. The rewards to an achieved level of education are also partly dependent upon the sector. Further analyses show that income differences between educational levels are especially pronounced among those with some form of medical education, and—albeit to a lesser extent—among those with a service, business, or engineering education, while those with a liberal arts or general education receive especially low financial returns to education (Erikson and Jonsson 1996c).

Roughly half the impact of type of education on prestige stems from the fact that it channels individuals into different industrial branches, which in turn have different opportunity and reward structures. This channelling must to a large extent be assumed to have been anticipated by the students in their choice of educational sector—many choose their education in order to find employment of a specific type and in a specific job sector. Yet, even controlling for branch of industry and grade-point averages, type of education has a non-trivial effect on labour-market outcomes for people at the same qualification level. This may come about because some types of education are, at a given point in time, in greater demand than others. Furthermore, type of education may carry information about personal characteristics of the students, much the same way as the level of education is normally assumed to do. For example, some educational programmes at secondary and tertiary level have a reputation of being very demanding, thus indicating special qualities among those who have successfully completed them. Some courses may also signal particular configurations of cultural capital or life-style which employers may regard as 'appropriate' for jobs at the higher echelons of the social structure (cf. Bourdieu 1984; Collins 1971).

Fourth, we found some support for the contention that the allocation process is more dependent on education in some industrial sectors, but in the main our expectations about sectoral differences in the occupational returns to education were not borne out.

Our results suggest that future studies of how the allocation of individuals to positions are structured by factors other than the amount of education have the potential of increasing our understanding of the social stratification process. At the same time, we can interpret our findings as supporting the view that a person's level of education is so crucial for his or her occupational attainment, that the structuring variables we have added are of only moderate relevance.

Fifth, education is a somewhat more crucial resource in the labour market for women than for men, in that the association between formal qualifications and class position is stronger among women. As expected, this is partly because men have better chances of promotion. It appears that few young women make a career on the job—their occupational positions are determined by educational level to the same extent at the age of 35 as at 25—while men make more occupational moves between these ages. Interestingly, while promotion is less common among women, they face lower risks of ending up in a social-class position 'below' what could be expected from their level of education.

Our analyses suggest that both these results can be explained by sex differences in the choice of what type of studies to pursue and the subsequent sex segregation in the labour market. If men and women had been equally distributed across educational sectors and industrial branches, the pattern and strength of the education position association would in fact have been very much the same. This result is important because it indicates that it is not primarily discrimination against women in promotion decisions that produce attainment differences between young men and women. Rather, to the extent that discrimination is at work, it takes effect at the entrance to the labour market, where employers in some sectors may prefer to employ men; or it works as adding a negative weight to some occupational or sectoral choices among women, for instance by constraining such choices since some careers appear incompatible with maternity and childbirth. It can be noted that our results are in accordance with the interpretation that women's educational and occupational preferences can partly be explained by the fact that their best strategy for 'getting ahead' will be to acquire educational credentials directed towards industrial branches where merit counts highly—the 'costs' of a loose connection to the labour market and of sex discrimination is probably less in occupations where formal requirements on merit are great.

Our results thus suggest that sex differences in attainment can be partially explained by preferential choices. It may be that women end up in the health care and educational labour-market sectors because they, compared to men, prefer a *maximin* income strategy, i.e. they choose an education that leads to a labour-market sector where they feel assured that they can find a safe job with an acceptable salary; or, they may sacrifice monetary rewards for other preferable job characteristics, such as intrinsic job values, opportunities to work with people, to work part-time, etc.

The sex differences in the allocation to social-class positions are not replicated in our analysis of occupational prestige, that is, the association between level of education and prestige is about the same for men and women. This may follow from the association between class and prestige being clearly higher among men than among women while the effect of education on prestige, given class, is about the same for the two sexes. It may be that the prestige of an occupation is determined by the education normally held by its incumbents to such a large extent that the association between education and prestige is about the same regardless of how the occupations are distributed among the social classes.

Sixth, we find compelling evidence to suggest that even by the end of the twentieth century social origin affects class destinations for young people at the same level of education, with the same type of education and with similar grades. This is, as expected, most evident in the primary sector of the economy and for the self-employed. Furthermore, we find clear evidence of a sex difference in the origin effects, indicating that there is still a predominantly patrilineal inheritance of class positions among young people. Moreover, the effect of class origin is stronger for young people at lower levels of education. This could indicate that for privileged families, educational attainment is only one strategy for securing the future of their children—other strategies might involve transferring capital, thereby facilitating self-employment, and helping children to positions with advantageous promotion prospects, e.g. by utilizing social networks. Further analyses actually suggest that the value of qualifications at tertiary and higher levels in achieving an upper service class position is almost entirely meritocratic—among young employees, both origin effects and sex differences appear to be wiped out by the credential value (Jonsson 1996*b*).

Thus, in this analysis we have once again demonstrated some of the standard results of stratification research, that there is strong association between level of education and social position, and that education mediates a large part of the effect of social origin on social destination, while a direct effect of origin on destination still remains. However, we have also been able to show some results that appear less often in the stratification literature. Hence, we have shown that, in Sweden at least, the association between level of education and class position is stronger among women than among men, and that it is slightly stronger among those from lower social origins and whose parents have less education than among higher classes and groups with higher education. Furthermore, we have demonstrated what is often assumed but seldom shown, namely that not only level, but also sector, of education, is important for occupational attainment.

We have, however, only been able to hint at the mechanisms that account for these associations and effects. Generally, we believe that they are built up from intentional actions by individuals—students, job seekers, and employers—within the structural constraints prevailing in Swedish society, especially in the labour market and within firms. Students can be assumed to choose level and type of education partly because of interests and partly because of labour-market prospects.[19] These choices have consequences for future job careers, regardless of how they are motivated, since allocation agencies apparently distinguish between job applicants with regard to both level and type of education. Hence, abilities, interests, preferences, expectations, and prejudices of young people and of employing agents in firms and organizations together structure the transitions from school to work.

NOTES

Financial support from the Swedish Council for Research in the Humanities and Social Sciences (HSFR, Grant F 903/94) is gratefully acknowledged. We thank Johan Fritzell and Carl le Grand and other participants in the sociology seminars at Stockholm University for helpful comments on an earlier draft.

1. The various aspects of Swedish society described here relate to 1990, the point in time to which our data refer. Since then changes have occurred, especially in the educational system, which makes parts of this description slightly outdated.

2. Some industrial sectors, such as banking and insurance, complement the public educational system with internal training.

3. The state unemployment agency has managed to cover such a great part of the labour market by way of the fact that the unemployed must register with it in order to claim unemployment benefits.

4. Two subjects, English and mathematics, normally had one less demanding and one more demanding section, in grades 7–9. What section a pupil ended up in was a matter of choice, which made social origin an influential predictor. In addition, there was one subject of the pupil's own choice, where the main alternatives were a second foreign language, technical education and economics. Though there have been no formal barriers since the mid-1980s, those who did not choose the more demanding courses in English and mathematics, and an additional language as the extra course, in practice reduced their opportunities of continuing onto the academic branches at secondary level.

5. One additional option is to leave before finishing secondary school. In the cohorts born 1956–1965, about one-third took this option and around one-quarter took academic examinations, while around 30 per cent completed vocational studies, and just over 10 per cent completed semi-vocational courses of study.

6. Type and level of education may also interact. Teacher training, for instance, only occurs at the tertiary level.

7. The original sample consists of 25 per cent of all those resident in Sweden born between 1943 and 1974. In our cohorts, slightly less than 20 per cent had no job at the time of the 1990 census, and are therefore excluded. Although we have no information on their activities, students and parents with small children will be the most common categories excluded. Unemployment rates were still very low in 1990.

8. The final grades from secondary school are used. We have no information on grades for those who finished after primary school. For this group of school-leavers we imputed the average final grades from primary school collected from another large data-set for a corresponding group (cf. Erikson and Jonsson 1993).

9. We are unable to distinguish those with incomplete education. This does not constitute a problem, however, as the percentage in our cohorts with incomplete compulsory schooling is very low, at around 2 per cent.

10. Class-origin effects are somewhat stronger for men than for women, but educational origin effects are slightly weaker. We believe that the combined effect of class and education in the family of orientation is about the same for the two sexes, and that the differences in the effects generated by this data-set should not be substantively interpreted (cf. Erikson and Jonsson 1993).

11. This is according to the standard interpretation in the Blau and Duncan (1967) tradition. We can also interpret the part of the educational effect on occupational prestige that is due to an association between origin and education as being in one respect 'ascribed'.

12. This decrease in the effect of level of education appears when GPA *alone* is added to the independent factors in Model 1.

13. This assumption is, on the other hand, partially supported by the result that the prestige gain for additional educational attainment is relatively high in the professional and administrative branches of the public service sector.

14. We should note, however, that the conclusions reached on the basis of Table 12.2 depend on the age selection of our respondents. Origin effects may increase over careers, and the same may apply for sector effects and work-life experience.

15. The model can be written SEX*EDUC+SEX*CLASS+SEX*LEVELS. The G^2 will obviously be equal to the sum of the G^2s resulting from the levels model fitted separately to the tables for men and women, as reported in Model C of Table 12.4. The G^2 of the combined model is thus 515.2 with 32 degrees of freedom and the index of dissimilarity is 1.1.

16. To take two examples: the odds ratio for the association between lower and higher tertiary education and positions in Classes I and II drops from 6.55 to 6.11 for men, and from 27.7 to 26.0 for women; and that relating educational levels 2a and 2c to Classes IIIa and VI drops from 9.39 to 8.0 for men, and from 6.17 to 6.05 for women.

17. Note that an education at level 2c could often be regarded as higher than one at level 3a for those in the parental generation.

18. The G^2 should be expected to be slightly greater for men because of the difference in sample sizes. A comparison that adjusts for this difference may be based on $G^2(S)$ (Erikson and Goldthorpe 1992: 88). If the sample size for men is adjusted to equal that for women, the resulting $G^2(S)$ is 578, which should be compared to a value of 438 for women.

19. See Erikson and Jonsson (1996*b*) for a discussion of the choice of level of education.

13

The Transition from School to Work in Switzerland

Do Characteristics of the Educational System and Class Barriers Matter?

MARLIS BUCHMANN AND STEFAN SACCHI

INTRODUCTION

This chapter examines the effects of social origin and educational attainment on occupational outcomes at the time of labour-market entry in Switzerland. This country constitutes an interesting case because the transition from school to work is largely unexplored. Given the strong occupational orientation of the Swiss educational system, which is, with the notable exceptions of Germany and Austria, unique in the industrialized world, the investigation of the extent to which, and the ways in which, occupation-specific credentials condition the allocation of persons to jobs will shed light on the significance of institutional factors in this process. It is of special interest whether particular educational qualifications generate credential-specific chances of labour-market allocation, which cannot be assessed by simply conceiving of education as an individual human-capital resource. With respect to social origin, similar issues arise. Beside the fact that remarkably little is known about the association between family background and occupational outcomes in Switzerland, the question arises as to whether particular origin classes are associated with specific mobility chances in the labour market. By exploring the nature of this association we will gain some insights into both the intergenerational reproduction of social inequality and the process of social mobility prevailing in Switzerland. We will thus be able partially to answer the question of whether class origin is associated with specific mobility chances, which cannot be accounted for by conceptualizing social origin exclusively in terms of individual (economic and cultural) resources. Against this backdrop, the main purpose of this chapter is to

identify the extent to which, and the ways in which, institutional characteristics of the educational system and class barriers shape the effects of social
origin and education on occupational outcomes at labour-market entry.

In addition to the importance of understanding the institutional context
within which the transition from school to work occurs, we also focus on other
macro-level factors, such as the economy. In a booming economy, for example, the demand for labour differs greatly from that in times of economic
recession. The employers' quantitative and qualitative demands for labour are
therefore likely to affect the association between educational qualifications and
occupational outcomes. In addition to individuals' educational attainment and
their social origin, we attempt to assess the effects of the demand for labour
at the time of labour-market entry on occupational allocation.

In order to gather some basic evidence regarding the associations between
social origin, education, and occupational outcomes at the time of labour-
market entry, our analyses will be based on a representative survey of Swiss-
German men and women born around 1950 and 1960. Before turning to the
empirical analysis, we will first outline the ways in which the linkages
between social origin, education, and allocation in the labour market may be
conceived. We will then describe the structure of the Swiss educational system, emphasizing its institutional characteristics and suggesting how these
features may affect the allocation process. Next, we will turn to the Swiss
class structure and provide some suggestions as to how particular social
classes either provide mobility chances or convey mobility barriers to their
sons and daughters.

DISCRETE AND GRADATIONAL PROCESSES GOVERNING FIRST ALLOCATION IN THE LABOUR MARKET

There are various ways of conceiving of the process by which social origin
and educational qualifications are converted into hierarchically ordered occupational positions. We distinguish between two types of conversion.

The first type is gradational in nature. In abstract terms, this implies that
differences in both social origin and educational qualifications can be mapped
on a continuum in such a way that higher standings indicate better chances
of being assigned to higher positions in the labour market and vice versa.
Thus, the underlying assumption is a gradational conversion of social origin
and education into occupational outcomes. The empirical investigation of
this type of process presupposes the existence of some kind of gradational
measures that might be used to characterize the standing of individuals with
respect to social origin and educational qualifications.

The second type of process by which positions in the labour market are assigned is discrete in nature. The basic assumption here is that both individuals' social origin and educational qualifications may be mapped into mutually exclusive and exhaustive categories. Each category is associated with particular mobility chances or barriers regarding allocation in the labour market. This approach to the conversion process assumes that structural and institutional factors are at work that either promote or limit the degree of mobility associated with particular categories. The identification of these factors is a prerequisite to the definition of such discrete measures.

With respect to social origin, the gradational and discrete approaches to the conversion process can be associated with the two main stratification paradigms, the status-attainment model (Blau and Duncan 1967), and the class-mobility model (Goldthorpe 1980; Erikson and Goldthorpe 1992, 1994). One way of capturing the role of education in the two alternative conceptions of the conversion process described above is by associating them with two different approaches, the *human-capital* approach (G. Becker 1975), and the *institutional* approach (Buchmann and Charles 1995; Buchmann and Sacchi 1995*b*; Charles and Buchmann 1994; König and Müller 1986; Maurice, Sellier, and Silvestre 1979, 1982; Müller 1994; Müller and Karle 1993). Below, we shall elaborate on the basic assumptions of these models, apply them to the Swiss case, and derive some hypotheses about the significance of these models in Switzerland, starting with the role of education regarding labour allocation.

THE SWISS EDUCATIONAL SYSTEM: THE IMPACT OF INSTITUTIONAL CHARACTERISTICS ON LABOUR-MARKET OUTCOMES

The role attributed to education for allocating people to jobs greatly depends on the selection of the theoretical framework. Within the framework of human-capital theory (G. Becker 1975), education is regarded as an individual investment and, consequently, as an indicator of the individual's productivity regarding market work. His or her productivity increases with the number of years spent in school, or in the educational system, where human capital is acquired. Upon labour-market entry, this is converted into a particular position in the labour-market hierarchy. According to this line of argument, educational qualifications constitute individual assets or resources. The more individuals invest in the acquisition of human capital, the more assets they acquire, and the higher the returns on their investments. In other words, their chances of obtaining higher positions in the labour-market hierarchy increase. Thus, the conversion of educational qualifications into occupational outcomes is gradational in nature. Accordingly, the gradational measure of educational qualifications is years of schooling.[1]

Within the framework of the institutional theory of education (J. Meyer 1977; Müller 1994), the characteristics of the educational system and the nature of the links between the educational system and the labour market affect the association between educational qualifications and occupational outcomes. In this theoretical framework, it is essentially the institutional arrangements within which the conversion process occurs that shape the association between education and occupational destination. Crucial institutional characteristics of the educational system that vary greatly among industrialized countries are educational differentiation and educational standardization (Allmendinger 1989*b*) as well as the linkage between the educational system and the labour market (Buchmann and Charles 1995; Charles and Buchmann 1994). In order to understand the ways in which the educational system mediates the conversion process in the Swiss case, below we present some basic information about the institutional arrangements of the Swiss educational system and its institutionalized links with the labour market.

The Swiss Educational System

The Swiss educational system is federalist in structure, with a high level of differentiation at the secondary level, and a strong vocational orientation (see Buchmann and Charles, with Sacchi 1993). First of all, the institutional arrangements of the educational system greatly vary by language region. In the French- and Italian-speaking parts of Switzerland, some structural elements of the educational system resemble those of the neighbouring countries of France and Italy, thus setting them apart from the characteristics of the Swiss-German educational system. In this chapter, we focus primarily on the latter given that Swiss-Germans constitute the great majority of the Swiss population (approximately 65 per cent), and also because our empirical analyses are based on data for two Swiss-German birth cohorts. However, the educational systems of the three language regions also show some commonalities, especially with regard to vocational orientation and, hence, the strong connectedness with the labour market. Moreover, the structure of the educational system in the German-speaking part of Switzerland varies greatly by canton.[2] Again, despite differences in the cantonal educational structures, we find similarities with respect to two major institutional characteristics, namely, the high level of differentiation and the strong vocational orientation.

Educational sorting processes (i.e. tracking) begin early for children in the German-speaking part of Switzerland (see also Buchmann and Charles, with

Sacchi 1993). Depending upon the canton, children attend primary school for four to six years before making the major transition to one of the three types of secondary school (*Realschule, Sekundarschule, or Gymnasium*). The range of options offered by these three types greatly varies. On completion, the *Gymnasium* includes the broadest range of options, followed by the *Sekundarschule* and the *Realschule*. The great majority of men and women completing the *Gymnasium* go on to university. While some of the school-leavers from the *Sekundarschule* and *Realschule* transfer to the *Gymnasium*, most of them serve a traditional apprenticeship. This involves a two-to-four-year training programme, combining some formal vocational education in a state-run school with practical on-the-job training in a firm or organization in the private or public sector. Those who complete an apprenticeship receive official certification of having acquired the skills necessary to practice a particular occupation. The Swiss system of vocational training encompasses several hundred vocational credentials, which documents the high level of differentiation and occupational specialization prevailing in Switzerland. For young men and women who serve an apprenticeship, the end of formal schooling occurs with the acquisition of an occupation-specific credential. The general structure of the educational system in the German-speaking part of Switzerland is represented in Figure 13.1 (taken from Buchmann and Charles, with Sacchi 1993).

The overwhelming majority of young Swiss men and women serve an apprenticeship. In 1990, for example, 80 per cent of school-leavers aged 15–17 years were enrolled in traditional apprenticeship programmes (Buchmann 1994). Given the great quantitative significance of this type of education, the role of occupation-specific credentials for allocating people to jobs deserves special attention. The system of vocational training involves the institutionalization of formal educational requirements for practice in many occupations. It is worth noting that, despite the federalist structure of the Swiss educational system, vocational education is defined nationwide for the great majority of occupations. Curricula, examinations, and certificates of vocational education are stipulated by the respective professional associations, employers, cantons, and the federal administration. There is, therefore, a high level of standardization across cantons which in turn guarantees the mobility of workers across the boundaries of the cantonal labour markets. Given this strong emphasis on vocational education and occupation-specific educational requirements, access to the great majority of medium- and high-status occupations is limited to those who have acquired the corresponding vocational credential (Charles and Buchmann 1994). In contrast to most other advanced industrialized countries, where educational systems emphasizing general knowledge prevail, Switzerland is characterized by an occupation-based educational system. This implies that the occupational

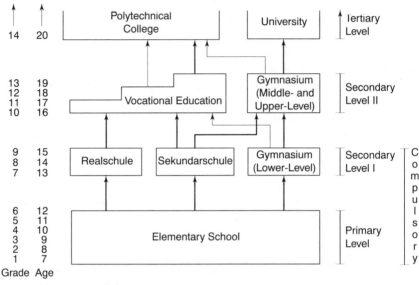

Note: Adapted from Bundesamt für Statistik 1987.
Source: Shavit and Blossfeld (1993: 178).

FIG. 13.1. *The Swiss educational system*
From *Persistent Inequality: Changing Educational Attainment in Thirteen Countries,*
ed. Yossi Shavit and Hans-Peter Blossfeld. Copyright © 1993 by WestviewPress.
Reprinted by permission of WestviewPress.

segmentation of the labour market is built into the Swiss educational system, thus generating extremely tight linkages between the educational system and the labour market. Educational requirements for most jobs are clearly defined by the vocational training programmes and the respective examinations for acquiring occupation-specific credentials. In the Swiss labour market, employers rely heavily on these credentials for allocating people to jobs. It is only in times of labour shortage that jobs are filled by people who are not certified to have successfully completed the particular occupation-based training. In times of plentiful labour supply, by contrast, the prospects of labour allocation are particularly bleak for those with only compulsory schooling; that is, those who have not acquired an occupation-specific credential. Given the importance of occupation-specific credentials for occupational allocation, we may conclude that, in the Swiss case, educational qualifications are associated with credential-specific chances of job allocation.

Against this background, we examined how the institutional arrangements of the Swiss educational system shape the association between educational qualifications and occupational outcomes upon labour-market entry. Given the highly differentiated educational system which involves early selection processes, we expect a relatively strong overall association between educational attainment and first allocation in the labour market. In comparison to countries in which the national educational system emphasizes general knowledge, we expect the association to be stronger in the Swiss case. In this respect, Charles and Buchmann (1994) have argued that in less differentiated educational systems based on general knowledge large segments of the population do not differ in terms of education, thus making educational sorting processes in the labour market less pertinent. It is not only the high level of differentiation, but also the close institutional linkages between the educational system and the labour market that account for the strong association between education and occupational outcomes in Switzerland. For example, the first job of many young men and women who completed vocational training is in the firm where the apprenticeship was served, thus documenting the strong organizational link between education and the labour market. Overall, the institutionalization of educational requirements for the practice of the great majority of occupations is responsible for strong educational sorting processes at the time of labour-market entry.

Moreover, we expect the conversion of educational qualifications into occupational positions in Switzerland to be a partially discrete process. The prerequisite of this type of conversion is a highly differentiated educational system characterized by tracks and respective educational certificates that are differently valued in the labour market. Although particular educational tracks may not vary greatly in the years of schooling they require for completion, the corresponding educational certificates are associated with different chances of occupational allocation. In other words, it is also the *type* of educational track completed that counts for the future location in the labour-market hierarchy, and not only the amount of educational investment. In particular, we distinguish between three aspects of the conversion of educational qualifications into first occupational allocation. The first aspect refers to the average returns which school-leavers of given educational tracks can expect on the basis of their human-capital investments. The second aspect is defined as the institutionally determined extra returns or losses of particular educational tracks. Third, the strength of the institutional link between educational tracks and particular segments of the labour market. Based on these three aspects of the conversion process we propose the following three expectations:

• We expect that the average human capital investments associated with particular educational tracks determine to a large extent the returns on given educational qualifications.

- In relation to the human capital investments, we can expect, (a) the prestigious academic track (i.e. university degree) to be associated with high extra returns in the labour market because at the tertiary level this track is still taken by only an elite few, thus guaranteeing especially profitable returns in the labour market; (b) that basic secondary level schooling and/or minimum vocational training are linked with relative losses, partially because the occupations to which these types of schooling provide access are predominantly female; and (c) the conversion rate of intermediate level general education with 'matriculation' to be associated with relative losses because this type of education does not provide occupation-specific skills.
- The institutional links between educational tracks and the labour market are expected to be strongest for vocational training primarily because most apprenticeships are confined to particular segments of the labour market. Moreover, there is a strong organizational link between this type of education and the labour market. Similar arguments hold for technical college certificates and a considerable proportion of university degrees.

THE STRUCTURE OF SOCIAL STRATIFICATION AND ITS IMPACT ON LABOUR-MARKET OUTCOMES

Stratification systems in advanced industrial societies may be characterized in various ways (Blau and Duncan, with Tyree 1994). One aspect involves their contours (see e.g. Grusky 1994). Applied to the stratification system and inter-generational social-mobility regime, the differentiation between discrete (or categorical), and gradational processes described above, corresponds to the well-known distinction between approaches referring to classes and those referring to gradational status groupings. As Grusky (1994: 16) maintains, the basic assumption of discrete models of stratification is that people can be sorted into mutually exclusive and exhaustive categories, usually referred to as classes. Classes are separated by boundaries, which exert constraints on mobility between them (Mayer and Carroll 1990). These constraints may vary in nature. By contrast, gradational models of stratification dispute the existence of such boundaries. In this perspective, the stratification system is vertically differentiated without being subdivided into distinct and exclusive groups.

According to these two types of stratification model, the mobility chances associated with one's social origin are either gradational or discrete. Within the framework of the status-attainment model, the circumstances of social origin represent the advantages or disadvantages in terms of socio-economic and cultural resources that the family conveys to children. Within this research tradition, the resources provided by the family background are measured either by socio-economic status (see e.g. Blau and Duncan 1967), or occupational scales of prestige (see e.g. Treiman 1977). According to these gradational measures of social origin, the assumption is that the greater the individual advantages, the better the opportunities for being allocated to a higher position in the labour-market hierarchy. Class-mobility models, by contrast, depart from the assumption that class boundaries limit or enhance mobility chances. Family background is not just conceived as a context providing resources to a greater or lesser degree, but is associated with the constraints or opportunities associated with particular class locations. These classes constitute social milieux characterized by particular value orientations, world-views, social networks, scope of actions, etc., which convey specific mobility chances or barriers to offspring. Both approaches assume, to a greater or lesser extent, that the effects of social origin on occupational outcomes are mediated by the offspring's educational attainment.

For Switzerland, we assume that class-specific mobility chances are at work at the upper and lower ends of the class structure. Among professionals especially, there is a great willingness and ability to promote their offspring's occupational careers, be it indirectly through the promotion of the children's educational aspirations and educational attainment, or directly through the use of their networks, access to information, control of resources, and so forth. By contrast, a working-class background is likely to be associated with mobility barriers, especially because the major channel of upward mobility, namely education, is still not highly valued in this social milieu. This is especially true for daughters from working-class backgrounds. Finally, the class of unskilled manual workers constitutes a social milieu in which the accumulation of social disadvantages generates mobility barriers, thus considerably limiting the offspring's opportunities for occupational attainment.

THE EFFECTS OF THE DEMAND FOR LABOUR ON THE TRANSITION FROM SCHOOL TO WORK

Several studies have shown that labour-market conditions at the time of labour-market entry affect the allocation of people to jobs (see e.g. Blossfeld 1985*b*, 1989). With an expanding labour market, the chances of being allocated to a higher position in the labour market hierarchy increase, and when the labour market shrinks, these chances diminish. Several macro-level indicators may be used to measure labour-market conditions. For our purposes, we selected the change in the total number of labour-force participants referring to the year of the individuals' labour-market entry and the year immediately preceding it. This indicator is a direct measure of the expansion or shrinkage of the labour force at the time when individuals' allocation to jobs is at stake. Based on this measure, we advance the hypothesis that the more the labour force expands, the better the opportunities for being allocated to a higher position in the labour-market hierarchy become.

DATA AND METHODS

Data for the analyses are taken from a 1989 mailed survey of two Swiss-German birth cohorts—one born between 1949 and 1951, and the other between 1959 and 1961 (Buchmann and Sacchi, forthcoming). The survey includes detailed biographical information on the educational, occupational, and family careers. The sample was drawn by a two-stage method whereby 100 communities (broken down by region and community size) were selected. Cohort members residing in the selected communities were then randomly sampled on the basis of information provided in the official register of community residents. The sample was limited to Swiss citizens. The final response rate was approximately 45 per cent, which is relatively high for a mailed survey of this length. Participation rates do not significantly differ by sex, cohort, type of labour market, region, and community size. Comparisons with available statistics also indicate that the samples are representative with the exception of a slight under-representation of men and especially women who have completed only compulsory schooling. The distribution over the other levels of schooling is consistent with available aggregate statistics. The analyses presented here are based on a sample weighted to be proportionally representative for the two birth cohorts and to correct for the under-representation of lower educational strata.

In order to test whether institutional arrangements of the educational systems and class-related mobility barriers affect occupational outcomes at labour-market entry, we compute two types of model.[3] The first is a multiple regression for estimating the effects of respondents' social origin and educational qualifications on the status of their first job (i.e. entry status)[4] The second is a multinomial logistic regression (Hosmer and Lemeshow 1989) for estimating the effects of the same variables on the class allocation of their first job (i.e. entry class). For entry status, we use Treiman's (1977) occupational prestige scale as our indicator. The correspondent dependent variable of the respondent's entry class is measured by Goldthorpe's class schema (Erikson and Goldthorpe 1992), which was slightly adapted for the Swiss case.[5] The following explanatory variables are included in both models. Respondent's education measured on the basis of the CASMIN educational classification (Erikson and Goldthorpe 1992; Müller and Karle 1993; Müller 1994), which was also slightly adapted to reflect the institutional particularities of the Swiss educational system.[6] In an additional model, we substitute the CASMIN schema by years of schooling (defined as the average number of years required for completing a given educational track) as a gradational measure of the respondent's education. Social origin is indicated by three variables. First, we include parent's education. This variable is measured as years of schooling corresponding to the highest level of schooling attained by one of the parents. Second, father's occupational prestige based on Treiman's (1977) occupational prestige scale is included as a gradational measure of social background. The third variable to represent social origin is father's class, which is again measured by Goldthorpe's class schema. Both father's occupational prestige and father's class represent the status and class position held at the time when the respondents were 15 years of age. The demand for labour is indicated by the (percentage) difference in the total number of Swiss labour-force participants between the year of the respondent's labour-market entry and the previous one. Cohort membership is indicated by a dummy variable, whereby cohort members born between 1959 and 1961 are coded as 1, those born between 1949 and 1951 as 0. In the models presented below, the reference categories used are Class VII (i.e. unskilled manual workers) for class origin, the educational category 2a (i.e. vocational training) for the respondent's education, and the cohort 1949–1951 for cohort membership.

Before presenting the results, we briefly discuss the implications of limiting the analysis to Swiss natives.[7] Given the relatively high proportion of foreign workers in Switzerland, the exclusion of this group of labour-market participants results in a considerable under-representation of the lower strata of the occupational hierarchy.[8] For the time period of interest here, namely the 1970s and 1980s, the overwhelming majority of foreign workers in Switzerland attended school in the countries of origin and entered the Swiss labour market as unskilled or semi-skilled workers. Under these conditions, Swiss natives were channelled into higher positions in the occupational system, thus profiting from what is called the *Unterschichtung* of Swiss society by foreign workers. Against this background, and in view of the process of interest here, namely the relationship between educational qualifications and occupational destinations, the exclusion of foreign workers is likely to result in an underestimation of the effects of education on the first allocation in the labour market. This will be especially true for the negative effects of the lower levels of education.

Marlis Buchmann and Stefan Sacchi

RESULTS

Entry Status

We begin by discussing the results of the multiple regression equations, which refer to the effects of social origin, education, demand for labour, and cohort on the respondent's entry status (see Table 13.1). Pooling the sample by cohort and splitting it by sex, two separate models were run—one for men and one for women. For both men and women, the variables included in the model account for approximately 47 per cent of the status differences at labour-market entry. Respondent's education exerts the strongest effect, whereby the three main levels of the CASMIN educational classification (i.e. level 1 (1a, 1bc); level 2 (2a, 2b, 2c); and level 3 (3a, 3b)) account for the major differences in status attainment. For example, the entry status of men

TABLE 13.1. *Multiple regressions of social origin, education, labour demand, and cohort on entry status*

	Men (N = 861)			Women (N = 760)		
	b	(se)	β	b	(se)	β
Constant	32.88**	(1.94)		35.73**	(2.15)	
Cohort (1959–1961)	−1.79**	(0.62)	−0.07	−1.90**	(0.68)	−0.07
Occupational status father	0.10**	(0.03)	0.11	−0.03	(0.04)	−0.03
Parent's education	0.13	(0.12)	0.04	0.21	(0.12)	0.06
Father's class:						
I	0.40	(2.07)	0.00	4.97*	(2.07)	0.06
II	1.32	(1.31)	0.03	2.87*	(1.45)	0.05
IIIab	−0.26	(1.69)	−0.00	2.59	(1.79)	0.04
IVabc	−1.11	(1.02)	−0.03	−0.59	(1.09)	−0.01
V + VI	1.34	(0.98)	0.03	0.32	(1.03)	0.01
Education:						
1a	−6.79**	(1.29)	−0.13	−10.14**	(1.09)	−0.25
1bc	−5.95**	(1.09)	−0.14	−5.20**	(0.89)	−0.15
2b	−1.87	(1.81)	−0.03	5.43**	(1.79)	0.08
2c	4.08*	(1.69)	0.06	2.39	(1.45)	0.04
3a	15.63**	(1.46)	0.27	14.79**	(1.34)	0.29
3b	21.51**	(1.16)	0.46	23.36**	(2.06)	0.30
Labour demand	1.51**	(0.45)	0.09	1.84**	(0.43)	0.13
Explained variance	47.52			47.42		

Significance levels of 5 and 1 per cent   are marked with one or two stars, respectively. Standardized co-effcients represent semi-partial correlations in the case of dummy variables (cf. Hardy 1993: 18).

who have acquired a university degree is, ceteris paribus, 21.5 prestige points above that of the reference category (2a) (i.e. respondents having completed vocational training). By contrast, the entry status of those who have only completed basic secondary level schooling and/or minimum vocational training (1bc) is about 6 prestige points below that of the reference category.

With respect to the effects of educational qualifications, the question arises as to whether the coefficients of the educational categories represent a linear pattern, which would suggest a gradational conversion of education into occupational outcomes at labour-market entry. If so, it is primarily the average investment in human-capital acquisition that determines the returns on educational qualifications likely to be realized in the labour market. At first sight, the coefficients do not appear to deviate much from linearity. A substantial loss of the model's explanatory power occurs, however, when substituting the categorical measure of education (i.e. the CASMIN classification) with the gradational measure of years of schooling (table not shown). It amounts to 4.4 per cent for men and 3.3 per cent for women. The corresponding F-test (Hardy 1993: 78) shows that the model fit declines significantly ($p = .001$). Hence, the returns on education for the first allocation in the labour market are not only determined by human-capital investment, but also by the educational track completed. This suggests that institutional factors characterizing the Swiss educational system affect the conversion rate of education into occupational outcomes. Particular educational tracks seem to provide returns that are either above or below what can be expected on the basis of the average human-capital investment. Table 13.1 shows that, for men, the returns of the educational category 2b (i.e. intermediate level of general education without the matriculation diploma) is 1.9 prestige points lower than those provided by the reference category (2a), which represents standard vocational training. This effect, however, misses the significance level of 5 per cent. For women, the category 2c (i.e. intermediate level of general education with the matriculation diploma) represents an educational credential that is not easily converted into first occupational positions that match the human capital investment. Although this effect is not significant, the pay-off on this educational investment is considerably lower compared to that of the educational track representing intermediate-level general education without the matriculation diploma (2b). On average, the entry status of women having acquired the educational credential of matriculation (2c) is only 2.4 prestige points above the entry status of the reference group (i.e. those who have completed standard vocational education). By comparison, the entry status of women whose educational qualifications represent intermediate-level general education without matriculation (2b) is 5.20 prestige points higher compared with the reference group. These findings suggest that, relative to human-capital investment, standard vocational education

(2a) seems to be highly profitable for men, whereas intermediate-level general education without matriculation (2b) is profitable for women. In general, the educational category 2c (intermediate-level general education with matriculation) is associated with relatively meagre returns. Given the strong vocational orientation of the Swiss educational system and the tight links between this system and the labour market, it is not surprising that the returns for intermediate-level general education are relatively small (with the exception of 2b for women). Men and women who have completed these tracks have neither acquired occupation-specific skills nor entered the prestigious academic track at the tertiary level (i.e. university). For this reason, their educational qualifications do not match the educational requirements according to which the Swiss labour market functions. Given the strong educational sorting processes prevalent in the Swiss labour market, it is likely, however, that these men and women may compensate for the initial losses later in their occupational career. Furthermore, Table 13.1 shows that, for both men and women, the returns of a university degree (3b) are especially high. Compared to respondents who have acquired a vocational credential (i.e. the reference group), the entry status of men with a university degree is (all other things being equal) 21.5 prestige points higher, and 23.4 points higher for women. Given that the academic track at the tertiary level is still taken by an elite few, this group seems to be able to secure disproportionately high returns for their educational investments. At the lower end of the educational categories, the bare completion of compulsory schooling is highly disadvantageous for women. The prestige level of their first jobs is 10.1 points below that of the jobs held by women who have acquired a vocational credential (2a).

The three variables indicating social origin show either no, or only weak, direct effects on the offspring's entry status. For men, only father's occupational status significantly affects occupational outcomes at the time of labour-market entry, and only father's membership in either Class I or Class II for women. When running a model that only includes the social origin variables, the effects of family background account for approximately 12 per cent of the status differences at labour-market entry (see Table 13.A1 in the Appendix). This holds for men as well as for women. Thus, the major portion of the social-origin effects is mediated by the respondent's education. This becomes evident when comparing Table 13.1 with Table 13.1A: almost all direct effects of family background collapse when respondent's education is included in the model. This is especially true for the strongest predictor of social origin, namely, parents' education. This is in line with findings reported by Buchmann and Charles, with Sacchi (1993), that show a relatively strong association between family background and offspring's educational attainment. Interpreting the significant direct effects of father's membership in Class I or Class II on women's entry status, we may maintain that these two top classes, which include among others the large group of professionals, represent social milieux where parents are especially eager (and able) to promote the occupational careers of their offspring. For women, this favourable social milieu seems to provide disproportionately high class-specific mobility chances.

Table 13.1 also shows a statistically significant effect of the demand for labour on entry status. This holds for both sexes. When the demand for labour expands, the occupational prestige of both men's and women's first jobs is significantly higher. These findings provide further support for the importance of the often neglected *period effects*. With respect to the transition from school to work, it is not only education that accounts for difference in first status allocation, but also the situation on the labour market that affects people's opportunities for occupational outcomes.

Referring to cohort membership, Table 13.1 reveals that men and women of the younger cohort (1959–1961) start their occupational careers, *ceteris paribus*, with a significantly lower entry status than their older counterparts (cohort 1949–1951). Comparing Table 13.1 and Table 13.A1, it is worth noting that the effect is only significant when controlling for respondent's education. This suggests that the younger cohort receives lower returns for their—on average—higher educational investments. In this context, the question arises as to whether the effects of education, in particular, and the other variables included in the model are stable across cohorts. In order to answer this question we tested cohort differences for entry status by running separate models for men and women and including, in addition to the model variables, interaction terms between cohort and all predictor variables (Jaccard, Turrisi, and Wan 1990).[9] For both men and women, the main effect of cohort is not significant and, with one exception, no interaction term is significant (table not shown).[10] This indicates the stability of the model presented in Table 13.1 across cohorts. We may thus conclude that the ways in which education differentiates job opportunities are the same for men and women in the older and younger cohort. The fact that the members of the younger cohort across all levels of education obtain a little less prestige in their first job relative to their educational investments may be interpreted in two ways.[11] With the expansion of the Swiss educational system in the years after the older cohort's labour-market entry and before the younger cohort's entry, the greater supply of educational certificates under conditions of more or less constant demand may have led to a devaluation of given educational credentials in the labour market (Buchmann 1989; Handl 1996). The other interpretation relates to the presence of foreign workers in the Swiss labour market. Given that our data only cover Swiss nationals, we may advance the hypothesis that differences in the number of unskilled and semi-skilled foreign workers in the Swiss labour market at the times when the members of the older and younger cohorts obtained their first jobs resulted in unequal profits from *Unterschichtung*. Around 1970, when the majority of the older cohort entered the labour market, the influx of foreign workers was much stronger than a decade later (around 1980) when most members of the younger cohort obtained their first jobs.[12] In 1970, consequently, the lower positions in the occupational hierarchy were filled by foreign workers to a much greater extent than in 1980. This second interpretation, however, does not account for the fact that the effect of interest is only significant when controlling for respondent's education. We therefore prefer the first interpretation provided above.

Table 13.1 furthermore shows a great similarity between the male and female models in the parameter estimates. In order to test gender difference in the effects of the predictors of entry status we estimated a pooled model (gender and cohort), adding interaction terms between gender and all predictors to the model.[13] Referring to the main effects in this model, it is important to point out that the effect of gender is not significant (b = 1.06; t = 0.52; p = .604) (table not shown). This means that, all other things equal, men's and women's chances of attaining a given entry status do not differ. However, when referring to the interaction effects, three parameter estimates differ significantly, indicating lower chances for women. First, the occupational prestige of first jobs is significantly lower for women who have only completed compulsory schooling (1a). Second, the pay-off for the educational investments is higher for women who have completed intermediate-level general education without matriculation (2b). And third, father's occupational prestige exerts a stronger effect for men (although the respective coefficient for women is not significant).

Entry Class

Before discussing the results of the multinomial logistic regression on entry class, we shall present the cross-tabulation of education and entry class by gender in Table 13.2.[14] For each level of schooling, the transition matrix shows men's and women's chances of entering a given class.[15]

Table 13.2 documents that almost all levels of education are closely linked with particular entry classes. Note the substantial gender differences in entry class by given levels of education. For example, women whose educational attainment ends with compulsory schooling (1a) predominantly enter Class IIIb, which includes non-manual routine employees, whereas their male counterparts are employed as unskilled manual workers and enter Class VII. The overwhelming majority of men who completed standard vocational training (2a) enter Classes V and VI (58.9 per cent). Women who have

TABLE 13.2. Cross-tabulation of education and entry class by gender

Level of education	Class I Men	Class I Women	Class II Men	Class II Women	Class IIIa Men	Class IIIa Women	Class IIIb Men	Class IIIb Women	Class V + VI Men	Class V + VI Women	Class VII Men	Class VII Women
1a			0.7 (1)	4.0 (6)	4.8 (4)	8.2 (12)	7.2 (6)	45.0 (67)	26.6 (22)	7.2 (11)	60.7 (50)	35.6 (53)
1bc		0.8 (1)	10.7 (9)	3.4 (6)	17.4 (15)	39.9 (72)	1.2 (1)	31.3 (56)	21.4 (18)	4.2 (8)	49.3 (42)	20.4 (37)
2a			7.1 (42)	12.6 (44)	12.3 (73)	34.3 (119)	3.3 (19)	30.7 (107)	58.9 (348)	17.6 (61)	18.4 (109)	4.7 (17)
2b	5.9 (1)		11.9 (3)	51.4 (16)	14.7 (3)	35.7 (11)	1.2 (0)	3.6 (1)	42.8 (11)	3.7 (1)	23.4 (6)	5.6 (2)
2c	10.3 (3)	6.5 (3)	33.6 (10)	22.6 (12)	33.7 (10)	21.9 (11)	8.2 (2)	32.6 (17)	4.0 (1)	2.5 (1)	10.3 (3)	13.8 (7)
3a	3.7 (2)	2.8 (2)	88.1 (37)	84.1 (48)	2.7 (1)	1.6 (1)		1.8 (1)	1.7 (1)	8.7 (5)	3.8 (2)	1.0 (1)
3b	72.9 (56)	60.8 (13)	18.8 (14)	32.6 (7)	6.3 (5)	1.5 (0)		5.1 (1)			2.0 (2)	

Note: Number of weighted cases in parentheses.

acquired a vocational credential predominantly enter either Class IIIa (34.3 per cent) or Class IIIb (30.7 per cent). At the tertiary level of schooling, the links with class allocation are even tighter and gender differences decline. This is especially prominent among men and women with advanced vocational certificates (3a) who enter almost exclusively Class II (88.1 per cent and 84.1 per cent), whereas those with university degrees (3b) are predominantly allocated to Class I (72.9 per cent and 60.8 per cent). Notable exceptions to these tight links between level of schooling and class allocation at the time of labour-market entry are the educational category of intermediate-level general education with matriculation (2c) and, for women, the educational category including intermediate-level general education without matriculation (2b), and basic secondary level education and/or minimum vocational training (1bc). Moreover, typical male and female transitions differ predominantly at the lower and intermediate levels of educational credentials. We attribute these differences to the high level of occupational sex segregation prevalent in the Swiss labour market which is built into the sex-typed apprenticeships (Charles 1992; Charles and Buchmann 1994). Moreover, intermediate-level general education without matriculation (2b) is more important for women as it provides access to a number of female-dominated occupations. All in all, Table 13.2 shows that the overwhelming majority of transitions are located along the diagonal, which is in line with arguments stressing the importance of human-capital investments for job allocation in the labour market. However, the transition matrix also shows a considerable number of empty or almost empty cells, indicating that particular transitions from school to work are not possible for institutional reasons. These findings thus provide support for the claim that the occupational differentiation built into the Swiss educational system tends to enforce transitions to particular entry classes. Because of its high level of institutional differentiation, almost all vocational credentials (2a), advanced vocational certificates (3a), and many university degrees (3b) are tailored to particular segments of the labour market, thus constituting extremely tight links between school and work.[16] Moreover, the transitions mentioned above that deviate from the diagonal (1bc and 2b for women, 2c for both sexes) indicate either extra returns or relative losses associated with particular educational tracks and credentials. In this respect, intermediate-level general education without matriculation is especially profitable for women; not, however, for men. The returns on intermediate-level general education with matriculation appear to vary widely: some individuals (especially men) are able to realize extra returns, whilst others (especially women) have to cope with major losses in relation to their human capital investment.

Similar conclusions can be drawn when examining the transition probabilities presented in Table 13.3. This table shows the multinomial logistic regression models for men and women (see Hosmer and Lemeshow 1989).[17] Given a particular level of education, the probabilities of entering a given class vary tremendously, even when other possible influences are controlled.[18]

For example, compared to men who served an apprenticeship (2a), the probabilities of entering Class I (instead of Class VII) are 602 times higher for men who acquired an advanced vocational credential (3b).[19] And compared to women who acquired a vocational credential, the estimated probabilities of entering Classes V and VI (instead of Class VII) are almost ten times lower for women whose education ended with compulsory schooling. For both men and women who only obtained basic secondary level schooling and/or minimum vocational training (1bc), the probabilities of entering Classes V or VI (instead of Class VII) are approximately 7.4 times lower than for the counterparts with a standard vocational credential (2a). The findings are in line with the results presented in Table 13.2.

These transition probabilities also raise the question of whether they represent a gradational or a discrete process. In the latter case, the extra returns (or relative losses) for educational investments would be attributable to institutional factors of the educational system, conditioning the transition from school to work. In order to examine this question, we computed an additional model, substituting the categorical measure of education (i.e. the CASMIN schema) by a gradational measure (i.e. years of schooling). If the transition in question does indeed represent a gradational process, we would expect that a gradational coding of education would *not* result in a substantial reduction of the model fit. It turns out that there is a huge reduction of the model Chi-square, which drops by 148.5 points for men and 129.6 points for women in comparison to a loss of 20 and 25 degrees of freedom, respectively.[20] This provides strong support for the assumption that the *type* of educational certificate conditions the effects of education on occupational outcomes. We drew the same conclusion above when discussing the findings of the multiple regression model based on entry status. In the case of entry class, the relative loss of education's explanatory power is, however, much greater.[21] This suggests that by measuring first occupational destination by entry class we are able to capture particular linkages between educational tracks and occupational positions which we would miss by exclusively focusing our analysis on entry status.

To assess the overall effect of education on entry class we computed a model excluding education. Comparing the two models with the help of a Likelihood-Ratio-Test, Table 13.4 shows that education makes *the* substantial contribution to the model's explanatory power. Repeating the same procedure for all other predictors, Table 13.4 furthermore documents that, by comparison, all other predictors make significant, although relatively weak

TABLE 13.3. *Multinomial logistic regression of social origin, education, labour demand, and cohort on entry class*

Coefficients (standard errors)	Entry class: men (N = 861)				Entry class: women (N = 760)				
	I	II	IIIab	V & VI	I	II	IIIa	IIIb	V & VI
Constant	−11.49**	−4.44**	−1.88*	1.77**	−18.73**	−1.08	0.87	2.23*	0.80
	(2.83)	(1.06)	(0.86)	(0.67)	(250.1)	(1.17)	(0.91)	(0.88)	(1.05)
Cohort (1959–1961)	−0.76	−0.55	−0.66*	−0.29	0.11	−0.82*	−0.72*	−0.01	−0.07
	(0.56)	(0.32)	(0.28)	(0.21)	(0.96)	(0.35)	(0.29)	(0.27)	(0.33)
Occupational status father	0.05	0.06**	0.02	0.02	−0.17**	−0.00	−0.01	−0.02	−0.02
	(0.03)	(0.02)	(0.01)	(0.01)	(0.05)	(0.02)	(0.02)	(0.02)	(0.02)
Parent's education	0.17**	0.11	0.04	−0.06	0.48**	0.08	0.08	0.05	0.07
	(0.10)	(0.06)	(0.05)	(0.04)	(0.18)	(0.06)	(0.05)	(0.05)	(0.06)
Father's class:									
I	−0.02	−1.47	0.20	−0.57	3.41	2.29*	−0.18	−0.04	0.21
	(1.79)	(1.05)	(0.91)	(0.83)	(2.48)	(1.09)	(0.90)	(0.90)	(1.14)
II	0.42	−0.40	0.27	−0.10	2.26	2.08*	1.50*	0.25	1.28
	(1.41)	(0.65)	(0.55)	(0.46)	(1.77)	(0.91)	(0.73)	(0.75)	(0.81)
IIIab	1.32	−0.68	−0.29	−0.72	1.85	1.54	0.55	−0.13	1.00
	(1.65)	(0.82)	(0.68)	(0.57)	(2.10)	(1.06)	(0.87)	(0.87)	(0.91)
IVabc	−0.24	−1.65**	−1.00*	−0.85*	0.96	1.23	−0.11	−0.19	−0.10
	(1.31)	(0.56)	(0.43)	(0.32)	(1.48)	(0.66)	(0.43)	(0.39)	(0.49)
V & VI	0.50	−0.21	−0.39	0.01	−4.27*	0.88	0.00	−0.43	−0.11
	(1.28)	(0.51)	(0.42)	(0.32)	(1.96)	(0.64)	(0.40)	(0.37)	(0.46)

Education.

1a	-9.32 (418.6)	-2.82* (1.32)	-1.62* (0.60)	-2.36** (0.39)	-0.60 (500.9)	-3.66** (0.75)	-2.86** (0.48)	-1.92** (0.41)	-2.29** (0.49)
1bc	-8.05 (229.3)	-0.41 (0.45)	-0.61 (0.39)	-2.04** (0.33)	11.18 (250.1)	-2.86** (0.57)	-1.13** (0.39)	-1.91** (0.39)	-2.05** (0.46)
2b	4.83** (2.24)	0.45 (0.79)	-0.07 (0.72)	-0.32 (0.56)	-0.59 (942.9)	0.86 (0.89)	-0.24 (0.89)	-2.55* (1.27)	-1.83 (1.27)
2c	5.98** (2.19)	2.15** (0.74)	1.67* (0.71)	-1.44 (0.93)	13.26 (250.1)	-1.06 (0.64)	-1.82** (0.62)	-1.17* (0.59)	-3.11** (1.04)
3a	6.40** (2.33)	4.51** (0.90)	0.39 (1.29)	-1.64 (1.44)	15.00 (250.1)	2.97* (1.36)	-1.86 (1.71)	-1.46 (1.67)	1.05 (1.04)
3b	9.98** (2.21)	3.32** (0.94)	1.88* (0.99)	-12.33 (230.9)	34.91 (1295)	15.28 (1271)	11.52 (1271)	12.44 (1271)	13.63 (1271)
Labour demand	0.60 (0.32)	0.34 (0.22)	0.90** (0.23)	0.22 (0.17)	1.60* (0.79)	0.38 (0.23)	0.53** (0.19)	-0.26 (0.15)	-0.02 (0.20)

Log-likelihood -850,9   -952,6
Chi² 735,9, df:60, Significance: .0000   548,4, df:75, Significance: .0000

contributions—with the exception of the demand for labour, which is quite substantial for both sexes (p = .001). We shall discuss in detail the effects of social origin, cohort, and demand for labour below.

For both sexes, social origin exerts a significant overall effect on entry class—net of all other effects. This is true for origin class and father's occupational status. The overall effect of parents' education on entry class is not significant for women, however. Note that the chances of entering Class I, especially, increase with parents' education (see Table 13.3). This parameter estimate is also significant for women. We interpret this particular finding by suggesting that the social milieu of highly educated parents provides a context that greatly enhances the mobility chances of their children. This is in line with the expectations advanced above. With respect to father's occupational status, sons' opportunities for entering Class II or Class I (although this coefficient is not significant due to low testing power) increase with father's status.[22] The effects of entry class vary by gender. For men, it should be noted that the probability of entering either Class I or Class VII increases for the sons of self-employed fathers. In other words, they are allocated either at the top or the bottom of the class structure. At present, we cannot assess whether those who are allocated to Class VII at the time of labour-market entry are able to move up later on in their occupational career by taking over a family or parental business or whether they have been affected by downward mobility risks. Among women, daughters of social-origin Class I or Class II seem to enjoy higher chances of entering these classes (although not all coefficients are significant, probably again due to testing power). Moreover, entrance in Class IIIa is another typical transition for these women. Finally, women from (skilled) working-class backgrounds (Classes V and VI) are affected by significantly lower chances of entering Class I compared to the daughters of unskilled manual workers (Class VII). This might be due to traditional gender images prevalent in this social milieu, which is accompanied by a low appreciation of educational investments.

With respect to the nature of the effects of social origin, the question arises as to whether these effects are mediated by the respondent's education. Comparing this model with the one that excludes respondent's education (see Table 13.A2), we find that the effect of parents' education is substantially reduced when controlling respondent's education. This corresponds to the finding regarding entry status, suggesting that social-origin effect pertaining to parents' education is mediated by the respondent's education. In contrast to the findings related to entry status, some effects of father's occupational status and father's class on the offspring's chances of entering particular classes either remain stable (e.g. father's occupational status and most sons' or daughters' entry classes) or even increase (e.g. father's

TABLE 13.4. *Likelihood-ratio tests for the overall significance of the predictors*

	Men				Women			
	χ^2-Diff.	(df)	Sig.	Reduction of model-χ^2 (%)	χ^2-Diff.	(df)	Sig.	Reduction of model-χ^2 (%)
Cohort (1959–61)	6.7	(4)		2.5	17.1	(5)	**	3.1
Occupational status father	12.4	(4)	*	1.6	14.5	(5)	*	2.6
Parent's education	13.4	(4)	**	1.8	10.0	(5)		1.8
Father's class	34.7	(20)	*	4.7	48.1	(25)	**	8.8
Education	509.4	(24)	***	69.2	354.7	(30)	***	64.7
Labour demand	32.3	(4)	***	2.5	32.3	(5)	***	5.9

Note: The percentage reduction of the model-Chi^2 refers to the full model shown in Table 13.3.
Significance levels are 5, 1, and 0.1 per cent

Class I and daughters' entry to Classes I or II; father's Class IVabc and sons' entry to Class II). These effects seem to indicate the presence of some direct effects of social-origin variables, thus pointing to the existence of some group-specific, non-meritocratic chances of class allocation.

Assessing the effects of the demand for labour on entry class, we find that when the labour force expands, the chances of entering Class IIIa (instead of Class VII) increase significantly for both sexes. In the time period under investigation, the economy was profoundly restructured. In this context, the general dynamics towards a service economy observed in Switzerland resulted primarily in the creation of jobs in Class IIIa. Furthermore, it is important to note that women's chances of entering Class I significantly increase in times of labour-force expansion. We may conclude that women only enjoy these chances when the 'supply' of men suitable for entering this class is exhausted! All in all, these findings confirm that period effects (which appear to be shaped by the class structure) constitute an important—albeit often neglected—aspect, profoundly conditioning the transition from school to work.

Referring to cohort membership, Table 13.3 shows that the chances of entering Class II and Class IIIa (instead of Class VII) are much lower for women of the younger cohort; the same holds for men of the younger cohort with regard to Class IIIab. According to the Likelihood-Ratio-Test, however, the overall significance of cohort membership only holds for women (see Table 13.4). This suggests that the opportunity for entering Class IIIa has declined across cohorts. Interestingly enough, the effect is only significant when controlling for the respondent's education—a finding also reported above with respect to entry status (see Table 13.A2). We may thus draw the same conclusion as above. That is, in relation to their educational investments, members of the younger cohort receive a lower pay-off. By using entry class as a dependent variable, we gain some additional information about this process, however. We are able to identify specific classes that are more difficult to enter.

To answer the question of whether the effects of the predictors included in the model are stable across cohorts, we ran separate models for men and women including, in addition to the model variables, the respective cohort interaction terms. In order to avoid overparametrization of the model, we separately included two sets of interaction for the social-origin variables and the other predictors, respectively. Because of the relatively low testing power, we used the aggregated version of entry class (for the coding of this variable, see Table 13.A3 in the Appendix). Nevertheless, testing power is still relatively low for numerous coefficients with the consequence of large standard errors. For this reason, we do not want to overinterpret the findings and report them in a summary fashion. For men, the effects are stable across cohort; the Likelihood-Ratio-Test indicates no significant cohort differences, neither for the origin nor for the other variables (Chi-square = 25.2, df = 21, p < .05; Chi-square = 27.2, df = 21, p < .05). For women, by contrast, we find significant changes with regard to both the model including the interaction terms with social origin (Chi-square = 38.6, df = 21, p = .01) and the model including the interaction terms with respondent's education and the demand for labour (Chi-square = 41.7, df = 21, p < .005). Overall, the findings show that the effects of father's class and respondent's education have somewhat declined across cohort.[23] In relation to the degrees of freedom, the changes in the model Chi-square are rather small, however, so that the aggregation of the cohorts is justified.

We also examined the question of whether the effects of the model variables differ by gender. Based on the aggregated version of entry class, the analogous interaction models, this time pooled across cohort and gender, and Likelihood-Ratio-Tests were run. As expected, the main effect of gender was very strong—highly significant for entry Classes I and II (b = -0.58; t = 2.33; p = .004), and for entry to Class IIIab (b = 2.47; t = 10.5; p = .004). It was not significant, however, for entry to Classes V and VI. This finding points to the great differences in men's and women's chances of entering particular classes. This is not surprising, given that some classes include occupational groups that are highly sex-typed. It is in contrast, however, to the finding regarding entry status, where the main effect of gender was not significant. This difference again stresses the importance of including both entry status and entry class into the analysis in order to better understand allocation processes in the labour market. The results further reveal that social-origin effects, especially, differ between men and women (Chi-square = 339.3, df = 21, p = .000).[24] The effects of respondent's education and of the demand for labour differ significantly as well (Chi-square = 74.1, df = 21, p < .001). Testing power, however, is not always sufficient to secure differences between singular effects statistically. Nevertheless, we find the following three significant differences: compared to their male counterparts, lower chances for women who only completed compulsory schooling (1a) regarding entrance in Classes IIIab or V and VI (instead of Class VII); lower chances for women who obtained basic secondary level education and/or minimum vocational training with regard to entering Classes I, II, and IIIab; and lower chances for women who completed intermediate-level general education with matriculation (2c) regarding entry to Class I and Class II. These findings indicate that the returns on particular *types* of educational investments are lower for women than for men. This suggests gender differences in the ways in which institutional factors affect first allocation in the labour market, probably related to the worse consequences of a missing occupation-specific credential for women.

CONCLUSION

The major purpose of this chapter has been to examine the ways in which social origin and education shape the first allocation of men and women to jobs in Switzerland. In particular, we have attempted to assess the relevance of institutional characteristics of the educational system and class barriers for the transition from school to work. We started from the assumption that the conversion of educational qualifications into occupational outcomes may be conceived of as a gradational, or a discrete, process. In the former case, education assumes the role of an individual investment in human-capital acquisition, which largely determines the returns on educational qualifications in the labour market. In the latter case, by contrast, educational qualifications are linked to their institutional context of production. Consequently, the conversion of education into occupational outcomes is shaped by the type of educational track completed. This implies that, in relation to the human-capital investment, particular educational certificates provide institutionally-determined extra returns or losses in the labour market. It further implies that the strength of the institutional link between educational tracks and particular segments of the labour market affects the conversion of educational qualifications into occupational outcomes.

With respect to social origin, mobility chances do not only depend on the economic and cultural resources the family conveys to its offspring, but also on class membership. Particular origin classes are associated with either mobility constraints or opportunities that result in less favourable or more favourable labour-market allocations than can be expected on the basis of the economic and cultural resources provided by the particular social origin alone.

Given the particular characteristics of the Swiss educational system—a high level of differentiation, strong vocational orientation, and tight linkages between education and the labour market—we expected the transition from school to work to be strongly conditioned by the institutionally-determined evaluation of educational qualifications in the labour market. The high level of differentiation and standardization prevalent in the Swiss educational system and the strong vocational orientation coupled with close institutional links to the labour market are mainly responsible for the significance of institutional factors in the first allocation of persons to jobs. The results show that, although the first allocation in the labour market is largely determined by human capital investments, institutionally-determined effects are also at work. This is evident when measuring first allocation in the labour market by entry status and when measuring it by entry class.

With regard to entry status, we find that the three main levels of the CAS-MIN educational classification account for the major differences in status returns—a finding that corresponds with arguments related to human-capital investments. However, when the specific returns of individual tracks are not taken into account as well, the explanatory power is considerably reduced for both sexes. This suggests that the returns on education for the first allocation in the labour market—measured as the occupational prestige of the first job—are not only determined by educational investments, but also by the educational track completed. Examining the returns on particular educational credentials, we find that, in relation to the acquisition of human capital, a university degree provides very high returns for both sexes. Standard vocational training brings disproportionately good returns for men, whereas for women, it is intermediate-level general education without matriculation that provides extra returns. For both sexes, intermediate-level general education with matriculation is associated with relatively meagre returns. The pay-off on compulsory schooling is extremely low for women.

Similar conclusions can be drawn by examining the transitions from level of schooling completed to entry class. The general pattern of transitions is in line with arguments stressing the importance of human-capital investments for the allocation in the labour market. However, when ignoring the specific returns of educational certificates, the model fit is greatly reduced, considerably surpassing the loss of explanatory power related to the neglect of the particularities of educational credentials in the case of entry status. This difference suggests that by conceiving of first occupational destination as a discrete process (i.e. entry class), we are able to capture particular linkages between educational tracks and occupational positions which we would otherwise miss. Moreover, the transition matrix shows a considerable number of empty or almost empty cells. This indicates that particular transitions from school to work are not possible for institutional reasons. Particular transitions also show extremely high or low transition probabilities net of all other effects, which stresses the significance of institutional factors affecting the allocation of persons to jobs. As discussed above, transitions shown in the cross-tabulation of education and entry class that deviate from the diagonal indicate either extra returns or relative losses associated with particular educational tracks and credentials. In this respect, and in line with the findings regarding entry status, intermediate-level general education without matriculation is especially profitable for women, but not for men. With respect to intermediate-level general education with matriculation, we are able to specify the results based on the multiple regression analysis. Men and women who enter the labour market with this type of educational credential vary widely in their class allocation, with men tending to gain, and women to lose, on their human-capital investment.

Comparing the effects of social origin on occupational outcomes at the time of labour-market entry by type of model applied, we find interesting differences. Based on the offspring's entry status, we find weak direct effects of the three variables indicating social origin. The major proportion of the social-origin effects is mediated by the educational attainment of children. This is especially true for the strongest predictor of social origin, namely parent's education. Based on offspring's entry class, the effect of social origin when measured by parents' education is also mediated by his or her education. However, with regard to other measures of social origin, namely father's occupational status and father's class, we find some stable, and even some increasing, effects when controlling for offspring's education. These latter findings confirm the presence of particular class-specific inter-generational mobility chances, which are obscured when conceiving of the transition from school to work exclusively as a gradational process.

Our analyses furthermore show that another contextual factor, namely the demand for labour, shapes the transition from school to work, stressing the importance of the often neglected period effects. When the labour force expands, the occupational prestige of both men's and women's first job is significantly higher. With regard to entry class, an expanding labour force increases the chances of entering particular classes: the class of routine non-manual employees of higher grade for both sexes and the class of higher-grade professionals for women. By taking into account labour-market opportunities, we are able to substantially improve our knowledge about the first allocation of men and women in the labour market. In addition, using entry class as a dependent variable, we can identify class positions with increasing entry opportunities in times of intensive demand for labour.

A similar conclusion can be drawn with respect to cohort membership. Referring to entry status, our findings show that men and women of the younger cohort (1959–1961) start their occupational careers with a lower entry status than their older counterparts (1949–1951). With respect to entry class, we are able to identify the specific classes for which entry chances have declined: the chances of entering the class of routine non-manual employees of higher grade are much lower for both younger men and women. Since the chances of the younger cohort have declined, not in absolute terms, but in relation to their educational investments, we interpret these findings as a powerful manifestation of the expansion of the educational system and the concomitant credentials inflation.

Given our samples of two cohorts, we were also interested in answering the question of whether the influences of education, social origin, and demand for labour are stable across cohorts. With regard to gender, we asked the corresponding question about the equality of the effects for men and women. In both instances, the differences seem to be small.

In sum, our results show that not only individual resources, but also structural barriers, affect the first labour-market allocation in Switzerland. In particular, the allocation is shaped by institutional characteristics of the educational system, the opportunity structure imposed by the demand for labour, and class origin, but these barriers only become visible when considering the discrete nature of the conversion process both on the input and output side.

TABLE 13.A.1. *Multiple regression of social origin and cohort on entry status*

	Men (N = 861)			Women (N = 760)		
	b	(se)	β	b	(se)	β
Constant	24.93**	(2.31)		20.63**	(2.43)	
Cohort (1959–1961)	−1.06	(0.77)	−0.05	0.65	(0.83)	0.03
Occupational status father	0.14**	(0.04)	0.15	0.04	(0.05)	0.04
Parent's education	0.59**	(0.14)	0.16	0.83**	(0.15)	0.23
Father's class:						
I	3.49	(2.61)	0.04	3.11	(2.54)	0.04
II	3.49*	(1.67)	0.07	4.93**	(1.78)	0.09
IIIab	2.40	(2.17)	0.04	5.57*	(2.18)	0.09
IVabc	−0.86	(1.30)	−0.02	−0.45	(1.36)	−0.01
V + VI	1.84	(1.26)	0.05	1.43	(1.27)	0.04
Explained variance	12.38			11.96		

Note: Significance levels of 5 and 1 per cent are marked with one or two stars, respectively. Standardized coefficients represent semi-partial correlations in the case of dummy variables (cf. Hardy 1993: 18).

TABLE 13.A.2. *Multinomial logistic regression of social origin and cohort on entry class*

Coefficients (standard errors)	Entry class: men (N = 887)				Entry class: women (N = 798)				
	I	II	IIIab	V + VI	I	II	IIIa	IIIb	V + VI
Constant	-7.67**	-4.89**	-2.32**	0.09	-9.21**	-4.87**	-2.00**	0.12	-1.80*
	(1.26)	(0.81)	(0.73)	(0.55)	(1.88)	(0.92)	(0.74)	(0.71)	(0.86)
Cohort (1959–1961)	-0.10	-0.36	-0.16	-0.09	1.04	0.06	-0.18	0.19	0.19
	(0.32)	(0.25)	(0.24)	(0.18)	(0.59)	(0.28)	(0.24)	(0.25)	(0.29)
Occupational status father	0.03*	0.05*	0.01	0.01	-0.02	0.01	-0.01	-0.02	-0.01
	(0.02)	(0.01)	(0.01)	(0.01)	(0.03)	(0.02)	(0.01)	(0.01)	(0.02)
Parent's education	0.23**	0.16**	0.09*	0.03	0.42**	0.21**	0.20**	0.10*	0.15**
	(0.06)	(0.05)	(0.04)	(0.03)	(0.10)	(0.05)	(0.05)	(0.04)	(0.05)
Father's class:									
I	1.52	-0.90	0.48	-0.58	0.51	1.16	-0.73	-0.22	-0.69
	(1.22)	(0.89)	(0.83)	(0.76)	(1.49)	(0.93)	(0.84)	(0.83)	(0.98)
II	1.72	0.27	0.50	-0.04	1.47	2.34**	1.43*	0.22	0.92
	(1.00)	(0.56)	(0.51)	(0.42)	(1.27)	(0.83)	(0.70)	(0.73)	(0.76)
IIIab	1.58	0.35	0.21	-0.23	2.01	1.98*	0.39	-0.19	0.66
	(1.12)	(0.68)	(0.64)	(0.53)	(1.29)	(0.88)	(0.75)	(0.77)	(0.79)
IVabc	0.48	-0.92*	-0.88*	-0.82*	0.15	1.03	-0.29	-0.32	-0.55
	(0.94)	(0.47)	(0.40)	(0.28)	(1.05)	(0.59)	(0.40)	(0.38)	(0.46)
V + VI	1.02	0.16	-0.20	0.08	-1.36	1.10	-0.11	-0.34	-0.29
	(0.93)	(0.44)	(0.39)	(0.28)	(1.35)	(0.57)	(0.37)	(0.35)	(0.42)
Log-Likelihood	-1173.4				-1215.0				
Chi²	170.3, df: 32, Significance: .0000				155.2, df: 40, Significance: .0000				

TABLE 13.A.3. *Multinomial logistic regression of social origin, education, labour demand, and cohort on entry class*

Coefficients (standard errors)	Collapsed entry class: men (N = 861)			Collapsed entry class: women (N = 760)		
	I + II	IIIab	V + VI	I + II	IIIab	V + VI
Constant	-4.65**	-1.83*	1.76**	-0.90	2.39**	0.83
	(1.05)	(0.86)	(0.67)	(1.13)	(0.83)	(1.05)
Cohort (1959–1961)	-0.59	-0.66*	-0.29	-0.65	-0.25	-0.02
	(0.32)	(0.28)	(0.21)	(0.34)	(0.25)	(0.32)
Occupational status father	0.05**	0.02	0.02	-0.01	-0.01	-0.02
	(0.02)	(0.01)	(0.01)	(0.02)	(0.01)	(0.02)
Parent's education	0.12*	0.04	-0.06	0.10	0.07	0.08
	(0.06)	(0.05)	(0.04)	(0.06)	(0.05)	(0.06)
Father's class:						
I	-1.29	0.18	-0.56	2.25*	-0.00	0.16
	(1.03)	(0.91)	(0.83)	(1.05)	(0.82)	(1.13)
II	-0.36	0.27	-0.10	2.07*	0.98	1.28
	(0.65)	(0.55)	(0.46)	(0.88)	(0.69)	(0.82)
IIIab	-0.51	-0.32	-0.71	1.44	0.14	0.96
	(0.80)	(0.68)	(0.57)	(1.02)	(0.82)	(0.91)
IVabc	-1.54**	-1.01*	-0.85**	1.13	-0.21	-0.11
	(0.56)	(0.43)	(0.32)	(0.63)	(0.37)	(0.50)
V + VI	-0.18	-0.39	0.01	0.67	-0.27	-0.12
	(0.51)	(0.42)	(0.32)	(0.60)	(0.35)	(0.46)
Education:						
1a	-2.82*	-1.63**	-2.35**	-3.59**	-2.20**	-2.31**
	(1.33)	(0.60)	(0.39)	(0.75)	(0.39)	(0.50)
1bc	-0.37	-0.62	-2.04**	-2.70**	-1.56**	-2.10**
	(0.45)	(0.39)	(0.33)	(0.54)	(0.36)	(0.46)

TABLE 13.A.3. *cont.*

Coefficients (standard errors)	Collapsed entry class: men (N = 861)			Collapsed entry class: women (N = 760)		
	I + II	IIIab	V + VI	I + II	IIIab	V + VI
2b	0.82	-0.07	-0.32	0.82	-0.88	-1.80
	(0.72)	(0.72)	(0.56)	(0.89)	(0.88)	(1.26)
2c	2.41**	1.67*	-1.44	-0.79	-1.47**	-3.11**
	(0.72)	(0.71)	(0.93)	(0.62)	(0.56)	(1.03)
3a	4.56**	0.40	-1.64	3.01*	-1.61	1.06
	(0.90)	(1.29)	(1.44)	(1.36)	(1.52)	(1.40)
3b	4.93**	1.79*	-12.10	11.87	7.62	9.12
	(0.89)	(0.98)	(214.2)	(142.7)	(142.7)	(142.7)
Labour demand	0.38	0.89**	0.23	0.27	-0.02	-0.07
	(0.21)	(0.22)	(0.17)	(0.22)	(0.14)	(0.19)
Log-likelihood	-802,2			-687,4		
Chi²	609,1, df: 45, Significance: .0000			373,2, df: 45, Significance: .0000		

TABLE 13A.4. *Multinomial logistic regression of social origin, education, labour demand, and cohort on women's entry class*

Coefficients (standard errors)	Collapsed entry class: women (N = 760)		
	I + II	IIIab	V + VI
Constant	−0.88	2.39**	0.83
	(1.13)	(0.83)	(1.04)
Cohort (1959–1961)	−0.64	−0.25	−0.02
	(0.34)	(0.25)	(0.32)
Occupational status father	−0.01	−0.01	−0.02
	(0.02)	(0.01)	(0.02)
Parent's education	0.10	0.07	0.08
	(0.06)	(0.05)	(0.06)
Father's class:			
I	2.21*	−0.01	0.17
	(1.05)	(0.82)	(1.13)
II	2.03*	0.97	1.31
	(0.88)	(0.69)	(0.82)
IIIab	1.44	0.14	0.96
	(1.02)	(0.82)	(0.91)
IVabc	1.10	−0.21	−0.09
	(0.62)	(0.37)	(0.49)
V + VI	0.64	−0.28	−0.11
	(0.60)	(0.35)	(0.46)
Education (collapsed):			
1a	−3.60**	−2.20**	−2.30**
	(0.75)	(0.39)	(0.50)
1bc	−2.71**	−1.56**	−2.10**
	(0.54)	(0.36)	(0.46)
2b	0.81	−0.88	−1.80
	(0.89)	(0.88)	(1.26)
2c	−0.79	−1.47**	−3.11**
	(0.62)	(0.56)	(1.03)
3ab	3.46*	−1.02	1.31
	(1.36)	(1.45)	(1.39)
Labour demand	0.25	−0.02	−0.07
	(0.22)	(0.14)	(0.19)

Log-likelihood −688,1
Chi² 371,7
df: 42
Significance: .0000

NOTES

1. The arguments pertaining to human-capital theory presented here are based on the assumption that an additional year of education across all types of educational tracks will yield the same increase in productivity. This assumption is consistent with the basic model of man underlying human-capital theory, namely that of the rational actor. If an additional year of schooling in some educational tracks yielded lower returns, i.e. lower increases in the individual's productivity regarding market work, it would be difficult to explain within the theoretical framework of human-capital theory, why people choose educational tracks yielding lower returns. This implies the rather simplifying assumption that the returns on educational investments do not depend on the completion of a given track.

2. In the Swiss political system, the cantons constitute one of the three levels of political administration.

3. We do not run a third model for estimating the effects of social origin and education on present employment status because this involves a distinction between information on youth unemployment has only been available for the last few years.

4. First job is defined as the first employment episode of more than four months in which work is considered to be the respondent's main activity.

5. Father's class membership and respondent's entry class (Goldthorpe's Class Scheme). Class I includes higher-grade professionals, administrators, and officials; managers in large industrial establishments; large proprietors. Class II— lower-grade professionals, administrators, and officials; higher-grade technicians; managers in small industrial establishments; supervisors of non-manual employees. Class IIIa—routine non-manual employees; higher grade (administration and commerce). Class IIIb—routine non-manual employees; lower grade (sales and services). Class IVabc—petty bourgeoisie; small proprietors and artisans, etc., with and without employees; farmers and smallholders and other self-employed workers in primary production. Classes V/VI—skilled workers: lower-grade technicians; supervisors of manual workers; skilled manual workers. Class VII (used as a reference class) unskilled manual workers.

6. CASMIN Educational Classification Scheme adapted for Switzerland (1b and 1c collapsed): 1a compulsory schooling; 1bc basic secondary level schooling, basic vocational training; 2a (used as a reference category) standard vocational training: traditional apprenticeship and full-time vocational schools; 2b intermediate-level general education without matriculation; 2c intermediate-level general education with matriculation; 3a advanced vocational training; 3b university.

7. The sample was limited to Swiss citizens for three reasons. First, due to financial restrictions, we were not able to provide translations of the questionnaire for all the languages spoken by foreign workers in Switzerland in order to secure a sufficiently high response rate. Second, given the diversity of foreign workers in Switzerland, analyses by country of origin would have been mandatory, thus demanding large oversamples of country-specific groups of foreign workers. Third, the interpretation regarding the transition from school to work would

have been difficult, given that the overwhelming majority of foreign workers attended school in their native countries.

8. In the mid-1980s, foreign workers represented about 21 per cent of the total work force in Switzerland.

9. The problem of multi-collinearity was handled by centring the continuous variables before computing the interaction terms (see Jaccard, Turrisi, and Wan 1990: 31, 43).

10. The only exception refers to the negative effect of the educational category 1bc including basic secondary level education and/or minimum vocational training, which has significantly declined for men.

11. The interpretations offered here are tentative, since we cannot test them directly with our data.

12. The findings related to the class analysis presented below (see Table 13.3) are consistent with this interpretation. For all class contrasts, there is a negative effect—significant in some instances only. This means that, controlling for education and other variables, men and women of the younger cohort ran a greater risk of starting their occupational career as unskilled workers rather than any other class.

13. Given that only one minor significant interaction effect was detected in the previous model, we do not include interaction terms between cohort and predictor variables in the present model.

14. For the assignment of Roman figures to the individual cases, see note 5.

15. Class IVab was omitted from the analysis because the transition from school to self-employed is almost completely absent in Switzerland.

16. The link between educational and occupational systems would be even tighter had we not only considered the vertical differentiation of entry positions. Training programmes at the same educational level may be linked to particular segments of the labour market. This is especially true for educational categories 2a, 3a, and—albeit to a lesser degree—3b.

17. The programme LIMDEP6 was used for parameter estimation. As discussed above, Class IVab was excluded from the analysis. Moreover, Classes IIIa and IIIb were collapsed for men as the latter category does not include men.

18. Unfortunately, some standard errors are large and, hence, the precision of some parameter estimates is low. In some instances, the number of cases per cell is insufficient due to the very low probability of a given transition. In other instances, the cells are empty due to 'structural zeros'. This means that a given transition is not possible by definition. Nevertheless, we decided not to raise the level of aggregation because of the loss of important information. The example of women's entry Class I, which is especially plagued by large standard errors, shows that some parameter estimates may be interpreted. For comparison, we include Table 13.A3 in the Appendix, showing a model in which entry classes are collapsed (I and II, IIIab, V and VI, VII). We also add Table 13.A4 to the Appendix where the educational categories 3a and 3b have been collapsed for women because of large standard errors related to category 3b.

19. The estimated probabilities are computed by raising the coefficient to the exponential power (see Hosmer and Lemeshow 1989).

20. Even if a Likelihood-Ratio-Test is not quite permissible—because the two

models compared are not entirely nested—the reduction of the model fit is impressive.

21. Given that the total explanatory power (Chi-square) of education amounts to 509.4 points for men and 354.7 points for women (see Table 13.4 discussed below), about 29 per cent (148.5 points) for men and about 37 per cent (129.6 points) for women are allotted to the categorical measure of education (i.e. the CASMIN scheme). With regard to entry status, by contrast, only 12.8 per cent for men and 9.8 per cent for women can be apportioned to the categorical measure for education.

22. With regard to Class I, we find the opposite effect for women. It is questionable, however, to interpret this finding because of the small number of cases.

23. In particular, we find the following declining effects across cohorts: the negative effect of social-origin Class II on women's chances of entering Class I; the negative effect of compulsory education (1a) on the chances of entering Class IIIab; the negative effect of basic secondary education and/or minimum vocational training (1bc) on the chances of entering Classes V and VI.

24. The large Chi-square difference does not result from the main effect of gender, since our baseline model includes this effect. This very large difference is astonishing. However, the social-origin effects presented in Table 13.3 and the respective interpretation document that these effects are sex-typed.

14

The Transition from School to Work in Taiwan

SHU-LING TSAI

INTRODUCTION

All industrial societies use educational and labour-market mechanisms to channel young people towards adult positions in the stratification system, yet the nature of these sorting mechanisms vary across societies (see e.g. Ishida, Müller, and Ridge 1995; Kerckhoff 1995, 1996; König and Müller 1986; Maurice, Sellier, and Silvestre 1986). Most of our existing knowledge of the nature of the education—labour-market linkage pertains to more developed countries, and to bridge the gap, we explore the experience of Taiwan after the extension of compulsory education from six to nine years in 1968.

Throughout the research our main concern has been, to what extent can labour-market position at entry be predicted by level and type of education, and how current employment status is conditioned by educational attainment. After outlining the policies and practices governing the Taiwanese school-to-work transition, we present the main issues and hypotheses before reporting and discussing the empirical results.

THE CONTEXT

As a newly industrializing society, the case of Taiwan is interesting in three respects vis-à-vis an examination of the association between educational attainment and initial labour-market position. First, because throughout the twentieth century, we can observe a long-term expansion in educational enrolment for both men and women (Yu 1988; Tsai, Gates, and Chiu 1994). Second, because from 1966 onwards, this expansion has been guided by a series of Manpower Development Plans (Y.-R. Yang 1994). And third, because Taiwan is one of the most successful cases of post-war Asian economic growth on record (Fei, Ranis, and Kuo 1979; Barrett and Whyte 1982; Wade 1990).

In the next section we elaborate the basic characteristics of Taiwan's school system, the role played by the state in shaping the structural conditions for social exclusion, and the nature of its labour market.

COMPETITION IN A STRATIFIED SCHOOL SYSTEM

Taiwan's educational system was initially developed by the Japanese (1895–1945), and subsequently expanded by the Chinese Nationalist regime. In 1968 compulsory education was extended to the level of junior high schools. Beyond compulsory education, transitions to advanced school levels are controlled by Taiwan's rigid entrance examination system, which has in turn led to a highly selective system of education—primarily public at the compulsory level, with standardized curricula in both public and private schools, dramatic educational watersheds at post-compulsory levels, tracking on the basis of examination results, and a clear hierarchy of schools at the same level.

In Taiwan, education from kindergarten to graduate school spans a minimum of twenty-two years (see Figure 14.1). Normally, it includes two years of pre-school education, six years of elementary school, three years of junior high school, three years of senior high school, two to seven years of undergraduate education, one to four years of graduate study for a master's degree, and two to seven years' study for a doctoral degree (Ministry of Education 1995: p. xviii).

Early social selection in schools characterizes Taiwan's stratification processes. Marked inequality of opportunity appears in attaining the middle level of the educational hierarchy (Hsieh 1987; Tsai and Chiu 1993; Y. Yang 1994). Graduates from junior high schools take competitive examinations and are assigned to tracked schools on the basis of the results.[1] The goal is entry to a 'good' senior high school which will prepare adolescents for success in the next contest for higher education three years later. Each major city has its own 'best' senior high schools for boys and girls. Competition at the senior high school level caused by excess demand generates competition at the junior high school level.

Under the tremendous pressure of matriculation competition, junior high schools are evaluated on the basis of their success rates for the joint entrance examination to local public high schools. According to Hsieh (1987: 215–17), in 1970 the Ministry of Education enforced a policy of 'two-level grouping by ability' which allowed junior high schools to sort students into high and low ability groups. The detrimental impact of this was so obvious that the

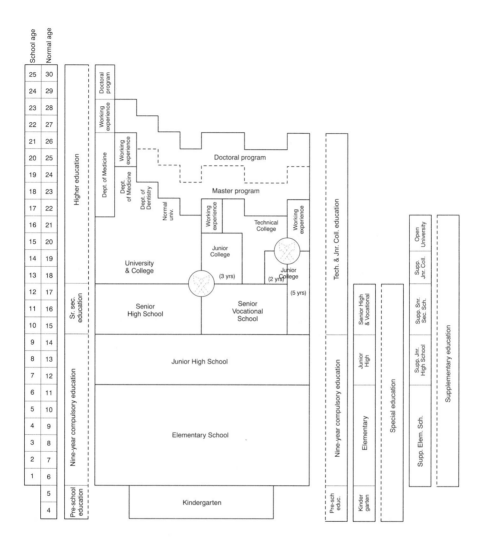

Fig. 14.1. *Structure of Taiwan's current educational system*

Ministry of Education attempted to limit the practice in 1979, and again in 1985, but most junior high schools continue to use ability grouping as a device to discourage 'bad' students from taking the public high school entrance examination, in order to maintain high examination results.

Students with insufficient grades for entry to public senior high schools usually take entrance examinations for other kinds of schools (private senior high schools, public/private vocational schools, junior colleges, and night schools).[2] Those who fail all the examinations either leave school altogether or attend tutorial schools and retake the examination the following year. Thus, through the operation of the examination system, Taiwan's society measures and labels an individual's ability as early as adolescence.

Since examination performance is the single criterion for school selection, both the ranking of students and the hierarchical ordering of schools at the same level are clear. In addition to prestige, senior secondary schools are differentiated by function. Generally speaking, senior high schools prepare students for higher education, and senior vocational schools train students in a marketable skill.

A great leap—the national joint entrance examination—takes students from high school to university or college. In 1994, of the 124,786 students taking this examination, only 44 per cent passed (Ministry of Education 1995: 36). The press prints the standard required by each university department or college, together with the names of the students accepted. The prestige or stigma attached respectively to success and failure, lead many parents to put pressure on their children to excel academically, with scant attention being paid to individual needs and talents (Lucas 1982: 212). Competition in entrance examinations for senior school is thus intense.

Under excess demand for higher education, it is commonly believed that the higher a school's success rate, the better the quality of education it produces. Accordingly, the success rate of students passing the examination largely determines the prestige ranking of senior high schools. By the same token, the lowest grades acceptable for entrance determines the hierarchical ordering of departments within and between universities and colleges. National universities are overwhelmingly higher in ranking than private colleges.

On the other hand, the main purpose of senior vocational schools is to turn students into 'basic skilled workers' with occupational ethics (Ministry of Education 1995: p. xxiii). There are seven categories of senior vocational schools, specializing in agriculture, industry, commerce, marine products, nursing and midwifery, home economics, and opera and the arts. The distribution of students by gender among the various types of vocational education is presented in Table 14.1. As shown in the table, during the academic year of 1994/5, an overwhelming majority (79 per cent) of male students enrolled in vocational-industrial schools,[3] whereas over half (58 per cent) of the female students were in commercial education.[4]

Graduates from senior vocational schools are supposed to engage in actual production activities with vocational knowledge and skills. Therefore, their curricula emphasizes practical vocational training. For instance, historically, workshop training had been reckoned to be one of the most important activities in Taiwan's vocational-industrial schools (Jeng 1980: 142). More gen-

TABLE 14.1. *Distribution of student enrolments in senior vocational schools, 1994–1995*

Type of vocational school	Total number of students	%	Male number of students	%	Female number of students	%
Agriculture	19,215	3.7	9,153	3.7	10,062	3.6
Industry	225,529	43.0	192,731	78.7	32,798	11.7
Commerce	197,659	37.7	36,089	14.7	161,570	57.9
Home economics	48,014	9.2	1,156	0.5	46,858	16.8
Marine products	8,035	1.5	4,521	1.8	3,514	1.3
Nursing and Midwifery	23,850	4.6	720	0.3	23,130	8.3
Opera and Arts	1,680	0.3	434	0.2	1,246	0.4
TOTAL	523,982	100.0	244,804	100.0	279,178	100.0

Source: Educational Statistics of the Republic of China 1995: 92.

erally speaking, the curricula of senior vocational schools standardized by the Ministry of Education require a 20–30 per cent focus on general studies, 30 per cent on specific vocational studies, and 40–50 per cent on workshop practice.

Besides joining the labour market, graduates from senior vocational schools may continue in higher education after passing the relevant entrance examinations. But, their success rate is limited. In 1994, only 16 per cent of senior vocational school graduates—boys and girls—entered advanced educational levels. This figure is much lower than the 56 per cent of boys and the 59 per cent of girls passing from senior high schools to university or college (Ministry of Education 1995: 29).

Students whose grades are insufficient for entry to university or college usually attend one of the two kinds of junior or technical colleges: one admitting junior high school graduates and lasting five years; and the other admitting senior high school graduates and lasting two to three years. Both kinds of college train students as skilled technicians. Junior college graduates and senior vocational school graduates may apply for admission to institutes of technology for advanced study.

Thus we can see that in a situation of excess demand for education, a primary function of Taiwan's stratified educational system is allocative, conferring success on some and failure on others. Although this mechanism is very rigid, educational selection based on examination merit appears to justify its highly competitive nature to the public, mainly because it is commonly believed to be the fairest system (Y.-H. Chang, Hsieh, and Huang 1995).

THE EFFECT OF STATE CONTROL ON EDUCATION

Taiwan's education system is centralized and state-managed, and even private schools are tightly controlled by the Ministry of Education. There are many expressions of state influence—from the number and type of schools built or licensed, to more subtle mechanisms, such as the timing of examinations, tuition levels, employment of teachers, and curricula.

The most pronounced state influence on the regulation of the transition from school to work is the introduction of compulsory education and optional further education (Mayer and Schoepflin 1989). Earlier studies on educational stratification (see e.g. Tsai and Chiu 1993; Tsai, Gates, and Chiu 1994) show that after the extension of compulsory education, the transition from junior high to post-compulsory school appear to be most selective, upgrading the most significant inequality in access to education—by social origin—to that level.

In addition to the extension of compulsory education, the state has shaped the structural conditions for social inclusion and exclusion by imposing a policy against the general trend whereby 'vocational education, as a share of secondary education, has declined in almost every educational system in the world' (Benavot 1983: 63), and has expanded secondary education by shifting the emphasis from general to vocational education at post-compulsory levels.[5] Since 1966 the state has encouraged expansion of the vocational sector while limiting the expansion of academic institutions,[6] so as to meet the growing demand for skilled workers generated by industrialization.[7] As a result, post-junior high school enrolments in academic institutions, raising the proportion from 39:61 in 1966 to 68:32 in 1994 (Ministry of Education 1995). By 1994 the ratio of the total number of senior high school students to senior vocational school students was 31.92 vs. 68.08 (Ministry of Education 1995: p. xxiii). In other words, the entire school system expanded over the past three decades, but the 'best' schools—those with preferential access to universities—did not.

We should emphasize that this approximately 30:70 ratio was not the natural result of educational supply and demand, but the product of deliberate government intervention; the Economic Construction Commission set this ratio as a policy goal (Y.-R. Yang 1994: 13–14). The restriction on the relative share of senior high schools in secondary education induces fierce competition among junior high school students, and school life is dominated by examinations. No wonder there has been a strong and increasing tendency towards going abroad for higher education, accompanied by the earlier brain-drain phenomenon, and more recently selective waves of out-migration.

State influence on the role played by education as a mechanism of social mobility is also worth noting. The policy of low tuition costs is designed to reduce social inequalities in educational attainment by lowering the economic barrier to access education. The first nine years of compulsory education are free, and beyond that, costs are 'moderately low for public high schools, moderately high for private high schools, very low for third-tier public schools, but very high for private higher education' (Cheng 1992: 65). Without the freedom to adjust to the equilibrium of costs and benefits and with the limited financial state support, private schools have been caught in a vicious cycle, and tend to be at the lower end of the prestige and quality scale.

Meanwhile, Taiwan's examination system favours those from advantaged socio-economic backgrounds or superior academic preparation (Lucas 1982). Take, for example, the joint entrance examination for universities and colleges. Candidates from middle and upper-middle income groups are disproportionately represented as regards both enrolments and success rates (Lucas 1982: 215). The combination of educational selection by examination results, and the low-cost tuition policy produces the observable 'unjust' distribution of educational resources. It appears that children from more advantaged backgrounds attend public high schools and then national universities, which are both better and cheaper, while children from poorer families either have no schools to attend, or are forced to enter the lower tracks in the more expensive private sector. Hence, it appears that Taiwan's educational policies tend to maintain the prevailing system of social stratification and reproduce class inequality,[8] rather than promoting equality of educational opportunity.

Drastic educational reforms have been demanded for decades (see e.g. Taiwan Research Fund 1994), yet debate on the scope and priorities of further educational expansion continues unabated. The controversy has centred on the functions of education in a society with two related issues: whether vocational secondary education is a crude mechanism of social exclusion, or a safety-net to prevent some students dropping to the bottom of the labour queue (Arum and Shavit 1995), and whether the expansion of higher education generates unemployment for college graduates which leads to wastage of resources and social instability. Both issues are empirically explored in the present analysis.

INDUSTRIALIZATION AND THE LABOUR MARKET

Since World War II, land-reform policy, import-substitution and export-oriented industrialization have delineated the historical stages of state development strategies in Taiwan (Hsiao 1986). Following the post-war land reforms, the agrarian class structure was transformed. Over the period of industrialization, new technology has been introduced in Taiwan, and the economic structure began to change as a result. As Taiwan changed from a domestic market-directed, import-substitution industrial programme to a labour-intensive, export-oriented manufacturing one in the mid-1960s, success for this development strategy depended on a marriage of cheap, disciplined local labour with international technology, capital, and markets (Deyo 1987; Bello and Rosenfeld 1990).

Most of the economic literature on the 'Taiwan miracle' portrays it as the result of an almost totally free market (Fei 1983), although the role played by the state has gone well beyond the principles of neo-classical economics (Wade 1990). According to Hamilton and Biggart (1988: S78–9), in the past three decades, Taiwan has moved away from the strong state model to the strong society model of state/business relations, promoted 'virtually free trade conditions' (Little 1979: 475), and carried out 'planning within the context of a free economy' (Myers 1984: 522). Although the state stills owns and manages a range of public enterprises, the public sector has steadily decreased in importance (Gold 1986; Myers 1984).

Free markets are also the basis of youth employment policy so that 'The labour market in Taiwan is as close to a textbook model of a competitive labour market as one is likely to find. The price of labour has adjusted passively to market conditions of price and productivity' (Wade 1990: 55). Institutional factors which intervene between buyers and sellers of labour are limited in Taiwan. Prior to 1987, strikes were illegal under martial law, and even today labour unions and other conventional methods of collective bargaining are still weak. Although the control of labour in Taiwan initially had political rather than economic-strategic roots, it has remained enterprise centred (Deyo 1987; Haggard 1990).

In Taiwan, the family firm and the business group are the dominant organizational forms throughout the economy, especially in the export sector (Hamilton and Biggart 1988: S60). The firm is embedded in a network of institutional relationships (such as satellite factory systems and sub-contracting systems based on personal ties) that give Taiwan's economy a distinctive character. According to Shieh (1992: 213), 'Taiwanese export-oriented capitalism has three characteristics: that the orders, which originate in the advanced core countries, are huge and fluctuate widely; that the industries it brings about are light, and thus divisible in their production processes; and that these industries are labour-intensive, which requires an abundant supply of cheap labour.' In short, Taiwan's industrialization is sustained through labour network processes (i.e. the subcontracting processes) and a micro-entrepreneurial mechanism which is unfolded in network labour processes (Shieh 1992). The small-to-medium size, single-unit, family-run firms predominate, comprising 98 per cent of all industrial enterprises (Lu 1996).

In summary, flexibility is the basic ingredient of Taiwan's economy. Because uncertainty is a constant feature in Taiwan's economic environment, the ability to respond to the economic opportunities on the world market is essential to entrepreneurial success (Hamilton and Biggart 1988; Ka 1993; Shieh 1992; Wade 1990). Although Taiwan's Government develops economic plans, state planning has 'no importance' (Little 1979: 487) in determining economic behaviour (Hamilton and Biggart 1988: S79).

ISSUES AND HYPOTHESES

We often assume that educational expansion has made an important contribution to Taiwan's rapid economic growth by enhancing the quality of human resources and by furthering the introduction of more productive technology.[9] This idea has been particularly popular among technocrats and scholars who incline to refer to Taiwan as a case of successful planning. Woo (1991), for instance, maintained that Taiwan's education system was planned to grow in a manner that closely matched the changing functional requirements of the growing economy. Nevertheless, there are reasonable doubts as to this success story (Y.-R. Yang 1994; Taiwan Research Fund 1994). We should look beyond the so-called economic miracle.

As discussed earlier, the transition from school to work in Taiwan involves a rigid, state-controlled examination system of education, a flexible, free market-oriented economy, and limited institutional linkage between them. On the one hand, we believe that schools can easily serve as sorters and signallers in youths' competition for jobs (Spring 1976; Thurow 1975). Irrespective of whether or not Taiwan's manpower planning was successful, Taiwan's educational system has a capacity to structure the flow of young people into the labour force. In a rigidly stratified school system, higher education certified with nationally recognized credentials are highly valued, especially under excess demand. Parents pressure their children to continue their studies as far upwards as possible (Lucas 1982: 212). 'Stigma is strongly attached to failure and often affects the "life chance" of those who fail the examination,' argued Cheng (1992: 65). It is commonly anticipated that students should move into adult labour-force positions whose stratified levels are highly correlated with levels of educational attainment.

On the other hand, in contrast with the case of Japan in which a 'job-referral system' operates between school and the labour market (Brinton 1988, 1993; Okano 1995; Rosenbaum and Kariya 1989; Rosenbaum et al. 1990), there is limited formal linkage between schools and employers in

Taiwan, and graduates usually seek jobs on their own. Most jobs in Taiwan clearly specify the required minimum level of education for the applicant. Educational or occupational credentials obtained from passing formal quali- fication examinations are essential in competition for jobs.

Meanwhile, and again in contrast to Japan, where firm internal labour markets prevail, Taiwan's small to medium-sized, flexibility-oriented, fam- ily-run firms require very little research and development, but cheap skilled labour and technicians. Vocational training is not widely practised in the booming private sector. Firms realize that productivity can be improved through more qualified workers, but hesitate in conducting vocational train- ing because opportunity cost of training may increase due either to the investment or to the high labour turnover rate (San 1990). Hence, among those with secondary education as their highest level of education, graduates from vocational schools with some specific job skills are preferred over senior high school graduates whose diplomas are not directly linked to specific job- types. School education prepares senior high school graduates for competi- tion in the entrance examinations of higher education, rather than providing preparation for labour-force participation. If unable to transit to higher edu- cation, senior high school graduates carry a mark of 'limited ability', in addi- tion to a label of 'lack of vocational training', which might discount their value in the labour market.

Finally, the state is certainly one of the agencies which impose regularity on the link between educational attainment and labour-market placements (Mayer and Schoepflin 1989). We wonder if the pronounced shift towards dual-stream, segmented secondary school has gone against social demand (albeit in favour of some industrial needs), for academic high schools are the main route to universities, and university degrees confer higher rates of return and prestige. Hence, the present analysis pays special attention to the roles played by vocational schools and higher education in determining cur- rent employment status.

DATA AND VARIABLES

The data for this analysis are taken from the Second Survey of Social Changes in Taiwan, 1990–1994.[10] This is a five-year project covering the main themes of Taiwan's changing society, based on representative samples. There are two types of questionnaire for each year investigated, focusing on two different themes. After a careful selection, the present analysis uses information ascertained from the following three data-sets: 1992 (I), 1994 (I), and 1994 (II). All three types of questionnaire asked for respondent's edu- cation, first job, current employment status, parental education, father's class and occupational status. More importantly, they all made a clear distinction between senior high school and senior vocational school at the secondary level, whereas earlier databases collapsed them into a single category. Since this study focuses on the experience of recent labour-force entry cohorts, we limit our analysis sample to respondents born after 1960; this sample should have entered junior high school after the extension of compulsory education.

The present analysis uses two dependent variables: first job[11] and current employment status. First job is measured in two ways: scaling in a two-digit Taiwanese version of socio-economic index constructed by Tsai and Chiu (1991); and using an eight-category version of the EGP class schema (Erikson, Goldthorpe, and Portocarero 1979). Our eight classes are: higher-grade service class (I); lower-grade service class (II); routine non-manual class (IIIa); personal service working class (IIIb); the petty bourgeoisie (IVab); skilled manual working class (V + VI); unskilled manual working class (VIIIab); and the farming class (IVc). Later, due to the sample-size limitations of the data analysed, Classes I and II were collapsed into a single category in the analysis, as were Classes IIIa and IIIb.

With respect to current employment status, we use a nominal measure consisting of three categories: unemployment, not in the labour force (students or housewives), and employed. But, again, we have combined the first two categories to solve the identification problems caused by the small sample size used in the estimation of multinominal logit models.

On the other hand, three types of independent variables are considered in this study: demographic characteristics such as sex and age; social origins-ethnicity,[12] father's class and occupational status, and parental education—the higher of father's and mother's education; and educational attainment.

Educational attainment is measured in two ways—years of education and educational qualifications. Because of the extension of compulsory education to nine years, respondents and their parents experienced different school systems. Accordingly, 'primary' education pertains to junior high school education for the respondents, whereas it means six years of education for their parents. More precisely, parental education is measured on a scale of three categories: primary (elementary school), secondary (junior and senior high school), and post-secondary (post-high school). Respondent's educational qualification is measured on a CASMIN scale of five categories: (1a) inadequate completion of compulsory education, (1b) completed compulsory education (junior high school), (2a) completed vocational education at secondary level, (2b) completed senior high school, (3a) attended vocational education at post-secondary level, (3b) attended university or college.

EMPIRICAL RESULTS

Our major analytical objective is to assess the extent of association between educational attainment and labour-market positions at entry. This part of the analysis relies on information from 1,581 respondents aged 21 to 34 for whom data were available on all variables included in the regressions. The total analysis sample consists of 667 men and 914 women.

Differential Achievements

It is constructive to give a general picture of educational and occupational selections by presenting some descriptive statistics. Table 14.2 reports the mean years of schooling completed by men and women from a variety of social origins, together with their mean SEI of first jobs and the distributions of sample. While the mean level of education attained by women is lower than men, the statuses of women's first jobs are on average higher than those of men. Although gender differences in both aspects are small, they are statistically significant at the level of $\alpha = .05$. This finding is consistent with past research based on the Wisconsin longitudinal data (Sewell, Hauser, and Wolf 1980). Also, similar to the American case, the variability in the initial occupational statuses of women is restrictive relative to that among men.

Up to a point, ethnic and class differences in educational attainment are parallel to those in initial occupational status. Consistent with the results of our earlier studies (see e.g. Tsai 1992), Mainlanders are more advantaged in the attainment of schooling and first job than other groups, whereas the Aborigines are the most disadvantaged. This pattern holds for both men and women. When class origins are taken into account, we find that the higher the level of parental education, the higher children's educational and occupational achievements. By the same token, children from lower classes attain a lower level of achievement than members of other classes.[13]

The Education-First Job Association

In the relationship between educational attainment and initial occupational achievement the zero-order correlation between years of schooling and status of first jobs is generally higher among women (.58), than among men (.52). Table 14.3 presents means and standard deviations of years of schooling by class position at entry to the labour market, together with the sample distributions for men and women.

While men and women have similar distributions of father's class (see Table 14.2), there are some differences between the sexes with respect to the allocation of entry class. As we can see in Table 14.3, the major gender differences pertain to the high proportion of women in Class IIIa+b (routine non-manual jobs), and their under-representation in Class VIIa+b (unskilled manual jobs) relative to men. The index of dissimilarity measuring the extent of sex segregation indicates that to equalize the distribution of men and women across the eight classes considered, 24.7 per cent of the women (or men) would require reclassification.[14]

The means and standard deviations of initial occupational statuses by educational qualifications are reported in Table 14.4. We can observe a monotonous increase in status of first job as one moves upward along the tripartite hierarchy of education, irrespective of sex. As expected, the average SEI of the occupations of those with university degrees is higher than that of people who obtained other types of credentials. Meanwhile, there is no substantial sex difference in SEI of occupations at the tertiary level, regardless of types of education.

On the other hand, among respondents who attained secondary education as their highest level of education, there is no significant difference in early occupational achievements between vocational school graduates and those with matriculation diplomas. This pattern holds for both sexes. But, men and women differ in the SEI of occupations when first entering the world of work, with men losing out to women with the equivalent of secondary education.

The Role of Education in First Occupational Attainment

We now turn to the causal analysis of education—first-job linkage by taking such background variables as age, ethnicity, and social origins into account. In this part of the analysis, we address two issues: the relative importance of education and ascription in the determination of initial occupational status; and whether, and to what extent, education serves as a mediating mechanism between origin and destination in the process of status attainment.

Using either years of schooling or dummy variables measuring educational qualifications, we estimate several pairs of regression equations predicting the SEI of initial occupational status by a variety of independent variables for men and women. Comparisons across these pairs of equations estimated, based on results not shown here, indicate that the categorical measurements of educational qualifications explain more variance in the SEI of first job than does an interval scale of schooling, regardless of sex. Moreover, the coefficients of determination reveal that the OLS regression equations are more powerful in accounting for initial occupational status among women than among men.

Table 14.5 presents results of two pairs of equations measuring father's

TABLE 14.2. *Mean years of education and mean SEI of first job by social origins and gender*

Social origins	Men				Women			
	Schooling	SEI	Cases	%	Schooling	SEI	Cases	%
TOTAL	12.22 (2.54)	62.73 (4.98)	667	100.0	11.74 (2.80)	63.61 (4.23)	914	100.0
Ethnicity								
Aborigine	10.90 (2.56)	61.07 (4.57)	10	1.5	8.71 (3.55)	62.81 (4.82)	17	1.9
Hokkien	12.05 (2.65)	62.51 (4.94)	458	68.7	11.49 (2.82)	63.30 (4.26)	655	71.7
Hakkas	12.30 (2.19)	62.29 (4.82)	107	16.0	12.22 (2.28)	63.84 (4.19)	125	13.7
Mainlanders	13.11 (2.10)	64.56 (5.10)	92	13.8	13.02 (2.50)	65.20 (3.66)	117	12.8
Parental education								
Primary (elementary school)	11.75 (2.64)	62.10 (4.88)	456	68.4	10.98 (2.86)	62.65 (4.10)	614	67.2
Secondary	13.02 (1.91)	63.81 (4.78)	168	25.2	13.07 (1.85)	65.34 (3.64)	239	26.1
Tertiary	14.05 (1.86)	65.30 (5.41)	43	6.4	14.16 (1.91)	66.53 (4.26)	61	6.7

Class origin								
I + II: Service class	13.77 (1.81)	65.32 (4.99)	110	16.5	13.30 (2.31)	65.88 (3.93)	173	18.9
IIIa+b: Routine non-manual workers	11.75 (2.70)	63.94 (4.94)	36	5.4	13.29 (2.18)	64.78 (3.82)	52	5.7
IVa+b: Petty bourgeoisie	13.01 (1.84)	63.67 (4.96)	123	18.4	12.06 (2.38)	64.64 (4.10)	195	21.3
V + VI: Skilled workers	12.33 (2.34)	62.28 (4.91)	84	12.6	11.37 (2.79)	62.69 (3.93)	110	12.0
VIIa+b: Non-skilled workers	11.62 (2.71)	61.94 (4.48)	130	19.5	10.95 (2.76)	62.39 (3.86)	155	17.0
IVc: Farmers	11.22 (2.64)	61.09 (4.60)	184	27.6	10.63 (2.92)	62.02 (4.00)	229	25.1

Note: Figures in parentheses are standard deviations.

TABLE 14.3. *Years of education by entry class and gender*

Entry class	Men			Women		
	Mean	Cases	%	Mean	Cases	%
I+II: Service class	14.05 (1.62)	168	25.2	13.77 (1.66)	170	18.6
IIIa+b: Routine non-manual workers	13.34 (1.64)	82	12.3	12.78 (2.09)	339	37.1
IVa+b: Petty bourgeoisie	12.05 (2.16)	21	3.1	10.56 (2.92)	16	1.8
V + VI: Skilled workers	11.59 (2.24)	219	32.8	10.00 (2.71)	253	27.7
VIIa+b: Non-skilled workers	10.91 (2.68)	159	23.8	9.90 (2.66)	132	14.4
IVc: Farmers	9.44 (2.85)	18	2.7	12.25 (2.36)	4	0.4
TOTAL	12.22 (2.54)	667	100.0	11.74 (2.80)	914	100.0

Note: Figures in parentheses are standard deviations.

TABLE 14.4. *SEI of first job by educational qualification and gender*

Educational qualification	Men			Women		
	Mean	Cases	%	Mean	Cases	%
Primary						
1ab: Compulsory education and below	59.22 (2.35)	156	23.4	60.02 (2.16)	263	28.8
Secondary						
2a: Vocational school at secondary level	61.85 (4.23)	227	34.0	63.97 (3.73)	290	31.7
2b: Senior high school	61.82 (4.60)	87	13.0	63.45 (3.56)	126	13.8
Tertiary						
3a: Vocational school at post-secondary level	66.10 (4.57)	131	19.6	66.68 (3.56)	150	16.4
3b: University and higher	68.63 (4.19)	66	9.9	68.32 (3.32)	85	9.3
TOTAL	62.73 (1.98)	667	100.0	63.61 (1.13)	914	100.0

Note: Figures in parentheses are standard deviations.

TABLE 14.5. *OLS regressions of the SEI score of first job*

Independent variables	Equations			
	(1)	(2)	(3)	(4)
	Men (N = 667)		Women (N = 914)	
Age	.11*	.04	−.06	.01
	(.05)	(.04)	(.03)	(.03)
Ethnicity (relative to Hokkien)				
Aborigine	−.53	.11	.23	1.65*
	(1.53)	(1.29)	(.96)	(.80)
Hakkas	−.26	−.33	.48	−.00
	(.52)	(.44)	(.38)	(.32)
Mainlanders	.91	.73	.62	.14
	(.58)	(.49)	(.42)	(.35)
Parental education (Relative to elementary)				
Secondary	.59	−.17	1.67*	.36
	(.47)	(.40)	(.33)	(.28)
Tertiary	.92	−.49	2.12*	−.00
	(.88)	(.74)	(.63)	(.53)
Father's class (relative to non-skilled workers)				
I + II: Service class	2.89*	.61	2.31*	1.01*
	(.67)	(.59)	(.49)	(.41)
III: Routine non-manual workers	1.61	1.12	1.57*	.10
	(.91)	(.77)	(.64)	(.53)
IVa+b: Petty bourgeoisie	1.59*	.21	1.98*	1.25*
	(.61)	(.52)	(.42)	(.35)
V + VI: Skilled workers	.36	−.08	.22	−.06
	(.67)	(.56)	(.49)	(.40)
IVc: Farmers	−.71	−.47	−.10	−.12
	(.55)	(.47)	(.41)	(.34)
Education (relative to primary)				
2a: vocational school at secondary level		2.49*		3.69*
		(.44)		(.29)
2b: Senior high school		2.34*		3.10*
		(.55)		(.37)
3a: Vocational school at post-secondary level		6.53*		6.18*
		(.51)		(.36)
3b: University and higher		8.98*		7.75*
		(.64)		(.45)
Constant	58.71*	58.27*	63.75*	59.31*
	(1.56)	(1.38)	(1.02)	(.90)
R^2	.10	.37	.16	.43

Note: Parenthetic entries are standard errors.
* Significant at the level of $\alpha = .05$

class on the EGP schema, for men and women. Each pair consists of a short equation (ascribed variables only), and a long one (ascribed variables and educational qualifications). Comparisons across these two equations highlight the role of educational attainment in mediating the effects of status ascription on early occupational achievement. Next, we report some results evident in this part of the analysis. Sex differences mentioned in the following are all statistically significant beyond the probability level of $\alpha = .05$ in a two-tailed test.

Educational attainment—measured by either interval or categorical approaches—proves to be the most powerful predictor of one's SEI of early occupation, irrespective of sex. Despite sex similarities in the patterns of differential SEI return to education, men and women differ in the pay-off for various educational qualifications. Comparisons of estimated coefficients across equations 2 and 4 in Table 14.5 reveal two opposite patterns of sex differences. With a secondary education, women obtain a higher status return to either vocational or academic tracking than men; with a tertiary education, men obtain a higher pay-off than women. However, among those with less than a tertiary education, it is senior vocational school, rather than senior high school, that brings a higher return of status in first jobs. This is true for both men and women.

Regarding the role played by education in mediating the effects of ascription on occupational achievement, let us start with ethnic effects. We find that for men and women, ethnicity is not an important determinant of the SEI of occupations at entry to the labour market, with or without controls for education.[15] The ethnic differences in the SEI of initial occupations reported earlier can be accounted for by their differential socio-economic backgrounds.

With respect to parental influences, we find that without controls for education, parental years of schooling exert a greater effect on women's statuses of first jobs than on those of men. But, the effects of parental years of schooling disappear when men's years of schooling or women's educational qualifications have been taken into account. On the other hand, the effects of father's occupational status remain significant among women, with controls for either levels or types of educational attainments. Among men, status ascription in the SEI is substantially mediated by educational qualifications. Men and women also differ in the ways that class of origin influences initial occupational status. Fathers in advantaged classes transmit direct benefits to their daughters in gaining prestigious jobs, but not to their sons. The intergenerational association between father's classes and sons' occupational statuses are substantially mediated by sons' educational qualifications.

The Role of Education in Entry Class Allocation

Having explored the dual role played by education in the attainment of initial occupational status, we examine the allocation of class positions by education. Multinominal logit regressions have been used to estimate the effects of educational qualifications on the propensity of entry into a certain class, net of background variables. Class VIIab (unskilled workers) is used as the reference group. Tables 14.6 and 14.7 report the estimated coefficients for men and women.[16]

TABLE 14.6. *Multinominal logit of entry class contrasted with Class VIIa+b (non-skilled workers) for men* (N = 649)

Independent variables	Entry class			
	I + II	III	IVa+b	V + VI
Intercept	−7.045*	−6.101*	−3.824	4.333*
	(2.158)	(2.293)	(4.346)	(1.799)
Age	0.057	−0.028	0.127	−0.061*
	(0.037)	(0.042)	(0.077)	(0.031)
Parental education (relative to elementary)				
Secondary & higher	0.559	0.744*	0.665	0.878*
	(0.323)	(0.359)	(0.627)	(0.293)
Father's SEI	0.029	0.067*	−0.054	−0.045
	(0.028)	(0.030)	(0.060)	(0.026)
Father's class (self-employment)	0.273	0.243	0.806	−0.088
	(0.272)	(0.312)	(0.540)	(0.220)
Education (relative to primary)				
2a: Vocational school at secondary level	2.962*	1.561*	−0.058	0.198
	(0.752)	(0.579)	(0.716)	(0.253)
2b: Senior high school	3.347*	1.819*	1.904*	0.462
	(0.802)	(0.668)	(0.656)	(0.361)
3ab: Tertiary	5.193*	3.220*	1.296	0.414
	(0.778)	(0.616)	(0.767)	(0.386)

* Significant at the level of $\alpha = .05$

Tables 14.6 and 14.7 reveal that highly qualified people are advantaged in access to professional and managerial positions, irrespective of sex. The higher the level of educational qualification attained, the greater the chance of being recruited into the service class. This is especially true for women with tertiary education. Besides, when contrasted against those with a primary education, vocational secondary education provides women with a

TABLE 14.7. *Multinominal logit of entry class contrasted with Class VIIa+b (non-skilled workers) for women* (N = 910)

Independent variables	Entry class			
	I + II	III	IVa+b	V + VI
Intercept	−7.765*	−5.247*	−15.836*	0.384
	(2.240)	(1.956)	(4.774)	(1.961)
Age	−0.029	0.009	0.278*	0.003
	(0.037)	(0.032)	(0.097)	(0.030)
Parental education (relative to elementary)				
Secondary and higher	0.131	0.360	0.477	−0.322
	(0.352)	(0.311)	(0.693)	(0.331)
Father's SEI	0.088*	0.068*	0.080	0.004
	(0.031)	(0.028)	(0.058)	(0.029)
Father's class (self-employment)	0.709*	0.178	0.099	−0.184
	(0.288)	(0.241)	(0.578)	(0.224)
Education (relative to primary)				
2a: Vocational school at secondary level	3.071*	2.111*	0.348	0.131
	(0.571)	(0.299)	(0.773)	(0.268)
2b: Senior high school	2.813*	1.713*	1.337	0.115
	(0.620)	(0.359)	(0.717)	(0.335)
3ab: Tertiary	7.304*	5.265*	2.963*	1.873
	(1.138)	(1.034)	(1.359)	(1.062)

* Significant at the level of $\alpha = .05$

higher chance in access to the service class than does senior high school education; the opposite is true for men. The same pattern of sex differences holds in access to the routine non-manual class, with educational qualifications lessening their effects. It seems evident that vocational secondary education benefits women more than men, as far as the inclusion of white-collar classes is concerned. Regarding the odds of recruitment into the petty bourgeoisie relative to becoming unskilled workers, the probability is greatest for male senior high school graduates relative to other men. In contrast, women with a tertiary education are more likely to start their careers as petty bourgeoisie than other women.

On the other hand, men and women diverge in the effects of social origin on the allocation of class positions in several ways. For a man, the likelihood of having a professional or managerial first job is solely determined by his education. For a woman, the propensity is influenced by her father's SEI and self-employment in addition to education. After controlling for educational qualification, the effects of father's SEI on the likelihood of being employed in routine non-manual jobs remain significant for both sexes, but parental education also exerts a direct effect among men (albeit not among women). Sons of parents with more than primary education are somewhat protected from starting a job as unskilled workers; they are more likely to enter the labour force as routine non-manual workers or as skilled workers. This is especially true among men in the working class, in which the distinction between skilled and unskilled workers depends primarily on parental education and age. Education is irrelevant for access to the skilled working class.

Education and Current Employment Status

The final task of this analysis is to examine the relationship between educational qualification and current employment status. We focus on two issues: whether vocational school in secondary education increases or inhibits an individual's likelihood of being employed; and whether higher education leads to higher unemployment. Our analysis is based on a sub-sample of 612 men and 740 women aged 25 to 35 for whom complete information was available for all variables in the multinominal logit regressions presented here.[17]

About 96 per cent of men, and almost 70 per cent of women, in our sample are currently employed. The unemployment rate is very small (3.3 per cent for men and 1.4 per cent for women) because Taiwan's labour market has cleared since the end of the period of labour surplus at the end of the 1960s (Wade 1990: 57). Most of the women currently not in the labour force are housewives, while their male counterparts are mostly students.

Table 14.8 presents the distribution of current employment status by educational qualification for men and women separately. As can be seen, men who attained at least a university education have a higher unemployment rate and a lower employment rate than other men, while women college graduates have a higher employment rate than other women. In order to see whether this implies that higher education leads to higher unemployment among men we used multinomial logit regressions contrasting current unemployment and being out of the labour force with employment for both sexes. Some of the parameters, however, cannot be identified due to the small size of the sample, and we modified the model specification by collapsing unemployment and not in the labour force into a single category (see Table 14.9).

Table 14.9 indicates that among men, none of the variables considered exerts a significant direct effect on current employment status. With a very high employment rate, men aged 25 to 35 tend to have an equal opportunity

Shu-Ling Tsai

TABLE 14.8. *Current employment status by educational qualification and gender*

Educational qualification	Current employment status							
	Men (N = 612)				Women (N = 740)			
	(1)	(2)	(3)	Total	(1)	(2)	(3)	Total
1ab: Compulsory education and below	7 (4.6)	0 (—)	144 (95.4)	151 (100.0)	2 (0.9)	98 (42.4)	131 (56.7)	231 (100.0)
2a: Vocational school at secondary level	7 (3.9)	1 (0.6)	173 (95.6)	181 (100.0)	6 (2.8)	62 (28.6)	149 (68.7)	217 (100.0)
2b: Senior high school	2 (2.6)	0 (—)	76 (97.4)	78 (100.0)	0 (—)	28 (29.5)	67 (70.5)	95 (100.0)
3a: Vocational school at post-secondary level	0 (—)	1 (0.8)	123 (99.2)	124 (100.0)	2 (1.8)	15 (13.2)	97 (85.1)	114 (100.0)
3b: University and higher	4 (5.1)	5 (6.4)	69 (88.5)	78 (100.0)	0 (—)	12 (14.5)	71 (85.5)	83 (100.0)
TOTAL	20 (3.3)	7 (1.1)	585 (95.6)	612 (100.0)	10 (1.4)	215 (29.1)	515 (69.6)	740 (100.0)

Note: Parenthetic entries are percentages. The three categories of current employment status are: (1) unemployment; (2) not in labor force; (3) employment.

TABLE 14.9. *Logit regression contrasting currently not employed (unemployed or out of the labour force) with currently employed*

Independent variables	Men (N = 612)	Women (N = 740)	Total (N = 1352)
Intercept	3.061	0.358	1.124
	(3.630)	(1.530)	(1.405)
Age	−0.125	0.041	0.016
	(0.076)	(0.032)	(0.029)
Ethnicity (relative to Hokkien)			
Aborigine	1.122	−0.964	−0.600
	(1.139)	(0.677)	(0.598)
Hakkas	−0.694	−0.562*	−0.562*
	(0.762)	(0.268)	(0.249)
Mainlanders	0.289	−0.204	−0.087
	(0.576)	(0.276)	(0.250)
Gender (male)			−2.240*
			(0.215)
Parental education (relative to elementary)			
Secondary	0.295	0.399	0.385
	(0.509)	(0.233)	(0.210)
Tertiary	−0.691	0.415	0.113
	(1.160)	(0.457)	(0.419)
Father's SEI	−0.040	−0.031	−0.033
	(0.048)	(0.020)	(0.018)
Father's self-employment	−0.253	−0.003	−0.021
	(0.425)	(0.176)	(0.161)
Education (relative to primary)			
2a: Vocational school at secondary level	0.098	−0.470*	−0.429*
	(0.553)	(0.212)	(0.195)
2b: Senior high school	−0.651	−0.570*	−0.566*
	(0.836)	(0.275)	(0.256)
3a: Vocational school at post-secondary level	−1.699	−1.440*	-1.444*
	(1.104)	(0.315)	(0.297)
3b: University and higher	1.099	−1.494*	−0.828*
	(0.595)	(0.379)	(0.309)

* Significant at the level of α = .05

of being employed. In contrast, there is an ethnic difference among women: other things being equal, Hakka women have a higher propensity of being employed relative to Hokkien women. Moreover, female labour-force participation is determined by education to a significant extent—the higher the level of education, the higher a woman's likelihood of being employed. In addition, female senior high school graduates are more likely to be currently employed than women from vocational schools at the same level. Thus, it appears that ethnicity and education exert direct effects on female patterns of labour-force participation, while the selectivity bias is minimal for men.

CONCLUSION

Most recent comparative research on the school-to-work transition focuses on the roles of institutional arrangements in the stratification processes in the core industrial societies (see e.g. Erikson and Jonsson 1996*a*; Kerckhoff 1996). It has been argued that Germany and France represent two ideal types of mobility space, respectively: qualificational space where vocational qualifications are used by employers to organize jobs and to allocate individuals among them, and organizational space where job skills are obtained from firm-specific on-the-job training (Maurice, Sellier, and Silvestre 1986; König and Müller 1986). Different from either Germany or France, Taiwan as a newly industrializing country has some distinct characteristics in shaping the school-to-work transition. Excess demand for secondary and higher education is a main difference between Taiwan and the core industrialized countries discussed in this book. Through the operation of the examination system, credentialism is embedded in Taiwan's matriculation competition. Although Taiwan has a rigid educational system developed by the Japanese, in contrast with Japan, the formal links between students and employers are limited.

In this analysis we have focused on the Taiwan experience after the extension of compulsory education, and, given the complexity of social stratification processes, have examined the structure and articulation between the educational system and the labour market using interval scaling and categorical measurements. Our empirical findings can be summarized as follows.

Consistent with our hypothesis, Taiwan's highly stratified educational system functions as a sorting and allocating mechanism. In conditions of excess demand, higher educational credentials confer a higher return of occupational status. The variance in early occupational achievement is more predictable among women than among men. Not only are women more restricted in the world of work relative to men, but they appear to be more meritocratic in the process of occupational attainment, on the one hand, and more responsive to ascriptive factors, on the other. As regards secondary vocational education, it appears to give individuals—irrespective of sex—a higher return of status in first jobs than senior high school education, and it is women who obtain a greater benefit from secondary vocational education, as far as entry into white-collar classes is concerned. Moreover, there is no substantial evidence indicating that higher education leads to higher unemployment. Finally, ethnicity is not a salient factor in the transition from school to work.

Sex differences in the school-to-work linkage can be partially attributed to compulsory military service for boys,[18] but male students enrolled in formal school can postpone military service until they leave school irrespective of the level of educational attainment. Compulsory military service significantly interrupts men's integration of sequential social roles in life course. Most regular jobs specify the completion of military service as a precondition for male applicants.

The role of ethnicity in the process of status attainment merits some discussion. It has been argued that Taiwan's economy has two modes: state-owned enterprises which are mostly monopolies, and a large sector consisting of private medium and small-sized enterprises and that these two modes correspond to two roads to career mobility, each 'loosely' associated with a different ethnic group (M.-K. Chang 1994: 118). According to Greenhalgh (1984: 537), Taiwanese tend to climb up through small-scale business and then larger-scale entrepreneurship into the commercial and industrial elite, whereas Mainlanders tend to exploit contacts in the bureaucracy and higher education to obtain tenured white-collar positions in the public sector.

We are interested in the differential pathways to success taken by different ethnic groups, but in the databases analysed, only the 1992 (I) survey included information on first job by labour-market sector. An examination of the available data provided by 188 men and 283 women appears that the distinction between the public and private sector is important for men.[19] Without controlling for this distinction, we are unable to clarify the relative importance of a variety of educational qualifications in alternative career paths. In our future study of ethnic differences in the process of status attainment, we will continue to explore if the booming private sector provides for Taiwanese specific education–occupation linkages, in which the role played by credentialism is not as important as it is in the public sector and in which a vocational education is preferred to a high-school diploma.

TABLE 14.A.1 Frequencies cross-classified by qualifications, entry class, and gender

Educational qualifications	Entry Class							
	I	II	IIIa	IIIb	IVa+b	V + VI	VIIa+b	IVc
Men (N = 667)								
1ab: Compulsory education & below	0	2	0	4	5	69	66	10
2a: Vocational school at secondary level	2	38	1	25	4	93	61	3
2b: Senior high school	2	15	0	10	8	30	17	5
3a: Vocational school at post-secondary level	10	50	4	27	3	23	14	0
3b: University & higher	10	39	1	10	1	4	1	0
Woman (N = 914)								
1ab: Compulsory education & below	0	4	6	26	6	141	79	1
2a: Vocational school at secondary level	1	44	74	65	3	67	34	2
2b: Senior high school	0	19	26	24	5	34	18	0
3a: Vocational school at post-secondary level	5	51	46	36	2	8	1	1
3b: University & higher	2	44	10	26	0	3	0	0

NOTES

This research was supported by a grant from the National Science Council of the ROC (NSC-85-2412-H-001-007). The author thanks Ying-Hwa Chang, Chih-Ming Ka, Walter Müller, Yossi Shavit, Gwo-Shyong Shieh, and Clare Tame for comments and suggestions, and Chun Lin for research assistance.

1. The two metropolitan municipalities of Taipei and Kaohsiung have recently implemented a trial 'Voluntary Program for Junior High Graduates to Continue Education', which assigns students to preferred senior high schools on the basis of academic performance, rather than examination results.
2. These examinations are held shortly after local newspapers publish the names of all students who passed the public high school entrance examination.
3. The vocational–industrial schools provide a wide variety of specialized training, including aeroelectronics, airplane maintenance, applied electronics, car maintenance and mechanics, casting, chemical analysis, civil and construction engineering, communication of electronics, computer science, constructional drafting, control engineering, dyeing and finishing, electrical appliance and freezing, electrical engineering, electronic equipment repair, electronics, fine-arts and craft, foundry, furniture carpenter, interior design, machine, machine repair building, machinery, mechanical and electrical engineering, mechanical drafting, mechanical wooden mould, mould, pipe fitting, printing, refrigerator and air-conditioning, repair and maintenance of engineering machinery, sheet metalworking, surveying, textile knitting, textile spinning, and textile weaving.
4. The specific training provided by vocational–commercial schools include: accounting affairs, advertisement, beauty art, business affairs, business English, business Japanese, clerical affairs, comprehensive business, data processing, gardening management, international trade, restaurant management, and tourism industry.
5. This is similar to the Israeli case where the proportion of vocational track students has risen considerably in the past three decades (Shavit 1984: 211).
6. After the extension of compulsory education in 1968, junior vocational schools stopped accepting new enrolments. Meanwhile, vocational classes were affiliated to some senior high schools, and by 1994, 84 senior high schools had vocational classes attached to them (Ministry of Education 1995: p. xxiii).
7. In the period 1971–1982, the number of senior high students was gradually reduced, while that of senior vocational school students grew in order to meet the growing demand for skilled workers generated by economic development. Since 1982, the demand for technicians has increased due to industrial upgrading, and as a result, the policy has changed slightly, leading to a gradual growth in the number of senior high students (Ministry of Education 1995: p. xxiii).
8. In addition, state policy appears to maintain educational stratification by ethnicity. This is especially notable among the lower socio-economic classes: 'native Taiwanese are on average more likely to come from a farming or manual background. Farmers and manual workers are economic and political minority groups who are disadvantaged in the allocation of educational resources' (Tsai and Chiu 1993: 218).

9. Several cross-national comparative studies (see e.g. Cheng 1992; Lee, Liu, and Wang 1994) indicate that despite similarities between the two countries, Taiwan's economic growth relied heavily on human-capital enhancement, whereas that of South Korea relied on technical progress.
10. The Survey consists of a series of islandwide longitudinal surveys sponsored by the National Science Council of the ROC.
11. First job is defined as 'the first formal (regular) job in which the respondent worked at least six hours a day after the completion of education' (Chiu 1992: 33). Despite some ambiguities, this operational definition has been adopted in the use of the first-job variable, we assume the transition is from school to work.
12. There are four ethnic groups in contemporary Taiwan—Aborigines, Hokkien, Hakkas, and Mainlanders. Aborigines are mostly scattered throughout the central mountains and remote villages on the eastern part of the island. Hokkien and Hakkas, descended from early Chinese immigrants, are differentiated primarily by dialect and ancestral continental origin. By contrast, Mainlanders are post-war immigrants and their Taiwan-born offspring. The ethnic composition of the analysis sample shown in Table 14.1 is close to that of the total population.
13. Daughters of Class III origin obtaining the same average level of schooling as those of Class I + II is a curious finding.
14. Counts of three-way cross-classification by gender, entry class, and educational qualification are presented in Appendix Table 14.A.1.
15. The exception is constituted by a few cases of Aborigine women included in the analysis.
16. Here we exclude twenty-two cases initially employed in the farming class, due to the problems of parameter identification. For the same reason we use dummy variables to measure father's class (scored 1 for self-employed, 0 otherwise), and parental education (scored 1 if the highest level of elementary school, 0 otherwise). Moreover, post-secondary vocational education and university education are collapsed into the tertiary level. Finally, ethnic differences are not considered because they are not statistically significant based on results not shown here.
17. In the 1992 (I) survey, students were excluded from the sample (Chiu 1992: 18), this might produce a potential—albeit slight—bias in the estimates when the compiled databases are used.
18. Military service is compulsory for boys aged 18 for two to three years.
19. We find that almost 6 per cent of the male respondents, and 8.5 per cent of women were employed in the public sector at the time of labour-market entry, whereas 94.1 per cent of men and 91.5 per cent of women were employed in the private sector. A Chi-square test on these figures reveals that the association between Mainlanders and public sector is significant among men, but not among women. Unfortunately, we have insufficient cases to carry out further analysis, and future surveys would be well advised to collect additional information along the line of the two-sector political economy.

15

The Early Returns

The Transition from School to Work in the United States

RICHARD ARUM AND MICHAEL HOUT

INTRODUCTION

Human-capital theory approaches educational stratification from the point of view of investments and returns: young people invest in themselves and their futures by enrolling in school, and reap the returns on those investments in the labour market (Becker 1972). While the key issue for theorists is the return to this investment over the individual's whole lifetime, many young people have a much shorter planning horizon. They want to know about the immediate returns to their education. In particular, they want to know if staying in school will 'pay-off' with a good job right after leaving. Theory has begun to catch up with this reality. Manski (1993) proposes a model that explicitly addresses the 'stay in school or go to work now' choice that young people make. In particular, he notes that students assess their prospects and choose according to what they know about those prospects, their sense of their academic ability, and how much they enjoy school.

The contributions of the human-capital investment perspective to understanding educational stratification cannot be denied. Nor should they be exaggerated. In particular, the human-capital investment perspective encourages us to look at education as a fungible linear accumulation, much like a financial investment. This is not the case. Students who opt for 'school' enrol not only in a particular school, but also in a curriculum within that school. The actual course of study depends on the choices that students make and institutional constraints such as admission standards and enrolment limits imposed by the capacities of teaching staffs, classroom size, and budgets for supplies and equipment. This differentiation in educational systems complicates the human-capital account of educational stratification and challenges other kinds of theorizing as well.

In the United States the differentiation comes in the form of academic and vocational tracking in secondary schools and the proliferation of non-traditional programmes in two-year community and junior colleges. These institutional arrangements offer an array of choices and constraints that defy the simple linear formulations found in most theoretical models. To attend to the differentiation of the educational system it is necessary to include track or higher educational sector in the measurement of educational investment and to look for links between each educational sector and particular occupational and wage outcomes.

Differentiation in the US educational system is modest in comparison with those of many other post-industrial societies (Müller and Karle 1993). Thus comparative research must attend to cross-national differences in the extent of curricular and institutional differentiation. And because the transition from school to work can be much more closely regulated in some of these institutional arrangements, we must also develop theories and models of special school-to-work channels (see e.g. Rosenbaum et al. 1990).

As long as it does not obscure the realities of educational differentiation, an investment-centred approach to educational decisions can resolve a problem that has vexed researchers who have focused on that differentiation. Most sociologists of education approach differentiation from an institutional perspective that asks about the 'effectiveness' of various departures from a standard academic curriculum. Conclusions about the effectiveness frequently turn on the way the contrasts are drawn in a way that could be framed as a 'compared to what?' dilemma. The effectiveness of vocational high-school programmes is usually judged relative to secondary school general curriculum programmes (R. Meyer and Wise 1982; Grasso and Shea 1979), but critics often compare them to academic tracks (see e.g. Gamoran and Mare 1989). Scholars have recently reached a consensus on the implications of differentiating academic and non-academic tracks (Gamoran 1996), but recent work has highlighted how vocational programmes are more effective than general track programmes in facilitating employment in desirous occupations, particularly for women (Arum and Shavit 1995; also see Rumberger and Daymont 1984; Kang and Bishop 1989). Research on post-secondary education replicates the 'compared to what?' dilemma. Young people who complete degree programmes at two-year colleges do better in the labour market than those who stop after high school but not as well as those who earn degrees at four-year colleges (Monk-Turner 1983; Dougherty 1987; Brint and Karabel 1989).

An investment approach provides researchers with objective criteria for choosing a basis for their comparisons. From an investment perspective, the question of whether the pay-off to a two-year post-secondary degree is 'appropriate' depends on whether it is proportionate to the investment it requires (greater than a high-school diploma and less than that required for a four-year post-secondary degree). In addition to the obvious time difference between a two- and four-year degree, each year at a four-year institution costs more money than a year at a two-year community or junior college. The NLSY data-set we use does not contain tuition information, so we cannot fully implement the investment approach, but we address the returns to two-year degrees with both the time and money differentials in mind. If we find that the rewards to two-year degrees are midway between those of an academic secondary diploma and a four-year college degree, we will conclude that the investment is worthwhile. Those with the two-year degree break even on time and are ahead on money. We will draw a less sanguine conclusion if it turns out that the rewards to a two-year degree are closer to those of an academic secondary diploma than to a four-year degree.

The investment perspective makes more sense in the United States than it might elsewhere. In the United States education is undertaken by individuals; employers and unions have few institutional ties to schools. Like the investor who pays now in the hope of uncertain future gain, the American student spends time and money on skills that may or may not 'pay-off' in higher lifetime occupational success or earnings. In Japan, Germany, and elsewhere, as we have seen in other chapters, schools and employers cooperate with employers. They attempt to match the skills that they teach to the employers' needs; they also establish stronger institutional linkages that match graduates to jobs through work-experience programmes and informal networks (Rosenbaum et al. 1990; S. Hamilton and Hurrelmann 1994; Kerckhoff 1995; Kariya this volume). The institutional ties give employers a stake in the students' training and reduce students' risks.[1] With few exceptions, the United States lacks this kind of institutionalized cooperation between schools and employers. In the absence of these stable institutional linkages, students take courses that lack real-world content, train on outmoded equipment, and graduate with little knowledge of their prospective employers' needs. That makes the initial labour-market experiences of young adults unstable—marked by high rates of job turnover in non-unionized employment situations.[2]

RESEARCH DESIGN

As our contribution to the international project designed to go beyond simple linear formulations, we employ a version of the CASMIN educational scheme (Ishida, Müller and Ridge 1995) to model the links between class destinations and educational niches defined in terms of educational level and academic content. We supplement these analyses with a refined set of educational contrasts that take advantage of special features of the US data. Given the weak institutional linkages between schools and employers in the United States (with some exceptions that are notable but not observed in our data), we expect the association between Müller's differentiated educational measure and first job to be weaker than it is in societies with strong institutional linkages. On the other hand, we expect the association between Müller's measure and first class to be stronger than the association between a more conventional measure of education and first class. Our supplementary analyses show that the returns to vocational preparation depend on the substantive content. Broad vocational programmes yield almost no return on the time invested in them, while trade, technical, business, and commercial programmes have positive returns.

DATA

We analyse data from the cross-sectional representative sample of the National Longitudinal Study of Youth (NLSY). The cross-sectional sample consists of data on 6,111 individuals aged 14 to 22 years in 1979. They were re-interviewed annually throughout the 1990s, so they were 26 to 34 years old at the last contact. We use data up until 1991, the last year for which data is currently publicly available.

Dependent Variables

First job can mean many things, and its definition influences the outcome of the study. Among the available definitions the one that poses the fewest problems for a study of school-to-work transitions selects the first job a person takes after leaving school for the last time. We could implement this definition for 97.9 per cent of the sample (assuming the last transition from school to labour market occurred prior to age 26—the age of the youngest members of the NLSY cohort at the last interview in 1991). An additional 0.7 per cent of the respondents were in school until the age of 26 but left before 1991; we included them in the analysis. For the eighty-two individuals (1.3 per cent of the sample) still unable to be classified, eleven cases were 'chronic' students—enrolled in school all survey years; the remaining seventy-one cases were unclassified as a result of missing data due to non-interviews.

We coded first job into classes according to a protocol suggested by Müller and Shavit (1994) that modifies the EGP standard class schema (Erikson and Goldthorpe 1992): I–II—all managerial and professional occupations; IIIab—routine non-manual occupations; IVabc—self-employed, non-professional occupations; V–VI—technical, supervisory, and skilled manual occupations; VIIab—unskilled manual occupations. Within the NLSY data-set occupations are coded according to the 1970 US Census classification scheme. We used a transformation file provided by Harry Ganzeboom to map these American codes into the EGP scheme.[3]

We supplement the analysis that treats first class as a categorical outcome with one based on Duncan SEI scores and Hourly Wages for first jobs. The Duncan SEI uses the same information as first class; it transforms the detailed occupational information into a unidimensional measure of socio-economic standing. For respondents who made their school-to-work transition during the course of the study (i.e. between 1979 and 1991), we could calculate hourly wage at first job from the data on the annual wage and salary income of the respondent divided by the annual total number of hours worked. This calculation overstates first wages among workers who earned raises during their first year. For respondents who made their school-to-work transition prior to 1979, the NLSY asked the respondents to estimate their wages on their first job; we substitute that subjective estimate for respondents who had already left school permanently before 1979. We transformed wages into 1990 US$ by multiplying the observed wage rate by the ratio of average wages for US workers in 1990 to average wages for US workers in the year in question. The usual practice is to adjust for cost-of-living, but doing so conflates standard of living with an individual's relative placement within the labour queue. Adjusting for relative wages keeps the annual fluctuations in standard of living out of the comparisons.

Current (1990) Work Status was based on 1990 interviews and coded: (1) employed; (2) unemployed (looking for work); (3) not in labour force; and (4) in active armed services. Individuals in the armed service were omitted from all OLS and logistic regressions. They are included in descriptive statistics that are reported by work status.

Independent Variables

Educational Attainment is the key independent variable, of course. It is measured at the time of school-to-work transition and coded to Müller's specifications. In the United States that amounts to:

- 1—left school prior to receiving a high-school diploma;
- 2a—high-school diploma, but no subsequent college degree, and self-reported enrolment in a vocational high-school programme;
- 2b—high-school diploma, no college degree and self-reported enrolment in high-school general curriculum programmes;
- 2c—high-school diploma, no college degree and self-reported enrolment in an academic (college-preparatory) high-school programme;

- 3a—at least one year of college and attained an Associate of Arts degree;
- 3b—at least three years of college and a Bachelor of Arts or higher graduate school degree.

This schema, by concatenating track and niche within the measure itself, affords the opportunity for comparative work among countries with diverse institutional settings and employment climates. Requiring reports of successful attainment of a high-school diploma for educational categories 2a–2c, an Associate of Arts degree for educational category 3a, and a Bachelor of Arts degree for category 3b, provides a strict constraint on entry into the advanced educational categories. Thus students who left school and later by their own initiative obtain a Graduate Equivalent Degree (GED) remain in the 1 category. In much the same way, high-school graduates who attend college but leave with only some type of educational or occupational certificate and not at least an AA remain at the CASMIN educational 2 level.

We supplement the analysis of CASMIN categories with information that sheds light on the special features of the US context. The CASMIN scheme takes for granted that all vocational programmes have substantive content. That is not true in some US high schools, so we differentiate among vocational track high-school graduate categories, making three sub-parts of the original 2a classification. Based on respondents' self-reports of the vocational programme they completed, we distinguish among:

- 2a–bc, high-school diploma, but no subsequent college degree, and self-reported enrolment in business and commercial vocational high-school programme;
- 2a–tt, high-school diploma, but no subsequent college degree, and self-reported enrolment in trade and technical vocational high-school programme;
- 2a–ov, high-school diploma, but no subsequent college degree, and self-reported enrolment in all other vocational high-school programmes.

Stronger effects of high-school curriculum, particularly for male trade and technical track students, occur when one measures high-school curriculum on the basis of coursework (results available upon request of the authors). This study relies on self-reports to remain consistent with the cross-national coding and classification schema used in this project.

Parental education is the higher of the mother or father's educational completed years of schooling. Individuals with at least one parent who had completed at least one year of college are coded 'tertiary level'; individuals with at least one parent who had completed twelfth grade (the normal level of secondary school completion) are coded 'secondary level'; persons with parents who completed less than twelve grades of education are coded 'primary level'. *Father's occupation Duncan SEI Score* is the Duncan SEI score of the reported occupation of the parent when the individual was age 14.

In the US context, *race and ethnicity* contribute independently to variation in school-to-work transitions. To control for these effects we use dummy variables (coded 1) for African-American and Latino respondents with whites as the reference category (other minorities are deleted from the analysis).

We use additional controls for *region, type of place*, and the *local unemployment rate*. These controls are measured at the time of school-to-work transition for all regressions except the regression on current (1990) work status for which we used comparable 1990 data. We identify four regions— north-east, north central, south, and west—and use three dummy variables with north central as the reference category. Type of place is measured with dummy variables (coded 1) for 'not in a Standard Metropolitan Statistical Area (SMSA)', 'SMSA, central city', and 'SMSA, specific place unspecified' with 'SMSA, not central city (that is, suburb)' as the reference category.[4] We define local unemployment rate as a continuous variate by assigning midpoint values to a categorical NLSY variable that identifies six levels of unemployment in three percentage-point increments (unemployment rates of greater than 15 per cent, the highest NLSY value, were coded 16.5). Due to space limitations, coefficients for the added controls of *region, type of place*, and *local unemployment rate* are not shown, but are available upon request.

MODELS AND MODELLING

We begin our analysis with a simple loglinear model for the three-way cross-classification of education by first job by gender. It expresses the association between education and first job as the interaction of a hierarchy effect, an affinity between four-year university education and professional employment, and a separate affinity between vocational and/or two-year post-secondary education and skilled manual and technical employment. The model for expected counts under this simple model is given by the formula:

$$\ln F_{ijk} = \lambda_0 + \lambda_i^E + \lambda_j^C + \lambda_k^S + \lambda_{ik}^{ES} + \lambda_{jk}^{CS} + \lambda_h^{Hier} + \lambda_p^{HiEd\,Prof} + \lambda_v^{VocSkil} \qquad (1)$$

where the λ-terms are normalized in a convenient way to allow for maximum likelihood estimation, and the covariates (*Hier, HiEdProf*, and *VocSkil*) are defined in the first panel of Table 15.1.

This simple explanatory model does not fit the data adequately, so we follow our Israeli colleagues and employ their preferred model (Table 15.1). The Israeli model (IS) has an embedded three-way interaction among all three factors in the model, that is, by specifying separate design matrices for men and women, the IS model is not nested under the model of no three-way interaction. After viewing the results of fitting the Israeli model to the American data, we modify the model to produce two variants that fit the three-way association acceptably well (Table 15.1).

After modelling the gross association (net of gender), we add several key independent variables and specify a multinomial logistic regression model of the effects of education on occupational outcomes net of the other independent variables. The general form of the multinomial logistic regression model is given by the formula:

$$y_{jt} = \beta_{j0} + \sum_{i=1}^{5} \beta_{ji} Ed_{it} + \sum_{p=6}^{P} \beta_{jp} Z_{pt} \qquad (2)$$

for class contrast j ($j = 1,..., 4$), person t ($t = 1,..., N$), and independent variables (including dummy variables and interaction terms) p ($p = 1,..., P$). We use Class VIIab as the reference category, so the four contrasts are (I–II vs. VIIab), (IIIab vs. VIIab), (IVabc vs. VIIab), and (V–VI vs. VIIab).

After completing our analysis of occupational placement, we turn to four other indicators of the school-to-work transition as dependent variables. The first two indicators are features of the first job. We use the same independent variables as in the occupational placement regressions to explore the determinants of, first, the socio-economic status of the first job and, second, the hourly wages earned in the first year of working. These two aspects of the first job capture the key socio-economic dimension of employment. They miss the class-of-worker distinction (that is, self-employed persons are not treated separately) and the blue-collar/white-collar distinction. The analyses of SEI and wages at first job will be misleading to the extent to which the 'non-vertical' aspects of career beginnings are crucial for social stratification (Hout and Hauser 1992; Erikson and Goldthorpe 1992). We use ordinary least squares (OLS) regression for these analyses.

The final dependent variable is employment status: employment, unemployment and non-employment. The contrasts are 'unemployed vs. employed' and 'not in the labour force vs. employed'. For this analysis we use multinomial logistic regression to estimate the effects of school-to-work contingencies and other factors on unemployment and non-employment early in the career. To do so we use employment status in the most recent period for which we have data.

TABLE 15.1. *Design matrices for topological models of the association between education and first occupation*

Covariates model
Hier + HiEdProf + VocSkil

Hier

	I-II	III	IV	V-VI	VII
1	0	1	1	1	2
2a	0	1	1	1	0
2b	0	1	1	1	0
2c	0	1	1	1	0
3a	0	1	1	1	0
3b	2	1	1	1	0

HiEdProf

	I-II	III	IV	V-VI	VII
1	0	0	0	0	0
2a	0	0	0	0	0
2b	0	0	0	0	0
2c	0	0	0	0	0
3a	0	0	0	0	0
3b	1	0	0	0	0

VocSkil

	I-II	III	IV	V-VI	VII
1	0	0	0	0	0
2a	0	0	0	0	0
2b	0	1	1	2	0
2c	0	0	0	0	0
3a	0	3	3	4	0
3b	0	0	0	0	0

Israeli preferred model (Is)

Men

	I-II	III	IV	V-VI	VII
1	1	1	1	1	4
2a	1	1	1	2	3
2b	1	1	1	1	2
2c	3	2	1	1	2
3a	4	3	1	4	1
3b	5	3	1	1	1

Women

	I-II	III	IV	V-VI	VII
1	1	1	1	1	4
2a	1	1	1	2	3
2b	1	1	1	1	2
2c	3	2	1	1	2
3a	5	3	1	2	1
3b	5	3	1	2	1

Adaptations of Is (AH1 and AH2)

AH1

	I-II	III	IV	V-VI	VII
1	1	1	1	1	4
2a	1	1	1	2	3
2b	1	1	1	1	2
2c	3	2	1	1	2
3a	5	3	1	4	1
3b	6	3	1	1	1

AH2

	I-II	III	IV	V-VI	VII
1	1	1	1	1	4
2a	1	1	1	2	3
2b	1	1	1	1	2
2c	3	2	1	1	2
3a	5	3	1	1	1
3b	6	3	1	1	1

FINDINGS

Descriptive Results

Men's and women's educational experiences differ slightly but significantly (as seen in Table 15.2). While men dropped out of high school before obtaining a diploma more often than women (21 per cent compared to 18 per cent), women attained junior college Associate of Arts degrees without continuing on to successfully gain more advanced post-secondary degrees (7 per cent compared to 5 per cent for men). Among high-school graduates with a vocational background, specialities are sex-typed; men enrolled in trade and technical programmes (7 per cent), while women enrolled in business and commercial programmes (7 per cent).

Despite their high levels of education, men and women in this cohort started out with humble occupations. More than half of the men started their work lives in blue-collar occupations (41 per cent in Classes VIIab and 19 per cent Classes V–VI); the women started out in clerical and sales positions (51 per cent in Classes IIIab). Very few of these young people had the resources to set themselves up in business; witness the negligible self-employment rate. Women hold a slight edge in professional and managerial occupations (22 per cent for women, 19 per cent for men in Classes I–II).

Race and ethnicity play a part in educational and early occupational success (Figure 15.1.a). Over 30 per cent of high-school drop-outs are either African-American or Latino (32 per cent for men, 33 per cent for women, compared to their overall representation in the sample of 19 per cent of men and 20 per cent of women). Interestingly, African-Americans are less prevalent among both the male and female vocational track high-school graduates (category 2a). African-American and Hispanic men are more likely to end up in educational category 2c (high-school graduates from academic college preparatory tracks who have not gone on to attain further post-secondary school degrees) than either white men or female non-whites. While female non-whites are equitably represented in the junior college 3a category, they are significantly under-represented in the four-year college degree 3b category (Hauser 1993). Non-white men are disproportionately absent from both post-secondary educational categories; they make up only 10 per cent of 3a graduates and only 8 per cent of 3b graduates (Hauser 1993).

While the expansion of American higher education has spurred a significant amount of educational 'structural mobility' (Hout 1996), parental education remains a prime contingency in a young person's own educational attainment. We will see the evidence for this below in the multivariate analyses, but it is also evident in the social composition of the six CASMIN educational categories (Figure 15.1.b). For persons who failed to attain a

TABLE 15.2. *Descriptive statistics by gender of those aged 26–34, 1990*

Continuous variables	Males			Females		
	Means	SD	N	Means	SD	N
Father's occupational Duncan SEI score	40.499	13.997	2,733	39.845	13.592	2,760
Unemployment rate at transition	7.921	3.331	2,728	7.879	3.340	2,973
Unemployment rate (1990)	5.599	1.938	2,541	5.578	1.935	2,771
First occupation hourly wages (adj.)	6.725	6.419	2,376	5.711	5.162	2,382
First occupation Duncan SEI score	33.158	14.137	2,878	36.046	13.663	2,993

Categorical variables	Males		Females	
	%	N	%	N
Parents education:		2,917		3,032
Primary level	22.6%		24.9%	
Secondary level	43.1%		43.0%	
Tertiary level	34.3%		32.1%	
Race:		3,003		3,108
African–American	11.5%		13.0%	
Hispanic	7.3%		7.3%	
White	81.2%		79.7%	
Region (at transition):		2,923		3,040
South	32.3%		34.3%	
West	17.8%		17.0%	
North-east	19.7%		19.0%	
North Central	30.1%		29.7%	

TABLE 15.2. *cont.*

Categorical variables	Males			Females		
	Means	SD	N	Means	SD	N
Region (1990):						
South		29.8%	2,629		36.6%	2,807
West		18.1%			17.3%	
North-east		18.6%			17.3%	
North Central		31.4%			28.3%	
SMSA (at transition):						
Not in SMSA		26.7%	2,717		25.3%	2,956
SMSA not in Central City		31.4%			32.1%	
SMSA Central City DK		25.2%			26.5%	
SMSA Central City		16.7%			16.0%	
SMSA (1990):						
Not in SMSA		23.6%	2,449		22.4%	2,666
SMSA not in Central City		33.0%			33.6%	
SMSA Central City DK		29.8%			31.9%	
SMSA Central City		13.6%			12.0%	
Educational attainment:						
1 (less than HS grad)		21.3%	2,950		17.8%	3,057
2a (HS grad - vocational)		11.1%			11.9%	
2a-i (business/commercial)		(0.7%)			(6.9%)	
2a-ii (trade/technical)		(7.0%)			(0.8%)	
2a-iii (other voc. programs)		(3.5%)			(4.3%)	
2b HS grad - general		29.9%			31.1%	
2c H.S. grad - academic		12.8%			12.7%	
3a two year college degree		4.8%			7.3%	
3b four year college degree		20.0%			19.3%	

First occupation:	2,881	2,977
Classes I–II	19.0%	22.1%
Classes IIIab	17.6%	51.5%
Classes IVabc	3.9%	1.9%
Classes V–VI	18.7%	3.9%
Classes VIIab	40.7%	20.6%
Current (1990) work status:	2,664	2,834
Employed	87.3%	71.6%
Unemployed	3.4%	4.6%
Not in labor force	6.4%	23.4%
Armed forces	2.9%	0.4%
Self-reports of reasons for school–work transition	2,370	2,502
Received degree	60.8%	61.5%
Chose to work	7.2%	4.5%
All other reasons	32.0%	34.1%
School-to-work transition prior to 1980	3,003	3,108
Yes	43.0%	47.8%
No	57.0%	52.2%
School enrolment 1990–1991:	2,759	2,908
Yes	8.5%	10.6%
No	91.5%	89.4%
Number of school-to-work transitions 1979–1991	3,003	3,108
0	1.5%	1.2%
1	80.1%	77.4%
2	16.5%	19.1%
3	2.2%	1.9%
4	0.1%	0.1%

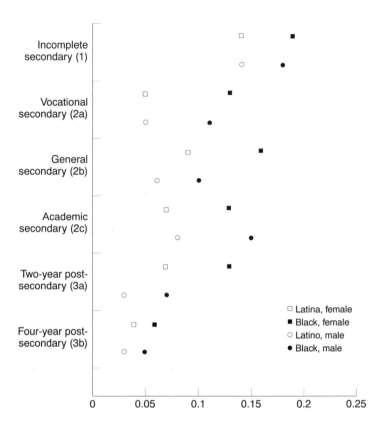

F<small>IG</small>. 15.1.a. *Educational attainment of individuals by racial and ethnic composition*

high-school diploma (1), one-half have parents with similarly low education backgrounds (compared to one-fourth of the sample as a whole). For men and women who attained a four-year college degree two-thirds are from similar backgrounds (compared to one-third in the sample as a whole).

Men and women earn higher wages at higher levels of education, as expected. Men earn about 50 cents more than women with the same level of education.[5] This gender gap of 50 cents is less than the widely cited 'sixty-nine cents on the dollar' women's wage, which would imply $3.45 per hour if men earned $5 per hour. However, recent data show that the gender gap iu uluuing in the wuikforcc as a whole, especially among younger cohorts (Spain and Bianchi 1996), so these data are not out of line with other recent statistics. The median hourly wage of women with incomplete secondary

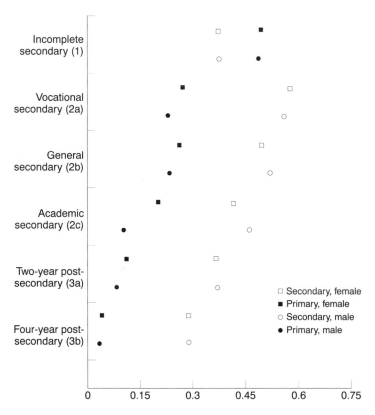

Fig. 15.1.b. *Educational attainment by parental education*

education is slightly less than $4; for men it is $4.50. College graduates earn $2 more per hour (on average) than high-school drop-outs of the same sex. Wages vary more within levels of education than between them, however, indicating a high degree of uncertainty in the early returns to education. The interquartile range of wages within each level of education exceeds $2 and the range from the 10th to the 90th percentile spans $7 at the lowest level of education and $12 among college graduates. The lower tails of the college-educated categories' (3a and 3b) distributions are not much higher than those of the high-school educational categories (particularly for men). These long tails indicate low initial monetary pay-offs for a small subset of the highly educated.

Women's first jobs have slightly higher status than the men's jobs, despite women's lower wages. The interquartile half of women (indicated by the boxes) have higher Duncan SEI scores than do men for all educational

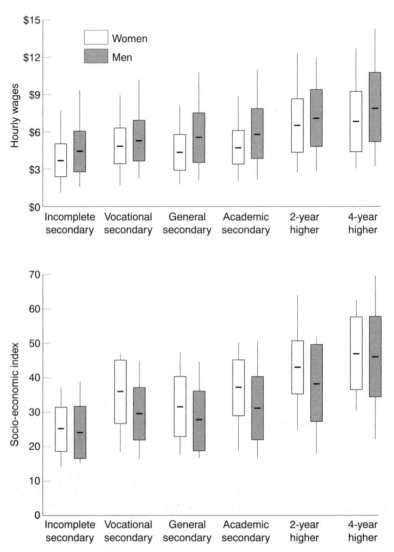

NOTE: Hourly wages are calculated in 1991 US$ (adjusted for change in annual average rate of pay); socioeconomic status is measured on the Duncan scale.

FIG. 15.2. *Distribution of wages and socio-economic status by gender, for those aged 26–34, 1991*

categories. Among secondary school graduates, the prevailing occupations for women are in the routine non-manual class (III) which has always traded off clean working conditions and the freedom from shift work for lower wages. The blue-collar jobs that male high school-graduates take pay more but offer less prestige and more varied schedules. Among college graduates, men and women are matched at the 75th percentile; the difference comes in the long lower tails to the men's distributions (and long upper tail for men with four or more years of college and a degree). Women have more discretion over whether or not to participate in the labour force. They can use that freedom of choice to hold out for an 'appropriate' job longer than their male counterparts. College-educated men accept first occupations with Duncan SEI scores that are lower than the jobs taken by half of the high-school educated men, as is shown in the lower edge of the college men's boxes and the long whiskers that show how the 10th–25th percentiles of college-educated men reach below the median status of high-school graduates' first jobs. For those men who attain a four-year college degree, the long upper whisker (spanning from the 75th to the 90th percentile), highlights that the relatively rare first jobs with the highest status (over 60 on the Duncan scale) go to men.

The fluid boundaries of the US educational system allow individuals to move easily in and out of school throughout at least their first decade of labour-market experience. One young person in five takes advantage of this institutional laxity: 19 per cent of the men and 21 per cent of the women had more than one school-to-work transition before age 26, that is, approximately one-fifth of the respondents moved from school into the labour force, back into school and back into the labour force between 1979 and 1991. Another 8 per cent of the men and 11 per cent of the women reported being enrolled in school in either 1990 or 1991, when they were between 25 and 33 years old. Of the people in school in 1990–1991, 27 per cent of the men and 38 per cent of the women had already made a school-to-work transition a decade earlier. The 11-point gender gap suggests that child-rearing responsibilities add special contingencies to women's school-to-work transitions.

The low-cost junior and community colleges promote fluidity: 44 per cent of women and 45 per cent of the men with a two-year college experience as their highest level of achievement have made more than one school-to-work transition. This finding suggests that the 'cooling out' function attributed to two-year colleges (Karabel 1972) is not the product of a progressing, creeping educational chill, but rather often involves a period of students testing the waters both in the labour market and in post-secondary institutions. Many young people who left high school for work came back: 24 per cent of women and 23 per cent of men with academic secondary education made two or three school-to-work transitions and 18 per cent and 19 per cent of women and men with complete vocational education did so (Figure 15.3). Relatively few of the people who go back to school fail to complete their high-school education; 86 per cent of men and 91 per cent of women with incomplete secondary education have not been back to school (that is, have made just one school-to-work transition).[6]

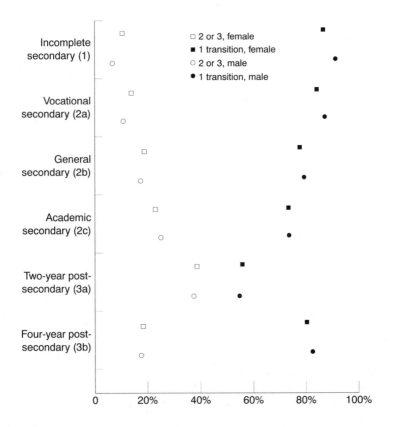

FIG. 15.3. *Number of school-to-work transitions before age 26 by gender*

Determinants of the Class of First Job

Class of First Job and Education by Gender: Bivariate Results

We begin our analysis by modelling the association between class of first job and education using the model in equation (1) and three topological models. The design matrices for the topological models are in Table 15.1 above. We conduct the analysis on two 6 × 5 tables (one for men and one for women). The results of the search for an acceptable model are summarized in Table 15.3.

The association between education and first job is substantial, as revealed by the large residual deviance from the null model (model 0 in Table 15.3): roughly 2,000 on a sample of 5,836 cases. Model 1, the CASMIN-like model (Erikson and Goldthorpe 1992) that includes the covariates Hier, HiEdProf, and VocSkil, captures three-fourths of the gross association but still leaves a significant residual deviance. The results from the other models confirm that the problem with this model is analogous to the problem with the original CASMIN model; the Hier term misspecifies the functional form of the relationship between high educational credentials and high status occupations (see Hout and Hauser 1992). We return to this point in the discussion below.

The succession of topological models begins where the Israeli analysis leaves off (Krause et al. this volume). The IS model, when fit to the US data, improves substantially over Model 1, but still does not attain an adequate fit. We made scatter-plots of observed and expected logits by educational attainment and examined the residuals. These plots indicated that the gender interaction implicit in the IS model was not appropriate for the American data, that the specification of level 4 need not include the combination of skilled blue-collar work and two-year college, and that the professional and managerial occupations got a substantial boost from four-year education (necessitating the creation of a new higher level—6). These improvements result in models AH1 and AH2. The AH2 variant with gender interaction is preferred under *Bic* and accounts for 92 per cent of the association between education and class of first occupation.

The parameter values for the IS, AH1, and AH2 topological models (with gender interactions) are shown in Table 15.4. They indicate a high degree of differentiation among the levels. To more readily see the substantive implications of these results, we present the logits for each of four independent contrasts between the higher classes and Class VIIab (see Figure 15.4). The expected logits for professional and managerial employment (relative to unskilled manual employment) curve sharply upward for both men and women. The academic secondary graduates are markedly above the other secondary graduates, the two-year college graduates are markedly above the academic secondary graduates, and the four-year university graduates are substantially above all others in the odds on professional or managerial employment. There is also a significant, appreciable slope to the curve relating education to routine white-collar employment, especially among men. Again, it is the academic outcomes that have the largest pay-offs, especially for men. The other two slopes are much shallower. The only significant

Richard Arum and Mike Hout

TABLE 15.3. *Goodness-of-fit statistics for three-way association among gender, education, and first occupations for those aged 26–34, 1990*

Model	L^2	X^2	df	Bic	% of baseline explained
0. Edu*Gender + Job*Gender	1,998.12	2,073.75	40	1,651	0%
1. Model 0 + Hier + HiEdProf + VocSkil	512.96	541.95	36	201	74%
2. Model 0 + IS.Linear	492.04	492.69	39	154	75%
3. Model 0 + IS	251.85	258.12	36	−60	87%
4. Model 0 + IS + IS.Gender	222.57	227.24	32	−55	89%
5. Model 0 + AH1	213.30	217.27	35	−90	89%
6. Model 0 + AH1 + AH1.Gender	180.57	184.35	31	−88	91%
7. Model 0 + AH2 + AH2.Gender	166.97	166.84	31	−102	92%
8. Model 0 + AH2	193.51	196.31	35	−110	90%

Note: All residual Chi² values (L^2 and X^2) are significant at the .05 level; furthermore, all differences among nested models are significant at the .05 level (using an L^2 or X^2 difference test).

...timates of the parameter of the Israeli preferred model and two American variations (AH1 and AH2) for persons aged 26–34, 1990

Education (CASMIN category)	Class of first job: men					Class of first job: women				
	I–II	IIIab	IVabc	V–VI	VIIab	I–II	IIIab	IVab	V–VI	VIIab
Israeli preferred model (IS):										
1 (less than HS grad)	0.	0.	0.	0.	1.291	0.	0.	0.	0.	1.344
2a (HS grad – vocational)	0.	0.	0.	.636	1.012	0.	0.	0.	.376	.468
2b (HS grad – general)	0.	0.	0.	0.	.636	0.	0.	0.	0.	.376
2c (HS grad – academic)	1.012	.636	0.	0.	.636	.468	.376	0.	0.	.376
3a (two-year college degree)	1.291	1.012	0.	1.291	0.	2.836	.468	0.	.376	0.
3b (four-year college degree)	2.748	1.012	0.	0.	0.	2.836	.468	0.	.376	0.
American variant 1 (AH1)										
1 (less than HS grad)	0.	0.	0.	0.	1.165	0.	0.	0.	0.	1.344
2a (HS grad – vocational)	0.	0.	0.	.596	1.082	0.	0.	0.	.376	.468
2b (HS grad – general)	0.	0.	0.	0.	.596	0.	0.	0.	0.	.376
2c (HS grad – academic)	1.082	.596	0.	0.	.596	.468	.376	0.	0.	.376
3a (two-year college degree)	2.563	1.082	0.	1.165	0.	2.563	.468	0.	1.344	0.
3b (four-year college degree)	3.086	1.082	0.	0.	0.	2.836	.468	0.	0.	0.
American variant 2 (AH2)										
1 (less than HS grad)	0.	0.	0.	0.	1.346	0.	0.	0.	0.	1.344
2a (HS grad – vocational)	0.	0.	0.	.633	1.056	0.	0.	0.	.376	.468
2b (HS grad – general)	0.	0.	0.	0.	.633	0.	0.	0.	0.	.376
2c (HS grad – academic)	1.056	.633	0.	0.	.633	1.344	.376	0.	0.	.376
3a (two-year college degree)	2.127	1.056	0.	0.	0.	2.127	.468	0.	0.	0.
3b (four-year college degree)	3.034	1.056	0.	0.	0.	2.836	.468	0.	0.	0.

Note: The standard errors for the four main levels effects in the IS model are: .088, .090, .117, and .180. The standard errors for the five main levels effects in the AH1 model are: .088, .090, .117, .205, and .132; for the gender interaction terms the four standard errors are: .112, .122, .147, and .180. The standard errors for the five main levels effects in the AH1 model are: .088, .090, .117, .205, and .132; for the gender interaction terms the five standard errors are: .113, .123, .149, aliased, and .187. The standard errors for the five main levels effects in the AH2 model are: .088, .090, .117, .202, and .132; for the gender interaction terms the standard errors are: .112, .122, .156, aliased, and .187.

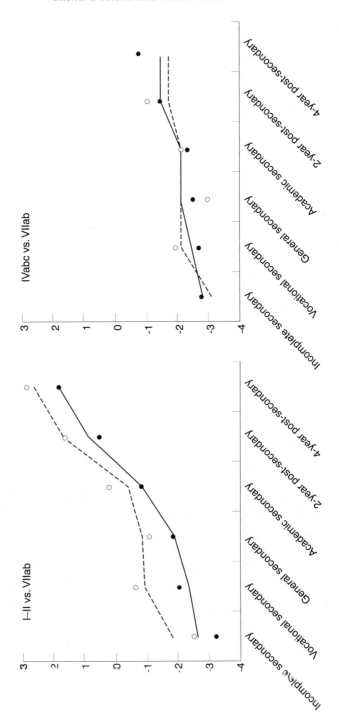

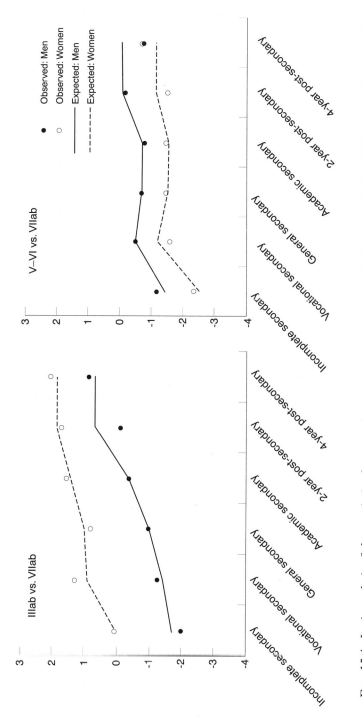

Fig. 15.4. *Logit analysis of the association between education and first occupation for those aged 26–34, 1990 (expected under AH2)*

contrast in the skilled vs. unskilled regression is between high-school drop-outs and all others.

These results fail to find much reward to non-academic education—except for women pursuing vocational secondary education as a path to clerical employment. We do find significant reward for non-traditional academic education in the form of two-year post-secondary degrees. Of course not all those who take a two-year post-secondary education opt for academic courses. Many of these programmes have a vocational emphasis. Nonetheless, they reward their graduates with chances of white-collar employment that are higher than those whose highest credential is an academic secondary diploma.

The next step in modelling could well be to explore Goodman's (1979, 1984, 1991) 'RC' model, as Hout and Hauser (1992) recommend for the CASMIN data itself. We do not, because in this analysis the five categories of first job capture relatively little of the variance in occupational status of first jobs. One alternative would be to expand the classification to more categories. Instead, we drop the categorical approach and use the detailed SEI scores and wages as our indicators of 'vertical' stratification. Before doing so, however, we explore the extent to which the gross education effects we have estimated here are either indirect or spurious due to the influence of other factors.

Class of First Job and Education: Multivariate Results

Having explored the bivariate relationship between schooling and employment closely, we turn to the effect of education net of other significant factors. Results of the multinomial logistic regression predicting class of first occupation are presented in Table 15.5 for the overall CASMIN educational categories and for the classification scheme that differentiates more fully for vocational programmes. A young man's odds of having a professional or managerial first job (Class I or II, relative to Classes VIIab) increase with each advance in education. Vocational education has virtually no professional pay-off; the vocational and general track high-school graduates have essentially the same odds on high status outcomes. Education affects the odds of routine non-manual (Class IIIab) employment also, although the gaps between general and vocational education (2a–2b) and between academic secondary and two-year post-secondary education (2c–3a) are not significant for men. Two- and four-year college degrees increase the likelihood of self-employment (Classes IVabc) for men, relative to all other educational categories with similarly low odds of self-employment. Finally, skilled manual occupations (Classes V–VI) are more likely than unskilled ones only for male high-school graduates or those with two-year college degrees relative to high-school drop-outs; no other comparison (when we use the cross-nationally comparable, but undifferentiated educational classification) is statistically significant.

For women, the pattern of effects of education on the likelihood of obtaining a first occupation in Classes I–II is similar to that of men: the odds increase at each subsequent educational level, with the exception of 2a and 2b which have similar odds. In distinction from four-year college graduates, vocational or academic high-school graduates and those with two-year college degrees, have similar chances of being in routine non-manual occupations (IIIab). Both general track high-school graduates and high-school drop-outs are less likely to have this rather typical occupational outcome than women with more or more-focused education. Furthermore, high-school drop-outs have statistically lower odds of attaining an occupation in Class III (relative to Class VII) than any other educational category. The pattern of educational differences in self-employment are exactly the same as the pattern with respect to routine white-collar work, even though self-employment is extremely rare and routine white-collar work the first occupation of a majority of these women. Finally, a woman's odds of being in a skilled manual occupation are significantly lower for a high-school drop-out than for a four-year college graduate; there are no statistically significant differences among the four intermediate educational categories on this destination.

When we elaborate the educational categories to include more detail about the vocational programmes we see that women with business and commercial high-school backgrounds have significantly higher odds of obtaining a first job in Classes I–II and in Class III occupations than do ordinary high-school graduates. Men in vocational programmes improve their odds of attaining a first job in Classes V–VI only in trade and technical programmes. Other vocational programmes do not improve their odds relative to other high-school graduates.[7]

Determinants of Occupational Status and Wages

Table 15.6 provides a similar set of regressions with Duncan SEI of first job as the dependent variable. The OLS estimates show clearly that the variables measuring educational attainment strongly affect first-job outcomes (on the socio-economic status dimension). Model (1) includes only variables measuring personal background of the individual (parent's educational level, race, and the Duncan SEI score of father's occupation). Model (2) adds the CASMIN educational categories (with Ed3b omitted). Model (3) adds social context measures of region, residence, and local unemployment rate. Model (4) contains the same variables as the previous model, but differentiates among vocational programmes. Models (3) and (4), in particular, indicate

TABLE 15.5. ML estimates of the effects of determinants of the class of first job relative to Class VIIab for those aged 26-34, 1990

	Males (N = 2,364)				Females (N = 2,482)			
	I–II	IIIab	IVabc	V+VI	I–II	IIIab	IVabc	V+VI
Intercept	1.080* (0.420)	0.122 (0.397)	-1.269 (0.680)	-0.676 (0.422)	2.680* (0.492)	1.752* (0.419)	-2.603* (1.078)	-0.855 (0.794)
Parent education:								
Primary level	-0.070 (0.256)	-0.614* (0.222)	-0.209 (0.393)	0.193 (0.196)	-0.542* (0.251)	-0.607* (0.182)	-0.888 (0.613)	0.211 (0.357)
Secondary level	-0.233 (0.171)	-0.246 (0.156)	0.109 (0.280)	0.045 (0.158)	-0.187 (0.192)	-0.252 (0.157)	0.032 (0.413)	-0.040 (0.314)
African-American	-0.655* (0.275)	-0.021 (0.204)	-0.492 (0.460)	-1.312* (0.267)	-0.479 (0.269)	-0.178 (0.184)	-1.011 (0.779)	0.234 (0.343)
Hispanic	-0.083 (0.315)	0.084 (0.267)	0.567 (0.453)	-0.211 (0.255)	0.120 (0.316)	0.222 (0.229)	-0.953 (1.053)	-0.744 (0.565)
Father's occupation Duncan SEI score	0.011 (0.006)	0.001 (0.005)	0.027* (0.009)	0.007 (0.005)	0.009 (0.006)	0.010 (0.005)	0.022 (0.014)	0.014 (0.010)
1 (less than HS graduate)	-4.497* (0.331)	-2.585* (0.260)	-1.522* (0.395)	-0.506 (0.293)	-4.743* (0.375)	-1.633* (0.295)	-1.543* (0.605)	-1.318* (0.528)
2a (HS grad. vocational track)	-3.674* (0.324)	-1.874* (0.264)	-1.666* (0.450)	0.208 (0.294)	-3.176* (0.349)	-0.573 (0.309)	-0.763 (0.616)	-0.824 (0.573)
2b (HS grad. general track)	-3.413* (0.226)	-1.687* (0.213)	-1.426* (0.343)	0.009 (0.272)	-3.621* (0.296)	-0.973* (0.280)	-1.793* (0.563)	-0.531 (0.480)

2c (HS grad. academic track)	-2.429* (0.236)	-1.115* (0.232)	-1.407* (0.427)	0.081 (0.300)	-2.380* (0.330)	-0.353 (0.314)	-1.489* (0.750)	-0.389 (0.551)
3a (two-year college degree)	-1.141* (0.305)	-0.834* (0.343)	-0.269 (0.509)	0.602 (0.388)	-1.312* (0.377)	-0.368 (0.377)	-0.472 (0.718)	-0.861 (0.767)
Comparisons with differentiated vocational category:								
1 (less than HS graduate)	-4.487** (0.331)	-2.572** (0.260)	-1.515** (0.395)	-0.502 (0.293)	-4.735** (0.375)	-1.622** (0.295)	-1.535* (0.605)	-1.294* (0.528)
2a-i (business and commercial)	-a-	-1.054 (0.621)	-a-	0.119 (0.684)	-2.884** (0.402)	-0.301 (0.347)	-0.681 (0.729)	-0.988 (0.708)
2a-ii (trade and technical)	-3.363** (0.357)	-2.100** (0.328)	-1.422** (0.490)	0.330 (0.312)	-4.024** (0.841)	-1.999** (0.591)	-1.234 (1.188)	-1.309 (1.168)
2a-iii (other vocational programmes)	-4.241** (0.625)	-1.772** (0.358)	-2.055** (0.782)	-0.041 (0.373)	-3.408** (0.478)	-0.656 (0.366)	-0.753 (0.787)	-0.511 (0.677)
2b (HS grad. general track)	-3.408** (0.226)	-1.688** (0.213)	-1.421** (0.343)	0.012 (0.272)	-3.624** (0.296)	-0.977** (0.280)	-1.798** (0.563)	-0.547 (0.480)
2c (HS grad. academic track)	-2.427** (0.236)	-1.110** (0.232)	-1.407** (0.427)	0.081 (0.300)	-2.381** (0.330)	-0.350 (0.314)	-1.489* (0.750)	-0.380 (0.551)
3a (two-year college degree)	-1.139** (0.305)	-0.828* (0.343)	-0.268 (0.508)	0.603 (0.388)	-1.316** (0.377)	-0.381 (0.377)	-0.477 (0.718)	-0.861 (0.767)

$*p < .05$ $**p < .01.$

-a- insufficient cases to estimate

that young people attain first jobs with higher Duncan SEI scores when they have obtained a four-year college degree than when they have earned only a two-year college degree. Similarly, high-school graduates obtain more desirable first jobs than high-school drop-outs, and first jobs that are significantly less desirable than those of persons who enter the job market with two-year college degrees. Among high-school graduates, the graduates of the general curriculum track do not do as well as male vocational trade and technical graduates and female business track students. While graduates of the college preparatory high-school track do better than general track students (reaping the expected positive return to their academic education even if they do not earn a junior college or higher degree), differentiating types of vocational programmes demonstrates that there are no significant differences in effects between academic curriculum and either male trade and technical programmes or female business and commercial ones.

The inter-generational transmission of advantage and disadvantage appears here in the positive effect of father's occupational status on the Duncan SEI score of the young man's first job. The total effect of father's SEI is .195 for men and .135 for women. These coefficients imply that two men with origins separated by 50 points can expect to have first jobs 9.75 points apart; their sisters can expect their first jobs to differ by 6.75 points. Considering that 21 SEI points separate professionals (SEI = 75) and managers (SEI = 54) in Class I, clerical workers in Class IIIa rank another 22 points down the scale (SEI = 33), and unskilled workers in Class VIIa are the lowest (SEI = 21), the coefficients reflect a modest level of stratification. By comparison, the coefficient in Blau and Duncan's (1967) classic study of men aged 25 to 64 years old in 1962 yielded an estimate more than twice as large (.42) for the same total effect. Most of the effect of father's SEI is mediated by education; 55 per cent of the total effect on men is indirect via education and 65 per cent of the total effect on women is indirect.

Young men who are African-American, in rural or non-Southern locations, and in areas of high unemployment are further disadvantaged. Young women in these categories do not obtain first jobs that are significantly worse than those of other women with the same social origins and education.

Table 15.7 presents OLS estimates of the determinants of hourly wages of first job (calculated in 1990 US$ and adjusted for changes in the annual average rate of pay). Examining the R^2 for the three models shows that adding educational attainment to the model has a greater impact on regressions run for women than it does for men; adding social context, however, has a greater impact on regressions run on men.

Obtaining a university degree pays off (Model 1). Persons who attained a two-year or four-year college degree earn higher wages than high-school graduates who in turn earn higher wages than high-school drop-outs. For men, surprisingly, little else matters; there are no statistically significant differences among high-school graduates from different curricular tracks nor between young men with two- or four-year college degrees. Women who attended a general curriculum track in high school, however, receive significantly lower wages than those who had attended business and commercial vocational programmes. In fact, they do no better than women who dropped out of high school. More surprisingly, women enrolled in business and commercial programmes also earn significantly higher wages than young women who completed their education in an academically oriented secondary programme (but did not go on to college). Thus the differentiation in the American educational system gives an unexpected boost to the initial wages of those educated in the non-traditional tracks. The supposed monetary advantages of academic education are not realized in the initial phase of labour-market activity unless it is followed by further education.

Neither parental education nor father's occupational status affect the initial wages of women and men from this cohort that left school in the 1980s. That does not mean that origins, more broadly conceived are unimportant. Parental income has strong indirect and direct effects on young people's experience with being in poverty (C. Fischer et al. 1996). By extension it presumably also affects their initial wages.[8]

Racial differences in earnings, thought to be declining, continue to contribute to stratification in the United States. African-American men received 15 cents less per hour than white men; the racial difference is smaller for women (a race–gender interaction that holds throughout the career, e.g. Farley and Allen 1987). This level of racial difference confirms both the persistence of race and its diminished quantitative importance, as the 15-cent difference is less than its magnitude in previous cohorts (J. Smith and Welch 1986).

Men living outside metropolitan labour markets received 11 cents less per hour than young men who made the school-to-work transition while living in a suburban location (that is, in an SMSA, but not in a central city). Other geographical contrasts are not significant. A high unemployment rate in the local economy also depresses wage rates of first jobs slightly (more for men than for women). The range from the tightest to the most depressed labour markets in the United States in 1990 was about 6 percentage points; the expected difference in wages between those two places then would be about 15 cents per hour for men (about $312 in a year of working 40 hours per week) and half that much for women.

TABLE 15.6. *OLS estimates of the determinants of the Duncan SEI score of first job by gender for those aged 26–34, 1990*

	Males (N = 2,360)				Females (N = 2,493)			
	(1)	(2)	(3)	(4)	(1)	(2)	(3)	(4)
Intercept	28.944*	43.223**	46.010**	46.009**	34.161**	45.468**	46.473**	46.406**
	(1.260)	(1.275)	(1.514)	(1.514)	(1.192)	(1.213)	(1.466)	(1.465)
Parent education								
Primary level	−5.912**	−0.472	−0.323	−0.434	−7.710**	−2.037*	−1.814*	−1.853*
	(0.887)	(0.834)	(0.843)	(0.845)	(0.819)	(0.776)	(0.780)	(0.780)
Secondary level	−4.645**	−1.177	−0.957	−0.973	−3.782**	−0.261	−0.172	−0.207
	(0.687)	(0.631)	(0.634)	(0.634)	(0.644)	(0.603)	(0.602)	(0.602)
African-American	−3.546**	−3.057**	−3.560**	−3.526**	−0.991	−0.870	−1.481	−1.444
	(0.942)	(0.844)	(0.878)	(0.879)	(0.872)	(0.785)	(0.826)	(0.826)
Hispanic	1.338	1.657	1.300	1.193	2.600*	2.413*	1.860	1.811
	(1.169)	(1.046)	(1.073)	(1.079)	(1.093)	(0.985)	(0.999)	(1.009)
Father's occupation Duncan SEI score	0.195*	0.084**	0.075**	0.074**	0.135*	0.047*	0.041*	0.041*
	(0.023)	(0.021)	(0.021)	(0.021)	(0.022)	(0.021)	(0.021)	(0.021)
1 (less than HS graduate)		−18.854**	−18.917**	−18.901**		−19.308**	−19.248**	−19.219**
		(0.882)	(0.885)	(0.885)		(0.877)	(0.887)	(0.886)

	(1)	(2)	(3)	(4)	(5)	(6)	(7)	(8)
2a (HS grad. vocational track)		−15.235** (0.955)	−15.006** (0.954)			−11.412** (0.907)	−11.254** (0.907)	
2a-i (business and commercial)				−18.413** (3.032)				−9.228** (1.068)
2a-ii (trade and technical)				−13.418** (1.108)				−18.450** (2.737)
2a-iii (other vocational programmes)				−17.473** (1.440)				−13.311** (1.282)
2b (HS grad. general track)		−16.323** (0.749)	−16.092** (0.756)	−16.088** (0.756)		−14.196** (0.717)	−13.964** (0.722)	−13.964** (0.720)
2c (HS grad. academic track)		−13.638** (0.887)	−13.528** (0.883)	−13.524** (0.882)		−10.661** (0.859)	−10.463** (0.859)	−10.464** (0.857)
3a (two-year college degree)		−7.565** (1.236)	−7.515** (1.231)	−7.507** (1.231)		−4.327** (1.014)	−4.259** (1.013)	−4.285** (1.013)
R^2	0.114	0.297	0.309	0.311	0.089	0.266	0.273	0.277

$* p < .05$ $** p < .01$

TABLE 15.7. OLS estimates of the determinants of hourly wages of first job (1990 US$ adjusted for change in annual gender-specific average rate of pay) for those aged 26–34, 1990

	Males (N = 1,995)				Females (N = 2,020)			
	(1)	(2)	(3)	(4)	(1)	(2)	(3)	(4)
Intercept	1.647**	1.908**	2.133**	2.133**	1.448**	1.770**	1.821**	1.812**
	(0.073)	(0.080)	(0.095)	(0.095)	(0.074)	(0.081)	(0.098)	(0.097)
Parent education								
Primary level	−0.250**	−0.129*	−0.094	−0.095	−0.258*	−0.097	−0.088	−0.087
	(0.053)	(0.055)	(0.055)	(0.055)	(0.052)	(0.053)	(0.054)	(0.053)
	−0.063	0.005	0.030	0.030	−0.098*	0.006	0.012	0.011
	(0.039)	(0.040)	(0.040)	(0.040)	(0.039)	(0.040)	(0.040)	(0.039)
Secondary level								
African-American	−0.149**	−0.135*	−0.150**	−0.150**	−0.088	−0.094	−0.142*	−0.145*
	(0.056)	(0.055)	(0.058)	(0.058)	(0.059)	(0.058)	(0.060)	(0.060)
Hispanic	0.012	0.026	−0.016	−0.021	0.078	0.066	0.028	0.009
	(0.067)	(0.067)	(0.068)	(0.068)	(0.073)	(0.071)	(0.072)	(0.072)
Father's occupation								
Duncan SEI score	0.003*	0.001	0.001	0.001	0.003*	0.001	0.001	0.001
	(0.001)	(0.001)	(0.001)	(0.001)	(0.001)	(0.001)	(0.001)	(0.001)
1 (less than		−0.434**	−0.437**	−0.437**		−0.533**	−0.535**	−0.520**
HS graduate)		(0.058)	(0.058)	(0.058)		(0.066)	(0.066)	(0.066)

	(1)	(2)	(3)	(4)	(5)	(6)
2a (HS grad. vocational track)	−0.280** (0.059)	−0.258** (0.059)		−0.341** (0.059)	−0.331** (0.059)	
2a-i (business and commercial)			−0.035 (0.196)			−0.209** (0.068)
2a-ii (trade and technical)			−0.217** (0.068)			−0.735** (0.171)
2a-iii (other vocational programmes)			−0.385** (0.090)			−0.468** (0.085)
2b (HS grad. general track)	−0.283** (0.046)	−0.274** (0.047)	−0.275** (0.047)	−0.447** (0.047)	−0.435** (0.047)	−0.438** (0.047)
2c (HS grad. academic track)	−0.279** (0.054)	−0.271** (0.054)	−0.271** (0.054)	−0.372** (0.056)	−0.361** (0.056)	−0.361** (0.055)
3a (two-year college degree)	−0.095 (0.077)	−0.089 (0.076)	−0.089 (0.076)	−0.073 (0.065)	−0.071 (0.065)	−0.072 (0.064)
R^2	.029	.085	.087	.084	.094	.099

*$p < .05$ **$p < .01$

The Risk of No Return Investment: Unemployment

Education is an antidote to the risk of unemployment (Table 15.8). The US economy was just beginning to stall in 1990, following significant growth from 1984 to 1989. The NLSY cohort was 25 to 33 years old in 1990; thus they were vulnerable to seniority-based layoffs. In that context, general or academic secondary education and post-secondary education reduced unemployment and increased labour-force participation of men (relative to male high-school drop-outs and graduates of vocational programmes). The pay-off comes rather early in the educational career; unemployment and non-participation among male high-school graduates from the academic track are not significantly higher than among the graduates of two- or four-year colleges. The higher wages of vocational graduates relative to other secondary school graduates (Table 15.7) do not translate into a reduced risk of unemployment; they might even make them more vulnerable. On the other hand, their vulnerability might be overstated; they are more likely to define periods of not working as 'unemployment' while others report similar spells as periods of being out of the labour force.

Female high-school drop-outs are also vulnerable; they are more likely to be either unemployed or not in the labour force relative to all other educational categories. Women with four-year college degrees are less likely to be unemployed than either general or academic track high-school graduates. Unemployment is not significantly higher among women with vocational-track secondary training than among college-educated women, although they are more likely to be out of the labour force. The general track, a disadvantage relative to other forms of secondary education on some outcomes, is an advantage with respect to unemployment and non-participation.[9]

CONCLUSION

American educational institutions have differentiated what they have to offer since the 1950s. Programmes of secondary and post-secondary education have increasingly come to mark themselves as vocational or academic. The rationale is to tailor the education of students to the needs and opportunities of the labour market. This differentiation has affected the early careers of women and men in this cohort that left school and started work in the 1980s. In particular, vocational offerings of substance—business and commercial high-school programmes for women and some trade and technical programmes for men—have brought about a clear and consistent pattern of positive outcomes. Graduates of these programmes had higher initial wages than their counterparts in both the general and academic curricula. They also had first jobs with higher Duncan SEI scores and better odds of being in either Classes I–II or Class III than their general curricular track counterparts.[10]

A two-year post-secondary degree rewards its holder with employment prospects, occupational status, and pay that are intermediate between the rewards of an academic secondary diploma and a four-year bachelor's degree. This is strong confirmation of the 'investment' perspective we have taken and human-capital theories of educational stratification in general. It calls into question those theories based on the 'diverted dream' metaphor (Brint and Karabel 1989). On the other hand, the two-year degree may not be an orderly transition point. Both men and women with two-year college degrees had lower odds of reporting leaving school because they had received a degree, suggesting that they attempted to go on but failed in the attempt. Surprisingly, two-year degree holders and four-year degree holders do not differ significantly in initial hourly wages.

We emphasize at this point that we are analysing 'early returns'. The early labour-market outcomes highlighted in this analysis are significant for understanding the beginnings of careers. They take on added significance in the light of previous research which has demonstrated that an individual's first job has long-term effects on their occupational trajectory (Blau and Duncan 1967; Sewell, Hauser, and Wolf 1980; Hauser and Carter 1995). Nonetheless, we remain cautious in assessing these findings because the human capital associated with an individual's educational attainment also has effects later in the individual's occupational career. In particular, the educational advantages of university graduates (and those with advanced degrees) tend to come later in the career when promotions to positions of higher authority differentiate men and women within the same initial occupational group (Wright, Baxter, and Birkelund 1995; Althauser 1989).

The promising results of two-year colleges indicate that the tension between 'channel of opportunity' and 'cooling-out function' has tipped in favour of opportunity just at a point when the two-year colleges are about to be swamped by demographic changes (Hout 1996). In particular, the 'echo' of the post-war baby boom will drive up the number of students seeking post-secondary education by 30 per cent at a time when public resources to support two- and four-year colleges and universities are shrinking. The data show clearly that education mediates entry into white-collar positions, especially the professional and managerial ranks (Figure 15.4). In that sorting, academic education is more important than other types. A differentiated vocational high-school curriculum, however, affects occupational outcomes for those that have not been singled out as the most likely candidates for the mental labours of the upper white-collar stratum. They earn higher wages when they are employed. To the extent that this curriculum specializes in

Table 15.8. *ML estimates of determinants of current unemployment and labour-force participation for those aged 26–34, 1990*

	Males (N = 2,145)				Females (N = 2,309)			
	(1)		(2)		(1)		(2)	
	unemployed	not in labour force	unemployed	not in labour force	unemployed	not in labour force	unemployed	not in labour force
Intercept	-3.795**	-4.907**	-4.038**	-4.134**	-5.168**	-2.681**	-4.023**	-2.503**
	(0.838)	(0.688)	(0.841)	(0.698)	(0.821)	(0.340)	(0.876)	(0.343)
Parent education								
Primary level	-0.188	0.050	-0.174	0.156	0.150	0.051	0.314	0.062
	(0.408)	(0.303)	(0.419)	(0.311)	(0.336)	(0.167)	(0.348)	(0.167)
	-0.030	-0.077	-0.015	-0.076	-0.183	-0.184	-0.102	-0.137
Secondary level	(0.334)	(0.262)	(0.346)	(0.275)	(0.297)	(0.135)	(0.312)	(0.135)
African–American	0.861*	0.670**	-0.364*	-0.447**	1.140**	0.053	-0.561**	0.021
	(0.348)	(0.255)	(0.179)	(0.132)	(0.288)	(0.183)	(0.144)	(0.092)
Hispanic	0.636	0.163	0.729	0.294	0.046	-0.087	0.078	-0.049
	(0.460)	(0.348)	(0.465)	(0.362)	(0.443)	(0.219)	(0.446)	(0.218)
Father's occupation	-0.010	0.003	-0.008	0.006	0.001	0.008	-0.002	0.005
Duncan SEI score	(0.011)	(0.009)	(0.011)	(0.009)	(0.010)	(0.005)	(0.010)	(0.005)

	(A)	(B)	(C)	(D)	(E)	(F)	(G)	(H)
1 (less than HS graduate)	1.317** (0.483)	2.190** (0.422)	1.376** (0.486)	2.210** (0.425)	2.621** (0.568)	1.627** (0.196)	2.788** (0.642)	1.771** (0.200)
2a (HS grad. vocational track)	1.222* (0.502)	0.580 (0.545)			1.211 (0.639)	0.800** (0.209)		
2a-i (business and commercial)			-a-	-a-			1.691* (0.738)	0.782** (0.250)
2a-ii (trade and technical)			1.603** (0.525)	0.816 (0.597)			-a-	1.259* (0.522)
2a-iii (other vocational programmes)			0.777 (0.729)	0.442 (0.817)			1.146 (0.941)	1.222** (0.275)
2b (HS grad. general track)	0.605 (0.471)	1.284** (0.414)	0.479 (0.483)	1.209** (0.419)	1.753** (0.552)	0.818** (0.172)	1.840** (0.628)	0.930** (0.177)
2c (HS grad. academic track)	0.013 (0.604)	0.748 (0.482)	0.035 (0.603)	0.313 (0.532)	1.580** (0.588)	0.409 (0.209)	1.819** (0.657)	0.537* (0.212)
3a (two-year college degree)	-0.439 (1.081)	0.190 (0.805)	-0.401 (1.082)	0.597 (0.692)	1.228 (0.684)	0.068 (0.266)	1.517* (0.744)	0.220 (0.264)

*$p < .05$ **$p < .01$
-a- insufficient cases to estimate

areas that are valued by employers, these programmes provide an alternative route to higher wages.

The weak to non-existent links between schools and employers make the transition to work uncertain for US school-leavers. Those who first leave school before completing high school or immediately upon leaving high school seldom receive any institutional support in their job search. Many are disappointed by the outcome of that search and return to school. Young people leaving the post-secondary system—on their first or second foray into the world of work—have more desirable credentials in hand, but little in the way of institutional support. Only those with post-graduate professional education can count on a circumscribed labour market to translate their credentials into an appropriate occupation. Even that narrowing of job tracks does not remove all of the uncertainties. The widest spread of earnings in first jobs is among the college graduates.

Does that produce more or less stratification in the United States than we would see if the structure were tighter? Comparing the United States to Germany suggests that looseness inhibits reproduction and stratification. The two-step chain of reproduction in Germany—the close association between origins and type of education and between type of education and first occupation—leads to a closer association between socio-economic origins and destinations in Germany than in the United States. Both links are weaker in the United States.

The 'diverted dream' approach to educational stratification in the United States has suggested, though, that the United States is more stratified than it might otherwise be if the educational system was less internally differentiated—in particular if there were no vocational tracks in secondary schools and no two-year colleges. Our results question that point of view. First of all, it is not clear that vocational track students would finish secondary school if they had to take more academic courses (Arum and Shavit 1995). Second, employers value the skills acquired in vocational tracks by paying higher wages to vocational graduates than to general graduates. Third, the occupational status and earnings of persons with diplomas from two-year colleges fall between those with no post-secondary credentials and those with bachelor's degrees. This indicates that the returns to two-year degree programmes are proportional to the time investment (and, given the low cost of these programmes, the financial return may exceed that of a bachelor's degree). The students in vocational programmes and two-year colleges are disproportionately from disadvantaged origins. By enhancing their graduates' chances for employment and their wages once they are employed, vocational programmes in secondary schools and two year colleges probably reduce the inter-generational transmission of inequality. They may also reduce the amount of inequality in outcomes by creating a valuable pool of non-academic human capital, as Labor Secretary Robert Reich (1991) argues, but that conclusion does not necessarily follow from our evidence of positive returns for these kinds of educational pursuits.[11]

NOTES

This paper was prepared for the School-to-Work Conference at the European University Institute, Florence in March 1995. We received financial support from the Survey Research Center and the Committee on Research at the University of California, Berkeley, and from the European University Institute. We would like to thank Yossi Shavit, Walter Müller, and Richard Breen for helpful comments on previous drafts.

1. There are some notable exceptions in the USA, where local schools and businesses have entered into partnership agreements (see e.g. Stern, Raby and Dayton 1992). The Federal government has recently provided limited funding to support, sponsor and develop such linkages (Smith and Scoll 1995).

2. Individuals in the NLSY report an average of eight different jobs in their first eight years after school. Unionization rates by 1990 had also fallen to low postwar levels. The percentage of unionized workers in 1990 in the NLSY sample by educational and occupational category were:

	Female	Male	Class	Female	Male
1	7	9	I–II	9	8
2a	9	17	IIIab	7	9
2b	8	17	IVabc	0	0
2c	7	16	V–VI	8	18
3a	9	11	VII	13	19
3b	9	6			

3. Although details of the US Census scheme and the Swedish and British official classification schemes on which EGP is based prevent an exact match (Erikson and Goldthorpe 1992: 50 ff.), the Ganzeboom transformation is useful for mapping to the level of aggregation employed here.

4. Some SMSAs are small enough that identifying whether the household is located in a central city or suburb will uniquely identify some individuals in the sample. To avoid the US Bureau of the Census suppressing the central city/suburb distinction for all cases in the SMSAs with less than 250,000 residents in both the central city and the suburbs.

5. Figure 15.2 presents box and whisker graphs of the percentile distribution of hourly wages (panel A), and socio-economic status of first job (panel B). Box and whisker plots show the 10th, 25th, 50th, 75th and 90th percentiles of a distribution (see Cleveland (1994) for a discussion of this and other ways of graphing data). The bottom of the box marks the 25th percentile. The top of the box marks the 75th percentile. The line inside the box marks the median. The tip of the line up from the bottom of the box marks the 10th percentile. The tip of the line up from the top of the box marks the 90th percentile. The lines are

called 'whiskers'. The advantage of a box and whisker plot over a simple line graph of means or medians is the ability of the box and whisker plot to communicate data on dispersion as well as data on central tendency in one image.

6. Recall that we did not 'give educational credit' for the GED, so some of these persons at the lowest level may have obtained a credential without actually returning to school, and some of those who did return may have obtained a credential through the examination process.

7. In weighted analysis using the entire NLSY sample these differences are significant at the $p < .01$ level.

8. Most sociologists prefer SEI and other indicators based on parental occupations to direct measures of parental income, in part because we think of occupation as a more reliable measure of 'permanent income' than high schoolers (or older peoples') reports of their parents' incomes while they were growing up. The results reported by C. Fischer et al. (1996) belie that conjecture. Despite the inaccuracies that undoubtedly infect the young people's reports of their parents' incomes, parental income is significant where neither SEI nor education are. The lesson is that we ought to be measuring parental income.

9. African-American men and women are more likely to be either unemployed or not in the labour force than otherwise comparable whites.

10. These results are particularly strong considering the methodology employed in this study. To remain consistent with the cross-national project, students from the general track who attended several years of college but did not attain a post-secondary degree were assigned back into 2b. The additional years of schooling many of them attained and their higher social origins may be responsible for their better outcomes. Finally, vocational curriculum was coded on the basis of self-reports; course transcripts provide more reliable information and are thus more strongly associated with occupational outcomes (Arum and Shavit 1995).

11. The large variance in wages within categories of educational attainment frustrates any attempt to derive the level of inequality implied by any pattern of returns to education.

REFERENCES

ABBOTT, A. (1988), *The System of Professions: An Essay on the Division of Expert Labor* (Chicago: University of Chicago Press).

ALESSI, T., and BRUNI, M. (1990), *Sistema formativo e professioni: Dalla disoccupazione intellettuale al deficit educativo* (Milan: Franco Angeli).

ALLMENDINGER, JUTTA (1989a), *Career Mobility Dynamics: A Comparative Analysis of the United States, Norway, and West Germany* (Berlin: Max-Planck-Institut für Bildungsforschung).

—— (1989b), 'Educational Systems and Labor Market Outcomes', *European Sociological Review*, 5: 231–50.

ALTHAUSER, ROBERT (1989), 'Internal Labor Markets', *Annual Review of Sociology*, 15: 143–61.

—— and KALLEBERG, ARNE (1990), 'Identifying Career Lines and Internal Labor Markets within Firms', in R. Breiger (ed.), *Social Mobility and Social Structure* (Cambridge: Cambridge University Press), 308–56.

AMANO, IKUO, DAIJIRO, HIDA, MIMIZUKA, HIROAKI, YUFU, SAWAKO, KARIYA, TAKEHIKO, IWAKI, HIDEO, SHIMIZU, KOKICHI, DONO, MICHIO, KOBAYASHI, MASAYUKI, IWANAGA, MASAYA, YOSHIMOTO, KEIICHI, KAWAKAMI, FUJIKO, HASHIMOTO, KENJI, and YOSHIDA, AYA (1988), *A Study of the Function of Graduates' Career Differentiation of Japanese High Schools*, Research Report financially supported by the Toyota Foundation III–036.

AMMASSARI, PAOLO (1969), 'La mobilità ascendente nella società avanzata', *Rassegna Italiana di Sociologia*, 10 (Jan./Mar.): 43–70.

ARUM, RICHARD, and SHAVIT, YOSSI (1995), 'Secondary Vocational Education and the Transition from School to Work', *Sociology of Education* 68: 187–204.

Australia (1985), *Essential Features of Australian Apprenticeship Systems, December 1984* (Canberra: Australian Government Printer; Commonwealth–State Training Advisory Committee).

Australian Bureau of Statistics (1986 and earlier), *Labour Statistics Australia* (ABS Catalogue No. 6101.0; Canberra: Australian Bureau of Statistics).

Australian Department of Employment, Education and Training (1991), *Retention and Participation in Australian Schools 1967 to 1990* (Monograph Series No. 6 (Apr.); Canberra: Australian Government Printing Service).

BARBAGLI, MARZIO (1974), *Disoccupazione intellettuale e sistema scolastico in Italia* (Bologna: Il Mulino).

BARON, J.N. (1984): 'Organizational Perspectives on Stratification' *Annual Review of Sociology*, 10: 37–69.

—— DAVIS-BLAKE, A., and BIELBY, W. T. (1986), 'The Structure of Opportunity: How Promotion Ladders Vary within and among Organizations', *Administrative Science Quarterly*, 31: 248–73.

BARRETT, R. E., and WHYTE, M. K. (1982), 'Dependency Theory and Taiwan: Analysis of a Deviant Case', *American Journal of Sociology*, 87: 1064–89.

BAUDELOT, CHRISTIAN, and GLAUDE, M. (1988), 'Les Diplômes se dévaluent-ils en se multipliant?', *Economique et Statistique*, 225 (Oct.): 3–16.

BECK, ULRICH (1984), *Risikogesellschaft: Auf dem Weg in eine andere Moderne* (Frankfurt: Suhrkamp).

BECKER, GARRY (1972), *Human Capital: A Theoretical and Empirical Analysis with Special Reference to Education* (New York: National Bureau of Economic Research).

—— (1975), *Human Capital* (New York: Columbia University Press).

BECKER, M., and CLOGG, C. (1989), 'Analysis of Two-Way Contingency Tables Using Association Models', *Journal of the American Sociological Association*, 84: 142–51.

BELL, DANIEL (1973), *The Coming of Post-Industrial Society: A Venture in Social Forecasting* (New York: Basic Books).

BELLO, WALDER, and ROSENFELD, STEFANIE (1990), *Dragons in Distress: Asia's Miracle Economies in Crisis* (San Francisco: Institute for Food and Development Policy).

BENAVOT, AARON (1983), 'The Rise and Decline of Vocational Education', *Sociology of Education*, 56: 63–76.

—— CHA, YUN-KYUNG, KAMENS, DAVID, MEYER, JOHN, and WONG, SUK-YING (1991), 'Knowledge for the Masses: World Models and National Curricula 1920–1986', *American Sociological Review*, 56: 85–101.

BENDER, S., and DIETRICH, H. (1994), 'Occupational Mobility in Germany: From Apprenticeship to Labour Market Integration', Paper presented at the workshop 'Determinants of Individual Success in Transitions to the Labour Market', Seelisberg, Switzerland, Sept. 1994.

BEN-PORATH, YORAM (1983), *Trends in the Labor Force Participation of Women 1955–1980* (Jerusalem: Falk Institute for Economic Research in Israel).

BERNSTEIN, DEBORAH (1991), 'Oriental and Ashkenazi Jewish Women in the Labor Market: Women in Israel', in Barbara Swirski and Marilyn P. Safir (eds.), *Calling the Equality Bluff: Women in Israel* (Oxford: Pergamon Press).

BLACKBURN, ROBERT M., JARMAN, JENNIFER, and SILTANEN, JANET (1993), 'The Analysis of Occupational Gender Segregation over Time and Place: Considerations of Measurement and Some New Evidence', *Work, Employment and Society*, 7 (3): 335–62.

BLAU, PETER M., and DUNCAN, OTIS D. (1967), *The American Occupational Structure* (New York: Wiley & Sons).

—— —— with TYREE, ANDREA (1994), 'The Process of Stratification', in David Grusky (ed.), *Social Stratification in Sociological Perspective* (Boulder, Colo.: Westview Press). 204–8.

BLOSSFELD, HANS-PETER (1985a), *Bildungsexpansion und Berufschancen: Empirische Analysen zur Lage der Berufsanfänger in der Bundesrepublik* (Frankfurt and New York: Campus).

—— (1985b), 'Berufseintritt und Berufsverlauf: Eine Kohortenanalyse über die Bedeutung des ersten Berufs in der Erwerbsbiographie', *Mitteilungen aus der Arbeitsmarkt- und Berufsforschung*, 18 (2): 177–97.

—— (1986), 'Career Opportunities in the Federal Republic of Germany: A Dynamic Approach to the Study of Life-Cycle, Cohort and Period Effects', *European Sociological Review*, 2: 208–25.

—— (1989), *Kohortendifferenzierung im Karriereprozess: Eine Längsschnittstudie über die Veränderung der Bildungs- und Berufschancen im Lebenslauf* (Frankfurt: Campus Verlag).

—— (1992), 'Is the German Dual System a Model for a Modern Vocational Training System? A Cross-National Comparison of How Different Systems of Vocational Training Deal with the Changing Occupational Structure', *International Journal of Comparative Sociology*, 23: 168–81.

—— (1993), 'Changes in Educational Opportunities in the Federal Republic of Germany: A Longitudinal Study of Cohorts Born between 1916 and 1965', in Yossi Shavit and Hans-Peter Blossfeld (eds.), *Persistent Inequality: Changing Educational Attainment in Thirteen Countries* (Boulder, Colo.: Westview Press), 51–74.

—— (1994), 'Different Systems of Vocational Training and Transition from School to Career: The German Dual System in Cross-National Comparison', in CEDE-FOP, *The Determinants of Transitions in Youth* (Papers from the 1993 ESF Network Conference on Transitions in Youth; Barcelona: CEDEFOP and GRET), 26–36.

—— and MAYER, KARL ULRICH (1988), 'Labour Market Segmentation in the Federal Republic of Germany: An Empirical Study of Segmentation Theories from a Life-Course Perspective', *European Sociological Review*, 4: 123–40.

—— and SHAVIT, YOSSI (1993), 'Persisting Barriers: Changes in Educational Opportunities in Thirteen Countries', in Yossi Shavit and Hans-Peter Blossfeld (eds.), *Persisting Barriers: Changes in Educational Opportunities in Thirteen Countries* (Boulder, Colo.: Westview Press), 1–23.

BOURDIEU, PIERRE (1984), *Distinction: A Social Critique of the Judgement of Taste* (Cambridge, Mass.: Harvard University Press).

—— and PASSERON, JEAN-CLAUDE (1977), *Reproduction in Education, Society and Culture* (Beverly Hills, Calif.: Sage).

BOWLES, SAMUEL, and GINTIS, HERBERT (1976), *Capitalist Schooling in America* (New York: Basic Books).

BRAUN, MICHAEL, and MÜLLER, WALTER (1997), 'Measurement of Education in Comparative Perspective', in Lars Mjoset, Fredrik Engelstad, Arnalug Leira, Ragnvald Kalleberg, and Grete Brochmann (eds.), *Methodological Issues in Comparative Social Science* (Greenwich, Conn.: JAI Press), 163–201.

BREEN, RICHARD (1984), *Education and the Labour Market: Work and Unemployment among Recent Cohorts of Irish School Leavers.* (General Research Series, Paper No. 119; Dublin: Economic and Social Research Institute).

—— (1991), *Education, Employment and Training in the Youth Labour Market* (General Research Series, Paper No. 152; Dublin: Economic and Social Research Institute).

—— and GOLDTHORPE, JOHN H. (1996), 'Class (and Gender) Differentials in Educational Attainment: Towards a Formal Theory', unpublished manuscript, Queen's University, Belfast, and Nuffield College, Oxford.

—— and WHELAN, CHRISTOPHER T. (1985), 'Vertical Class Mobility and Class Inheritance in the British Isles', *British Journal of Sociology*, 36: 175–92.

—— —— (1992), 'Explaining the Irish Pattern of Social Fluidity', in John H. Goldthorpe and Christopher T. Whelan (eds.), *The Development of Industrial Society in Ireland: Proceedings of the British Academy 79* (Oxford: Oxford University Press), 129–51.

514   *References*

BREEN, RICHARD and WHELAN, CHRISTOPHER T. (1993), 'From Ascription to Achievement? Origins, Education and Entry to the Labour Force in the Republic of Ireland during the Twentieth Century', *Acta Sociologica*, 36 (1): 3–19.

—— —— (1994), 'Modelling Trends in Social Fluidity: The Core Model and a Measured Variable Approach', *European Sociological Review*, 10 (3): 259–72.

—— —— (1996), *Social Change and Social Mobility in the Republic of Ireland* (Dublin: Gill and Macmillan).

—— HANNAN, DAMIAN F., and O'LEARY, R. (1995), 'Returns to Education: Taking Account of Employers' Perceptions and Use of Educational Credentials', *European Sociological Review*, 11 (1): 59–73.

—— —— ROTTMAN, DAVID B., and WHELAN, CHRISTOPHER T. (1990), *Understanding Contemporary Ireland: State, Class and Development in the Republic of Ireland* (London: Macmillan).

BRINT, STEVEN, and KARABEL, JEROME (1989), *The Diverted Dream: Community Colleges and the Promise of Educational Opportunity in America, 1900–1985* (New York: Oxford University Press).

BRINTON, MARY C. (1988), 'The Social–Institutional Bases of Gender Stratification: Japan as an Illustrative Case', *American Journal of Sociology*, 94: 300–34.

—— (1993), *Women and the Economic Miracle: Gender and Work in Postwar Japan* (Berkeley and Los Angeles: University of California Press).

—— and KARIYA, TAKEHIKO (forthcoming), 'Institutional Embeddedness in the Japanese Labor Markets', in Mary Brinton and Victor Nee (eds.), *The New Institutionalism in Sociology* (New York: Russell Sage).

BROOM, LEONARD, JONES, FRANK L., McDONNELL, PATRICK, and WILLIAMS, TREVOR (1980), *The Inheritance of Inequality* (London: Routledge & Kegan Paul).

BROWN, CHARLES, and MEDOFF, JAMES (1989), 'The Employer Size-Wage Effect', *Journal of Political Economy*, 97: 1027–59.

BÜCHEL, FELIX, and HELBERGER, CHRISTOF (1995), 'Bildungsnachfrage als Verischerungsstrategie: Der Effekt eines zusätzlich erworbenen Lehrabschlusses auf die beruflichen Startchancen von Hochschulabsolventen', *Mitteilungen aus der Arbeitsmarkt- und Berufsforschung*, 28: 32–42.

BUCHMANN, MARLIS (1989) *The Script of Life in Modern Society: Entry into Adulthood in a Changing World* (Chicago: University of Chicago Press).

—— (1994), 'Adolescence in Switzerland', in Klaus Hurrelmann (ed.), *International Handbook of Adolescence* (Westport, Conn.: Greenwood Press), 386–99.

—— and CHARLES, MARIA (1995), 'Organizational and Institutional Factors in the Process of Gender Stratification: Comparing Social Arrangements in Six European Countries', *International Journal of Sociology*, 25 (2): 66–95.

—— and SACCHI, STEFAN (1995a), 'Mehrdimensionale Klassifikation beruflicher Verlaufsdaten: Eine Anwendung auf Berufslaufbahnen zweier Schweizer Geburtskohorten', *Kölner Zeitschrift für Soziologie und Sozialpsychologie*, 35 (3): 413–42.

—— —— (1995b), 'Changing Patterns of Intragenerational Status Mobility: A Comparison of Germany and Switzerland', Paper presented at the Research Committee 28 of the International Sociological Association, Zürich, May 1995.

—— —— (forthcoming), *Berufsverlauf und Berufsidentität im soziotechnischen Wandel*, Final report to the Swiss National Science Foundation, Bern.

—— and CHARLES, MARIA with SACCHI, STEFAN (1993), 'The Lifelong Shadow: Social Origins and Educational Opportunity in Switzerland', in Yossi Shavit and Hans-Peter Blossfeld (eds.), *Persistent Inequality: Changing Educational Attainment in Thirteen Countries* (Boulder, Colo.: Westview Press), 177–92.

CALLAN, TIM, NOLAN, BRIAN, WHELAN, B. J., and HANNAN, DAMIAN F., with CREIGHTON, S. (1989), *Poverty, Income, and Welfare in Ireland* (General Research Series, Paper No. 146; Dublin: Economic and Social Research Institute).

CARLSSON, GØSTA (1958), *Social Mobility and Class Structure* (Lund: CWK Gleerup).

CARROLL, GLENN R., and MAYER, KARL ULRICH (1986), 'Job Shift Patterns in the Federal Republic of Germany: The Effects of Social Class, Industrial Sector, and Organizational Size', *American Sociological Review*, 51 (3): 323–41.

CASS, BETTINA (1988), 'Income Support for the Unemployed in Australia: Towards a More Active System', *Social Security Review* (Issues Paper No. 4; Canberra: Australian Government Publishing Service).

CBS (Central Bureau of Statistics), *see* Israel, Central Bureau of Statistics.

CEDEFOP (1991), *Vocational Training in the Federal Republic of Germany* (Luxembourg: Official Publications Office of the European Community).

CHANG, YING-HWA, HSIEH, C.-T., and HUANG, Y.-S. (1995), 'Tracking Effects on Attainment of Socioeconomic Status', Paper presented at the Conference on Educational Reforms, Taiwan, Sept. 1995 (in Chinese).

CHANG, MAU-KUEI (1994), 'Toward an Understanding of the Sheng-Chi Wen-Ti in Taiwan', in Chen Chung-Min, Chuang Ying-Chang, and Huang Shu-Min (eds.), *Ethnicity in Taiwan: Social, Historical, and Cultural Perspective* (Taipei: Institute of Ethnology, Academia Sinica), 93–150.

CHARLES, MARIA (1992), 'Cross-National Variation in Occupational Sex Segregation', *American Sociological Review*, 57: 483–502.

—— and BUCHMANN, MARLIS (1994), 'Assessing Micro-Level Explanations of Occupational Sex Segregation: Human Capital Development and Labor Market Opportunities in Switzerland', *Swiss Journal of Sociology*, 20 (3): 595–620.

CHENG, T.-J. (1992), 'Dilemmas and Choices in Educational Policies: The Case of South Korea and Taiwan', *Studies in Comparative International Development*, 27 (4): 54–79.

CHIU, HEI-YUAN (1992) (ed.), *A Project Report on the Second Survey of Social Changes in Taiwan: 1992* (Taipei: Institute of Ethnology, Academia Sinica).

CLEVELAND, WILLIAM (1994), *Visualising Data* (Summit, NJ: Hobart Press).

COBALTI, ANTONIO, and SCHIZZEROTTO, ANTONIO (1993), 'Inequality of Educational Opportunity in Italy', in Yossi Shavit and Hans-Peter Blossfeld (eds.), *Persistent Inequality: Changing Educational Attainment in Thirteen Countries* (Boulder, Colo.: Westview Press), 155–76.

—— —— (1994), *La mobilità sociale in Italia* (Bologna: Il Mulino).

COLE, ROBERT E. (1979), *Work, Mobility, and Participation* (Berkeley: University of California Press).

—— and TOMINAGA, KEN'ICHI (1976), 'Japan's Changing Occupational Structure and its Significance', in Hugh Patrick (ed.), *Japanese Industrialization and its Social Consequences* (Berkeley: University of California Press), 53–95.

COLLINS, RANDALL (1971), 'Functional and Conflict Theories of Educational Stratification', *American Sociological Review*, 36: 1002–19.

COLLINS, RANDALL (1979), *The Credential Society* (New York: Academic Press).

CONZE, WERNER, and KOCKA, JÜRGEN (1985) (eds.), *Bildungsbürgertum im 19. Jahrhundert. Teil 1: Bildungssystem und Professionalisierung in internationalen Vergleichen* (Stuttgart: Klett-Cotta).

CUMMINGS, WILLIAM K. (1980), *Education and Equality in Japan* (Princeton: Princeton University Press).

—— AMANO, IKUO, and KITAMURA, KAZUYUKI (1979) (eds.), *Changes in the Japanese University: A Comparative Perspective* (New York: Praeger).

DAHRENDORF, RALF (1992), *Der moderne soziale Konflikt* (Stuttgart: Deutsche Verlags-Anstalt).

DAR, YEHEZEKEL, and RESH, NURA (1991), 'Socioeconomic and Ethnic Gaps in Academic Achievement in Israeli Junior High Schools', in N. Bleichrodt and P.J.D. Drenth (eds.), *Contemporary Issues in Cross Country Cultural Psychology* (Amsterdam: Zeitlinger), 322–33.

DÄUMER, R. (1993), *Log-multiplikative Modelle zur Bestimmung der Assoziation zwischen qualitativen Variablen mit inkonsistent geordneten Kategorien*, Zentralarchiv für Empirische Sozialforschung an der Universität zu Köln ZA-Informationen, 33: 52–74.

DE GRAAF, PAUL M., and GANZEBOOM, HARRY B.G. (1993), 'Family Background and Educational Attainment in the Netherlands of Birth Cohorts 1891–1960', in Yossi Shavit and Hans-Peter Blossfeld (eds.), *Persistent Inequality: Changing Educational Attainment in Thirteen Countries* (Boulder, Colo.: Westview Press), 75–99.

—— and LUIJKX, R. (1995), 'Paden naar succes: geboorte of diploma's?', in J. Dronkers and Wout C. Ultee (eds.), *Verschuivende ongelijkheid in Nederland* (Assen: Van Gorcum), 31–45.

—— and VERMEULEN, H. (1997), 'Female Employment over the Life-Course in the Netherlands: Birth Cohorts 1925 to 1974', in Hans-Peter Blossfeld (ed.), *The Family Cycle and Women's Part-Time Employment in Europe* (Boulder, Colo.: Westview Press).

DE LILLO, ANTONIO, and SCHIZZEROTTO, ANTONIO (1982), 'Diseguaglianze educative e diseguaglianze occupazionali: Il caso italiano', in F. S. Cappello, M. Dei, and M. Rossi (eds.), *L'immobilità sociale* (Bologna: Il Mulino).

—— —— (1985), *La valutazione sociale delle occupazioni* (Bologna: Il Mulino).

Department of Education and Science (DES) (1965), Circular 10/65: 'The Organization of Secondary Education' (London: HMSO).

DEYO, FREDERIC C. (1987), 'State and Labor: Modes of Political Exclusion in East Asian Development', in Frederic C. Deyo (ed.) *The Political Economy of the New Asian Industrialism* (Ithaca, NY and London: Cornell University Press), 182–202.

DIGGLE, P., and KENWARD, MICHAEL (1994), 'Informative Drop-outs in Longitudinal Data Analysis', *Applied Statistics*, 43: 49–94.

Digitales Informationssystem (1995), *Digitales Informationssystem soziale Indikatoren für die Bundesrepublik Deutschland: Interaktives Informationssystem zum sozialen Wandel, der Entwicklung der Lebensbedingungen und der Lebensqualität in der Bundesrepublik Deutschland* (Mannheim: ZUMA, Abteilung Soziale Indikatoren).

DOUGHERTY, KEVIN (1987), 'The Effects of Community Colleges: Aid or Hinderance to Socio-Economic Attainment?', *Sociology of Education*, 60: 86–103.

DOWNING, R. I. (1973) (ed.), *The Australian Economy: A Manual of Applied Economics* (London: Weidenfeld and Nicolson).

DRONKERS, J. (1983), 'Have Inequalities in Educational Opportunity Changed in the Netherlands?', *Netherlands' Journal of Sociology*, 19: 133–50.

DUNCAN, OTIS D., and HODGE, R. W. (1963), 'Education and Occupational Mobility', *American Journal of Sociology*, 68: 629–44.

DURU-BELLAT, M., and MINGAT, ALAIN (1988), 'De l'orientation en fin de cinquième au fonctionnement du collège. 2. Progression, notation, orientation: l'impact du contexte de scolarisation', *Cahiers de l'IREDU*, 45 (Jan.).

ERIKSON, ROBERT, and GOLDTHORPE, JOHN H. (1992), *The Constant Flux: A Study of Class Mobility in Industrial Societies* (Oxford: Clarendon Press).

—— —— (1994), 'Trends in Class Mobility: The Postwar European Experience', in David Grusky (ed.), *Social Stratification in Sociological Perspective* (Boulder, Colo.: Westview Press), 289–316.

—— and JONSSON, JAN O. (1993), *Ursprung och utbildning: Social snedrekrytering till högre studier* (SOU 1993:85, Stockholm: Fritzes).

—— —— (1996*a*) (eds.), *Can Education be Equalized? The Swedish Case in Comparative Perspective* (Boulder, Colo.: Westview Press).

—— —— (1996*b*), 'Explaining Class Inequality in Education: The Swedish Test Case', in Robert Erikson and Jan O. Jonsson (eds.), *Can Education be Equalized?* (Boulder, Colo.: Westview Press), 1–63.

—— —— (1996*c*), 'Income Attainment among Young Employees in Sweden: The Importance of Credentials, School Performance, Job Matching, and Industrial Branch', Paper presented at the RC28 Spring meeting, Stockholm, Sweden, June 1996.

—— GOLDTHORPE, JOHN H., and PORTOCARERO, LUCIENNE (1979), 'Intergenerational Class Mobility in Three European Societies', *British Journal of Sociology*, 30: 415–41.

ESPING-ANDERSEN, GØSTA (1993) (ed.), *Changing Classes:Stratification and Mobility in Post-industrial Societies* (London: Sage).

EYRAUD, FRANÇOIS, MARSDEN, DAVID, and SILVESTRE, JEAN-JACQUES (1990), 'Occupational and Internal Labour Markets in Britain and France', *International Labour Review*, 129: 501–17.

FARLEY, REYNOLDS, and ALLEN, WALTER R. (1987), *Beyond the Color Line* (New York: Russell Sage).

FEATHERMAN, DAVID L., and HAUSER, ROBERT M. (1978), *Opportunity and Change* (New York: Academic Press).

FEI, JOHN (1983), 'Evolution of Growth Policies of NICs in a Historical and Topological Perspective', Paper presented at the Conference on Patterns of Growth and Structural Change in Asia's Newly Industrializing Countries (NICs) and Near NICs in the Context of Economic Interdependence, East–West Center, Honolulu, Apr. 1983.

—— RANIS, G., and KUO, S. (1979), *Growth with Equity: The Taiwan Case* (New York: Oxford University Press).

FELMLEE, D. H. (1993), 'The Dynamic Interdependence of Women's Employment and Fertility', *Social Science Research*, 22: 333–60.

FISCHER, CLAUDE, HOUT, MICHAEL, JANKOWSKI, MARTÍN SÁNCHEZ, LUCAS, SAMUEL

R., SWIDLER, ANN, and VOSS, KIM (1996), *Inequality by Design: Cracking the Bell Curve Myth* (Princeton: Princeton University Press).

FISCHER, W., and LUNDGREEN, P. (1975), 'The Recruitment and Training of Administrative and Technical Personnel', in Ch. Tilly (ed.), *The Formation of National States in Western Europe* (Princeton: Princeton University Press), 87–103.

FRANZ, WOLFGANG, and SOSKICE, DAVID (1994), 'The German Apprenticeship System' (Discussion Paper FS I 94–302; Berlin: Wissenschaftszentrum Berlin für Sozialforschung).

FREDLAND, ERIC. J., and LITTLE, ROGER D. (1985), 'Socioeconomic Status of World War II Veterans by Race', *Social Science Quarterly*, 66: 533–51.

GALLIE, DUNCAN (1995) (ed.), *Social Change and the Experience of Unemployment* (Oxford: Oxford University Press).

GAMORAN, ADAM (1996), 'Educational Stratification and Individual Careers', in Alan C. Kerckhoff (ed.), *Generating Social Stratification* (Boulder, Colo.: Westview Press), 59–74.

—— and MARE, ROBERT (1989), 'Secondary School Tracking and Educational Inequality: Compensation, Reinforcement or Neutrality', *American Journal of Sociology*, 54: 1146–83.

GANZEBOOM, HARRY B. G., and LUIJKX, R. (1995), 'Intergenerationele beroepsmobiliteit in Nederland: Patronen en historische veranderingen', in J. Dronkers and Wout C. Ultee (eds.), *Verschuivende ongelijkheid in Nederland* (Assen: Van Gorcum), 14–30.

—— —— and TREIMAN, DONALD J. (1989), 'Intergenerational Class Mobility in Comparative Perspective', *Research in Social Stratification and Mobility* 8: 3–84.

GARNIER, M. A., and RAFFALOVICH, L. E. (1984), 'The Evolution of Equality of Educational Opportunities in France', *Sociology of Education*, 57: 1–11.

GILMOUR, P., and LANSBURY, R. (1978), *Ticket to Nowhere: Education, Training and Work in Australia* (Middlesex: Penguin Books).

GOLD, T. B. (1986), *State and Society in the Taiwan Miracle* (New York: Sharpe).

GOLDTHORPE, JOHN H. (1980), *Social Mobility and Class Structure in Modern Britain* (Oxford: Clarendon Press).

—— and HEATH, ANTHONY (1992), 'Revised Class Schema 1992' (Oxford: Nuffield College, Joint Unit for the Study of Social Trends, Working Paper No. 13).

—— and HOPE, K. (1974), *The Social Grading of Occupations: A New Approach and Scale* (Oxford: Clarendon Press).

—— and PORTOCARERO, L. (1981), 'La Mobilité sociale en France 1953–1970, nouvel examen', *Revue Française de Sociologie*, 22: 151–66.

—— and PAYNE, CLIVE (1986), 'On the Class Mobility of Women: Results from Different Approaches to the Analysis of Recent British Data', *Sociology*, 20: 531–55.

—— with LLEWLLYN, CATRIONA, and PAYNE, CLIVE (1980), *Social Mobility and Class Structure in Modern Britain* (Oxford: Clarendon Press).

—— YAISH, MEIR, and KRAUS, VERED (forthcoming), 'Class Mobility in Israel: A Comparative Perspective', *Research in Social Stratification*, 15.

GOODMAN, T. A. (1979), 'Simple Models for the Analysis of Occupational Mobility Tables and Other Kinds of Cross-Classifications Having Ordered Categories', *Journal of the American Statistical Association*, 74: 537–52.

—— (1984), *The Analysis of the Cross-classified Data Having Ordered Categories* (Cambridge, Mass.: Harvard University Press).

—— (1987), 'New Methods for Analyzing the Intrinsic Character of Qualitative Variables Using Cross-Classified Data', *American Journal of Sociology*, 93: 529–83.

—— (1991), 'Measures, Models and Graphical Displays in the Analysis of Cross-Classified Data', *Journal of the American Statistical Association*, 86: 1085–1111.

GOUX, DOMINIQUE, and MAURIN, ERIC (1993), 'La Sécurité de l'emploi, une priorité croissante pour les diplômés', *Economie et Statistique*, 261: 67–77.

—— —— (1994), 'Education, expérience et salaire: tendances récentes et évolutions de long terme', *Economie et Prévision*, 1994/5: 155–78.

—— —— (1995a), 'Origine sociale et destinée scolaire: L'inégalité des chances devant l'enseignement à travers les enquêtes Formation-Qualification Professionnelle 1970, 1977, 1985 et 1993', *Revue Française de Sociologie*, 36: 81–121.

—— —— (1995b), 'Changes in the Demand for Labour in France: A Study for the Period 1970–1993', Paper presented at the OECD Expert Workshop on Technology, Productivity and Employment held in Paris.

—— —— (1997), 'Meritocracy and Social Heredity in France: Some Aspects and Trends', *European Sociological Review*, (13 (2).

GRADOLPH, R., and HOUT, MICHAEL (1994), 'The Gender Gap in Authority', Paper presented at the ISA World Congress, Bielefeld, Germany, July 1994.

GRASSO, JOHN, and SHEA, JOHN (1979), *Vocational Education and Training: Impact on Youth* (Berkeley: Carnegie Foundation for the Advancement of Teaching).

GREENHALGH, SUSAN (1984), 'Networks and their Nodes: Urban Society on Taiwan', *China Quarterly*, 99: 528–52.

GRUSKY, DAVID (1983), 'Industrialization and the Status Attainment Process: The Thesis of Industrialization Reconsidered', *American Sociological Review*, 48: 494–506.

—— (1994), 'The Contours of Social Stratification', in David Grusky (ed.), *Social Stratification in Sociological Perspective* (Boulder, Colo.: Westview Press), 3–35.

HAGGARD, STEPHAN (1990), *Pathways from the Periphery: The Politics of Growth in the Newly Industrializing Countries* (Ithaca, NY and London: Cornell University Press).

HAKIM, CATHERINE (1992), 'Explaining Trends in Occupational Gender Segregation: The Measurement, Causes and Consequences of the Sexual Division of Labour', *European Sociological Review*, 8: 127–52.

HALLER, MAX (1983), 'Klassenstrukturen und Beschäftigungssystem in Frankreich und in der Bundesrepublik Deutschland: Eine makrosoziologische Analyse der Beziehung zwischen Qualifikation, Technik und Arbeitsorganisation', in Max Haller and Walter Müller (eds.), *Beschäftigungssystem im gesellschaftlichen Wandel* (Frankfurt: Campus), 287–370.

—— KÖNIG, WALTER, KRAUSE, PETER, and KURZ, K. (1985), 'Patterns of Career Mobility and Structural Positions in Advanced Capitalist Societies: A Comparison of Men and Women in Austria, France, and the United States', *American Sociological Review*, 50: 579–603.

HALSEY, A. H. (1961), 'Sponsored and Contest Mobility: A Criticism of Turner's Hypothesis', *American Sociological Review*, 26: 454–5.

HALSEY, A. H. (1977), 'Towards Meritocracy? The Case of Britain', in Jerome Karabel and A. H. Halsey (eds.), *Power and Ideology in Education* (New York: Oxford University Press), 173–86.

—— HEATH, A. F., and RIDGE, JOHN M. (1980), *Origins and Destinations: Family, Class and Education in Modern Britain* (Oxford: Clarendon Press).

HAMILTON, G. G., and BIGGART, N. W. (1988), 'Market, Culture and Authority: A Comparative Analysis of Management and Organization in the Far East', *American Journal of Sociology*, 94 (Supp.): S52–S94.

HAMILTON, STEPHEN, and HURRELMANN, KLAUS (1994), 'The School to Career Transition in Germany and the United States', *Teachers' College Record*, 96: 329–44.

HANDL, JOHANN (1986), 'Zur Veränderung der beruflichen Chancen von Berufs- anfängern zwischen 1950 und 1982', in H. Franke, M. Kaiser, R. Nuthmann, and H. Stegmann (eds.), *Berufliche Verbleibsforschung in der Diskussion*, Beiträge zur Arbeitsmarkt- und Berufsforschung, No. 90.4 (Nürnberg: Institut für Arbeitsmarkt- und Berufsforschung), 13–48.

—— (1996), 'Hat sich die berufliche Wertigkeit der Bildungsabschlüsse in den achtziger Jahren verringert? Eine Analyse der abhängig erwerbstätigen, deutschen Berufsanfänger auf der Basis von Mikrozensusergebnissen', *Kölner Zeitschrift für Soziologie und Sozialpsychologie*, 48 (2): 249–73.

HANNAN, DAMIAN F., and SHORTALL, S. (1991), *The Quality of their Education: School Leavers' Views of Educational Objectives and Outcomes* (General Research Series, Paper No. 153; Dublin: Economic and Social Research Institute).

—— RAFFE, DAVID, and SMYTH, EMER (1996), 'Cross-National Research on School to Work Transitions: An Analytical Framework', mimeo.

HARDIMAN, NIAMH (1988), *Pay, Politics and Economic Permanence in Ireland* (Oxford: Clarendon Press).

HARDY, MELISSA A. (1993), *Regression with Dummy Variables* (Newbury Park: Sage).

HART, S. (1976), *Geschrift en getal* (Dordrecht: Historische Vereniging Holland).

HASHIZUME, SADAO (1976), 'Returns to Educational Credentials and Attitudes toward Credentials' in Sadao Hashizume (ed.), *Gakureki Hencho to sono Kozai* (Tokyo: Daiichi Hoki) (in Japanese).

HAUSER, ROBERT (1978), 'A Structural Model of the Mobility Table', *Social Forces*, 56: 919–53.

—— (1979), 'Some Exploratory Methods for Modelling Mobility Tables and Other Cross-Classified Data', in D. R. Heise (ed.), *Sociological Methodology 1980* (San Francisco: Jossey-Bass), 141–58.

—— (1993), 'Trends in College Entry among Whites, Blacks and Hispanics', in Charles Clotfelter and Michael Rothschild (eds.) *Studies in Supply and Demand in Higher Education* (Chicago: Chicago University Press), 61–104.

—— and CARTER, WENDY (1995), 'The Bell Curve as a Study of Social Stratification', Paper presented at the American Sociological Association Annual Meeting, Washington, DC.

HEATH, A. F., and McMAHON, D. (1997), 'Education and Occupational Attainment: The Impact of Ethnic Origins', in V. Karn (ed.), *Education, Employment and Housing among Ethnic Minorities in Britain* (London: HMSO), 91–113.

—— and RIDGE, JOHN M. (1983), 'Schools, Examinations and Occupational Attainment', in J. Purvis and M. Hales (eds.), *Achievement and Inequality in Education* (London: Routledge), 239–57.

—— MCMAHON, D., and ROBERTS, J. (1994), 'Ethnic Minorities in the Labour Market', Paper presented at the ECSR/ESF conference on Changes in Labour Markets and European Integration, Espinho, Portugal.

—— MILLS, C., and ROBERTS, J. (1992), 'Towards Meritocracy: New Evidence on an Old Problem', in Colin Crouch and A. F. Heath (eds.), *Social Research and Social Reform: Essays in Honour of A. H. Halsey* (Oxford: Oxford University Press), 217–43.

HEDSTRÖM, PETER (1988), *Structures of Inequality* (Stockholm: Almqvist & Wicksell International).

HENNING, HANS-JOACHIM (1984), *Die deutsche Beamtenschaft* (Stuttgart: Franz Steiner Verlag).

HIBBS, DOUGLAS A. (1991), 'Market Forces, Trade Union Ideology, and Trends in Swedish Wage Dispersion', *Acta Sociologica*, 34: 89–102.

HIDA, DAIJIRO (1983), 'Japanese High School Students and Labour Force Entry', in Hideo Iwaki and Hiroaki Mimizuka (eds.), *High School Students* (Tokyo: Shibundo), 184–92 (in Japanese).

HOSMER, D. W., and LEMESHOW, S. (1989), *Applied Logistic Regression* (New York: Wiley & Sons).

HOUT, MICHAEL (1981), *Mobility Tables* (London: Sage).

—— (1996), 'The Politics of Mobility', in Alan Kerckhoff (ed.), *Generating Social Stratification* (Boulder, Colo.: Westview Press), 293–316.

—— and HAUSER, ROBERT (1992), 'Symmetry and Hierarchy in Social Mobility: A Methodological Analysis of the CASMIN Model of Class Mobility', *European Sociological Review*, 8: 239–66.

HSIAO, HSIN-HUANG MICHAEL (1986), 'Development Strategies and Class Transformation in Taiwan and South Korea: Origins and Consequences' *Bulletin of the Institute of Ethnology*, 61: 183–217 (Taipei: Institute of Ethnology, Academia Sinica).

HSIEH, HSIAO-CHIN (1987), 'Ability Stratification in Urban Taiwanese Secondary Schools', *Bulletin of the Institute of Ethnology*, 64: 205–52 (Taipei: Institute of Ethnology, Academia Sinica).

HUIJGEN, F. (1989), *De kwalitatieve structuur van de werkgelegenheid in Nederland*, iii. *Bevolking in loondienst en functieniveaustructuur in 1977 en 1985* (Osa Voorstudie V33; The Hague: OSA).

ILO (1990), *International Standard Classification of Occupations (Revised 1988)* (Geneva: ILO).

INSEE (1992), *Nomenclature des professions et catégories socioprofessionnelles, index analytique*, i–ii (Paris: INSEE).

ISHIDA, HIROSHI (1993), *Social Mobility in Contemporary Japan: Educational Credentials, Class and the Labour Market in a Cross-National Perspective* (Stanford, Calif: Stanford University Press).

—— GOLDTHORPE, JOHN H., and ERIKSON, ROBERT (1991), 'Intergenerational Class Mobility in Postwar Japan', *American Journal of Sociology*, 96: 954–75.

—— MÜLLER, WALTER, and RIDGE, JOHN M. (1995), 'Class Origin, Class

Destination, and Education: A Cross-National Study of Ten Industrial Nations', *American Journal of Sociology*, 101 (1): 145–93.

ISHIDA, HIROSHI, SPILERMAN, SEYMOUR, and SU, KUO-HSIEN (1995), 'Educational Credentials and Promotion Prospects in a Japanese and an American Organization', Center on Japanese Economy and Business, Working Paper No. 92, Columbia Business School.

Israel, Central Bureau of Statistics (1988), *Statistical Abstracts of Israel 1988* (Jerusalem: CBS).

—— (1991), *Statistical Abstracts of Israel 1991* (Jerusalem: CBS).

—— (1992), *Statistical Abstracts of Israel 1992* (Jerusalem: CBS).

—— (1993), *Statistical Abstracts of Israel 1993* (Jerusalem: CBS).

IWANAGA, M. (1984a), 'The Organization of the Youth Labour Movement and School', *Kyouiku Shakeigaku Kenkyuu*, 38: 134–45 (in Japanese).

—— (1984b), 'Research on the Structure of the Labour Market for Graduates', *Osaka Daigaku Ningenkagakubu Kiyou*, 10: 247–76 (in Japanese).

JACCARD, JAMES, TURRISI, ROBERT, and WAN, CHOI K. (1990), *Interaction Effects in Multiple Regression* (Beverly Hills, Calif.: Sage).

JACKSON, E., and CROCKET, H. (Jr.) (1964), 'Occupational Mobility in the United States: A Point Estimate and a Trend Comparison', *American Sociological Review*, 29 (Feb.): 5–15.

JACOBS, J. A., and LIM, S. (1992), 'Trends in Occupational and Industrial Sex Segregation in Fifty-Six Countries, 1960–80', *Work and Occupations*, 19: 450–86.

JENG, R.Y.-C. (1980), 'Vocational-Industrial Education in Taiwan from 1945 to 1978', Doctoral dissertation (New York University).

JIANG, F.-F. (1990), 'The Role of Educational Credentialism in Taiwan's Labour Market: Do Diplomas or Human Capital Act as a Screening Device?', *Academia Economic Papers*, 18 (2): 129–78 (Taipei: Institute of Economics, Academia Sinica) (in Chinese).

—— (1995), 'Does Credentialism Play an Important Role in the Taiwan Labour Market: Evidence from the Period 1978–92', Working paper (Taipei: Institute of Economics, Academia Sinica) (in Chinese).

JIL (Japanese Institute of Labour) (1989), *International Comparative Study on Job Adjustment of Young Adults: The Bridge from School to Work* (Shokken Research Report No. 86).

JONES, FRANK L. (1989), 'Occupational Prestige in Australia: A New Scale', *Australian and New Zealand Journal of Sociology*, 25 (Aug.): 187–99.

—— (1992a), 'Common Social Fluidity: A Comment on Recent Criticisms', *European Sociological Review*, 8 (Dec.): 233–7.

—— (1992b), 'Sex and Ethnicity in the Australian Labour Market', Occasional Paper (Canberra: Australian Bureau of Statistics).

—— (1993), 'Unlucky Australians: Labour Market Outcomes among Aboriginal Australians', *Ethnic and Racial Studies*, 16 (July): 420–58.

—— KOJIMA, H., and MARKS, G. N. (1994), 'Comparative Social Mobility: Trends over Time in Father-to-Son Mobility in Japan and Australia, 1965–1985', *Social Forces*, 72 (Mar.): 775–98.

JÖNSSON, JAN O. (1993), 'Education, Social Mobility and Social Reproduction in Sweden: Patterns and Changes', in E. J. Hansen, Stein Ringen, Hannu Uusitalo, and Robert Erikson (eds.), *Welfare Trends in the Scandinavian Countries* (Armonk, NY: M. E. Sharpe), 91–118.

—— (1996*a*), 'Stratification in Post-Industrial Society: Are Educational Qualifications of Growing Importance?', in Robert Erikson and Jan O. Jonsson, *Can Education be Equalized?* (Boulder, Colo.: Westview Press), 113–44.

—— (1996*b*), 'Explaining Social Inequalities in Educational Attainment: Do Benefits from Educational Investments Differ according to Social Origin?', mimeo (SOFI: Stockholm University).

JUPP, JAMES (1964), *Australian Party Politics* (London: Cambridge University Press).

KA, C.-M. (1993), *Market, Social Networks, and the Production Organization of Small-Scale Industry in Taiwan: The Garment Industries in Wufenpu* (Taipei: Institute of Ethnology, Academia Sinica) (in Chinese).

KALLEBERG, ARNE, and SØRENSEN, AAGE B. (1979), 'The Sociology of Labor Markets', *Annual Review of Sociology*, 5: 351–79.

KANG, SUK, and BISHOP, JOHN (1989), 'Vocational or Academic Coursework in High School: Complements or Substitutes?', *Economics of Education Review*, 8: 133–48.

KARABEL, JEROME (1972), 'Community Colleges and Social Stratification', *Harvard Educational Review*, 42: 521–62.

KARIYA, TAKEHIKO (1988), 'Institutional Networks between Schools and Employers and Delegated Occupational Selection to Schools: A Sociological Study on the Transition from High School to Work in Japan', Ph.D dissertation (Department of Sociology, Northwestern University).

—— (1991), *A Sociology of School, Occupation and Selection* (Tokyo: Tokyo University Press) (in Japanese).

—— (1995) (ed.), *From College to Work* (Hiroshima: Hiroshima University, Research Institute for Higher Education) (in Japanese).

—— YUKI, OKITSU, YOSHIHARA, KEIKO, KONDO, HISASHI, and NAKAMURA, TAKAYASU (1993), 'The Transition from College to Work: Its Embeddedness in Alumni–Student Relations', *Tokyo University Faculty of Education Bulletin*, 32: 89–118 (in Japanese).

Keizai Doyukai (1975), *Kigyonai Shushokusha no Gakureki tou nikansuru Jittai Chosa* (Research on the Education of Employees in Firms. Survey Report) (Tokyo: Keizai Doyukai).

KELLER, SUZANNE, and ZAVALLONI, M. (1964), 'Ambition and Social Class: A Respecification', *Social Forces*, 43: 58–70.

KELLEY, JONATHAN, CUSHING, ROBERT G., and HEADEY, BRUCE (1987), *Australian National Social Science Survey, 1984 (User's Guide and Data File)* (Canberra: Social Science Data Archives, Australian National University).

—— BEAN, CLIVE, and EVANS, M. D. R. (1995), *Australian National Social Science Survey, 1986–1987: Role of Government [Computer File]* (Canberra: Social Science Data Archives, Australian National University).

KERCKHOFF, ALAN C. (1990), *Getting Started: Transition to Adulthood in Great Britain* (Boulder, Colo.: Westview Press).

—— (1995), 'Institutional Arrangements and Stratification Processes in Industrial Societies', *Annual Review of Sociology*, 15: 323–47.

—— (1996), 'Building Conceptual and Empirical Bridges between Studies of Educational and Labor Force Careers', in Alan C. Kerckhoff (ed.), *Generating*

Social Stratification: Toward a New Research Agenda (Boulder, Colo.: Westview Press), 37–56.

KIKUCHI, JOJI (1990) (ed.), *Education and Social Mobility*, iii (Tokyo: University of Tokyo Press) (in Japanese).

KIMURA, A., WATANABE, M., NAKAJIMA, F., HOTTA, C., MATSUMOTO, J., and IMADA, S. (1989), *International Comparative Study on Job Adjustment of Young Adults: The Bridge from School to Work* (Shokken Research Report No. 86).

KINNEY, CAROL (1995), 'From a Lower-Track School to a Low-Status Job? An Ethnographic Study of Two Japanese High Schools', Ph.D. dissertation (University of Michigan).

KOCKA, JÜRGEN (1987) (ed.), *Bürger und Bürgerlichkeit im 19. Jahrhundert* (Stuttgart: Klett-Cotta).

KOHLI, MARTIN, REIN, MARTIN, GUILLEMARD, ANNE-MARIE, and VAN GUNSTEREN, HERMAN (1991), *Time for Retirement: Comparative Studies of Early Exit from the Labor Force* (Cambridge: Cambridge University Press).

KOIKE, KAZUO (1988), *Understanding Industrial Relations in Modern Japan* (London: Macmillan).

—— and WATANABE, YUKIRO (1979), *The Illusion of the Educational Credential Society* (Tokyo: Toyo Keizai Shinposha) (in Japanese).

KONIETZKA, D., and SOLGA, H. (1995), 'Two Certified Societies? The Regulation of Entry into the Labour Market in East and West Germany', Paper presented at the workshop 'Transitions in Youth: Comparisons over Time and across Countries', Oostvoorne, the Netherlands, Sept. 1995.

KÖNIG, WOLFGANG (1990), *Berufliche Mobilität in Deutschland und Frankreich: Konsequenzen von Bildungs- und Beschäftigungssystemen für Frauen und Männer 1965 bis 1970* (Frankfurt: Campus).

—— and MÜLLER, WALTER (1986), 'Educational Systems and Labor Markets as Determinants of Worklife Mobility in France and West Germany: A Comparison of Men's Career Mobility, 1965–1970', *European Sociological Review*, 2 (1): 73–96.

—— LÜTTINGER, P., and MÜLLER, WALTER (1988), *A Comparative Analysis of the Development and Structure of Educational Systems: Methodological Foundations and the Construction of a Comparative Educational Scale* (CASMIN Working Paper No. 12; University of Mannheim).

KORPI, WALTER (1983), *The Democratic Class Struggle* (London: Routledge & Kegan Paul).

Koyo Shokugyo Sogo Kenkyusho (1989), *An International Comparative Study of Youth's Occupational Adjustment* (Tokyo: Koyo Shokugyo Sogo Kenkyusho) (in Japanese).

KRAUS, VERED (1976), 'Social Grading of Occupations', Doctoral dissertation (Jerusalem: Hebrew University) (in Hebrew).

—— (1992), 'The Role of Industrial and Economic Sectors on Gender Inequality in Earnings', *Research in Social Stratification and Mobility*, 11: 153–75.

—— and HODGE, ROBERT W. (1990), *Promises in the Promised Land: Mobility and Inequality in Israel* (New York: Greenwood Press).

—— and TOREN, NINA (1993), 'Changes in Opportunity Structure and Stratification Patterns in Israel 1974–1991: Trends in Mobility and Social Inequality', unpublished report for the Ford Foundation.

KURZ, K. (1995), 'Labour Force Exits Surrounding the Birth of a Child: A Comparison of German and American Women', in W. Voges and G. J. Duncan (eds.), *Dynamic Approaches in Comparative Social Research* (Aldershot: Avebury), 131–56.

—— and MÜLLER, WALTER (1987), 'Class Mobility in the Industrial World', *Annual Review of Sociology*, 13: 417–42.

LAGARDE, S., MAURIN, ERIC, and TORELLI, C. (1995), 'Flows of Workers, Internal Promotions and the Business Cycle: Some Evidence from French Plant Data 1987–1992', INSEE Working Paper, F9511.

LAUTERBACH, W. (1994), *Berufsverläufe von Frauen: Erwerbstätigkeit, Unterbrechung und Wiedereintritt* (Frankfurt: Campus).

LEE, M.-L., LIU, B.-C., and WANG, P. (1994), 'Education, Human Capital and Economic Development: Comparison between Korea and Taiwan', *Economics of Education Review*, 13 (4): 275–88.

LE GRAND, C. (1993), 'Karriär- och utvecklingsmöjligheter på de interna arbets-marknaderna', in C. le Grand, R. Szulkin, and M. Tåhlin (eds.),, *Sveriges arbet-splatser* (Stockholm: SNS), 48–83.

—— (1994), 'Löneskillnaderna i Sverige: Förändring och nuvarande struktur', in J. Fritzell and O. Lundberg (eds.), *Vardagens villkor* (Stockholm: Brombergs), 117–60.

LEPSIUS, RAINER M. (1987), 'Zur Soziologie des Bürgertums und der Bürgerlichkeit', in Jürgen Kocka (ed.), *Bürger und Bürgerlichkeit im 19. Jahrhundert* (Stuttgart: Klett-Cotta), 79–100.

LEWIN-EPSTEIN, NOAH, and SEMYONOV, MOSHE (1993), *The Arab Minority in Israel's Economy* (Boulder, Colo.: Westview Press).

LIGHT, I. (1984), 'Immigrant and Ethnic Enterprise in North America', *Ethnic and Racial Studies*, 7: 195–216.

LIJPHART, AREND (1968), *The Politics of Accommodation: Pluralism and Democracy in the Netherlands* (Berkeley: University of California Press).

LINDBECK, ASSAR (1993), *Unemployment and Macroeconomics* (Cambridge, Mass.: MIT Press).

LIPSMEIER, A. (1991) (ed.), *Berufliche Weiterbildung: Theorieansätze, Strukturen, Qualifizierungsstrategien, Perspektiven* (Frankfurt: Verlag der Gesellschaft zur Förderung arbeitsorientierter Forschung und Bildung).

LITTLE, IAN MALCOLM DAVID (1979), 'An Economic Reconnaissance', in W. Galenson (ed.), *Economic Growth and Structural Change in Taiwan* (Ithaca, NY: Cornell University Press), 448–507.

LOCKWOOD, D. (1958), *The Blackcoated Worker* (London: Allen & Unwin).

LU, Y.-H. (1996), 'Women and Work in Taiwanese Family Business', Paper presented at the workshop on Women and Work in Contemporary East Asia, Tokyo, May 1996.

LUCAS, C. J. (1982), 'The Politics of National Development and Education in Taiwan', *Comparative Politics*, 14 (2): 211–25.

LUSTICK, IAN (1980), *Arabs in the Jewish State* (Austin: University of Texas Press).

LYNN, RICHARD (1988), *Educational Achievement in Japan* (London: Macmillan).

MADDOCK, RODNEY, and MCLEAN, IAN W. (1987) (eds.), *The Australian Economy in the Long Run* (Cambridge: Cambridge University Press).

MANGUM, STEPHAN L., and BALL, DAVID (1987), 'Military Skill Training: Some Evidence of Transferability', *Armed Forces and Society*, 13: 425–41.

MANSKI, CHARLES (1993), 'Adolescent Econometricians: How do Youth Infer the Return to Schooling?', in Charles Clotfelter and M. Rothschild (eds.), *Studies of Supply and Demand in Higher Education* (Chicago: University of Chicago Press), 43–60.

MARE, ROBERT (1981), 'Change and Stability in Educational Stratification', *American Sociological Review*, 46: 72–87.

MARSDEN, DAVID (1990), 'Institutions and Labour Mobility: Occupational and Internal Labour Markets in Britain, France, Italy, and West Germany', in Renato Brunetta and Carlo Dell'Aringa (eds.), *Labour Relations and Economic Performance* (London: Macmillan).

MAURICE, MARC, SELLIER, FRANÇOIS, and SILVESTRE, JEAN-JACQUES (1979), 'Die Entwicklung der Hierarchie im Industrieunternehmen: Untersuchung eines gesellschaftlichen Effekts', *Soziale Welt*, 30: 295–325.

—— —— —— (1982), *Politique d'éducation et d'organisation industrielle en France et en Allemagne: Essai d'analyse sociétal* (Paris: Presses Universitaires de France).

—— —— —— (1986), *The Social Foundations of Industrial Power: A Comparison of France and Germany* (Cambridge, Mass.: MIT Press).

MAURIN, ERIC (1992), 'La Nomenclature française des catégories socioprofessionnelles: D'une construction pragmatique à une représentation théoretique de la société française', Paper presented at the CREST meeting at Nuffield College, Oxford.

MAYER, KARL ULRICH (1991), 'Berufliche Mobilität von Frauen in der Bundesrepublik Deutschland', in Karl Ulrich Mayer, Jutta Allmendinger, and Johannes Huinink (eds.), *Vom Regen in die Traufe: Frauen zwischen Beruf und Familie* (Frankfurt: Campus), 57–90.

—— BLOSSFELD, HANS-PETER (1990), 'Die gesellschaftliche Konstruktion sozialer Ungleichheit im Lebenslauf,' in P. A. Berger and S. Hradil (eds.), *Lebenslagen, Lebensläufe, Lebensstile* (Soziale Welt, Sonderband 7; Göttingen: Schwartz), 297–318.

—— and CARROLL, GLENN R. (1987/1990), 'Jobs and Classes: Structural Constraints on Career Mobility', *European Sociological Review*, 3: 14–38. Reprinted in Karl Ulrich Mayer and Nancy C. Brandon Tuma (eds.), *Event History Analysis in Life Course Research* (Madison: University of Wisconsin Press, 1990).

—— and SCHOEPFLIN, URS (1989), 'The State and the Life Course', *Annual Review of Sociology*, 15: 187–209.

MEYER, JOHN W. (1977), 'The Effects of Education as an Institution', *American Journal of Sociology*, 83 (July): 55–77.

—— RAMIREZ, FRANCISCO O., and SOYSAL, YASEMIN (1992), 'World Expansion of Mass Education, 1870–1980', *Sociology of Education*, 65 (2): 128–49.

MEYER, ROBERT, and WISE, DAVID (1982), 'High-School Preparation and Early Labor Force Experience', in R. Freedman and D. Wise (eds.), *The Youth Labor Market Problem: Its Nature, Causes and Consequences* (Chicago. University of Chicago Press), 277–339.

MINCER, JACOB (1974), *Schooling, Experience and Earnings* (Cambridge, Mass.: National Bureau of Economic Research).

Ministry of Education (Taiwan) (1995), *Education in the Republic of China* (Taipei: Bureau of Statistics, Ministry of Education).

MONK-TURNER, E. (1983), 'Sex, Educational Differentiation and Occupational Status', *Sociological Quarterly*, 24: 393–404.

MÜLLER, WALTER (1978), 'Further Education, Division of Labour and Equality of Opportunity', in R. Campiche, J. P. Hoby, and Ch. Lalive d'Epinay (eds.), *Effets economiques et sociaux de l'enseignement* (Vevey: Delta), 469–526.

—— (1986), 'Women's Labor Force Participation over the Life Course: A Model Case of Social Change?', in P. B. Baltes, D. L. Featherman, and R. M. Lerner (eds.), *Life-Span Development and Behaviour*, 7: 43–67 (Hillsdale).

—— (1994), 'Bildung und soziale Plazierung in Deutschland, England und Frankreich', in Hansgert Peisert and Wolfgang Zapf (eds.), *Gesellschaft, Demokratie und Lebenschancen: Festschrift für Ralf Dahrendorf* (Stuttgart: Deutsche Verlags-Anstalt), 115–34.

—— and HAUN, D. (1994), 'Bildungsungleichheit im sozialen Wandel', *Kölner Zeitschrift für Soziologie und Sozialpsychologie*, 46: 1–42.

—— and KARLE, WOLFGANG (1993), 'Social Selection and Educational System in Europe', *European Sociological Review*, 9 (1): 1–23.

—— and SHAVIT, YOSSI (1994), 'Educational Qualifications and Occupational Destinations', Project outline.

—— LÜTTINGER, PAUL, KÖNIG, WOLFGANG, and KARLE, WOLFGANG (1989), 'Class and Education in Industrial Nations', *International Journal of Sociology*, 19 (3): 3–39. Reprinted in M. Haller (ed.), *Class Structure in Europe: New Findings from East–West Comparisons of Social Structure and Mobility* (Armonk, NY: Sharpe), 61–91.

MYERS, RAMON H. (1984), 'The Economic Transformation of the Republic of China on Taiwan', *China Quarterly*, 99: 500–28.

NAOI, ATSUSHI (1979), 'The Construction of the Occupational Status Scale', in Ken'ichi Tominaga (ed.), *The Stratification Structure in Japan* (Tokyo: Tokyo University Press), 291–328 (in Japanese).

Nobi Nobi (1976), 'A Difficult Time to Find a Job', *Nobi Nobi*, 18–25 Jan., Asahi Shimbun-sha (in Japanese).

O'CONNELL, P., and LYONS, M. (1995), *Enterprise Related Training and State Policy in Ireland: The Training Support Scheme* (Dublin: Economic and Social Research Institute).

ODAKA, KONOSUKE (1984), *The Analysis of Labor Market* (Tokyo: Iwanami Shoten) (in Japanese).

OECD (1992), *Education at a Glance: OECD Indicators. Regards sur l'éducation, les indicateurs de l'OCDE* (Paris: OECD).

—— (1994), *Employment Outlook 1994* (Paris: OECD).

—— (1995a), *Education at a Glance: OECD Indicators* (Paris: OECD).

—— (1995b), *OECD Education Statistics* (Paris: OECD).

—— and Irish Government (1965), *Investment in Education* (Dublin: Stationary Office).

OGATA, KEN (1975), *Gakureki Shinko Shakai* (Society Believing Diplomas) (Tokyo: Jiji Tshushin-sha).

OKAMOTO, HIDEO, and HARA, JUNSUKE (1979), 'The Analysis of Prestige Evaluation of Occupations', in Ken'ichi Tominaga (ed.), *The Stratification Structure in Japan* (Tokyo: Tokyo University Press), 421–33 (in Japanese).

OKANO, KAORI (1993), *School to Work Transition in Japan* (Clevedon (UK): Multilingual Matters).

—— (1995), 'Rational Decision Making and School-Based Job Referrals for High School Students in Japan', *Sociology of Education*, 68: 31–47.

OPCS (1970), 'Classification of Occupations 1970' (London: HMSO).

ORMEROD, PAUL (1994), *The Death of Economics* (London: Faber & Faber).

OTTERSPEER, W. (1992), *De wiekslag van de geest; de Leidse universiteit in de negentiende eeuw* (The Hague: Stichting Hollandse Historische Reeks).

PAGAN, A. (1987), 'The End of the Long Boom', in R. Maddock and I. W. McLean (eds.), *The Australian Economy in the Long Run* (Cambridge: Cambridge University Press), 106–30.

PARKIN, FRANK (1979), *Marxism and Class Theory* (New York: Columbia University Press).

PROST, ANTOINE (1992), *Education, société et politiques: Une histoire de l'enseignement en France, de 1945 à nos jours* (Paris: Seuil).

RAGIN, CHARLES C. (1989), *The Comparative Method: Moving Beyond Qualitative and Quantitative Strategies* (Berkeley: University of California Press).

REGINI, MARINO (1996), 'Les Différentes formes de capitalisme en Italie', in Colin Crouch and Wolfgang Streeck (eds.), *Le Capitalisme en Europe* (Paris: Découverte), 139–56.

REICH, ROBERT (1991), *The Work of Nations* (New York: Vintage Books).

ROHLEN, THOMAS P. (1983), *Japan's High Schools* (Berkeley: University of California Press).

ROSENBAUM, JAMES E. and KARIYA, TAKEHIKO (1989), 'From High School to Work: Market and Institutional Mechanisms in Japan', *American Journal of Sociology*, 94 (6): 1334–65.

—— —— (1991), 'Do School Achievements Affect the Early Jobs of High School Graduates in the United States and Japan', *Sociology of Education*, 64 (2): 78–95.

—— —— SETTERSTEN, RICK, and MAIER, TONY (1990), 'Market and Network Theories of the Transition from High School to Work: Their Application to Industrialized Societies', *Annual Review of Sociology*, 16: 263–99.

RUMBERGER, RUSSELL, and DAYMONT, THOMAS (1984), 'The Economic Value of Academic and Vocational Training Acquired in High School', in M. E. Borus (ed.), *Youth and the Labor Market: Analysis of the National Longitudinal Study* (Kalamazoo, Mich.: W. E. Upjohn Institute for Employment Research), 157–91.

SAHA, LAWRENCE J., and KEEVES, JOHN P. (1990), *Schooling and Society in Australia: Sociological Perspectives* (Sydney: Australian National University Press).

SAKAMOTO, ARTHUR, and POWERS, DANIEL (1995), 'Education and the Dual Labor Market for Japanese Men', *American Sociological Review*, 60: 222–46.

SAN, G. (1990), 'Enterprise Training in Taiwan: Results from the Vocational Training Needs Survey', *Economics of Education Review*, 9 (4): 411–18.

SCB (Statistics Sweden) (1988), *Svensk utbildningsnomenklatur (SUN), 1 Systematisk version*, Meddelanden i samordningsfrågor 1988: 4 (Stockholm: SCB).

—— (1989), *Yrkesklassificeringar i FoB 85 enligt Nordisk yrkesklassificering (NYK) och Socioekonomisk indelning (SEI)*, *Alfabetisk version*, Meddelanden i samord-ningsfrågor 1989: 5 (Stockholm: SCB).

SCHADEE, H. M. A., and SCHIZZEROTTO, ANTONIO (1990), *Social Mobility of Men and Women in Contemporary Italy* (Trent: University of Trent, Department of Politica Sociale, Quaderno 17).

SCHIZZEROTTO, ANTONIO (1988), 'Il ruolo dell'istruzione nei processi di mobilità sociale', *Polis*, 2: 83–124.

—— and BISON, IVANO (1994), 'Gender Inequalities in Labour Market Participation and in Career Duration', Paper presented at the Espinho ESF Conference.

—— —— (1996), 'Mobilità occupazionale tra generazioni e mobilità di carriera: Un confronto internazionale', in G. Galli (ed.), *La mobilità della società italiana* (Rome: Sepi), 446–507.

SEBER, G. A. F. (1980), *The Linear Hypothesis: A General Theory* (2nd edn.; New York: Macmillan).

SEMYONOV, MOSHE, and COHEN, YINON (1990), 'Ethnic Discrimination and the Income of Majority-Group Workers', *American Sociological Review*, 55: 107–14.

SEWELL, WILLIAM H., HAUSER, ROBERT M., and WOLF, WENDY C. (1980), 'Sex, Schooling and Occupational Status', *American Journal of Sociology*, 86: 551–83.

SHAVIT, YOSSI (1984), 'Tracking and Ethnicity in Israeli Secondary Education', *American Sociological Review*, 49: 210–20.

—— (1989), 'Tracking and the Educational Spiral: A Comparison of Arab and Jewish Educational Expansion in Israel', *Comparative Education Review*, 33 (2): 216–31.

—— (1990a), 'Tracking and the Persistence of Ethnic Occupational Inequalities in Israel', in *International Perspectives on Education and Society 2* (Greenwich, Conn.: JAI Press), 23–37.

—— (1990b), 'Segregation, Tracking and the Educational Attainment of Minorities: Arabs and Oriental Jews in Israel', *American Sociological Review*, 55 (1): 115–26.

—— (1992), 'Arabs in the Israeli Economy: A Study of the Enclave Hypothesis', *Israel Social Science Research*, 7 (1 and 2): 45–66.

—— and HANS-PETER BLOSSFELD (1993) (eds), *Persistent Inequality: Changing Educational Attainment in Thirteen Countries* (Boulder, Colo.: Westview Press).

—— and WESTERBEEK, KARIN (1995), 'Stratification in Italy: An Investigation of Failed Reforms', European University Institute Working Paper SPS 96/1, Florence.

—— and ROSSTEUSCHER, S., and MÜLLER, WALTER (in progress), 'Educational Stratification in Six Countries: Testing the Institutional Perspective'.

—— MÜLLER, WALTER, KRAUS, VERED, and KATZ-GERRO, Tally (1994), 'Vocational Education and the Transition of Men from School to Work in Israel, Italy and Germany', Paper presented at the ESF workshop, Seeliberg, Switzerland.

SHEPHERD, P. (1995), 'The National Child Development Study: An Introduction to the Origins of the Study and the Methods of Data Collection', NCDS User Support Group, Working Paper 1.

SHIEH, GWO-SHYONG (1992), *'Boss' Island: The Subcontracting Network and Micro-Entrepreneurship in Taiwan's Development* (New York: Peter Lang).

SHIRAHASE, SAWAKO, and ISHIDA, HIROSHI (1994), 'Gender Inequality in the Japanese Occupational Structure: A Cross-National Comparison with Great Britain and the United States', *International Journal of Comparative Sociology*, 35: 188–206.

Shokugyo Kenkyujo (Research Instititue of Employment) (1981), *Survey Report of Recruitment Criteria of Firms* (Jigyosho no Saiyosenko Nikansuru Chosa Kenkyu Hokokusho), Shokken Research Report No. 15.

SIXMA, H., and ULTEE, WOUT C. (1984), 'An Occupational Prestige Scale for the Netherlands in the Eighties', in B. F. M. Bakker, J. Dronkers, and Harry B. G. Ganzeboom (eds.), *Social Stratification and Mobility in the Netherlands* (Amsterdam: Siswo), 29–39.

SMITH, JAMES, and WELCH, FINIS (1986), *Closing the Gap: Forty Years of Economic Progress for Blacks* (Santa Monica, Calif.: RAND Corporation).

SMITH, NARSHALL, and SCOLL, BRETT (1995), 'The Clinton Human Capital Agenda', *Teachers College Record*, 96: 389–403.

SØRENSEN A. B., and KALLEBERG, ARNE (1981), 'An Outline of a Theory of the Matching of Persons to Jobs', in I. Berg (ed.), *Sociological Perspectives on Labour Markets* (New York: Academic Press), 49–74.

SOSKICE, DAVID (1993*a*), 'Social Skills from Mass Higher Education: Rethinking the Company Based Initial Training Paradigm', *Oxford Review of Economic Policy*, 9 (3): 101–13.

—— (1993*b*), 'Product Markets and Innovation Strategies of Companies and their Implications for Enterprise Tenure: A Comparative Institutional Approach to Some Cross-Country Differences', unpublished manuscript, Berlin: Wissenschaftszentrum Berlin für Sozialforschung.

SPAIN, DAPHNE, and BIANCHI, SUZANNE (1996), *Balancing Act: Motherhood, Marriage and Employment among American Women* (New York: Russell Sage Foundation).

SPILERMAN, SEYMOUR (1977), 'Careers, Labor Market Structures and Socioeconomic Achievement', *American Journal of Sociology*, 83: 551–93.

—— and ISHIDA, HIROSHI (1996), 'Stratification and Attainment in a Large Japanese Firm', in Alan C. Kerckhoff (ed.), *Generating Social Stratification* (Boulder, Colo.: Westview Press), 317–42.

SPRING, J. (1976), *The Sorting Machine* (New York: David McKay).

STEADMAN, J. (1980) *Progress in Secondary Schools* (London: National Children's Bureau).

—— (1983), *Examination Results in Selective and Non-Selective Secondary Schools* (London: National Children's Bureau).

STEINMANN, S. (1994), 'Übergänge vom Bildungs- ins Erwerbssystem in Deutschland', unpublished manuscript, Mannheim Center for European Social Research, University of Mannheim.

STERN, DAVID, RABY, MARILYN, and DAYTON, CHARLES (1992), *Career Academies: Partnerships for Reconstructing American High Schools* (San Francisco: Jossey-Bass Publishers).

STOLZENBERG, R. (1978), 'Bringing the Boss Back in: Employer Size, Employee Schooling, and Socioeconomic Achievement', *American Sociological Review*, 43: 813–28.

STRATMANN, K., and SCHLÜTER, A. (1982) (eds.), *Quellen und Dokumente zur Berufsbildung 1794–1869* (Cologne: Boehlau).

STREECK, WOLFGANG, and HILDERT, JOSEF (1990), 'Die Rolle der Sozialpartner in der Berufsausbildung und der beruflichen Weiterbildung: Bundesrepublik Deutschland', in CEDEFOP (European Centre for the Development of

Vocational Training), *Die Rolle der Sozialpartner in der beruflichen Erstausbildung und Weiterbildung* (Luxembourg: Official Publications Office of the European Community), 43–55.

Taiwan Research Fund (1994), *Educational Reform in Taiwan* (Taipei: Chi-Wen Press) (in Chinese).

TAKEUCHI, YO (1981), *The Sociology of Competition* (Tokyo: Sekai Shisosha) (in Japanese).

—— (1995), *Japan's Meritocracy* (Tokyo: Tokyo University Press) (in Japanese).

TESSARING, MANFRED (1993), 'Das duale System der Berufsausbildung in Deutschland: Attraktivität und Beschäftigungsperspektiven', *Mitteilungen aus der Arbeitsmarkt- und Berufsforschung*, 20: 131–61.

THÉLOT, C. (1982), *Tel père, tel fils?* (L'oeil économique series; Paris: Dunod).

THUROW, LESTER C. (1976), *Generating Inequality: Mechanisms of Distribution in the US Economy* (London: Macmillan Press).

TÖLKE, A. (1989), *Lebensverläufe von Frauen: Familiäre Ereignisse, Ausbildungs- und Erwerbsverhalten* (Weinheim: Juventa).

TREIMAN, DONALD J. (1970), 'Industrialization and Social Stratification', in E. O. Laumann (ed.), *Social Stratification: Research and Theory for the 1970s* (Indianapolis: Bobbs Merrill), 207–34.

—— (1977), *Occupational Prestige in Comparative Perspective* (New York: Academic Press).

TREIMAN, DONALD J., and YIP, KAM-BOR (1989), 'Educational and Occupational Attainment in 21 Countries', in Melvin L. Kohn (ed.), *Cross-National Research in Sociology* (Newbury Park, Calif.: Sage), 373–94.

TSAI, SHU-LING (1992), 'Social Change and Status Attainment in Taiwan: Comparisons of Ethnic Groups', *International Perspectives on Education and Society*, (2): 225–56 (Greenwich, Conn.: JAI Press).

—— and CHIU, HEI-YUAN (1991), 'Constructing Occupational Scales for Taiwan', *Research in Social Stratification and Mobility*, 10: 229–53 (Greenwich, Conn.: JAI Press).

—— —— (1993), 'Changes in Educational Stratification in Taiwan', in Yossi Shavit and Hans-Peter Blossfeld (eds.), *Persistent Inequality: Changing Educational Attainment in Thirteen Countries* (Boulder, Colo.: Westview Press), 193–227.

—— GATES, HILL, and CHIU, HEI-YUAN (1994), 'Schooling Taiwan's Women: Educational Attainment in the Mid-Twentieth Century', *Sociology of Education*, 67: 243–63.

TURNER, R. H. (1960), 'Sponsored and Contest Mobility', *American Sociological Review*, 25: 855–67.

TUSSING, A. D. (1978), *Irish Educational Expenditures: Past, Present and Future* (General Research Series, Paper No. 92; Dublin: Economic and Social Research Institute).

TYREE, ANDREA (1981), 'Occupational Socioeconomic Status, Ethnicity, and Sex in Israel: Considerations in Scale Construction', *Megamot*, 27 (in Hebrew).

UJIHARA, SHOJIRO, and TAKANASHI, AKIRA (1971), *The Analysis of the Japanese Labor Market* (Tokyo: Tokyo University Press) (in Japanese).

UNESCO (1976), *International Standard Classification of Education (ISCED)* (Paris: UNESCO).

WADE, ROBERT (1990), *Governing the Market: Economic Theory and the Role of Government in East Asian Industrialization* (Princeton: Princeton University Press).

WALLERSTEIN, IMMANUEL (1974), *The Modern World-System: Capitalist Agriculture and the Origins of the European World-Economy in the Sixteenth Century* (New York: Academic Press).

WATANABE, SHIN (1987), 'Job-Searching: A Comparative Study of Male Employment Relations in the United States and Japan', Ph.D. dissertation (University of California, Los Angeles).

WEGENER, B. (1985), 'Gibt es Sozialprestige?', *Zeitschrift für Soziologie*, 14: 209–35.

WHELAN, CHRISTOPHER T. (1994), 'Modelling Trends in Social Fluidity: The Core Model and a Measured Variable Approach', *European Sociological Review*, 10 (3): 259–72.

—— BREEN, RICHARD, and WHELAN, B. J. (1992), 'Industrialization, Class Formation and Social Mobility in Ireland', in John H. Goldthorpe and Christopher T. Whelan (eds.), *The Development of Industrial Society in Ireland* (Oxford: Oxford University Press), 105–28.

WILLIAMSON, OLIVER E. (1975), *Markets and Hierarchies: Analysis and Antitrust Implications* (New York: Free Press).

WINFIELD, I., CAMPBELL, R. T., KERCKHOFF, ALAN C., EVERETT, D. D., and TROTT, JERRY M. (1989), 'Career Processes in Great Britain and the United States', *Social Forces*, 68: 284–308.

WOO, JENNIE HAY (1991), 'Education and Economic Growth in Taiwan: A Case of Successful Planning', *World Development*, 19: 1029–44.

WRIGHT, ERIK OLIN, BAXTER, JANEEN, and BIRKELUND GUNN (1995), 'The Gender Gap in Workplace Authority: A Cross-National Study', *American Sociological Review*, 60: 407–35.

XIE, Y. (1992), 'The Log-Multiplicative Layer Effect Model for Comparing Mobility Tables', *American Sociological Review*, 57: 380–95.

YAISH, MEIR (1995), 'Class and Class Mobility in Israel', MA thesis (University of Haifa, Department of Sociology and Anthropology).

YANG, YI-RONG (1994), 'Education and National Development: The Case of Taiwan', *Chinese Education and Society*, 27 (6): 7–22.

YANG, YING (1994), 'Reform of Secondary Education for the Equality of Educational Opportunities', *Chinese Education and Society*, 27 (6): 42–55.

YOGEV, ABRAHAM (1981), 'Determinants of Early Educational Career in Israel: Further Evidence for the Sponsorship Thesis', *Sociology of Education*, 54: 181–95.

YOSHIMOTO, KEIICHI, KOSUGI, R., YONEZAWA, A., MUROYAMA, H., and NAKAJIMA, F. (1992), *Job Placement Services in Universities and Early Stages of College Graduates' Careers* (Research Report No. 33; Tokyo: Japan Institute of Labour).

—— SATO, GUNEI, SENGOKU, TAMOTSU, TANAKA, KOICHI, HAYASHI, YOSHIKI, and YOSHIDA AYA (1984), *Education and its Effects* (Report on the Japanese High School and Beyond (HSB) data) (Tokyo: Nihon Seishonen Kenkyuujo) (in Japanese).

YU, C. M. (1988), *The Education of Women in Taiwan under Japanese Rule, 1895–1945* (Taipei: Institute of History, National Taiwan Normal University) (in Chinese).

NAME INDEX

SUBJECT INDEX

The index is organized by keywords and countries. Keywords with information for less than five countries are entered only under the respective countries.

educational policy:
  Britain 72–3; France 103, 105;
    Germany 145, 147; Israel 225;
    Netherlands 342–3, 345; Sweden
    372; Taiwan 448–9
educational system:
  centralization: Britain 3; France 108–9;
    Germany 145; Ireland 216; Israel
    38, 224; Sweden 372;
    Switzerland 410; Taiwan 448
  compulsory schooling (school leaving
    age): Australia 54; Britain 71–4, 77;
    France 105; Germany 145; Ireland
    189; Israel 222; Italy 253; Japan
    287; Netherlands 342; Sweden 379;
    Taiwan 444
  school differentiation 471; France 109;
    Israel 224; Japan 13, 287–9,
    298–304, 312, 315–17, 327–33;
    Switzerland 410; Taiwan 444–6;
    United States 472
  standardization 6–7, 9–10, 12–14, 21–3,
    26–8, 32–3, 37–40, 46 n., 48 n.;
    Britain 74; France 108; Germany
    144–6, 148, 151; Ireland 192; Israel
    224; Japan 287–8; Sweden 372;
    Switzerland 411, 432; Taiwan 411,
    446
  stratification 6–7, 9–10, 12–14, 21–3,
    26–8, 32–3, 37–40, 46 n., 48 n.;
    Britain 71, 73–5; France 106–8;
    Germany 144–5, 151; Ireland 192;
    Israel 224; Italy 259; Japan 287–9,
    308; Sweden 372; Switzerland 411,
    413; Taiwan 444–7; United States
    473–4, 478, 480, 489, 505, 508
  structure of 6–7, 9–10, 12–14, 21–3,
    26–8, 32–3, 37–40, 46 n., 48 n.;
    Australia 54–5; Britain 71–5;
    France 105–11; Germany 144–51,
    186 n.; Ireland 189; Israel 222–6,
    231; Italy 253–6, 279, 284 n.; Japan
    287–8; Netherlands 342–3; Sweden
    372–3; Switzerland 410–14, 424,
    432; Taiwan 444–9; United
    States 472, 476, 504
  vocational specificity 9–10, 12–14,
    21–3, 26–8, 30, 32–3, 37–41, 38 n.;
    Britain 71; France 107; Germany
    40–1; Israel 225–6; Italy 256,

    279–80; Netherlands 40–1, 341–2;
    Sweden 372, 398; Switzerland 40–1;
    Taiwan 446–7; United States 474,
    498, 504
elite schools, *see* France; Britain; Japan
employment:
  part time, *see* France; Netherlands;
    Sweden
  in private sector, *see* Italy; Sweden;
    Taiwan
  in public sector: France 110, 114;
    Germany 149–50; Italy 257, 260;
    Sweden 370–1, 394–6; Taiwan 467
  short-term contract, *see* France
  temporary, *see* Netherlands
equality of opportunity:
  in educational participation 5;
    France 105–6; Ireland 190, 194–8;
    Italy 283–4; Japan 287; Sweden 373;
    Taiwan 444, 449
  between generations 5; France 135;
    Germany 156; Japan 294–6; Sweden
    377, 399, 404; United States 508
  legislation, *see* Japan; Sweden
ethnicity 39
  Australia 15
  Israel 15, 46 n., 48 n., 221–2, 224–30,
    232–3, 236–7, 240–1, 245–50
  Switzerland 417, 421–2
  Taiwan 15, 454, 460, 463–7
  United States 15, 474, 480, 484,
    498–9, 510 n.
examinations 3, 38
  France 114
  Germany 150
  Ireland 189
  Italy 256–7
  Sweden 373
  Switzerland 412
  matriculation: Britain 71; France 105,
    108, 139–40; Germany 144–5;
    Ireland 216; Israel 223–5, 232–3,
    245–6; Japan 314; Sweden 373, 397;
    Switzerland 414, 419–20, 422, 424,
    431, 433; Taiwan 444–6
exclusion from labour force, *see*
  Germany; Italy; Taiwan

firm size:
  and education, *see* Japan